*Routledge Library Editions*

# THE ECONOMICS OF INFLATION



ECONOMICS

*Routledge Library Editions – Economics*

# MONETARY ECONOMICS
## In 4 Volumes

| | | |
|---|---|---|
| I | The Economics of Inflation | *Bresciani-Turroni* |
| II | The Economics of Repressed Inflation | *Charlesworth* |
| III | The Role of Money | *Soddy* |
| IV | Monetary Policy and the Development of Money Markets | *Wilson* |

# THE ECONOMICS OF INFLATION

## A Study of Currency Depreciation in Post-War Germany

COSTANTINO BRESCIANI-TURRONI

Routledge
Taylor & Francis Group
LONDON AND NEW YORK

First published in 1937

Reprinted in 2003 by
Routledge
2 Park Square, Milton Park, Abingdon, Oxon, OX14 4RN

Transferred to digital printing 2006

*Routledge is an imprint of the Taylor & Francis Group*

Printed and bound by Antony Rowe Ltd, Eastbourne



*British Library Cataloguing in Publication Data*
A CIP catalogue record for this book
is available from the British Library

The Economics of Inflation
ISBN 13: 9780415434621

Miniset: Monetary Economics

Series: Routledge Library Editions – Economics

# THE ECONOMICS *of* INFLATION

A STUDY OF CURRENCY DEPRECIATION
IN POST-WAR GERMANY

*by* COSTANTINO
BRESCIANI-TURRONI
PROFESSOR OF ECONOMICS IN THE UNIVERSITIES
OF MILAN AND CAIRO

*with a Foreword by*
LIONEL ROBBINS
PROFESSOR OF ECONOMICS IN THE UNIVERSITY
OF LONDON

*translated by Millicent E. Sayers*

LONDON
GEORGE ALLEN & UNWIN LTD

*The Italian original*

LE VICENDE DEL MARCO TEDESCO

*First published by Universita Bocconi in 1931*

FIRST PUBLISHED IN ENGLISH 1937

SECOND IMPRESSION 1953

THIRD IMPRESSION 1968

*The English edition has been substantially revised by the author*



SBN 04 332005 8

PRINTED IN GREAT BRITAIN

*by Photolithography*

BY JOHN DICKENS & CO LTD

NORTHAMPTON

# FOREWORD

THE depreciation of the mark of 1914–23, which is the subject of this work, is one of the outstanding episodes in the history of the twentieth century. Not only by reason of its magnitude but also by reason of its effects, it looms large on our horizon. It was the most colossal thing of its kind in history: and, next probably to the Great War itself, it must bear responsibility for many of the political and economic difficulties of our generation. It destroyed the wealth of the more solid elements in German society: and it left behind a moral and economic disequilibrium, apt breeding ground for the disasters which have followed. Hitler is the foster-child of the inflation. The financial convulsions of the Great Depression were, in part at least, the product of the distortions of the system of international borrowing and lending to which its ravages had given rise. If we are to understand correctly the present position of Europe, we must not neglect the study of the great German inflation. If we are to plan for greater stability in the future, we must learn to avoid the mistakes from which it sprang.

There is another reason why the history of this episode is peculiarly significant to students of the social sciences. Accidents to the body politic, like accidents to the physical body, often permit observations of a kind which would not be possible under normal conditions. In peaceful times we may speculate concerning the consequences of violent change. But we are naturally precluded from verifying our conclusions: we cannot upset the smooth current of things for the advancement of abstract knowledge. But when disturbance takes place, it is sometimes possible to snatch good from evil and to obtain insight into the working of processes which are normally concealed. No doubt there are dangers here. We must not ignore the possibility that the processes thus revealed are themselves abnormal: we must not infer, for instance, that propositions which apply to large inflations necessarily apply, without modification, to small inflations. But the dangers are clear: it is not difficult to keep them in mind and to guard against them. And the opportunities of fruitful research are enormous. In this matter of the depreciation of the mark, there is hardly any branch of the theory of economic dynamics which is not illuminated by examination of its grim events.

For both these reasons, therefore, I hope that this book will obtain a wide circulation among the English-speaking public. Its distinguished author, Professor Bresciani-Turroni, had very special opportunities for writing it; for he was working in Berlin during the years in which the events he describes took place: first as a member of the Reparations Commission, then as head of the Export Control, and finally as economic advisor to the Agent-General for reparations. As they peruse the chapters in which he develops his beautifully lucid and essentially catholic explanations, many readers, I think, will feel that these appointments were among the few fortunate events of those troubled times. I hope they will feel, too, a debt of gratitude to the trustees of the Sir Halley Stewart foundation for the generous grant which made it possible to make available in the English tongue the results of such valuable researches and to Mr. and Mrs. Sayers for the pains they have taken with the exacting and time-consuming task of translation.

LIONEL ROBBINS

THE LONDON SCHOOL OF ECONOMICS
*September 1937*

# CONTENTS

# LIST OF TABLES

# APPENDIX OF TABLES

# LIST OF DIAGRAMS

## CHARTS

# PREFACE TO THE ENGLISH EDITION

THE present book is a translation, with some modifications—changes in arrangement, omission here and there of redundant mention of sources, and the addition of an appendix to chapter two (formerly chapter three)—of the work *Le vicende del marco tedesco*. The Appendix is a translation of Chapter I of my work *Le previsioni economiche* (Nuova Collana di economisti italiani e stranieri. Unione Tipografica Editrice Torinese, Torino 1932, vol. vi).

In the analysis of the causes and effects of the depreciation of the German mark I have used, besides German official publications and economic articles in some of the leading newspapers (which are an important source of information), personal observations made during a long stay in Germany from 1920 to 1929, first as a member of Berlin staff of the Reparations Commission; then as head of the German Exports Control which was instituted in 1921 by the Committee of Guarantees; and lastly as economic adviser to the Agent-General of Reparations.

I acknowledge my debt to the Director of the Universitá Bocconi, who has kindly permitted the present translation and also to the Unione Tipografica Editrice Torinese. Particularly I am grateful to the Sir Halley Stewart Trust, which has greatly facilitated the appearance of the English edition by a generous grant for translation. I emphasize this the more because it seems to me to show that, far above ephemeral political disturbances, live and lasting forces are at work which assure the permanence of that bond between the nations which is created by the work of past generations. One of these live forces is the work of science.

I wish to take this opportunity of thanking Professor Robbins, who initiated the production of an English edition, and by whose valuable suggestions I have greatly profited.

C. BRESCIANI-TURRONI

CAIRO
*May 1937*

# THE ECONOMICS OF INFLATION

## CHAPTER I

## Foreign Exchanges and Internal Price Movements in Germany 1914 to 1923

### I. AN OUTLINE OF EVENTS

1. On the afternoon of July 31st, 1914, the Reichsbank, on its own initiative, suspended the conversion of notes, which in the preceding days had come, in great quantities, to its branches to be exchanged for gold, so that the gold reserve had already suffered a considerable decline. On August 4th the conversion of notes was suspended by law, with effect as from July 31st. Another law of the same date authorized the Reichsbank to discount short-term bills issued by the Treasury and to use them, together with commercial bills, as cover for notes.

According to the weekly statements of the Reichsbank, in the two weeks from July 24th to August 7th the quantity of Reichsbank notes in circulation increased by more than two milliard marks. Thus was initiated a monetary inflation which was without precedent in history. Actually the nominal value of Reichsbank bills circulating on November 15th, 1923, the day on which the inflation ended (on that day the discounting of Treasury bills by the Reichsbank ceased), amounted to 92·8 trillion paper marks (a trillion = $1{,}000{,}000^3$).

In the past the money which had suffered the greatest depreciation was probably the so-called "continental money," issued by the American Colonies during the War of Independence. In 1781 that money was worth a thousandth part of its original value.* The deprecia-

* Hock, *Die Finanzen und die Finanzgeschichte der Vereinigten Staaten*, Stuttgart, 1867, p. 403.

tion of the famous assignats was also less than that of the mark. On June 1st, 1796, a metal franc was worth 533 assignat francs.*

Among the currencies, other than the German mark, which depreciated enormously after the war, were the Austrian crown, the Hungarian crown, the Polish mark, and the Russian rouble. In January 1923 the depreciation of the German mark had already exceeded that of the Austrian and Hungarian crowns; towards the end of the first half of the same year it overtook and passed that of the Polish mark; and at the beginning of October the German mark was also more depreciated than the Russian rouble, a gold mark being worth 709 million paper marks, while a gold rouble was equivalent to 505 million old paper roubles.

After the stabilization of the exchanges the value of the most depreciated currencies in relation to gold was as follows: an Austrian gold crown was equal to a little more than 14,300 paper crowns; a Hungarian gold crown was worth a little more than 16,600 paper crowns; the value of a gold zloty was fixed at 1,800,000 Polish marks; the conversion rate of the paper rouble, fixed by the decree of March 7th, 1924, was 1 gold rouble = 50,000 roubles of the 1923 issue, that is 50 milliard of old Soviet roubles.

In the days preceding the monetary reform the quotations of the dollar at Berlin were as follows:

| | *Milliards of paper marks* |
|---|---|
| November 13th, 1923 .. .. .. | 840 |
| November 14th, 1923 .. .. .. | 1,260 |
| November 15th, 1923 .. .. .. | 2,520 |
| November 20th, 1923 .. .. .. | 4,200 |

But these were the official quotations. Actually in the open foreign market the dollar reached much higher rates. According to the figures referred to by Schacht in his book on the stabilization of the mark the dollar was quoted at 3,900 milliard paper marks at Cologne on November 13th, 1923; 5,800 milliards on the 15th; 6,700 milliards on the 17th, and 11,700 milliards on November 20th. This was the highest quotation.† The German monetary law of August 30th, 1924, fixed the conversion rate of the new Reichsmark (whose weight in fine gold was equal to that of the old mark) at a *thousand milliard* paper marks.

Out of curiosity I note the fact that on November 11th, 1923, notes

* Falkner, *Das Papiergeld der Französischen Revolution*, Leipzig, 1924, p. 49.

† H. Schacht, *The Stabilization of the Mark*, 1926, p. 102 (London: George Allen & Unwin, Ltd.).

for 1,000 milliards were issued. There followed notes for 2,000, 5,000, 10,000, and 100,000 milliards denominations. These last were the highest issued. They were stamped on one side only. Stuart Mill, speaking of the assignats, states that "it at last required an assignat of six hundred francs to pay for a pound of butter."* Now, towards the end of November 1923 a kg. of bread cost 428 milliard paper marks in Berlin, a kg. of butter 5,600 milliards, a newspaper 200 milliards, a tram ticket 150 milliards, the postage for an inland letter 100 milliards, and so on.

### II. 1914 TO THE ARMISTICE

2. The examination of the causes which provoked the depreciation and the collapse of the German mark must be preceded by an analysis of the statistics of the issues of paper money, the movement of the floating debt, the foreign exchange value of the mark, and the prices of various classes of goods. In the tables and diagrams included in this chapter I have endeavoured to depict certain fundamental facts which characterize the various periods into which the history of the German mark from 1914 to 1924 can be divided.

In the first period, that is from the outbreak of the World War until the Armistice, the depreciation of the German mark was relatively slow. In October 1918 a gold mark was worth 1·57 paper marks. More rapid was the rise of wholesale prices, from 1 (1913) to 2·34. In that period the issues of paper money increased more rapidly than the price of a gold mark expressed in paper marks and than the general prices of goods, as is shown in the following figures and in Diagram 1:

TABLE I

*(Annual Averages)*

| | *Value of the gold mark in terms of paper marks* | PRICES OF GOODS *Imported* | PRICES OF GOODS *Produced in Germany* | *Quantity of money† in circulation* |
|---|---|---|---|---|
| 1913 | 100 | 100 | 100 | 100 |
| 1914 | 102 | 102 | 106 | 116 |
| 1915 | 116 | 134 | 142 | 147 |
| 1916 | 131 | 141 | 154 | 172 |
| 1917 | 157 | 147 | 186 | 245 |
| Oct. 1918 | 157 | 214 | 239 | 440 |

* *Principles of Political Economy*, edited by Ashley, 1926, p. 548.

† The "Quantity of Money in Circulation" means the notes of Reichsbank and of the Private banks of issue (these last have not much importance); the notes of the

Together with the issues of paper money the current account deposits at the Reichsbank also grew rapidly, especially after 1915, thanks to the intense propaganda in favour of the substitution of the cheque for the banknote in payments.*

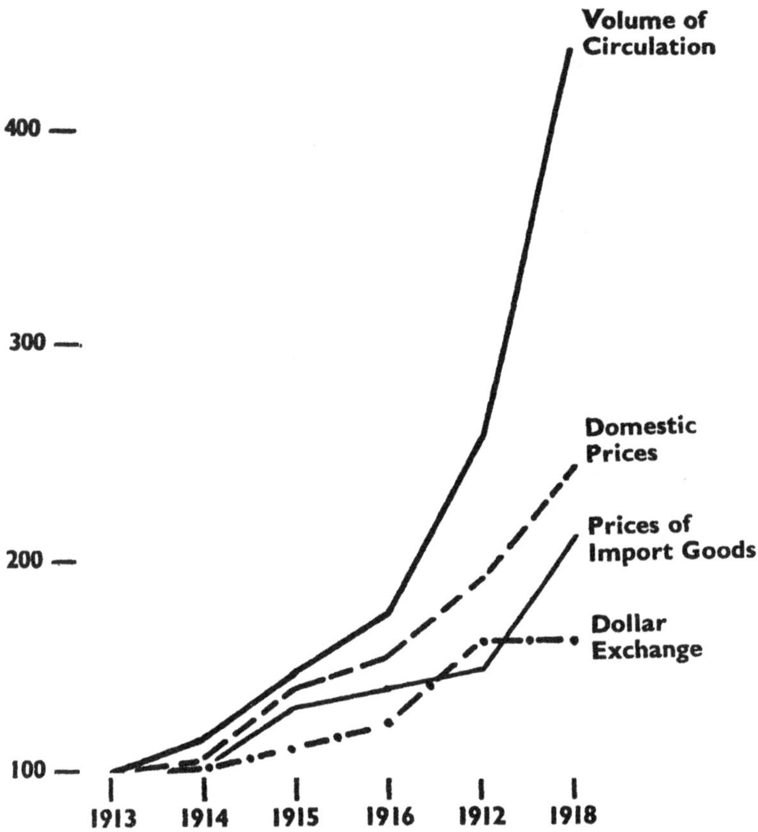


DIAGRAM I.—Basis of all curves: 1913 = 100

Reich ("Reichskassenscheine"); the notes issued by the Loan Offices which were created on August 4th, 1914; and metallic money.

I have calculated the indices contained in the present chapter from the data given in the official publication, *Zahlen zur Geldentwertung in Deutschland, 1914–1923*, Berlin, 1925.

* Current account deposits at the Reichsbank (in millions of marks):

| | | | |
|---|---|---|---|
| July 31st, 1914 .. .. | 1·3 | December 31st, 1916 .. | 4·6 |
| December 31st, 1914 .. | 1·8 | December 31st, 1917 .. | 8·1 |
| December 31st, 1915 .. | 2·4 | December 31st, 1918 .. | 13·3 |

The index numbers of prices, compiled by the Statistical Bureau of the Reich, are (1) of the wholesale prices of imported goods* and (2) of home-produced goods. The increase of the prices of goods of

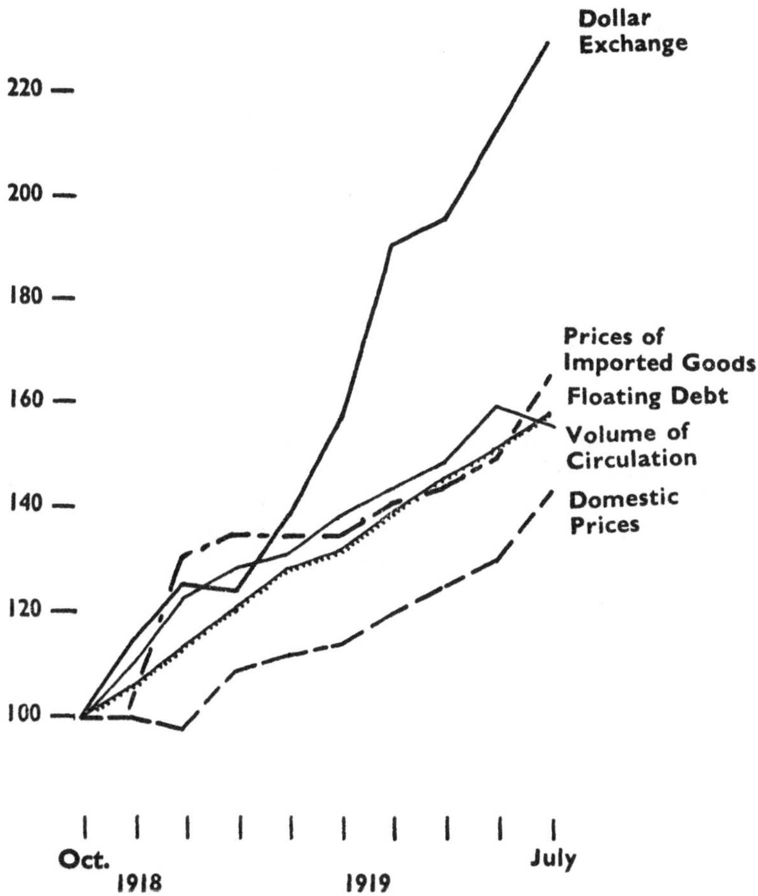


DIAGRAM II.—Basis of all curves: October 1918 = 100

the first category (index number 214 in October 1918) was less, during the war, than the increase of prices of goods of the second category (index number 239 in October 1918).

In the period indicated the floating debt of the Reich was enormously

* As to the items included in the "imported goods," see Chapter III, p. 129.

increased, having risen from 300 millions of marks in July 1914 to 55·2 milliards in December 1918. Towards the end of 1918 Treasury bills formed almost the entire portfolio of the Reichsbank and were also held outside the Reichsbank, especially by the great banks who had invested deposits in them.

Gold in the reserve of the Reichsbank amounted to 1,253 millions of marks on July 31st, 1914. The reserves were considerably augmented in the succeeding years, the Reichsbank having attracted to itself a great part of the gold which had formerly been in circulation. At the end of 1918 the Reichsbank had 2,262 million marks in gold.*

### III. FROM THE ARMISTICE TILL THE SIGNING OF THE TREATY OF VERSAILLES

**3.** In the next period (from November 1918 to July 1919) the velocity of the depreciation of the mark increased. In contrast to that which had occurred during the war years, the tendency to rise began to show itself in the dollar rate and in the prices of imported goods more rapidly than in internal prices.† As Diagram II and the following figures show, both the floating debt (issues of Treasury bonds) and the quantity of notes in circulation increased, in the period indicated, more rapidly than internal prices, but less rapidly than the dollar rate.

TABLE II

| | *Internal prices* | *Prices of imported goods* | *Circulation* | *Floating debt* | *Dollar rate* |
|---|---|---|---|---|---|
| October 1918 .. | 100 | 100 | 100 | 100 | 100 |
| November 1918 .. | 100 | 100 | 109·6 | 106·2 | 113·5 |
| December 1918 .. | 98·7 | 130·8 | 123·9 | 114·5 | 125·5 |
| January 1919 .. | 107·9 | 135·0 | 129·3 | 121·6 | 124·2 |
| February 1919 .. | 112·1 | 135·0 | 132·1 | 127·8 | 138·2 |
| March 1919 .. .. | 114·2 | 135·0 | 139·3 | 132·4 | 157·3 |
| April 1919 .. .. | 120·1 | 141·6 | 144·3 | 139·4 | 191·1 |
| May 1919 .. .. | 125·1 | 144·4 | 149·6 | 146·1 | 194·9 |
| June 1919 .. .. | 129·7 | 150·5 | 159·8 | 152·3 | 212·7 |
| July 1919 .. .. | 142·7 | 165·9 | 156·9 | 157·9 | 228·7 |

* Gold Reserves of the Reichsbank (in millions of marks):

| | | | |
|---|---|---|---|
| July 31st, 1914 .. .. | 1,253 | December 31st, 1916 .. | 2,520 |
| December 31st, 1914 .. | 2,092 | December 31st, 1917 .. | 2,406 |
| December 31st, 1915 .. | 2,445 | December 31st, 1918 .. | 2,262 |

† The expression "internal prices" signifies in this chapter prices of goods produced in Germany.

IV. FROM JULY 1919 TO FEBRUARY 1920

4. In the following period (July 1919 to February 1920) the various curves assumed characteristic positions. Those of the dollar rate and of the prices of imported goods are clearly detached from the other

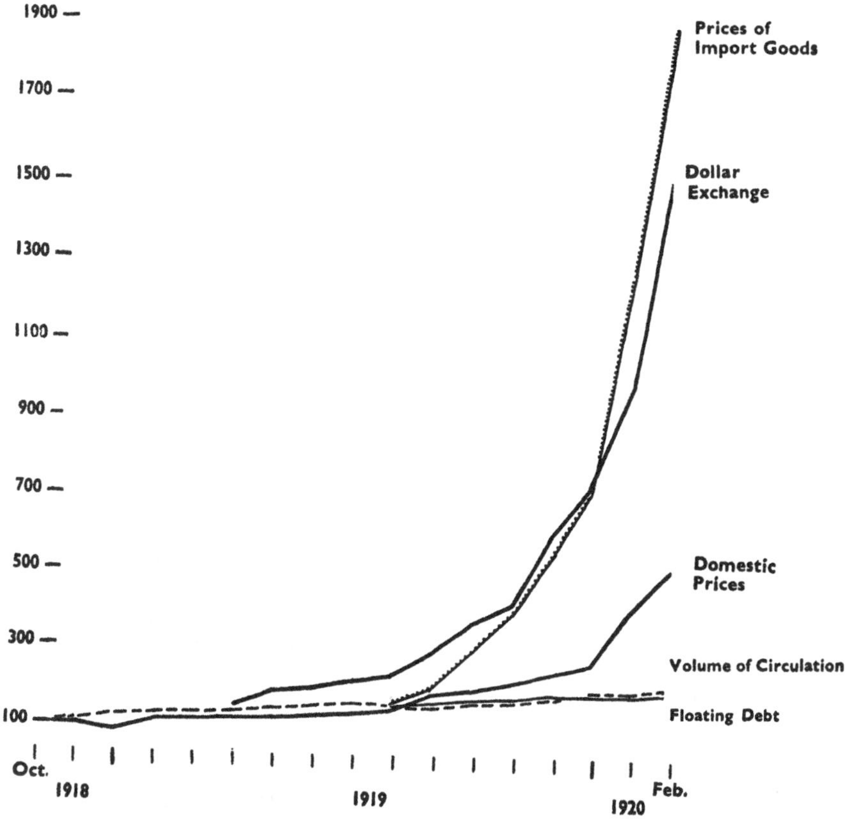


DIAGRAM III.—Basis of all curves: October 1918 = 100

curves. The curve of internal prices follows, but at some distance. Still less rapid was the increase of the circulation and of the floating debt. (Diagram III.)

In February 1920 the dollar rate was 23·6 times the former parity. As for prices, even in August 1919 the measure of the increase was still nearly equal for the home-produced goods and for those imported (4·24 and 4·29 respectively; 1913=1); but from August onwards the prices of imported goods underwent a rapid increase (relatively to the increase in the outside world) which carried the index number to 40·63 in February 1920; while in the meantime the index number of home-produced goods rose to 12·10 (1913=1).

TABLE III

| | *Internal prices* | *Prices of imported goods* | *Circulation* | *Floating debt* | *Dollar rate* |
|---|---|---|---|---|---|
| October 1918 .. | 100 | 100 | 100 | 100 | 100 |
| August 1919.. .. | 177·4 | 200·5 | 153·2 | 162·2 | 285·3 |
| September 1919 .. | 194·6 | 288·8 | 158·4 | 167·2 | 365·0 |
| October 1919 .. | 210·5 | 383·6 | 162·5 | 172·8 | 407·0 |
| November 1919 .. | 235·6 | 543·0 | 170·0 | 176·8 | 580·9 |
| December 1919 .. | 264·9 | 704·7 | 188·0 | 179·3 | 709·6 |
| January 1920 .. | 402·1 | 1,276·1 | 191·4 | 183·2 | 980·9 |
| February 1920 .. | 506·3 | 1,898·5 | 203·9 | 184·6 | 1,503·2 |

The total index number of wholesale prices in February 1920 was 16·85 times that of 1913. The Statistical Bureau of the Reich calculated, for the first time, for February 1920 an index number of the cost of living: 8·47 (1913=1) was the result.

### V. FROM FEBRUARY 1920 TO THE ACCEPTANCE OF THE ULTIMATUM OF LONDON

**5.** In the next period (February 1920–May 1921) at first a rapid improvement of the dollar rate showed itself; later there was once

TABLE IV

| | *Circulation* | *Dollar rate* | *Internal prices* | *Prices of imported goods* | *Cost of living (food)* | *Floating debt* |
|---|---|---|---|---|---|---|
| February 1920.. | 100 | 100 | 100 | 100 | 100 | 100 |
| March 1920 .. | 109·5 | 84·6 | 103·1 | 98·8 | 116·1 | 102·9 |
| April 1920 .. | 114·6 | 60·2 | 98·5 | 84·7 | 129·6 | 106·9 |
| May 1920 .. | 118·0 | 46·9 | 106·9 | 63·6 | 139·5 | 114·2 |
| June 1920 .. | 125·4 | 39·5 | 102·1 | 52·1 | 135·0 | 127·2 |
| July 1920 .. | 128·2 | 39·8 | 104·1 | 46·7 | 133·7 | 137·9 |
| August 1920 .. | 133·0 | 48·2 | 110·1 | 50·2 | 123·4 | 145·4 |
| September 1920 | 139·2 | 58·5 | 111·8 | 54·8 | 123·0 | 155·4 |
| October 1920 .. | 142·1 | 68·8 | 106·9 | 57·3 | 133·9 | 158·0 |
| November 1920 | 142·2 | 77·9 | 110·7 | 58·1 | 141·7 | 165·0 |
| December 1920 | 149·9 | 73·6 | 109·3 | 49·8 | 150·5 | 171·7 |
| January 1921 .. | 144·7 | 65·5 | 112·6 | 44·9 | 150·1 | 174·7 |
| February 1921.. | 147·1 | 61·9 | 109·1 | 40·9 | 143·7 | 181·8 |
| March 1921 .. | 147·7 | 63·0 | 105·9 | 39·7 | 142·6 | 187·0 |
| April 1921 .. | 149·1 | 64·1 | 105·8 | 38·4 | 140·7 | 194·0 |
| May 1921 .. | 150·1 | 62·8 | 104·6 | 37·5 | 139·2 | 198·5 |

again a progressive depreciation. But in May 1921 the dollar rate was still below the level which it had attained in February 1920. The prices of imported goods diminished considerably (a marked fall of prices took place in that period in the outside world). On the other hand,

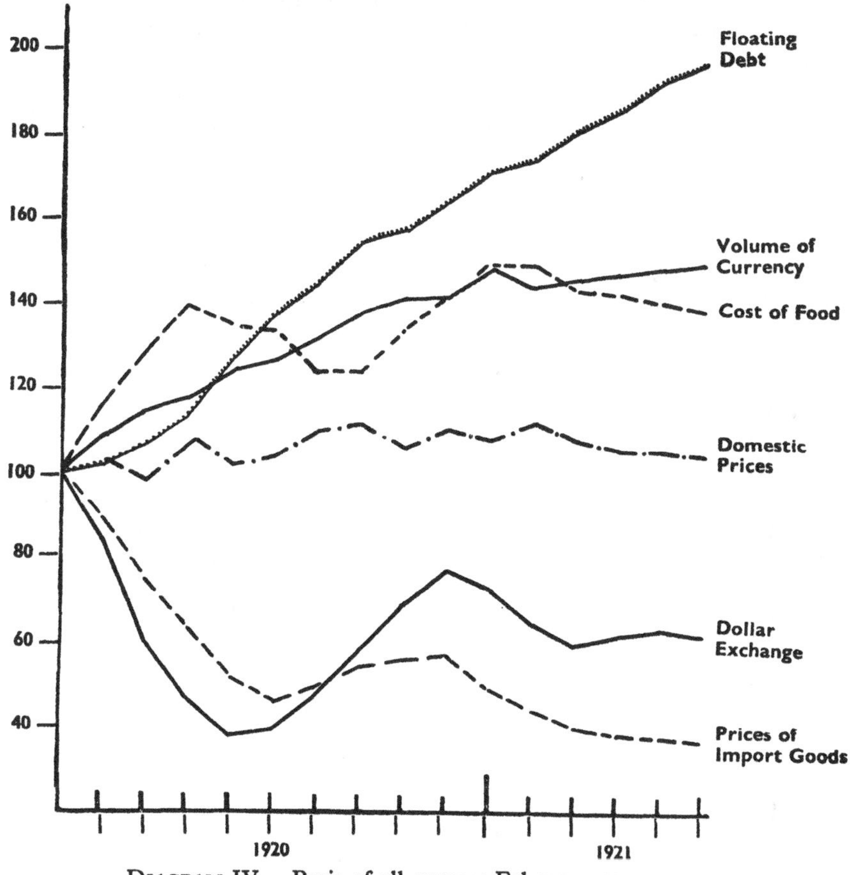


DIAGRAM IV.—Basis of all curves: February 1920 = 100

the increase of the floating debt was enormous (from 89 to 176·6 milliards) and so consequently was that of the circulation (from 54,456 millions to 81,735 millions). Internal wholesale prices were maintained at a fairly constant level; but the cost of living rose appreciably.

Diagram IV shows that in the period under examination the relative positions of the various curves were on the whole different from those which we have found in the preceding period. That of the floating debt rose much more rapidly than the other curves. The curves of circulation, of the cost of living, and of internal prices, followed. They continued to lag behind the prices of imported goods and the dollar rate. In May 1921 the dollar rate had risen to 14·83 times that of 1913; the complete index number of wholesale prices to 13·08 (imported goods 15·23; home-produced goods 12·66); the index number of the cost of food to 13·20. Once more was established an approximation to equilibrium between the purchasing power of the paper mark in Germany and its purchasing power abroad.

## IV. FROM MAY 1921 TO JULY 1922

**6**. In the months between May 1921 and July 1922 once more the various phenomena examined present some characteristic aspects

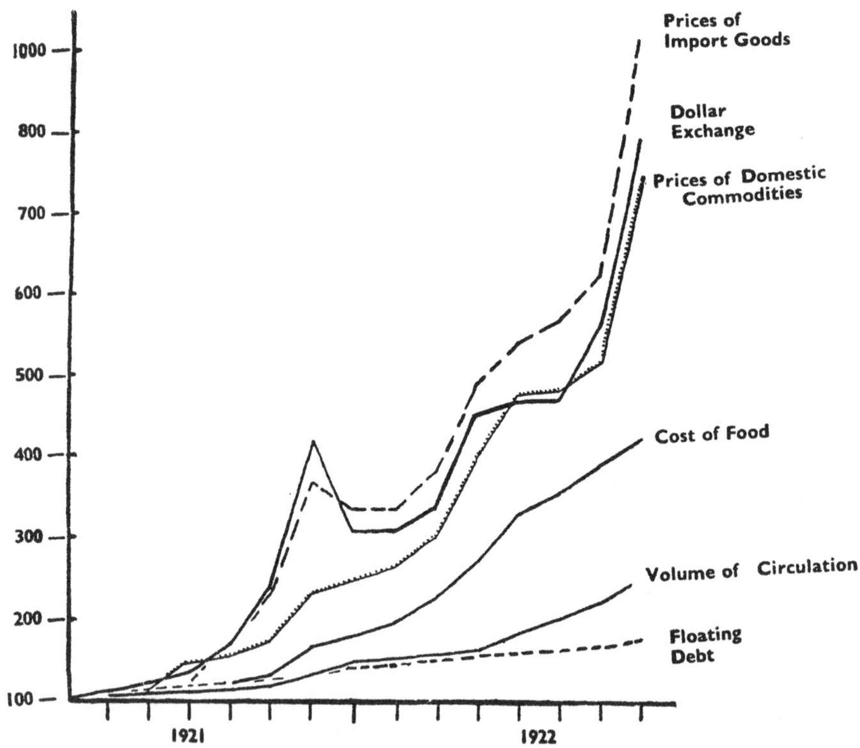


DIAGRAM V.—Basis of all curves: May 1921 = 100

which were different from those observed in the preceding period (see Diagram v).

TABLE V

| | *Circulation* | *Dollar rate* | *Internal prices* | *Prices of imported goods* | *Cost of living (food)* | *Floating debt* |
|---|---|---|---|---|---|---|
| May 1921 .. | 100 | 100 | 100 | 100 | 100 | 100 |
| June 1921 .. | 103·9 | 111·3 | 104·3 | 104·7 | 103·8 | 104·8 |
| July 1921 .. | 106·0 | 123·1 | 108·1 | 113·0 | 113·0 | 108·1 |
| August 1921 .. | 108·7 | 135·3 | 151·1 | 127·1 | 120·4 | 114·8 |
| September 1921 | 116·1 | 168·4 | 154·2 | 173·5 | 122·3 | 119·1 |
| October 1921 .. | 122·0 | 241·1 | 176·5 | 235·4 | 133·1 | 123·4 |
| November 1921 | 133·5 | 422·4 | 234·4 | 371·8 | 165·8 | 128·3 |
| December 1921 | 150·4 | 308·3 | 250·4 | 333·0 | 178·6 | 139·8 |
| January 1922 .. | 152·2 | 308·1 | 267·2 | 333·2 | 186·6 | 144·8 |
| February 1922 .. | 157·8 | 333·9 | 297·2 | 380·8 | 228·8 | 148·8 |
| March 1922 .. | 164·4 | 456·5 | 397·1 | 490·0 | 272·9 | 154·0 |
| April 1922 .. | 184·4 | 467·4 | 472·7 | 538·6 | 330·0 | 159·1 |
| May 1922 .. | 198·8 | 466·0 | 476·0 | 565·8 | 354·5 | 163·8 |
| June 1922 .. | 221·1 | 509·9 | 516·6 | 622·4 | 387·8 | 167·1 |
| July 1922 .. | 248·6 | 792·2 | 734·6 | 909·7 | 517·9 | 174·3 |

The most rapid increase was shown in the dollar rate and in the prices of imported goods. Internal wholesale prices followed, and especially from February 1922 they showed a tendency to adapt themselves to the dollar rate much more rapidly than was the case in the preceding period. The index number of the cost of living still lagged much behind; still more slowly the circulation and the floating debt increased. At this point the following facts deserve to be emphasized: in March 1922 the two curves of the circulation and of the floating debt, which till then had almost coincided, commenced to diverge from one another, and henceforth the circulation increased more rapidly than the floating debt. That is probably explained by the fact that in 1922 the Reichsbank considerably increased the circulation by commercial loans.

## VII. JULY 1922 TO JUNE 1923

7. The following table and Diagram VI show the behaviour of the various indices from July 1922 to June 1923. A tendency of the dollar rate to anticipate the movement of internal prices is frequently apparent. But the sensitiveness of internal wholesale prices as well as of the cost of living is more marked than in the preceding periods; and when, for a short time, the rise in the dollar rate was arrested (e.g. in the months of March and April 1923), the index numbers of internal

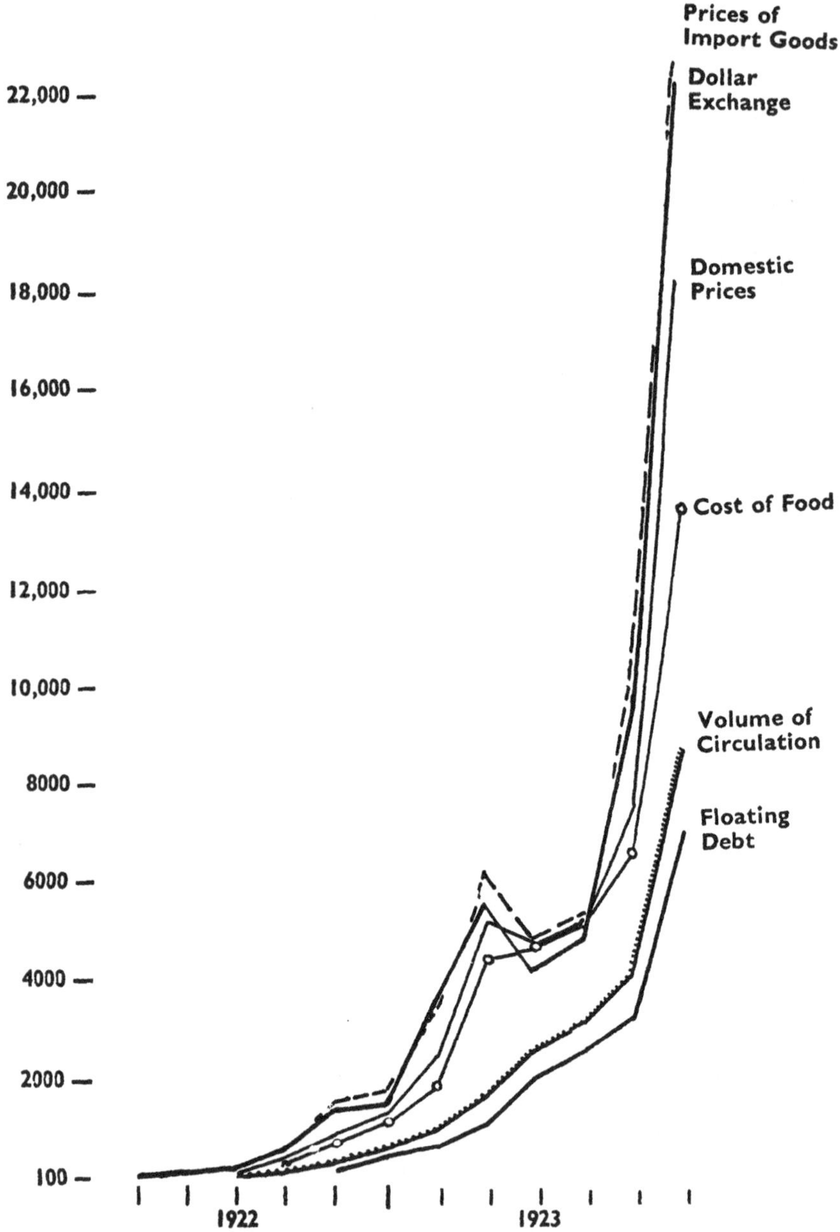


DIAGRAM VI.—Basis of all curves: July 1922 = 100

prices and the cost of living overtook and surpassed the index number of the dollar rate. After April 1923 the dollar rate again rose rapidly, leaving behind the index numbers of internal prices and of the cost of living. Throughout this period the floating debt and the circulation showed a continuous increase, as also in the period in which the dollar rate was stable. But over the year as a whole the circulation increased less than did prices.

TABLE VI

| | *Dollar rate* | *Internal prices* | *Prices of imported goods* | *Cost of living (food)* | *Circulation* | *Floating debt* |
|---|---|---|---|---|---|---|
| July 1922 .. | 100 | 100 | 100 | 100 | 100 | 100 |
| August 1922 .. | 230 | 177 | 234 | 143 | 124 | 108 |
| September 1922 | 297 | 276 | 311 | 225 | 164 | 146 |
| October 1922 .. | 645 | 533 | 652 | 389 | 238 | 196 |
| November 1922 | 1,456 | 1,018 | 1,545 | 804 | 379 | 272 |
| December 1922 | 1,539 | 1,371 | 1,756 | 1,180 | 637 | 485 |
| January 1923 .. | 3,644 | 2,553 | 3,420 | 1,998 | 984 | 676 |
| February 1923 | 5,661 | 5,280 | 6,349 | 4,656 | 1,741 | 1,165 |
| March 1923 .. | 4,297 | 4,811 | 4,920 | 4,849 | 2,727 | 2,143 |
| April 1923 .. | 4,959 | 5,087 | 5,389 | 5,120 | 3,250 | 2,741 |
| May 1923 .. | 9,665 | 7,569 | 9,817 | 6,758 | 4,223 | 3,336 |
| June 1923 .. | 22,301 | 18,194 | 22,496 | 13,673 | 8,557 | 7,149 |

## VIII. JUNE 1923 TO THE INTRODUCTION OF THE RENTENMARK

**8.** In the months which preceded the monetary reform the depreciation of the mark was so rapid that it is necessary to set the graphical representations on a logarithmic scale. Common use of these graphical representations, formerly to be found only in manuals of statistics, and regarded almost as curiosities, is due to the depreciation of the mark. The Statistical Bureau of the Reich made great use of them.

TABLE VII

| 1923 | *Prices of imported goods* (1913 = 1) (*Thousands*) | *Internal prices* (1913 = 1) (*Thousands*) | *Cost of living** (1913 = 1) (*Thousands*) |
|---|---|---|---|
| July 31st .. .. | 297 | 161 | 39 |
| August 7th .. .. | 855 | 409 | 71 |
| August 14th .. .. | 833 | 630 | 150 |
| August 21st .. .. | 1,575 | 1,180 | 437 |
| August 28th .. .. | 1,840 | 1,666 | 754 |

[continued

* Index number of the total cost of living.

TABLE VII—*continued*

| 1923 | *Prices of imported goods* (1913 = 1) (*Millions*) | *Internal prices* (1913 = 1) (*Millions*) | *Cost of living** (1913 = 1) (*Millions*) |
|---|---|---|---|
| September 4th .. | 3·8 | 2·8 | 1·2 |
| September 11th .. | 20·8 | 9·7 | 1·8 |
| September 18th .. | 49·5 | 33·3 | 6·1 |
| September 25th .. | 44·2 | 34·6 | 14·2 |
| October 2nd .. .. | 110·0 | 79·4 | 28·0 |
| October 9th .. .. | 395·9 | 289·8 | 40·4 |
| | (*Milliards*) | (*Milliards*) | |
| October 16th .. .. | 1·5 | 1·0 | 109·1 |
| October 23rd .. .. | 19·4 | 13·6 | 691·9 |
| | | | (*Milliards*) |
| October 30th .. .. | 23·6 | 17·7 | 3·0 |
| November 5th .. | 155·8 | 123·6 | 13·7 |
| November 13th .. | 305·0 | 257·8 | 98·5 |
| November 20th .. | 1,608·8 | 1,374·4 | 218·5 |
| November 27th .. | 1,627·0 | 1,382·0 | 792·8 |
| December 4th .. | 1,620·0 | 1,280·0 | 1,535·0 |
| December 11th .. | 1,557·0 | 1,217·0 | 1,515·0 |
| December 18th .. | 1,593·0 | 1,174·0 | 1,244·0 |
| December 27th .. | 1,577·0 | 1,125·0 | 1,200·0 |

| 1923 | *Dollar rate* (1913 = 1) (*Thousands*) | *Circulation* (*Billions*)† | *Treasury Bonds* (*Billions*) |
|---|---|---|---|
| July 31st .. .. | 262 | 43·6 | 55·7 |
| August 7th .. .. | 786 | 62·3 | 85·1 |
| August 15th .. .. | 643 | 116·4 | 194·2 |
| August 23rd .. .. | 1,210 | 273·9 | 587·0 |
| August 31st .. .. | 2,454 | 663·2 | 1,196·3 |
| | (*Millions*) | | |
| September 7th .. | 12·6 | 1,182·0 | 1,800·8 |
| September 15th .. | 21·5 | 3,183·7 | 3,984·4 |
| September 22nd .. | 26·2 | 8,627·7 | 12,379·6 |
| September 29th .. | 38·1 | 28,228·8 | 46,716·6 |
| October 5th .. .. | 142·9 | 46,933·0 | 73,450·7 |
| October 15th .. .. | 895·7 | 123,349·8 | 170,181·6 |
| | (*Milliards*) | | |
| October 23rd .. .. | 13·3 | 524,330·6 | 690,674·3 |
| | | (*Trillions*) | (*Trillions*) |
| October 31st .. .. | 17·3 | 2·5 | 6·9 |
| November 7th .. | 150·0 | 19·2 | 27·5 |
| November 15th .. | 600·0 | 92·8 | 191·6 |
| November 20th .. | 1,000·0 | — | — |

* Index number of the total cost of living.

† A billion = $1{,}000{,}000^2$; a trillion = $1{,}000{,}000^3$.

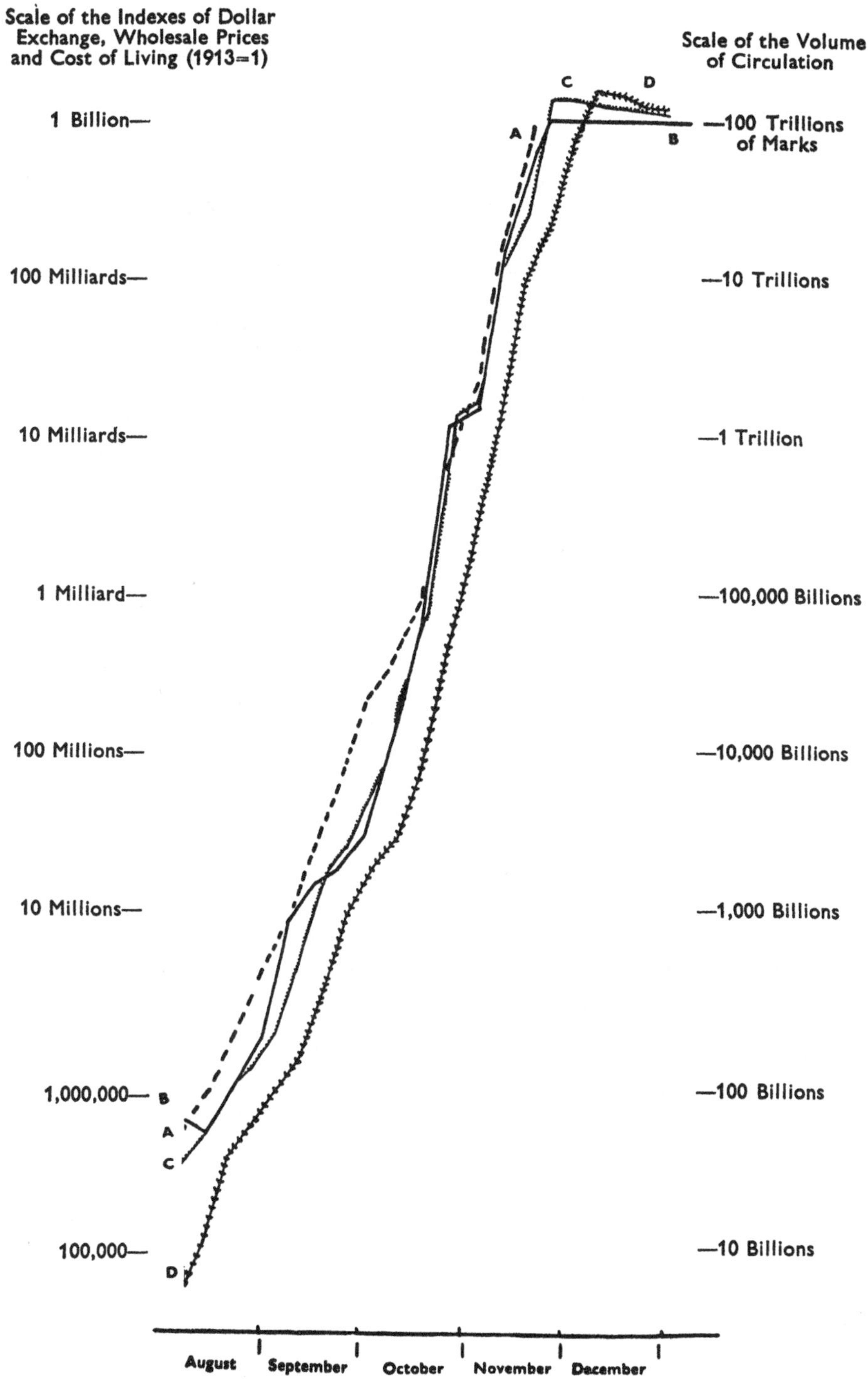


Diagram VII.—A = volume of circulation B = dollar exchange
C = domestic prices D = cost of living

These tables and Diagram VII show that in the last months of inflation a very close mutual dependence was established between the quantity of notes in circulation, the dollar rate, wholesale prices, and the cost of living. All the curves move in the same direction, forming a single group and clearly showing the tendency to reciprocal adaptation. The contrast between this diagram and Diagrams I–V, in which the various curves are disposed to spread fanwise, is obvious.

The increase of the dollar rate, having immediate repercussions on prices (and also on salaries and wages), stimulated the increase of the floating debt and of note-issues, and the torrent of new paper which proceeded uninterruptedly from the Reichsbank was, in turn, the cause of a further depreciation of the exchange rate. In that last phase of the depreciation of the German mark internal wholesale prices increased more rapidly than external prices and the dollar rate; so that on November 20th—the day on which the definite fixing of the dollar rate at 4,200 milliards of paper marks closed the story of the depreciation of the mark—the index of internal wholesale prices was 1,374 milliards, whilst the index of the dollar rate was 1,000 milliards. In the succeeding days the index of the cost of living rose to 1,535 milliards.

## IX. SUMMARY OF EXCHANGE RATES AND PRICES FROM 1914 TO 1923

**9.** Diagram VIII allows us to glance at the whole movement of the paper mark in terms of gold from 1914 to 1923. This diagram represents summarily the phases through which the German mark successively passed: slow depreciation during the years of the World War; rapid diminution of value during 1919; and relative stability, till the second half of 1921. Throughout this period the movement of the mark exchange was analogous to that of the other principal European exchanges, save for a greater amplitude of fluctuation. The Italian lira, for example, which after the end of the war was still kept at 80 per cent of its pre-war value in terms of the dollar, was scarcely worth 18 per cent of the gold parity in December 1920. But from the second half of 1921 onwards the curve of the mark was clearly detached from the group of the other principal European currencies. The German mark, the Austrian crown, the Hungarian crown, and the Polish mark formed a separate group. After the collapse of the autumn of 1921 the depreciation of the German mark became even more rapid. Diagram VIII—which is on a logarithmic scale—shows that from the end of 1921 onwards the rapidity of the depreciation of the mark was continually increasing.

**10.** Past experiences invariably show that the increase of the quantity of paper money provokes a diminution of the purchasing power of the money; not uniformly, but in varying degrees according to the various kinds of goods, services or productive resources exchanged for money.*

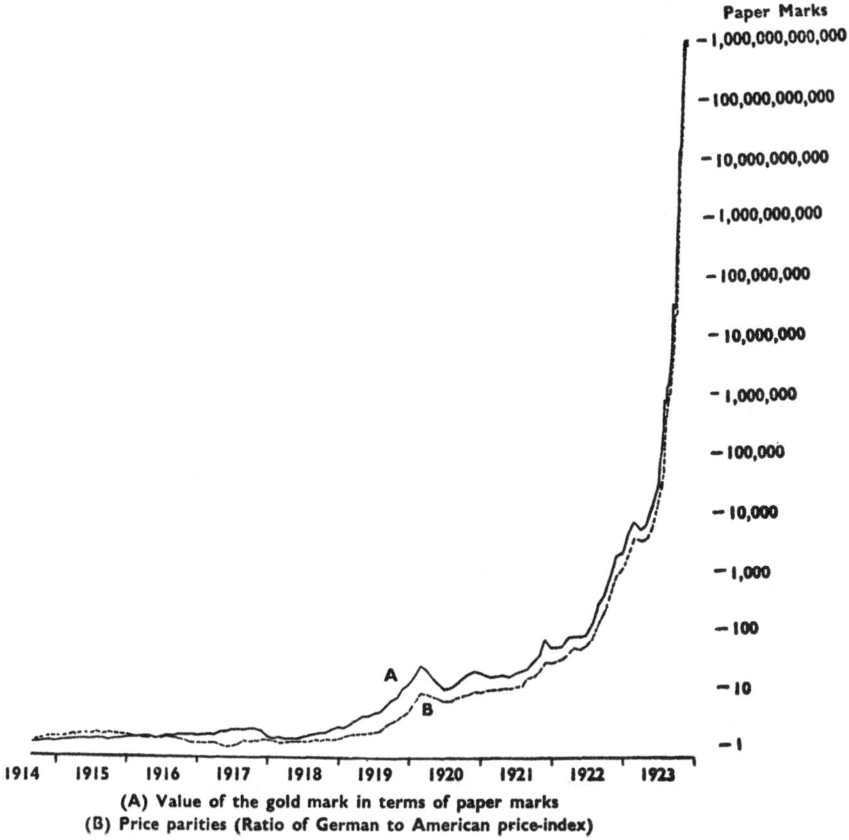


DIAGRAM VIII

In this matter the scale of depreciation which was compiled in 1864 by an American author for the greenbacks is of interest.† Supposing

* On the fluctuations of the different categories of prices in following the variations of the purchasing power of money *see* Mortara, "Effetti delle variazioni del potere d'acquisto dell'oro" (*Giornale degli Economisti*, 1931).

† Delmer, *The Great Paper Bubble*, 1864 (quoted by Hock, *Die Finanzen und die Finanzgeschichte der Vereinigten Staaten*, Stuttgart, 1867, p. 572).

the various prices equal to 100 before the inflation, they (expressed in paper money) were increased in the following manner:

| | |
|---|---|
| Stipend for intellectual work | 110 |
| Wages of unskilled operatives | 120 |
| Wages of skilled operatives | 130 |
| Land | 140 |
| Hand-made articles | 150 |
| Machine-made articles | 160 |
| Articles for direct consumption | 160 |
| Raw materials | 170 |
| Securities redeemable in paper | 180 |
| Securities redeemable in gold | 190 |
| Precious metals | 200 |

In Germany the increase of prices expressed in paper marks was most unequal in the various categories of economic goods. In Diagram IX I have represented the movement of certain characteristic prices. Since the graphical representation of prices expressed in paper marks could not be of much use, I have preferred to indicate the movement of prices converted into gold according to the dollar rate. These prices have been extracted from the official German publications.

The various curves of Diagram IX indicate: (*a*) The index number of prices in the outside world (as representative of these prices the index number compiled by the Bureau of Labour of the United States has been used); (*b*) the index number of wholesale prices in Germany; (*c*) the index number of the cost of living in Germany (i.e. cost of food; the official index number was first published, as I have already recorded, at the beginning of February 1920); (*d*) the index number of the real wages of miners; (*e*) the index number of the prices of the principal industrial and banking shares.

The diagram allows us to realize certain fundamental facts which characterized the German economy during the inflation and which will be amply illustrated in the succeeding chapters. Such are the divergence between the purchasing power of the mark in terms of foreign goods and its purchasing power in Germany; the great variability of German prices; the depression of real wages during the whole period of inflation; and the enormous diminution in the prices of industrial shares.

The level of the various curves has been supposed equal to 100 in 1913. The diagram shows clearly how the inflation provoked disequilibrium in the economic system, the various elements in the latter being disturbed in unequal measure.

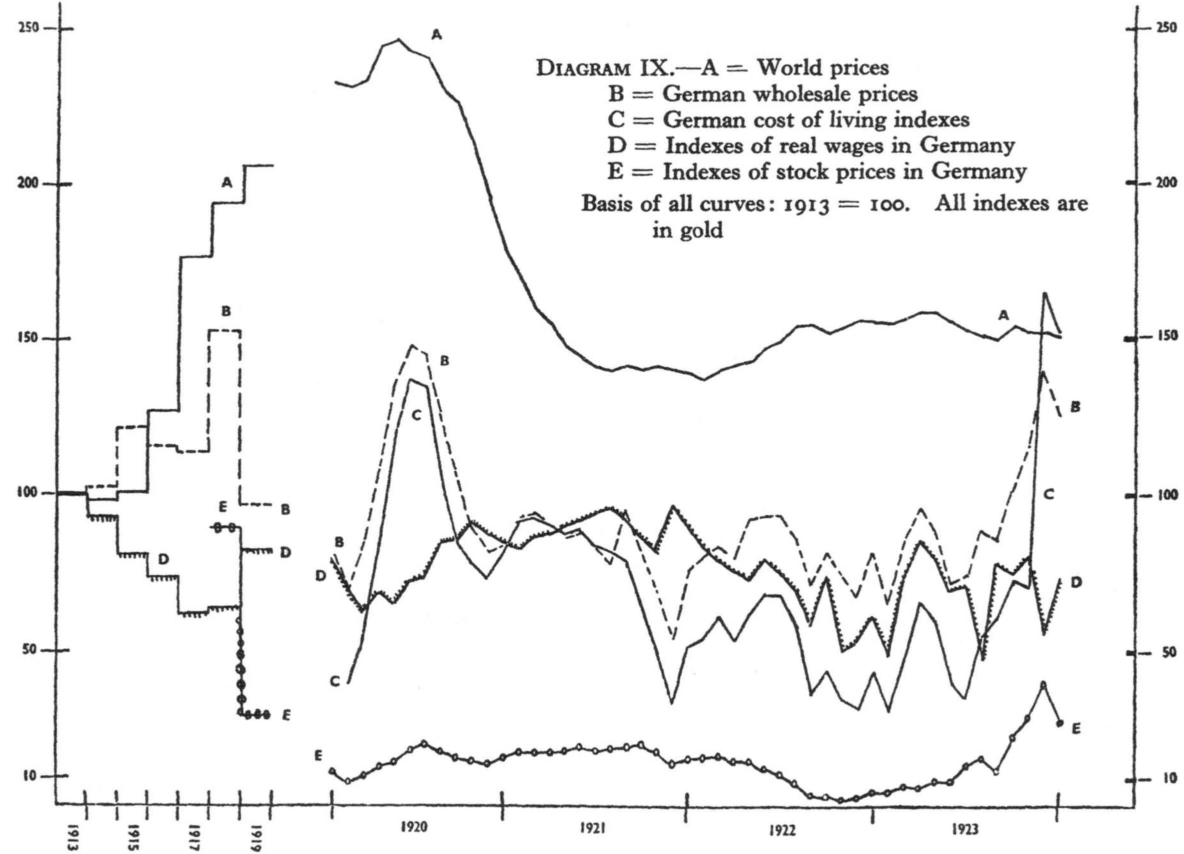


Diagram IX.—A = World prices
B = German wholesale prices
C = German cost of living indexes
D = Indexes of real wages in Germany
E = Indexes of stock prices in Germany
Basis of all curves: 1913 = 100. All indexes are in gold

B*

# CHAPTER II

# The National Finances, the Inflation and the Depreciation of the Mark*

## PART I

### I. THE HELFFERICH EXPLANATION OF THE DEPRECIATION OF THE MARK

**1.** The discussions provoked by the depreciation of the mark in Germany during the decade 1914–1923, present an interesting resemblance to the controversies in England in the years which preceded the publication of the Bullion Report. Throughout the period of the inflation the theory held by the Reichsbank, by successive German Governments, by the great bankers, by great industrialists, by German officials, and by a great part of the Press, was that the depreciation of the mark was caused by the state of the balance of payments. During the war Germany had a "passive" balance because of excess imports over exports; later it was accentuated by the effects of the payment of reparations and of the other burdens imposed by the Treaty of Versailles.

It would be exaggerating to affirm that this was also the point of view of all the German economists. Some of them, as Liefmann, Schlesinger, Pohle, Beckerath, Terhalle, and Lansburgh, clearly recognized the influence of the paper inflation on internal prices and on the exchange rate. But others refused to admit a relation of cause and effect between the increase of the quantity of paper money and the depreciation of the exchange, and they adhered to the "theory of the balance of payments."† This mental attitude, contrary to quantitative monetary conceptions, was the effect of the line of thought which was prevalent before the war, and which preferred that type of monetary approach which Altmann called "Qualitative" as opposed to the quantitative.‡ Writers were attempting to construct a "sociological"

* Originally published in *Economia*, 1924.

† According to Diehl (*Über Fragen des Geldwesens und der Valuta*, second edition, 1921, p. 63), "the theory of Liefmann, according to which the exchanges are in close relation to internal prices, has not been sustained lately; indeed, this conception has been decidedly discredited."

‡ In the volume *Die Entwicklung der deutschen Volkswirtschaftslehre im XIX. Jahrhundert*, 1928, vi, p. 4.

conception of money. Under the influence of these views, as opposed to the quantitative theory, such economists stressed the movement of the value of money as an "historical process," which is not simply a matter of comparing flows of money and of goods, but which demands the comprehension of the entire complicated economic structure. To this was added the influence of the work of Knapp, who diverted German studies from the analysis of the quantitative relations between money, prices, and exchange rates.

Dalberg* claims to have been the first to introduce into the post-1914 literature about monetary problems the theory that the diminution of value suffered by a currency in the internal market is the determining factor of the movement of the exchanges, i.e. of the "external value" of that money. In making this claim Dalberg disputes that of Liefmann, who had claimed that he himself first introduced this theory into Germany, though he did not claim to be the originator of the theory—the relation existing between "internal value" and "external value" being well known outside Germany. "The recognition of this relation," continues the same author, "has a decisive importance. The scientific value of all the publications of the first three years of the war is doubtful, for those works take no account of this relation; ignorance of it explains, moreover, many errors or omissions in German monetary policy."

2. To a great number of writers and German politicians the deficits in the budgets of the Reich and of the States, and the paper inflation, were not the cause, but the consequence of the external depreciation of the mark.†

* *Die Entwertung des Geldes*, second edition, 1919, p. 93.

† During the discussions of the "Commission on Socialization" (see *Verhandlungen der Sozialisierungskommission*, 1921, vol. i, pp. 148 and following) a great diversity of opinions about the causes of the depreciation of the mark was manifested. The following are typical opinions:

BERNHARD (Director of the *Vossiche Zeitung*): "If we had an active balance of payments it would be a matter of indifference whether the accounts of the State showed a deficit or no, as it would also be a matter of indifference whether this deficit were covered by loans or by an increase in the floating debt or by any other means."

EULENBERG: "A balancing of the Budget is entirely impossible as the exchange varies in the proportions which we see. First stabilization of the exchange and then stabilization of the national finances. There is no sense in wishing to take the Budget and its balancing as a starting-point."

DIETZEL: "I cannot but contradict the affirmations of my colleague Eulenburg. It is true that the disequilibrium of the balance of payments has an influence on the level of internal prices. But at the same time it is true that some price variations are entirely independent of this and are due to the forced issue of paper into the channels

The most authoritative representative of this theory is Helfferich, who expounded it in the sixth edition of his work *Das Geld* (Leipzig, 1923).

The increase of the circulation [affirms Helfferich] has not preceded the rise of prices and the depreciation of the exchange, but it followed slowly and at great distance. The circulation increased from May 1921 to the end of January 1923 by 23 times; it is not possible that this increase had caused the rise in the prices of imported goods and of the dollar, which in that period increased by 344 times.

That the collapse of the exchange rate was entirely disproportionate to the increase of the circulation also appears from the following argument: The circulation of the Reichsbank of January 24th, 1923, represented a value in paper marks of 1,654 milliards, but in gold only 330 millions; that is, no more than a twentieth of the value of the circulation in the period preceding the war. . . . It is not to be doubted . . . that the increase of the circulation did not even distantly keep pace with the depreciation of the mark abroad. The theory, according to which the inflation is the cause of the depreciation of the German mark, is based on the *petitio principi* that the external value of money (expressed by the foreign exchange rate) can only be determined by the quantity of paper money.

Now in the present case the causes of the collapse of the money are independent of the conditions of the paper circulation. These causes are obvious; on a country whose balance of payments was passive by about three milliards of gold marks, there was imposed the burden of the reparations bill, amounting annually to about 3·3 milliards of gold marks; to that was added the payments for the redemption of short-term debts; for the costs of occupation, etc., etc.

of circulation. And this issue is in turn due in a great part to the fact that we, up to now, have been unable to satisfy the needs of the Reich by taxation; for example, the need of money for the wages of railwaymen, which are enormously increased. The value of the paper mark depends on the quantity circulating at home: the home value as well as the foreign value. Until the Budget is balanced stabilization of the exchange remains simply impossible."

EULENBERG: "I believe that we need a larger quantity of notes and a bigger floating debt, because we have very high prices."

HILFERDING: "The conception of Bernhard, which holds possible a stabilization of the exchange in spite of the continuation of the unbalanced National Accounts and of the issues, is purely theoretical. It is an economic impossibility. For with the increase of the issues the balance of trade necessarily becomes passive. In effect, the issues increased internal prices, and that stimulated imports and impeded exports."

BERNHARD: "The primary phenomenon is the situation of the balance of payments. The moment we have an active balance, the internal value of money is entirely independent of the valuation which is given it abroad. The moment the demand in the foreign exchange market for the currency of a country surpasses the supply the question of the internal value of the money of that country comes no longer into consideration."

In Eucken's book, *Kritische Betrachtungen zum deutschen Geldproblem* (1923), the theory, according to which the depreciation of the mark was due to the disequilibrium of the balance of payments, is subjected to a sharp criticism.

According to Helfferich, the concatenation of the facts is as follows:

The depreciation of the German mark in terms of foreign currencies was caused by the excessive burdens thrust on to Germany and by the policy of violence adopted by France; the increase of the prices of all imported goods was caused by the depreciation of the exchanges; then followed the general increase of internal prices and of wages, the increased need for means of circulation on the part of the public and of the State, greater demands on the Reichsbank by private business and the State and the increase of the paper mark issues. Contrary to the widely held conception, *not inflation but the depreciation of the mark was the beginning of this chain of cause and effect*; inflation is not the cause of the increase of prices and of the depreciation of the mark; but the depreciation of the mark is the cause of the increase of prices and of the paper mark issues. The decomposition of the German monetary system has been the primary and decisive cause of the financial collapse.*

**3.** The ideas expressed by Helfferich were also common in the German Press.† The following opinions which were expressed by an authoritative periodical towards the end of 1922 are characteristic:

Since the summer of 1921 the foreign exchange rate has lost all connection with the internal inflation. The increase of the floating debt, which represents the creation by the State of new purchasing-power, follows at some distance the depreciation of the mark. . . . Furthermore, the level of internal prices is not determined by the paper inflation or credit inflation, but exclusively by the depreciation of the mark in terms of foreign currencies. . . . To tell the truth, the astonishing thing is not the great quantity but the small quantity of money which circulates in Germany, a quantity extraordinarily small from a relative point of view; even more surprising is it that the floating debt has not increased much more rapidly.

The theory formulated in German official circles, to explain the causes of the depreciation of the mark, is expounded with clarity also in the following passage from a memorandum of the Central Statistical Office.‡ "The fundamental cause of the dislocation of the German monetary system is the disequilibrium of the balance of payments. The disturbance of the national finances and the inflation are in their turn the consequences of the depreciation of the currency. The depreciation of the currency upset the Budget balance, and determined with an *inevitable necessity* a divergence between income and expenditure, which provoked the upheaval."

The conviction, so widely held, that the depreciation of the mark

* See also the article by Helfferich, "Das deutsche Finanzwesen," in *Börsen-Courier*, February 24th, 1924.

† An exception was the *Frankfurter Zeitung*, which always contested the policy of inflation.

‡ *Deutschlands Wirtschaftslage*, March 1923, p. 24.

was only the expression of the disequilibrium of the balance of payments for a long time prevented any serious consideration of monetary reform.

In the congress of German bankers which took place in September 1920, Warburg maintained that the exchange was the expression of the depressed economic, financial, and social conditions of Germany, and that an improvement (or a stabilization) of the exchange could not be achieved until the general situation had been improved from this threefold point of view. Until then every measure of monetary policy would be ineffectual.

In July 1922 the Minister of National Economy elaborated a project for monetary reform which, it was hoped, would have resulted in the stabilization of the exchange. But the project was not carried through, because of the opposition of the Reichsbank. During 1922 the management of the Reichsbank tenaciously refused to allow the gold reserve to be used for monetary reform. At the meeting on August 28th, 1922, of the Central Committee of the Reichsbank, Havenstein, the president, categorically stated that it was not possible to make even an attempt at the stabilization of the exchange while the principal cause of the German crisis remained, that is until Germany succeeded in obtaining a moratorium and a tolerable solution of the reparations question. Havenstein alluded to the failure of the recent intervention of the Reichsbank in the exchange market; 230 millions of foreign exchange had been uselessly sacrificed without the Reichsbank having succeeded in preventing the continued depreciation of the exchange. But Havenstein did not add that the action of the Reichsbank must necessarily be fruitless if at the same time it continued to issue new paper money.

Also in November 1922, after a committee of foreign experts called in by the German Government had declared the stabilization of the German exchange to be possible under certain conditions, the Reichsbank stuck firmly to its theory, according to which it was useless to attempt monetary reform. Fatalistic ideas dominated the governing circles. Once more I quote the opinion of Helfferich: "Inflation and the collapse of the exchange are children of the same parent: the impossibility of paying the tributes imposed on us. The problem of restoring the circulation is not a technical or banking problem; it is, in the last analysis, the problem of the equilibrium between the burden and the capacity of the German economy for supporting this burden."*

Opposed to the German theories were those which can be called the "English" (because vigorously upheld by the representatives of

* "Die Autonomie der Reichsbank" in *Börsen-Courier* of April 4th, 1922.

Great Britain in the Reparations Commission and in the Guarantees Committee) according to which the fundamental cause of the depreciation of the mark was the Budget deficit, which provoked continued issues of paper money. I hold this second theory to be essentially correct, although it is necessary to recognize that in the last stages of the depreciation of the mark the relations between the Budget deficit, the quantity of paper money, prices, and the exchange became more complicated, as we shall see in the course of the present enquiry.

In certain writings of American economists one encounters the influence of the argument advanced by the Germans. For example, according to Professor Williams the causal order of events was the following: "Reparation payments, depreciating exchanges, rising import and export prices, rising domestic prices, consequent budgeting deficits, and at the same time an increased demand for bank credit; and finally increased note-issue."* Commenting on the work of Professor Williams, Professor Angell observed that "The reality of the type of analysis which runs *from* the balance of payments and the exchanges *to* general prices and the increased issue of paper seems to be definitely established."†

## II. THE CONDITIONS OF THE NATIONAL FINANCES DURING THE WAR

**4.** Let us examine, in the light of the facts, the theory according to which the budget deficit was not the fundamental cause but the *effect* of the depreciation of the mark.

In the following table, in millions of marks, the total income and expenditure of the German Reich during the years 1914–1918 are indicated.‡

TABLE VIII

| *Financial years* | *Government expenditure* | *Ordinary and extra-ordinary income* |
|---|---|---|
| 1914 | 9,651 | 8,149 |
| 1915 | 26,689 | 23,207 |
| 1916 | 28,780 | 22,815 |
| 1917 | 53,261 | 35,215 |
| 1918 | 45,514 | 31,590 |
| | 163,894 | 120,976 |

* "German Foreign Trade and the Reparations Payments" (*Quarterly Journal of Economics*, 1922, p. 503).

† *The Theory of International Prices*, 1926, p. 195.

‡ *Statistisches Jahrbuch für das Deutsche Reich*, 1917–1921.

The income figures shown in the preceding table include the proceeds from the war loans, subscriptions to which amounted to about 98 milliards of marks. The result was, therefore, that scarcely one-eighth of the expenditure of the years 1914–18 was covered by ordinary income. The difference between the total expenditure and the total income was covered by means of the issue of Treasury bills. The discounting of the Treasury bills at the Reichsbank provided the channel for an inflation which in part is shown directly in the increase of notes in circulation, and in part remained latent for a certain time.

The method adopted by the German Government for financing the war* consisted in funding the floating debt by means of periodical issues of loans. But already by the autumn of 1916 the failure of the method was becoming patent. From then onwards the sums yielded by the loans were always less than the amount of the floating debt. At the end of September 1918, after the issue of the ninth war loan, the floating debt amounted to 48 milliards of marks.

The circulation was not increased in the same proportion, because about half of the Treasury bills had been taken up by the principal banks, public institutions, or some great private firms. From July 23rd, 1914, to October 31st, 1918, the paper circulation (notes of the Reichsbank and those issued by the Loan Office) was increased by 24·2 millions of paper marks.

**5.** The German Government thought, at first, that the war would be short.† Besides, Helfferich was sure that the conquered enemies would bear the burden of it. Only at the end of 1915 was it resolved to create new sources of ordinary income,‡ but the new taxes were entirely inadequate. The difficulty of increasing the income of the Reich was due also to the particular structure of the German financial system, which was founded on a tripartition of the income between

* Germany's war expenses (Helfferich, *Das Geld*, p. 209):

| | MILLIARDS OF PAPER MARKS | |
|---|---|---|
| *Year of the War* | *Annual total* | *Monthly Average* |
| 1st | 20·1 | 1·7 |
| 2nd | 24·1 | 2·0 |
| 3rd | 34·4 | 2·9 |
| 4th | 46·9 | 3·8 |
| August 1st, 1917–December 31st, 1918 | 21·8 | 4·4 |
| | 147·3 | 2·8 |

† Helfferich, *op. cit.*, p. 212.

‡ For particulars see the admirable book of C. Rist, *Les finances de guerre de l'Allemagne*, Paris, 1921, p. 125.

the Reich, the State, and the Municipalities, which did not provide the Reich with an income capable of being expanded and easily adapted to increasing needs. The defects of the fiscal organization, which lacked, at the centre, a fiscal system of the Reich, to which the fiscal administrations of the separate States ought to be subordinated, exercised a damaging influence on the financial policy of the war and the post-war years.*

If Helfferich affirmed that directly after the outbreak of the war it was necessary to provide, by issues of paper money, for the expenses of mobilization which amounted to two milliards of paper marks, and for the first expenses of the war, one must recognize that in this he was right. The Government would not have been able to finance the first phase of the war with taxes, because of the difficulty of obtaining a sufficient sum by contributions in a few days, nor with loans, because of the tension of the internal financial market.

But we should recognize that the financial policy followed later justified the harsh criticisms to which it was subjected in Germany itself. We may neglect the criticisms of the extreme parties which seem influenced by political passions. Yet eminent personalities of the Conservative parties have not spared the financial policy of the war some severe reproaches. Solmssen, director of the Diskonto-Gesellschaft, affirmed that the whole financial policy, on the base of which Germany conducted the war, was an error.† The German Government neglected to draw from taxation the means for continuing the struggle. The Reichsbank became a pliable instrument in the hands of the Minister of Finance and renounced the functions of a central organ whose business it is to regulate the circulation of the country.‡ The facility of creating the means for covering the expenses made possible a habit of extravagance not only in public finance but also by private persons, whose consumption was not limited by heavy taxes.

The fatal theory dominating governing circles and the Reichsbank,

* As a justification of the financial policy followed by him during the war, Helfferich has observed, in his book, that the ordinary account was balanced during the war. But Helfferich has not said that during the war the normal military expenses were entered in the extraordinary account and perhaps other expenses which ought to have figured in the ordinary account.

† *Das deutsche Finanzwesen nach Beendigung des Weltkriegs*, 1921, p. 8.

‡ Lotz (*Valutafrage und öffentliche Finanzen in Deutschland*, 1923, p. 7) contrasted the German policy with the more energetic financial and banking policy followed by England and France. It is remarkable that the Government did not endeavour to stimulate private investors to acquire Treasury bills; in that way the inflation would have been probably less.

the theory which affirmed that inflation did not exist in Germany and that, at any rate, the depreciation of the mark was not the effect of the increase of the circulating medium, made less acceptable the action which would have effectively bridled the increase of the issues. According to the Reichsbank, although the quantity of paper money in circulation increased, one could not speak of "inflation," because this paper money was covered by a one-third reserve. But this reserve included, besides gold, the notes issued by the "Loan Offices" created in August 1914!

Later the Reichsbank, to diminish the issues of notes, favoured the creation of bank deposits, in the belief that by substituting one form of new purchasing power for another inflation would be limited!

Inverting cause and effect, the Reichsbank indicated in its annual report, as a cause of the increasing issues of paper money, the rise of prices, provoked by the scarcity of goods. Helfferich writes in this connection (*Das Geld*, p. 462):

> The president of the Reichsbank, Havenstein—with whom the author was in continual contact during the years of the war (as Secretary of State to the Treasury and later as Secretary of State for Internal Affairs and representative of the Chancellor in the direction of the Bank)—has always upheld the opinion that one could not speak of inflation, when account was taken of the great quantity of money placed to the account of the military administration and of private firms, of the money circulating in occupied territories and of the increased need, which was due to an increase in prices and salaries independent of monetary conditions.*

**6.** During the war the depreciation of the mark was the consequence of the policy of financing the expenditure of the Reich by having recourse on a very large scale to the central note-issuing authority.†

* Also in "Memoranda on Economic Measures," presented by the Government to the Reichstag, it was maintained that the depreciation of the exchange was an effect of the causes which influenced the balance of payments, and had nothing to do with the diminution of the purchasing power of the mark in the home market. (Prion, *Inflation und Geldenwertung*, 1919, p. 48.) To excuse the Reichsbank it is necessary to add that the same erroneous ideas were also held by the issue banks of neutral countries. During the war, Cassel writes: "The central banks in the neutral countries gave earnest assurance that no depreciation in money was taking place, that the rise in the general price level was due to all other possible causes. . . ." (*Money and Foreign Exchange after 1914*, p. 122).

† Hilferding, *Verhandlungen der Sozialisierungskommission*, vol. ii, p. 228: "From 1914 onwards Germany did nothing serious to finance its expenses—not even after the war. In 1918, 1919, and 1920 we had not increased the Reich's income, instead it had diminished enormously in comparison with peace time; it was natural that the mark should fall."

However, the mark depreciated on the whole slowly during the war years. During the whole of that period monetary and financial phenomena developed according to the classical scheme. Budget deficit, increase of issues, increase of internal prices, i.e. diminution of the purchasing power of the paper money: a diminution which necessarily exercised a depressing influence on the exchange.

I have already noted in Chapter 1 that from 1914 to October 1918 internal prices increased less than the quantity of money existing in Germany. Some circumstances attenuated the influence of the increase of issues on prices (besides the demand for paper marks for circulation in occupied territory),* namely, the increased relative importance of payments in cash, the fact that many hoarded paper money in order to evade taxes or in the hope of an increase in its value after the war, or to have liquid resources in readiness at the coming of peace. It is necessary also to take account of the laws which fixed maximum prices for foodstuffs and for a series of raw or subsidiary materials (the laws of August 4th, 1914, modified by successive orders).

### III. INCOME AND EXPENDITURE OF THE REICH FROM 1919 TO 1923

7. In the months which followed the cessation of hostilities the upheaval of the national finances continued to be the principal cause of the increase of note-issues and of the depreciation of the exchange. In November and December 1918 paper circulation increased by about 6·5 milliards of marks, that is by 24 per cent over the level at the end of October 1918. Very heavy expenses burdened the Reich accounts. They were caused by the very heavy burdens imposed by the conditions of the Armistice, by the expenses of demobilization, by the disorder of all life, political, economic, and social, after the revolution of November 1918, by the maintenance of the unemployed, by the purchase of provisions for the people, and by the extravagances of those who were raised to new authority by the revolution. That phenomenon which Wagner had already affirmed to be the consequence of inflation had appeared, i.e. public administration is the less economical the more unlimited are the resources made available by the creation of new money. Wagner quoted† the following words of Hock in support of this: "Once the deficit has become the dominating feature of the situation and has reached a figure of many millions, all saving of small

* On this, see the observations of Cassel, who holds that this circumstance could only explain a small part of the increase of the circulation (*Money and Foreign Exchange*, etc., p. 41).

† *Russische Papierwährung*, Riga, 1868, p. 29.

amounts seems useless, it is believed that only great reforms could afford salvation and the financial administration is possessed by a spirit of dissipation and neglect."

To this was added the disorganization of the railway administration, of the post-office, and in general of all activities exercised by the State, all of whose accounts showed enormous deficits. Because of the wretched functioning of the bureaucratic machinery, of the decadence of State authority, and of the tenacious opposition of interested parties, taxes yielded little.

It is true that in the conditions existing after the Armistice it would have been difficult to raise by taxation the means necessary for satisfying the needs of the State. A bold financial reform would have been necessary; but the revolutionary Government either had not the courage to resort to decisive measures or it feared that this would have given a very grave shock to the already weakened political and economic structure of Germany. The increase of note-issues seemed the simplest method. It is curious to observe that it was actually a Socialist Government which resorted to the most traditional and unjust form of taxation.

Meanwhile the German people, impoverished by the blockade, felt the necessity of importing great quantities of foodstuffs and raw materials. For this purpose large credits abroad were needed; but the internal political situation was too uncertain, and foreign creditors did not wish to run the grave risk of lending money to these stricken Germans. The Reichsbank ought itself to have guaranteed such loans. But this was not possible, because in accordance with the financial agreement concluded between Germany and the Allies on December 13th, 1919, the Reichsbank had been forbidden to dispose of its gold reserve.*

In default of foreign credits, it was taking up of paper marks voluntarily by foreigners more confident than the Germans themselves in the future of Germany which made possible large purchases in foreign markets. In a certain sense, therefore, it can be admitted that the increase of the paper-money issues aided Germany in surmounting the post-war crisis; but opposed to this advantage what great dangers were involved!

There weighed also on the balance of payments expenditure on the service of debts to foreigners, contracted during the war. According to an estimate of Schacht,† in the two years between the end of 1918

* Elster, *Von der Mark zur Reichsmark*, 1928, p. 110.

† *Die Stabilisierung der Mark*, 1928, p. 25.

and the end of 1920 debts were paid to foreigners amounting to 900 million gold marks.

### IV. THE CAUSES OF THE DEPRECIATION OF THE MARK IN 1919

**8.** In Table I in the Appendix the expenditure and effective income of the Reich and the monthly increase of the floating debt from 1919 to the end of 1923 are shown. Since an examination of the Reich accounts continually adjusted to allow for the variations in the value of the mark cannot lead to any accurate conclusion, I consider that the variations of the floating debt are the best empirical index of the deficit of the Reich.

From the end of October 1918 to the end of March 1919 the floating debt rose by 15·6 milliards of paper marks, equal, according to the monthly average value of the dollar, to 7·741 millions of gold marks.* In the first three months of the 1919 financial year the deficit of the Reich amounted to 3·063 millions of gold marks. Throughout the period to the end of June 1919 the dollar rate constantly rose. But no one could reasonably assert that in that period the enormous deficit was the consequence of the depreciation of the circulating medium; instead it was certainly due to a fundamental defect in the national financial system in which the income was insufficient to cover the expenditure.

The following period, which began in July 1919, is from more aspects interesting for the study of monetary phenomena. In July 1919 the dollar curve, which in the preceding months had already begun to break away from the other curves, suddenly showed a very rapid increase (see Diagram III). The various curves are spread as a fan; the curve of the internal prices rises less than that of the dollar, and the circulation curve less than that of internal prices. The gold mark, which in October 1918 was worth, on the average, 1·57 paper marks, rose to 3·40 paper marks in July 1919; to 10·8 in December of the

* The increase which took place in the separate months may be seen from the following figures:

INCREASE OF FLOATING DEBT

| | *Paper marks* (*Milliards*) | *Gold marks* (*Millions*) |
|---|---|---|
| November 1918 .. | 3·0 | 1·695 |
| December 1918 .. | 4·0 | 2·030 |
| January 1919 .. .. | 3·4 | 1·743 |
| February 1919 .. .. | 3·0 | 1·382 |
| March 1919 .. .. | 2·2 | 0·891 |
| | 15·6 | 7·741 |

same year; and to 23·58 in February of the following year. Such a rapid depreciation had never been known in the past.

**9.** What is the explanation of this sudden depreciation of the German mark? The financial statistics show that the cause was not a sudden rise in the expenditure of the State. The curve of the floating debt (see Diagram III) shows a rise more or less uniform. Neither is there any indication of large payments having to be made to foreigners about that time. The coincidence of the signing of the Treaty of Versailles with the beginning of the sharp ascent of the exchange curve leads one to suppose that there was some connection between the two phenomena. But since the financial obligations imposed on Germany by the Treaty of Versailles could only have made their influence materially felt later, that connection can only be explained by the existence of psychological influences. Probably the signing of the treaty provoked a psychological crisis in certain German circles, lack of confidence in the future of Germany dominated the German mind and was manifested—for the first time in the history of the mark—in a "flight from the mark," i.e. in a demand for foreign exchange. Fear of revolutionary movements at home and the desire to avoid the heavy taxes with which the Government intended to balance the Budget also contributed to the "flight from the mark."*

In the figures shown in Table I of the Appendix we find evident repercussions of the depreciation of the mark. The gold value of the income was round about 300 million marks in the months April to July 1919. In the following months the gold value rapidly decreased (along with the depreciation of the mark) and touched a minimum in February 1920 (73·8 millions).

But the German authors, who have maintained that the depreciation of the mark was the cause of the disequilibrium between income and expenditure because, given the imperfect adaptation of income to the monetary depreciation, the yield was diminished, have not considered that in the period now under examination the depreciation of the mark influenced both income and *expenditure* in the same direction. Computed in gold marks, the total expenditure also diminished considerably from July 1919 to February 1920 and more rapidly than the income. But

* We must also take account of the following circumstance, recorded by Hawtrey (*Monetary Reconstruction*, London, 1923, p. 71). In January 1920 the fall of the mark and of the Austrian crown was made more rapid by the refusal on the part of the American banks to give credits to those exporters who used to sell in a depressed European money and to hold the proceeds of the sale.

since the significance of these figures, expressed in gold marks, which were in reality non-existent, could not be intelligible, I prefer to take into consideration the figures which show in paper marks the increase of the floating debt.

They are as follows:

TABLE IX

*Increase of Floating Debt*

(Milliards of paper marks)

| | | | |
|---|---|---|---|
| 1919 | | 1919 | |
| April | 3·4 | November | 1·9 |
| May | 3·2 | December | 1·4 |
| June | 3·0 | | |
| July | 2·7 | 1920 | |
| August | 2·1 | January | 1·9 |
| September | 2·4 | February | 0·7 |
| October | 2 7 | March | 2·6 |

We are therefore unable to deduce that the depreciation of the mark, which showed itself in the second half of 1919 and lasted until February 1920, was the cause of an increase in the difference between expenditure and income. On the contrary, never was this difference so small as in February 1920, that is in the month in which the dollar rate reached a maximum, relatively to the rates of 1919 and 1920.

## V. THE DEPRECIATION OF THE MARK DURING THE FINANCIAL YEAR 1920–21

**10.** In 1919 and 1920 numerous new laws were promulgated which radically transformed the German fiscal system by the creation of a great system of taxes imposed by the Reich—the States now passing into a completely subordinate position. These charges ought, on the one hand, to have assured to the central power a proper income, sufficient to cover the heavy expenses, and on the other hand to have contributed effectively to that consolidation of Germany which was one of the principal objects of the constitution of Weimar.

This was the famous fiscal reform which is linked with the name of Erzberger. But because of the profound change in the fiscal arrangements the assessment of the new taxes proceeded very slowly. It was a veritable maze of taxes, some of which were difficult to apply. Inspired partly by demagogic conceptions—Erzberger had proclaimed that in the future Germany the rich should be no more—the taxes met with lively opposition from the wealthy classes. The unduly high rates were a stimulus to evasion, and to "the flight of capital" abroad.

Yet the very high rates of the German taxes lose something of their significance if they are considered in relation to the method of valuing real property and industrial plant. The situation of the possessors of securities or of mortgages was very unfavourable as compared with that of the landowners and industrialists. In comparisons which have often been made between the fiscal burden which weighed on the German population and that supported by other countries, the fact that the rates of taxation are only one element in the fiscal burden has not been sufficiently appreciated; the methods of assessing the tax and of the valuation of property, the exemptions and rebates of taxes, the possibility of evasion, and delays in payment have, equally, a great importance.

**11.** In the financial year 1920-21, thanks to the influence, although slow, of the new fiscal laws, the Reich's income continually increased and reached 400–500 millions of gold marks in the months towards the end of the financial year. But expenditure grew more rapidly. The financial statistics of 1920 are worthy of attention, because study of them leads to the conclusion that even in that year the depreciation of the mark could not have any influence in the sense of provoking the deficit in the Reich accounts. In fact, in that year the value of money remained almost stable, for the gold mark was worth 14·2 paper marks in April 1920 and 14·9 in March 1921. In spite of that, the deficit in Reich accounts amounted to 6,050 millions of gold marks, that is 60 per cent of the total expenses, in the financial year 1920–21. The deficit was covered by the issue of Treasury bills. The circulation of paper money increased by about 20 milliards. Conditions which should conduce to a new fall of the mark were prepared. For the moment a part of the newly issued marks was sold abroad.

It was again possible for the German Government to place a considerable part of the Treasury bills outside the Reichsbank. In March 1921 of the total issue of 166·4 milliards of Treasury bonds, 101·9 milliards were still possessed by private banks, large firms, etc. There was still a check to the increase of note-issues.

As is shown in Diagram IV, in the period from February 1st, 1920, to May 1921 the increase of the floating debt was the factor which dominated and characterized the financial and monetary situation. The increase of the note-issues obviously provoked a continual rise in internal prices, as is particularly shown by the cost of living curve. The psychological crisis which had occurred in the second half of 1919 was gradually calmed, and it seemed that a certain faith in the mark was again established among the German population. In the first months of 1920 a reaction to the sharp depreciation of the preceding months appeared. As the Reichsbank observed in its Report for 1920, there was a tendency on the part of the German public to sell foreign exchange possessed by it; exchange which the Reichsbank willingly bought against marks. It would still have been possible to save the mark if the German Government had taken energetic measures to re-establish a balanced Budget instead of allowing Treasury bills to be discounted continually at the Reichsbank. It should be added that in the financial year 1920-21 the expenditure consequent on the application of the Treaty of Versailles was not relevant in the explanation of the deficit of the Reich.*

## VI. DISCUSSIONS CONCERNING THE FINANCIAL REFORM AND THE FINANCIAL COMPROMISE OF MARCH 1922

**12.** The acceptance of the Ultimatum of London (March 5th, 1921) now imposed on the Government the obligation to prepare a vast fiscal reform which would render existing taxes more productive and procure new receipts sufficient for the payment of reparations. In the following months a violent struggle arose between the different parties, representing definite socio-economic classes, a struggle which resembled the campaign provoked two years previously by the projects of Erzberger.

On one hand the Socialists energetically insisted on the necessity of compelling the wealthy classes to contribute to the expenditure which the State must incur to satisfy its obligations to the Allies. Property (it was said) can and should adapt itself to a sacrifice corresponding to its capacity to contribute. At a time of depreciation of the mark only a direct participation of the exchequer in the profits of industry and agriculture could prevent the continual diminution of the real yield of the taxes. Hirsch, the Secretary of State, published a memorandum proposing that mortgages in terms of gold in favour of the State should be imposed on all property. Interest payments could be made in paper money, on the basis of a coefficient which, for agriculturists, would vary with the price of cereals. It was also proposed

* See Part IV of the present chapter.

that a certain percentage of the capital of joint-stock companies should be ceded to the State. Only by such a method could a contribution be obtained from the proprietors of "real goods" and of "gold values" (Goldwerte) whom the methods of valuation of property, followed until then, had treated too lightly.

The representatives of the democratic parties also showed themselves favourable to the idea of obliging "capital" to support a much heavier fiscal burden than in the past.* They put it from a realistic point of view: Germany must pay reparations, and if this payment was not well arranged the confusion in economic relations and the depreciation of the exchange which would result would put the foreigner in a position to buy a part of German resources dirt cheap. The wealth of Germany would have been uselessly dissipated. Hence it would be better to regulate the transfer abroad of a part of the "substance" of Germany. Having created a direct participation for itself in agricultural property and industrial firms, the State would have been able to utilize the securities representing this co-proprietorship.

But all the parties on the Right were up in arms against these projects, which were denounced as the beginning of a socialization of the means of production. The Nationalists refused to support the new fiscal proposals, declaring that the attempt to satisfy the obligations imposed under the Ultimatum of London was a "stab in the back" of the German economy, which the parties of the Left apparently would like to disarm and to abandon to the enemy.

It was already clear in August 1921 that the adversaries of the "taxation of material wealth" were so strong as to be able to wreck, in the Reichstag, every project designed with this object. Faced by the violent opposition of the interested classes, the Government, in the fiscal projects published in August, definitely abandoned the idea of a mortgage title in favour of the Reich on rural and urban property and of a participation in industrial and commercial enterprises. The proposal of a new property tax and of a tax on increase in capital were no longer the kernel of the reform, as the Socialists wished, but a mere ornament beside the heavy taxes on consumption goods.

The struggle for fiscal reform continued in the succeeding months. In consequence of the continual modifications recommended by numerous commissions and sub-commissions, the fiscal projects were altered and

* An attempt—unsuccessful in practice—at a capital levy, had been made in 1919 with the introduction of "Reichsnotopfer" which should have been one of the cornerstones of Erzberger's reform.

mutilated. Representatives of the Labour parties complained that the new proposals struck especially at consumers, and endeavoured to reduce the burden of indirect taxes; while the wealthy classes attempted to undermine the efficiency of the proposals for new direct taxes. These classes were especially fighting the innovation involved in the proposals regarding the methods of valuing property, which were no longer to be based on "rent values" (Ertragswert), which experience had already shown to be inadequate, but on "selling" value.* Opposition was especially lively on the part of agriculturists, who denounced the method of valuing property according to "selling value" as an indirect way of making the Reich participate in the "gold value." They also contested any project whatever which was designed to increase the yield of a tax in proportion to the depreciation of the mark.

On the other hand, towards the end of 1921 the democratic party saw clearly that the depreciation of the mark threatened to make the proposed fiscal reform totally ineffective. It presented a proposal according to which the rates of the taxes should be fixed in gold, and they should be actually paid in paper marks, according to an index proportioned to the internal purchasing power of the mark. But the project was rejected by the Financial Sub-Commission of the Reichstag.

Finally on March 9th, 1922, a compromise was concluded between the parties on the base of an authorization given to the Government to impose a forced loan of a milliard gold marks. It was stipulated that the money received from this forced loan could not be used in payments in cash to the Allies but must serve only for internal payments, resulting from the peace treaty, such as the expenses of occupation, and, above all, the intended compensation to German industrialists for payments in kind.†

The wealthy classes, having been obliged to accept against their will the principle of a forced loan, immediately took their revenge on the problems of the application of the principle. They secured the concession that the loan should be payable in paper marks at the fixed rate of 70 paper marks to one gold mark. Consequently the successive declines in the value of the mark robbed the forced loan of all effect,

* The "rent value" is that which is obtained by capitalizing the return at the current rate of interest. According to German agriculturists the market value was notably superior to the capitalized value of current rentals, because of the over-valuation of land.

† The law which approved the new taxes—forty new taxes or modifications of existing ones—was promulgated on April 6th, 1922.

as it did of all the others, even the indirect taxes, regarding which the error of establishing fixed rates in paper marks had been committed.

### VII. THE CONDITIONS OF THE NATIONAL FINANCES IN 1921 AND 1922

**13.** After the acceptance of the Ultimatum of London on the part of Germany, the Reparations Commission created the so-called "Committee of Guarantees" whose function was to put into execution the plan of London. The Berlin Delegation of the Committee of Guarantees made agreements with the German Government and with the Reichsbank, and collaborated with the latter with the object of helping the collection of the foreign exchange necessary for the payment of reparations. The Reichsbank made many efforts in this matter. Exporters were obliged to hand over to the Reichsbank a part of the foreign exchange which came into their possession. At the same time the offices for the control of foreign trade made efforts in order to extend the custom among exporters of selling abroad for "appreciated" foreign currencies, rather than for paper marks.

**14.** In the first months of the financial year 1921 the mark, which, as we have seen in the preceding year, had shown a notable resistance, in spite of the continuous increase of the note-issue and internal prices, once more began to lose value in terms of the dollar. At the same time both the floating debt and the issues of paper money were increased continually. From August onwards, the depreciation became more rapid. A situation was produced analogous to that which we have already considered while studying the movement of the mark in the second half of 1919. The sudden collapse of the mark was not preceded by a sudden expansion of the circulation, such as would give a satisfactory explanation of the depreciation of the exchange. Diagram v shows that the dollar rate curve suddenly rose in the last months of 1921, much above the curves of the circulation and of the floating debt, apparently pulling up behind it the internal prices and the index number of the cost of living. The opinion generally held is that the cause of the rapid depreciation of the mark was the payment of the first milliard for reparations. We shall discuss this point presently.

**15.** During 1921, as had already happened in the second half of 1919, the depreciation of the mark considerably depressed the yield of taxation from about 400 million gold marks, which was the figure at the beginning of the financial year, to 113 million in November, in which month the depression of the exchange rate was greatest (1 gold mark = 63 paper marks). But even the expenditure, computed in gold marks, diminished in a parallel manner, so that not even for the financial year 1921 can it be affirmed that the budget deficit was provoked by the depreciation of the mark. Indeed, the increase of the floating debt did not show, after August 1921, an increase any more rapid than that of the preceding months.

**16.** In the period of relative stabilization of the exchange which occurred in the first months of 1922 the recovery of the national finances made some progress. The German Government adopted some financial measures to reduce expenditure (e.g. an increase in the "legal" price of bread) and to increase income (as, e.g., the increase of railway rates). A fleeting equilibrium was reached between income and ordinary expenditure; there was even a very small surplus which was set aside for the expenses arising from the Treaty of Versailles. An improvement was also shown in the railway accounts. The extraordinary Budget was not balanced; nevertheless, the increase of the floating debt slackened in the first months of 1922 and the percentage of the total expenditure which was covered by issues of Treasury bills declined.

But confidence in the mark, which the event of September 1921 had profoundly shaken, could not be re-established. On the contrary, after June 1922, a new wave of pessimism swept over Germany. German speculation renewed its attacks against the mark, which once again suffered a sharp fall. The number of people whose interests were favoured by a continuous depreciation of the mark, increased continually in Germany. Not only the great industries and the large merchant firms, but also very numerous classes of investors hoarded foreign bills or currency. The thoughts of all—from the great captain of industry to the modest typist—were concentrated on the dollar rate; and the face of the modest burgher was illuminated by a complacent smile when the daily bulletin, impatiently awaited, revealed to his greedy glance an increase in the dollar rate, while it was clouded if the official quotation showed an improvement in the mark. In a much-frequented cabaret the manager used to address the public in these words: "Many gentlemen are good-humoured this evening, that is to say, the dollar rises!"; or even: "Many people this evening have melancholy faces, that is to say, the mark rises!"

**17.** In the summer of 1922 there appeared for the first time a distinct reaction of the depreciation of the mark on the Reich Budget, in the sense that the deficit was aggravated. While in the preceding months the German Government had succeeded in making some progress towards the balancing of expenditure and income, after July 1922 the depreciation of the mark again profoundly disturbed the state of the national finances. The real yield of the receipts lessened rapidly. In September of that year it had fallen, in terms of gold, to less than 100 millions; in November to little more than 60 millions. On the other hand, expenditure was maintained at a high level. The depreciation of the mark, which originally had been the consequence of the dislocation of the national finances, now contributed very much to the aggravation of the disorder and progressive disintegration. It also accentuated the losses of the railway administration, since the rates had not been advanced in proportion to the depreciation of the mark, whilst expenses increased rapidly. The subsidy from the Reich, which had been reduced in the first months of the financial year 1922, had to be continually and considerably increased in the succeeding months.

## VIII. THE CONDITIONS OF THE REICH BUDGET AFTER THE OCCUPATION OF THE RUHR

**18.** In the first months of 1923 the occupation of the Ruhr gave the *coup de grâce* to the national finances and the German mark. Because of it some important sources of income were lost to the State: the tax on coal, export duties, custom-house dues, and railway receipts. In addition, the German Governments—renewing their wartime errors of financial policy—did not think to cover the heavy expenses caused by Passive Resistance with new taxes. It conceded very large credits to the Ruhr industry to put it in a position to continue production. The continued depreciation of the mark made these loans almost worthless, since only to a very small extent were they subject to the "Valorization Clause," i.e. the obligation on the part of the debtor to restore the real value received by him at the time of the loan.

It was only at the end of August 1923 that the "Ruhrabgabe" was created, that is the tax for the Ruhr, the yield of which was intended to meet the expenses of Passive Resistance.

The nominal value of the notes in circulation, which was 1,280 milliards at the end of 1922, increased to 1,984 milliards on January 31st, 1923; 3,513 on February 28th; 5,518 on March 31st, and 6,546 on April 30th. Whilst at the beginning of 1922 the Treasury bills issued were still placed in almost equal proportions in the portfolio of the Reichsbank and outside the Reichsbank; in 1923 the portion of new ones which was absorbed by the market decreased rapidly. At the end of April 1923 about three-quarters of them were held by the Reichsbank, and at the end of July 93 per cent. To every addition of Treasury bills there now corresponded an equivalent increase in the issues of notes.

The disastrous policy, which consisted in financing the Passive Resistance by means of printing notes, aroused sharp criticism in Germany itself.

Thus, contrary to the opinion of many writers,* the financial policy of the German Government was a fundamental factor also in the last phase of the depreciation of the mark.

**19.** It is evident that the consequence of that policy could not but be the continual depreciation of the mark, which the Reichsbank opposed in vain by adopting, in February 1923, action to support the mark. Indeed, in the second half of March it was already clear that the Reichsbank could no longer attempt to maintain the mark rate artificially while continuing the issues of paper money. The rise in internal prices, paralysing the export trade, threatened to aggravate the crisis provoked by the violent detachment of the Ruhr. Reserves of notes were collected by the German industrialists, and especially by those of the Ruhr, whom the Government had helped generously by subsidies, and were thrown on to the foreign exchange market. As Havenstein, the President of the Reichsbank, declared before the Committee for research into the causes of the depreciation of the mark: "On the 28th March began the attack on the foreign exchange market. In very numerous classes of the German economy from that day onwards thought was all for personal interests and not for the needs of the country."† The Reichsbank had to sell daily foreign exchange to the amount of about 20 millions of gold marks. But the demand for foreign exchange quickly became more intense and rose to 70 millions. The dam raised by the Reichsbank broke down on April 18th, the Reichsbank not being able any longer to sell foreign exchange at the official rate fixed for the dollar; the mass of paper money accumulated

* For example, Professor Angell, who says that "in the later stages of the German experience . . . the degree of the depreciation had absolutely no immediate relationship to Government finance."—*Op. cit.*, p. 446.

† Also Elster, referring to this episode, recognizes that the German industrialists refused to support the measures taken by the Reichsbank to stabilize the mark, and instead thought only of their private interests.—*Op. cit.*, p. 182.

in four months by the continual issues broke into the market and the dollar rate rose giddily.

## IX. THE INFLUENCES OF THE DEPRECIATION OF THE MARK ON THE RECEIPTS OF THE REICH

**20.** Having reached this point in our treatise, it will be convenient to pause a moment to examine more thoroughly the varied reactions which in the advanced stages of the inflation the depreciation of the mark exercised on the income and expenditure of the State.

(*a*) In the first place the depreciation of the mark rendered difficult—and, in times of the rapid depreciation of the currency, impossible—the formation of a budget of expenditure. Whatever estimate was made, it was exceeded in a very short time even before the estimate had been approved by the Reichstag! Thus arose the necessity for continual corrections and modifications: they were like a distorting veil which concealed the true financial situation.

(*b*) The assessment of certain taxes, for example that on income, met with very great practical difficulties. For example, how could depreciation be calculated in order to determine the "real" income and not only the "apparent" income of a firm?

(*c*) Since the nominal value of estates and nominal incomes normally increased with depreciation of the mark and the taxes were steeply progressive, there resulted an increase of the fiscal burden without a corresponding increase in the contributive capacity of the citizens. In the summer of 1919, when the preparatory work on the law regarding income tax was commenced, the mark was still worth 32 gold pfennigs; in December 1921, when the law was amended, the dollar was worth 180 paper marks; towards the middle of May 1922, when a plan for amending the law to the continuous monetary depreciation was presented to the Reichstag, the dollar was already worth 295 paper marks, and towards the end of July—soon after which the proposed amendments had been approved—it was quoted at 520 paper marks.

It was continually necessary to change the classes of income and estates, the regulations about the minimum income and estates exempt from taxation and the rebates of taxes, etc.

Thus was evolved a very great confusion in the financial laws, a continual succession of laws or ordinances which modified the preceding ones,* increasing difficulties of application, an increase of work in the Finance Office and therefore a delay in the assessment of taxes and greater facility for evasion.

(*d*) The basis of the fiscal system was unstable, since the yield of certain important taxes was closely connected with the fluctuations of the exchange and in a particular way with the continually varying phenomenon of the difference between the internal and external value of the paper mark. For example, the yield of the export taxes depended on that difference and should have been continually modified according to whether it rose or fell. But the modifications were always made too late and consequently occasioned disturbance in the economic life of the country. It was proposed to create export taxes towards the end of 1919, when the rapid depreciation of the exchange had increased the divergence between the external and internal value of the German currency. In fact, however, the export taxes were introduced only some months later, when a rise in the foreign exchange value of the mark on the one hand and the rise of internal prices on the other had noticeably diminished that difference. Owing to pressure from interested parties the taxes were perceptibly reduced in the summer of 1920; but they were again increased after a renewed depreciation of the currency. (In September 1923 they were finally abolished.)

Another example is the tax on coal, which had been introduced at a time when there existed a great difference between the German home price of coal and the price in the world market. Later, when the difference between the two prices was lessened, the tax on coal became too heavy for the German economy and threatened to diminish seriously the possibility of German competition in the foreign markets. The tax was first reduced and later, at the beginning of September 1923, when the price of German coal had already reached or surpassed the world price, it was completely abolished.

* For example, the law of July 20th, 1922, was the *sixth* amendment of the law of March 29th, 1920, which instituted the income tax.

**21.** But the most important influence exercised by the depreciation of the money on the fiscal system was this: Computed in paper money the yield from taxes might even increase; but the real income (the purchasing power of the sum received by the State) declined. This resulted from the following causes:

(*a*) The depreciation of the currency provoked a true and peculiar destruction of taxable wealth, since the income and property of many social classes were diminished and often completely annihilated. It is true that there was some, though not complete, compensation in the increase of the contributive capacity of the classes for whom the depreciation of the currency was the source of conspicuous profits. But the excess profits derived from the depreciation easily escaped the tax-collector.

Moreover, the continual depreciation of the national currency induced all classes of citizens to invest their savings in foreign currencies, bills, securities, etc., which were easily concealed. The "flight of capital," which in Germany assumed the importance of a "mass phenomenon" and which seemingly vigorous restrictions did not succeed in impeding, continually removed much taxable wealth from the power of the German Exchequer.

(*b*) Between the moment or period of time in which the transaction occurred which gave rise to any financial obligation, and the moment when the transaction was ascertained by the fiscal organizations and the tax was fixed in figures, and again between this moment and that at which the tax was actually paid, there passed varying intervals of time. If in the meantime the circulating medium depreciated, the tax-payers paid a sum whose real value was the lower the longer were the intervals. Acceleration of the assessment of the tax and shortening of the interval between that assessment and the actual payment reduced the loss suffered by the State; but the interval of time could not be completely eliminated; and in periods of very rapid depreciation even a short interval was enough to cause a grave loss to the Exchequer.

(*c*) The yield of the duties or taxes, reckoned in paper money, was imperfectly adapted to the currency depreciation. For this purpose it is possible to arrange the taxes in a scale of sensitiveness.

The case of taxes endowed with a maximum degree of sensitiveness, the yield from which varied exactly with the variations of the exchange rate, is exceptional. An instance of such sensitive taxes is given by customs duties, when they are fixed in gold and payable in paper at a "premium" which is fixed on the basis of the daily rate of exchange. When on the other hand, as was the case for a long time in Germany, the premium is fixed at shorter or longer intervals, the adaptation to the rate of exchange is imperfect, even for customs duties. Another example of a most sensitive fiscal income was the stamp duty *ad valorem* on the buying and selling of foreign exchange.

At the other end of the scale are found those taxes or duties which were completely insensitive to the depreciation of the money; for example, all the fiscal charges for legal documents, passports, etc.; all the indirect taxes fixed by the units of weight, volume, or number of packets of the taxed material (as, e.g., the tobacco, sugar, alcohol, and other taxes).

Between these extremes are a great number of taxes whose yield tended to vary with the variation of the internal value of the paper money, which value remained for some years perceptibly higher than the external value. But even here it is necessary to proceed to a subdivision, rendered necessary by the difference, often considerable, between the internal value of the mark, measured by the index number of the wholesale prices, or the internal value of the mark, measured by the index of the cost of living. The yield of some taxes tended to follow the increase in wholesale prices—for example, the income tax inasmuch as it was levied on the industrial or the commercial classes. The yield of other taxes, on the other hand, was adapted to variations in the cost of living, after a short or a long interval—e.g. income tax, inasmuch as it was levied on wages or stipends, which tended to vary with the variations of the index number of the cost of living.

## X. INFLUENCES OF THE DEPRECIATION OF THE MARK ON THE EXPENDITURE OF THE REICH

**22.** From the preceding analysis it may be seen how highly relevant was the divergence between the internal and external value of the mark to the management of the German tax system. Since the nominal incomes of numerous social classes were increased more or less in proportion to the diminution of the *internal* value of the mark; and since internal prices, which formed the basis of many taxes (for example, the "Umsatzsteuer"—turnover tax), were increased less than the dollar rate, it would not have been possible to obtain from existing taxes a constant yield, reckoned in gold. But it may be asked: "Was that necessary for the balancing of the Budget?" To reply to this question it is necessary to examine the relation between the monetary depreciation and the expenditure of the State. For expenses, as for receipts, we can make a scale according to their degree of sensitiveness to the depreciation of the mark.

Some expenses varied exactly with the variations of the exchange rate. Such were the expenses incurred by Germany in the payment of cash reparations for the clearing of pre-war debts and credits, for the purchase of cereals abroad, for the maintenance of representatives abroad, etc.

Other expenses increased in proportion to the rise of internal wholesale prices. The most important example is the expenses incurred by the railway administration in the purchase of coal and materials necessary for the renewal and extension of plant and for the purchase of rolling-stock.

Others tended to increase with the rise of the cost of living in Germany; such were expenditure on stipends and wages, and, in part, pensions.

Finally, certain expenses remained quite insensitive to the depreciation of the currency: the principal example is the interest on the public debt. The relief to the national finances on this account was very considerable. Later the State intervened to help financially the small bondholders ("Kleinrentner"), who were ruined by the depreciation of the currency; but the expenses incurred in these subsidies were not even remotely comparable to the burdens which the State Budget would have had to support if the depreciation of the currency had not occurred.

**23.** What is the final result of all these influences acting, on one hand on the income and on the other on the expenditure? *A priori* the final result cannot be foreseen since it depends on the effective composition of income and expenses according to the categories elucidated above.

As we have seen, the study of the German finances shows that in the second half of 1919 the depreciation of the mark not only produced a diminution of the real value of the receipts but also greatly reduced the expenses, computed in gold marks. That is explained by the fact that in 1919 by far the greater part of the expenditure of the Reich was internal expenditure. Now, prices and wages had not increased in proportion to the depreciation of the mark; indeed in February 1920 the index number of the prices of goods in the United States was more than three times that of gold prices in Germany. Besides, the payments which were constant in paper marks, i.e. the interest on the public debt and pensions, were still a substantial proportion of ordinary expenditure of the Reich.

But later, in the financial year 1922, the situation changed. As we have already observed, from that year onwards, in the periods of depreciation, the receipts reckoned in gold generally diminished more rapidly than the expenditure. The reaction of prices to the new issues of paper money always came quickly—this was especially true of wholesale prices—and therefore even the internal expenses rapidly reflected the influence of the depreciation of the currency, while the receipts increased later and more slowly. Payments of interest on the public debt had now become a negligible quantity. Therefore a disequilibrium between income and expenditure appeared which aggravated the original sad state of the national finances.

**24.** The facts just referred to also suggest the following considerations. In these years one often heard repeated the belief that Germany's capacity for paying reparations was measured by the mark rate. To this it was justly objected that a country's capacity for payment is measured not by the foreign exchange value of its money, but by its wealth in real goods, by its production, its exports, etc. However, as the question of reparations is not only a problem of the transfer of goods from one country to another, but also a problem of internal finance—it is certain that the depreciation of the mark, creating a divergence between the internal and external value of the German money, made it more difficult for the German Government to obtain from taxes the necessary sum in paper marks for the purchase of the foreign exchange required for the payment of reparations. There existed, therefore, a relation between the depreciation of the mark and the German Government's capacity to satisfy its obligations to the Allies.

### XI. THE ERRORS AND WEAKNESSES OF GERMAN FINANCIAL POLICY

**25.** But could not the German Government have freed the national finances from the effects of the depreciation of the currency, by "valorizing" the taxes from the beginning?

It is true that the incomes of certain social classes were less sensitive to the depreciation of the exchange, but for other classes the depreciation of the currency was the fount of considerable gains. Exporters sold to the State foreign bills of exchange at high prices, while their expenses were not increased in proportion. For many industrialists the rise in the price of foreign exchange implied a large customs protection which permitted them to raise their prices. Why did not the German State think from the beginning of making those classes who had derived great benefits from the depreciation contribute more largely to the public expenses? For a long time the democratic parties and representatives of workers' syndicates in vain demanded a reform in the method of imposing taxes, which would have saved the Exchequer from heavy losses. Instead, even towards the end of 1922 the Minister of Finance declared himself opposed to the introduction of a system which would permit the adaptation of the yield of taxation to the depreciation of the mark. In the succeeding months, after the very great fall in the exchange which followed the occupation of the Ruhr, the question was examined once more. On March 20th, 1923, a law was published on "the depreciation of money in relation to the fiscal laws." But, practically, this law did not give to the State efficacious means of defence against the effects of the depreciation of money, because it was limited to imposing a fine of 30 per cent of the amount of the tax on the taxpayer who delayed for more than three months the payment of tax owed and a fine of 15 per cent for delays less than three months.

Later other improvements were timidly undertaken; such as the change, in certain taxes on consumption goods, from fixed rates to a percentage of the value of the taxed object; the earlier dating of payments on account of income tax and the turnover tax, the abbreviation of the time allowed for payment, and the obligation to pay interest on sums paid late.

There were numerous cases of rates of taxes and tariffs which were in grotesque contrast to the rise in prices. For a long time some obviously ridiculous taxes and very low tariffs were maintained. For some time the German railways fixed very much lower fares for passengers, among whom were numerous foreigners, than those charged in any other country. For inexplicable motives the German postal authorities for some time charged less than a gold pfennig for the forwarding of letters abroad (letters sent for the most part by merchants, industrialists, and foreigners); and the natural consequence of that system was a very great fall in receipts.*

* From an official publication (*Zahlen zur Geldenwertung*, 1925) I have deduced the following tables which seem to me important documents of the financial policy followed by the German Government during the inflation.

*3rd Class Fare (in gold) for one Person, per Kilometre*

(1913 = 100)

| | | | |
|---|---|---|---|
| 1- 1-14—31- 3-18 | 79·2 | 1- 6-23—30- 6-23 | 6·4 |
| 1- 4-18—31- 3-19 | 73·9 | 1- 7-23—31- 7-23 | 5·9 |
| 1- 4-19—30- 9-19 | 41·5 | 1- 8-23—19- 8-23 | 2·3 |
| 1-10-19—29- 2-20 | 18·3 | 20- 8-23—31- 8-23 | 10·7 |
| 1- 3-20—31- 5-21 | 33·4 | 1- 9-23—10- 9-23 | 9·3 |
| 1- 6-21—30-11-21 | 21·9 | 11- 9-23—17- 9-23 | 7·3 |
| 1-12-21—31- 1-22 | 18·5 | 18- 9-23—24- 9-23 | 27·0 |
| 1- 2-22—30- 9-22 | 11·1 | 25- 9-23— 1-10-23 | 58·4 |
| 1-10-22—31-10-22 | 3·0 | 2-10-23— 9-10-23 | 21·1 |
| 1-11-22—30-11-22 | 2·6 | 10-10-23—12-10-23 | 6·9 |
| 1-12-22—31-12-22 | 5·0 | 13-10-23—17-10-23 | 12·4 |
| 1- 1-23—31- 1-23 | 4·7 | 18-10-23—24-10-23 | 7·7 |
| 1-2 -23—28- 2-23 | 6·0 | 25-10-23—28-10-23 | 10·7 |
| 1- 3-23—31- 5-23 | 10·8 | 29-10-23—31-10-23 | 41·0 |

This table shows that in certain periods the railway passenger fares were, in gold, scarcely 2–3 per cent of the pre-war fares! It was objected that it was difficult for the railways to adapt their tariffs to the rapid monetary depreciation. But other companies—e.g. the Berlin Electric Tram Company—adapted their tariffs, if not perfectly, at least in a large measure to the depreciation of the money; and it is impossible to understand why the railways could not do the same.

The following table shows that the postal tariffs for some time were, if reckoned in gold, 1 per cent of the pre-war tariff:

*Price (in gold) for Franking a Letter for Home Delivery*

(1913 = 100)

| | | | |
|---|---|---|---|
| 1- 1-14—31- 7-16 | 88·3 | 1- 7-23—31- 7-23 | 3·6 |
| 1- 8-16—30- 9-19 | 78·5 | 1- 8-23—23- 8-23 | 1·2 |
| 1-10-19— 5- 5-20 | 14·0 | 24- 8-23—31- 8-23 | 11·1 |
| 6- 5-20—31- 3-21 | 29·0 | 1- 9-23—19- 9-23 | 4·1 |
| 1- 4-21—31-12-22 | 21·3 | 20- 9-23—30- 9-23 | 7·4 |
| 1- 1-22—30- 6-22 | 31·8 | 1-10-23— 9-10-23 | 14·0 |
| 1- 7-22—30- 9-22 | 12·2 | 10-10-23—19-10-23 | 3·7 |
| 1-10-22—14-11-22 | 5·7 | 20-10-23—31-10-23 | 0·7 |
| 15-11-22—14-12-22 | 6·5 | 1-11-23— 4-11-23 | 1·4 |
| 15-12-22—14- 1-23 | 13·2 | 5-11-23—11-11-23 | 7·5 |
| 15- 1-23—28- 2-23 | 7·9 | 12-11-23—30-11-23 | 13·3 |
| 1- 3-23—30 -6-23 | 8·1 | 1-12-23—31-12-23 | 100·0 |

It was only on August 20th, 1923, that the system of increasing the railway fares little by little at varying intervals was abandoned. The multiplication system was adopted. But since a given multiplicator always remained in force for a certain number of days, it was reduced by lagging much behind the rise in the dollar. Railway fares fixed in gold and payable in paper marks at the rate of the previous day were only introduced on November 1st, 1923; tariffs of "constant values" were adopted for the telegraph and telephone services on November 15th, and for postal service on December 1st, 1923.

Even in the summer of 1923—at a time of a very rapid depreciation of the mark—the amount of the tax on wages remained on the average about a fortnight in the hands of the entrepreneurs before being paid into the Exchequer. The entrepreneurs thus used for their advantage a great part of the tax effectively paid by the working classes. The amount of the tax on turnover (Umsatzsteuer) which industrialists and merchants collected from the purchaser at the moment of the sale, was paid a month after the end of each quarter. Even in July 1923 the Railway Administration allowed frequent delays of payment. One must admit this policy of negligence and remissness in the face of the interests of influential groups did much to aggravate the inflation.

**26.** In the second half of August 1923 the Minister, Cuno, some days before his dismissal, presented some proposals for new taxes. It was a belated attempt to stop, by means of an increase of receipts, the fall of the mark and to repair the errors of the financial policy inaugurated after the occupation of the Ruhr, the policy which had neglected to create the sources of income necessary for financing Passive Resistance. The new "brutal" taxes (as they were called) at first aroused grave prejudice in industrial, commercial, and banking circles. Foreign exchange, securities, and goods were offered on the market by those who had not the liquid resources necessary for the payment of the new taxes. For a brief moment the dollar rate eased and prices of securities fell. But the continued increase of the note-issues and large concessions of credit on the part of the Reichsbank quickly robbed the fiscal reforms of their efficacy. The dollar rate renewed its upward swing and the real value of the sum due to be paid in taxes lessened daily, thanks to the very rapid depreciation of the currency. The last battle fought by the German Government on fiscal ground, to curb the descent of the mark, was definitely lost.

**27.** Only when the disintegration of the monetary system was already complete did the Government decide to "valorize" the payments of those taxes which were collected in arrear, it being prescribed that contributors should pay a sum in paper marks equivalent to the gold value due on the tax claim on the day the tax obligation was incurred. (Order of October 11th, 1923.) The coefficients by which the original sum had to be multiplied were fixed periodically. But even now the valorization was incomplete, since the coefficients were perceptibly below the level corresponding to the depreciation of the mark. For example, for the period from October 17th to 19th, the multiplicator was fixed at 1·08 milliards of paper marks, although the gold mark rate on October 17th was already 1·3 milliards and on the 19th about 2·9 milliards. Then on the insistence of the agriculturists the coefficient was reduced to 936 millions for the days October 20th to 23rd, although the gold mark rate had risen in the meantime to 13·3 milliards! On the 23rd the coefficient was raised to 13·3 milliards, but the gold mark rate was already 15 milliards. At the same time the Finance Officials wasted time and material in exacting very small amounts—amounts much less than the expenses of collecting the money. For example, in October 1923 a passport for the Polish frontier cost only two paper marks!!

In the last phase of the inflation the system of "coefficients" no longer protected the State against the diminution of receipts caused by the depreciation of the circulating medium; indeed, if payment should merely be delayed for a day or two, or if the marks received should remain for a short time in the State Treasury, the latter was bound to suffer heavy losses.

The German fiscal system continued to be based (except in cases cited in the footnote) on the paper mark until the Order of December 19th, 1923, which definitely substituted for it the gold mark, in the fixing of tariffs and in the valuation of taxable goods.*

* In this note are indicated the dates of the most important laws according to which the gold mark was gradually substituted for the paper mark in the German fiscal system.

The law of March 20th, 1923, marked the beginning of a long series of laws or decrees having as their object the adaptation of the fiscal system to the depreciation of the currency. We record the following measures: Decree of March 22nd on the surcharges on customs duties; decree June 5th on automobile tax; laws of July 9th regarding taxes on sugar, matches, beer, salt, and playing cards. Another law of July 9th fixed a system of co-efficients for applying to the interim payments of taxes; but they became insufficient almost at once because of the rapid depreciation of the mark. Also there were: the decree of July 9th regarding the assessment of taxes on export; the law of August 11th about the duties on beer, sugar, salt, matches, coal, mineral waters, etc.; the law of August 11th concerning the tax on industrial and

**28.** Do not let us under-estimate the difficulties with which an energetic policy would have had to contend at a time when the exchange rate of the mark was exposed to influence, independent of the financial policy, which provoked continual fluctuations in the exchange rate. But the weakness of the State in the face of the great economic groups, the complications of the German fiscal system, the delay in the collection of taxes and the lack of arrangement for the adaptation of the taxes to the depreciation of the mark, aggravated the financial situation. It is evident from the dates of the decrees referred to in the preceding paragraphs that the measures taken to obviate the dangerous repressions of the depreciation of the money on the income of the State were too late and incomplete.* Consequently, in October 1923 an extraordinary phenomenon in the history of the public finance appeared, *the complete atrophy of the fiscal system.* In the last decade of that month the ordinary receipts covered about 0·8 per cent of the expenses; the State now obtained money exclusively through the discount of Treasury bills.

In the December issue of *Wirtschaft und Statistik*, 1923, some interesting calculations were published of the amount in gold of the yield from taxes and of the other receipts of the State, derived from loans and by the discount of Treasury bills. For the period from 1914 to October 1923 the total results are as follows: taxes, 21·2 milliards; loans, 52·6 milliards; Treasury bills, 59·1 milliards. These statistics clearly display the financial policy followed by the German Government for ten years, which resulted in scarcely 15 per cent of the expenses being covered by means of taxes!

agricultural concerns, a tax payable in gold or in paper according to a co-efficient fixed every Thursday for the week and operating from the following Saturday (this was the first tax fixed on the gold basis); the law of August 11th regarding the increase of the co-efficients fixed for the interim payments of the tax on income and on companies; the decree of September 27th which suppressed, for delayed payments of taxes on income and on companies and for the Ruhrtax, the system of fixed co-efficients, substituting for it the system of a multiplicator fixed each week; the decree of October 11th on the valorization of debts of a fiscal character. The decree of October 17th fixed some specific rates of tax in gold marks on sugar, salt, matches, and playing cards. That of October 3rd decreed that the tax on tobacco should be reckoned and charged on the gold basis. Those of November 9th and 26th and December 7th put on a gold basis the taxes on automobiles, beer, business turnover, and the Ruhr tax. Finally, the decree of December 19th transformed the entire fiscal system, putting it on a gold basis both in assessment and in collection.

* An obscure point in the financial history of post-war Germany is the financial administration of the States. The Budgets of the States were not less disturbed than that of the Reich. The Reich had to intervene continually with subsidies and contribution of various kinds.

## PART II

### I. THE POLICY OF THE REICHSBANK

**1.** To the "governmental" inflation, provoked by continual demands made on the Reichsbank by the State, was added a second form of inflation, which Germans called "private," that is, the creation of paper money for business men.

The credit policy adopted by the Reichsbank was based on the idea that a "private" inflation could not occur if the Reichsbank remained faithful to the strict rule of allowing for discount only "commercial" bills, excluding "financial" bills. It would then be certain, it affirmed, that no notes or, in general, credit concessions, would be issued in a measure greater than was necessary and that a normal "reflux" of notes to the bank would be established. Thus old errors were revived.*

The Reichsbank did not recognize that, in a period of continuous "governmental" inflation, and consequently a rise in prices, the rigorous distinction between commercial and financial bills, even if it were practically possible, was not a sufficient guarantee against the danger of a "private" inflation. At a time when prices are rising because of the governmental inflation, the amount of notes issued by the Reichsbank to satisfy the demands of trade must surpass the reflux of notes previously issued. Let us suppose that when the price level is 100 the demand for short-term credit is 1,000. If prices rise later to 120, demand will tend to reach 1,200. At the same time notes for the amount of 1,000 are returned; the reflux will be lower by 200 than the new issues. Moreover, the demand for new credit is stimulated by the prospect of a continual rise in prices.

Consequently, the optimism with which the management of the Reichsbank for a long time considered the concession of credits to private individuals was quite unjustified. It did not realize that the extension of bank credits, like the issue of notes on account of the State, profited some classes and imposed loss on others. It did not realize that there was an abnormal demand for credit, to limit which

* Errors exposed by Thornton, *An Enquiry into the Nature and Effects of the Paper Credit of Great Britain*, London, 1802, p. 285.

it was necessary to adapt the discount rate to the rate of the depreciation of the paper mark.

The official discount rate in Germany had remained fixed (at 5 per cent) from 1915 until July 1922. Until the summer of 1922 the Reichsbank exercised, almost exclusively, the function of a State bank, discounting Treasury bills presented to it. The increasing needs of trade were satisfied by private banks, who secured the means by discounting at the Reichsbank the Treasury bills in which they had largely invested the money of depositors during and after the war. At the end of 1920, 25 per cent of the total value of Treasury bills was held by the eight great banks of Berlin, which had invested 60 per cent of their deposits in that way.

But in the summer of 1922 the Reichsbank began to supply directly to commerce and industry the financial means, the need of which, in that period of credit crisis, was urgently felt. To mitigate this crisis the Reichsbank insistently counselled the business classes to have recourse to the creation of commercial bills,* which it declared itself ready to discount at a much lower rate than the rate of the depreciation of the mark, and even than the rates charged by private banks.

Indeed the official discount rate was 6 per cent at the end of July 1922; it was raised to 7 per cent at the end of August; to 8 per cent on September 21st; 10 per cent on November 13th; 12 per cent on January 18th, 1923; and 18 per cent in the last week of April 1923. It is enough to compare these rates with the increase in the dollar rate (a gold mark was worth 160 paper marks at the end of July 1922; 411 paper marks at the end of August, 1,822 at the end of November; and 7,100 at the end of April 1923) to be convinced that the policy of the Reichsbank could not but give a strong stimulus to the demand for credit and to the inflation.† Here are some figures: on June 30th, 1922, the value of the commercial bills in the portfolio of the Reichsbank amounted to 4·8 milliard marks, while its holding of Treasury bills amounted to 186·1 milliard marks. On December 30th of the same year the total of commercial bills had risen to 422·2 milliards, representing about a third of the amount of the Treasury bills (1,184·5

* Since the outbreak of the war the commercial bill had fallen into disuse, owing to the spread of cheque payments.

† Prion, *Deutsche Kreditpolitik*, 1919–23—in "Jahrbuch" of Schmöller, 1924, vol. ii, p. 189.

milliards). On February 15th, 1923, the amount of commercial bills (1,345 milliards) had reached almost 60 per cent of the holding of the Treasury bills (2,301). Hence, besides the governmental inflation, there had developed a very great banking inflation. On November 15th, 1923, the value of the commercial bills in the portfolio of the Reichsbank amounted to 39·5 trillion marks (a trillion = $1{,}000{,}000^3$). At the same time deposits on current account at the Reichsbank had also increased very rapidly.*

2. In Reichsbank circles it was denied that a rise in the discount rate could exercise a depressing influence on the inflation, and on prices. On the contrary, such people were more ready to consider a rise in the discount rate as a cause of the rise in the costs of production and therefore of prices. Rather than raise the discount rate it was thought more appropriate to apply a certain rationing of credits, only the more deserving firms being allowed to benefit therefrom.† But such a method favoured a privileged class, to whom the Reichsbank presented enormous sums of money, to the detriment of classes to whom the depreciation of the mark was disadvantageous. People who enjoyed the favour of the Reichsbank could make sure of purchasing goods and foreign exchange. Speculation against the mark was in such ways financed by bank credits.‡ The credit policy adopted by the Reichsbank reinforced the effects of the "governmental" inflation and helped to accelerate the fall of the mark, which, indeed, had never been so rapid as it became after the summer of 1922.§

* Deposits on Current Account: 32·9 milliards on December 31st, 1921; 33·4 milliards on March 31st, 1922; 37·2 milliards on June 30th, 1922; 530·5 milliards on December 30th, 1922; 1,165 milliards on February 15th, 1922; 129·6 trillion on November 15, 1923.

† In the jubilee volume, *Die Reichsbank, 1901–1925*, Berlin, 1926, the Directors of the German note-issuing authority attempted to justify themselves against the accusation of having favoured inflation, by asserting that in 1922 and 1923 credit was made available to clients for economically profitable objects. Credits were not granted which would have been used to buy gold or foreign bills, with speculative intentions, or for the purpose of acquiring goods other than the normal necessities of business or to make up the deficiency of fixed capital. Experience showed that it was not practically possible to apply a rigorous distinction between legitimate and non-legitimate credits.

‡ "The Reichsbank was persuaded to give exceedingly liberal credit concessions by the laments of the industrialists, who stated that they could not otherwise pay the salaries and wages of their employees. But if those industrialists had not invested their available means in goods, securities, and foreign bills, they would not have been embarrassed."—Pinner in the *Berliner Tageblatt* of February 9th, 1923.

§ In Reichsbank circles it was maintained that the granting of credit to the manu-

To the credits granted by the Reichsbank it is also necessary to add those of the "Loan Offices" which at certain times were appreciable (they amounted to 252 milliard paper marks at the end of 1922).

**3.** The policy of the Reichsbank was severely criticized when a committee in the spring of 1923 investigated the causes of the fall of the mark.* The deputy Hertz calculated the presumed profits of those who had taken money on credit on January 1st, 1923, and restored the same after the collapse of the mark, and concluded that it was the Reichsbank itself which had offered to speculators the possibility of counteracting the action for the support of the mark.

It was suggested to the Reichsbank that it should remove the possibility of unjust profits for those to whom it advanced money by compelling the debtor to pay back a sum in paper marks having the same *real value* as the sum taken on loan. The real value could be calculated by means of the rate of exchange or the index number of wholesale prices. But only towards the middle of August 1923 did the President of the Reichsbank announce the adoption of the principle of loans at a "constant value," and commence to apply that principle. The debtor had then to restore the sum received plus four-fifths of the sum corresponding to the amount of the depreciation of the mark, which was calculated on the basis of the sterling exchange rate. If, for example, he had received 1,000 and the sterling exchange rate had risen from 100 to 150, he had to repay 1,400. The "depreciation clause," at first only applied to the advances, was extended, as from the beginning of December 1923, also to the discount of bills of exchange. Until at the

facturers was a compensation for the losses of working capital which they had suffered because of the depreciation of the mark. On this point it may be observed that in the summer of 1922, in general, business men had learned to discount in the paper prices the risk of the future depreciation of the paper mark. This is also the opinion of Professor Prion, who thus summarizes the methods adopted by German business men in the second half of 1922: (*a*) the fixing of sale prices on the basis of the cost of "reproduction"; (*b*) the purchaser was obliged to pay in cash on the consigning of the goods; (*c*) recourse, in a large measure, to credit from the Reichsbank. "In reality," concludes Prion, "the object of these methods, the preservation of working capital, was more than achieved, thanks to the courteous invitation of the Reichsbank to discount commercial bills" (Prion, *Deutsche Kreditpolitik*, 1919–23—in "Jahrbuch" of Schmöller, 1924, vol. ii, p. 195).

* An impressive criticism of the policy of the Reichsbank was made by Professor Hirsch in the article "Falsche Kreditpolitik" published in the review *Plutus* of August 1st, 1923.

end of January 1924 short-term credits of the Reichsbank were usually issued with this clause.*

Thus the banking policy also, like the financial policy, was characterized by errors in the interpretation of monetary phenomena, by excessive indulgence to the interests of influential groups, and by tardy—and consequently ineffective—innovations. Banking policy was a fundamental cause of the paper inflation and consequently of the depreciation of the mark.

## II. THE APPARENT SCARCITY OF THE CIRCULATING MEDIUM

**4.** The supporters of the theory that the depreciation of the mark was the consequence of events independent of the financial policy of the German Government and of the inflation, stated that the *chronological order* of the phenomena connected with the depreciation of the money confirmed their theories.

The depreciation of the German mark did not proceed in a uniform manner. There were times when depreciation was slow or the exchange was maintained almost stable. Suddenly, often following some political event, the demand for foreign currencies became intense and the exchanges rapidly depreciated. Then, unexpectedly, the money market would settle down and there would be a reaction in the exchange; but generally the latter would remain at a level appreciably higher than before. Then a new period of relative stabilization or of slow depreciation was recommenced, which later was followed by another sudden depreciation of the German currency. These sudden changes from a given level of the price of the dollar to a much higher one occurred, for example, in the autumn of 1921; in July 1922, and in January and

* According to the Reichsbank Report for 1923 the interest rates per annum charged in the second half of 1923 were as follows:

| *Discount on Bills* | *Advances* |
|---|---|
| (*a*) For credits without the "depreciation clause": August 2nd–September 14th, 30 per cent; September 15th–December 31st, 90 per cent. | (*a*) For advances without the "depreciation clause": August 2nd–September 14th, 31 per cent; September 15th–October 7th, 31 per cent (plus a commission of $\frac{1}{4}$ per cent per day); October 8th–December 31st, 108 per cent. |
| (*b*) For "stable value" credits from December 29th, 10 per cent. | (*b*) For "stable value" advances September 15th–December 28th, 10 per cent; from December 28th, 12 per cent. |

July 1923. The sudden falls of the mark which happened at these times were not *immediately* preceded by comparable increases of the issues of paper money.

We must admit that some of the facts which were observed in the last phases of the depreciation of the mark seem to give support to those who deny that the inflation was at the root of the matter.

The characteristic of those last phases was the very close connection between the exchange rate and domestic prices. (See Diagrams VI and VII.) A rise in the exchange spread almost immediately to all prices; not only to those of imported articles but also to purely domestic goods; and to both wholesale and retail prices. The sole preoccupation of industrialists, wholesale, or retail merchants at the time was the dollar rate. An increase in wages, salaries, and fees immediately followed the rise in prices.

**5.** So long as the disturbance of the exchange exercised only a slow and partial influence on prices, an improvement of the exchange itself was possible and was actually experienced sometimes. But when internal prices, thanks mainly to the influence of psychological causes, commenced to adapt themselves immediately to the sudden increases in the dollar rate, the depreciation of the exchange tended to become permanent because the rise of internal prices quickly established a new level of exchange equilibrium.

The sudden rise of prices caused an intense demand for the circulating medium to arise, because the existing quantity was not sufficient for the volume of transactions. At the same time the State's need of money increased rapidly. Private banks, besieged by their clients, found it practically impossible to meet the demand for money. They had to ration the cashing of cheques presented to them. On some days they declared that they were obliged to suspend payments or open their offices for a few hours only. Panic seized the industrial and commercial classes, who were no longer in a position to fulfil their contracts. Private cheques were refused because it was known that the banks would be unable to cash them. Business was stopped. The panic spread to the working classes when they learned that their employers had not the cash with which to pay their wages.

The economic system reacted to this scarcity of the circulating medium; new forms of credit were invented. In the summer of 1923, when the scarcity of money was most acute, the Berlin banks decided to issue a kind of cheque which was to be acceptable at their branches and which was also willingly accepted by the public, who were desirous of having any means of payment whatever. Private firms, industrial companies, combines, and public authorities issued every kind of provisional money.

But all these expedients were not sufficient to satisfy the great need of money provoked by the enormous rise in prices, and the eyes of all were turned to the Reichsbank. The pressure exercised on it became more and more insistent and the increase of issues, from the central bank, appeared as a remedy.

These phenomena, which appeared in Germany after a sharp rise in the exchange, made the increase of issues appear as unavoidable as the inevitable consequence of the rise of prices which had been provoked by the depreciation of the exchange. The opinion, on this subject, formed in administrative circles, is clearly expressed in the following words of Helfferich: "To follow the good counsel of stopping the printing of notes would mean—as long as the causes which are upsetting the German exchange continue to operate—refusing to economic life the circulating medium necessary for transactions, payments of salaries and wages, etc., it would mean that in a very short time the entire public, and above all the Reich, could no longer pay merchants, employees, or workers. In a few weeks, besides the printing of notes, factories, mines, railways and post office, national and local government, in short, all national and economic life would be stopped."*

The authorities therefore had not the courage to resist the pressure of those who demanded ever greater quantities of paper money, and to face boldly the crisis which (although painted in unduly dark colours by Helfferich) would be, undeniably, the result of a stoppage of the issue of notes. They preferred to continue the convenient method of continually increasing the issues of notes, thus making the continuation of business possible, but at the same time prolonging the pathological state of the German economy. The Government increased salaries in proportion to the depreciation of the mark, and employers in their turn granted continual increases in wages, to avoid disputes, on the condition that they could raise the prices of their products. A characteristic example of this is given by the discussions of the "Coal Council," where employers and employed easily came to agreement on the basis of higher wages and correspondingly higher coal prices.

Thus was the vicious circle established: the exchange depreciated; internal prices rose; note-issues were increased; the increase of the

* *Das Geld*, p. 650.

quantity of paper money lowered once more the value of the mark in terms of gold; prices rose once more; and so on.

### III. THE INCREASE IN THE ISSUES OF PAPER MONEY

**6.** Certainly the difficulties with which the Government and the Reichsbank had to wrestle in the last phases of the depreciation of the mark were very serious. It is certain that the rise in home prices, which was the immediate consequence of the depreciation of the exchange, had given a definite thrust to the increase of note issues and of the floating debt.

But it is important not to forget that that last stage of the depreciation of the mark was, in a great part, the direct consequence of an erroneous financial policy in the preceding years. Besides, the increase of the note-issues, following the increase of home prices, was not at all a *necessary* action, as some writers seem to believe. An energetic financial and monetary policy and a more circumspect banking policy would have broken the vicious circle; as in fact it was broken by the monetary reform of November 1923.

Instead, for a long time the Reichsbank—having adopted the fatalistic idea that the increase in the note-issues was the inevitable consequence of the depreciation of the mark—considered as its principal task, not the regulation of the circulation, but the preparation for the German economy of the continually increasing quantities of paper money which the rise in prices required. It devoted itself especially to the organization, on a large scale, of the production of paper marks.

Towards the end of October 1923 the special paper used for the notes was made in thirty paper mills. The printing works of the Reich, in spite of its great equipment, was no longer sufficient for the needs of the Reichsbank; about a hundred private presses, in Berlin and the provinces, were continually printing notes for the Reichsbank. There, in the dispatch departments, a thousand women and girls were occupied exclusively in checking the number of notes contained in the packets sent out by the printing press. One of the more extraordinary documents in the history of the German inflation is the memorandum of the Reichsbank, published in the daily papers of October 25th, 1923. In this the issuing institution announced that during the day notes to the total value of 120,000 billions of paper marks had been stamped (a billion $= 1{,}000{,}000^2$). But the demand during the day had been for about a trillion ($1{,}000{,}000^3$). The Reichsbank announced that it would do its utmost to satisfy the demand and expressed the hope that towards the end of the week the daily production would be raised to half a trillion!

## PART III

### I. THE DEPRECIATION OF THE MARK AND THE DISEQUILIBRIUM OF THE BALANCE OF TRADE

**1.** I have already said that, according to an opinion widely held in Germany, the passive balance of trade was the first and fundamental cause which during the war had already provoked the depreciation of the value of the mark in terms of foreign currencies. After the outbreak of the war the publication of trade statistics ceased; but the Government did not refrain from informing the public that the balance of trade showed a grave disequilibrium.

Later, the excess of imports over exports (including the imports effected on account of the allies) was valued by the Statistical Bureau of the Reich at 15 milliard gold marks, for the period from August 1st, 1914, to the end of 1918.

Obviously, in this argument and in this pretended statistical proof there is much confusion of ideas. If at a given exchange rate between the mark and foreign money the demand for the latter exceeds the supply, the mark is depreciated, and that tends, other things being equal, to re-establish the equilibrium between imports and exports. If, instead, statistics show that for the whole of a long period imports have exceeded exports, it shows that the excess has been compensated for by other items in the balance of payments, such as foreign credits, and sale of stocks and shares; for how, otherwise, could the excessive imports have been paid for?

On the other hand, not even the "Purchasing Power Parity Doctrine" (although certainly more satisfactory than the "adverse balance of payments theory") gives a complete explanation of the foreign exchanges. (See Appendix to this chapter.)

The principal point on which one must insist is this: In a great country like Germany, endowed with vast resources and with a great variety of imports and exports—on which variety was based, even during the war, a considerable elasticity of foreign demand for German products, and of German demand for foreign goods*—a depreciation of the exchanges, when it is provoked only by an increase in the demand for foreign goods, cannot go beyond a certain limit (let us say 15, 20, or 30 per cent of parity) because compensatory forces which the

* Rist, *op. cit.*, p. 178.

depreciation raises prevent it from passing beyond this limit. Although the increase in the demand for foreign goods may be the cause of an initial depreciation of the market exchange, it cannot explain the *continual* depreciation. To explain the *continual* depreciation in this fashion it would be necessary to assume that the real demand curve for foreign goods was moved continually towards the right (see diagrams in the aforesaid Appendix). But that is scarcely probable; besides, the reactions which would arrest the depreciation of the exchange would quickly appear.

2. It is impossible to prove how far the excess of imports over exports during the war was caused by *independent* movements of the international demand for goods; and how far, on the other hand, the movements of Germany's demand curve for foreign goods and of the foreigners' demand curve for German goods were the effect of a rise in the German home prices, provoked by the monetary inflation (see Appendix).

It is doubtful if the theoretical scheme, described in the Appendix, is applicable to the abnormal conditions of the German economy during the war. It may, however, be observed that even at a time when goods traffic and foreign transactions are controlled and limited by restrictions,a disequilibrium between internal and external prices cannot but exercise an influence on the exchange rate. As Diehl (a writer who would not admit the influence of the inflation on the exchange) himself observed, after the outbreak of the war: "*Thanks to the rising prices of many goods in Germany, it was profitable to buy these goods in neutral countries and resell them in Germany.* German buyers went to the neutral countries, carrying with them great quantities of German notes, with the object of doing business of this kind and in this way they depressed the German exchange."*

Those who deny the influence of the rise in home prices on the mark exchange maintain that the causes which determined the prices of goods and the exchange rate respectively were completely different. They argued: the Swiss, Danes, Dutch, etc., who bought marks on the exchanges, did so, not in order to buy German goods but to satisfy their obligations to Germany. Hence these people were not affected by the general level of prices in Germany; the price of bills of exchange payable in marks depended on the demand and supply of those bills.

The weakness of this argument is obvious: the supply and demand

* Diehl, *Ueber Fragen des Geldwesens und der Valuta*, Jena, 1921, p. 46.

for foreign bills of exchange, existing at a given moment, were the result of preceding transactions; and exports from Germany were the more discouraged and imports were the more stimulated the higher rose the level of German prices.

Further, it is not true that neutrals bought marks only to pay the debts they owed to Germans. From the outbreak of the war Germany began to pay for her imports partly with marks, which the vendor put aside, hoping for a future rise in the German exchange. Or he opened a credit account in marks at a German bank. As Professor Beckerath rightly observes,* for the foreigner the value of the German mark, now off the gold standard, was measured by the quantity of goods which he could buy with marks, that is, it depended on the German prices of exportable goods. Indeed, many foreign speculators, who had acquired large quantities of marks, proposed to keep them in the hope of the mark exchange rate improving, but to change them quickly for German goods directly the rate had shown signs of depreciating. Thus the internal value of the mark had to be taken into consideration by those speculators. If, for example, German home prices had increased from 100 to 120, the foreign exporter could no longer sell his goods at 100, but had to raise his price in proportion. But that meant a depreciation of the mark relatively to foreign money.

**3.** According to the Statistical Bureau of the Reich the principal items of the balance of payments during the war were as follows:

TABLE X

*Debit Items*

(Milliards of gold marks)

| | |
|---|---|
| Imports of goods into Germany | 23 |
| Imports on account of Allied countries | 4 |
| | 27 |

*Credit Items*

(Milliards of gold marks)

| | |
|---|---|
| Exports of goods | 12 |
| Exports of gold | 1 |
| Sales of German securities | 1 |
| Sales of foreign securities | 3 |
| Credits (of which 3 to 4 milliards in terms of foreign currency, the rest in marks) | 10 |
| | 27 |

* *Die Markvaluta*, 1920, p. 11.

## II. THE BALANCE OF PAYMENTS AFTER THE END OF THE WAR

**4.** The German trade journals relate that in the months following the Armistice there was a "goods famine." Great quantities of foodstuffs and raw materials were imported, and therewith stocks, which after the long war were totally exhausted, were replenished. To the imports recorded in the official statistics must be added an unknown but certainly a considerable quantity of goods (especially luxury articles such as cigarettes, chocolates, wines, spirits, etc.) which penetrated into Germany through the "hole" which the occupation of the Rhineland made in the German customs belt. On the other hand the political disorder caused by defeat and revolution, the difficulties of re-establishing commercial relations which the economic blockade had broken, and the impossibility of reorganizing in a day the great industries which for many years had directed all their energy to the production of war goods, impeded in the first months of 1919 a rapid renewal of exports.

Towards the end of 1919 and in the following years, exports increased, but on the whole slowly. According to an estimate of the Statistical Bureau, the disequilibrium between imports and exports amounted, in the four years 1919–1922, to 11 milliard gold marks.

To the disequilibrium between imports and exports was added the influence of the payments which Germany had to make for reparations, for the settlement of private debts and credits, for various inter-allied commissions, and for the repayment of old loans, etc. Moreover, all those credit items (particularly the income from German foreign investments, estimated at about 25 milliard marks) which before the war covered the deficit in the balance of trade, had either diminished or completely disappeared.

In the absence of foreign credits the deficit in the balance of payments was covered, for the most part, by the sale of marks, which for a long time, in spite of bitter past experience, foreign speculators bought in considerable quantities, thinking that the extreme limit of the depreciation was reached. The reports of the banks showed, for the beginning of 1919, great sales of marks and a continuous and very marked rise in deposits by foreigners.* It was the creation of new

* The Committee of Experts which, in 1924, made an investigation of the mark credit balances on foreign account in the principal banks of Germany from the end of 1918 to the end of 1923, found that there had been during this five-year period more than a million individual accounts of this kind (*The Experts' Plan for Reparation Payments*, published by the Reparations Commission, p. 125).

marks which made it possible to purchase goods abroad beyond the limit set by the value of exports. When foreigners ceased to buy German marks the excess of imports rapidly diminished.*

**5.** It is not possible to say, on the basis of German trade statistics (which, as we shall see later, are most inaccurate), when the equilibrium of Germany's trade balance was re-established. In 1922 imports, calculated on 1913 prices, amounted to 6·211 million gold marks and exports to 6·199 millions.

From many facts and from opinions of competent authorities it appears that in 1922 (a year in which reparation payments were very small and when exports had increased) the condition of the balance of payments became favourable,† thanks to the expenditure of the numerous travellers who visited Germany in that year, to the activities of the shipping companies, and to the sale of securities, mortgages, houses, land, *objets d'art*, etc. At that time the depreciation of the mark not only continued but did so more rapidly than ever before.

In the months of January to October 1923, according to the calculations of the Statistical Bureau of the Reich, imports amounted to 5,155 million marks and exports to 5,024 millions. But these figures are incomplete, because they include the foreign trade of the occupied territories only in so far as goods destined for them, or provided by them, had to cross non-occupied territory.

### III. ABNORMAL CONDITIONS OF THE FOREIGN EXCHANGE MARKET

**6.** It was alleged in Germany that the favourable conditions of the balance of payments in 1922 could not exercise a beneficial influence on the German exchange because a great amount of foreign exchange was hoarded instead of being offered on the market. To this abnormal shortening of the supply of foreign bills there corresponded a similar abnormal expansion in the demand.

* Even in 1922, despite the fact that the great depreciation of the mark had already caused enormous losses to foreign possessors of German money, the sales of marks abroad continued. According to a German official publication (*Deutschlands Wirtschaftslage*, Berlin, 1923), even in October 1922 the quantity of paper marks sold through some few foreign banking houses amounted to 22 milliards.

† See *Plutus* of August 1st, 1923. Also Eucken, *Kritische Betrachtungen zum deutschen Geldproblem*, 1923, p. 15, and Lansburg, "Die Zahlungsbilanz," in *Bank*, July 1923. The latter maintains that in 1922, after exports, the expenditure by foreign travellers represented the most important credit item of the German balance of payments.

The disequilibrium between the demand and supply of foreign bills was the result of the following factors:

(*a*) Having little faith in the political and economic future of Germany and desiring to avoid taxes, German industrialists formed the habit of leaving abroad a part of the profits from exports; that is, the difference between the cost of production and the price which they received by selling abroad.

(*b*) Even a great part of the foreign money which was obtained by the sale of securities, houses, land, etc., was either left abroad (the "flight of capital") or hoarded at home, so that it did not come on to the exchange market.

(*c*) The numerous decrees which surrounded the buying of foreign exchange with difficulties, helped to lessen the supply because the possessor of foreign exchange would not give it up at any price, fearing that he would be unable to re-purchase it later when the need arose. If the authorities wished to relieve the foreign exchange market by prohibiting the purchase of foreign exchange by persons who were not traders, it was necessary to supplement the measures restricting the purchase of foreign exchange by issuing stable value securities which would offer to possessors of paper marks the possibility of investing their savings safely. This was the opinion of financial writers: but the proposal was not accepted because it was feared that, following a further depreciation of the mark, the Reich would have to bear at that too heavy a burden when it had to redeem the securities. But this argument was groundless, because the issue of a stable-value loan should have formed part of a general plan for the stabilization of the mark.

(*d*) There was a brisk demand for foreign exchange on the part of German possessors of paper marks. More and more, as the mark depreciated, the phenomenon was understood by the public and the mark ceased to be wanted as a "store of value." The mark balances of industrial firms and even of private persons were converted into shares and into foreign exchange. A considerable amount of foreign exchange was therefore continually withdrawn from the market for the purpose of more or less permanent investment. At certain times, as in October 1921, July and August 1922, and in January 1923 after the occupation of the Ruhr, the purchase of foreign exchange by the public assumed the proportions of a pathological phenomenon. The feverish acquisition of foreign exchange explained in great part the rapid fall of the mark which occurred at these periods. The situation of the foreign exchange market then appeared completely dominated by the purchases of the public, which were the consequence of the panic created by political events.

The very rapid and sharp depreciation of the mark was mainly at those times due to psychological causes, operating especially in Germany. Indeed, it was observed at those times that the impetus for the rise of the dollar originated in the German bourses and not in foreign markets, where the mark was generally quoted at a rate somewhat higher than that in Berlin. No one could blame the German investors, who sought to escape the consequences of the depreciation of the mark, by buying foreign exchange. After the "slaughter of the innocents" occasioned by the depreciation of the currency, it could not be expected that the public should continue to deposit their own money in the savings banks or invest it in Government bonds.

(*e*) As depreciation progressed, the mark was continually rendered more unfit for the function of the circulating medium, and for this purpose foreign exchange took the place of German money. In this way a part of the foreign currencies came to be permanently diverted into the channels of internal circulation.

(*f*) The depreciation of the mark stimulated an ever-growing speculation in foreign exchange. In this way a certain quantity of foreign currency which passed continually from hand to hand in speculating circles, was diverted from the money market.

(*g*) The purchase of foreign exchange was a method frequently used by "real" trade for diminishing the risks arising from the fluctuations of the exchange. Merchants who sold goods for future delivery for payment in paper marks protected themselves against the risk of the future depreciation of the mark by buying, at the time the contract was concluded, a corresponding quantity of foreign exchange. The practice of calculating prices in foreign money, which became widespread in the second half of 1922, as a protection against the risks of the depreciation of the paper mark, also resulted in a marked rise in the demand for foreign exchange, because merchants who assumed the obligation of paying a sum in paper marks, varying according to the rate of exchange on the day of payment, had to protect themselves against eventual losses by buying foreign exchange. This practice of insuring against the risk of the depreciation of the mark, which became more and more common towards the end of 1922, contributed therefore to the deterioration of the situation in the foreign exchange market.

In certain branches of industry, in which it was necessary to take account of risks arising from obligations contracted in foreign money, it was felt to be desirable to counteract these risks with guarantee funds in foreign exchange. That happened, for example, in assurance firms.

Hence, under conditions of the depreciation of the circulating medium, the foreign exchange market presented an altogether extraordinary appearance. When the currency is stable the demand for foreign exchange is determined by the necessity of making payments abroad. But in Germany, to this normal demand was added an entirely abnormal demand, which was principally provoked by the desire to invest savings securely in foreign exchange. It is worth mentioning that for a long time there was also a brisk demand for marks by foreigners who speculated for a rise in German money, while in Germany many people speculated for a fall. The large purchases of marks by foreigners for some time checked the rise of the exchanges. But when foreigners ceased to buy marks and a great part of the marks (either notes or bank deposits) possessed by them were offered in Germany for foreign exchange, shares, houses, goods, etc., the depreciation of German money in terms of foreign currencies and goods in the home market was intensified.

**7.** There is no doubt that the abnormal demand for foreign exchange on the part of the German public who determined to take part in the flight of capital must cause a depreciation of the exchange. This depreciation, however, could not go beyond certain limits if the quantity of marks had not been increased. In fact, the increase in the prices of foreign currencies had immediate effect on the prices of imported goods, and that—had the money income of consumers remained stable—would have meant that prices which passed a certain limit would quickly become prohibitive. It was only due to the rise in money incomes, which was the consequence of the increase in the circulation, that it was possible that imported goods, which were sold at rising prices because of the depreciation of the exchange, could find buyers.

Besides, if the amount of the circulation and the volume of credit did not increase, there would be limits to the supply of paper marks in the foreign exchange market, and, on the whole, this supply could not be very large. The great mass of the public could not much lessen their normal purchases of consumption goods in order to buy foreign money; and manufacturers needed their money, especially for buying raw materials, paying workers, etc.* When the public sold securities, houses or land in large quantities with the object of buying foreign money with the receipts from the sales, obviously such sales were only possible while there were people with sufficient means for buying those goods and securities. If the original value (according to the cost of production or of purchase) of the goods or securities offered for sale exceeded the amount of the money saved, then either (*a*) the vendors must sell at a lower cost and suffer losses, which, if they went beyond a certain limit, would check sales, and therefore also the flight of capital; or (*b*) the purchasers must buy the goods and securities with the aid of bank credits. But in this second case it is the bank credits which stimulate the flight of capital abroad; and credit restriction would, therefore, be an efficacious obstacle to this flight.

Sometimes it happens that the demand for foreign money on the part of certain classes in country X is so *inelastic* that the total sum spent, in the money of X, in the purchase of foreign money increases when the currency of X is depreciated. Something like this situation arises in practice when an increase in the price of foreign currencies, instead of reducing purchases of foreign goods, induces importers to anticipate their purchases. If, besides, exports are also rather inelastic, it may be said that the depreciation of the exchange, rather than provoking reactions which re-establish the equilibrium, tend, instead, to increase the disequilibrium of the balance of payments and to accentuate the depreciation of the currency. But even in this case, if the quantity of money in the country with depreciating exchange, and therefore the money incomes of its people, *is not increased*, the rise in the value of foreign currencies will not go beyond a certain limit. In fact, the people of that country cannot spend more than a certain sum on foreign goods and on the purchase of foreign currencies. Besides, depreciating exchange will stimulate foreigners to purchase shares, houses, and land, so that for this reason also the depreciation cannot go beyond a certain limit.

Also, it is most improbable that the *total* curve of the demand for foreign money on the part of a country will remain inelastic for a long time. As soon as the public realizes that the Government has firmly decided not to increase the note issues, confidence in the national currency is re-established and the abnormal demand for foreign currencies ceases. In fact, when the mark was finally stabilized in

* The influence of an increase in the velocity of circulation will be examined in Chapter IV.

November 1923, the demand for foreign exchange was immediately reduced, and the only demand in the market was that occasioned by the normal needs of trade.

Hence, in order that the abnormal demand for foreign exchange for hoarding should exercise a detrimental influence for a long time on the national paper money (as happened in Germany), it is necessary that this demand should be fed, continually, by new issues of paper money, which also cause distrust to spread continually.

## PART IV

### I. PAYMENTS UNDER THE TREATY OF VERSAILLES

**1.** A special item in the German balance of payments was the payment of reparations. Numerous German economists and politicians have stated—an opinion accepted also by several economists outside Germany*—that the principal cause of the depreciation of the mark in the post-war years was the necessity for the German Government to create new money to pay reparations, or, more generally, to satisfy the financial obligations arising from the Treaty of Versailles. In his recent work Elster says that "the stages in the progress of the mark towards depreciation were the same stages which characterized the development of the arrangements between the Allies and the German Government with regard to reparations. . . . The ruin of the German mark was the work of the Allies, while the United States Government looked on in silence."†

Doubtless, the burdens imposed on Germany by the Treaty of Versailles contributed to the deficit shown in the financial years 1920–1923, but as may be seen from German sources, they were not the only causes and never the most important.

In the following table‡ the figures of the deficit are shown (measured

TABLE XI

(*Millions of gold marks*)

| *Financial year* | *Total* | *Expenses under the Treaty of Versailles* |
|---|---|---|
| 1920 | 6,053·6 | 1,850·9 |
| 1921 | 3,675·8 | 2,810·3 |
| 1922 | 2,442·3 | 1,136·7 |
| 1923 (April–December) | 6,538·3 | 742·4 |
| | 18,710·0 | 6,540·1 |

* For example, Cassel, *op. cit.*, p. 191.

† *Op. cit.*, pp. 130 and 214. On the other hand, it should be mentioned that some German writers expressed moderate judgment on the influence of reparations on the foreign exchanges—as, e.g., Professor Hirsch (*Deutschlands Währungsfrage*, 1924, p. 12). Also Professor Mises wrote: "The progressive depreciation of the mark could not be the effect of reparations payments; it is simply the result of the Government's financing itself by issuing additional notes" ("Die geldtheoretische Seite des Stabilisierungsproblems," *Schriften des Vereins für Sozialpolitik*, vol. 164, part ii, p. 31).

‡ See art. "Die Reichseinnahmen und Ausgaben in Geldmark" in *Wirtschaft und Statistik*, No. 9 of 1924.

by the increase in the floating debt) and those of the total expenses borne by the German Treasury under the Treaty of Versailles.

As one may see, even according to German statistics the cost of the application of the Treaty of Versailles could not explain more than a third of the total difference between expenditure and income which existed in the four financial years 1920–1923. Besides, as has already been stated, in the eight months from November 1918 to the end of June 1919, that is *before the signing of the treaty*, the deficit in the Reich Account amounted to a good ten milliard gold marks!

Certainly the expenses imposed on Germany by the treaty and by successive agreements regarding reparations were most considerable, but other countries also came out of the war with a balance of accounts weighted by the formidable burden of interest on debts contracted during the war. In Germany itself, at the end of the war, the public debt, funded and floating, amounted in round figures to 75 milliard gold marks. The service of the debt probably required three or four milliard gold marks a year. Thanks to the depreciation of the mark which occurred in 1919 that burden had been consistently reduced by 1920, when the expenses of the treaty began.

The consolidated public debt of the Reich amounted to 58·5 milliard gold marks at the end of March 1918, to 33·7 milliards towards the end of March 1919, and to 5·4 milliards a year later.*

Let us suppose that the Allies had refrained from imposing any financial burdens whatever on Germany. It is suggested that then the mark would not have depreciated. But the German Government were bound to pay interest on the public debt. There would be two possible courses: either the German Government, finding it impossible to collect the necessary sum by means of taxes, would have to resort to the issue of paper money, and the mark would depreciate even without the influence of the Treaty of Versailles; or it would have to cut down expenses and increase the fiscal burden of the German population: but if it had energetically stated the necessity for this policy in 1920, it would have prevented the further depreciation of the mark in spite of the treaty, so that that cannot have been the fundamental cause of the depreciation of the German mark.

2. Alternatively it is sometimes suggested that the German mark depreciated because the German Government had to buy foreign exchange in order to be able to make reparation payments. Actually

* See the official publication: *Deutschlands Wirtschaft, Währung und Finanzen*, 1924, p. 29.

payments in foreign exchange had little relevance until August 31st, 1921. They consisted almost exclusively (in addition to the maintenance of the various commissions instituted by the Treaty of Versailles) of the clearing of pre-war credits and debits resulting from relations between German citizens and those of the allied countries; the balance being adverse to Germany necessitated a payment in foreign money by Germany. On this account Germany had to pay 600 million gold marks before the end of 1922.

According to some writers, among whom was Cassel, it was the attempt made by Germany to fulfil her obligations imposed by the Ultimatum of London of May 1921 which provoked the collapse of the mark. In accordance with the clauses contained in the ultimatum Germany paid, towards the end of August 1921, in foreign money, a milliard gold marks and on November 15th another instalment of 500 million marks.

These were the only disbursements of cash made by Germany under the said ultimatum. On December 14th, 1921, the German Government informed the Reparations Commission that it would not be in a position to pay the instalments due on January 15th and February 15th, 1922. The Commission decided that Germany should continue the payments in kind and every ten days should pay 31 million gold marks in cash. Moreover, the Reparation Recovery Act remained in force. As a result of further negotiations it was agreed that the German Government should pay during 1922 50 million gold marks each month beginning from May 15th and 60 million on the 15th of November and December. But in July 1922 the Government declared that it could not continue to pay even this reduced amount. The last payment was made on July 15th. On August 17th the Government suspended, also on its own initiative, the payments arising from the settlement of private credits and debits.

## II. THE INFLUENCE OF REPARATION PAYMENTS ON THE VALUE OF THE MARK

**3.** According to official documents the milliard gold marks paid by Germany on August 31st, 1921, was collected in the following manner: Foreign exchange bought on the market or remitted by the Reichsbank, 541 million gold marks; credits conceded by Dutch banks, 270 millions; silver pledged by the Reichsbank, 58 millions; gold bought in the country, 15 millions; credit by the Bank of Italy,

32 millions; loans conceded by German banks, 16 millions; consigned in gold, 68 millions.

One must admit that the payment of this milliard exercised an appreciable influence on the German exchange, because an excess of exports over imports did not exist. The German exchange remained relatively stable after the summer of 1920. But a slow depreciation appeared once more after the acceptance of the ultimatum. It became more rapid during October 1921, when the German Government had to repay at short notice the credits which it had contracted in Holland on onerous terms.

But those who attributed the rapid rise in the price for foreign exchange which occurred in the autumn of 1921 only to the demand for foreign exchange provoked by the payment of the first milliard, were in error. An even greater influence was exercised by the panic which spread in Germany when the decision of the Council of the League of Nations relating to the division of Upper Silesia was known. German politicians and the more authoritative Press had proclaimed for months that the detachment of Upper Silesia meant the economic ruin of Germany. When the separation was decided, alarm seized the German public, who attributed to it a greater importance than it really had. On October 17th in the Berlin foreign exchange market there was a panic of overwhelming violence.

**4.** The events which occurred in September 1921 have never been clearly analysed. There is no doubt that in that month there began a violent attack on the mark in the German Bourse. Was this attack the effect of the spontaneous action of speculators who discounted the urgent need for foreign exchange on the part of the Government for reparation payments and who, considering the difficulties arising from the arrangement of Dutch credits, foresaw a further depreciation of of the mark? Was a concerted and systematic attack organized by the adversaries of the "fulfilment policy" to show that every attempt by Germany to pay reparations necessarily conduced to the collapse of the mark?

In those days even the Chancellor of the Reich publicly reproached the want of patriotism in those who, profiting from the fact that the Government had urgent need of collecting a considerable quantity of foreign exchange in a short time, had organized an active speculation on a continual rise in the dollar. According to statements appearing in the more reliable German Press, which severely criticized the actions of the speculators, the fall of the mark did not originate in New York and was therefore not provoked by foreign speculators; but the origin of the movement was the Berlin Bourse, where, in fact, the quotations were generally more unfavourable to the mark than in New York.

The rise in the dollar rate spread panic among German and foreign holders of paper marks. In the first days of November the lack of confidence became more serious. The "flight from the mark" became general. Those who were in Berlin in those days tell of shops besieged by a crowd ready to buy any object at any price, in order to get rid of paper marks as quickly as possible. The demand for industrial shares was very active and the price of them rose rapidly.

That German speculation exaggerated the exchange rates of the dollar is obvious from the fact that the dollar, which had been pushed beyond 300 marks at the beginning of November, fell precipitously on December 1st to 190; industrial share prices following. The result was an indescribable panic among the mass of small capitalists who had speculated on the fall of the mark or bought industrial shares at high prices.

**5.** A part of the responsibility for the fall of the mark which occurred in September 1921 also rests on those banks which had supported numerous purchasers of foreign exchange by means of credits.

That the great German industries were in a position to supply the Government, owing to the credit they enjoyed abroad, with the foreign exchange necessary for the payment of reparations is clear from the offer which the Association of German Industries made to the Government on September 28th, 1921. But this offer was based on conditions so difficult and humiliating—among other things the great industries demanded the control of the railways—that the Government had to reject the proposal.

**6.** As has been said, in July 1922 reparation payments in foreign exchange were suspended. In spite of this the depreciation of the German exchange continued; one of the periods of most rapid depreciation of the mark was the time between July 15th and August 31st, 1922. Even Elster is obliged to acknowledge that the fall of the mark experienced in those days could not be explained by payments under the Treaty of Versailles. "Nevertheless," he suggests, "the cause still rests in the treaty, whose very existence represented for German economy such a heavy burden that confidence in an improvement of the governmental finances and of the currency must continually decline."* I willingly admit that the Treaty of Versailles created psychological influences unfavourable to the mark. But, in his study of the consequences of the payments made in 1921, Elster neglected the fundamental question: why were those consequences so serious?

The answer is as follows. The German Government bought foreign exchange with paper money which was not purchasing power collected from German citizens by taxes, but new purchasing power created by the discounting of Treasury bills at the Reichsbank, that is by the increase of note-issues.† If, on the other hand, the quantity of paper money had not been increased, the depreciation of the mark, caused by the payment of reparations, would not have gone beyond a certain limit, which it is reasonable to suppose would have been quickly reached—given the reactions which would have shown themselves in an elastic demand for foreign exchange and in the export of goods and services, and, moreover, in the sale to foreigners of houses, shares, and other parts of the national wealth of Germany. Hence a more energetic financial policy would at least have lessened the effects of reparation payments on the German exchange. But as we have seen in the preceding paragraphs, the wealthy classes were tenaciously opposed to an effective financial reform which would have given the Government the means to begin fulfilling the obligations assumed by the acceptance of the Ultimatum of London.

Certainly, the ultimatum had imposed on Germany the payment of sums which far exceeded her contributive capacity; as was recognized later by the allied countries and was implicit in the celebrated report of the Dawes Committee. It was impossible to squeeze each year from the German people two milliard gold marks, plus a sum equivalent to 26 per cent of the value of exports (five milliard gold marks in 1920); and besides this the expenses arising from occupation, the numerous control commissions, etc. It was not possible for exports to develop so rapidly as to exceed imports by several milliards and to create the source from which the German Government normally had to draw the foreign exchange necessary for reparation payments.

But in Germany the supporters of the so-called "Fulfilment policy"

* *Op. cit.*, p. 166.

† One may read on page 14 of the Report of the Deutsche Bank for 1921 that the German Government procured more than a quarter of the sum due to the Allies by means of credits contracted abroad. "To the fact that these credits were covered *by the sale of paper marks abroad*, in default of foreign exchange offered by exporters, was due the rapid depreciation of the mark in the short period from August to November."

wanted the German people to make a great effort to pay the *first instalments*, thus showing their good faith; in the meantime world opinion would become more favourable to Germany, the occupation of the Ruhr would be avoided, and the Allies would be persuaded, little by little, of the necessity of alleviating the burdens imposed by the Ultimatum of London. Many people in Germany believed that the first instalments could be paid without excessive difficulty, partly by increasing taxes on income and capital and partly by an internal loan, subscriptions to which should be payable partly in foreign exchange.

But the opposers of the "Fulfilment policy" started from a different premise. In was an illusion to believe—they contended—that the payment of the first instalments would induce the allied Governments to mitigate the hard conditions imposed by London; on the contrary, the idea held abroad that Germany's capacity to pay had not been over-estimated at London would be strengthened. Then to what purpose fling into the bottomless well of reparations some milliards which might be so useful for the economic reconstruction of Germany? Also, if Germany did make an effort to pay some milliards, she could only succeed in covering a part of the interest on the sum fixed in London! Then before continuing reparation payments it was necessary to obtain from the Allies a moratorium of some years and a considerable reduction of the German debt.

It is also worth mentioning that the solution of the reparations question was impeded by those groups of industrialists among the Allies who were opposed to reparations in kind.

As the head of the French Government stated in the House of Deputies in the session of June 19th, 1924, there had been assigned to France for 1922 goods in kind worth 950 million gold marks. Actually, in that year France received only 179 million marks' worth of goods, almost exclusively coal and coke, and that was because certain French industrial groups used their influence to stop the supply of goods which would have competed with their products. At the same session the head of the French Government cited the case of an order for motor cars worth 117 million francs which they were forced to renounce because of the opposition of the French manufacturers.

## PART V

### I. THE INFLUENCE OF SPECULATION ON THE VALUE OF THE MARK

**1.** The German Governments were often accused of having wanted the depreciation of the mark in order to show that it was impossible for Germany to pay reparations.

To this accusation Stresemann replied in one of his speeches that a ministry which had "provoked by design the fall of the mark would have been an arch-criminal."

Actually it cannot be admitted that a Government, conscious of the very serious losses which the depreciation of the mark involved to numerous classes of society and of the profound moral disturbance which the experience caused in the whole of the German people, organized the collapse of the mark. Moreover, the manœuvre would have been aimless since it would have been easy for the Allies to tell the German Government that Germany's capacity for payment was not measured by the conditions of the currency but by the other much more important indices, such as her general wealth, the activity of her industries, the amount of her exports, the importance of foreign credits, etc.

For these reasons I cannot consider that accusation seriously. Neither shall I consider another accusation, often raised in Germany itself, according to which the depreciation of the mark was the effect of a conspiracy arranged by the reactionary and nationalist parties, who sought thereby to disorder German finances, to bring discredit on the republican régime and to undermine its (still insecure) foundations, in order to be able to restore the old régime on the ruins of the young republic.*

**2.** The accusation that the collapse of the German exchange was provoked by bold groups of professional speculators seems better founded. The objection to that is that speculation cannot be the original cause of the depreciation of the currency of a country. On the contrary, speculation appears when for certain reasons, such as the Budget deficit, the continual issues of paper money, the disequilibrium of the balance of trade, and the political situation, the exchanges are unstable. Speculation weakens and eventually disappears when the causes which

* See on this point the article of Professor Valentin in *Börsen-Courier* of August 21st, 1923.

provoked the original depreciation of the currency become less. Speculation in Austrian crowns flourished so long as that currency was unstable; but it disappeared as soon as the stabilization plan was adopted. Directly the monetary reform of November 1923 made the German exchange stable, speculation ceased, after some fruitless attempts to prevent the success of the operation. The well-known movements of international speculators are significant: they first fixed their abode in Vienna; later they passed to Berlin, and after the German monetary reform they transferred their activities to Paris, where the situation of the French franc promised to open for them a field of further activities.

But although the origin of the depreciation of the German mark cannot certainly be traced to the manœuvres of speculation, it appears possible to state that at a certain stage of the depreciation of that currency, speculation played an important part. Recent monetary experiences, in Germany and elsewhere, show that the theories of some economists on the influence of speculation are too optimistic. According to economists, speculators foreseeing the future variations of exchanges and anticipating them with their transactions, lessen the fluctuations themselves. But this theoretical conception often does not correspond to reality. Speculation has continually produced enormous fluctuations in the exchange rates for the German mark. Speculation often anticipated the future variations but exaggerated them, partly because its action was extraordinarily reinforced by the operations of the public, who followed more or less blindly the example of a few professional speculators. The dollar rate was increased rapidly from one day to the next and even from one hour to the next by the expectation of a future rise. But often the rates which had been pushed to a level not corresponding with the fundamental conditions could not be maintained; the first liquidation on the part of wise speculators spread panic among the public, who hastened to sell foreign exchange; hence a fall in the rates as sudden and sharp as the preceding rise had been.

For some time it was foreign speculation (foreigners possessed large sums of marks) which provoked the great fluctuations of the exchanges. In February 1920 the mark had fallen to 4 per cent of its gold parity; in May of the same year it rose again to 12 per cent; and that was mainly due to foreign speculation.* Later the speculation of Germans assumed greater importance.

On November 29th, 1921, the dollar was quoted at 276 marks; on

* Deutsche Bank, Report for 1920, p. 13.

December 1st it fell sharply to 190. By August 1922 the dollar rate had risen beyond 1,900 marks; but a violent reaction set in and the dollar fell to little more than 1,200 marks. On November 1st, 1922, it was quoted at 4,465 marks; November 7th, 8,068; two days later, 6,711; November 21st, 6,791; and on November 28th, 8,480 marks. On December 11th, 1922, it was at 8,337 marks; December 16th, 5,380; and on the 27th, 7,522 marks. Towards the middle of August 1923 the dollar rate rose giddily to 1, 2, 3, and 5 million marks; later falling suddenly to 3 millions. These examples, which could be multiplied, show that speculation did not exercise a stabilizing influence on the exchanges, but had rather the opposite effect.

**3.** The theorists also maintain that speculation cannot exercise an influence which manifests itself constantly in the same direction. For example, speculation cannot provoke a permanent and continuous rise of the exchanges. In fact, the speculator for a fall in the mark would act in the first place by buying foreign exchange, thus causing a rise in the price thereof; but later would come the moment at which he must sell the foreign exchange and his demand for marks would cause an improvement in the German exchange.

Without doubt this argument is valid for an early phase of the depreciation of the paper mark, when there was no intimate connection between the exchange rate and domestic prices. But in a later phase, when the depreciation of the exchange had immediate effect on prices, the consequences of the operations of speculators were more serious and lasting. In fact, the rise in prices, as we have seen above, was a potent stimulus to the increase of the inflation, as the Government and the Central Bank had not sufficient strength to oppose the demands of business men. Hence the new level of the exchange, provoked by speculators, tended to be justified by internal developments. Subsequent dealings of speculators, who offered on the market the foreign exchange earlier acquired by them, could not depress the exchange rate to its former level, because the foreign exchange was bought with the aid of the new issues of paper money, and a new equilibrium of the exchange was established corresponding to the new level of internal prices.

Experience showed that—whilst every depreciation of the exchange had immediate repercussions on internal prices—an improvement, on the other hand, only exercised a weak and slow influence in lowering the level of prices. As von Siemens, President of the Administrative Council of Siemens and Halske, has observed on this subject: "The internal value of the mark always adapted itself more rapidly to the depreciation of the external value, sometimes it even anticipated it; but when the exchange improved, human nature impeded the adaptation of prices." It is true that the prices of raw materials and foodstuffs decreased; but the vast majority of internal prices remained more or less unaffected. Manufacturers and wholesale merchants preferred not to sell goods rather than adapt themselves to a fall in prices.

Therefore, taking account of these circumstances: (*a*) the great sensitiveness of internal prices to a depreciation of the exchange; (*b*) the great inertia with which they met an improvement in the exchange; (*c*) the scarcity of foreign exchange which was always evident in the German Bourse at times of an increase in the dollar rate; and (*d*) the increase of the inflation which immediately followed the rise in prices—it is obvious that speculators could exercise a great influence in the way of stimulating a continual depreciation of the mark. But it is certain that a financial and banking policy which did not regard the increase of note-issues as an inevitable consequence of the rise in internal prices, would have been able to arrest the effects of speculation on the fall of the mark. In fact the energetic policy, followed after the stabilization of the mark, knocked the bottom out of speculation against the German mark.

### II. THE INFLUENCE OF CERTAIN CLASSES OF GERMAN INDUSTRIALISTS ON THE DEPRECIATION OF THE MARK

**4.** The actions of groups of speculators, unsolicitous for the interests of their own country,* were reinforced by the influence exercised by certain classes of producers.

* The *Berliner Börsen-Courier* of September 12th, 1921, states that "according to all appearances the fall of the mark did not have its origin in the New York exchange, from which it may be concluded that in Germany there was active speculation directed towards the continual rise of the dollar." Also the *Berliner Tageblatt* of September 14th, 1921, laments that "the increase in the number of those who speculate on the fall of the mark and who are acquiring vested interests in a continual depreciation."

The *Frankfurter Zeitung* of September 5th, 1922, condemns the frenzied speculation in foreign currencies. "The enormous speculation on the rise of the American dollar is an open secret. People who, having regard to their age, their inexperience, and their lack of responsibility, do not deserve support, have nevertheless secured the help of financiers, who are thinking exclusively of their own immediate interests."

On the influence of German speculation on the exchanges see Müller (ex Under-Secretary of State) in *8 Uhr Abendblatt* of May 22nd, 1923: "Those who have studied seriously the conditions of the money market state that the movement against the German mark remained on the whole independent of foreign markets for more than six months. *It is the German bears, helped by the inaction of the Reichsbank, who have forced the collapse in the exchange.*"

The example of all countries with a depreciated currency shows us that the depreciation of money creates a vast net of interests vested in the maintenance and continuation of the depreciation itself; interests which are disturbed by the possibility of a stabilization of the exchange and which, therefore, are assiduously opposed to the return of normal monetary conditions.

Seventy years ago Wagner wrote: "Powerful groups are interested in the maintenance of the premium on gold and even in its increase. If steps are taken for the improvement of the circulation, the powerful party of the protectionists opposes them with all the means at its disposal. Bankers and industrialists are in agreement. This has been proved every time in the numerous attempts made in Austria to re-establish the currency; the same thing happened in Russia in 1862. In the United States the attempt to eliminate the premium was opposed with veritable fanaticism. The adversaries of paper money and of protection are called traitors by the company of industrial egoists."*

This is just what happened in Germany. There is no doubt that the paper inflation would not have assumed such vast proportions if it had not been favoured in many ways by the people who drew a large profit from it. It is clear from the discussions held in 1922 and 1923 in the "Economic Council of the Reich," that representatives of those classes used their influence on the Government to impede the reform of the public finances and to sabotage all proposals for the stabilization of the German exchange, which they only accepted when, at last, an economic catastrophe threatened Germany and it was evident that the consequences of the inflation would rebound against their authors. Without making the exaggerated statement that the depreciation of the mark was due to a conspiracy of the industrial classes, it is certain, nevertheless, that they contributed largely to it, aided by the agriculturists who saw the lightening of the burden of their mortgages, which before the war was very heavy, and by all the other people who prospered owing to the continued depreciation of the national money. Such obvious and conspicuous advantages for producers could be derived from this phenomenon, that naturally they became the most convinced supporters of monetary inflation.† While sale prices rapidly

* Wagner, *op. cit.*, p. 105.

† Moulton (*Germany's Capacity to Pay*, London, 1923) refutes the accusation that the industrialists favoured the depreciation of the mark, observing that it was not in their interests to cause misery to vast numbers of German citizens, that is to consumers of the products of industry. Moulton's argument would have been just if based on the hypothesis that man is always wise enough to resist the temptation of an immediate advantage which involves a future danger.

approached world prices the industrialists paid wages which for a long time increased only at a great distance behind the rise in sale prices; other elements in the cost of production, such as transport expenses, declined in importance. The fiscal burden was continually lightened, and in addition the payment of certain taxes which industry had to pay into the exchequer, collecting them from others, became for the entrepreneur a source of conspicuous excess-profits. Mortgage debts were rapidly cancelled; bank credits, cleverly used, made possible the acquisition of foreign exchange, freehold property, etc.; and the difference between internal and external prices was a source of considerable gains for exporters.

The Dawes Committee also observed, in its Report, that the wealthy classes in Germany had not, in the last years, borne a fiscal burden adequate to their means. Nothing exasperated and irritated the lower classes so much as the state of affairs in which those who were the strongest economically, and who by the general ruin had been able to reap great advantages, contributed to the payment of taxes less than all the others.

**5.** Suddenly a theory of the depreciation of the mark was formed which lauded it as a great blessing. By stimulating exports, it revived industrial activity. Industrialists accustomed themselves to consider the depreciation of German money, with the consequent divergence between its internal and external values, as a condition without which industry could not continue to be productive. The possibility of an improvement in the value of the mark was viewed with grave apprehension, because—as Klöckner, a great industrialist observed—"the consequence would be a disaster of incredible magnitude." Another representative of the industrial classes added: "An appreciable and unforeseen improvement in the mark would paralyse the export trades and provoke vast unemployment. But even if it were gradual, any further improvement in our exchange would be a catastrophe."

In June 1922 Stinnes declared himself against a foreign loan "which would raise the exchange rate of the mark to a level which German economy could not endure." Against Stinnes, whom public opinion considered as one of the principal supporters of the depreciation of the mark, Georg Bernhard launched this virulent attack:*

He has woven intrigues against every Government which he was afraid would put in order the internal conditions of Germany. Every time any problem

* See *Vossische Zeitung*, October 18th, 1923.

whatever was considered—whether it were the question of reparations or that of German finances—he has always raised his voice and declared that the premises necessary for the solution of that problem did not yet exist. He attacked Rathenau after the conclusion of the Wiesbaden Agreement. . . . The classes on which he exercised a great influence opposed in a most violent way all attempts to reconstruct the finances and restore the currency by the issue of a gold loan or in any other way. . . . By means of credits amounting to milliards, whose value was continually reduced by inflation, he bought one firm after another in every possible branch of industry, he appropriated banks, financed shipping firms, acquired participations abroad and controlled numerous commercial enterprises. And all this he co-ordinated with the system of his politics, which aimed at the maintenance of inflation and disorder.

In a memorandum of the German Workers' Association, published in 1925, it is recorded that after the invasion of the Ruhr the great industries continued to buy foreign exchange, thus provoking the anger of Havenstein, the President of the Reichsbank, and succeeded, thanks to the rapid depreciation of the currency, in practically avoiding the payment of taxes. In fact, in March 1923 95 per cent of the total yield from income tax was paid by wage-earners and salaried workers. But the credits conceded by the Government to the industrialists constituted the most scandalous chapter in the history of that unhappy period. The sums received, which were intended to serve to finance Passive Resistance, were partly employed in the purchase of foreign exchange or for the construction of new machinery.

# APPENDIX TO CHAPTER II

# The Foreign Exchanges under Conditions of Inconvertible Paper Money

## I. THE DETERMINATION OF EXCHANGE RATES

**1.** The doctrine according to which, in the case of paper standards, "the rate of exchange between the monetary standards is determined, essentially, by the quotient of the purchasing powers of these standards in their respective countries" (Cassel), is based on the hypothesis that gold prices of goods tend, in various countries, to a uniform level. Thornton and Wheatley, who were the originators of the Purchasing Power Parity Theory, were also supporters of the theory of the international equalization of commodity prices. The Purchasing Power Parity Theory, if it is to be anything more than a mere truism, must be interpreted thus: Both country X and country Y produce, say, iron, whose price expressed in the respective currencies is, in conditions of equilibrium, $p_x$ in X and $p_y$ in Y. Suppose that iron can be easily transported from X to Y and vice versa, the price of iron in the currency of X ought to be equal to that in the currency of Y multiplied by the exchange rate (neglecting transport costs). We have therefore:

$$p_x = p_y C_x \quad \ldots \ldots \ldots \ldots \quad (1)$$

where $C_x$ is the price of the monetary unit of Y in terms of the currency of X. Hence the exchange rate is equal to the ratio between the prices.

But actually different international commodities are produced, for the most part, in different countries, as the theory of international trade shows. And then, if X produces and exports, say, cotton, and Y produces and exports iron, equation (1) loses all significance. If $p_x$ and $p_y$ are supposed to indicate, not the *absolute* prices of cotton and iron, but, respectively, the variations of the prices of these two goods, then equation (1) can have a significance which, however, requires some proof, as it is by no means obvious.

**2.** When these considerations are borne in mind it is apparent that the theory of foreign exchanges under conditions of inconvertible paper money must be placed on a more secure basis than that given by a conception so vague and uncertain as that of the international equalization of commodity prices. It is necessary to adopt another method of approach, which is indicated by the theory of international prices.

Let us assume that two countries, say Egypt and Germany, trade exclusively with one another, and that only one commodity is exported from each, namely, cotton from Egypt and iron from Germany.* Let us suppose further that each country has an independent paper standard: paper marks in Germany and paper piastres in Egypt. It is clear that the Egyptian demand for German iron will depend on the price, *in terms of Egyptian money*, which must be paid for it. Indeed, the price in terms of marks acquires a meaning for Egyptians only after it has been converted into their currency, which is for them the standard of value. In the same way the German demand for Egyptian cotton will vary according to the price *in terms of marks.*

Let us take an easy arithmetical example. Suppose that the Egyptian and German demands are represented, respectively, by the equations:

$$N = \frac{A}{P^x} \quad . \quad . \quad . \quad . \quad . \quad . \quad . \quad . \qquad (2)$$

and

$$M = \frac{B}{Q^y} \quad . \quad . \quad . \quad . \quad . \quad . \quad . \quad . \quad . \qquad (3)$$

Where $A$, $B$, $x$, and $y$ are constants and $P$ and $Q$ are, respectively, the price of iron in terms of Egyptian money and the price of cotton in terms of German money. If we further indicate by $I$ the price of iron expressed in marks and by $R$ the number of piastres that are given for one mark, we have $P = IR$. In the same way we may write: $Q = \frac{C}{R}$, $C$ being the price of cotton in terms of Egyptian money.

On the assumption of constant costs, $I$ and $C$ are not influenced in equilibrium conditions by international demand, but are separate and independent factors.† Other things remaining equal, they will depend on the monetary conditions in each country. If these conditions are arbitrarily assumed and if, therefore, $I$ and $C$ are supposed to be known, and to remain constant, it follows that both the Egyptian demand for iron and the German demand for cotton will only depend on the rate of exchange between marks and piastres.

If we multiply the quantity of iron demanded by Egypt at various prices by these prices, we have a schedule of money totals which indicate the amounts of piastres that Egyptian consumers of iron are willing to spend on this commodity, at the various prices in terms of Egyptian currency. From the demand function we may therefore derive the *aggregate expenditure function*, $Z = NIR$. On the other hand, the amounts of marks which German consumers of cotton are willing to spend are indicated by the aggregate expenditure function $W = M\frac{C}{R}$. Expressed in terms of Egyptian money, the sum spent by Germans is $MC$.

Obviously in *equilibrium conditions* the total value of Egyptian exports, in

* Each commodity is supposed to be made exclusively from the exporting country's materials and labour. Transport costs are neglected; they will be taken into consideration later.

† This assumption is also made by Professor Taussig. See Chapter 26 of his *International Trade.*

terms of Egyptian money, must be exactly equal to the total value of imports into Egypt, in terms of the same money. This condition is expressed by the equation*

$$CM = INR \quad . \quad . \quad . \quad . \quad . \quad . \quad . \quad . \quad . \quad (4)$$

In equation (4) there are three unknown quantities,† namely the exchange rate $R$ and the quantities of iron ($N$) and cotton ($M$), which are exchanged for one another. These unknown quantities are simultaneously determined by three equations, namely the two demand functions and the conditions embodied in

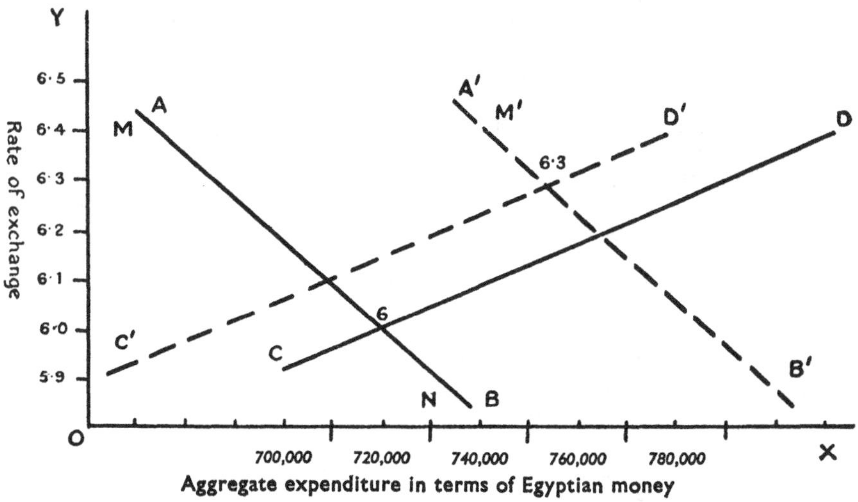


CHART I

* It follows from equation (4), if we divide both sides by $R$, that the value of exports from Germany, in terms of German money, is equal to the value of imports into Germany in terms of the same money.

† As Professor Ohlin observes (*Interregional and International Trade*, Cambridge, Harvard University Press, 1933, pp. 575–81), the assumption that the prices of imported and exported commodities are not affected by variations in the quantities of imports and exports is often not in accordance with actual price movements. If in equation (4) $C$ and $I$ are not supposed to be known, but are determined together with the other quantities by all conditions of international trade, we have five unknowns instead of three. But, on the other hand, we shall add to the three equations (1), (2), and (3) the two export supply functions $M = f\ (C)$ and $N = f\ (I)$, which may also be written $C = \phi\ (M)$ and $I = \phi\ (N)$. The equations express the relation between prices and quantities of exports under some arbitrarily assumed monetary conditions. Therefore we have five unknowns and five equations and the rate of exchange $R$ is determined together with the other unknowns by the conditions of international trade and by the monetary conditions in the countries concerned. (See, for a developed mathematical treatment of the problems of international trade, T. O. Yntema, *A Mathematical Reformulation of the General Theory of International Trade*, Chicago, 1932.)

equation (4). If we put, in the above equations, $A = 43{,}200{,}000$, $B = 2{,}000{,}000$, $x = 2$, $y = 2$, $C = 100$, $I = 10$, we have, solving equations (1), (2), and (3),

$$M = 7{,}200;\; N = 1{,}200;\; R = 6.$$

The curves AB and CD of Chart I represent, respectively, the aggregate expenditure schedules of Egypt and Germany.*

**3.** Let us suppose now that, following a currency inflation, the price of cotton in Egypt increases from 100 to 105. The consequences on the foreign exchange market will be as follows:

In the previous example it was assumed that, say, at the rate of 1·709 iron units for 1 cotton unit Egypt was willing to exchange 7,385 cotton units (whose price per unit in Egypt was 100) for 12,623 iron units. If Egypt is still willing to give 7,385 cotton units for 12,623 iron units, that means she will give for this quantity of iron 775,400 units of her money instead of 738,500; that is to say, she is willing to buy the same quantity of iron as before at a rate of exchange between Egyptian and German money which is 5 per cent less favourable than before (German prices in terms of marks remaining unchanged). Proceeding in this way, we may easily calculate the new aggregate expenditure curve. (See curve A′B′ of Chart.) As regards Germany, it is quite plausible to assume that the demand for cotton remains unchanged, in terms of German money. That means that, say, at a price of 17·1 marks Germany will continue to be willing to buy 6,844 of Egyptian cotton. When cotton prices stood at 100 Germany was willing to buy 6,844 of cotton (and consequently to spend 684,400 units of Egyptian money on it) if the rate of exchange was 5·85. Now that cotton prices stand at 105 Germany will buy 6,844 of cotton and spend

* Some possible values of these functions are indicated in the following table:

| *Egypt's Demand for Iron* | | | | *Germany's Demand for Cotton* | | | |
|---|---|---|---|---|---|---|---|
| $R$ | $IR$ | $N$ | $NIR$ | $R$ | $\frac{C}{R}$ | $M$ | $MC$ |
| 5·85 | 58·5 | 12,623 | 738,500 | 5·85 | 17·1 | 6,844 | 684,450 |
| 5·90 | 59·0 | 12,410 | 732,200 | 5·90 | 16·9 | 6,962 | 696,200 |
| 5·95 | 59·5 | 12,201 | 726,050 | 5·95 | 16·8 | 7,080 | 708,050 |
| 6·00 | 60·0 | 12,000 | 720,000 | 6·00 | 16·7 | 7,200 | 720,000 |
| 6·05 | 60·5 | 11,803 | 714,070 | 6·05 | 16·5 | 7,320 | 732,050 |
| 6·10 | 61·0 | 11,610 | 708,200 | 6·10 | 16·4 | 7,442 | 744,200 |
| 6·15 | 61·5 | 11,422 | 702,430 | 6·15 | 16·3 | 7,564 | 756,450 |

The equilibrium exchange rate is obviously 6, because only at this rate is the money value of imports into Egypt (720,000) equal to the money value of exports from Egypt. It may also be observed that the equilibrium exchange rate is that value of $R$ which makes the quantity of cotton demanded by Germany exactly equal to the quantity which Egypt is willing to supply, and the quantity of iron demand by Egypt equal to the quantity supplied by Germany.

If the demand curves of the two countries intersect at more than one point, to every such point there corresponds an equilibrium rate of exchange between the two currencies. The equilibrium will be *stable* at some points and at others *unstable*. But as Marshall observes, the "Normal Class" of demand curves (that is to say, curves which intersect in only one point) "is the only one which has any real importance" (*Money, Credit, and Commerce*, 1923, p. 335).

718,600 units of Egyptian money, if the rate of exchange is 6·14. In this way we may construct Germany's new aggregate expenditure curve (curve C′D′ on Chart I). The new equilibrium rate of exchange is then 6·30, that is to say the exchange rate will have risen exactly in proportion to the rise in cotton prices, in terms of Egyptian currency. But this conclusion presupposes that the *real demand* for iron by Egypt has remained unaltered after the inflation.

Now, in fact, inflation does not equally affect the money incomes of all social groups, but the incomes of some will rise more, and those of others less, than the general average. It is possible that this influences the demand for foreign goods. It is true that in the long run there will be a tendency for the money incomes of all classes to adjust themselves to the degree of inflation; but some permanent effects on the demand for foreign goods will remain. If, however, it can be presumed that these effects are comparatively slight, it follows that the changes in the ratio of price indices will tend to be accompanied by about equal changes in exchange rates, when the conditions of trade are not changed by *other* causes.

**4.** A change in the position of the curves of aggregate expenditure may be simply the consequence of currency inflation, as in the case represented by Chart I. But it may also be due to *independent* variations in the real demand for goods. This is a point generally neglected by supporters of the Purchasing Power Parity theory. They consider the variations of the supply and demand for foreign bills as a phenomenon determined purely, in the final analysis, by the state of the circulation.

But it is obvious, in our example, that Egypt increases its demand for German iron if it needs more iron than formerly (e.g. to construct railways) independently of the state of the circulation in Egypt. If these variations of demand are temporary, the influence on the exchanges will pass. If they are permanent it will not be so.

An increase in Egypt's demand (in the "schedule sense," to use Professor Fisher's expression) means a movement of Egypt's aggregate expenditure curve towards the right (Chart II). This will result in a rise in the price of marks in terms of Egyptian money. For instance, it follows from the above equations, putting $A=45{,}000{,}000$ (an increase of $A$ obviously means a rise in the demand schedule), and leaving the values of the other constants unchanged:

$$N = 12{,}164; \quad M = 7{,}399; \quad R = 6{\cdot}082.$$

In this case Egypt's aggregate expenditure curve takes the position A′B′ (Chart II). It will be observed that $\frac{7{,}399}{12{,}164} > \frac{7{,}200}{12{,}000}$. An increase in Egypt's demand therefore results, other things being equal, in (*a*) a depreciation of the rate of exchange between her goods and foreign goods, and (*b*) in a diminution of the external value of her currency.*

* Let us consider briefly the case when $C$ and $I$ depend on the quantities exported. Let us add, then, to the previous equations (1), (2), and (3) the two following equations:

$$C = 0{\cdot}01389\,M \text{ and } I = 0{\cdot}000833\,N$$

Solving this system of five equations we have $R = 6$, $C = 100$, $I = 10$, $M = 7{,}200$,

To put this in a more general form, let the following equation express a new position of equilibrium between Egyptian exports and imports:

$$C'M' = N'I'R' \qquad \ldots \ldots \quad (5)$$

From equations (4) and (5) we have, putting $\frac{M}{N} = B$; $\frac{M'}{N'} = B'$; $\frac{C'}{C} = S$; $\frac{I'}{I} = U$,

$$\frac{R'}{R} = \frac{U}{S} \cdot \frac{B'}{B} \qquad \ldots \ldots \quad (6)$$

that is to say, *the index of exchange rates is equal to the ratio of purchasing powers (in terms of export prices) multiplied by the index of the barter terms of trade.* Therefore, this formula, which could be called *the equation of foreign exchanges* under a régime of independent paper standards, clearly shows that the index of exchange rates depends not only on the ratio of price levels, but also on the conditions of international demand, as expressed by the second factor $\frac{B'}{B}$.

It is easy to see that, if we indicate by $E$ the index of cotton and iron prices in terms of Egyptian money and by $G$ their index in terms of German money, we have, neglecting costs of transport:

$$\frac{E}{G} = \frac{R'}{R} \qquad \ldots \ldots \quad (7)$$

whatever may be the changes occurring in the barter terms of trade.

Obviously formula (7) holds true for any number of commodities, provided they are the same in each country. It should be observed, however, that, in order that formula (7) should be valid, either $E$ and $G$ must be *unweighted* averages, or the weights assigned to each commodity must be the same in all countries.

## II. INFLUENCE OF NON-MERCHANDISE TRANSACTIONS ON EXCHANGE RATES

**5.** So far I have neglected non-merchandise transactions such as loans, tributes, interest payments, tourist expenditure, and the like. It can be easily shown that these transactions do not affect the essentials of the problem.

In the example taken above Egypt was supposed to exchange cotton for

$N = 12{,}000$. Now let us suppose that Egypt's demand for iron increases, other conditions remaining equal, and that the new demand is expressed by the equation $N = \frac{50{,}000{,}000}{I^2 R^2}$. Solving the new system of equations we have:

$$R = 6{\cdot}36; \quad C = 104; \quad I = 10{\cdot}1; \quad M = 7{,}486; \quad N = 12{,}118.$$

The rate of exchange has changed, though the monetary conditions (which might be expressed by an index of domestic commodities) have been supposed to remain constant. The index of exchange rates $\left(\frac{6{\cdot}36}{6} \times 100 = 106\right)$ *is not equal* to the ratio of the indices of export prices $\left(\frac{104}{101} \times 100 = 103\right)$.

iron. Now suppose that Egypt has to pay every year a certain sum to Germany, as a tribute, or as interest on debt incurred there, or from any other cause. In conditions of equilibrium Egypt will export a certain quantity $T$ of cotton, whose value will be exactly equal to the payments $D$ arising from non-merchandise transactions. Let us suppose that these payments are fixed in terms of Egyptian money.* In equilibrium conditions, total payments to Egypt in terms of Egyptian money must be equal to total payments, in terms of the same money, by Egypt. This equilibrium of Egypt's balance of payments will be expressed by the equation

$$(M' + T)C = N'IR' + D \quad . \quad . \quad . \quad . \quad . \quad . \quad (8)$$

Again in the above formula we have three unknown quantities, $M'$, $N'$, and $R'$, which are determined by the two demand curves and by the condition expressed by equation (8). It should be observed that the ratio of the new exchange rate $R'$ to the old rate $R$ is equal—assuming price levels in both countries have remained unchanged—to the ratio of the new net barter terms of trade $\frac{M'}{N'}$ to the old terms $\frac{M}{N}$.

If we assume, for instance, that Egypt has to pay regularly to Germany a sum of £ 120,000, then, the demand curves being those indicated by equations (1) and (2), in the new equilibrium conditions $R$ will be equal to about 6·333 instead of 6, as previously. In these conditions Egypt exports about 8,021 cotton, of which 6,821 are exchanged for 10,771 iron and 1,200 offset the tribute payments. The barter terms of trade have turned against Egypt, and, it will be observed, exactly in the same proportion as the price of marks in terms of piastres has increased.†

There is another possibility, that is, Egypt may offset, through a deflation policy which results in a diminution of $C$, the influence of the tribute payments on the exchange rates. In this case also there would be no exact correspondence between purchasing power parities and exchange rates.

Graphically the non-merchandise payment by Egypt means that her aggregate expenditure curve AB shifts uniformly to the right while that of Germany does not move (Chart 11). The degree of depreciation of the Egyptian pound will

* Under this assumption $T$ is known beforehand; if, on the contrary, Egypt has to pay a fixed sum $O$ of German money, then we shall put in equation (8) $D = OR$ and $T = \frac{OR}{C}$. $T$ is then determined simultaneously with the rate of exchange.

† *If it is assumed that the debtor country is able to pay in any case in goods and services*, the money in which the remittances have to be made is a matter of little concern. If in our examples we suppose that Egypt has to pay Germany 20,000 units of German money (if $R = 6$; 120,000 units of Egyptian money are equivalent to 20,000 units of German money) then in the new equilibrium conditions we should have $R = 6{\cdot}35$ (instead of $R = 6{\cdot}333$), that is to say, the Egyptian currency would depreciate a little more than in the case when Egypt had to pay 120,000 units of her money.

But if the adjustment of the debtor country's trade balance is slow, then serious difficulties may arise when the remittances are to be made in a foreign currency. Then it is no longer true that, as Professor Taussig writes (*op. cit.*, p. 359), the payment is made "by a stroke of a pen."

then depend (*a*) on the elasticities of the two demand schedules for commodities, (*b*) on the absolute amount of the payments, (*c*) on the volume of trade before the payments were begun. The less the absolute volume of trade, the less elastic Egypt's aggregate expenditure curve will become as a consequence of

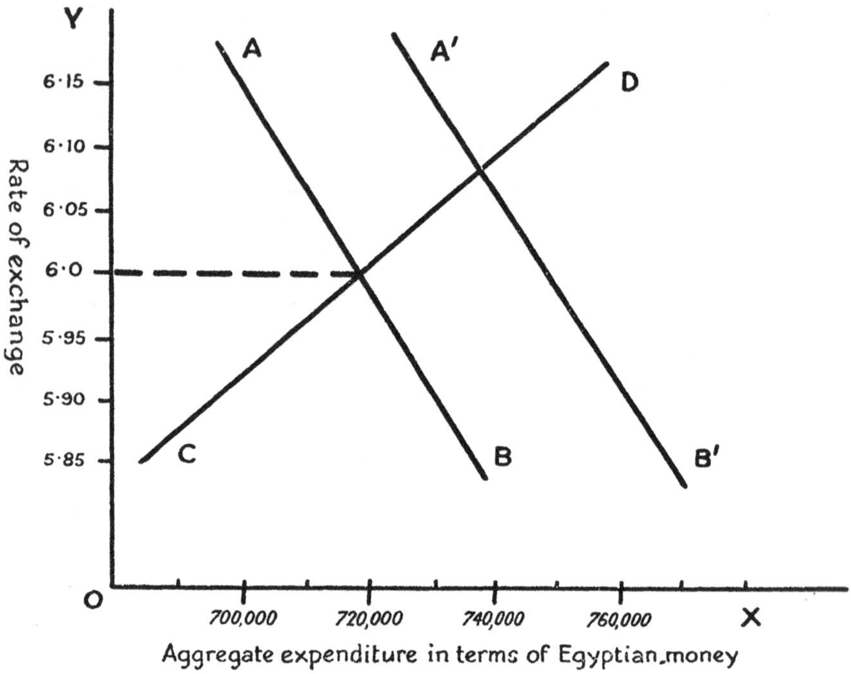


CHART II

the payments and the more, therefore, will a given amount of payments depress the external value of the debtor country's currency.*

III. THE INFLUENCE OF TRANSPORT COSTS

**6.** In the previous analysis I have neglected transport costs. However, the consideration of these does not affect the essentials of the problem we are examining.

Following Marshall, we may consider them as an element of the total supply prices of the goods concerned.† If *C* and *I* are, respectively, the domestic prices

* Suppose that in equilibrium conditions 3,600 units of cotton were exchanged for 6,000 of iron, the volume of trade being thus reduced by one-half compared with the former assumed conditions. Let us suppose, as before, $R = 6$, and the same elasticity for both demand curves ($= -2$). The payment of 120,000 units of Egyptian money by Egypt to Germany would then cause the exchange rate to increase from 6 to about 6·67.

† *The Pure Theory of Foreign Trade* (Series of reprints of scarce tracts: London School of Economics, vol. i, 1930, p. 2).

for cotton and iron, and $xC$ and $yI$ are the cost of transporting a unit of each commodity, then the total supply prices will be $C(1 + x)$ and $I(1 + y)$. If, further, we suppose that each country carries its own goods to the other country, equation (4) may be written in a slightly modified form:

$$C(1 + x)M = I(1 + y)NR \quad . \quad . \quad . \quad . \quad . \quad . \quad . \quad (9)$$

We have, therefore:

$$R = \frac{C}{I} \cdot \frac{M}{N} \cdot \frac{1 + x}{1 + y} \quad . \quad . \quad . \quad . \quad . \quad . \quad . \quad . \quad (10)$$

This equation shows that $R$ depends also on the ratio of transport costs. The real terms of trade are not $\frac{M}{N}$ but $\frac{M(1 + x)}{N(1 + y)}$. The factors $\frac{M}{N}$ and $\frac{(1 + x)}{(1 + y)}$, however, are not independent. If, for instance, $x$ increases, it means that the supply price of cotton delivered in Germany increases. This will affect $\frac{M}{N}$, in different measures according as Germany's demand for cotton has an elasticity equal to, greater than, or less than, unity. In the first case the value of $\frac{M(1 + x)}{N(1 + y)}$ remains unchanged, and the value of $R$ is therefore not affected by the change in the cost of transport. In the second case the value of $\frac{M(1 + x)}{N(1 + y)}$ increases, and Egypt's money depreciates in terms of marks; while the converse happens in the third case.*

It will be observed that the expression $\frac{IN(1 + y)}{M}$ indicates the price of cotton in Germany, in terms of German money. Indeed, for Germans, the price of one cotton unit is equal to the price of one iron unit (including transport costs) multiplied by the number of iron units which must be given for one cotton unit. From equation (10) we have, therefore, if the price of cotton in Germany in terms of German money is indicated by $C_m$,

$$R = \frac{C}{C_m}(1 + x) \quad . \quad . \quad . \quad . \quad . \quad . \quad . \quad . \quad (11)$$

that is to say the rate of exchange between piastres and marks is equal to the ratio of the price of cotton in terms of piastres to the price of cotton in terms of marks, allowing for cost of transport.†

## IV. EXCHANGE RATES IN THE CASE OF VERY ELASTIC SCHEDULES OF INTERNATIONAL DEMAND FOR COMMODITIES

7. Up to this point we have considered two countries which, by hypothesis, produced and exported *different* commodities. We have seen that variations

* It is obvious that not only changes in transport costs, but any other non-monetary cause resulting in changes in supply prices, will affect $R$ in the sense described in the text.

† Formula (10) is given by Professor Pigou in "The Foreign Exchanges" (*Quarterly Journal of Economics*, November 1922, p. 37). As shown in the text this can be easily deduced from Formula (9).

in the international demand for goods, or payments caused by non-merchandise transactions, can cause considerable divergences between the internal and external value of a currency. When, as actually happens, many countries trade together and the transactions cover a great variety of goods, the variations of the foreign exchange of a country, caused by fluctuations in the home demand for a given commodity, provoke reactions in the international demand for other goods, which puts a limit to the variations of the factor $\frac{B'}{B}$ in equation (6) and therefore to the variations of the exchange rate. Moreover, if the variations of factor $\frac{U}{S}$ are much greater—as happened in many countries during and after the World War because of the monetary inflation—the variations of the second factor of equation (6) can be regarded as insignificant as compared with those of the first factor.

8. Now there is a further problem. It may be that country X produces some goods of international character which are identical with those produced by other countries. If the exchange rate of X is permanently depreciated it means that prices, computed in gold, of these goods will be permanently lower in X than in the world market. But how is this possible in view of the tendency for the equalization of world prices?

To this one can reply that often the various countries which produce goods of the same name actually produce different articles.* That applies especially to manufactured articles but often, also, to products of the soil. Egyptian cotton is different from that of America and India. Now, it is true that a correlation exists between the prices of all varieties of the same commodity, but experience shows that differences in prices between single varieties can fluctuate considerably, more or less in proportion to the possibility of substituting one kind for another. For example, the depreciation of Egyptian money after September 1931 resulted in a fall in the gold price of Egyptian cotton. This fall was smaller in the price of that variety of cotton (Ashmouni) which is most nearly interchangeable with American cotton.

If different countries produce the same goods, then the articles in question are often produced under conditions of increasing cost. Let us suppose that the marginal cost of wheat in Egypt in Egyptian money is 120 and in Germany in German money, 20. If, following a rise in the Egyptian demand for iron, the external value of Egyptian money falls, the export of wheat from Egypt to Germany will be stimulated. The production of wheat will be increased in Egypt and lessened in Germany; therefore the marginal cost rises in the former country and falls in the latter. In the new situation of equilibrium we shall have, for example, the price of wheat in Egypt: 121·5; in Germany, 19·6; exchange rate, 6·20. (In this argument no account is taken of transport costs.)

It will be observed that, again, the German price is equal to the Egyptian price multiplied by the rate of exchange. But the statement, which is often made, that the Purchasing Power Parity doctrine is valid for international commodities, would be rather misleading in the case just considered. The

* Taussig, *Principles of Economics*, New York, 1925, vol. i, p. 492.

essence of this doctrine is to show, in the words of the Bullion Report, that the course of exchange with foreign countries forms "the best general criterion from which any inference can be drawn as to the sufficiency or excess of paper money in circulation." Now, in the case of international commodities the equivalence between exchange rates and price ratios always holds true (ignoring costs of transport and other expenses); but if the conditions of international demand vary, exchange rates will also vary, even when the monetary conditions of the countries concerned remain constant, so that exchange rates are no longer the index of these conditions.

**9.** Moreover, the fact that a country, X, produces—or is able to produce—in large quantities goods of an international character which are similar to those produced by other countries, has a great influence on the foreign exchange value of that country's currency. Indeed, it makes more elastic the foreign demand for goods produced by X as well as the demand for foreign goods by X. Consequently, as soon as X's money falls in external value, owing to an increase in the demand for some foreign goods by X or following the payment of a tribute, a big rise in the foreign demand for goods from X is stimulated and at the same time the demand for *other* foreign goods by X is restricted. These reactions tend to moderate the effects on the barter terms of trade and on the foreign exchanges of the initial disequilibrium of the balance of payments. However, the *original rate of exchange will not be restored.* For at this rate the country under consideration would again have an unfavourable balance of trade, which would again bring about a depreciation of her currency. The increase in the demand for foreign goods, which we assumed at the outset, will therefore exercise a *permanent* influence on the barter terms of trade and on exchange rates. This influence, which had been ignored by the supporters of an extreme Purchasing Power Parity doctrine, has been well pointed out by Professor Taussig and other economists. But it seems to me that too little stress has been laid by some critics of Cassel's theory on the fact that the shifts in exchange rates will be kept within narrow limits when international demand schedules are very elastic. In many countries the great bulk of exports and imports consists of competitive articles. Therefore the elasticities of *international* demand will tend to be very high even if the articles concerned (wheat, cotton, sugar, etc.) are of such a kind that the domestic demand for them has little elasticity.

Also in the case when a country on a paper-money basis has to make remittances abroad arising out of non-merchandise operations as interest payments, war indemnities, loans and the like, neither the barter terms of trade nor the exchange rates will be substantially affected in the long run (even if the debtor country has to transfer large sums), when the foreign demand for the goods of the country concerned and its own demand for imported goods are very elastic. Now, as Marshall showed, this is the case for a great modern industrial country—Germany is one such—with great resources. In this case the Purchasing Power Parity theory is *approximately* valid, when it refers to exportable commodities.

In conclusion, there is a fundamental difference between the methods of action of the two factors which influence foreign exchanges in the case of a paper standard. A fall in the internal value of a currency tends to be reflected to its full extent, without any modification, on the foreign exchanges. A change of the balance of payments, on the other hand, provokes compensations which substantially limit the effect of it on the exchanges.

### V. RELATIONS BETWEEN EXCHANGE RATES AND PRICES OF DOMESTIC COMMODITIES

**10.** No explicit mention has been made so far of *domestic* commodities. It is clear that there is no necessary relation between exchange rates and the *absolute* prices of such domestic commodities as, owing to difficulties of transport or from other causes, have but a local market. However, if we compare, not absolute exchange rates and absolute commodity prices, but *indices* of exchange rates and prices, which measure percentage changes from the positions of a base year, it might be asked whether formula (6) holds good, when we substitute indices of domestic prices for those of export prices.

It is clear that this substitution involves the assumption that, when the price-level of a country varies from monetary causes, both the prices of domestic and of exported commodities are affected in a uniform way, so that their percentage changes are the same.

Now, as Mr. Keynes observes, in the assumption that different price-levels will move in the same way, there is "an important element of truth, when the initial disturbance has been of a monetary character."* In fact, when the prices of export goods rise more than those of domestic goods, labour and capital will shift towards the production of the former class of goods; and the converse will happen when prices of export goods are lower than those of domestic goods. But—though the direction of the changes in the prices of both categories of goods will tend to be the same—the extent of the change will generally be different, even if the conditions of international demand do not change. The reasons for the failure of different price-levels to move together are clearly explained by Mr. Keynes.

We may therefore conclude that, generally speaking, formula (6) will be at best only approximately valid if we substitute for $U$ and $S$ the indices of domestic prices (for instance cost of living indices) in the countries concerned, or a compound index of general prices (prices of domestic and export commodities jumbled together).

**11.** In conclusion, there is no doubt that an appreciable divergence can be established in certain conditions and maintained even for a considerable time between the external value of a paper currency and its internal value, measured by the prices of domestic goods. This divergence is, besides, often the symptom of a situation which, though it may last for a considerable time, is likely in the long run to develop some counteracting tendencies. Suppose that X exports only one commodity, the foreign demand for which diminishes. The external value of X's currency will fall substantially, owing to the fact that X does not produce other goods suitable for export. Wages and prices of domestic commodities will be comparatively low in X, in terms of foreign currencies. As long as deficiency of technical knowledge, transport difficulties, the inability of X's

* *A Treatise on Money*, vol. i, p. 91.

producers to adapt their articles to the requirements of foreign purchasers, lack of an export organization and of foreign knowledge of X's articles, or many other possible causes, prevent an expansion of X's exports, the situation described above will last; but it will surely change little by little under the stimulus of low wages and low domestic prices. That is to say, little by little X will attempt to develop new branches of economic activity, thus replacing more and more, on the one hand, foreign commodities by domestic ones, and, on the other hand, exporting new articles. (Something like that is now happening in Egypt.) It may also be that X becomes a promising field for investment. In this way, by degrees, exchange rates will become less unfavourable to X and its prices in terms of foreign currencies will be brought nearer to the level of foreign prices.

We may therefore conclude that as long as there is a considerable discrepancy between exchange rates and price parities, there is no really stable equilibrium either in trade or in production or as regards the international value of the paper standards. While the Purchasing Power Parity doctrine proves quite inadequate to describe the facts observed in short periods, it acquires more significance when we consider it as the expression of fundamental forces acting for longer periods.*

* For a more detailed treatment of the subject of this Appendix the reader is referred to the author's paper, "The Purchasing Power Parity Doctrine" (*Egypte Contemporaine*, vol. xxv, Cairo, 1934).

## CHAPTER III*

# The Divergences between the Internal Value and the External Value of the Mark

### I. SOME HISTORICAL EXAMPLES

**1.** Even before the World War there had often existed some divergence between the purchasing power of a depreciated paper currency in the country in which it was issued (its internal value) and the purchasing power of the same money in terms of gold (or silver) and foreign goods (its external value).† During the period of the notorious assignats it was observed that the internal value of the paper money surpassed its value in terms of precious metal.

> La baisse de l'assignat [wrote Thiers] commençait d'abord à la bourse par rapport au numéraire et à toutes les valeurs mobiles. Elle avait lieu ensuite par rapport aux marchandises, qui renchérissaient dans les boutiques et les marchés. Cependant les marchandises ne montaient pas aussi rapidement que le numéraire, parce que les marchés sont éloignés de la bourse, parce qu'ils ne sont pas aussi sensibles et que d'ailleurs les marchands ne peuvent pas se donner le mot aussi rapidement que des agioteurs réunis dans une salle. La différence determinée d'abord à la bourse ne se prononçait donc ailleurs qu'après un temps plus ou moins long; l'assignat de 5 francs qui déjà n'en valait plus de 2 à la bourse, en valait encore 3 dans les marchés . . .‡

Consequently, those who possessed metallic money could then live cheaply at Paris, just as after the World War the possessors of foreign exchange could live cheaply in Vienna or Berlin. A speculator who had spent 1,000 paper francs (i.e. 4 gold francs and 16 sous) on a dinner declared that formerly he never spent less than 12 francs on his dinner. Even in that episode shrewd business men had converted their paper money into metallic money in time.

* From a memorandum by the author, "Studi sul deprezzamento del marco tedesco —Il valore 'interno' e il valore 'esterno' del marco," published in the *Giornale degli Economisti*, 1924.

† Galiani had observed that paper money declined in value more slowly in the country of issue than abroad (Gonnard, *Précis d'Economie Monetaire*, Paris, 1930, p. 206). The expressions "Internal Value" (Binnenwert) and "External Value" (Aussenwert) were introduced by Lexis (see article "Papiergeld" in *Handwörterbuch der Staatwissenschaften*).

‡ *Histoire de la Révolution française*, Brussels, 1884, vol. i, p. 379.

On the other hand, in England during the régime of the Bank Restriction Act, according to Walker* the purchasing power of paper money in terms of goods in the home market "depreciated much more than its purchasing power in terms of gold." Palgrave also expressed the opinion (supported by the researches of Tooke and by the index numbers calculated by Jevons) that "the inflation resulting from the over-issues of paper currency during the period of bank restriction in Great Britain must have been very great and that it must have largely exceeded the difference between the value of gold and that of the currency." The purchasing power of the paper pound in terms of foreign goods cannot be measured, owing to the absence of information about Continental prices.†

During and after the World War, which provoked, in varying degrees, the depreciation of the currencies of several countries, much data on the phenomenon of the divergence between the internal and external values of depreciated currencies, as on other monetary changes, became available.

The study of the German mark in particular reveals the following important circumstance: the successive phases of the currency depreciation were distinguished from each other, in this case, by certain characteristic phenomena. The relations between the National Budget, paper inflation, exchange rates, wages, prices, and employment conditions were not the same in the various phases. Also the divergences between the internal and external values of the currency were different according to the phase of the depreciation, as will appear in the following discussion.

## II. THE VARIOUS MEASURES OF THE DEPRECIATION OF A PAPER CURRENCY

2. In an investigation into the fluctuations of the value of the mark (or of any other paper currency) it is necessary to distinguish clearly the three following ideas:

(*a*) *the depreciation of the purchasing power of the paper mark in terms of goods in the home market*. Assuming 100 as the level of German prices, say, in July 1914, and $p_1, p_2, p_3, \ldots$ the successive levels of

* Cited by Palgrave in his dictionary, article on "Inflation."

† On the relation between prices of goods, foreign exchanges, and circulation in England during the period 1797–1821 see Appendix A of Angell, *op. cit.*, where the more recent studies of the argument are summarized.

prices in paper marks, the successive depreciations of the purchasing power are measured by the ratios:

$$\frac{p_1 - 100}{p_1} \qquad \frac{p_2 - 100}{p_2} \qquad \ldots$$

(*b*) *the discount of the paper mark against the gold mark.* In practice it was usual to measure this fall on the basis of the quotations of the Bourse of the paper mark expressed in *dollars*. The dollar was considered as representing gold. Assuming $C_1$, $C_2$, etc., as the exchange rate for the paper mark expressed in dollars, and 0·2382 being the mint par of the gold mark in dollars, the discount is measured by the ratios:

$$\frac{0{\cdot}2382 - C_1}{0{\cdot}2382} \qquad \frac{0{\cdot}2382 - C_2}{0{\cdot}2382} \qquad \ldots$$

(*c*) *the depreciation of the purchasing power of the paper mark in terms of foreign goods*. If 100 is the level of prices in the world market in July 1914, and $P_1$, $P_2$ . . . the price indices in gold at successive dates, the depreciation of the purchasing power of the paper mark is measured thus:

$$\frac{0{\cdot}2382P_1 - 100C_1}{0{\cdot}2382P_1} \qquad \frac{0{\cdot}23820_2 - 100C_2}{0{\cdot}2382P_2} \qquad \ldots$$

**3.** According to the Purchasing Power Parity doctrine, *if gold prices in the world market are assumed to remain unaltered*, the discount of the paper mark against gold is equal to the depreciation of its purchasing power in the home market. Wagner, the first writer on monetary subjects who investigated systematically the relations between the depreciation of value and the discount against gold of a paper currency, based his research on this hypothesis.* Wagner's hypothesis was clearly justified by conditions at that time; in fact he studied the phenomena relating to the depreciation of the currency of a country which had relations with other countries where the level of gold prices was stable, or practically so. Obviously that hypothesis was no longer valid for the years after 1914, when the level of gold prices in the world market was different from that before the war.

But Wagner shows in his inductive investigations that although a reciprocal connection exists between the "depreciation of value" of the paper currency (Wertverminderung) and the "discount" (Entwertung),

* *Russische Papierwährung*, Riga, 1868, p. 80.

actually an equality does not exist—in time or in space—between the two quantities.* They can differ according to the conditions of time or space, and in very different degrees. The study of the causes and effects of this disparity constitutes the most interesting part of Wagner's researches.

The premium on gold tends to make itself felt on internal prices, but, according to Wagner, the adaptation of the latter to the discount of the currency is not generally complete, and hence internal prices tend to remain lower (if computed in gold) than those of the world market. Several characteristic phenomena arise from this divergence, such as the "export premium" and the protection of home industry.

**4.** If, however, gold prices in the outside world rise, the discount of the paper currency in terms of gold is no longer equal to the depreciation of its purchasing power in terms of goods in the home market.

According to the Purchasing Power Parity Doctrine, *in conditions of equilibrium*, the depreciation of the purchasing power of a paper currency in the home market is equal to the depreciation of the purchasing power it suffers in terms of foreign goods; that is, in the case of the paper mark, we have:

$$\frac{p - 100}{p} = \frac{0{\cdot}2382P - 100C}{0{\cdot}2382P} \quad . \quad . \quad . \quad . \qquad (1)$$

From (1) we have the equation:

$$\frac{P}{p} = \frac{C}{0{\cdot}2382} \quad . \quad . \quad . \quad . \quad . \quad . \quad . \qquad (2)$$

(1) and (2) obviously *presuppose* that the indices of gold prices in the world market and those of Germany, converted into gold, are equal in conditions of equilibrium.†

The ratio

$$\frac{0{\cdot}2382P}{pC} = D$$

may be defined as the "coefficient of divergence" between the actual exchange rate of the mark and the "price parities," or between the depreciation of the purchasing power of the paper currency in the home

* *Op. cit.*, p. 113.

† This hypothesis, which is the basis of the Purchasing Power Parity theory, is discussed in the Appendix to Chapter II.

market and its depreciation in terms of foreign goods. Obviously *D* also shows the ratio between the index numbers of prices in the world market and those of German prices converted into gold (taking the same base year)

### III. SOME OPINIONS ON THE RELATIONS BETWEEN THE INTERNAL AND EXTERNAL VALUES OF THE MARK

**5.** Many statistical investigations have shown, though only with that broad approximation which is inevitable in such investigations, that the ratio between the gold value of a depreciated currency and the gold mint par tends to equal the ratio between the gold prices of the world market and home paper prices. But in this equation which is the "active" element and which the "passive"? In other words, is it the price-level in a country with a depreciated currency which fixes the exchange rate (supposing the price-level in the world market to be constant) or, on the other hand, do the home paper prices depend on the exchange rate?

This question was discussed by German economists. Ignoring the opinions of those who deny any connections whatever between internal and external value, it may be said that three theories on this problem have been expounded by economists.

(*a*) The price-level in a country with a depreciated currency is the fundamental and dominant fact. This opinion was expressed by Lexis before the war. He writes: "The relevant variations of the internal value are transmitted more or less completely to the external value, sometimes in greater, sometimes in lesser, degree. But the repercussion of independent movements of the external value on the internal value is, in general, slower and weaker; and it often happens that a clear examination reveals an independent movement of the internal value which was the cause and not the effect of the external value."*

Among the few German writers who after 1914 accepted this point of view was Dalberg. He writes: "When Germany experienced a greater general rise in prices than occurred abroad, the exchange of goods with other countries could only be continued on condition that that rise was compensated for by a depreciation of the exchange. To judge from the available facts which is 'cause' and which 'effect' it is necessary to remember that the general level of prices of a country is deeply embedded in the economic structure of the country itself, and cannot, therefore, be altered so rapidly by external influences, as can

* Lexis, "Papiergeld" in *Handwörterbuch der Staatwissenschaften*, p. 903.

the exchange rate and the balance of payments. It is itself the phenomenon towards which the other facts gravitate."*

(*b*) The foreign exchange rate having moved, as a result of changes in the balance of payments, brings about a change in the internal value. This doctrine, to the substance of which Wagner adheres† in the work cited above, became, as we have seen, prevalent in Germany. In an official publication it was stated: "If the dollar is quoted at Berlin above its purchasing power parity, German internal prices rise, and this movement is limited only by the inertia of certain prices. If the dollar falls below this parity, the possibility of foreign competition provokes a fall in home prices."

(*c*) Between internal and external value there is an *interdependence*, and according to circumstances the one or the other is the prevailing factor. Professor Angell‡ writes that this idea has in these last few years increased in favour among students of monetary problems.

## IV. DIFFICULTIES IN ASCERTAINING EXCHANGE RATES AND INTERNAL PRICES IN GERMANY

**6.** Tables IV to VII in the Appendix show: (1) the monthly average values of the gold mark, expressed in paper marks, according to the daily quotations of the dollar at Berlin; (2) the ratios between the monthly index numbers of German wholesale prices, in paper marks, and the index numbers of American prices, according to the Bureau of Labour; (3) the "coefficients of divergence" between the internal and external values of the mark; the external value being calculated (*a*) on the basis of the index numbers of the Bureau of Labour and (*b*) on the basis of the index numbers of the gold prices of goods imported into Germany.

The data referred to in the tables cover the period August 1914–June 1923. The calculation of the *average* level of the dollar exchange rate and of German prices presents some difficulties in the period of the very rapid depreciation of the currency which commenced in June 1923.§ For that period I have, therefore, preferred to use not the monthly

* Dalberg, *Die Entwertung des Geldes*, 1919, p. 96. Also Pohle (*Geldenwertung, Valutafrage und Währungreform*, 1920) recognizes that the purchasing power of the mark in the home market is the primary and fundamental factor.

† In expressing this opinion Wagner was probably much influenced by the work of Hock, *Die Finanzen und die Finanzgeschichte der Vereinigten Statten*, Stuttgart, 1867, where it is stated that in America, during the inflation of the greenbacks, the prices of imported goods rose first and later the rise spread to internal prices.

‡ *Op. cit.*, p. 197.

§ See Appendix to the present chapter.

averages but the indices calculated for a given day of the week, which are more worthy of attention. They are combined in Table XII.

Besides some technical difficulties regarding the determination of the average level of gold prices and of the dollar exchange rate, it is of interest to notice that in the last phase of the depreciation of the mark, which began in the summer of 1923, the purchasing power of the paper mark, *at a given moment*, in terms of gold or of domestic goods, was also uncertain.

Until then, the quotations of the paper mark on the various German and foreign exchanges had generally not been very diverse. But in the summer of 1923, as a result of the intervention of the Reichsbank in the foreign exchange market and of the numerous decrees restricting business in foreign exchange, there were some remarkable differences between the quotations of the various German bourses, between these and the quotations at New York, and between the official rates and those of the free market. For example, on August 17th the dollar was quoted at 3·2 million marks at Berlin, 4·2 at Frankfurt, 4·4 at Cologne, 3·97 at Hamburg, and 3·85 at Danzig. On October 1st the value of the dollar in the above exchanges was: 242, 345, 380, 285, and 275 million marks. The quotations at Cologne were generally highest at that time for three reasons: the abundance of paper marks created by the excessive "Ruhr credits"; the lack of confidence in the paper mark (always more emphasized in the occupied territories than in other parts of Germany); and of the French monetary policy which tended to drive the paper mark out of circulation.

At the beginning of November 1923 the official foreign exchange rates were fixed in Germany at a noticeably lower level than the foreign quotations and those of the "black bourses." Later, following the suspension, on November 15th, 1923, of the discounting of Treasury bills by the Reichsbank, the paper mark improved somewhat and the foreign quotations approached the official German rates.

Finally, in the last phase of the depreciation of the mark, regular transactions in paper marks ceased in the foreign markets and the rates of those markets gradually lost importance. "Transactions in marks are limited to casual business or to speculation," wrote the *Frankfurter Zeitung* of November 7th, 1923, and "therefore the prices quoted cannot represent a correct valuation of the paper mark." This was also shown by the enormous difference between the buying and selling rates for marks. For example, at Zürich, on November 5th, the paper mark was quoted (for a billion marks) 0·50 francs to buyers and 3·50 francs

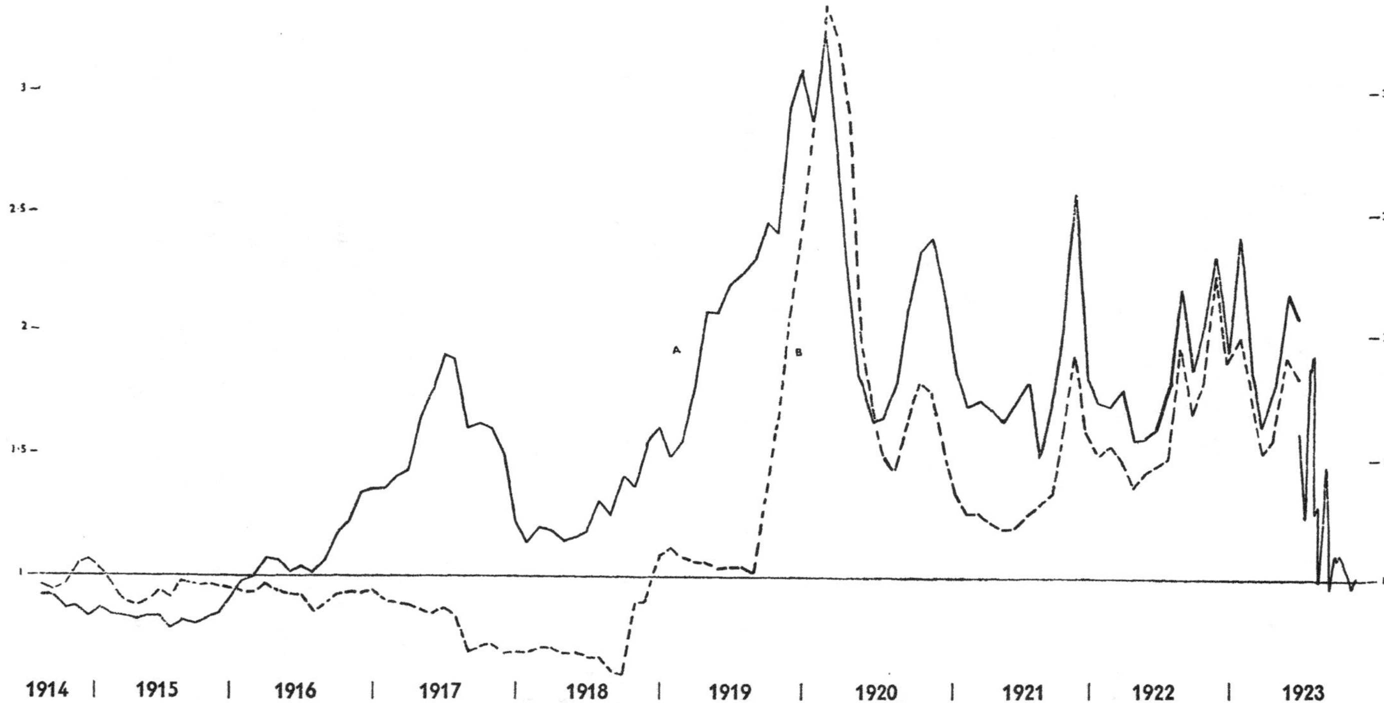


DIAGRAM X.—Coefficients of divergency between the external and the internal value of the mark. A According to America's wholesale prices. B According to the prices of goods imported into Germany

to sellers. At New York (according to the correspondent of the *Frankfurter Zeitung*) the exchange rate of the paper mark was fixed by a small group of speculators who met round a table in a café!

In the weeks which preceded the introduction of the Rentenmark and the final and general adoption of gold prices, even the purchasing power of the paper mark in the home market was uncertain. The very great difference between the prices in paper marks of the same article, at a given moment, in different places,* and the enormous fluctuations which the same prices underwent in very short periods of time show that the paper mark had already ceased to function as a measure of the value of goods. The process of the decomposition of the monetary system was already complete.

In Diagram VIII, Curve A shows the movements of the exchange rates of the gold mark expressed in paper marks; and Curve B shows the "price parities," i.e. the ratio between German prices in paper marks and American (Bureau of Labour) prices.

Diagram X shows the movements of the coefficients of divergence for the whole period of the inflation.

The coefficients of Curve A, beginning from July 1923, were calculated on the base of the *weekly* index numbers of German prices published by the *Berliner Tageblatt*.

Three distinct periods appear in the diagram: (*a*) the war period; (*b*) a second period, in which the external value of the paper mark was considerably lower than the internal value; and (*c*) a third period which closed the inflation, in which the internal value approached the external value and tended to equal it.

We now proceed to examine in detail the characteristics of these three periods.

## V. THE WAR PERIOD

**7.** It is not possible to give a satisfactory measure of "price parities" for the period of the war. Generally, in the studies which have been made of the movements of the German exchange, price parities have been calculated by using the ratio between German and American prices. Now—at least after America entered the war and became a closed market for Germany—these price parities have little significance. Besides, the German official index numbers only included the prices of

* According to official calculations the average variability of the Cost of Living Index from place to place (measured by means of the average relative deviation) in September 1921 was 8·16 per cent, in September 1922, 9·56 per cent, in June 1923, 17·64 per cent, and in September 1923, 30·4 per cent.

raw materials and semi-finished goods, whilst those of the Bureau of Labour also included prices of finished products. One must also remember the tendency on the part of Germany during the inflation to purchase foreign goods of a quality inferior to those imported before the war.

In German official statistics there is an index of prices of imported goods which was calculated, separately, in paper and in gold. In the Italian edition of this book the opinion was expressed that this index constitutes a good measure of the variations of the external value of the paper mark during the war. But from information subsequently obtained from the Statistical Bureau of the Reich it appears that, for the war period, this index was calculated on the base of prices of four commodities only, i.e. lead, copper, zinc, and tin, so that this index has little real value.

The conclusions suggested by the examination of the tables and diagrams are somewhat uncertain. According to the indices of import prices, during the whole war period the exchange rate of the mark increased *less* than in proportion to the increase of the ratio between German paper prices and external gold prices; but, for the reason now shown, this conclusion rests on an uncertain basis.

If the external value of the mark is measured by means of the American indices then the internal value of the paper mark remained lower than the external value in 1914, 1915, and in the first two months of 1916. The monetary inflation, begun in Germany directly after the outbreak of the war, together with other secondary causes, immediately provoked a rise in the general level of prices. At the end of 1914 the index number of German paper prices already exceeded the American index number by 29 per cent; and in July 1915 there was a difference of 49 per cent. In this first period the exchange rate of the mark was imperfectly adapted to the price parities and consequently German gold prices were higher than American prices.*

* *Gold Prices of Goods*

| | 1914 | | 1915 | | 1916 | |
|---|---|---|---|---|---|---|
| | *Germany* | *Labour Bureau* | *Germany* | *Labour Bureau* | *Germany* | *Labour Bureau* |
| January .. | — | — | 114·8 | 99 | 118 | 114 |
| February .. | — | — | 118·6 | 100 | 118 | 117 |
| March .. .. | — | — | 121·2 | 100 | — | — |
| April .. .. | — | — | 123 | 100 | — | — |
| May .. .. | — | — | 121 | 101 | — | — |
| June .. .. | — | — | 120 | 100 | — | — |
| July .. .. | — | — | 128 | 101 | — | — |
| August .. | 109 | 100 | 125 | 101 | — | — |
| September .. | 111 | 103 | 125 | 101 | — | — |
| October .. | 113 | 97 | 127 | 104 | — | — |
| November .. | 112 | 98 | 125 | 105 | — | — |
| December .. | 117 | 97 | 120 | 109 | — | — |

**8.** Towards the middle of 1916 the exchange rate of the gold mark expressed in paper marks was about equal to the "price parities." But later it became noticeably higher than the ratio between German and American prices because of the rapid rise in the latter, which was not followed (as theory would suggest) by an improvement of the German exchange. On the contrary, during the first nine months of 1917 the German exchange depreciated continually, moving in the reverse direction to the price parities.

A sudden and heavy fall in the price of the gold mark (in paper marks) occurred after November 1917 (October 1917, 174; January 1918, 124) and was probably due to the success of Caporetto which, by causing some expectation of an issue from the war favourable to the Central Powers, provoked a demand for German money in neutral markets. In this way, the exchange rate of the mark was raised to the neighbourhood of the level of the price parities. In June 1918 the coefficient of divergence (calculated on the basis of American prices) was 1·18. But in the second half of 1918 the exchange rate of the mark once more depreciated considerably and the coefficient of divergence increased (October 1918, 1·36).

On the whole, it may be said that during the war period, save for temporary fluctuations, there was not much difference between the exchange rate of the mark and the "price parities"; whilst in the following years, as the diagrams show, the divergence was much greater.

In the years 1914–18 the value of the gold mark in paper marks increased *less* than the level of German prices (see Diagram 1). A plausible explanation of this is the fact that, in that period, prices in terms of gold also rose in foreign markets.

From the beginning of 1917 the German Government adopted a series of measures to obstruct the depreciation of the exchange. On March 24th, 1917, it announced its intention to demand from German citizens the surrender, for paper marks, of foreign securities possessed by them,* and in June of the same year it began to sell the securities abroad. At the same time it sought to encourage the obtaining of foreign loans by means of direct negotiations with neutral Governments and by inducing German importers to obtain credit from their foreign supply merchants. Simultaneously the control of imports and of the purchase of foreign exchange was continually made stricter. (The "Central Office for Foreign Exchange" had been created on January 28th, 1916.) Moreover, in the autumn of 1917 the Reichsbank bought

* Rist, *op. cit.*, p. 200.

considerable quantities of marks in neutral markets. It is necessary to take account also of the exports of gold for the purpose of purchasing foreign goods. Because of these exports of gold in the third week of June 1917 the gold reserve of the Reichsbank for the first time showed a fall; and there was a further sharp drop in the third week of July.

It is obvious that the desire to support the exchange by selling foreign securities or selling gold abroad, while the internal monetary inflation exercised a continual pressure on it, was a mistaken policy. If it is impossible or undesirable to stop the inflation it is better to allow the exchange to depreciate and natural corrections will develop (such as the automatic limitation of imports and, if special conditions do not impede it, the expansion of exports) which tend to re-establish the equilibrium in the balance of trade.

## VI. RELATIONS BETWEEN THE EXTERNAL AND INTERNAL VALUES OF THE MARK AFTER 1918

**9.** The years following 1918 lend themselves more to the study of the relations between the external and internal values of the mark than does the exceptional period of the World War.

The index number of prices of imported goods from January 1920 onwards was a more reliable measure than formerly of the purchasing power of the paper mark in terms of foreign goods. In fact from that time onwards the index was calculated on the base of twenty-two imported goods; later the number was raised to thirty-five. Yet among these goods were included not only articles imported from abroad, but also some things such as yarns and sheet iron made at home with imported raw materials. That partly explains why the index numbers of the prices of imported goods, calculated by the Statistical Bureau of the Reich, are generally lower than those of American prices.

After the Armistice a new phase in the evolution of the mark was begun. The external value of the German currency fell well below its internal value and remained lower until September 1923. The coefficient of divergence between the exchange rate of the gold mark in terms of paper money and the price parity, which was 1·36 in October 1918, had become 3·25 in February 1920. This was the highest figure reached by the coefficient of divergence. During this period the index number of American prices rose from 202 to 232; and that of the German paper prices from 233 to 1,685. The theoretical index number of the exchange rate of the gold mark, corresponding to the ratio between the level of German prices and that of American prices in February 1920, was 726, while the actual index number of the exchange rate was 2,360.

Later, a sharp improvement in the exchange—the index number fell from 2,360 in February to 932 in June 1920—once more noticeably lessened the divergence between the two values of the German paper money, the divergence in June 1920 being measured by the coefficient 1·71.

In the whole of the period under examination the coefficient of divergence oscillated continually. Every depreciation of the exchange tended to lessen the external value and to increase the divergence between this and the internal value. The sharp falls of the exchange which occurred in October and November 1921, in August and November 1922, and in January and July 1923, are characteristic instances.

But every time the increase in the disparity between the two values provoked a reaction. The reaction consisted, not in an improvement of the exchange, and hence in an approach of the external to the internal value of the mark, but, because of the continual note issues, in a rise in the internal price-level, that is, in a fall of the internal value of German money.

These facts lead to the conclusion that in the period under discussion the new incessant issues of paper money acted *first* on the exchanges and afterwards on internal prices, whether as a result of speculation or because some of the new money was employed directly by the German Government to purchase foreign exchange. Later the money came into the internal circulation, provoking a rise in the prices of goods; but at the same time new issues of paper money, which went directly into the foreign exchange market, caused a new depreciation of the exchange.

These conditions explain why, during almost all the period under examination, the prices in paper money of imported goods remained higher than internal prices. (Diagrams II, III, V, VI.)

**10.** The reaction of internal prices was slow at first. In the field of economics Germany preserved for a long time, even after the end of the war, her war restrictions. A system of "maximum prices" and of coercive measures (Zwangswirtschaft) prevented a rapid adaptation of home prices to the exchanges. In particular internal prices were kept down by the following causes:

(*a*) The "political price" of bread. Agriculturists were obliged to sell a part of their cereal crops (2·5 million tons in 1921–22) at legal prices. Besides, the State sold at a heavy loss the cereals which the "Reichsgetreidestelle" imported from abroad;

(*b*) For a long time the price of coal remained well below the "world" price;*

(*c*) The rents policy, thanks to which, at times of a rapid depreciation of the mark, the cost of house rent became a very small fraction of the income of a family;†

(*d*) The regulation of railway rates, which remained much lower than before the war.

To these must be added a cause of a monetary nature; in numerous classes of society, especially in the country in 1919 and also in the following years, in spite of the continual depreciation of the currency, great quantities of notes were continually hoarded. Even in September 1922 a bank director‡ asserted that "the German population preserves considerable quantities of notes." By such means the rise of internal prices was retarded.§

## VII. THE SENSITIVENESS OF THE VARIOUS CLASSES OF PRICES

**11.** The Italian economist Messedaglia, noticing many years ago that prices followed the exchange slowly, refers to a "coefficient of inertia" of prices.|| Also in Germany well-known psychological causes

* During the depreciation of the mark which occurred from May to October 1921, the paper prices of coal and iron ore remained unchanged, i.e. prices in gold fell. In November 1921 a ton of coal cost 4 gold marks (in 1913, 12 marks), and a ton of steel 34 marks (74 in 1913).

† Expenses of a family of three persons, according to the *Wirtschaftskurve* (1923, fasc. ii, p. 25), in the fourth quarter of 1922:

| | |
|---|---|
| Rent | 0·4 |
| Food | 64·7 |
| Light and heating | 15·7 |
| Sundry expenses | 19·2 |
| | 100·0 |

‡ *Berliner Tageblatt*, September 20th, 1922.

§ According to *Bergwerkszeitung* (No. 166, July 1922), "because of the hoarding of great quantities of notes the internal depreciation of the currency was not completely shown in internal prices as compared with the external depreciation."

|| *Opere scelte di economia*, 1922, vol. ii, p. 508. The same idea was also found, among others, in several earlier economists. Hüfeland (*Die Lehre vom Gelde und Geldumlauf*, Giessen, 1819, p. 426) observes that in periods of monetary inflation the small merchants and producers hesitate to ask for higher prices, while the great merchants hasten to raise them. Also Helfferich (*Von den periodischen Schwankungen im Werte der Edelmetalle*, 1843) and Kries (*Das Geld*, Berlin, 1873, p. 141) speak of

acted, thanks to which, in the first phases of the depreciation of a currency, the merchants tended to correlate the sale price to the cost of the purchase or of the production of the article, and not to the cost of "repurchase" or "reproduction." The idea of the cost of reproduction as a measure of selling price made slow progress in Germany. Opposed at first by the law as a form of usury the practice of calculating the price of "repurchase" only spread towards the end of 1921, and it had already become general in the second half of 1922. For example, in the ready-made clothing trade attempts were made to measure the weekly variations of the value of the currency by means of a composite index, calculated on the base of the following elements: (*a*) the exchange rate of the dollar; (*b*) the official premium on gold fixed by customs officers; (*c*) the index number of wholesale prices for textile products; and (*d*) the weekly wage of a workman in the Berlin ready-made clothing trade.

In the meantime the war restrictions were relaxed little by little. Consequently, from the second half of 1921 onwards, the reaction of the internal value of the mark to the depreciation of the exchange was more rapid. Scarcely did a sudden depreciation of the mark separate the external value from the internal value before the fall of the latter quickly tended to bring the two values together again.

**12.** Statistics of German internal prices in the advanced phases of the inflation clearly show the tendency in wholesale prices to approach the level of world prices, after a sudden fall of the mark had separated those two price levels. This tendency appeared very quickly in the prices of imported goods—copper, cotton, lard, etc.—and after some time lag, in the prices of goods produced at home. But even after these latter the connection with external prices was obvious. If a depreciation of the exchange increased, say, the price of Dutch margarine or of American corn, the supply of German butter or of home-grown cereals immediately falls and the price increases. The more home production is insufficient for the needs of the market, the more rapid is the repercussion of the depreciation of the exchange. As for wheat prices, it was observed that they tended to decrease, generally, from west to east, which is explained by the fact that the western provinces had a dense population which was dependent for a great part of its food on imports.

a *vis inertiae* of prices and of the frictions which the variations of the ratio between the demand and supply of money must overcome in order that a movement in the level of prices may be produced.

Obviously, prices of articles quoted at the Bourse were adapted to the dollar exchange rate more rapidly than prices fixed, at intervals, by national or local authorities.

The measure of the increase of general prices was very different in various parts of Germany, according to their different economic characteristics. Germany's experiences confirmed much that was written many years before by Wagner with regard to Russia.* "The premium on gold was reflected on prices especially in the great ports and in centres of great commercial activity. Its influence spread along the great communication routes into the interior of the country. If, however, the rise in prices does not proceed from the premium on gold, but from the increasing issues of paper money, it could make itself felt from other directions, for example starting from the centres of production."

From the index numbers of the *Berliner Tageblatt*, which include 117 articles and seem to be among the best, it appears that in the summer of 1923 the rise in prices:

(*a*) Was greatest in the prices of imported goods;

(*b*) Was almost equal, to the maximum rise, for the most important raw materials produced at home (these would largely be raw materials produced by the great syndicates, who regulated the internal prices according to the external);

(*c*) Was less for home-produced foodstuffs;

(*d*) With regard to industrial articles produced internally the rise was more marked in the prices of producers' goods than in the prices of articles for direct consumption.

For a long time public opinion in Germany would not admit that prices of articles exclusively produced at home should vary with the dollar exchange, and salesmen who took the exchange as a guide were described as usurers. Even in September 1922 those men who, at the Leipzig Fair, sold wood from their forests at a price regulated by the exchange rate of the dollar, were subjected to public reproach. It was objected that the price of timber ought not to be related to the external value of the mark, because the timber merchants had no need of foreign exchange to pay for imports.

* *Op. cit.*, p. 83.

### VIII. THE RAPID ADAPTATION OF INTERNAL PRICES TO THE VARIATIONS OF THE EXCHANGE IN THE LAST PHASES OF THE DEPRECIATION OF THE MARK

**13.** In consequence of the facts to which I have alluded, in the last phases of the depreciation of the mark the adaptation of home prices to exchange rates tended to become continually more rapid. A reputable commercial paper observed on this point, in the autumn of 1922, "the effects of the fall of the mark are now different from those observed last year. Now every depreciation of the external value is reflected *much more rapidly* on the internal. After each new fall of the mark the wave of rising prices, starting from prices of raw materials and of foreign foodstuffs, spreads to all home prices. Wages and salaries follow these more quickly than they did last year."

Later, the adaptation of home prices to the exchange rate tended to become automatic, that is the paper prices were the result of two factors: the base prices and the "multiplier," the "index" which varied in more or less strict relation to exchange rates.* But for a long time the sensitiveness of internal prices was not so great as to cause the ratio between the internal and external values of the mark to become unity.

But though the equalization of the internal and external values of the mark was not reached before the summer of 1923, the tendency to adaptation was always present, and was a force which for four years kept in a continual state of agitation prices of goods, security prices, wages, salaries, railway rates, and the rates of taxes, and provoked a series of conflicts between various social classes, each of which strove to avoid the disadvantages of the depreciation of the currency. The disparity between the internal and external values of the mark was, therefore, one of the central facts of the economic life of Germany from 1919 to 1923, which explains many characteristic aspects of German economy and finance during that period.

**14.** In the summer of 1923 a new phase may be clearly traced. Internal prices in that period reached the level of world prices. Once more the sudden falls of the exchange thrust them every time below that level; but each time the reaction was immediate. The habit of calculating the cost of replacement became general. The merchant,

* In Austria also as the devaluation of the crown proceeded, the connection between prices and exchange became continually stricter, especially after the application of the "index law" of June 28th, 1922.

overcoming the psychological inertia of the past, calculated the price of his merchandise in gold and fixed the prices in paper according to the exchange rate. Wages, salaries, and fees were also based on the system of the "index" and of the "multiplier" which was generally the index number of the cost of living, published by the Statistical Bureau, each announcement of which was awaited with great impatience by the employers and employees. This index has been defined as "the principal axis around which all German life gyrated." Methods were devised for adapting wages not only to the immediate depreciation but also to the probable future depreciation of the mark.

**15.** The movement of prices and of the exchange beginning from July 1923 may be seen in the following table. As the index numbers of

Table XII

| | A The ratio between paper prices in Germany and prices in the United States (Bureau of Labour) | B Exchange rate of the gold mark expressed in paper marks |
|---|---|---|
| July 3rd | 22,400 | 38,095 |
| July 10th | 32,200 | 44,405 |
| July 17th | 28,100 | 51,905 |
| July 24th | 52,600 | 98,571 |
| July 31st | 121,500 | 261,905 |
| August 7th | 322,300 | 785,714 |
| August 14th | 442,600 | 714,286 |
| August 21st | 831,100 | 1,309,524 |
| August 28th | 1,130,100 | 1,523,809 |
| September 4th | 1,936,000 | 3,095,238 |
| September 11th | 7,476,100 | 15,761,905 |
| September 18th | 23,382,600 | 35,714,286 |
| September 25th | 23,506,500 | 28,809,524 |
| October 2nd | 54,870,100 | 76,190,476 |
| October 9th | 199,610,400 | 285,714,286 |
| October 16th | 709,610,400 | 976,190,476 |
| October 23rd | 9,480,519,000 | 13,333,333,333 |
| October 30th | 12,142,857,000 | 15,476,190,475 |
| November 6th | 83,225,806,000 | 100,000,000,000 |
| November 13th | 170,967,740,000 | 200,000,000,000 |
| November 20th | 911,870,960,000 | 1,000,000,000,000 |
| November 27th | 918,000,000,000 | 1,000,000,000,000 |
| December 4th | 868,441,560,000 | 1,000,000,000,000 |
| December 11th | 827,597,400,000 | 1,000,000,000,000 |
| December 18th | 808,181,818,000 | 1,000,000,000,000 |
| December 27th | 779,220,780,000 | 1,000,000,000,000 |

[continued

C—RATIO BETWEEN UNITED STATES PRICES AND GOLD PRICES IN GERMANY

(*a*) *According to official index numbers*

| | |
|---|---|
| July 3rd | 1·70 |
| July 10th | 1·38 |
| July 17th | 1·36 |
| July 23rd | 1·87 |
| July 31st | 2·15 |
| August 7th | 2·44 |
| August 14th | 1·61 |
| August 21st | 1·58 |
| August 28th | 1·35 |
| September 4th | 1·60 |
| September 11th | 2·11 |
| September 18th | 1·53 |
| September 25th | 1·22 |
| October 2nd | 1·39 |
| October 9th | 1·43 |
| October 16th | 1·38 |
| October 23rd | 1·41 |
| October 30th | 1·28 |
| November 6th | 1·20 |
| November 13th | 1·17 |
| November 20th | 1·10 |
| November 27th | 1·09 |
| December 4th | 1·15 |
| December 11th | 1·21 |
| December 18th | 1·24 |
| December 27th | 1·28 |

(*b*) *According to index Numbers of the "Berliner Tageblatt"*

| | |
|---|---|
| July 3rd | 1·51 |
| July 10th | 1·35 |
| July 17th | 1·26 |
| July 23rd | 1·41 |
| August 1st | 1·87 |
| August 7th | 1·92 |
| August 14th | 1·27 |
| August 21st | 1·31 |
| August 28th | 1·00 |
| September 4th | 1·13 |
| September 11th | 1·47 |
| September 18th | 1·22 |
| September 25th | 0·96 |
| October 2nd | 1·08 |
| October 9th | 1·11 |
| October 16th | 1·08 |
| October 23rd | 1·10 |
| October 30th | 1·09 |
| November 6th | 1·08 |
| November 13th | 1·04 |
| November 20th | 1·02 |
| November 27th | 0·96 |
| December 4th | 0·97 |
| December 11th | 0·99 |
| December 18th | 1·01 |

prices calculated by the Statistical Bureau of the Reich have been subjected to various criticisms I have taken account also of the indices published by the *Berliner Tageblatt*, which seem to represent more adequately the rise in prices experienced during the summer of 1923.

According to these indices in October and November 1923, i.e. in the last stage of the German inflation, the gold index number of prices in Germany generally reached, and in some weeks surpassed, the index number of the United States.

The continuous and acute oscillations which the index number of gold prices, of goods imported into Germany, showed in the second half of 1923, make it doubtful whether this index was any longer a reliable measure of the level of gold prices outside Germany.

Other statistics show that in August 1923 the prices of some important commodities such as coal, iron, and semi-finished iron goods had passed the level of the world market. In the following months this occurred for several other articles, such as skins, rye, wheat, meat, and zinc.*

According to the Statistical Bureau of the Reich, the index numbers of gold prices of some kinds of goods, in the second half of 1923, were as follows:†

TABLE XIII

(*1913 = 100*)

| 1923 | *Coal* | *Machines* | *Iron goods* | *Hosiery* | *Textile goods* |
|---|---|---|---|---|---|
| July .. .. .. | 112 | 118 | 81 | 100 | 100 |
| August .. .. | 223 | 176 | 113 | 133 | 131 |
| September .. .. | 212 | 186 | 152 | 125 | 117 |
| October .. .. | 259 | 178 | 177 | 161 | 166 |
| November .. .. | 208 | 160 | 201 | 187 | 201 |
| December .. .. | 193 | 167 | 188 | 157 | 185 |

The great rise in prices in October and November and the fall in December were obvious.

According to data contained in the review *Wirtschaft und Statistik* (No. 23, December 1923, and following numbers), in order to purchase 100 kg. of each of the following goods—wheat, wheat flour, barley, oats, beef, pork, butter, coffee, cotton, iron, zinc, lead, and coal—it was necessary to spend in the three countries named below the following sums of gold marks:

TABLE XIV

(*Gold marks*)

| *In the months of* | *Germany* | *England* | *France* |
|---|---|---|---|
| October 1923 .. .. | 1,660·6 | 1,435·2 | 1,437·5 |
| November 1923 .. | 2,331·4 | 1,451·3 | 1,414·1 |
| December 1923 .. | 1,719·3 | 1,477·7 | 1,455·7 |
| January 1924 .. .. | 1,601·7 | 1,449·5 | 1,330·6 |

According to these figures, German gold prices exceeded English gold prices in October 1923 by 15·7 per cent, and in November 60·6 per cent. A considerable drop in prices occurred in the following December.

Other official figures show that the German index numbers of prices

* Elster, *op. cit.*, p. 275.

† *Wirtschaft und Statistik*, 1924, No. 1.

of industrial raw materials exceeded those in England, France, and the United States by the following amounts:*

TABLE XV

| *In the months of* | *England per cent* | *France per cent* | *United States per cent* |
|---|---|---|---|
| August 1923 | 1·2 | 4·4 | —15·8 |
| September 1923 | 16·0 | 18·3 | 2·2 |
| October 1923 | 19·7 | 19·6 | 6·4 |
| November 1923 | 10·4 | 14·7 | —1·3 |

Finally, according to the *Frankfurter Zeitung*, in November 1923, at the time of the monetary reform, the index of *wholesale* prices of 10 food commodities was 2·046 milliards (prices about the middle of 1914 = 1). Hence gold prices were 2·05 times pre-war prices. For *retail* prices of the same goods the rise was even more considerable: 2·39 times 1914 prices. Until November 1923 retail prices had increased less than wholesale prices. But during November the former increased by 89 times and the latter only 28 times.

**16.** The preceding facts confirm the view that the index number of general prices, compiled by the Statistical Bureau of the Reich, imperfectly represents the movement of German internal prices in the summer and autumn of 1923. Numerous other data deduced from various official and private sources agree in testifying to an extraordinary rise in prices in Germany, not *after* the monetary stabilization, as happened in other countries, but during the last phase of the paper inflation. The phenomenon is also confirmed by many other characteristic and notorious facts, such as the exodus of foreigners from Germany because of the extraordinary rise in the cost of living and, by contrast, the affluence of Germans in Czechoslovakia, Switzerland, and Italy, where, by their extravagant expenditure (lamented by the Press), they did bad service to the German cause.

According to authoritative opinions, this rapid rise of prices was partly the consequence of the fall in the productivity of labour.

For some time the advantages derived by German industrialists from the depreciation of the mark—fall in real wages, low price of coal, low railway rates, reduction of real interest on mortgage debts, contracted before the war, and fiscal evasion resulting from a system of taxes which were not adapted to the depreciation—were so conspicuous

* *Materials pour servir a l'étude de la situation de l'Allemagne,* Berlin, January, 1924.

as to exceed the increase in costs due to less rational production. But as the depreciation proceeded the advantages decreased and the limiting influence which it exercised on production became continually more apparent.

Over and above this decline in productivity there were the following influences of a monetary character. In the summer of 1923, owing to the difficulty of fixing prices on the basis of the "cost of production," the practice rapidly spread of taking as a "price-basis" the pre-war prices of goods, to which was applied a coefficient which took account of the increase in prices in the outside world. The German Press, in the summer of 1923, described the various stages of the "general march towards peace-time prices."

But very quickly the merchants recognized that not even the system of fixing prices in gold, while the means of payment remained the paper mark, could guarantee them from heavy losses at a time of the rapid depreciation of the currency. For them losses could be very considerable, because the manufacturing firms used to credit their clients with the value which the paper marks, received in payment, had at the time when they were effectively converted into foreign exchange. And it was not always easy to secure foreign exchange quickly.

In order to eliminate merchants' losses—it being impossible to increase the multiplier arbitrarily—the basic prices had to be increased. The total price in paper marks therefore included a sum representing the premium against the risk of the future depreciation of the currency.

This fact is characteristic because a contrast to the phenomena which appeared during the first phases of the depreciation of the currency. In those phases the prospect of an increase of the circulation acted more rapidly on the exchanges than on prices, and home prices remained lower than external prices; but in a later phase of the depreciation a future depreciation of the exchange was allowed for in the present prices, and home prices tended to exceed external prices.

In the autumn of 1923 the rise in the basic prices was also a result of the arbitrary fixing of the rate of foreign exchange at a lower price than that quoted abroad. The merchant who was obliged to adopt the official multiplier was exposed to the risk of receiving a quantity of marks very much smaller than that necessary to replace his goods. He protected himself by increasing the basic price. This is one of the reasons why gold prices in November 1923, if computed on the basis of the official dollar exchange rate, appeared much higher than those in the world market.

## IX. MONETARY PHENOMENA OBSERVED DURING THE LAST PHASE OF THE DEPRECIATION OF THE MARK

**17.** Many facts prove the existence of a characteristic phenomenon which has been mentioned, i.e. the custom of allowing for the *future* depreciation of the currency in the fixing of *present* prices. For example, the fact that in the last phase of the inflation retail prices increased much more rapidly than wholesale prices is explained by the fact that retail prices contained a "premium against the risk of monetary depreciation" much higher than that in the prices of wholesale trade, where it was usually the custom to pay in foreign exchange or in other money on "stable value" terms.

A "surcharge for the depreciation of the currency" (Geldentwertungszuschlag) was officially established in August 1923 on the prices of coal, to guarantee the producers against the losses caused by the depreciation which the currency suffered in the interval between the payment by the consumers and the receipt of the money by the producers. At first this surcharge was calculated in gold marks at 4·15 per ton (price of a ton, 27·95 gold marks). By such means the price of coal was raised to 34 gold marks; the increase in the price entailing a corresponding increase in the coal tax. In practice the surcharge proved to be insufficient.

That prices contained a high premium against the risk of depreciation was obvious in all those cases where, for the same commodity, there was a different price according to the nature of the means of payment. For example, the manufacturers of rubber goods exacted, on the basic prices fixed in gold marks, a supplement of 50 per cent if payment was made in paper marks. The suppliers of wood for cigar boxes allowed the following discounts on their basic prices: 20 per cent if the payment was made in gold loan bonds (Goldanleihe); 30 per cent if the purchaser paid with "Dollarschatzanweisungen"; and 45 per cent if with "appreciated" foreign exchange. Another example of official recognition of the inclusion in the sale price of a premium against depreciation was a decree of the Hamburg Police authority, which settled that when the base price was justly calculated (that is, equal to pre-war price plus 30 per cent) the vendor could exact a supplement of 30 per cent if the payment was made in paper marks.

As a result of the return to peace-time gold prices as the basic price and of the adaptation of *present* prices to the *future* exchange rate, in a more advanced stage of the monetary depreciation, *the rise of internal prices was more rapid than the rise of foreign exchange rates.* "The principal characteristic of the last phase of the monetary depreciation in Germany," writes Kuczynski, "was the rise of internal prices, which from 60 per cent, round about the world level, as they were at the end of 1922, rose at least to 110 per cent of the world level towards the autumn of 1923."*

Although the phenomenon now under consideration (i.e. the tendency of internal prices to be adapted no longer to the exchange rate of the day on which the goods were sold, but to the probable future rate, that of the day on which the money received by the vendor was spent) was probably the more obvious in Germany, it could also be observed in other countries with a much depreciated currency. Thus "Austrian merchants had formed the habit of increasing sale prices by a certain percentage to guarantee themselves against losses caused by the depreciation of the currency, since it was possible that paper money received in payment might decline in value an hour after the sale."†

From private information it appears that the practice of including in the sale price a certain margin for the risk of the immediate depreciation of the money received was also common in Poland towards the end of 1923. Finally, in Bolshevik Russia it was observed that "the goods market adjusts itself to *future* note-issues, *by anticipating the rise in prices*."‡

When in the second half of November and during December 1923 the paper mark was stabilized, "the premium against the rise of depreciation" tended to disappear and prices fell, as the statistical data referred to shows.§

**18.** Let us formulate our conclusions. In an early phase the external value of the mark was dominated mainly, in its general movement, by the fall of the purchasing power of the mark in the home market.

In a later phase the movements of the internal value and of the

* *Deutsch-Französische Wirtschaftskorrespondez*, No. 10, of 1924.

† De Bordes, *The Austrian Crown*, London, 1924, p. 211. In Austria towards the end of 1921 the exchange rate of the gold crown had increased by 1,700 times (compared with 1913) and prices (cost of living) by 800 times. Towards the end of August 1922 (i.e. in the last phase of the depreciation of the Austrian crown) the price of the gold crown had increased 16,000 times and prices by 11,000 times, i.e. during 1922 these last had increased more rapidly than the rate of foreign exchange.

‡ Milentz, *Die Neuorientierung der bolschewistischen Finanzpolitik*, Stuttgart, 1923, p. 46.

§ Similarly in Austria the first effect of the stabilization of the exchange was the fall in prices because merchants no longer had any need to allow in their prices for the risk of a future monetary depreciation (Herz, "Wie Oesterreich saniert wurde," in *Berliner Tageblatt*, No. 423, of September 9th, 1923).

external purchasing power of the German mark appeared determined mainly by the exchange rate of the dollar expressed in paper marks. The exchange rate of the dollar varied primarily under the action of causes which directly influenced it; these variations provoked corresponding movements in the internal purchasing power, but the reaction was not, generally, immediate, hence the external value remained lower than the internal.

In an early phase of the depreciation there existed a "system" of internal prices, the rigidity of which presented a great contrast to the very sharp variations of the exchange rate and tended to lead the latter back towards equilibrium, despite the influence of causes directly affecting the exchange rate in causing a movement from equilibrium.

Later this system of internal prices was disorganized. On the one hand was the lack of control first imposed by public authority; on the other, the influence of psychological causes, which curbed the rise of prices, was continually weakened. Prices became more and more sensitive to the variations of the exchange. Movements in the exchange rate caused an immediate movement in certain prices, the disturbance spreading slowly to other prices; but this process of diffusion became more rapid as the situation developed. A "system" of internal prices, which represented a kind of centre of gravity of the oscillations of the exchange and which determined the "equilibrium price" of the latter (the current market price representing only an ephemeral movement), no longer existed. Internal prices became unstable and, together with wages and salaries, they became subject to every breath in the exchange market.

These German experiences apparently confirm the point of view of those writers who have recently criticized the Quantity Theory of money in its application to the theory of foreign exchanges. Professor Aftalion writes that in a country with a paper currency it is "the exchange which dominates internal prices . . . the action of the exchange rate on prices throws a great light on what must be the true theory of money, the theory which must be substituted for the quantitative theory."* If, continues Aftalion, in France the franc depreciates in terms of the dollar, there will be increases in the money incomes of exporters, of their workmen, of owners of foreign securities, and of importers who have bought (and paid for) goods before the depreciation of the franc. All these people are disposed to pay more francs than before for the goods they purchase; in other words, their demand for

* *Monnaie et industrie*, 1929, p. 2.

goods increases and prices rise, not only those of imported and exported goods but also of those produced at home.

Aftalion's argument does not take account of the fact that, if money incomes had not increased owing to an increase in the quantity of money in circulation, to the rise in the demand for foreign exchange provoked by an intenser need for foreign goods, or by making foreign payments resulting from "non-merchandise transactions," there must correspond a lesser demand for home-produced goods. Those who produced these goods, suffering losses, restrict production and dismiss workmen; hence the fall in the demand for goods tends to be accentuated. On the other hand, exporters invest their profits in extending the production of goods for export, and their demand for labour increases. In the last analysis, the prices of goods for internal consumption tend to be maintained at the former level, and the depreciation of the exchange rate only has a permanent influence on prices of imported goods, and a temporary influence on those of exported goods. Therefore, internal prices can only be displaced under the pressure of the depreciation of the exchange in so far as there is a continual issue of paper money.*

Together with the dominant influence of the German monetary inflation on the exchange rate of the mark, but entirely secondary, was that of the variations of gold prices in the world market. It may be observed that this influence does not appear always to have been that indicated by the Purchasing Power Parity doctrine, which is a theory of foreign exchanges in "the long run," rather than a description of what happens "in the short run." When the prices of goods in foreign countries vary, and the demand of the country with the paper currency does not react immediately, or the reaction is weak, it may happen that the first effect of a fall (or a rise) in world prices may be a rise (or a fall) in the foreign exchange value of the money of that country. For example, in 1919 the rise in gold prices in the world market probably contributed to the *depreciation* of the foreign exchange value of the paper mark, because at that time the German demand for more foreign goods (which were urgently required in Germany) was rather inelastic. On the contrary, in the second half of 1920 the fall in world prices probably helped the improvement of the German mark.

* The influence of a rise in the velocity of the circulation of money is studied in Chapter IV.

# APPENDIX TO CHAPTER III*

# On Certain Methodological Questions regarding the Calculation of the Depreciation of the Mark

## I. ARITHMETIC AND HARMONIC AVERAGES OF THE VALUE OF THE GOLD MARK EXPRESSED IN PAPER MARKS

**1.** In Chapter III I have referred to certain difficulties and uncertainties which occur if one wishes to calculate, on the basis of daily statements indicating the level of prices and the rates of exchange, an average of prices, in paper or gold, and of exchange rates.

During 1923 differences appeared between the numerical results arrived at by the Accountancy Office of the Reparations Commission at Paris on the one hand and the Berlin Delegation of the Committee of Guarantees on the other, with regard to the calculation of the monthly *average* exchange rate of the dollar, expressed in paper marks. The Paris office based its calculations on daily quotations in New York, while the Berlin office used those of the Berlin Bourse; but this could not explain the difference between the averages, because the daily quotations of the two markets were not substantially different. What, then, were the reasons for the difference which, more and more as 1923 passed, tended to increase in each successive calculation of the monthly averages of the daily exchange rates? This question was put to the author of this book when he was technical consultant to the Committee of Guarantees. It was the origin of the following study.

**2.** The daily exchange rate between paper marks and dollars can be expressed in two ways: (*a*) in the form of a fraction of the dollar (or of the gold mark) as, e.g., on January 3rd, 1923, the rate of exchange of the paper mark in New York was 0·000134 dollars; (*b*) by means of a figure which indicates the quantity of paper marks equal to a dollar (or a gold mark, which is equal to $\frac{1}{4{\cdot}20}$ of a dollar). The mint par of the mark being 0·2382 dollars, on January 3rd, 1923, a gold mark was worth $\frac{0{\cdot}2382}{0{\cdot}000134} = 1{,}778$ paper marks. Thus the exchange rate of the paper mark expressed in gold marks is reciprocal of the exchange rate of the gold mark expressed in paper marks.

The following summary shows (*a*) the quotations of the paper mark in New

* In this appendix I have joined two articles, "La misura del deprezzamento di una moneta cartacea" and "Media aritmetica, armonica e geometrica dei corsi di una moneta deprezzata." The former was published in *Rivista Bancaria*, 1923, and the latter in *Metron*, 1924.

York in January 1923, and (*b*) the corresponding values of the gold mark expressed in paper marks:

| *Day* | (*a*) | (*b*) | *Day* | (*a*) | (*b*) |
|---|---|---|---|---|---|
| 2nd | 0·000139 | 1,714 | 17th | 0·000054 | 4,411 |
| 3rd | 0·000134 | 1,778 | 18th | 0·000045 | 5,294 |
| 4th | 0·000124 | 1,921 | 19th | 0·000050 | 4,764 |
| 5th | 0·000118 | 2,019 | 20th | 0·000051 | 4,671 |
| 6th | 0·000116 | 2,054 | 22nd | 0·000046 | 5,179 |
| 8th | 0·000103 | 2,313 | 23rd | 0·000051 | 4,671 |
| 9th | 0·000098 | 2,431 | 24th | 0·000048 | 4,963 |
| 10th | 0·000095 | 2,507 | 25th | 0·000048 | 4,963 |
| 11th | 0·000095 | 2,507 | 26th | 0·000043 | 5,540 |
| 12th | 0·000096 | 2,481 | 27th | 0·000036 | 6,617 |
| 13th | 0·000093 | 2,561 | 29th | 0·000029 | 8,214 |
| 15th | 0·000073 | 3,263 | 30th | 0·000022 | 10,828 |
| 16th | 0·000063 | 3,781 | 31st | 0·000021 | 11,344 |

Now the question arises: what was the *average* number of paper marks equal to a gold mark in January 1923?

We can answer this question in one or other of the following ways:

(*a*) The arithmetic mean of the daily rates of the paper mark, expressed in dollars, can be calculated; the reciprocal of this average (multiplied by 0·2382) is the average rate required. On the basis of this calculation we have for January 1923: 1 gold mark = 3,276 paper marks. This was the method followed by the Accountancy Office at Paris.

(*b*) The arithmetic mean of the daily rates of the gold mark, expressed in paper marks, can be calculated. According to this method, in January 1923: 1 gold mark = 4,338 paper marks. This was the method followed by the Berlin Office.*

**3.** The results of the two methods are very different. And they must necessarily differ.

In effect if:

$$k_1, k_2, \quad . \quad . \quad . \quad k_n$$

are the exchange rates of a gold monetary unit expressed in the depreciated currency, and

$$\frac{1}{k_1} = x_1, \quad \frac{1}{k_2} = x_2 \quad . \quad . \quad . \quad \frac{1}{k_n} = x_n$$

are the exchange rates of a depreciated currency expressed in fractions of a gold monetary unit, the quantity

$$\frac{k_1 + k_2 + \quad . \quad . \quad . \quad + k_n}{n} = M_1$$

* Applying this method to the quotations in Berlin, for January 1923 we have an average rate of 4,281 paper marks for 1 gold mark. This was the rate given by the Statistical Bureau of the Reich. On the other hand, according to the Federal Reserve Bank of New York, the average rate was 3,275 paper marks for 1 gold mark.

cannot be equal to the quantity:

$$\frac{n}{\frac{1}{k_1}+\frac{1}{k_2}+\;.\;.\;.\;+\frac{1}{k_n}}=M_2$$

It is obvious that, while $M_1$ is the *arithmetic* mean of the rates, $k_1$, $k_2$, . . . $k_n$, $M_2$ is their *harmonic* mean. Now, it is known that the arithmetic mean of a series of terms is a different sum from the harmonic mean and that, precisely, the former is always higher than the latter.

**4.** I have also found some great differences between the average exchange rates of the gold mark or the dollar, expressed in paper marks, which were published by various Statistical offices or banks (such as the Federal Reserve Bank of New York).

For example, in No. 13 of 1923 (page 413) of the review *Wirtschaft und Statistik* (published by the German Statistical Bureau) one reads that in 1922 the average exchange rate of the gold mark was 449·2 paper marks. But the monthly *Statistical Bulletin* of the League of Nations (1923, No. 3, p. 29) shows the average exchange rate for 1922 to be 101·2 paper marks for a gold mark.

When the differences between the single terms are very small the harmonic mean approaches the arithmetic mean. Therefore, before the war, when the fluctuations of the exchange were very small (except for some countries) it was a matter of indifference whether the arithmetic or harmonic mean of a series of quotations was calculated. Examining post-war statistics one finds that the difference between the results, arrived at by calculating one average instead of the other, was not significant either for the Italian lira or the French franc, at least until 1923, as the following example shows:

AVERAGE EXCHANGE RATE OF THE DOLLAR

| | *In Italian lire* | | | *In French francs* | | |
|---|---|---|---|---|---|---|
| | 1920 | 1921 | 1922 | 1920 | 1921 | 1922 |
| Method (*a*).. | 20·6 | 23·3 | 21·0 | 14·5 | 13·2 | 12·2 |
| Method (*b*).. | 21·5 | 23·5 | 21·1 | 14·7 | 13·3 | 12·3 |

Thus the question has special significance for the calculation of the average depreciation of paper money, which suffers heavy and sharp falls in value, as did the German mark, the Polish mark, and the Austrian crown. For the German mark, the difference between the results obtained by the two methods increased in 1921; it became more considerable in the period of rapid depreciation from August 1922 to January 1923; it grew less in the months of the relative stability of the exchange rates of the mark (January–July 1922 and March–April 1923).

**5.** Certainly in business life the daily exchange rates are the important rates. But even for certain practical purposes it can be useful to know with some accuracy the average of a series of daily exchange rates. For example, in German statistical sources figures regarding various economic and financial phenomena—Government expenditure, yield of taxes, railway receipts, increases in the capital of limited companies, bank deposits, etc.—are shown in paper marks. It is necessary to know what average coefficient of depreciation should be used to obtain, with sufficient approximation, the amount of gold marks equivalent to those sums of paper marks.

Let us suppose that a certain sum $S$, expressed in the depreciated currency which refers to a certain period, say a month, must be converted into gold terms. If we do not know how that sum is distributed between the days, so that we could apply to each part the relevant daily rate, it will be necessary to have recourse to a summary method, using an *average* of the exchange rate. Then we should find that, say, $T$, who lives in New York and has before him the lists of that Stock Exchange where it is customary to quote the *paper mark* in fractions of a dollar, will think he is following the less arbitrary proceeding by multiplying $S$ by the arithmetic average of the exchange rates of the paper mark expressed in gold. $Z$, on the other hand, who lives at Berlin and is accustomed to the methods of the Bourse, where the exchange rate of the *dollar* is quoted in paper marks, naturally proceeds to divide $S$ by the arithmetic average of the exchange rates of the gold mark expressed in paper. The two calculations do not agree.

**6.** Which is the correct method? In January 1923 was the average value of the paper mark $\frac{1}{3276}$, or only $\frac{1}{4317}$ of the mint par?

On the whole, we may say that neither of the two methods can give an exact result. The *exact* measure of the average depreciation of the paper mark compared with gold could only be calculated if the amount of paper marks exchanged for foreign currencies, during the period to which the calculation refers, is known. Let us suppose that in a given period the total sum of $S$ paper marks has been exchanged for a certain quantity of bills and foreign currency equivalent to $O$ gold marks. The quotient:

$$C = \frac{S}{O}$$

shows how many paper marks were exchanged, on an *average*, for a gold mark, that is, it gives the *exact* average value of a gold mark in paper marks. The average exchange rate of the paper mark in gold marks is given by the reciprocal of $C$, that gives:

$$C^1 = \frac{O}{S}.$$

In practice, the amount of the transactions being unknown, we cannot but determine $C$ *approximately*. For that purpose, let us analyse the quantities $S$ and $O$. Quantity $O$ results from the sum of the quantities $o_1, o_2 \ldots o_n$, which have been exchanged respectively for the quantities $s_1, s_2 \ldots s_n$, of paper marks on each of the days which compose the total period, to which the average $C$ refers. Indicating with $k_1, k_2 \quad . \quad . \quad . \quad k_n$, the average value of the gold mark in paper marks on each of these days, we have:

$$s_1 = o_1k_1; \quad s_2 = o_2k_2; \quad . \quad . \quad . \quad s_n = o_nk_n$$

Therefore we can write:

$$C = \frac{k_1o_1 + k_2o_2 + \quad . \quad . \quad . \quad + k_no_n}{o_1 + o_2 + \quad . \quad . \quad . \quad + o_n}$$

Hence the *exact* average exchange rate of the gold mark in paper marks is equal to the *weighted arithmetic average* of the daily exchange rates of the gold mark. The weights are given by the quantity of gold marks which have been exchanged daily for paper marks.

Now to determine the numerical value of $C$ it is necessary to have recourse to one of the following hypotheses:

*Hypothesis I.*—Let us suppose that *the number of paper marks* which, each day, have been exchanged for gold marks, remains constant; let us assume, that is: $k_1o_1 = k_2o_2 = \quad . \quad . \quad . \quad k_no_n$. Then we have:

$$C = \frac{n}{\frac{1}{k_1} + \frac{1}{k_2} + \quad . \quad . \quad . \quad + \frac{1}{k_n}}$$

that is, the average exchange rate is equal to the harmonic average of the daily exchange rates of the gold mark in terms of paper marks, or, what is the same thing, to the reciprocal of the arithmetic average of the daily exchange rates of the paper mark expressed in gold marks.

*Hypothesis II.*—Let us suppose that *the number of gold marks* which are daily exchanged for paper marks remains constant; that is, let $o_1 = o_2 = \quad . \quad . \quad . \quad o_n$. Then we have:

$$C = \frac{k_1 + k_2 + \quad . \quad . \quad . \quad + k_n}{n}$$

that is, the average exchange rate is equal to the arithmetic average of the daily exchange rates of the gold mark.

7. Thus we have found the formulae for $M_2$ and $M_1$. Method (*a*) is based on the first hypothesis; the second justifies method (*b*). The problem is thus reduced to this question: which is nearer to reality, the first hypothesis or the second?

If it can reasonably be supposed that in each of the partial periods which make up the total period, the *quantities of paper marks* forming the total sum remains constant, this sum will be divided by the reciprocal of the arithmetical average of the quotations of the paper mark in terms of gold marks. If, instead, it is to be supposed that in each of the partial periods the *quantities of gold marks* corresponding to the partial figures of the paper marks remains constant, the total sum of paper marks will be divided by the arithmetic average of the quotations of the gold mark expressed in paper marks.

The first hypothesis is rarely applicable to real facts, when it is a question of a rather long period of time. The value in paper marks of imports and exports, Clearing House returns, bank deposits, Government expenditure, the sums paid in wages, the yield from many taxes, etc., tended to adapt themselves to the depreciation of the mark, that is, the quantities of paper marks corresponding to the partial periods which form the total period, tended to increase in proportion to the loss in value suffered by the paper mark.

Nor does the second hypothesis, on which is based method (*b*), accord perfectly with reality. The total quantity of gold marks, which, in a given period, was exchanged for paper marks, was not distributed uniformly over the time; in other words, the *weights* of the single exchange rates of the gold mark expressed in paper marks, on the basis of which we wish to calculate the average exchange rate, are not equal. But the second hypothesis is much nearer to reality than is the first.

For example, in 1922 German exports amounted to 1,732,093 millions of paper marks. If the monthly figures are unknown and we wish to convert the aggregate figure of paper marks into gold, by dividing this figure by 101·2 (average exchange rate of the gold mark according to the League of Nations' *Bulletin*), we should arrive at an absurd result: 17,116 millions of gold marks. In fact, the figure arrived at by the German Statistical Bureau, by converting the figures month by month, was 3,970 millions of gold marks. By dividing the aggregate sum of paper marks by the arithmetic average of the exchange rates of the gold mark (449·2) we have a result which approaches reality, that is, 3,865 million gold marks. This coincidence is explained by the fact that the gold value of exports had not been subject to great fluctuations from month to month in 1922 (except in the months of August and December).

## II. THE GEOMETRIC MEAN OF THE DAILY EXCHANGE RATES OF THE GOLD MARK

**8.** The contrast between the results obtained by working on the bases of the two methods indicated would be eliminated if the geometric mean of the exchange rates were used; that is, the quantity

$$\sqrt[n]{k_1 k_2 \quad . \quad . \quad . \quad k_n} = M_3$$

or the quantity:

$$\sqrt[n]{x_1 x_2 \quad . \quad . \quad . \quad x_n} = M_4.$$

Actually

$$M_3 = \frac{1}{M_4}$$

Is, therefore, the use of the geometric mean of the daily exchange rates more suitable? That is our next problem.

In the following table are indicated the arithmetic, harmonic, and geometric *monthly* averages of the *daily exchange rates of the gold mark expressed in paper marks* (that is, the quantities $M_1$, $M_2$, and $M_3$). The daily exchange rates of the gold mark have been calculated on the base of the daily quotations of the paper mark in New York.

| 1923 | *Arithmetic average* | *Harmonic average* | *Geometric average* |
|---|---|---|---|
| January .. .. | 4,338 | 3,275 | 3,737 |
| February .. .. | 6,616 | 6,209 | 6,403 |
| March .. .. | 5,066 | 5,060 | 5,053 |
| April .. .. | 5,909 | 5,759 | 5,832 |
| May .. .. | 11,147 | 10,641 | 10,891 |
| June .. .. | 26,244 | 24,194 | 25,195 |
| July .. .. | 100,153 | 70,072 | 81,329 |
| August .. .. | 1,053,843 | 702,113 | 881,681 |
| September .. | 26,022,000 | 12,666,000 | 19,833,000 |
| October .. .. | 7,450,000,000 | 353,000,000 | 1,675,000,000 |
| November .. | 961,368,000,000 | 552,599,000,000 | 796,081,000,000 |
| December.. .. | 1,065,000,000,000 | 1,051,000,000,000 | 1,057,000,000,000 |

As may be seen, the arithmetic, the harmonic, and the geometric means differed appreciably in January 1923 (when a sharp depreciation of the mark occurred) and later, at the beginning of June, when following unsuccessful action on the part of the Reichsbank to sustain the mark, the dollar rate once more rose rapidly.

In December the three averages differed little from one another, thanks to the stabilization of the rates of the paper mark, which was the consequence of monetary reform.

Let us fix our attention on October, which is the month for which the greatest divergences between the averages appear. According to the arithmetic average the average exchange rate of the gold mark was 7,450 million paper dollars, to the geometric it was 1,675 millions, and to the harmonic it was 353 millions.*

**9.** An inductive verification of these results can be given in the following manner. Opposite are the German statistics (unpublished) which give the *daily* increase of the floating debt, in paper marks. The figures relate to October 1923, and have been converted into dollars according to the daily exchange rate of the dollar on the Berlin Bourse.

The floating debt increased because of the rise in the expenses of the German Government, which, in their turn, were a function of the exchange rate of the dollar and of the index number of internal prices.

Therefore, dividing the figure which gives the total amount, in paper marks, during the month of October by the corresponding value in gold (1,071 million gold marks), we have an approximate measure of the average value of the gold mark in October.

This average value—7,801 million paper marks for one gold mark—is much nearer to the *arithmetic average* of the daily exchange rates than to the geometric

* The figure 353 millions was given by the *Bulletin mensuel de Statistique*, published by the League of Nations, November 1923. But, according to the German Statistical Bureau, which, as I have said, considered as the average exchange rate of the gold mark the arithmetical average of the daily exchange rates of the gold mark (according to quotations of the dollar at Berlin), the average value of the gold mark was, in October 1923, 6,017 million paper marks (*Wirtschaft und Statistik*, 1923, p. 708).

or harmonic averages. It is evident that this indirect determination somewhat exaggerates the average value of the gold mark, because the Government expenses, computed in gold, increased particularly in the last days of the month when the value of the paper mark was more depressed.*

Hence the geometric average gives for the gold mark a value in paper marks

DAILY INCREASE OF THE FLOATING DEBT

| Day | *Billions of paper marks* | *Millions of dollars* |
|---|---|---|
| 1st | 3,143 | 12·9 |
| 2nd | 3,175 | 9·9 |
| 3rd | 2,326 | 5·3 |
| 4th | 2,084 | 3·8 |
| 5th | 8,510 | 14·2 |
| 6th | 6,726 | 11·2 |
| 8th | 4,212 | 5·0 |
| 9th | 4,753 | 3·9 |
| 10th | 9,280 | 3·1 |
| 11th | 17,128 | 5·6 |
| 12th | 21,027 | 5·2 |
| 13th | 33,605 | 8·4 |
| 15th | 28,756 | 7·6 |
| 16th | 29,887 | 7·3 |
| 17th | 33,565 | 6·1 |
| 18th | 56,983 | 7·0 |
| 19th | 88,466 | 7·3 |
| 20th | 125,500 | 10·4 |
| 22nd | 157,334 | 3·9 |
| 23rd | 223,500 | 4·0 |
| 24th | 346,889 | 5·5 |
| 25th | 602,517 | 9·2 |
| 26th | 778,360 | 11·9 |
| 27th | 1,384,185 | 21·3 |
| 29th | 1,187,538 | 18·3 |
| 30th | 1,693,847 | 26·0 |
| 31st | 1,502,319 | 20·7 |
| | 8,355,615 | 255·0 |

which is very much lower than the ratio between the sum of the daily figures of paper marks and that of the daily figures of gold marks.

* Other examples of indirect determination of the average value of the paper mark in October may be found in article cited ("Media aritmetica, armonica e geometrica dei corsi di una moneta deprezzata," *Metron*, 1924).

That it must be so is easily explained on the basis of a mathematical relation explained by Fechner.* We can have

$$\frac{s_1 + s_2 + \quad . \quad . \quad . \quad + s_n}{o_1 + o_2 + \quad . \quad . \quad . \quad + o_n} = \sqrt[n]{k_1 k_2 \quad . \quad . \quad . \quad k_n}$$

only when the relative standard deviation† of the values $s$ from their arithmetic average is equal to the relative standard deviation of the values $o$ from their arithmetic average. As Fechner showed, according as the dispersion of the values $s$ is greater or less than that of values $o$, the geometric average of the ratios $\frac{s}{o}$ (equal in our case to $k$) is smaller or greater than the ratio between the two sums.

In our case the variability of the values $s$ is much greater than that of values $o$,‡ and this explains why the geometrical average is an erroneous measure of the value average of the gold mark expressed in paper marks.

A problem analogous to that now studied arises when we wish to calculate an average of a series of price indices of goods, computed during a period of rapid depreciation of a currency. In Germany the arithmetic average is generally used. This proceeding is justified by the tacit hypothesis that at the various times, to which the individual determinations refer, the quantity of goods exchanged for money remains constant. This hypothesis hardly accords with the facts; but in a period of rapid depreciation of the mark it is more plausible than that which is based on the harmonic average, which presupposes that the *quantities of paper marks* exchanged for goods remain constant. Also the geometric average of the indices of prices would give erroneous results, because at a time of monetary inflation and of great fluctuations in the value of money, the variability of the sums of paper money exchanged daily for goods is much greater than the variability of the quantities of goods.§

* See Fechner, *Kollektivmasslehre*, Leipzig, 1897, p. 361. Fechner observes that the relation referred to in the text—which is a consequence of the relation between the arithmetical and geometrical averages shown by Scheibner—is only approximate, but that it does not alter the results appreciably.

† That is, the standard deviation divided by the arithmetic average of the values $s$.

‡ The standard deviation is 165·2 per cent of the arithmetic average for values $s$, and 62·5 per cent of the arithmetic average for values $o$.

§ The calculation of an average index of prices in gold may lead to erroneous results when it is based on an average of price indices in paper and an average of exchange rates. For example, according to the *Bulletin mensuel de Statistique* of the League of Nations, issue of November 1923, p. 18, the index number of goods prices in paper was on an average in October 1923, 7,095,000,000 (1913 = 1). According to the same publication (p. 28) the average exchange rate of the gold mark expressed in paper marks was 353,000,000. Dividing the first figure by the second, we obtain the result that in October the average level of prices in gold was twenty times the pre-war level! This absurd result is explained thus: the first figure is an arithmetic average of a series of index numbers of prices, while the second is a harmonic average of a series of quotations of the mark exchange.

CHAPTER IV

# Relations between the Total Value and the Quantity of Paper Money in Circulation*

## I. AN ECONOMIC SOPHISM

**1.** During 1923, when in Germany every obstacle to the issue of paper money had been removed, and the circulation was rising to increasingly fantastic figures, eminent financiers and politicians maintained and endeavoured to show that there was neither monetary nor credit inflation in Germany.

The argument on which the pretended demonstration was based is an example of an interesting economic sophism. It admitted that the nominal value of the paper money issued was certainly enormous; but the "real" value, that is the gold value according to the exchange rate, of the mass of notes in circulation, was much lower than that of the money circulating in Germany before the war. For example, on August 7th, 1923, the note-issues amounted to 62,338 milliard paper marks. On the same day a gold mark was worth 783,000 paper marks. The "real," "intrinsic" value of the paper money in circulation was scarcely 80 million gold marks! How could it be stated that there was inflation in Germany?

**2.** The principal and most authoritative supporter of the strange theory in Germany was Helfferich, who expounded it in June 1923 before the "Committee of Inquiry into the causes of the Fall of the Mark." The former Minister of Finance and celebrated economist categorically affirmed that in Germany there was no inflation, since the total value, in gold, of the paper money in circulation was covered by the gold in the Reichsbank in a considerably higher proportion than before the war.

Later Helfferich expounded the same theory, again supporting it

* In this chapter I have used (amplifying considerably) two articles: "C'è stata inflazione in Germania?" and "La rapiditá di circolazione di una moneta deprezzata," the former published in *Rivista Bancaria* of 1924 and the latter in *Giornale degli Economisti* of 1925.

with other arguments and data, in the new edition of his well-known work on money.*

Before the same Committee Havenstein, then President of the Reichsbank, explained an analogous notion. He asserted that the cause of the fall of the mark was not the "so-called inflation," but that "the impulse to monetary depreciation had always come from abroad." In a later discussion on August 25th, 1923, Havenstein denied that there was a credit inflation in Germany. Defending the policy of the Reichsbank against the ever lively attacks made by a part of the German Press, Havenstein tried to show that the Central Bank had not been generous with credits, observing that the portfolio of the Reichsbank was worth, in gold marks (computing the value of the separate bills at the moment of discounting), much less than half the value of the 1913 portfolio.

These erroneous interpretations of monetary facts had very serious practical results, since they helped to stop the responsible authority from setting a limit to the issues of paper money.

**3.** That there had been no inflation in Germany was believed to be proved, not only by the modest figure which was obtained when the total nominal value of the notes in circulation was converted into gold, but also from the fact that the increase of this nominal value was less rapid than the increase of prices (especially from the second half of 1922 onwards). In the summer of 1922 Professor Julius Wolf wrote: "In proportion to the need, less money circulates in Germany now than before the war. This statement may cause surprise, but it is correct. The circulation is now 15–20 times that of pre-war days, whilst prices have risen 40–50 times. The decline in transactions cannot explain the difference."† Later an economic journal wrote:‡

> The Press of the Allied countries states that Germany has ruined her exchange since the war by gigantic note issues. Now, in Germany, everyone knows that for some months already the note issues of the Reichsbank have been nominally most gigantic, but actually they are small, very small (!) if account is taken of their real value, as may be seen by comparing the rise of the note issues with the rise of prices. Not even the most faithful followers of the quantitative theory will maintain that the relatively small increase in the quantity of paper money has provoked the rise in prices, which has been much more considerable.

* Helfferich, *Das Geld*, 1923, p. 646.

† *Markkurs, Reparationen und russisches Geschäft*, Stuttgart, 1922, p. 10.

‡ *Wiederaufbau*, October 13th, 1922.

Similarly, in his recent work on the German mark, Elster states that "however enormous may be the apparent rise in the circulation in 1922, actually the figures show a decline" !*

The same ideas may also be found in official publications. For example, in the pamphlet *Deutschlands Wirtschaftslage*, edited by the Statistical Bureau of the Reich in March 1923, one reads (p. 28) that "in Germany at the end of 1922 the quantity of paper marks in circulation was *scarcely* equal to 160 times the quantity of money circulating before the war and that cannot be considered high if compared with the rise in prices. Already in December 1922 wholesale prices were 1,475 times and retail prices 685 times pre-war prices."

The Statistical Bureau of the Reich has calculated, for a series of countries, the real value of the quantity of paper circulating in each. This was obtained by dividing the total nominal value of the paper money by the index number of wholesale prices (index number of 1913 = 1). The figures for each country have been converted into gold marks. The following table, reproduced from *Wirtschaft und Statistik*, gives the real value of the circulating medium divided by the number of inhabitants.†

TABLE XVI

| *Country* | *Gold marks per person* | | |
|---|---|---|---|
| | 1913 | 1920 | 1922 |
| Australia | 45·33 | 107·04 | 122·96 |
| Belgium | 116·76 | 140·53 | 193·33 |
| Bulgaria | 35·58 | 23·27 | 25·71 |
| Canada | 72·36 | 55·45 | 49·43 |
| Denmark | 58·97 | 54·12 | 87·94 |
| Germany | 44·71 | 87·63 | 17·92 |
| England | 13·18 | 84·40 | 110·73 |
| France | 116·87 | 180·05 | 229·90 |
| British India | 2·79 | 3·59 | 4·27 |
| Italy | 64·96 | 70·13 | 72·53 |
| Japan | 17·96 | 26·00 | 23·95 |
| Low Countries | 89·49 | 119·56 | 145·15 |
| Norway | 50·83 | 56·54 | 73·85 |
| Sweden | 47·82 | 48·47 | 73·05 |
| Switzerland | 66·84 | 89·49 | 103·33 |
| Spain | 79·80 | 73·43 | 90·99 |
| United States of America | 48·10 | 101·35 | 97·66 |

The preceding table is interesting because it shows what strange conclusions may be reached if it is admitted that the "real" value of

* Elster, *op. cit.*, p. 167.

† *Wirtschaft und Statistik*, 1923, No. 1.

a paper currency, related to the number of inhabitants, can indicate the degree of inflation of the circulation in various countries at a given moment, or at different times in the monetary history of one country.* For example, it may be deduced from the table that the degree of inflation had been very much greater in England (110·7 gold marks per person at the end of 1922) than in Germany (17·9 gold marks). Of all the countries, except India, that with the slightest inflation was Germany itself, where the degree of inflation had declined from 1920 (87·6 marks per person) to 1922, whilst in other countries which after the war had practiced a strict policy of deflation the inflation had increased!

### II. THE FALL OF THE TOTAL VALUE OF THE PAPER MONEY IN CIRCULATION IN AN ADVANCED PHASE OF INFLATION. EXPLANATIONS GIVEN BY KEYNES AND MARSHALL

**4.** Without doubt, the contrast between the enormous nominal value of the mass of notes in circulation and their very small total "real" value constitutes one of the most curious facts which were observed in the last phase of the German inflation which began with the second half of 1923. Because of the sudden and considerable fluctuations of the exchange, if the total nominal value of the paper money were converted into gold the figures would vary very much; but they would oscillate round a level which was very low compared with the total value of the German circulation on the eve of the war (about 6 milliard marks). According to *Wirtschaft und Statistik* the total value of Reichsbank notes was 482·8 million gold marks on July 17th, 1923; 79·3 on August 7th; 181 on August 15th; 226·4 on August 23rd; 93·6 on September 7th; 740·7 on September 30th; 328·4 on October 7th; 39·3 on October 23rd; and 144·6 at the end of October. On November 15th—on the eve of the cessation of the discount of Treasury bills by the Reichsbank—based on the *official* value of the gold mark (six hundred milliard paper marks), the total value of notes of the Reichsbank in circulation was 154·7 million gold marks. But based on the exchange rate of the paper mark in New York the total value was as low as 97·4 million gold marks.

The facts, to which the German economists quoted above directed attention, are clearly established; but their interpretation of those facts is obviously mistaken. They did not mention the analogous experi-

* *Berliner Tageblatt*, September 3rd, 1922. By similar reasoning it is possible to argue that the inflation in Faance in July 1922 was greater than that in Germany!

ences of the past. According to Thiers, in 1795 the assignats which were circulating in France had a total nominal value of 20 milliards of francs, but their total real value amounted to less than 200 million gold francs.* In the "greenbacks" period in America some argued that the depreciation of the paper currency was not due to the increase in the quantity in circulation, and it was argued that the main cause was the decline in production and the fall in the supply of labour.† It was on that occasion that Carey, in a letter to the Secretary to the Treasury, insisted that it could not be true that there was too much money in circulation; indeed, he added, in France the circulation was 30 gold dollars per head, in England 25 dollars, and in the United States only 12½.‡

**5.** Whilst in Germany itself economists and financiers thought they had found in the fall of the total value of the circulating money the proof of the non-existence of the "so-called inflation," outside Germany the scientific explanation of the phenomenon was given. I refer to a famous article by Keynes in which he shows that in an advanced phase of monetary inflation new note-issues are accompanied by an increase in the *velocity of the circulation* of the currency, and that the influence exercised by the velocity of circulation on prices and the exchange can be greater than that of successive issues of paper money.§

Marshall expounded some other interesting considerations in his work *Money, Credit and Commerce*, published in 1923.‖ The observations of Marshall are concerned with the conception of "total value" of the quantity of money and explain the continual fall of this total value in a period of continual depreciation of the monetary unit. Every individual invests a certain proportion of his income in "ready purchasing power," i.e. money available for spending. The total value of the money circulating in a country will tend to equal the sum of the real values of the quantities of money which every individual wishes to keep available, because in such a way "every one will be able to have as much ready purchasing power at command as he cares to

* *Histoire de la Révolution française* (Brussels, 1844), vol. ii, p. 254.

† Hock, *Die Finanzen und die Finanzgeschichte der Vereinigten Staaten* (Stuttgart, 1867), p. 556.

‡ Hock, *op. cit.*, p. 556.

§ Keynes, "Inflation as a Form of Taxation," *The Reconstruction of Europe*, *Manchester Guardian* Supplement, pamphlet v.

‖ See also Cannan, "The Application of the Theoretical Apparatus of Supply and Demand to Units of Currency," *Economic Journal*, 1921, p. 453. This author writes: "Experience seems to show that the unit of currency falls to zero long before the supply of the currency reaches infinity."

have." In other words, if every person decides to keep for himself, in the form of money, a tenth of his income, the total value of the sum of money in circulation will tend to equal a tenth of the national income.

Therefore "the less the proportion of their resources which people care to keep in the form of currency, the lower will be the aggregate value of the currency, that is, the higher will prices be with a given volume of currency." . . . "The total value of an inconvertible paper currency therefore cannot be increased by increasing its quantity; *an increase in its quantity, which seems likely to be repeated, will lower the value of each unit more than in proportion to the increase.*"*

### III. RELATIONS BETWEEN THE QUANTITY OF PAPER MONEY, PRICES AND THE FOREIGN EXCHANGE RATES IN AN ADVANCED PHASE OF MONETARY DEPRECIATION

**6.** Statistics relative to monetary facts which occurred during and after the World War, like statistics regarding earlier episodes, show that in an advanced stage of a monetary depreciation the foreign exchange rates and prices increase more rapidly than the quantity of legal paper money in circulation, whose total "real" value continually decreases in consequence.

This phenomenon may be described as one of the outstanding features of the circulation in countries with a much depreciated currency, in contrast to those States where the depreciation proceeds more slowly.

A classic example of the phenomenon is given by the "assignats" of the French Revolution, to which I have already referred.

In an early stage of the depreciation of the assignats, at the end of May 1794, the exchange rate of metallic money, expressed in paper, had increased in much the same proportion as the issues of paper money. In May 1794 the quantity of money in circulation had a nominal value equal to less than three times the value of the circulation at the beginning of the revolution. On the other hand, 100 metal francs cost 278 assignat francs. The total *real* value of the circulation had remained almost constant.

But later the depreciation of the assignats became more rapid than

* Marshall, *op. cit.*, chapter iv; see also Pigou, *Essays in Applied Economics*, 1923, chapter xvi; Robertson, *Money*, chapter ii; Keynes, *A Treatise on Money*, vol. i, chapter xiv. Senior had observed that the quantity of money which a country needs depends also "on the average proportion of the value of his income which each individual habitually keeps by him in money" (*Three Lectures on the Value of Money*, London School of Economics reprint, p. 11).

the increase of money in circulation. This may be seen in the following table:*

TABLE XVII

| | *Nominal value of assignats in circulation (in thousands of francs)* | | *Exchange rate of metallic money (100 francs) in paper* | |
|---|---|---|---|---|
| May 1st, 1794 .. | 5,891,479 | 100 | 278 | 100 |
| January 1st, 1795 .. | 7,228,519 | 123 | 476 | 171 |
| July 1st, 1795 .. | 12,338,144 | 209 | 2,085 | 750 |
| January 1st, 1796 .. | 27,565,237 | 458 | 22,857 | 8,213 |
| June 1st, 1796 .. | 35,427,369 | 601 | 53,333 | 19,185 |

Compared with May 1794, in June 1796 the quantity in circulation was six times as much; but the price of metallic money was 190 times.

**7.** The phenomenon was reproduced in several countries after the World War.

Based on the facts collected by De Bordes† I have compiled the following table for Austria:

TABLE XVIII

| *End of* | *Indices‡* of the quantity of paper money | *of the prices of goods* | *of the exchange rate of the crown* |
|---|---|---|---|
| | *Austria-Hungary* | | |
| January 1915 .. | 2·02 | 1·34 | 1·10 |
| July 1915 .. .. | 2·50 | 1·73 | 1·35 |
| January 1916 .. | 2·85 | 2·78 | 1·65 |
| July 1916 .. .. | 3·34 | 3·96 | 1·63 |
| January 1917 .. | 4·30 | 6·59 | 1·91 |
| July 1917 .. .. | 5·15 | 8·17 | 2·29 |
| January 1918 .. | 7·29 | 8·31 | 1·65 |
| July 1918 .. .. | 9·83 | 14·34 | 2·00 |
| November 1918 .. | 13·17 | 16·40 | 2·90 |
| | *Austrian Republic* | | |
| January 1920 .. | 26·5 | 49·22 | 55·0 |
| December 1920 .. | 61·3 | 62·2 | 133·6 |
| June 1921 .. .. | 99·4 | 85·3 | 142·9 |
| December 1921 .. | 348 | 450 | 1,117 |
| June 1922 .. .. | 1,110 | 1,789 | 3,837 |
| August 1922.. .. | 2,707 | 7,422 | 15,663 |
| December 1922 .. | 8,160 | 11,683 | 14,207 |
| June 1923 .. .. | 10,866 | 12,391 | 14,346 |
| December 1923 .. | 14,251 | 13,600 | 14,328 |

* Falkner, *Das Papiergeld der französischen Revolution*, Leipzig, 1924, p. 49.

† *The Austrian Crown*, 1924.

‡ The index number of the quantity of paper money was calculated by De Bordes, by supposing that the average circulation before the war was 2,500 million crowns in Austria-Hungary, and 500 million crowns in the territory of the actual Austrian Republic.

This table shows that in the period of the most rapid depreciation of the Austrian crown, that is from June 1921 to August 1922, the real value of the paper circulation fell rapidly. Towards the end of August 1922 the quantity of paper money had increased as from 1 to 2,707; prices had risen from 1 to 7,422; and the exchange rate of the gold crown from 1 to 15,663. Calculated on the basis of the index number of prices, the real value of the circulation was reduced to about 180 million crowns, and on the basis of the dollar exchange rate to about 90 million crowns. After the stabilization of the exchange the total value of the circulation rose once again.

The examination of German statistics leads to analogous conclusions. The following table is based on official publications:

TABLE XIX

*Germany*

| | | *Indices* | | | |
|---|---|---|---|---|---|
| *End of* | *Currency circulation (millions of marks)* | *of the currency circulation* | *of the dollar exchange rate* | *of the wholesale prices* | *of the cost of living* |
| 1913* | 6,070 | 1 | 1 | 1 | 1 |
| 1914 | 8,703 | 1·43 | 1·07 | 1·25 | — |
| 1915 | 10,050 | 1·65 | 1·23 | 1·47 | — |
| 1916 | 12,315 | 2·04 | 1·36 | 1·50 | — |
| 1917 | 18,458 | 3·04 | 1·35 | 2·02 | — |
| 1918 | 33,106 | 5·45 | 1·97 | 2·46 | — |
| 1919 | 50,173 | 8·26 | 11·14 | 8·03 | — |
| 1920 | 81,628 | 13·5 | 17·4 | 14·4 | 11·58 |
| 1921 | 122,963 | 20·3 | 45·7 | 34·9 | 19·28 |
| 1922 | 1,295† | 213·3 | 1,807·8 | 1,474·8 | 685 |
| 1923‡ | 2·5§ | 413‖ | 17·3† | 18·7† | 3·0† |

The real value of the quantity of paper money in circulation increased during the period in which the depreciation of the mark was moderate (until the Armistice); but later it fell. But after some oscillations, in the summer of 1921 the total value of the circulation was once more equal, within a little, to the pre-war value (about six milliard gold marks). After July 1921 an increasingly rapid decline began. At the end of September 1921 the total value was (according to the index number of wholesale prices) 4,560 million marks; at the end of November 3,175 millions.

* Yearly average. † Milliards.
‡ End of October. § Trillions. ‖ Millions.

The fall of the value of the circulation continued during 1922 and was particularly rapid at the beginning of July in that year. Towards the end of June the outstanding paper money was worth 2,560 millions in gold. At the end of 1922 the real value of the circulation was 880 million gold marks (according to price indices) and 670 millions according to the exchange index. During 1923, as we have already seen, the real value of paper money oscillated irregularly round about a very low level.

If the real value of the total circulation is calculated on the basis of the cost-of-living index numbers, the fall of the real value appears slower than when the calculations are based on wholesale prices. At the end of 1921 the cost-of-living index had increased almost at the same rate as the circulation index; after that the difference between the two indices went on increasing.

The reduction suffered by the aggregate value of the circulation was more acute in Germany than in Austria, in proportion to the greater monetary depreciation. To find another example of so conspicuous a contraction of the circulation it is necessary to look at Russia:

TABLE XX

*Russia**

| | *Indices* | |
|---|---|---|
| | *of the quantity of money* | *of prices (Moscow)* |
| 1913–14 | 1 | 1 |
| January 1916 | 2·35 | 1·41 |
| January 1917 | 3·84 | 2·72 |
| October 1917 | 7·65 | 7 |
| January 1918 | 11·71 | 23 |
| July 1918 | 18·43 | 103 |
| January 1919 | 25·53 | 229 |
| July 1919 | 43·04 | 657 |
| January 1920 | 93·8 | 3,400 |
| July 1920 | 213·2 | 9,390 |
| January 1921 | 499·9 | 20,339 |
| July 1921 | 1,103 | 70,021 |

From the statistical researches of Milentz it appears that in Russia also (as in Austria and Germany) in an early period prices increased less rapidly than the quantity of money. At the beginning of 1917 the aggregate value of the circulation was noticeably higher than before the war. But after the advent of the Kerenski Government prices

* The figures are extracted from Milentz, *op. cit.*

increased rapidly; and even more after the Bolshevik revolution. The divergence between the movement of prices and of the note issues was continually accentuated. At the end of July 1921 the circulation had increased by 1,103 times and prices by 70,021. The aggregate value of the paper money in circulation was reduced to a very low figure, as the following table shows:

TABLE XXI

*Russia*

| | Nominal value of the circulation (Milliards of roubles) | Real value according to the cost of living index number (Millions of roubles) | Real value according to the official exchange rate of the rouble (Millions of roubles) |
|---|---|---|---|
| July 1st, 1914 .. .. | 2·28 | 2,285 | 2,280 |
| January 1st, 1917 .. | 9·13 | 4,210 | — |
| January 1st, 1918 .. | 27·9 | 1,660 | 1,177 |
| January 1st, 1919 .. | 61·2 | 590 | 266 |
| January 1st, 1920 .. | 225·0 | 135 | 65–71 |
| January 1st, 1921 .. | 1,168·6 | 91 | 44 |
| January 1st, 1922 .. | 17 billions | — | 103 |
| October 1st, 1923 .. | 22·701 billions | — | 41 |

Analogous phenomena were experienced in other countries with much depreciated currencies. The quantity of paper money circulating in Hungary still had, in June 1921 (according to the rate of exchange), a total value of 365 million gold crowns. In December 1922 it was only 162 millions, and in June 1923, 107 millions.*

The aggregate value of notes circulating in Poland amounted to 405 million gold marks at the end of 1921 (according to the index number of prices). The catastrophic depreciation of the Polish mark reduced the real aggregate value of the circulation to 146 millions in July 1923 and to 89 in December of the same year, although the nominal value of the circulation from the end of 1920 to the end of 1923 had increased from little more than 49 milliard marks to 125,372 milliards.†

The countries cited, where the aggregate real value of the quantity of paper money in circulation diminished enormously during the

* *Wirtschaft und Statistik*, 1923, p. 671.

† *Wirtschaft und Statistik*, 1923. See also *Memorandum sur les Monnaies* (League of Nations), p. 19.

inflation, constituted a group clearly distinct from other countries with a depreciated currency.*

* Here are some facts relevant to other countries:

ITALY

| End of | *Index numbers* of the paper circulation | of the price of the gold lira | of the prices of goods |
|---|---|---|---|
| 1913 | 1 | 1 | 1 |
| 1914 | 1·29 | 1·02 | 0·95† |
| 1915 | 1·81 | 1·27 | 1·33† |
| 1916 | 2·27 | 1·32 | 2·00† |
| 1917 | 3·65 | 1·59 | 3·06† |
| 1918 | 4·98 | 1·22 | 4·09 |
| 1919 | 6·67 | 2·51 | 4·57 |
| 1920 | 7·90 | 5·53 | 6·55 |
| 1921 | 7·72 | 4·35 | 5·95 |

† Average of the year.

FRANCE

| End of | *Index numbers* of the paper circulation | of the price of the gold franc | of the prices of goods (July of each year) |
|---|---|---|---|
| 1913 | 1 | 1 | — |
| 1914 | 1·76 | 0·99 | 1 |
| 1915 | 2·33 | 1·13 | 1·43 |
| 1916 | 2·92 | 1·13 | 1·88 |
| 1917 | 3·91 | 1·10 | 2·73 |
| 1918 | 4·29 | 1·05 | 3·44 |
| 1919 | 5·52 | 2·07 | 3·56 |
| 1920 | 5·57 | 3·26 | 5·06 |
| 1921 | 5·37 | 2·46 | 3·37 |

HOLLAND

| End of | *Index numbers* of paper circulation | of price of gold florin | of prices of goods |
|---|---|---|---|
| 1913 | 1 | 1 | 1 |
| 1920 | 3·59 | 1·30 | 2·30 |
| 1921 | 3·32 | 1·11 | 1·95 |

SWITZERLAND

| End of | *Index numbers* of paper circulation | of price of gold franc | of prices of goods |
|---|---|---|---|
| 1913 | 1 | 1 | 1 |
| 1920 | 3·26 | 1·22 | 2·38 |
| 1921 | 3·21 | 0·99 | 1·78 |

## IV. VARIATIONS IN THE VELOCITY OF CIRCULATION OF THE GERMAN MARK—1914–22

**8.** For some time after the outbreak of the war it was observed in Germany that not all the paper money issued remained effectively in circulation. During the war and also after the Armistice paper money was extensively hoarded, especially in the country. Calculations, of whose accuracy it is difficult to be certain, conclude that the nominal value of notes withdrawn from circulation at the end of 1920 had risen to 10 milliard paper marks, that is to about one-seventh of the total issues. In addition a considerable quantity of marks had found their way abroad.

The notes which were not in circulation could not influence prices.

Later, when the continual depreciation of the German currency undermined the confidence of even the most obstinate speculators for a rise in the mark, the hidden marks flowed into the market, both from the interior of Germany and from abroad, intensifying the rise of prices.

At the same time, *pari passu* with the progressive depreciation of the mark, the demand for money (as cash or bank balances) by the Germans—employers and workers alike—for personal needs and for business purposes, rapidly diminished.

In the summer of 1923, when the mark was losing value day by day—even between morning and afternoon—everybody tried to get rid of marks as soon as they were received.

This increase in the velocity of the circulation was the expression of the fact that the population lived from day to day, without keeping any cash reserves. In Germany, indeed, common observation showed that hardly a retailer or workman existed who possessed liquid balance greater than that necessary for two or three days.*

**9.** We can attempt to measure in a rough way the variations of the velocity of the circulation which occurred in Germany after 1914. Suppose that before the beginning of the inflation we had the following equation of exchange:

$$MV = p_1a + p_2b + p_3c \quad . \quad . \quad . \qquad (1)$$

where $M$ is the quantity of money issued, $V$ the velocity of the circulation, $a$, $b$, $c$, . . . the quantities of goods exchanged and $p_1$, $p_2$, $p_3$ . . . the respective prices. Suppose that the quantity of goods and their

* Lansburgh in the *Bank* of September 1923.

velocity of the circulation remains constant and that only the quantity of money and the velocity of its circulation change. In the next period we should then have the following equation of exchange:

$$M'V' = p'_1a + p'_2b + p'_3c \quad . \quad . \quad . \qquad (2)$$

From these two equations we have

$$\frac{M'V'}{MV} = P \quad . \quad . \quad . \qquad (3)$$

where $P$ shows the arithmetical weighted average of the variations of prices, the weights being given by the quantities of goods in the base year. The approximate values of $P$ are given by statistics and so, moreover, are the values of $M'$ and $M$; (as has been said, $M$, in 1913, was equal, in round figures, to 6 milliard marks). Hence it is easy to calculate $\frac{V'}{V}$, i.e. the variations in the velocity of the circulation of money.* The values of $\frac{V'}{V}$ are given in the table on page 168. I have calculated two series of values; in the first $P$ is taken as an index of wholesale prices, in the second as the index of retail prices (cost of food).

The indices of the preceding tables are certainly very rough. The real income of the German population during the years 1914–23 was lower than the pre-war income; and there were other considerable changes.

The figures of the table indicate the variations of the velocity of the circulation of money apart, for the most part, from the variations of the velocity of the circulation of goods.†

The significance of the indices of the table lies in the following considerations. The *same* money can be considered from two different aspects: (1) as money capital at the disposal of the entrepreneurs,

* It can be easily seen that, if we start from Professor Pigou's or Mr. Robertson's "cash balances equations" (instead of Professor Fisher's equation of exchange), we get the same numerical results as regards the variations of the velocity of circulation of the mark.

† The elimination of the influence exercised by the variations of the velocity of the circulation of goods is not complete because it is uncertain what effect these variations could have exercised on prices. The researches of Marget and Marschak tend to show that these variations are not necessarily "neutral" with regard to prices. (A. W. Marget, "The Relation between the Velocity of Circulation of Money and the Velocity of Circulation of Goods," *Journal of Political Economy*, August 1932, p. 502. J. Marschak, "Volksvermögen und Kassenbedarf," *Archiv für Socialwissenschaft und Sozialpolitik*, January 1933, p. 409).

and (2) as the money income of those people who sell them their services. At the beginning of a "circulating period"* the working classes

TABLE XXII

*Variations of the Velocity of Circulation of Money in Germany* (1913 = 1)

(*A*) *Based on Wholesale Prices*

| | |
|---|---|
| 1914 | 0·92 |
| 1915 | 0·94 |
| 1916 | 0·87 |
| 1917 | 0·72 |
| 1918 (nine months) | 0·61 |
| October 1918 | 0·52 |
| November 1918 | 0·48 |
| December 1918 | 0·45 |

| | 1919 | 1920 | 1921 | 1922 | 1923 |
|---|---|---|---|---|---|
| January | 0·46 | 1·47 | 1·10 | 1·77 | 8·45 |
| February | 0·46 | 1·85 | 1·03 | 1·91 | 9·59 |
| March | 0·44 | 1·72 | 1·00 | 2·32 | 5·35 |
| April | 0·45 | 1·51 | 0·98 | 2·53 | 4·79 |
| May | 0·45 | 1·41 | 0·96 | 2·39 | 5·74 |
| June | 0·43 | 1·21 | 0·96 | 2·33 | 6·77 |
| July | 0·49 | 1·18 | 0·99 | 2·97 | 10·34 |
| August | 0·62 | 1·23 | 1·30 | 4·57 | 8·57 |
| September | 0·70 | 1·18 | 1·31 | 5·18 | 5·14 |
| October | 0·78 | 1·13 | 1·48 | 6·99 | 17·79 |
| November | 0·89 | 1·17 | 1·88 | 9·01 | — |
| December | 0·96 | 1·06 | 1·70 | 6·85 | — |

(*B*) *Based on Retail Prices*

| | 1920 | 1921 | 1922 | 1923 |
|---|---|---|---|---|
| January | — | 1·10 | 1·20 | 4·15 |
| February | 1·05 | 1·03 | 1·42 | 5·46 |
| March | 1·12 | 1·02 | 1·55 | 3·63 |
| April | 1·19 | 1·00 | 1·75 | 3·21 |
| May | 1·25 | 0·98 | 1·74 | 3·22 |
| June | 1·14 | 0·98 | 1·72 | 3·26 |
| July | 1·10 | 1·04 | 2·04 | 6·11 |
| August | 0·98 | 1·08 | 2·34 | 6·08 |
| September | 0·93 | 1·03 | 2·81 | 3·72 |
| October | 1·00 | 1·07 | 3·33 | 10·43 |
| November | 1·05 | 1·21 | 4·34 | — |
| December | 1·06 | 1·16 | 3·78 | — |

receive from their employers a certain quantity *M* of money. During the circulating period this money is spent in the purchase of con-

* For this expression see Pigou, *Industrial Fluctuations*, p. 136.

sumption goods and flows gradually into the tills of the retailers. From these the money passes to the wholesalers and, successively, to the producers of finished or semi-finished articles, and of raw materials, and becomes the money capital of various kinds of entrepreneurs. The expenses of these last are reduced in the last analysis to wages for workmen and profits for the producers of various intermediate goods, besides interest, rents, etc.; in short, to money incomes of all those who render productive services.

In its way through the various stages of production the quantity of money $M$ serves as base, during a certain period $R$, for a certain (money) volume of transactions $Q$. The ratio $Q/M$ gives the velocity of the circulation of the monetary capital. If—the number of the stages of production remaining the same—retailers, wholesalers, producers, etc., *hasten* the purchases of finished and semi-finished goods, raw materials, etc., the velocity of the circulation of money capital increases. The indices of Table (A) give an approximate measure of these variations. The velocity of the circulation of money varies also if the number of stages of production varies; but, as was said above, of this second kind of variation no account was taken in the table.

The ratio between the total money income of this given period $R$—which is equal to the quantities of goods and services consumed multiplied by the respective retail prices—and the quantity of money $M$, gives the velocity of circulation of money, in the sense of the number of times the same unit of money becomes an element of income ("income-velocity" according to Schumpeter and Pigou*). The velocity of the circulation of money, thus defined, depends on two factors: (*a*) the length of the circulating period of the money $M$—the velocity of the circulation during the period $R$ evidently the greater, the shorter the circulating period; (*b*) the ratio between the aggregate income and quantity of money $M$ during the circulating period. These two quantities are not necessarily equal, because salaried workers, wage-earners, and entrepreneurs spend a part of their money income on *services*, thus creating new incomes. If $M$ is equal to 100,000, but during the circulating period 10,000 is spent not on goods but on services—and if those who render the services spend their income during the circulating

* *Industrial Fluctuations*, p. 152. Keynes criticizes the conception of Pigou and Schumpeter of the velocity of the circulation of money, for which he wishes to substitute the more precise idea of the velocity of the circulation of "business deposits" and of "income deposits." It seems to me that good arguments may be used to justify one as much as the other of these conceptions of the velocity of the circulation of money.

period—the velocity of the circulation of money during the circulating period is not equal to unity but to 1·1.

During the inflation, the fact that the demand for the services of doctors, lawyers, teachers, etc., gradually diminished, causing a very great reduction in their incomes, should have caused a fall in the velocity of the circulation of money *within* each circulating period. On the other hand the rise in the number of intermediaries who bought goods to retail them should have tended, inasmuch as they created new profits and new incomes, to increase the velocity of the circulation of money within the circulating period.

The values of $V'/V$ given in Table (B) may be considered as an approximate measure of the "income-velocity" of money. Between the two kinds of the velocity of the circulation of money, distinct in the preceding table, there is naturally an intimate connection. A rise in the velocity of the circulation of money capital tends—when it is not due simply to an increase in the intermediary stages of production—to provoke a rise in wholesale prices, which tends to react on retail prices. The real income of the working classes then falls; and the workers demand a rise in money wages which either provokes new issues of paper money, or, if the quantity of paper money remains constant, can only be obtained by means of a rise in the income velocity of money, that is by shortening the interval between the successive payments of wages.

**10.** The preceding figures are represented in Diagram 11. This diagram is of certain interest because it is an index, however rough, of the degree of confidence which the German population placed in the national currency, and also it shows the psychological crises which the nation passed through. The fall in the velocity of circulation of money during the war shows that throughout that period complete confidence in the mark was maintained in Germany. This confidence was not even shaken by the military defeat, signalized by the unfavourable terms of the Armistice, and by the serious internal disturbances which upset Germany at the beginning of 1919. On the contrary, large amounts of marks were hoarded.*

From the diagram it would appear that the first occurrence of loss of confidence was in July 1919, after the Treaty of Versailles was

* "A repetition of the hoarding mania on quite a large scale appears to have occurred in Germany in connection with the revolution, and it is believed that considerable amounts of notes remained for a long time in private possession, particularly in that of the present population" (Cassel, *Money and Foreign Exchanges after 1914*, London, 1922, p. 39).

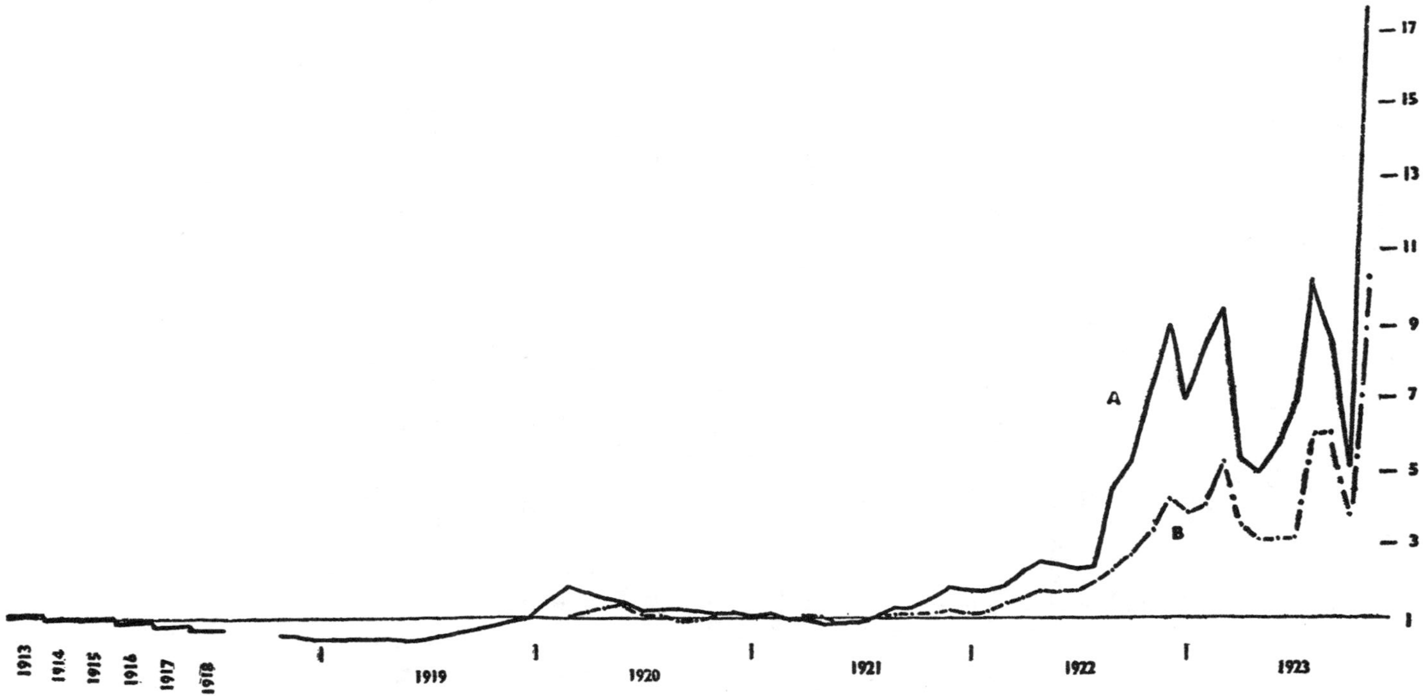


Diagram XI.—Velocity of circulation of money (1913 = 1)
A. According to wholesale prices.
B. According to retail prices.

signed. Our calculations probably supply an indirect statistical documentation of the abandonment of the mark, which began to be evident in that period, by the upper classes of the German population. It is not possible that the sudden fall in the total value of the German currency, which occurred in the second half of 1919, could be an expression of the fall in production, since the latter probably became more active in that period.

But, according to the graph, in 1920 the psychological crisis provoked by the imposition of the Treaty of Versailles was weakened and little by little confidence in the German currency was re-established; in fact, the velocity of circulation of the mark fell. Another index of this renewed confidence was the fact that in 1920, and in the first months of 1921, the Reichsbank could place with the public in an increasing measure the Treasury bonds issued.*

The sudden rise in the velocity of the circulation after July 1921 indicates the outbreak of a new crisis of doubt. The flight from the mark was renewed and became continually quicker.† In contrast to what had happened before, the psychological crisis was not of short duration, but became continually more intense. The continual drop in the real value of the total amount of money in circulation was certainly the consequence of the rise in the velocity of the circulation and cannot be attributed to the fall in the quantity of goods produced, because it is known that, on the contrary, thanks partly to the stimulus given by the monetary depreciation, economic production increased after the autumn of 1921 and in 1922 probably reached 70–80 per cent of the pre-war level. But the total real value of the currency in the middle of 1922 was hardly a third of the pre-war value.

A comparison of the two indices, which it is possible to make from 1920, shows that the velocity of the circulation of the money among business firms rose *before* the velocity of circulation among consumers rose. And that is quite plausible. Beginning from the second half of 1921 the indices of Table XXII (A) are considerably higher than those of Table XXII (B).

* MILLIARDS OF PAPER MARKS

| | *February* 1920 | *December* 1920 | *April* 1921 |
|---|---|---|---|
| Treasury bonds issued .. .. | 89·0 | 152·8 | 172·7 |
| Retained by the Reichsbank .. | 38·1 | 57·6 | 58·8 |
| Placed outside the Reichsbank .. | 50·9 | 95·2 | 113·9 |

† In Chapter IX I refer to numerous other facts which prove the flight from the mark.

Besides, the tendency is shown for the indices of the two tables to approach each other in the periods of relative stabilization of the mark (e.g. second half of 1920–first half of 1921); while the distance between the two indices is accentuated in the periods of rapid depreciation of the mark (e.g. second half of 1922).

## V. THE TOTAL REAL VALUE OF MARKS IN CIRCULATION IN 1922 AND 1923

**11.** According to the preceding tables, the rise in the velocity of the circulation of money continued (subject to fluctuations) until the end of the inflation. The highest index was for October 1923. But as regards the last phase of the inflation I believe that the increase in the velocity of the circulation, which is the phenomenon to which Keynes and other economists have referred, does not completely explain the very great reduction of the total real value of the paper money.

According to experiences also in other countries with a depreciated currency, in the last phases of the monetary depreciation the difference between the rise in prices and the increase of the circulation was connected with the variations suffered by another element of the equation of exchange, that is with the decline in the quantity of goods.

This decline depends on two kinds of causes:

(*a*) The depreciation of the currency in an early stage does, in a way, stimulate production; but in a later phase it acts as an increasingly serious obstacle to production, which it disorganizes. Hence a fall in production occurs, as was evident in Germany in 1923, in Poland and in other countries having a currency which was depreciating rapidly.

(*b*) It is also necessary to take account of the fall in the quantity of goods which were exchanged for paper money.

At a certain stage of the depreciation of a paper currency this ceases to exercise the function of a store of value, and is replaced by foreign exchange. At a further stage, when the depreciation is very rapid, the depreciated paper is also more and more replaced by foreign exchange in its function as a "means of payment." This happened to the German mark. First in foreign trade, then in internal wholesale trade, and later in retail trade, the practice of making payments in foreign money spread rapidly. Every new issue of notes, by continually weakening confidence, always restricted the "field of circulation" (as it could be called) of the paper mark, and therefore the monetary unit was depreciated (that is prices in paper marks increased) more than in proportion to the increase of note-issues.

In August 1923 the value of the paper money in circulation amounted on some days to scarcely 80 million gold marks. However much the velocity of the circulation of the paper mark was increased, it is difficult to admit that so very small a quantity of money sufficed for the needs of German trade, which in 1913 required 6 milliards. The explanation is given precisely by the fact that alongside the paper mark there circulated a large quantity of foreign exchange and of "emergency money" (Notgeld).

Furthermore, the risk of transactions effected by payment in paper marks became so great in the summer of 1923 that many producers and merchants preferred not to sell at all, rather than accept in exchange a money subject to rapid depreciation. Agriculturists refused to sell their crops (if the purchaser had no foreign exchange); industrialists and wholesale merchants jealously guarded their goods; and retail merchants tried to limit sales by the reduction of the hours for which their shops were open.

Hence, because of the repudiation of paper money, the continually increasing quantities of new money which were put in circulation were concentrated on a continually lessening quantity of goods.

**12.** Examining the monetary events which occurred in Germany, we may, I believe, come to these conclusions: (*a*) in an early stage, which was the longest, monetary depreciation was mainly in proportion to the quantity of paper money; (*b*) in the next period, that is from the summer of 1921 to the summer of 1922, the influence of the new note-issues was intensified by the increase of the velocity of circulation, by the return of marks sold abroad and by the efflux of marks from hoards; (*c*) after the summer of 1922 a new influence was added to provoke a fall in the value of the monetary unit more than proportional to the increase in the quantity of paper money, for the place of the paper mark was taken by foreign exchange and by other means of payment. This fact recalls some analogies with the past. The history of the assignats also showed that the phase, characterized by a depreciation of the assignats more rapid than the increase of the quantities issued, coincided with the reappearance and growing diffusion of metallic money in the circulation. Hence in monetary conditions characterized by a great distrust in the national money the principle of Gresham is reversed, and *good money drives out the bad*, and the value of the latter continually depreciates.

While in normal conditions the variations of the quantity of money modify neither the velocity of the circulation of the money itself nor of the quantity of goods, in the abnormal conditions created by a rapid depreciation of money the increase of note-issues, spreading the lack of confidence in paper money, provokes an increase in the velocity of the circulation of money and a fall in the supply of goods.

### VI. BORTKIEWICZ'S VIEWS ON THE CAUSES OF THE INCREASE OF THE VELOCITY OF THE CIRCULATION OF THE PAPER MARK

**13.** In a memorandum read during a meeting of the "Verein für Sozialpolitik"* Bortkiewicz opposed the theory—supported by many economists and also accepted by the present author—according to which expectation of an ultimate depreciation, by inducing possessors of money to dispose of it quickly, provokes an increase in the velocity of the circulation of the currency.

To simplify the problem Bortkiewicz supposes that there were only entrepreneurs and wage-earners, and that the latter used their wages in purchasing goods produced and sold by the former. The money, which the entrepreneurs gave their workmen as wages at the beginning of the "productive cycle," gradually returned to the tills of the entrepreneurs, if the workmen made their purchases little by little, distributing them at uniform intervals of time between one pay-day and the next. Suppose now that the workmen, fearing a future monetary depreciation, concentrate their purchases at the beginning of the productive cycle. It is true that in such a case the money will return more quickly to the producers, but it will remain in their tills until the beginning of a new productive cycle because there will be no more goods on the market. The velocity of the circulation of money is certainly increased by the working classes, but it is correspondingly lessened by the entrepreneurs. From the point of view of the entire economy the velocity does not change, as Bortkiewicz also shows by means of an arithmetical example.

Therefore, concludes Bortkiewicz, it is not true that the purchases anticipated by consumers, who wish to dispose of their money, increase the velocity of the circulation of this money.

Bortkiewicz does not deny that, in the abnormal monetary conditions created by the depreciation of the circulating medium, the velocity of

* "Die Ursachen einer potenzierten Wirkung des vermehrten Geldumlaufs auf das Preisniveau" (*Verhandlungen des Vereins für Sozialpolitik*, Stuttgart, September 24th–26th, 1924, vol. 170, p. 256).

the circulation of money increases, but he gives the following explanation of the phenomenon:

At a certain stage of the inflation it is the "external value" of the depreciated money which determines the "internal value," that is the level of prices expressed in that money. Lack of confidence in money, above all, depresses the value of that money in terms of foreign currencies; internal prices increase; "the rise in internal prices which, however, have increased in a greater proportion than the quantity of existing money, provokes a scarcity of the circulating medium, which people endeavour to relieve by modifying the systems and methods of payment and by increasing in one way or another the velocity of the circulation of the money" (p. 266). The increase in the velocity of circulation is not the *cause* which accelerates the monetary depreciation but the expression of an adjustment to the new necessities created by the rise in prices, which, in its turn, is the consequence of the continual depreciation of the exchanges.

It may be observed, at this point, that the perfecting of the systems of payment is not an *automatic* consequence of the rise of prices. The scarcity of money which was experienced in Germany at every fresh wave of rising prices proved that it was not easy to modify rapidly methods of payments; most times new forms of bank money or of emergency money were created.

### VII. OBJECTIONS TO THE BORTKIEWICZ THEORY

**14.** Let us note particularly that it appears even in this theoretical scheme of Bortkiewicz that the purchases of goods anticipated by consumers will in all probability exercise important *indirect* influences on the value of the money. In fact, producers will not leave idle in their tills the money which rapidly flows there, but will endeavour to guarantee themselves against the risk of a future depreciation. Since, according to the hypothesis of Bortkiewicz, there are no more goods on the market, these having been entirely bought up by consumers, the producers will purchase foreign exchange. The external value of the money falls, prices rise, and the crisis is aggravated. These consequences are not imaginary. Probably the great flow of paper money into the foreign exchange market, which was observed in Germany at certain periods, was also due to the fact that at certain times producers disposed of large liquid resources, thanks to consumers having anticipated their purchases.

But, leaving these indirect influences, let us examine more thoroughly the scheme of Bortkiewicz.

In constructing his theory, Bortkiewicz takes no account of one circumstance, which I think cannot be neglected. If the workmen, who at first distributed their purchases uniformly over a period, say, of three months, later spend all their wages in five days (I am following the numerical example given by Bortkiewicz), the consequences of the sudden increase in the supply of money cannot but be a rise in prices. Anyone who was in Berlin or Vienna in the days of a monetary panic could give evidence of how the sudden influx of buyers into the shops induced the vendors to raise the prices of all goods at once, provided that legal restrictions (often easy to evade) did not prevent them. In Berlin prices rose on the days when employees received the longed-for payment of a quarter's salary, which they hastened to spend on purchases of food, clothing, etc., putting, by such means, a great quantity of money on the market.

Hence we must admit that wage-earners supplying to the goods market in five days the quantity of money which formerly was spent a little at a time over three months, provoked a rise in prices. Suppose that prices were doubled. That would mean that the purchasers could acquire only half the goods existing on the market. The money returns to the producers. These spend it once again and exchanging it between themselves acquire the other half of the goods, which had remained unsold. Hence the velocity of the circulation of the money is doubled, in spite of the fact that the interval between successive payments of wages remains the same.

It seems, from a passage in the memorandum cited, that Bortkiewicz also had considered the eventuality of a rise in prices as a consequence of the purchases anticipated by consumers. However, he states that the consumption of monetary reserves collected by these consumers cannot exercise any lasting influence on prices, "because these reserves are quickly exhausted." But it may be observed that though the reserves of some classes of consumers are exhausted, the same money is once more offered by other classes, so that a new equilibrium may be established, characterized by a contracting of the monetary reserves held by private individuals (that is, a greater supply of money on the market), by a higher level of prices, and by an increased velocity of the circulation of money, as well as by a restriction of working-class consumption and by an expansion of the entrepreneurs' consumption.

Let us also take the hypothesis that the workmen, not adapting themselves to a permanent fall in their standard of living, obtain (from the producers) an increase in their nominal wages. If the quantity of money remains constant, the rise in wages can only be effected by means of more frequent payments of the same sum of money. It is known that in Germany during the last phases of the depreciation of the mark, the interval between the dates of payment of wages was continually reduced.

In short, whether the producers spend to their own advantage the money which returns quickly to their tills because of the purchases hastened by workmen, or instead return the money to the latter, the consequence of those purchases is always a rise in the velocity of the circulation of the money itself.

**15.** Let us illustrate the argument by an arithmetical example. Suppose the existing quantity of money $M$ is 3,000 units. Every day one-third of this total is offered in the market in exchange for 10 units of goods. The price of each unit of goods will be 100. Suppose also, following the scheme propounded by Bortkiewicz (though this scheme is rather unreal), a "production cycle" of six days, and that at the end of every production cycle a quantity $S$ of 60 units of goods comes on to the market. In a period of, e.g., 12 days, the total payments amount to 12,000 units of money; and since we have assumed the stock of money equal to 3,000 units, the velocity of circulation of money is 4. In the period considered there are two production cycles—that is to say, $S$ is renewed twice.

Common observation suggests that normally every day a certain fraction of $M$ is exchanged against a certain fraction of $S$. In normal conditions these fractions do not vary much from one day to another (apart from the recognized "purchasing cycles," such as weekly, monthly, and seasonal cycles). Let us suppose that the money $M$ is spent in $a$ days, that $S$ is exhausted in $b$ days, and that every day a certain amount of money equal to $\frac{1}{a}M$ is exchanged against a certain quantity of goods equal to $\frac{1}{b}S$. Suppose further that the goods change hands once only. For each day, then, the "equation of exchange" will be :

$$\frac{1}{a}M = \frac{1}{b}S\,P \text{ (}P\text{ being the price)} \quad . \quad . \quad . \quad . \quad . \quad (4)$$

Now, if during a given period of time the quantity of money $M$ has changed hands $r$ times, and $S$ has been replaced $v$ times, for that period we should have the equation of exchange:

$$Mr = SvP \quad . \quad . \quad . \quad . \quad . \quad . \quad . \quad (5)$$

from which may be derived the equation:

$$r = \frac{b}{a}v \quad . \quad . \quad . \quad . \quad . \quad . \quad . \quad . \quad (6)$$

Hence the velocity of circulation of the money is equal to the rapidity of replacement of $S$—that is to the number of "production cycles" in the given period of time—multiplied by the ratio between the number of days after which $S$ is exhausted and the number of days during which the money $M$ is spent.

In our numerical example $b = 6$, $a = 3$, and $v = 2$, whence $r = 4$.

**16.** Let us now suppose that every day 1,500 units instead of 1,000 units of money come on to the market. Then if prices remain unchanged (because prices have been fixed by law), then each day 15 units of goods will be exchanged for 1,500 units of money. $S$ will be exhausted in four days, and for two days of the six there will be no goods in the market. In a period of twelve days the total value of transactions will be, as in the preceding case, equal to 12,000 units of money, and the velocity of circulation will remain unchanged. And this is the case considered by Bortkiewicz.

Now let us suppose instead that, following the increase in the supply of money, prices rise to 150. Every day 10 units of goods are exchanged for 1,500 units of money. $S$ is exhausted in 6 days; the total value of transactions rises in the period considered to 18,000 units of money, and the velocity of circulation becomes 6.

In our formula, in the first case, $b = 4$, $a = 2$, $v = 2$, and consequently $r = 4$; in the second case $b = 6$, $a = 2$, $v = 2$, and therefore $r = 6$. More generally, if $a$ decreases, i.e. if the fraction of the existing money, which is offered each day for goods in the market, increases, and if $b$ decreases proportionately, which is possible only if the increased supply of money has no effect on prices, the velocity of circulation does not change.

But as we said above, it is much more probable that the increase in the supply of money will cause a rise in prices. In that case, $b$ decreases less than in proportion to the decrease in *a*—which means that the velocity of the circulation increases.*

The preceding observations show the errors into which Havenstein fell when he made the statement referred to at the beginning of this chapter. The fact is that the Reichsbank, by keeping the rate of discount too low, stimulated an expansion in the demand for short-term credits and an increase in the issues of notes. Suppose that the nominal value of the commercial bills of exchange in the portfolio of the Reichsbank increased from 100 to 200, then the increase in the issues of notes provoked a more than proportional rise in the prices of goods, because the velocity of the circulation of money increased at the same time. The real value of the portfolio—that is the nominal value divided by the index number of prices—decreased: Havenstein concluded that the Reichsbank had followed a restrictive credit policy!†

* Professor Marget, although he admits equation (6) to be a "correct formulation" (see p. 310 of the article quoted above), makes certain objections. He writes: "Let $k$ equal the number of days in the period for which $V$ and $v$ are being computed. . . ." Obviously, if $a$ equals the number of days required to give $M$ a velocity of $V$ (i.e. $k$ days will equal $aV$), "hence, $V = \frac{k}{a}$, and, by the same reasoning, $v = \frac{k}{b}$. It is obvious that, since $k$ is a constant, $a$ cannot vary without $V$ varying, nor $b$ vary without $v$ varying."

On that point one may observe that, according to Bortkiewicz, if $a$ drops, say, from 20 to 10 days, $V$ does not increase during period $k$, because in every cycle the *money will remain idle for 10 days*. Similarly, if $b$ decreases, $v$, which is the number of "productive cycles" contained in $k$ and *which depends on the technical conditions of production*, does not increase. According to Bortkiewicz, the consequence of the decline of $b$ is only that during a part of the cycle there are no more goods on the market.

According to our formula the case considered by Bortkiewicz is that in which the ratio $b/a$ is constant; but that presupposes, as is seen in the text, that the prices of goods do not vary when the fraction of the stock of money which is offered each day in the market increases.

I believe that this footnote also replies to the objections made by Holtrop to the formula given in the text. In the article cited Marget shows that the formula is also valid when $S$ and $v$ have the significance, respectively, of a stock of goods and of velocity of the circulation of goods.

† It was realized even in 1923 that the average term of the bills of exchange in the portfolio of the Reichsbank was much less than in 1913, as may be seen in the following figures, which have been extracted from various Reports of the Reichsbank.

*The Proportion of Internal Bills of Exchange in the Portfolio of the Reichsbank, with their Terms*

| | *Up to* 15 *days* | 16–30 *days* | 30–90 *days* |
|---|---|---|---|
| 1913 | 35·3 | 16·8 | 47·9 |
| 1923 | 97·1 | 1·3 | 1·6 |

In 1923 97·1 per cent of the bills of exchange were for terms of about 15 days; in 1913 only 35·3 per cent.

**17.** In conclusion, I believe that the observations of Bortkiewicz, however interesting, do not show that the opinions of those economists who stated that consumers, by spending their money incomes more rapidly, increased the velocity of the circulation of money, were unfounded. It is true, however, that the phenomenon has been explained sometimes in a manner not altogether correct. It is inaccurate to say that prices increase more rapidly than the quantity of money *because* the velocity of the circulation increases. Instead, the relation existing between the phenomena in question is as follows (as explained by Marshall): the fraction of their incomes or wealth which individuals are, on the whole, disposed to hold in the form of "available money," diminishes, therefore the quantity $\frac{1}{a}M$ increases; prices rise; and money circulates more rapidly.

But many experiences have shown that this rise in the velocity of the circulation, which is the consequence of the flight from the depreciated money, is only a temporary phenomenon, if the public knows that the Central Bank, in spite of the pressure of interested persons, stands fast and does not increase the note-issues. If a shortage of the circulating medium is then felt, the rise in prices is arrested, confidence returns, and spreads gradually among the public, consumers recover the habit of spending their money incomes gradually, and the velocity of the circulation of money slackens once more.

As we shall see in a later chapter, after the stabilization of the mark exchange (November 1923) the velocity of the circulation of money lessened immediately.

Numerous other authors, besides Bortkiewicz, contend that the depreciation of the exchange provoked an increase in the prices of goods, and that from that followed a rise in the velocity of circulation of money, which was sufficient to support the new high level of prices. With the aid of this argument writers have sought to show that the internal value of a paper currency is independent of monetary and banking policy and is, on the contrary, dominated by the state of the balance of payments.

Also, by bringing into prominence the factor "velocity of the circulation of money," it apparently breaks down the argument of Taussig* and other economists, according to whom a general rise of prices in a country with a paper currency is not possible if the quantity of money does not vary—because in such a case the total monetary income of

* *International Trade*, p. 354.

the population remains constant. To this it may be objected that the total monetary income does not depend solely on the quantity of money, but also on its velocity of the circulation. In my opinion, it is necessary to distinguish between the indirect and the direct effects of a depreciation of the exchange. Indirectly, the depreciation of the exchange, by creating the expectation of future rises in prices, and therefore inducing consumers and merchants to hasten purchases, helps to provoke a rise in the velocity of the circulation of money. But, as was said above, these effects are purely temporary if the exchange does not continue to depreciate.

As for the *direct* effects of the rise of prices, provoked by the depreciation of the exchange, on the velocity of the circulation of the money, it may be observed that until the public has lost confidence in the money, the depreciation of the exchange, due to a disturbance in the balance of payments, only influences the prices of imported and exported goods. If the quantity of money does not vary, the profits of some classes of merchants correspond to the losses of other classes. In every way, even if new incomes are created, they are only a very small matter compared with the mass of existing monetary incomes; and the influence on the income velocity of the money and on general prices could only be very slight.

The situation is different when, in an advanced phase of the inflation, a depreciation of the exchange reacts immediately, mainly for psychological reasons, also on the prices of goods of purely domestic character, and the rise of prices becomes general. Then the income velocity of money tends to increase as a direct consequence of the depreciation of the exchange, either because obvious profits are created to the advantage of producers—profits which they invest in the purchase of goods—or because the working classes and salary-earners whose real incomes are lessened obtain the payment of wages and salaries at shorter intervals.

But that, I repeat, occurs only in that last phase of the monetary depreciation which the excessive issues of paper money have caused; hence monetary and banking policy always remains the dominating factor.

CHAPTER V*

# The Influences of the Depreciation of the Mark on Economic Activity

## I. THE OPINIONS OF THE CLASSICAL ECONOMISTS ABOUT THE EFFECTS OF THE MONETARY INFLATION ON PRODUCTION

**1.** Most varied and contradictory opinions were expressed in Germany and elsewhere regarding the effects which the depreciation of the mark exercised on German economy.

It was often affirmed that only the inflation made it possible for German industry to continue to produce, there being the exceptional and interesting spectacle of extraordinary activity and prosperity in Germany at a time of general crisis in business in other countries, and especially in some of those who were victorious in the Great War.

To this view others objected that it was a question only of an "apparent prosperity," which concealed the real and continual loss of capital, the disintegration of productive apparatus, the increasing poverty of many classes of society, and the symptoms of a crisis, which, after having remained latent for a long time, burst forth with unparalleled violence in the last months of 1923.

In reality, from the Armistice onwards the economic and social situation of Germany remained extraordinarily complex. Light and shade, alternating phases of depression and prosperity, a strange combination of disintegrating forces and constructive energy, almost unforeseen changes of the situation, and apparently inexplicable contradictions characterize post-war German economy.

Before analysing the influences which monetary inflation exercised on German production we must discuss some theoretical considerations. On this question, as on many others, there is a striking contrast between the economists and the practical men. The latter have always asserted that the increase of the quantity of money, provoking an increase in prices, stimulated production, favoured exports, strengthened the productive equipment of the country and gave birth to new industries, which were put in a position to meet foreign competition. In short,

* Part of this was originally published in *Rivista Bancaria* (1924) and part in *Economia* (1925).

it exercised influences mainly favourable to the general economy of the country, even if some classes with fixed incomes undeniably suffered from the effects of monetary depreciation.

**2.** To the theory, according to which the increase of the quantity of money stimulates production—a theory supported, as is well known, by Hume—the classical school is opposed. "However abundant may be the quantity of money or bank-notes," wrote Ricardo,* "though it may increase the nominal prices of commodities; though it may distribute the productive capital in different proportions; though the Bank, by increasing the quantity of their notes, may enable A to carry on part of the business formerly engrossed by B and C, nothing will be added to the real revenue and wealth of the country. B and C may be injured and A and the Bank may be gainers, but they will gain exactly what B and C lose. There will be a violent and an unjust transfer of property, but no benefit whatever will be gained by the community."

Combating the opinion of Attwood, who contends that the increase of prices provoked by the new issues of paper money stimulated every producer to maximize his efforts, Mill observed that the expectation, on the part of traders, of still higher real profits (that is the command of a greater quantity of goods) must necessarily be illusory "since, all prices being supposed to rise equally, no one was really better paid for his goods than before."†

**3.** The classical theory, according to which the increase of the issues of paper money cannot provoke an increase of the total production of the country, was expounded, in a form which may be called final, by Wagner in his work on "Russian Paper Money." The results of Wagner's research are summarized in this proposition: "Paper-money is capital from the point of the private trader, but it is not so for the national economy."‡

Total production depends on the quantity of concrete means of production existing at a given moment, and not on the quantity of monetary capital. If new money is created, which enters into competition with the money previously circulating, for the purchase of the

* "The High Price of Bullion," *Works*, edited by McCulloch, p. 286.

† *Principles of Political Economy*, edited by Ashley, London, 1926, p. 550. An interesting analysis of Attwood's idea is made by R. G. Hawtrey, *Trade and Credit*, pp. 64 and following.

‡ *Op. cit.*, p. 16.

existing means of production or consumption goods, then the consequence will be a rise in prices. If paper money is issued in a quantity larger than the amount of metallic money which formerly circulated, and for which the paper money is substituted, its sole effect is to direct the employment of existing resources into different channels. This change in the direction of production explains the variations and apparent expansions of production which were often observed after the issue of paper money. The entrepreneurs who came into the possession of newly issued paper—these were usually producers of war materials—attracted to themselves a part of the existing real resources, but this caused a shortage in other industries, which were therefore obliged to limit production. The quantity of goods existing at the time of the issues remained unchanged and therefore it is clear that the greater purchase of the means of production by one set of people must correspond to a reduced purchase by another set of people. The apparent prosperity of industry is only partial. It is true that new firms are established, but the articles which they make only take the place of other goods which would have been produced in normal conditions. To the prosperity of some regions or great towns, to which flowed the new paper money, there corresponds a depression in other places, just as prosperity of some social classes corresponds to the poverty of others.

These are the ideas of Wagner, which are not substantially modified by certain observations with which he tempered a little the rigidity of the theory. He observes that total production could increase, following the issue of paper money, only in the case in which new firms, created by the inflation, were more productive than those whom the inflation had caused to restrict their output. It may be said that this happened, but, adds Wagner, "it may also be said that the contrary happened."* Repeating a discussion by Mill, Wagner observes moreover that if in the country where the paper money is issued gold is still in circulation, that gold is displaced gradually by the paper money and exported abroad in exchange for raw materials, machines, foodstuffs for the working classes—in short, in exchange for material goods which increase the available resources in the country with paper money. In another case the issue of paper money can provoke, indirectly, an increase of real resources and hence of total production, that is in the case of a country which has paper money and succeeds in inducing foreigners to accept notes in payment of goods. Therefore, according to Wagner,

* *Op. cit.*, p. 25.

the Russian policy which prohibited the exportation of paper money was not very wise. The two cases described by Wagner also applied to Germany during the depreciation of the mark.

**4.** The theory, according to which monetary inflation provoked not an increase but only a change of direction in economic production, was generally accepted by economists. It is true that Thornton had already expounded a contrary opinion, studying the problem from a dynamic point of view and using in evidence the slow adaptation of salaries to the increase of prices;* but the authority of later economists prevailed, and Thornton's important discussions were forgotten.

After the World War it was noticed that in some countries with depreciated currencies unemployment was very slight, while countries with stable or less depreciated currencies were troubled by a vast amount of unemployment. Now, the number of workers employed being an index of the total volume of production, it seemed clear that, contrary to the opinion prevailing among economists, inflation acted as a stimulus to production. There appeared to be further proof of this conclusion, when it was noticed that some countries suffered much unemployment after monetary stabilization.

## II. "FORCED SAVING" IMPOSED ON SOME CLASSES BY THE INFLATION, AS THE SOURCE OF THE NEW RESOURCES

**5.** In practice, passing from one given level of prices and wages, corresponding to a given quantity of money, to a higher level, *time* is required, and during this interval some very interesting phenomena develop.

Even the case here examined reveals one of the fundamental characteristics and, if we like, one of the defects of the classical theories. Ricardo and Mill do not take account of the period of transition from one position of equilibrium to another. Now, periods of transition, as recent monetary experiences have shown, can be very long, and to neglect them and simply banish them into the category of "disturbing" circumstances is to wander too far from real life.

Let us suppose, following Böhm-Bawerk, that all the working capital

* "It must be admitted that, provided we assume an excessive issue of paper to lift up, as it may for a time, the cost of goods, though not the price of labour, some augmentation of stock will be the consequence: for the labourer, according to this supposition, may be forced by this necessity to consume fewer articles, though he may exercise the same industry" (*An Enquiry into the Nature and Effects of the Paper Credit of Great Britain*, London, 1802, p. 263).

of manufacture is spent in wages. With a money capital of 100,000, for example, they pay in a given period for the work of 1,000 men who in their turn are able to buy 1,000 units of goods. The capitalists and other classes of consumers have, let us say, 20,000 units of money with which they buy 200 units of goods. (Let us suppose, for simplicity, that the velocity of circulation of money equals unity.) If, now, the money capital of the manufacturers becomes 120,000, thanks to new bankers' credits or to profits derived from governmental inflation, and wages increase only, let us suppose, from 100 to 110, the manufacturers could absorb into their service, besides the 1,000 men previously employed, 91 other individuals in search of work. The total sum of the wages is offered by the workers in the market for goods where, as formerly, there are 1,200 units of goods, and where the workers newly employed enter into competition with the old workers and other classes of consumers. The new distribution of goods will be different from the former. The prices being raised from 100 to 116·7 the group of old workmen will secure 942·8 units of goods (instead of 1,000: in other words their real income has diminished); the other classes of consumers will be able to buy 171·4 units instead of 200; and the newly employed workers will take 85·7 units. The share enjoyed by the entire working class is increased, to the detriment of that obtained by classes with fixed incomes.

**6.** In the preceding example we have supposed that at the moment at which the issues of paper money are increased there exists a certain number of unemployed workers. If, instead, the entire supply of labour is occupied—a hypothesis too rigorous and unreal, because there is always a reserve of the forces of labour, constituted by the numbers of workers' families, by small proprietors and small rentiers who would become labourers if the rise of the cost of living seriously diminished their incomes; besides, a man's working hours can be prolonged by means of "overtime"—the phenomena are more complicated, but the result is not substantially different. If the real wages of the worker diminish as a result of the inflation, it means that for the reproduction of the "subsistence fund" for the working classes, it is sufficient to employ a smaller sum of productive energies than before; that is, a part of the productive energies of the country can be employed in other ways, for example, in the creation of new and more efficient "means of production," which at a future time will make possible an ampler production of consumption goods. Hence prices will fall once more and the real wage of the workman, which has been temporarily depressed, will rise once more.

Then if we consider the relations between paper inflation and the means of production from a static point of view, as did the classical economists, it is certain that inflation does not increase the quantity of machines, industrial buildings, etc., which exist at a given time in a country. But from the dynamic point of view the conclusion is different. Thanks to the "forced saving" which paper inflation, by provoking an increase of prices, imposed on the workers previously employed, and on the classes of society with fixed incomes, it is quite possible that the total economic production is increased.*

This obviously presupposes that the wages are at the outset above the "minimum," and that the working classes are not willing to, or cannot effectively, oppose the reduction of real wages.

### III. RELATIONS BETWEEN THE DEPRECIATION OF THE MARK AND UNEMPLOYMENT

**7.** Now let us examine the actual facts. According to official statistics the number of unemployed, which was high at the beginning of 1919, decreased continually in Germany—if we exclude temporary fluctuations to which we shall refer later—until the middle of 1922. It is true that there was for a long time in Germany *latent* unemployment. After the Armistice, when it was necessary to prevent the danger of grave troubles, large numbers of the unemployed were absorbed in national enterprises. In 1920 the personnel of the railway exceeded 1,100,000 individuals, whereas it numbered scarcely 700,000 before the war. The personnel of the postal and telegraphic administrations was increased by about 120,000 new employees. The demobilization laws put many limits to the liberty of employers in dismissing men when there was insufficient work; before dismissing it was necessary to introduce the system of short-time. I must also mention the influence of the eight-hour-day law, promulgated in November 1918.

* The conception of "forced saving" is implicit in some arguments which Mill produced when discussing his proposition that "industry is limited by capital." Mill in fact writes: "If the labourers were reduced to lower wages, or induced to work more hours for the same wages, or if their families, who are already maintained from capital, were employed to a greater extent than they are now in adding to the produce, a given capital would afford employment to more industry" (*op. cit.*, p. 65). In another passage Mill observes that there are "privations which though essentially the same with saving, are not generally called by that name, because not voluntary." They are "a kind of compulsory saving" (*op. cit.*, p. 69).

In the summer of 1922 unemployment practically disappeared. It appears that—in spite of the gaps caused by the war in the ranks of the working population—the total number of individuals occupied in industry, agriculture, commerce, public services, etc., was greater in 1922 than before the war.

In the following diagram (XII) the continuous line shows the dollar rate, and the two broken lines represent the percentage of unemployed

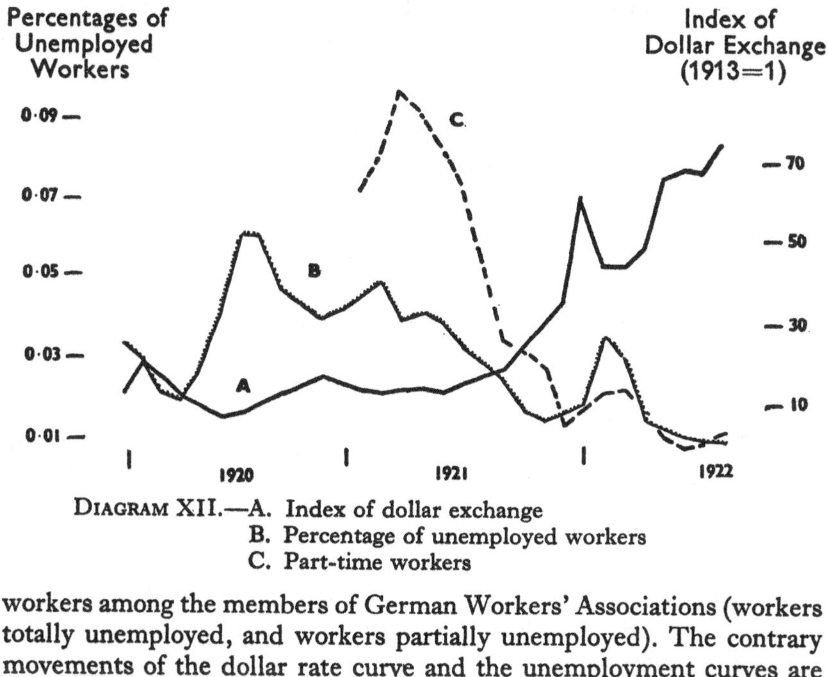


DIAGRAM XII.—A. Index of dollar exchange
B. Percentage of unemployed workers
C. Part-time workers

workers among the members of German Workers' Associations (workers totally unemployed, and workers partially unemployed). The contrary movements of the dollar rate curve and the unemployment curves are evident from the second half of 1921, when the German mark, after a period of relative stability, began to depreciate rapidly.

The diagram also offers proof of a characteristic connection between the variations of the exchange rate and the variations of unemployment. The fluctuations of the mark caused a continual instability in the conditions of German production, an alternation of periods of feverish activity and periods of restraint and business crises. It may be seen that, generally, to every improvement of the mark there corresponded an increase of unemployment (March–July 1920; November 1920–February 1921; December 1921–January 1922), and that every depreciation of the exchange was followed by an improvement in the conditions of the labour market (January–February 1920; July–November 1920; April–November 1921; and then during the first half of 1922).

At the times of the depreciation of the mark the foreign and home demands for goods were intensified. Foreign purchasers wanted to profit by the greater purchasing power of their own money in the German market; and even at home the prospect of continuous increases in prices was an inducement to anticipate purchases or to buy goods as a means of investing money which continually lost value. On the other hand, in the periods when the mark improved, foreign demand declined, and at home there occurred what in the summer of 1920 was called "the buyers' strike."

The statistical relations between real wages and the inflation will be studied in another chapter.

### IV. ECONOMIC ACTIVITY IN GERMANY FROM OCTOBER 1921 TO THE SUMMER OF 1922

**8.** It is not possible to give an exact picture of economic production in the years 1919–23 because the German statistics are incomplete. It can, however, be said that these statistics and the economic journals of that period show that total production increased from 1919 until towards the end of 1922. Certainly it would be erroneous to attribute this increase exclusively to the influence of the monetary depreciation; because in a great measure it was the expression of the progressive reconstruction of German economy after the turmoil produced by the war and the revolution. But it was probably due to the currency depreciation that Germany, which the depreciation of the mark had isolated from the outside world, was spared the grave crisis which various other countries suffered in 1920.

**9.** The period between October 1921 and the summer of 1922 is specially important for the study of the relations between monetary depreciation and economic activity. On the events of that period I have collected evidence from which may be drawn the following conclusions.

In the German Press the industrial and commercial situation was often described by the expression "general liquidation." The shops were denuded of goods. Foreigners, favoured by the superiority of their money, made important acquisitions. Germans, greatly agitated by the fall of the mark, bought whatever they could at any price simply in order to exchange their money for "material values." At the beginning of November 1921 the flight from the mark assumed the nature of a panic, which rapidly spread through all classes of society.

All information regarding the condition of the principal industries in the month of November shows that the depreciation of the mark provoked a considerable increase of orders. The metallurgical industries were working at full pressure so that they had to introduce overtime, and they refused to accept new orders. Even the automobile industry had a peak of prosperity then. The textile trade was assured work for several months; the cotton firms were for some time unable to undertake new engagements; the woollen industry of München-Gladback had work for four or five months; in the silk industry delivery dates were six months after orders; the linen industry had sold its output until the spring of 1922 and would not accept new orders.

The hosiers could no longer keep pace with the demands of their customers. The chemical industry profited by the prosperity of the textile firms. The paper mills had a period of intense activity, thanks mainly to important orders from abroad. Even the potteries experienced good conditions.

From November 26th to December 1st, 1921, the price of the dollar rate fell sharply from 293 to 190 paper marks. There was a moment of suspense in the business world. The Press declared that the improvement of the mark had been a catastrophe for German industry. Trade orders rapidly diminished.

From economic information relating to December 1921 and January 1922 it is obvious that the oscillations of the dollar rate, which occurred in these months, created a state of grave uncertainty in German industry. However, the factories continued to work intensely thanks to the previous orders.

In February 1922 the dollar began to rise, and on March 7th was quoted at 262 paper marks. A new wave of commercial and industrial activity was the result. The volume of business done in the great spring fairs was an obvious indication of the new lease upon which economic life had entered. Illustrating the intensity of the demand for goods which was shown in March at Leipzig Fair, the *Berliner Tageblatt* wrote: "It is no longer simply a zeal for acquiring, or even a rage: it is a madness." It was a demand provoked by panic. Merchants bought for fear that if they waited the stocks would be exhausted. The Fairs of Breslau and Frankfort were brilliant successes, and again traders showed great impatience to purchase. "Germany is craving, hungering for goods," wrote the *Frankfurter Zeitung*, "and he who possesses goods is master of the situation." The *Berliner Tageblatt* added: "Business has reached a maximum of intensity. Buyers care nothing about prices. There is a general rush for goods." This expression of feverish activity given by the great Fairs was confirmed by information about the great industries, every one of which showed a great number of new orders. It was expected that the factories would have work for many months. The *Lokal Anzeiger* described the situation thus: "The mad activity of industry and commerce makes one giddy."

## V. CERTAIN STATISTICS OF PRODUCTION IN GERMANY IN THE YEARS 1920–23

**10.** However, these statements, suggested by the impressions of the moment, were somewhat exaggerated. Even many foreigners, who regarded the "prosperity" of Germany with envy, exaggerated the influence exercised by the depreciation of the mark on German production. An examination of the statistics allows us to give a more balanced judgment. From the most important statistical indices—agriculture statistics; production and consumption of coal, iron, and steel; imports of industrial raw materials; quantities of goods transported by railways and inland waterways, etc.—it appears that in 1922 (which was the year of greatest economic expansion after the war) total production probably reached no more than 70–80 per cent of production in 1913 in the present territory. The impression produced by the very low unemployment figure is, therefore, somewhat impaired.*

* I give here certain summary data on German production during the inflation period. Most remarkably the official statistics show a great decrease in *agricultural production*, though lack of comparability has probably led to the exaggeration of the whole of this important phenomenon.

*Production in Thousands of Tons in the Post-War Territory*

| | 1913 | 1921 | 1922 | 1923 |
|---|---|---|---|---|
| Rye .. .. | 10,130 | 6,798 | 5,234 | 6,682 |
| Wheat .. .. | 4,046 | 2,933 | 1,958 | 2,897 |
| Potatoes .. .. | 44,013 | 26,149 | 40,661 | 32,580 |

We must not forget that 1913 was a year of exceptional harvests. But even if we take as our base the average of several pre-war years, a considerable decrease in production is shown, the causes of which—having their roots in the war—have often been illustrated by German writers.

As for industrial production, the most important indices are given by the production of coal, iron, and steel, some non-ferrous metals, and by the importation of raw materials.

The production of coal amounted in 1913, in German post-war territory, including Polish Upper Silesia, to 172·5 millions of tons; and without Upper Silesia to 140·9 millions. In 1922, 130·3 million tons was produced (the production of Upper Silesia is included in this figure for the first five months of the year). To appreciate fully the importance of carboniferous production it is necessary to include lignite, which,

## VI. DISTURBANCE IN THE DIRECTION OF ECONOMIC ACTIVITY

**11.** The depreciation of the mark provoked some disturbance, worthy of note, in the direction of economic activity.

converted into coal at the official coefficient of 2/9, gives 19·4 million tons for 1913 and 30·5 for 1922. Moreover, even the utilizing of water power made perceptible progress during the inflation. Among the most important works executed after the war must be mentioned the construction of the electricity centres of Bavaria, which *The Times* described as a "monument of the inflation." They represented the harnessing of about 1,865,000 horse-power; that is, nearly 30 per cent of the available hydraulic power.

According to the figures supplied by the "Coal Council of the Reich" in 1913, the quantity of coal available for German industry, deducting the consumption of the mines and the coal given to miners (Deputatkohle), amounted to 122·8 million tons in the present confines of Germany (plus Upper Silesia). In 1921 the quantity available for industry was reduced to 88·5 million tons (72·1 per cent of the consumption of 1913).

According to my calculations, in 1922 the total consumption of combustibles reached the figure of 1913, taking account of the loss of territory. It is, however, necessary to observe that in 1922 (*a*) the consumption of the mines was greater; (*b*) the quantity of coal given to miners was greater; (*c*) the percentage of other substances found in the coal was higher. Hence the quantity available for industry was really less than in 1913.

The production of iron and steel is shown by the following figures:

| (*For* 1913 *in the present confines of Germany*) | *Iron* (*Millions of tons*) | *Steel* |
|---|---|---|
| 1913 | 10·9 | 11·9 |
| 1920 | 6·4 | 8·5 |
| 1921 | 7·9 | 10·1 |
| 1922 | 9·4 | 11·7 |
| 1923 | 4·9 | 6·3 |

The consumption of certain metals—as copper, lead, zinc, tin, and aluminium—is a significant index of the general situation of industrial production. According to the statistics of *Metallbank* and *Metallgesellschaft* of Frankfort the figures for Germany are as follows:

| *Consumption of* | 1913 | 1919 | 1920 (*Millions of kilos*) | 1921 | 1922 | 1923 |
|---|---|---|---|---|---|---|
| Lead .. .. .. | 230·4 | 60·0 | 67·5 | 101·4 | 143·0 | 59·3 |
| Copper .. .. | 259·7 | 24·0 | 73·7 | 126·5 | 148·1 | 96·1 |
| Zinc .. .. .. | 232·0 | 60·0 | 71·8 | 64·2 | 75·7 | 66·1 |
| Tin .. .. .. | 19·9 | 4·4 | 7·3 | 11·3 | 12·2 | 7·9 |
| Aluminium .. .. | 20·7 | 41·8 | 35·2 | 16·0 | 27·0 | 27·0 |

The figures for aluminium include the production of Germany, Switzerland, and other European countries, excluding France, Italy, and England.

There are very few statistics of the production of semi-finished or finished industrial goods. But the knowledge at our disposal enables us to discover this phenomenon in many cases: on the one hand, the *capacity for production* increased compared with pre-war days; on the other, *effective production* was less than that of 1913. An example of this is given by the dyestuffs industry. According to statistics published by the Department of Commerce at Washington, even in 1922, which was economically the most active post-war year, production did not exceed two-thirds of the quantity

There was often observed in Germany a characteristic contrast between industrial activity, which at certain times was intense, and made before the war, and in 1923 it was about 50 per cent. In the meantime the capacity for production had increased from 20 to 25 per cent.

Here are figures of imports of certain of the most important materials consumed by industry (tons):

| | 1913 | 1922 | 1922 (1913 = 100) |
|---|---|---|---|
| Raw cotton .. .. | 429,573 | 218,312 | 58·8 |
| Raw wool .. .. | 183,407 | 184,241 | 100·5 |
| Raw silk .. .. .. | 4,131 | 1,652 | 40·0 |
| Linen .. .. .. | 70,834 | 12,715 | 17·9 |
| Jute .. .. .. | 162,063 | 102,631 | 63·3 |
| Ox hides .. .. | 167,641 | 78,944 | 47·1 |
| Calf skins .. .. | 39,230 | 15,213 | 38·8 |
| Copper .. .. .. | 225,392 | 177,930 | 56·8 |
| Rubber .. .. .. | 28,995 | 33,450 | 115·4 |
| Rough or sawn wood .. | 4,522,980 | 1,923,398 | 42·5 |
| Tin .. .. .. | 14,261 | 8,276 | 57·7 |
| Petrol .. .. .. | 745,466 | 192,681 | 25·8 |

In one special field German industry showed great activity; that is, in the reconstruction of the mercantile marine. More even than by the indemnities paid by the Government after the war, it was favoured by great profits realized by the navigation companies whose incomes were provided, in great part, by foreigners.

*Shipping Tonnage (in thousands of tons) Launched in the Years*

| | |
|---|---|
| 1913 .. .. | 459 |
| 1920 .. .. | 326 |
| 1921 .. .. | 446 |
| 1922 .. .. | 625 |
| 1923 .. .. | 418 |

According to Lloyd's the German Mercantile Marine had, on June 30th, 1924, a tonnage of 2,856,000 and so had reached 55 per cent of pre-war tonnage. Germany also concentrated its energy on the reconstruction of its inland shipping which the cessions at the end of the war to the Allied countries (France, Belgium, Italy, Portugal, Czechoslovakia, and Poland) had gravely reduced. On December 31st, 1912, official statistics registered a tonnage of 7,394,467 tons. The German writer "Nauticus" calculated for December 1921 a tonnage of 6,868,709.

That total production, during the period of inflation, was on a lower level than that reached before the war is shown also by statistics of goods transported by railway or inland waterways.

*Tons of Goods Transported on German Railways (Monthly Average in Millions of Tons)*

| | |
|---|---|
| 1913 (without Alsace-Lorraine) | 44·9 |
| 1922 .. .. .. .. | 32·3 |
| 1923 .. .. .. .. | 20·8 |

The following figures show the *movements at German ports* in thousands of tons:

| | *Ships entering* | *Ships cleared* |
|---|---|---|
| 1913 | 34,772 | 34,922 |
| 1920 | 12,545 | 12,360 |
| 1921 | 19,169 | 19,114 |
| 1922 | 25,488 | 26,350 |
| 1923 | 30,860 | 30,899 |

In 1923 in the two largest German ports, Hamburg and Bremen, the pre-war

the standard of living of large sections of the population, which remained relatively low. "Produced" income appeared to be much greater than "consumed" income.

Many different explanations were suggested. The thesis supported for propaganda purposes by those who asserted that Germany worked for the Allies, was obviously an exaggeration. Leaving aside the parts of national property handed over, it is certain that the demands made by Germany on her annual income to satisfy her obligations to the Allies only represented, in the years 1919–23, a modest fraction of that income.

The explanation given by Lansburgh* is also too one-sided. It affirmed that the contrast between the continual increase of German production and the low average income of the population was due to the fact that Germany, because of the depreciation of the mark, purchased abroad at very high prices, whilst selling at very low prices. Part of the normal price of German products was absorbed by the exchequer of importer countries under the form of differential customs duties.

**12.** A more plausible explanation seems to be that the low standard of life of a great part of the German population was due, above all, to the deficiency in agricultural production. Owing to the lack of certain chemical fertilizers, of the dearth of the forces of labour, and of the fall in the intensity of labour in the years 1919–23 agricultural production was much lower, as we have seen already, than before the war. There was also a certain disequilibrium in the distribution of agricultural products; particularly the great cities suffered from obvious scarcity.

Furthermore, the activity of industry was especially directed to the production of the means of production.†

movement was surpassed (Hamburg: ships entering in 1913, 14,185 thousands of tons; in 1923, 15,344 thousands. Bremen: 5,251 and 5,818 thousands). But these figures show the *tonnage* of the ships, not the *quantity* of goods effectively embarked and disembarked. It is known that after the war the shipping statistics for Hamburg were swollen by the fact that that port was touched by many ships belonging to foreign companies established there after the war. But the great movement of ships was not a sign of a corresponding movement in goods. Besides, the increase of traffic in 1923—in a year of economic depression—was mainly due to the increase of the imports of English coal, rendered necessary by the occupation of the Ruhr.

(The preceding data have been extracted, unless otherwise stated, from *Statistisches Jahrbuch für das deutsche Reich* and from the review *Wirtschaft und Statistik*, published by the Statistical Office of the Reich.)

* See *Die Bank*, issue of April 1922.

† This is confirmed by the more recent enquiries of R. Wagenführ. See *Die Industriewirtschaft* (edited by the Institut für Konjunkturforschung), Berlin, 1933, p. 26.

This was due, essentially, to causes of two kinds:

(*a*) to the direct action of the State. It was natural that, after the end of the war, German Governments should be preoccupied with the reconstruction of Germany's productive apparatus.

For example, after the war, the German Government constructed canals, inland ports, and great electricity centres; on behalf of the railway administration it placed large orders for railway materials,* and reconstructed the existing equipment which had been worn out by the long war; granted compensation to the shipping companies, which, profiting also from other revenues, reconstructed in a few years a substantial part of the fleet; similarly, it paid appreciable sums to entrepreneurs who had been compelled to give up their establishments in Lorraine and obliged them to reconstruct their plant on German soil.

Therefore, a part of the new issues of paper money for Government purposes was immediately transformed into a demand for instrumental goods.

(*b*) To the indirect influence of the inflation. The inflation restricted the real incomes of numerous classes of consumers. Their demand for consumption goods was therefore lessened. For example, for some time in Berlin there remained every day some thousands of pints of milk, in spite of the fact that the production was much less than that of pre-war days.†

On the other hand, inflation on Government account, provoking an increase of prices, created exceptional profits for certain kinds of entrepreneurs. Inflation has been defined by some writers as a tax.‡ But the characteristic of this tax is that, at the same time as the State is taking a part of the national income for itself, it imposes on some classes of society a levy in favour of other classes.

To give a rough idea of the importance of the sums which inflation can put at the disposal of the entrepreneurs in a large country, I shall give certain figures. The annual salaries and wages paid before the war in Germany probably aggregated about twenty-five milliard marks;

* Railway rolling-stock in 1913, with Alsace-Lorraine: locomotives, 29,100; passenger coaches, 65,150; goods trucks, 669,457. After the Armistice Germany found her stock extremely reduced in number and in very bad condition. On October 1st, 1920, she possessed 30,000 locomotives, 60,000 passenger coaches, and 546,800 goods trucks.

At the beginning of 1924 the quantity of rolling-stock had surpassed that of 1913 (locomotives, 29,966; passenger coaches, 67,800, and trucks, 723,100).

† *Der Wiederaufbau*, Berlin, 1922–23, p. 479.

‡ Wagner, *op. cit.*, p. 14.

a diminution of only 10 per cent or 20 per cent of the *real* wages (actually the depression during the inflation was greater) would signify profits of several milliards! According to official calculations, before the war house rents totalled five milliard marks, of which probably three milliards were paid by the working classes. During the inflation rents were reduced almost to zero, which permitted employers to reduce nominal wages accordingly.

The profits of the inflation originated a demand for "producers'" goods.* Part of the short-term bank credits could be employed in long-term investments, because, thanks to the increase of prices, the debtor repaid only a part of the original real value of the credit.

To that was added the influence of an economic conception, which is widely held in countries with depreciated currencies, that is the myth of "real value" or "intrinsic value." It was thought that even if for the time being the entirely new equipment was not utilized, it nevertheless always represented an "intrinsic value," a "substance" as it was called in Germany. In that country, as a German writer observed, the savings of entrepreneurs were crystallized into iron and stones. In the acutest phase of the inflation Germany offered the grotesque, and at the same time tragic, spectacle of a people which, rather than produce food, clothes, shoes, and milk for its own babies, was exhausting its energies in the manufacture of machines or the building of factories.

An example is given by the proved facts of German agriculture. To avoid the effects of the monetary depreciation, German agriculturists continued to buy machines; the "flight from the mark to the machine," as a German author wrote,† was the most convenient and the easiest means of defence against the depreciation of the currency. But towards the end of the inflation, farmers realized that a great part of their capital was sunk in machines, whose number was far above what would ever be needed.

## VII. THE PRODUCTION OF INSTRUMENTAL GOODS

**13.** Thanks to the intense demand for "instrumental" goods, the engineering industries received a great stimulus during the depreciation

* The tendency of monetary or credit inflation to alter the preceding distribution of demand between consumption goods and producers' goods is brought into evidence by Schumpeter in his classic article "Das Sozialprodukt und die Rechenpfennige" (*Archiv für Sozialwissenschaft und Sozialpolitik*, 44 Bd., 1917–18). See also the criticisms of Budge (*Waren-oder Anweisungstheorie des Geldes*, *idem* 46 Bd., 1918–19).

† Beckmann, "Kapitalbildung der deutschen Landwirtschaft während der Inflation" (*Schmöller's Jahrbuch*, 1924, p. 123).

of the mark. In certain branches of the engineering industry the expansion of equipment was enormous; as in the dockyards, whose capacity for production was doubled; a characteristic example, wrote a financial journal, of a mistaken estimate of the post-war economic situation on the part of German entrepreneurs.

Ultimately the demands for "instruments of production" all converged on the market for iron, and so on coal. The "forced saving" of numerous classes of society went above all to the advantage of the iron and steel and mining industries, which could exploit the situation thanks to the monopolistic position which their powerful syndicate had been able to obtain. Under the stimulus of the intense demand for iron, the iron and steel firms continually extended their works, consuming themselves a great part of the iron produced. The capacity for the production of steel, which was nearly 12 million tons in 1913, in the present German territory, rose during the inflation to more than 15 millions. The monthly averages of the production of steel were as follows:

TABLE XXIII

(*Thousands of Tons*)

| | 1920 | 1921 | 1922 |
|---|---|---|---|
| 1st quarter .. .. | 660 | 813 | 961 |
| 2nd quarter .. .. | 747 | 758 | 972 |
| 3rd quarter .. .. | 812 | 839 | 974 |
| 4th quarter .. .. | 873 | 922 | 998 |

The total production in 1922 (11·7 million tons) equalled the production in 1913 in the present German territory.

The development of the iron and steel industry naturally intensified the demand for, and the production of, coal. In 1922 Germany produced about 160 million tons of combustibles (including lignite reduced to anthracite equivalent), that is about 90 per cent of the quantity extracted in 1913 in the same area. But this quantity was insufficient for their needs, because a part had to be supplied to the Allies. Thus arose the fierce struggle among the iron and steel firms for the possession of the coal mines. Mines of low productivity, abandoned for a long time, were reopened; the production of substitutes for coal (lignite, water power, petrol) was increased; the technique of the systems of utilizing combustibles was continually improved (Wärmewirtschaft), succeeding, according to the opinions of competent people, in reducing consumption by 10 per cent. In the inflation years there arose the causes of overproduction of coal which was shown in 1924 and 1925.

The continual movement of resources from industries producing direct consumption goods to those producing the means of production, is clearly illustrated in the statistics. As Professor Hirsch writes, "from 1919 to 1921 an industrial migration occurred with a rapidity which had no precedent in history; more than 200,000 new workers were employed in the mines."* The highest number was reached towards the end of December 1922.

According to the figures published by the north-west group of the Union of German iron and steel manufacturers, the total of the number of men employed varied from 1913 onwards in the following manner:

TABLE XXIV

| | *Firms* | *Number of workers* |
|---|---|---|
| 1913 | 291 | 178,500 |
| 1921 | 267 | 223,000 |
| 1922 | 256 | 249,425 |
| 1923 | — | 250,000–260,000 |

As was seen above, the production of steel was greatly increased in the second half of 1921 and during 1922, that is in a period of a rapid depreciation of the mark. In that period, on the other hand, because of the diminution of internal consumption itself, and of the exports, the production of the cotton industry was very depressed, since it was estimated that it equalled less than 60 per cent of the pre-war production (if imports of raw cotton are taken as an index and the part consumed by Alsace-Lorraine is deducted from the 1913 figure). The period which commenced with the second half of 1922 was characterized by a considerable diminution of popular consumption. Based on official data I have constructed Diagrams XXIII–XXV, which show the consumption of meat,† beer, sugar, and tobacco,‡ and the net imports of coffee. The most marked fall in consumption was observed in 1923. Directly after the monetary stabilization consumption increased; but we will return to this matter. (The diagrams will be found on pp. 379–81.)

* *Magazin der Wirtschaft* of September 10th, 1925. In all the German mining districts 578,895 workers were employed towards the end of 1913 and 887,285 towards the end of March 1922.

† The figures do not include the entire consumption, but only the consumption of meat from animals slaughtered in public slaughter-houses plus the net imports (i.e. 80 per cent of the total consumption).

‡ The diagram indicates a sharp rise of consumption in October 1925, followed by a heavy fall. These variations are mainly due to the changes in the tax on tobacco which occurred at that time. The diagram does not show the actual consumption but the quantities of tobacco taxed each month.

**14.** The contrast between the consumption of "producers' goods" and that of final goods was also shown by the alterations manifested during the inflation in the composition of the foreign trade of Germany. That part of the production of consumers' goods which exceeded home consumption (which latter was diminished by the contraction of the purchasing power of numerous classes of society) sought an outlet abroad and consequently we find that certain kinds of finished products were often preponderant in the total exports, while, for the same reasons, imports of these goods declined. Even food imports were extraordinarily reduced.* As for steel products, with respect to which the home demand remained very brisk, the fraction of production which was consumed at home was higher than before the war. Likewise the export of machines and coal was checked by the keen internal demand.

On the other hand foreign iron was imported in great quantities, home production being insufficient to satisfy the intense demand. But the increase in the imports of coal which was shown in 1922 is especially characteristic, in that year Germany being changed from a mainly exporting country to an importing one.†

**15.** The intense demand for the instruments of production which existed in Germany during the period of the rapid depreciation of the mark, is revealed in the disparity between the movement of prices for consumers' goods and those for producers' goods. On this we may refer to the interesting statistics published by the *Frankfurter Zeitung*.‡

* Total net imports of foodstuffs (according to official statistics) 63·3 million quintals in 1913; 36·3 in 1922.

† *Foreign Trade in Coal (Thousands of Tons)*

| 1922 | *Imports* | *Exports* |
|---|---|---|
| January .. .. .. | 194 | 752 |
| February .. .. | 163 | 669 |
| March .. .. .. | 285 | 795 |
| April .. .. .. | 337 | 796 |
| May .. .. .. | 334 | 702 |
| June .. .. .. | 783 | 529 |
| July .. .. .. | 1,539 | 198 |

The figures for July are influenced by the detachment of Upper Silesia. But even from January to June there was a considerable increase of imports. Reparations in kind are not included in the export figures.

‡ See issue i, 1924, of *Wirtschaftskurve*, published by *Frankfurter Zeitung*. In the category of producers' goods are included: finished steel products, motors, boilers, machine oil, semi-finished wool materials, leather, wagons, cement, bricks, etc.; in the list of consumers' goods are included: foodstuffs, firewood, linen wear, stockings, shoes, stoves, etc.

The depreciation of the mark, which was intensified in the summer of 1921, provoked a more rapid increase in the prices of producers' goods than in those of consumers' goods. The disparity between the two price curves was increased during the whole of 1922; an obvious symptom of the industrial expansion which characterized that year. The divergence continued and increased even after the occupation of the Ruhr, in spite of the grave blow which that gave to German economy. The industry of the non-occupied territory did not at once feel the damaging effects of the French sanctions, but it was first favoured by an enormous increase of the issues of paper money and by the influence of the orders which had formerly been placed with firms in the Ruhr.

## VIII. THE EXPANSION OF GERMANY'S PRODUCTIVE EQUIPMENT DURING THE INFLATION

**16.** I reproduce from my collection of documents certain authoritative evidence, which confirms the view that during the depreciation of the mark numerous German industries not only reconstructed but also considerably enlarged their productive apparatus.

The organ of the great Rhineland industry, the *Bergwerkszeitung*, wrote in its issue of July 1st, 1922: "It is obvious that the iron and steel industry itself uses great quantities of iron, since it is attempting, in increasing measure, to renew completely and to modernize its plant. The profits of the industry are employed primarily for this object. . . . Besides the consumption of the industry itself there is the increased consumption of the railways. The demand for rolling-stock and sleepers has also increased extraordinarily, thanks to the construction of sidings for private firms. The technical improvements introduced by the great agricultural concerns, the needs of the mines, the construction of canals and highways has created an extraordinary demand for iron and steel products."

The issues of June 1st, 1922, June 4th, 1922, and July 1st, 1922, of the *Frankfurter Zeitung* gave some interesting accounts of the grandiose constructions and transformations carried out by the principal German industrial groups, and especially by Rhenish-Westphalian industry. The efforts were obviously made with the object of systematically developing the concerns, modernizing them in all particulars, and creating an efficient sales organization. The perfecting of the productive machinery was an object of the first importance on the part of all the iron and steel trusts.

The intense activity in the construction for industrial purposes had already created, in the summer of 1922, a scarcity of labour and had provoked an increase in wages; many workmen, therefore, abandoned other less remunerative occupations.

In the report of the Siemens Group (Siemens and Halske A.G. and Siemens-Schuckertwerke G.m.b.H.) for the year ending September 30th, 1922, one reads: "German industry aims at improving the productive processes. The desire to render efficient and to complete industrial plant is shown above all in the numerous orders for plant, largely for extensions, from the iron and steel and mining industries. Similar developments have affected the demand for spindles and looms, and even for machinery for the cement, leather, gum, paper, and pen trades. The chemical industry has commissioned us to construct plant for progressive exploitation of methods for extracting atmospheric azote. Numerous enlargements of electricity stations, which provide lighting for the public, are also noted." On the subject of agricultural conditions the *Frankfurter Zeitung* of March 2nd, 1924, wrote: "Even agriculture has employed in a large measure the money which accrued to it and the paper credits which it obtained (it has generally appeared as able as industry to secure these credits) for the purpose of augmenting its equipment. The yield from the soil and the condition of the cattle have not, on the average, completely returned to the pre-war level. On the other hand, the buildings and machines are much improved and are more abundant than formerly. Capital is at least preserved, and among many farmers has increased."

The opinion expressed by Professor Wolf before the Commission for socialization is worthy of mention.* "I believe it is known that the equipment of German factories has, for comprehensible reasons, undergone an extraordinary improvement in the course of the last two years. The reason was simply this: it was not desirable to show unduly high net profits and therefore those profits were invested in such a manner as to escape the duties of the Exchequer."

"The great poverty of the Reich" (observed a Berlin journal of November 26th, 1921) "did not actually imply the impoverishing of German economy. It is a characteristic fact that the spirit of initiative and the enormous push in industrial and banking expansion had never been so great as in the days when the dollar oscillated between 250 and 300 marks." And another financial journal affirmed that "Germany had come out of the inflation period with a greater quantity of the

* See *Verhandlungen der Sozialisierungskommission*, vol. i, 1921, p. 71.

means of production than she had possessed when the inflation commenced." We shall see below that in part these investments were lost, and that substantially the process of the rationalization of German industry commenced only after the monetary stabilization.

### IX. THE FORMATION OF THE GREAT POST-WAR INDUSTRIAL GROUPS

**17.** In close relation with the facts just illustrated is the phenomenon of industrial concentration which made remarkable progress during the depreciation of the German mark.

It is of course true that industrial concentration was not a new phenomenon in Germany. It was known before the war, when it usually appeared in the form which was called later "horizontal concentration" (a union of firms sharing the same stage of an industry)—the Rhenish-Westphalian coal syndicate is a classical example. Even the forces which stimulated a "vertical" concentration, i.e. the combination of firms producing raw materials with those producing semi-finished or finished articles, were clearly evident before the war.*

* Generally writers on economic subjects, studying the different features of the pre-war and post-war phases of industrial concentration, state that before the war in Germany the "syndicate" predominated (in contrast to the United States, where "trusts" had sprung up) and, further, that concentration was then "horizontal," while after the war the prevailing form was "vertical" concentration. These statements, which have now become commonplaces, only contain part of the truth. In fact, even before the war some great German syndicates had become in practice true and proper "trusts" dominated by a very small number of powerful firms. The evolution of the great Rhenish-Westphalian coal syndicate is characteristic. In 1893 there were 96 members of it who had a total participation of 33·5 million tons, that is on the average 336,614 tons each. On the eve of the war, the number of members had decreased to 62, while the total production had increased to 88·5 million tons, i.e. an average of 1,428,763 tons each. But no less than 41 associated firms had a share much below the average. The greatest part of the production was already concentrated in a minority of great firms. For example, a share of about 10 millions belonged to "Gelsenkirchener"; about 8 million was controlled by "Harpener"; and 3·6 by "Deutsch-Luxemburg." (See Ufermann and Hüglin, *Stinnes und seine Konzerne*, 1923, p. 22.) The Rhenish-Westphalian syndicate, which according to the agreement of 1893 ought to have represented the interests of all the associated firms, had become instead substantially the organ of a single group of firms and particularly of the "mixed firms." As Ufermann writes, it formed the basis of actual industrial concentration. It was the basis of the power of the few "coal magnates" who became the most outstanding protagonists of an aggressive imperialism.

Analogous phenomena had appeared in the iron and steel industries. The steel syndicate did not support the weakest firms against the strongest; on the contrary, it continued the process of the absorption of the weak by the strong.

Even before the war, alongside the "horizontal" concentration, the tendency towards "vertical" concentration was becoming more and more marked, and it had led to the creation of grandiose productive organizations—such as those of Krupp and

It was frequently remarked that in the smaller and impoverished Germany of post-war years had arisen industrial organizations much more complex and stronger than those which existed in Germany in 1913, when the country was at the zenith of its commercial, financial, and political power.

**18.** Let us analyse briefly the causes of these characteristic phenomena. Besides the causes which were operating even before the war, it is necessary to take account of the peculiar new conditions created by the war and the Treaty of Versailles.

(*a*) Already before the war the strength of the mutual attraction of coal and iron was manifest. After the war the scarcity of coal, caused by the cessions of territory, by tributes to the Allies, and by the diminished production made the demand for fuel on the part of the iron and steel trades very keen. A struggle began for the purchase of the coal mines. The combination of the mines with the fuel-consuming industries often made possible a more rational utilization of fuel. But yet other firms besides the iron and steel firms sought to acquire control over the coal mines; e.g. there was the participation in the "Rheinische Stahlwerke," acquired by the "dyestuffs group" with the object of securing the option on coal belonging to those steel works in the Rhenish-Westphalian syndicate.

(*b*) As may be seen from the declarations made many times before shareholders' meetings, often the principal motives stimulating agreements between producers, or leading to the fusion of firms, were the possibilities of acquiring raw materials in common and of working them according to a uniform plan, the saving of the greatly increased general expenses, specialization, and at the same time integration of the work of the associated firms, the elimination of intermediaries, and the diminution of the expenses of production made possible by

Thyssen. The "mixed" firm showed itself to be very much superior to the "simple" firm from both economical and technical points of view. The vicissitudes of the struggle between the "pure" mines and the mines with furnaces (Hüttenzechen) in the coal syndicate, and between the "pure" ironworks (reine Walzwerke) and the "mixed" ironworks (gemischte Walzwerke), are well known. The "pure" firms had either to become "mixed" firms or to be absorbed in the "mixed" firms.

During the war industrial concentration made perceptible further progress (Pilotti: "La Concentrazione industriale in Germania," Roma, 1918; a series of articles extracted from *Corriere Economico*), partly under the influence of the new conditions created by the war, i.e. the deficiency of raw materials, of coal, and manual labour, the necessity of reducing transport, various difficulties of production, etc. In some cases amalgamation of firms was imposed by the State.

combining the successive stages of a productive process under one management.

In the brewing industry a stimulus to concentration had been given in the first place, at a time of very low production, by the desire of the large brewers to secure the quota belonging to the small firms. Production had been divided, by authority, between the various breweries, and to each had been assigned a maximum output. But later one of the principal causes of the increasing prevalence of great breweries was that the small firms found it impossible to supply their output on credit to their clients, who had generally fallen into financial difficulties.

(*c*) The scarcity of iron and steel induced numerous firms producing finished articles to ally themselves with iron and steel companies, which assured them a regular supply of semi-finished goods. On the subject, the words of Stinnes in a speech before the Economic Council of the Reich on November 9th, 1922, are worthy of note: "*Vertical* organizations are a product of our time and so also indeed are *horizontal* organizations. When there is neither money nor goods vertical organizations are formed in order to save money and raw material. When there is abundance, as may happen again one day, horizontal organizations will again be established."

On the other hand, at a time, such as was the post-war period in Germany, of continual and sharp changes in market conditions, it was important even for the great iron and steel firms to assure themselves of a regular sale for their own products. Therefore agreements were concluded with firms producing finished goods, or these were compelled to combine with the iron and steel group.

For similar reasons the great iron and steel groups wished to control or to establish the shipyards, which, thanks to the reconstruction of the German mercantile fleet, were among the best purchasers of semi-finished goods.

(*d*) The Treaty of Versailles had given a severe blow to the German iron and steel industry. The iron mines and the huge modern plant of Lorraine were lost. In fact, the treaty forced the liquidation of all property belonging to Germany in Lorraine. The organisms of the great German firms—such as Deutsch-Luxemburg, Gelsenkirchener, Thyssen, Röchling, etc.—were at one blow stripped of their vital parts. The firms of the Luxemburg and the Saar were voluntarily ceded. The dismembered organizations were reconstructed either by the union of the very great firms which were mutually complementary

(Deutsch-Luxemburg and Gelsenkirchener) or by the acquisition of other plant and mines, or by the construction of new plant in the territory remaining to Germany.

On the one hand there was the scarcity of goods and disposable capital, and on the other the necessity to restore German economy, profoundly shaken by the war and by the consequences of the Treaty of Versailles. The great reconstruction works demanded the collaboration of the great firms.

Another example is given by the reconstruction of the mercantile navy. It required much capital. The compensation paid by the Reich was shown to be insufficient because of the depreciation of the mark. Capital was sometimes provided by the iron and steel groups. For example, the Funke iron and steel group secured the majority of the shares of the Kosmos Shipping Company and then forced the amalgamation of this company with the Deutsch-Austral Company. The Funke group was in a position to speed up the reconstruction of the ships of these two companies, not only by granting them financial aid, but also by favouring, in the supply of steel plates and other materials, the shipyards which worked for those companies.

There was also the necessity of using to the utmost and in the most rational manner the existing tonnage and of distributing in an agreed way the compensation paid by the Reich. The conventions between the various companies which were to eliminate competition helped to attain those ends.

(*e*) Industrial concentration was also favoured by certain arrangements of the Rhenish-Westphalian syndicate, which granted to the mixed firms the right to the direct consumption of a certain proportion of the coal produced (Selbstverbrauchrecht). Under the influence of the large firms, the conception of "direct consumption" was continually enlarged. It came to include the consumption of the firms in which the associated mine had some participation. At first an 81 per cent participation at least was necessary, then 50 per cent sufficed, and at last (from 1922 onwards) 35 per cent. In 1924 the coal consumed directly by the firms associated in the syndicate represented 30 million tons, that is a third of the total production of that syndicate. Since the firms using coal, who did not possess their own mines, had to pay the sale price of the syndicate for it, the existence of a margin between the sale price and the cost of production gave the firms who used their own coal a very great advantage. It was, therefore, natural that the possibility of enjoying this privilege was a motive which stimulated industrial concentration. In the years immediately following the war, when coal was scarce, concentration was favoured by the fact that the mixed firms possessed the precious fuel; later it was more than anything else the lower price of coal which put them in a condition to undercut firms without their own mines.

(*f*) In certain cases concentration was compulsory under special laws. This was so for the potash industry, which after the war passed through a grave crisis, mainly because of the heavy fall in exports, as compared with pre-war days. A law of October 1921 prohibited any increase in capacity, the object being to prevent a useless consumption of resources and a prejudicial overproduction. Also the law guaranteed a share in the profits to those firms which had undertaken to stop production voluntarily. By such methods it aimed at consistently concentrating production in the most profitable firms, and at improving, through a more rational production, the competitive position of an industry which, because of the war, had lost its former position of monopoly in the world market.

(*g*) In the end, even financial legislation had an influence which cannot be neglected on the concentration of firms. I allude to the tax on business turnover (Umsatzsteuer) which did not apply to exchanges effected between the firms belonging to a given group. Therefore the independent firms, which had to pay this very heavy tax on all the supplies received from other firms, were in a most disadvantageous position.

(*h*) Even the occupation of the Ruhr, by creating very great difficulties for many of the weaker firms, while the strong ones were able to profit largely from the Government subsidies, favoured concentration. According to testimonies of that period, the occupation of the Ruhr, owing to the economic crisis which it caused, brought annihilation to many small business men who were formerly independent.

## X. THE INFLUENCES OF THE MONETARY INFLATION ON INDUSTRIAL CONCENTRATION

**19.** In the light of the preceding review it cannot be asserted that industrial concentration, which constituted one of the most interesting aspects of German economy in the years which followed the end of the war, was the effect of a single cause: inflation. But it is also certain that the monetary depreciation gave a very strong impetus to the centralization of industry, powerfully favouring the action of other causes working in the same direction. Those favoured by the inflation secured enormous sums of paper marks. The inflation worked to the advantage of the great firms, which could profit more easily from the changeable conditions of the market, adapting sale prices to the monetary depreciation, using bank credit, and directing to their own advantage the economic and financial policy of the State.

As is well known, in Germany the prices of real estate and industrial stocks, if reckoned in gold, remained very low for a long time. Thanks to having exported goods, or in consequence of their forced liquidation or sale of businesses in Lorraine, the Saar and Luxemburg, great firms had secured considerable quantities of foreign exchange, and these, profiting by the high purchasing power of foreign exchange in Germany, bought under favourable conditions industrial companies, packets of shares, land, and buildings.

The sudden depreciations of the mark often created serious embarrassments for the smaller firms. The commercial houses which did not know how to or could not guarantee themselves against the risk of a future fall, by raising prices or by other means, found themselves with a working capital insufficiently replaced by the sale of goods. Often these firms were then bought by big manufacturers, who, wiser or more fortunate, had survived the tempest let loose by the sharp fall of the exchange. As was observed in a financial journal, "in periods of a shortage of money the small or average concerns lost the ability to live on their own means, and they became the easy and inexpensive prey of the large firms."

The depreciation of the mark had enormously increased the nominal value of raw and subsidiary (fuel) materials, rendering it constantly more difficult for some commercial houses to maintain the stocks necessary for the regular working of their businesses. Thanks to their close union with the iron and steel companies and the mines, which assured a regular supply of raw materials and coal, firms producing finished articles could reduce their stocks and thus disinvest a part of their working capital. An example of this was given in the balance sheet of Siemens and Schuckert. At the end of July 1919 the stocks of raw material were worth 46·5 millions of paper marks, and at the end of September 1920 145·1 million. Thanks to the "community of interest" created later with the Stinnes group, in September of 1921 the value of the stocks had been reduced to 106 million of paper marks, in spite of the monetary depreciation which had occurred in the meantime.

From many facts observed during the inflation it is apparent that one of the motives which induced firms to unite themselves in "vertical" groups was the desire to exploit systematically the monetary depreciation. The associated business firms provided each other with raw materials, semi-finished or finished products, and thereupon drew on each other bills which were presented to the Reichsbank or to other banking institutions for discount. Credits in paper marks procured large profits thanks to the depreciation of borrowed money. Later the issue of "emergency money" became a source of conspicuous gains, which, naturally, the great associated industries could put into circulation more easily than the commercial houses of minor importance.*

The concentration of firms was also facilitated by the fact that, during the inflation, very many individual concerns were transformed into joint-stock companies. The principal cause of this transformation was the continual depreciation of the money, which imposed on the firms the necessity of increasing their working capital. Now, the legal form of the joint-stock company made it easier to procure new capital, either by the issue of shares or by the negotiation of loans.

**20.** Whoever examines the various industrial groups which appeared after the end of the war will see that they can be divided into two categories: some are simply aggregates of dissimilar firms, whilst others were established by *systems*, these latter being, it is true, more or less perfect according to the circumstances which allowed some sort of order in the control of the various firms.

The influence of the inflation was mainly evident in the formation of the "aggregates." Financial rather than economic motives led to the creation of these groups and the spirit of speculation, that is the consideration of the gain derived from the transformation into "material" goods of a capital of paper marks, possessed by the speculator or by those prepared to lend.

Sometimes the rearrangement of the firms, that is the transformation of an aggregate into a system, was the consequence of purchases made, in the first place, with a purely speculative object. The financier who found himself in possession of the most heterogeneous businesses as a rule did not think of anything but reselling them at the next favourable occasion; but sometimes, instead, he endeavoured to form a system

* Moeller, "Die Progression in der Geldentwertung," *Schmöller's Jahrbuch*, 1924, vol. i, p. 88.

by completing his possession with other purchases, this time not affecting them from simple motives of a financial character.

Therefore, these motives were sometimes combined with those of an economic character. For example, the increasing interest of the iron and steel industry in ocean shipping was in part determined simply by the fact that the purchase of ships, whose price had been depressed by the crisis of maritime transport, constituted an excellent employment for available capital. But at the same time it was advantageous for the great iron and steel companies, which bought abroad great quantities of iron ore, to be able to effect their transports in their own ships or in those belonging to a company over which they exercised control.

Some characteristic examples of the concentration of firms, effected during the inflation, are quoted in the footnote.*

* In the summer of 1920 Stinnes created the "Rhein-Elbe-Union," which was the union of two of the greatest firms existing in the mining and iron and steel industries: the Gelsenkirchener Bergwerks-Ges. and the Deutsch-Luxemburg. The purchase of the majority of the shares in another great iron and steel firm, "Bochumer Verein," allowed Stinnes to gather even this one into his group. Thanks to the "community of interest" contracted later with Siemens-Schuckert, Stinnes transformed the Rhein-Elbe-Union into the "Siemens-Rheinelbe-Schuckert-Union," the electric iron and steel trust which became the greatest industrial group in Germany.

Stinnes also continually enlarged his own "private" group, that is the group formed from those enterprises which depended directly on him and which for the greater part was based on the "Joint-Stock Company of Hugo Stinnes for maritime navigation and overseas commerce." It was especially in the private Stinnes group that the prevalence of financial motives over those of an economic character was revealed. It was in the formation of this combine, which included most dissimilar firms, that Stinnes was revealed as "the greatest profiteer of the inflation." The Stinnes private group even acquired important participation and firms abroad (see the book, already cited, of Ufermann und Hüglin, *Stinnes und seine Konzerne*; according to these authors, before his death Stinnes had a more or less large share in 1,535 principal firms, with 2,888 plants or secondary concerns).

In the years following the war (1920 and 1921) the Stumm group was reorganized and developed. For some time the Berlin Exchange was under the influence of the purchases which the Stumm group made with the money received as compensation for the loss of their Lorraine businesses and for the cession of a 60-per-cent share of the firms in the Saar. The purchases were not made by chance: they were made with the object of giving an organic structure to the group. Coal and iron mines constituted the basis of it. The ores were dealt with in the great furnaces belonging to the group, which produced various grades of iron and steel. The fundamental activity of the group was the production of semi-finished articles; but they were concerned also with numerous factories which manufactured finished articles; engineering industries, makers of lorries, agricultural machines, and electrical fittings, and with shipyards.

The Klöckner group was also enlarged and reorganized in 1920. Towards the end of December 1920 Klöckner could announce that now the firms under his management were assured a share of 5 million tons from the production of the Rhenish-Westphalian syndicate; that the group was in a position to produce the great quantities of steel

**21.** The concentration made rapid progress, especially in the iron and steel and mining industries. It may be stated that towards the end of the inflation six or seven groups monopolized the production of coal and steel, thus exercising a very great influence on the engineering industry.

According to the data of 1924, a share in the coal syndicate, equal to 18·9 per cent of the total production, belonged to the Stinnes group.* It had now left the other groups a long way behind it. Among these, Krupp and Haniel each had a share nearly equal to 6·9 per cent; Phönix participated to the extent of 5·4 per cent; Hoesch to 5·1 per cent; and Thyssen to 4·6 per cent. Hence these groups among them monopolized about 50 per cent of the production of the syndicate. Nearly 30 per cent belonged to eight other great firms (among which were two great "pure" firms, i.e. Harpener and the fiscal administration); and the rest was divided between twenty-five other small and medium firms which formed part of the syndicate. Hence, compared with 1913, the concentration of the mines was much greater, and a far greater influence was exercised by the great iron and steel groups.

necessary as raw material for associated firms; that already all iron articles, even the most refined (with the exception of tubes), could be manufactured in works dependent on the group. In 1923 the six principal firms of the Klöckner group were amalgamated, creating the new Klöckner-Werke A.G. Company.

Another important group was formed by Otto Wolff. Even the industrial groups existing before the war did not remain inactive. The financial journals of 1920 show the continual enlarging and rearranging of the groups of Krupp, Allg. Elek. Ges., Haniel, etc.

In 1921 the Krupp firm greatly enlarged its coal basis. Thanks to closer relations with certain mining firms the share of Krupp in the production of the Rhenish-Westphalian syndicate was raised from 4·7 to 8·6 million tons. The manufacture of locomotives and railway trucks was increased; a yard for building ships for inland navigation was built at Kiel, and the production of textile machinery, automobile, agricultural machines, etc., was started.

The centre of gravity of A.E.G. was in the electricity industry. This gigantic organism was developed after the war in various directions. On the one hand, A.E.G. endeavoured to enlarge its basis by acquiring a control over firms producing raw materials. On the other, it was forced into the engineering industry (by the agreements with the Linke-Lauchhammer firms) and into a series of other industries producing finished articles.

The internal structure of the groups was very diverse. Some were the result of a true and proper amalgamation of firms. Others, instead, were joined by the more or less close bond of the "community of interest" (Interessengemeinschaft) and were combined for a determinate period of time (for example, for the firms of "Siemens-Rhein-Elbe-Schuckert-Union" it was for eighty years, until September 30th, 2000).

The numerous aggregations of firms which occurred during the inflation have no interest from a scientific point of view. From their very nature, they were continually changing.

* Tross, *Konzerne der Schwerindustrie*, 1924.

Of the shares assigned to the iron and steel firms united in 1924 in the great new raw steel syndicate, the great groups, Stinnes, Thyssen, Krupp, and Phönix, were apportioned an aggregate quota of 6·3 million tons, equal to 47 per cent of the entire output. Four other groups each controlled quotas amounting in all to 25 per cent.

The influence of a few great groups prevailed not only in the mining and iron and steel industries, but also in the electrical, chemical, and potash industries,* in certain important branches of the engineering industry (for example, locomotives), and in the shipbuilding industry.† In other industries either "vertical" or "horizontal" concentration made rapid progress from 1919 to 1923. We may mention the brewing industry (amalgamation of the great breweries of Schultheiss and Patzenhofer); the coal by-products industry (e.g. the trust of Upper Silesia); the cigarette industry; the insurance companies, and the great shops (Karstadt). Karstadt, the proprietor of about forty great shops, applied the principle of vertical concentration, acquiring numerous participations in the cotton industry, in the making of linen and clothes, and in the manufacture of carpets, furs, etc.

## XI. THE SITUATION OF THE PRIVATE CREDIT BANKS DURING THE INFLATION

**22.** On the whole, concentration in banking during the period of the inflation made less rapid progress than was evidenced in other

* At the beginning of 1922 two great groups, "Deutsche Kaliwerke" and "Wintershall," fiercely disputed about the control of the Glückauf-Sonderhausen Company. In March 1922 the disputants came to an agreement and formed a grandiose "trust" to which the Ronnehberg Company also adhered. The trust enjoyed a share of 40·286 per cent in the production of the potash syndicate. The Salzdefurth-Aschersleben-Westeregeln-Leopoldshall group followed, with a quota of 16·973 per cent. Hence, even in the potash industry the syndicate had not been able to assure independence to the medium firms; on the contrary, a process of selection had appeared, thanks to which the less productive firms had been eliminated.

† The great iron and steel groups wished to extend their influence to the shipping companies, and they accordingly nominated their representatives in the administrative councils of numerous companies controlling maritime traffic or ship-building. But on the whole the shipping companies were opposed to the tendency which aimed at adding them to the great industrial groups. The biggest firms preserved their independence. Some minor companies were absorbed by other more powerful ones (e.g. the Hamburg-Amerika Line in 1920 annexed the Deutsche-Levante Line); others were formed into very close "community of interests," equivalent in practice to a complete amalgamation (the most important example was the agreement concluded in 1921 between "Kosmos and the Deutsch Austral"); finally, others agreed to a common control of certain lines or to divide certain services among themselves in a manner which avoided costly competition.

fields of economic activity. Banking concentration was already much advanced before the war. After the war the provincial banks resisted the tendency to centralization at Berlin. We may instance the group of provincial banks whose centre was the "Allg.-Deutsche Credit-Anstalt" of Leipzig. The cases of concentration more worthy of note were: the amalgamation of the Darmstädter Bank with the Nationalbank für Deutschland; the absorption, by the Deutsche Bank, of the Hannoversche Bank, the Braunschweiger Privatbank, and the Privatbank zu Gotha towards the end of 1920, and later of the Württembergische Vereinsbank and the Essener Kreditanstalt. Also worth mentioning was the increasing concentration of mortgage banks.

Further, one of the characteristic phenomena of the inflation was the rise of numerous new banks, owned by private bankers who hitherto had had no experience in this business.

As is well known, before the war the influence of the great banks in German economic life was very great, for they had available their own gigantic capital and milliards of their deposits. The great banks often provided the impulse to great transactions and to industrial concentrations.

But even before the war, an attentive observer of economic phenomena could see the tendency on the part of some large groups (the most important example was given by A.E.G.) to make themselves independent of the banks by creating their own "finance companies."

After the war several large industrial groups, thanks to the profits due mainly to their monopolistic position and to the inflation, became so strong financially that they no longer had any need for banks. Therefore these lost a large part of their influence. On the other hand, because of the continual depreciation of money, the real value of deposits rapidly diminished. The banks ceased to be the safe-deposits in which formerly a great part of the disposable capital of the nation had been collected.

When, in an advanced phase of the inflation, the Reichsbank became the only institution for the distribution of credit, the banks were transformed into simple intermediaries who transmitted to their clients the money received from the note-issuing institution; and since they had to charge more and more for their services, the large groups wished to make themselves independent of the banks, intending to profit directly from the credit of the Reichsbank.

When later, in the last phase of the inflation, even the banking system of payments could no longer function because of the very great rapidity of the monetary depreciation, the importance of the banks declined still more.

The tendency to become independent of the banks was shown, on the part of the great industrial groups, by the foundation of their own banks which executed the financial transactions of the groups and generally all their banking operations. Further, the industrial groups extended their control upon banks previously independent. Thus was evolved a process opposite to that which was known before the war: the influence of the great industries on the banks, the "scaling of the banks." Examples are the participation of Stinnes in the Berliner Handelsgesellschaft and the Barmer Bankverein; and the acquisition of the majority of the shares in the Deutsche Länderbank by the Badische Anilin- und Soda-Fabrik.

The absorption of the banks by the industrial groups made some progress even after the stabilization of the German exchange, when numerous banks found themselves in grave financial difficulties because of the losses suffered during the inflation. The Michael group then acquired control over several banks.

Thus on the whole the banks were weakened by the inflation. They lost a considerable part of their capital and reserves, as was shown after the compilation of the "gold balance sheet." As a result of the diverse influence exercised by the monetary depreciation on the banks and on the great industrial firms their relative positions were profoundly changed. The banks did not succeed in protecting themselves efficaciously against the effects of the monetary depreciation. At the end of the inflation the resources of the great banks, such as Diskonto-Gesellschaft, the Dresdner Bank, and the National- und Darmstädter Bank, were much less than those imposing accumulations of resources which were owned by the electric iron and steel group, by A.E.G., and by the chemical industry groups.

## XII. THE INFLUENCE OF THE INFLATION ON ECONOMIC PRODUCTION IN AN ADVANCED PHASE OF THE DEPRECIATION OF THE MARK

**23.** As we have seen, in 1922 German economy had the appearance of great activity. Minimum unemployment figures, production which in some branches of industry approached pre-war figures (though the total remained below), the prosperity of some classes, the fervour of new initiative, and the creation of great industrial groups—some "economic duchies" according to Rathenau's phrase—which by the power of capital, the multiplicity of manufactures, and the competitive spirit appeared to attest the vigour of German industry.

Not enough importance was attached to the other effects of the depreciation, which affected production adversely. The example of Germany seems interesting to me, because it shows that influences which limited production remained latent at first and were overshadowed by contrary influences, but made themselves felt more and more when the depreciation continued and became more rapid.

These influences were especially noticeable from the second half of 1922. Our next task is to examine them in detail.

## XIII. THE INCREASE OF UNPRODUCTIVE WORK

**24.** Owing to the effect of the monetary depreciation *unproductive work* acquired ever increasing proportions. It appeared in various characteristic forms:

(*a*) *The hypertrophy of commercial organization.*—The number of middlemen increased continually at a time when the buying and selling of goods, thanks to the very rapid increase of prices, created the possibility of quick profits. Besides legitimate commerce which already comprised a very long chain of middlemen, there grew and blossomed in the hothouse of the currency depreciation clandestine commerce, which was devoted to bargaining in all sorts of foodstuffs, useful articles, artistic objects, gold and silver goods, etc.

We can see from the statistics of the joint-stock companies that their increase was most rapid in commerce; the number of joint-stock companies in this branch of economic activity (including the banks) jumped from 933 to 4,226 in the period 1919–25, that is from 10·3 per cent to 29·6 per cent of the total number. The foundation of companies of this nature was made very easy during the period of inflation; the law required only a small capital.* Similar developments appeared in the number of limited liability companies.

(*b*) *The hypertrophy of the banking system.*—For reasons easy to understand, a great number of new small banks grew up in Germany during the inflation. The number of private foreign exchange firms was multiplied. Even the existing banks increased the number of their branches, especially in new localities. They extended their premises

* *Wirtschaft und Statistik*, 1926, p. 321.

or even constructed imposing new palaces, continually employing new people. Here are some figures:*

Table XXV

| | *Establishment of New Banks* | *Numbers employed in the "D" banks*† |
|---|---|---|
| 1914 | 42 | 14,223 |
| 1919 | 49 | 23,339 |
| 1920 | 65 | 30,489 |
| 1921 | 67 | 36,608 |
| 1922 | 92 | 45,430 |
| 1923 | 401 | 59,833 (autumn) |
| 1924 | 74 | 30,266 (end of year) |

It was estimated that the number of persons employed in all the banks jumped from about 100,000 in 1913 to 375,000 in the autumn of 1923.

The increase in banking business was not the consequence of a more intense economic activity. The work was increased because the banks were overloaded with orders for buying and selling shares and foreign exchange, proceeding from the public which, in increasing numbers, took part in speculations on the Bourse. The banks did not help in the production of new wealth; but the same claims to wealth continually passed from hand to hand.

An index of this increase in banking activity is given by the very great increase in the number of current accounts during the inflation. When the money was stabilized, the number of current accounts rapidly diminished, as the following figures (which refer to the three biggest "D Banks") show:

Table XXVI

| *End of year* | *Number of Current accounts* |
|---|---|
| 1913 | 552,599 |
| 1919 | 1,227,934 |
| 1920 | 1,489,497 |
| 1921 | 1,609,572 |
| 1923 | 2,500,000 (estimated figure) |
| 1924 | 646,229 |

(*c*) *The pathological development of speculation.*—On the spread of speculation in goods, securities, and foreign exchange in countries with a depreciated money I need not write many words.

* *Jahrbücher für Nationalökonomie*, 1926, p. 318.

† Deutsche Bank, Diskonto-Gesellschaft, Darmstädter Bank, Dresdner Bank.

(*d*) *The increase of unproductive labour in individual businesses.*—This increase was mainly the consequence of calculations which became longer and longer and were necessary because of the increase of the nominal figures of transactions; the continual conversions of foreign exchange into paper marks or vice versa; the application of very complicated taxes; the computation of pay supplements, of advance payments, and of various deductions. Besides, the numerous controls of an economic and financial character obliged the entrepreneur to divert many employees from productive labour.* General expenses increased, and the economic machine partly worked unproductively. The incessant disputes between employers and representatives of the working class about the increase of wages and salaries caused much loss of time and prevented the managers from thinking of the real interests of the business.

On this point some figures published by the Borsig and Siemens-Schuckert firms are of interest. According to Borsig, the diminution of the productivity of the business, which was evident in 1922 compared with 1913, was not so much due to less efficiency in the work of productive labourers as to the increase of the number of "unproductive" workmen. In 1913 there were 66 workmen of this second category for every 100 productive workmen; in 1922 there were 120.

We may add the analogous conclusions of Siemens-Schuckert. In 1914 for every productive workman 0·537 was employed in the office, and in 1923 0·766, which was an increase of 42·6 per cent in the relative number of employees. The increase was mainly the consequence of the increase in accountancy necessitated by the monetary inflation. Later, in an account of the year 1925, the same source observed that "the inconveniences of the preceding years caused by continual discussions regarding labour conditions—discussions which were provoked by the monetary depreciation and the rise of prices—which had disturbed the managers of industry, had ceased," and therefore "it was possible for the managers to concentrate their attention on technical work and on the administration of the business."

## XIV. THE DECLINE IN THE INTENSITY OF LABOUR

**25.** One very important circumstance which influenced production was the diminution of the intensity of labour, which was evident in

* The Diskonto-Gesellschaft writes in its *Report* for 1921, p. 13, that out of one hundred employees not less than ten were exclusively occupied in work ordered by the financial authorities.

Germany in the advanced phases of the monetary depression. The phenomena had various causes:

(*a*) As will be explained in a later chapter, the inflation provoked a diminution of real wages, in such a manner as to allow some productive energy, which formerly had been used for the production of consumption goods, to be employed in the production of new capital goods. But if the reduction of wages goes beyond a certain limit, or lasts too long, the physical energies of the working classes are affected. The lowering of the standard of living diminished the capacity for work, simply because wages were insufficient to provide the means of recuperation for worn-out human machines.

In another chapter I shall refer to some wage statistics which show that during the monetary depreciation the variability of the worker's income increased considerably.

This had some important psychological consequences. They are less obvious but they probably had great influence on production. The continued depreciation of the currency and the uncertainty of the future, which it caused, produced a depression of working-class spirit, and the will to work declined.

The "dollar rate" was the theme of all the discussions among employees or workers. Their thoughts were concentrated on the problems of meeting their own needs with a money which lost value from hour to hour, and of spending their wages and salaries quickly in order to reduce their losses to a minimum. The productivity of labour suffered seriously from this psychological disturbance. Workers became less careful and materials such as coal and oils were wasted. The labourer's energies were partly used in the dispute for an increase in his nominal wage. Even before the war it had been observed that the intensity of the labour of the workmen was reduced in the periods when they were negotiating with their employers for an increase in wages.

We have, unfortunately, few statistics regarding the average production per workman during the inflation. But these few, and more still the unanimous observations of employers, agree in suggesting that during the last phases of the inflation, which were characterized by a rapid depreciation of the mark, the anxiety of the working classes made the average return per man decrease, and also lowered the standard of what work he did. Moreover, anyone could see in Germany at that period that a state of nervous irritation had taken possession of all classes of society.

For example, the production of coal in the Ruhr district, which in 1913 had amounted to 928 kg. per miner, had decreased to 585 kg. in 1922.*

With regard to the quality of the work, there are the results of an enquiry made by the *Frankfurter Zeitung*,† which constructed an index of the quality of certain products. Suppose this index equal to 1 on April 1st, 1921, then by October 1922 it had decreased to 0·82 and to 0·64 in October 1923. Directly after the monetary stabilization, thanks to the return of calm to the workman's mind, the quality index rose to 0·99 (January 1924). In April of the same year it was 1·24.

### XV. THE SUSPENSION OF THE NATURAL SELECTION OF FIRMS

**26.** The inflation profoundly altered the distribution of social saving. It is true that at first a certain mass of "forced saving" was created. But it cannot be said that these savings became available to the most productive firms and to those entrepreneurs who were most able to employ rationally the capital at their disposal. On the contrary, inflation dispensed its favours blindly, and often the least meritorious enjoyed them. Firms socially less productive could continue to support themselves thanks to the profits derived from the inflation, although in normal conditions they would have been eliminated from the market, so that the productive energies which they employed could be turned to more useful objects.

One of the most characteristic phenomena of the German inflation was the almost complete disappearance of bankruptcies in advanced phases of the monetary depreciation. In 1913 there were, on an average, 815 bankruptcies a month. They had decreased to 13 in August 1923; 9 in September; 15 in October; and 8 in November! This fact was often interpreted as an index of industrial prosperity; rather it was a symptom of the *malaise* of the economic system, since it showed that the inflation had suspended the natural process of the selection of firms. Moreover, the ease with which quick profits could be made induced many rash and astute people to create new firms which were mostly formed on an unsound basis and represented a waste of social energy. As we shall see in another chapter, for the most part these firms were wrecked by the stabilization crisis.

* The Deutsche Bank writes in its *Report* for 1921 (p. 14) that the number of men employed in the Rhenish-Westphalian coal industry had increased by 46 per cent since 1913, while production had fallen by 21·7 per cent.

† *Wirtschaftskurve*, 1926, p. 71.

## XVI. THE DIFFICULTIES OF RATIONAL PRODUCTION

**27.** The inflation which considerably reduced labour costs for the manufacturer weakened the stimulus to seek more effective methods of production. Also the continual and very great fluctuations in the value of money made it very difficult to calculate the costs of production and prices, and therefore also made difficult any rational planning of production. The entrepreneur, instead of concentrating his attention on improving the product and reducing his costs, often became a speculator in goods and foreign exchanges.

It is clear that, during the inflation, capital investments greatly increased; but in many cases it was a question of an extension of plant rather than an intensification of production and a perfecting of technical methods. Many of the great industrial groups which grew up during the inflation did not represent superior forms of economic organization, as was at first erroneously believed. They were only a means, in the hands of able speculators, of profiting by the favourable conditions created by the inflation.

These last considerations lead us to record another influence, of the inflation, contrary to the progress of economical production. The selection of captains of industry came about in an entirely peculiar manner. Success was the lot not of him who increased the productivity of society's efforts, thus contributing to the increase of general welfare, but to him who had the capacity for organizing and directing great speculations on the exchange and for using wisely, with the object of personal gain, the variations of the value of money.

The inflation exercised contradictory influences on the structure of production. On the one hand the exceptional profits of certain industries and the decline of the real rate of interest stimulated the demand for capital goods; but on the other hand the low wages deterred many entrepreneurs from improving their machinery, which remained old and inefficient, compared with that of other countries.

The diminution of the purchasing power of vast numbers of consumers caused in some spheres a retrograde movement in methods of production. A curious example was the reappearance in the streets of Berlin of old and rickety carriages in the place of the taxis which had become too expensive for the public.

## XVII. THE ECONOMIC CRISIS CAUSED BY THE INFLATION IN 1923

**28.** For all the reasons referred to above, some of which will be further studied in the chapter on the effects of the monetary stabilization, that stimulus which the inflation in Germany had given in an initial stage to production was weakened subsequently. In 1923 inflation disorganized all economic life. The fountain it created, that is the "forced saving," was entirely dried up when in an advanced stage the adjustment of wages to the depreciation of the mark was made more and more rapidly. At the same time voluntary saving decreased rapidly. Many classes of society, who formerly had maintained the stream of new capital with their savings, now ceased to save, as is shown by the statistics of the savings and deposit banks. They preferred to spend as soon as they received it, money which after a few days was less valuable.

As statistics regarding the increases of capital of the joint-stock companies show, the resources which the companies could draw from the capital market were reduced to very low figures in 1923. By using the method of issuing "loans at a stable value"* it was still possible to satisfy the more urgent needs of capital on the part of industry; as, for example, for the utilization of hydraulic power and the construction of electricity centres.

**29.** The occupation of the Ruhr and the consequent "Passive Resistance" certainly aggravated the economic crisis which occurred in Germany in the second half of 1923; but they were not the only nor even the principal causes of that crisis. For a certain time the occupation of the Ruhr even gave a stimulus to industries in the non-occupied territory.† But in the course of 1923 the disorganization of the German economy made rapid progress. Because of the continual increase of general expenses, the lowering of the intensity of work and the increase of risks, the cost of production, and with it prices, rose rapidly. The gap between prices in Germany and those in world markets lessened and finally disappeared.

In some branches of industry internal prices tended to surpass those of the outside world. Consequently the foreign demand for German products decreased. Unemployment in Germany increased. Unquestionable indications of this changing situation were already

* These loans were first issued in 1922 by industrial companies, states, and municipalities. The first form assumed by the stable-value loan was that of mortgage titles based on the value of rye. Loans based on the values of coal, potash, etc., followed. Loans in gold or foreign exchange were introduced later (see *Wirtschaft und Statistik* of 1924, No. 3).

† Lansburg, "Die deutsche Krisis," in *Bank*, January 1924. See also the *Report* of Diskonto-Gesellschaft for 1923, p. 10.

manifest after the summer of 1922. For the first time unemployment was increasing in spite of the rapid depreciation of the mark.

**30.** At a time of rapid currency depreciation business houses had to make great efforts to conserve their working capital. The producer protected himself by forcing his customers to pay in foreign money, or amounts in paper marks which were computed at the rate of the day on which the producer could convert them into foreign money. The retail trader at that time tried to protect himself by fixing a basic price in gold marks or dollars which he converted into paper marks at the daily rate. But the practical application of these principles met with great difficulties. For example, on November 1st, 1923, the official dollar rate on the Berlin Exchange was 130 milliards of paper marks. This rate had to be the rate used as a basis for sales which were to be effected in the twenty-four hours following the time of the fixing of that rate. Hence, on the morning of November 2nd, prices in the shops were fixed thus: basic price in gold marks $\times \frac{130}{4 \cdot 2}$ milliards. In the afternoon of the same day the shopkeepers learned with sad surprise that the dollar rate had risen to 320 milliards. The paper money which they had received in the morning had lost 60 per cent of its value! After that the shopkeeper had to convert that paper money into foreign exchange in order to be able to pay the wholesaler, or remit it to him and wait till the wholesaler had credited him with the sum actually received by the conversion. In the meantime the paper money had suffered a further depreciation.

The retail trader had, therefore, to increase his basic price considerably. In fact, prices in October and November 1923 were very high. The stoppage of sales was the consequence. Businesses and great shops were deserted. The personnel was greatly reduced. Moreover, the country customers were absent, because the farmers would not sell their products for a money which depreciated from hour to hour.

The drop in sales resulted in the impossibility of replacing working capital; production ceased, and unemployment increased. On September 1st, 1923, in unoccupied territory there were 249,192 unemployed, supported entirely by the State; on October 15th, 696,922; on November 15th, 1,265,218, and on December 15th, 1,485,014.* To this figure

* The number of unemployed workmen in occupied territory was estimated at two millions.

must be added the great number of those who were working short-time (1,813,169 on November 15th, 1923).

In the end the ever grave menace of an imminent economic crisis induced the German Government to end their delays and to carry through a monetary reform which put an end to the inflation and quickly relieved the very grave economic crisis in which the inflation had culminated.*

* In Austria the economic developments showed stages substantially similar to those which were observed in Germany after 1919. At first, the difficulty of securing supplies of coal and raw materials having been overcome, the inflation gave a stimulus to certain industrial groups. But already towards the end of 1921 and in 1922 the rapid depreciation of the crown set in action influences which limited production, and the "Inflationskonjunktur" ended. The crown was stabilized towards the end of 1922 and the economy of the country had to pass through a stabilization crisis. From the spring of 1923 onwards signs of an improvement were perceptible. (See on this subject, *Geldentwertung und Stabilisierung, etc.*, and the report of Rist and Layton, *Situation économique de l'Auttriche*, League of Nations, 1925.)

## CHAPTER VI

# The Depreciation of the Mark and Germany's Foreign Trade*

### I. DIFFERENCES OF OPINION BETWEEN ECONOMISTS ABOUT THE INFLUENCE OF THE PAPER INFLATION ON THE BALANCE OF TRADE

**1.** The classical school was more concerned with determining the conditions of a given static equilibrium than with studying the period of transition between one static equilibrium and another. On the foreign trade of a country and monetary depreciation the statement of Stuart Mill is characteristic: "The imports and exports are determined by the metallic prices of things, not by the paper prices . . . a depreciation of the currency does not affect the foreign trade of the country: this is carried on precisely as if the currency maintained its value."†

The effects of the currency depreciation on foreign trade subsequently formed an object of investigation by many economists; among those in the first rank Wagner must be mentioned.

**2.** In the opinions of writers there have appeared two diverse conceptions of the relations between paper circulation and the balance of trade.

(*a*) Goschen writes:‡ "It will be easily seen why it is possible to assume that a country in which a depreciated currency and a prohibition to export bullion exist, is likely to be importing more than it is exporting. . . . Sometimes Governments, simply for their own purposes, issue a quantity of paper money: the natural consequence will be over-importation; prices will rise in consequence of the increase in circulation, and accordingly attract commodities from other markets, while the exports, having risen also, will be less easy of sale abroad."

But this conception is contradicted by the fact that in countries experiencing a progressive depreciation of money,

* Memorandum published for the first time in *Giornale degli Economisti*, 1924.

† *Op. cit.*, pp. 634–5. Compare, on this point, the observations of Taussig, *International Trade*, 1927, p. 339.

‡ *The Theory of the Foreign Exchanges*, third edition, pp. 72–3.

internal prices computed in gold were generally *less* than gold prices in the world market.

(*b*) But there is an alternative line of argument. The increase of note-issues influences the foreign exchanges *before* internal prices. Internal gold prices fall below those in the outside world; exports are stimulated and imports are discouraged. Hence in countries with a depreciated circulation forces would constantly be in operation tending to produce an active balance of trade, and not a passive one, as would result in the preceding theoretical scheme. As Fanno writes: "The high cost of foreign exchange in countries with inflation, causes an abnormal contraction of imports and an abnormal expansion of exports."*

## II. RELATIONS BETWEEN INFLATION AND THE BALANCE OF TRADE IN VARIOUS PHASES OF THE DEPRECIATION OF THE MARK

**3.** Germany's case is interesting because it is possible to study the relations between foreign trade and the depreciation of the currency in various phases of that depreciation. Besides, Germany was the first example of a great country with an enormously depreciated currency exporting industrial products on a vast scale.

(*a*) Currency and credit inflation began in Germany directly after the outbreak of the World War. Paper prices in the home market increased in the course of a year by 50 per cent (according to the indices of the Central Office of Statistics) and gold prices remained for a long time above those abroad. The first of the two theoretical schemes under consideration was probably applicable in that first phase (taking into account the restrictions due to the war and the economic policy of the time): the disparity between home and foreign prices stimulated imports† and together with other causes contributed to the disequilibrium of the balance of trade.

(*b*) In a second phase—note-issues continually increasing and a distrust in German money beginning to spread—the foreign exchanges felt the influence of causes tending to a continual depreciation of the mark before internal prices did so.

* Fanno, "Circolazione cartacea e commercio internazionale," *Economia*, 1924, p. 312.

† See facts related in the third chapter of the present volume.

"From the middle of 1918 onwards," writes Dalberg,* "this typical phenomenon appeared: the depreciation of the exchange preceded by some time the depreciation of the internal value of the mark, and therefore the level of internal prices was much lower than that of world prices. Exports were stimulated." This was the period of "exchange dumping" (Valutadumping). The second of the above theories became applicable, but with modifications, as we shall now see.

(*c*) In the last phase the inflation, which proceeded with fantastic rapidity, provoked a series of economic and psychological phenomena, thanks to which the internal price-level increased enough to reach and even to surpass the world price-level. This disparity of prices favoured imports and it was solely owing to the restrictions imposed on these that Germany was not flooded with foreign goods. Export trades, on the other hand, were threatened with a grave crisis, to prevent which German industrialists were obliged in many cases to sell abroad at prices much lower than those prevailing in the home market. It was no longer a question of "exchange dumping"—which had been consistent with export prices higher than those at home—but there was a return to the true, classical "dumping." In the second half of August 1923, especially under the influence of the increase in coal prices which rose perceptibly above those of English coal, the level of internal prices rose rapidly. The blow to the export trades was immediate, as the decrease in the number of "export licences" showed.

At the beginning of December 1923, after the stabilization of the paper money, internal prices decreased once more. But the adjustment to the level of world prices required much time. In the following spring, the results of the Leipzig Fair obviously showed, to judge by the business done, that the prices of many industrial goods were still too high.

Of the three phases referred to, the most important for the economic life of Germany—and even the most interesting from a scientific point of view, for the manifold variety of phenomena to which it gave rise—was the second.

* *Banko-Mark im Aussenhandel*, 1922, p. 13.

## III. INFLUENCES OF THE DEPRECIATION OF THE MARK ON THE VOLUME OF EXPORTS

**4.** In investigating the relations between foreign trade and the exchange rate it is necessary to keep absolutely distinct from each other the influences of the exchange on the physical *volume* of imports and exports and those it exercised on the *value*.

With regard to volume, the most obvious symptom of these influences was the *continuous instability of imports and exports*, especially of the latter.

From 1919 onwards the foreign trade of Germany did not develop in a uniform manner, but irregularly. Periods of relatively rapid increase were followed by periods of stagnation or by a fall in exports.

This had, of course, been true of pre-war days. Foreign trade varied with the trade cycles, which subjected many aspects of economic life to periodic fluctuations. But the period was then relatively long; a complete cycle generally lasting from seven to nine years. Germany's post-war foreign trade, on the other hand, showed a rapid alternation of phases of expansion and of depression; and these sometimes lasted no longer than a few months. Of this phenomenon trade statistics give an imperfect picture only; a thorough investigation would require statistics of orders, or, at least, of licences issued by the Foreign Trade Control Offices. The actual export and import of goods in many cases takes place in a month later than that of the order; moreover, the interval is very variable and therefore the statistics may underestimate the variations in orders. To that must be added the inaccuracy, often inevitable, of official statistics; for example, exports effected in a certain month are attributed to a later month.

After the outbreak of the war the publication of German trade statistics stopped. They were only renewed in 1920. For 1919 there is some data (communicated to the financial conference at Brussels in 1920). About the quantities and values of imports and exports no data exist for the first four months of 1921.

**5.** In Diagram XIII the unbroken line represents the coefficient of the divergence between the purchasing power of the mark in terms of imported goods and its purchasing power in terms of goods made in Germany;* the broken line indicates the quantities exported. The

* I.e. the relation between the index number of imported goods and that of home-produced goods, to the end of July 1923; the relation between the index numbers of American prices and German prices in gold, for the following period (see also Diagram X).

DIAGRAM XIII.—A. Coefficients of divergency between the internal and the external value of the mark
B. Exports

general impression given by this diagram is that of sufficiently obvious correlation between the *fluctuations* of the quantities exported and those of the coefficient of divergence till the middle of 1922. After that the contact between the two curves is broken. In the second half of 1922 the third phase, referred to above, began.

In the last months of 1919, after Germany had with difficulty reopened trade relations with other countries, exports were suddenly increased in quantity, thanks to the sharp depreciation of the mark, which caused an increase in the divergence between the internal and external value. From 3·2 million quintals in January 1919, exports jumped to 12·0 millions in August, and to 27·6 in December. That period was described by Germans as the "general liquidation" of Germany, because every kind of product was exported. Germany became in those months—as one may read in a Deutsche Bank report* —the great "fair" for the purchasers of every country. It is known that the German Government had to intervene, organizing a control over exports.

In March 1920 the mark rose and the divergence between its internal value and its external value diminished. A severe business crisis was the result; a crisis which lasted throughout the summer, until in the winter the renewed slow depreciation of the mark gave a new impetus to exports, which slowly revived during 1921.

In the autumn of 1921, when the depreciation of the mark developed into a sudden collapse, a fresh spurt of activity was apparent in the export trade. The quantities exported rose from 11·4 million quintals in May to 19·7 in October 1921. According to the commercial journals of October and November 1921, foreign demand for German goods was so intense that many industrial concerns announced that goods ordered could not be delivered for several months.

The relative stabilization of the mark in the first months of 1922, accompanied by a rise in home prices, which tended to adjust themselves to the level of world prices, aroused misgivings among German exporters. The trade journals of that period agree in showing that the fall of the dollar rate occurring after December 1st, 1921, caused a slackening in orders from abroad—the margin between home and foreign prices being lessened—and even in the home market purchasers seemed less eager to buy. This was a fresh illustration of the disadvantageous effects of a sudden improvement of the mark on German industry. The quantities exported fell to 17·5 million quintals in

* *Report* for 1920, p. 14.

February 1922, but on the whole they were maintained at a relatively high level through the first half of 1922. A further cause of the diminution in total exports in the second half of 1922 was the decrease in exports of coal following the loss of Upper Silesia.

The sharp fall in the exports curve at the beginning of 1923 was a result of the occupation of the Ruhr. For the remainder of 1923 the volume of exports was, on the whole, unaffected by the very great depreciation of the mark.

Hence, from the Armistice onwards, the German export trade was continually in an unstable condition owing to the frequent fluctuations of the mark. A paradoxical situation arose in which an improvement in the mark was feared as a catastrophe while the hope of renewed expansion appeared to depend on a continual depreciation of German money.

## IV. INFLUENCES OF THE DEPRECIATION OF THE MARK ON THE VOLUME OF IMPORTS

**6.** It is less easy to gather from statistics the influence of the fluctuations of the mark on the quantities imported. The following are reasons for this.

(*a*) Imports were dominated by Germany's urgent need of purchasing abroad foodstuffs for her population and raw materials for industries, stocks of which had been completely exhausted during the war. For this reason imports increased, even in periods of rapid depreciation of the mark, as in 1919 (1·7 million quintals imported in January, 10·2 millions in July, 8·2 in December); or in 1921 (12·9 millions in May, 21·7 millions in October); or in 1922 (19·2 millions in January, 29·8 in July, 32·7 in October).

(*b*) The continuous issues of paper money—which for some years foreigners accepted willingly—gave German individuals and the Government new purchasing power which could be employed for the purchase of goods abroad. The disequilibrium in the balance of trade was thus a consequence of the inflation, not because the inflation had raised the level of internal prices above the level of prices in the outside world (indeed the contrary was the case), but because the inflation made possible the acquisition of foreign raw materials and foodstuffs to the value of several milliards of gold marks.

(*c*) The reaction on imports of a fall in the foreign exchange value of the currency can be immediate and quite appreciable in those countries in which there is little or no connection between exports and imports. For example, in Russia during the depreciation of the rouble, a case studied by Wagner, exports were agricultural products and raw materials and imports were manufactured goods. In these conditions a fall in the exchange rate immediately placed an obstacle in the way of imports, while giving an immediate stimulus to exports. But the case of Germany is different; and the traditional picture in economic science, which was modelled on the experiences of agricultural countries with depreciated currencies, could only be applied to the German case with some modification. German industry works largely with foreign raw materials. If, in order to profit by the depreciation of the mark, it wanted to increase its own exports, it had first to import raw materials, except to the extent that the increase in exports corresponded with a decline in internal consumption. Hence the phenomenon, at first sight paradoxical, which was constantly observed in Germany; the first effect of a depreciation of the mark was an increase in orders placed abroad, not only because purchases were being anticipated, but also because an increase in the activity of German industry was foreseen. During 1919, writes the Deutsche Bank, even in the periods of most serious depreciation of the mark, merchants were buying foreign goods on an enormous scale, paying any price—thus intensifying the fall in the exchange.* Contrariwise, the opposite phenomenon appeared at times when the exchange rate improved. When, after the steep decline of the autumn of 1921, the mark rose, German business men suspended their purchases of raw materials, fearing the fall in the value of these goods which would immediately follow a further rise of the mark. Moreover, German industry had habituated itself to thinking of the depreciation of the mark as being the essential condition of its being able to continue to produce.

(*d*) The purchase of foreign goods was one of the means of investing a money whose value was threatened with rapid diminution. Business men who had the disposal of some paper

* *Report* for 1919, p. 14.

marks built up their stocks of foreign goods even if, for the time being, they did not need them for their business. This phenomenon was maintained also in the report of Vissering, Dubois and Kamenka (November 8th, 1922) on the stabilization of the mark. It was shown in that report that there was an abnormal development in imports due to distrust in the paper mark which induced industrialists to invest available funds in foreign goods. It was stated that the stabilization of the exchange, causing a renewal of faith in the national money, would remove this stimulus to imports.

## V. INFLUENCES OF THE DEPRECIATION OF THE MARK ON THE COMPOSITION OF THE EXPORT AND IMPORT TOTALS

**7.** In order to investigate more fully the influence of the depreciation of the mark on the quantities of goods exported, it is necessary to distinguish *stocks already existing* at the time of a sudden depreciation of the exchange from *goods which were not yet produced.*

The first influence of a sudden increase in the divergence between the internal and external value of the mark showed itself—especially on the first occasions when the reaction of internal prices was slow and incomplete—in an increased demand by foreigners for goods actually in the shops and warehouses of merchants and producers. The Germans sold foreigners goods of any description, goods entirely produced at home or partly made with foreign raw materials or even of genuine foreign origin, because the selling price assured them what seemed to be a suitable profit. Some even sold the machinery of their own works!

**8.** As regards the goods produced *during the existence of a divergence between internal and external values of the mark*, it is necessary to distinguish according to whether (*a*) the proportion of the total cost of the product spent on raw materials is high, or (*b*) it is low and the greater part is spent on wages.

The stimulus given to exports by the depreciation of the exchange is weaker as the proportion of raw materials employed in the production of a given article is higher. For obvious reasons that was true, before all, in the case where the raw materials were imported from abroad. But in Germany even the prices of important raw materials produced at home—after being for some time below world prices—showed in an advanced stage of the inflation a tendency to increase rapidly in periods of the depreciation of the mark, and to rise to the level of foreign prices.

On the other hand, German wages always remained much below those paid in the great industrial countries. Careful investigations made in 1922 by the United States Tariff Commission led to the conclusion that "German manufacturers had a great advantage in world trade because of the prevailing low wages" (about 10 cents an hour in Germany as against 50 to 75 in the United States).*

**9.** As a result of these facts, the depreciation of the mark tended to provoke in German foreign trade certain characteristic changes when compared with the period preceding the World War. It became more and more desirable for German industry to export the finished article rather than semi-finished, as the difference between the cost of production and the world price for the former was greater. Indeed, statistics show that the proportion of manufactured products in the total of German exports continually increased (in 1913, 63·3 per cent of the total value; 78 per cent in 1923 on the price basis of 1913). In spite of the fact that in 1922 Germany exported, on the whole, much less than formerly, the export of some manufactured articles had not undergone a great fall, or had even increased.† The export of semi-finished articles had fallen very much (for example, iron goods: 5,700 thousands of quintals exported in an average month in 1913; 2,551 in 1922).‡

Contrary phenomena were apparent in the import figures. Imports

* *Depreciated Exchange and International Trade*, Washington, 1922, p. 65. The advantage of the German manufacturer was not equal to the whole difference between the money wages, for account has to be taken of the difference between the productivity of labour in the two countries.

† In 1922 the volume of goods exported by Germany (assessing their value by 1913 prices) was little more than 60 per cent of the 1913 exports; but taking account of the single class, *manufactured products*, in 1922 a volume of exports equal to 75 per cent of the 1913 volume was reached. The following figures show the average monthly exports (in thousands of quintals) of certain goods.

| | 1913 | 1922 |
|---|---|---|
| Machines .. .. | 698·8 | 577·1 |
| Paper .. .. .. | 452·2 | 412·3 |
| Rubber goods .. .. | 16·4 | 14·1 |
| Leather .. .. .. | 45·4 | 42·9 |
| Glass .. .. .. | 204·2 | 119·3 |

‡ The fall was also due to the cession of Lorraine.

of manufactured goods were reduced and the proportion of raw materials imported increased.*

In 1913 raw and semi-finished materials were 57·8 per cent of the total imports; in 1922, according to 1913 prices, 64·5 per cent. If the category of finished products shows a small increase in 1922 (15·1 per cent) compared with 1913 (13·8 per cent), this was due to the fact that Germany, owing to the cession of Alsace-Lorraine, imported considerable quantities of finished iron products and textile goods. In the machine class, imports dropped from 85·9 thousands of quintals in 1913 to 17·6 in 1922; leather goods dropped from 12·5 to 7·1, and rubber goods from 3·5 to 0·3, etc. Naturally, legal restrictions of various kinds contributed to the fall in imports. But even without them imports of manufactured goods would have been reduced by the monetary causes mentioned above, which gave a very great advantage to German industries producing finished goods in competition with foreign industries.†

### VI. THE SUPPOSED "INVASION" BY GERMAN GOODS

**10.** The statistics show us that on the whole the rise in exports was not so conspicuous as *a priori* would have been anticipated, given the

* *Values Calculated to the Base of Price Units of* 1913

*Total Foreign Trade in Millions of Gold Marks*

| | *Imports* | | *Exports* | |
|---|---|---|---|---|
| 1913 | 10,769·7 | 100·0 | 10,097·2 | 100·0 |
| 1922 | 6,302·8 | 100·0 | 6,181·5 | 100·0 |
| | | *Finished Products* | | |
| 1913 | 1,384·3 | 13·8 | 6,396·3 | 63·3 |
| 1922 | 953·3 | 15·1 | 4,463·6 | 78·7 |
| | | *Raw Materials* | | |
| 1913 | 4,990·9 | 46·3 | 1,518·1 | 15·0 |
| 1922 | 2,960·4 | 47·0 | 407·4 | 6·5 |
| | | *Semi-finished Materials* | | |
| 1913 | 1,233·5 | 11·5 | 1,139·5 | 11·2 |
| 1922 | 1,005·0 | 17·5 | 658·5 | 10·6 |
| | | *Foodstuffs and Cattle* | | |
| 1913 | 3,061·0 | 28·4 | 1,043·3 | 10·4 |
| 1922 | 1,384·1 | 20·4 | 252·0 | 4·1 |

† Not only were the imports of foreign finished goods decreased but Germany *exported* goods which formerly had usually been imported. E.g. before the war Holland supplied Germany with large quantities of cigars, while Germany exported to Holland only very small quantities. In 1920 the situation was reversed. Other examples are watches, formerly imported from Switzerland, watch glasses and watchmakers' instruments (Schultze, *Not und Verschwendung*, 1924, p. 525).

continuous depreciation of the German exchange rate. During the inflation exports from Germany always remained much below those of 1913.* In 1920 Germany sold abroad a quantity of goods equivalent, at 1913 prices, to 3·7 milliard gold marks. In the eight months from May to December 1921 (figures for the first four months have not been published) exports reached, at 1913 prices, 3 milliards in round figures, that is, probably 4½ milliards for the whole of 1921. Thus the increase was not very conspicuous compared with the earlier year, despite the fact that the dollar rate had passed from 80 marks on the average, in May 1921, to 300 marks at the beginning of November of the same year. In 1922 exports (always at 1913 prices) were a little more than 6 milliard gold marks.

**11.** The fact is important because it contradicts the statements which were made and often repeated about the "invasion" by German goods of foreign markets. These statements aroused the suspicion that German statistics were seriously inaccurate and the suspicion was strengthened by the contrast between the relatively small export figures and the activity of German industry. Now an examination, undertaken by the present writer, of the trade statistics published by the principal countries importing German goods, has confirmed that:

(*a*) In the years following the World War the quantities of articles of German origin were often far less than the quantities imported in 1913. The diminution is particularly striking in iron goods, chemical products, agricultural products, and textile goods. The diminution was generally less marked in engineering products. Only imports of certain secondary goods, such as toys, musical instruments, wooden articles, and a few others, sometimes were above those of 1913.

* According to the calculations of the Statistical Bureau of the Reich, the weighted index numbers of the quantities imported and exported are as follows:

| | *Imports* | *Exports* |
|---|---|---|
| 1913 | 100 | 100 |
| 1920 | 35 | 36 |
| 1921 | 51 | 44 |
| 1922 | 57 | 61 |
| 1923 | 43 | 52 |

The 1913 figures are for the 1913 territory. These figures have been calculated by applying the prices of 1913 to the quantities imported and exported, for every article.

(*b*) Imports of German origin generally bore a *smaller* proportion to the total of imported goods than they had done in 1913.*

It is undeniable that the depreciation of the mark was a means of commercial penetration by Germany, who wished to recover her position in international markets. It even gave a great impulse to the mercantile marine, thanks to the profits of ships which carried goods for foreigners. But trade statistics show that there was no "invasion" by German goods of foreign markets after the war.

The disturbance of international trade, which doubtless was at times a serious phenomenon, however exaggerated by those interested, was due, not so much to the quantity of German goods, as to their low prices and to the continual oscillations of the mark exchange which made difficult any forecasts regarding the possibility of German competition.

## VII. CAUSES WHICH LIMITED THE EXPANSION OF GERMAN EXPORTS DURING THE DEPRECIATION OF THE MARK

**12.** German exports were bound to suffer from the influence of some causes which tended to depress them:

(*a*) Germany lost Lorraine, which had contributed largely to the exports of iron products, Alsace which was an important centre of the textile industry, Posnania and other regions of the East where the sugar industry had been situated. Besides, the peace treaty obliged Germany to supply coal and other products which necessarily lessened the quantity available for export. It should be observed that reparations

* In the official memorandum, *Matériel pour servir à l'étude de la situation monétaire et financière de l'Allemagne* (Berlin, January 1924), the following figures appear:

*Percentage of Trade with Germany to the Total Foreign Trade of the Following Countries*

| | Imports | | Exports | |
|---|---|---|---|---|
| | 1913 | 1922 | 1913 | 1922 |
| Belgium .. .. .. | 15·7 | 13·3 | 25·3 | 14·0 |
| France .. .. .. | 12·8 | 5·4 | 12·6 | 8·5 |
| Italy .. .. .. | 16·8 | 8·0 | 13·7 | 10·4 |
| Great Britain .. .. | 10·5 | 2·6 | 9·5 | 6·0 |
| U.S.A. .. .. .. | 10·3 | 3·8 | 14·2 | 8·2 |

These figures are open to the objection that after the war German foreign trade was diverted from ex-enemy countries towards ex-neutral countries. But the statistics even of these latter countries show that, in general, except for Holland, imports of German goods were below the 1913 levels. In 1913 Germany's share in the total foreign trade of the thirteen principal countries (including Germany) was 18·2 per cent, and in 1923 it was 9·3 per cent (*Wirtschaft und Statistik*, 1924, p. 103).

in kind are not included in the official statistics of foreign trade, published in the inflation period. Also, during the invasion of the Ruhr the foreign trade of the occupied territory was no longer included, practically speaking, in the official figures compiled by the Bureau of the Reich.

(*b*) In 1922, and still more in 1921, German industrial production was appreciably lower than that of 1913 (in spite of symptoms of an intense and often feverish activity).*

(*c*) For a number of causes, other than monetary ones and legal restrictions, imports remained, after the end of the war, below those of 1913. For example, before the war Germany received from her foreign investments an income of a milliard or a milliard and a half marks which compensated for an equivalent value of imported goods. Those foreign investments being lost, Germany had to restrict her imports. In part the consumption of articles which were formerly imported, diminished; and in part these goods were replaced by goods of home production (which were frequently of a lower quality). The amount of production available for export was therefore lessened. Agricultural products are an example of this. In 1913 Germany imported, as a monthly average, 22,179 thousand quintals of agricultural products; in 1922 only 9,016. Corresponding with this fall was a similar drop in exports from 5,552 thousand quintals to 1,368. The same may be said of a variety of industrial goods, or even of raw materials.

(*d*) Exports were subject to limits of various kinds and to control exercised by the "Aussenhandelstellen" (Foreign Trade Bureau).† But it is uncertain to what point these controls were efficacious. It seems that able merchants had no difficulty in eluding them. It is said, besides, that the "Aussenhandelstellen" were none other than the instruments of influential industrial groups, and that by fixing minimum prices for export goods too high, they sought to

* See Chapter v of this volume.

† Between the autumn of 1919 and the spring of 1920 a new system of export control, which was exercised by the so-called "Aussenhandelstellen," was elaborated to prevent merchants and industrialists from selling to foreigners at extremely low prices. Minimum selling prices were fixed. See a description and justification of this policy in Trendelenburg (Commissioner for Import Licences), *Weltwirtschaftskrise und Aussenhandel*, 1921.

eliminate the competition in the foreign market of firms not belonging to the group, those groups selling at prices which were lower than official prices.

(*e*) Exports of certain goods could not rise rapidly because of the obstacles which impeded an increase of production, i.e. the lack of coal (especially of the better qualities) and, at certain times, transport deficiences and the difficulty in importing raw materials.

(*f*) Furthermore, the urgent necessity of providing for the needs of the home market made the proportion of goods available for export much smaller, preventing this proportion from increasing rapidly with the depreciation of the mark. Germany had come out of the war having lost almost her entire merchant navy; with a network of railways worn out by four years of very hard wear; with a very small number of locomotives, because 5,000 had been ceded to the Allies and most of the remainder were in need of repairs; with an insufficient number of trucks*—hence in 1919 a catastrophe threatened the collapse of the entire German system of transport—and with industrial plant and machinery which must be repaired or replaced.

### VIII. INFLUENCES OF THE DEPRECIATION OF THE MARK ON INVISIBLE EXPORTS

**13.** However, the depreciation of the mark was one of the causes which allowed Germany to maintain her exports at a modest figure at a time of economic depression in world trade, in 1920 and 1921. Perhaps, if the depreciation had not existed, that figure would have been even lower.

Also, official statistics do not include all the goods exported from Germany. An unknown but probably appreciable part escaped official recording. This part included goods smuggled out of the country or exported under false declarations (smuggling was stimulated by the legal limitations imposed on exports); articles bought by the armies of occupation; the so-called "small trade of the frontier," which at certain times of rapid depreciation of the mark was anything but insignificant (e.g. purchases by the Swiss, Danes, and Dutch).

* See p. 196.

**14.** Finally, the depreciation of the mark exercised an appreciable influence on two other kinds of exports, to which we allude briefly.

(*a*) *Services for foreigners:* For example, for a long time German railway charges for the transport of goods did not increase in proportion to the depreciation of the mark. Therefore trade routes were diverted across Germany, whose through traffic increased. The expenses of unloading, commissions of various kinds, etc., at Bremen and Hamburg were lower than in other ports, and that caused foreign goods to be brought continually to these ports; for example, goods directed to Czechoslovakia passed through Hamburg, and many goods which formerly had been sent to the ports of Rotterdam or Antwerp were now sent across Germany via Bremen.

The foreign demand for the services of the German mercantile marine was also increased. It is for this reason that from 1920 to 1922 the mercantile marine found itself in favourable circumstances while a heavy depression was experienced by the merchant navies of other countries. Also foreign merchants sent their ships to German docks for repairs because, owing to the depreciation of the mark, wages were much lower in Germany than elsewhere.

An important part of the "invisible exports" consisted of goods consumed by foreigners during their residence in Germany and their payments for the use of resources (hotels, means of transport, etc.) put at their disposal and for personal service.

From German statistics a correlation between the oscillations of German prices (in gold) and the movements of visitors may be clearly seen. The statistics of the State of Hamburg are typical on this point:

| *Of every* 100 *visitors in* | *were foreigners* |
|---|---|
| 1919 | 3·7 |
| 1920 | 12·3 |
| 1921 | 21·1 |
| 1922 | 29·5 |
| 1923 | 20·7 |
| 1924 | 12·0 |

The relative number of foreigners increased continually during the inflation and reached its maximum in 1922; later, following the rise of German gold prices, the influx of foreigners lessened considerably.*

(*b*) *Export of part of national property:* The influence exercised by the depreciation of the mark on the purchases made by foreigners, of industrial or bank shares, houses, and, in a lesser degree, of land, was manifest. The Statistical Bureau of the Reich calculated in 1923 that a tenth of the total value of the share capital of German businesses was owned by foreign capitalists. Kuczinski's statistics show that purchases of houses by foreigners varied in close relationship with the fluctuations of the mark.† At pre-war prices the total value of houses sold to foreigners was very considerable: it amounted to many milliards of gold marks. According to information collected in 1927 by a Commission of Enquiry into the economic conditions of Germany, in Berlin during the inflation about 25,000 houses were bought for foreigners. At 1927 prices the total value of those houses was estimated at 2 milliard marks.

## IX. RELATIONS BETWEEN EXPORTS AND PRODUCTION DURING THE MONETARY DEPRECIATION

**15.** The *relations between exports and production* deserve to be considered in greater detail. Three principal cases may be considered:

(*a*) The increase of exports of a given article, which is the consequence of the divergence between the internal and external values of the national money, is not followed by an increase in the production of that article. The rise in exports signified in this case a corresponding fall in the quantity formerly consumed at home.

(*b*) The possibility of increasing the exports of a given article provoked an increase in the production of it, but at the expense of other articles, the export of which is less attractive.

* *Hamburger Statistische Monatsberichte*, July 1st, 1926.

† See *Vierteljahreshefte deutscher Städte*, 1921, fasc. 1, p. 34; also Moulton and McGuire, *Germany's Capacity to Pay*, 1923, p. 91.

On the whole, the production of the country is not increased; only the *direction* of economic activity is changed.

(*c*) The rise in exports is accompanied by an increase in the total production of the country with a depreciated currency.

The first case appears when a divergence between the internal and external values of money occurs suddenly and after a short time stops. The influence of that divergence is shown only in the sale of goods *already* in the warehouses; given the brief duration of the phenomenon, production in general does not feel it.

The second and third cases are seen when the divergence between the internal and external values of the money lasts for some time. But in a country where plant is already fully occupied, where unemployment does not exist, and where available resources are scarce, the effects on total production cannot be very considerable. If the divergence continues, a displacement of production is slowly produced: capital and labour move towards the production of those goods for which the divergence is most conspicuous (case (*b*)).

On the other hand, in a country where only a part of the machinery is occupied and where there is a considerable number of unemployed, a depreciation of the exchange, by stimulating foreign demand, can really provoke an increase in the total production. Let us suppose, for example, that at a given moment, in the world market, a machine costs £50 sterling, equivalent to fifty thousand marks at the rate of a thousand paper marks per pound sterling. Suppose that this figure represents within a little also the price at which German industrialists can supply their machines. Suddenly there is a depreciation of the German exchange and the pound sterling is worth 1,100 marks. If internal prices and wages are not increased in proportion the industrialist could offer his machines, while making a profit, at a lower price than £50 sterling; so he could overcome foreign competition and extend his sales, using his own plant more and increasing the number of his employees. The depreciation of the mark by such means makes profitable an increase in production above its former level. And doubtless that was true of Germany. For some time the fall of the external value of the mark below its internal value, stimulating foreign demand, gave ample occupation to industry and contributed to a decrease in unemployment.*

* See the facts referred to in Chapter v of this work.

## X. ERRORS IN GERMAN STATISTICS OF THE AGGREGATE VALUE OF EXPORTS

**16.** Before analysing the connections between the depreciation of the currency and the prices of exported goods we must deal briefly with a preliminary question. Are the German statistics reliable so far as the *values* of the goods exported are concerned?

The values were calculated on the basis of the declarations furnished by the exporters, which were examined and eventually corrected by the Statistical Bureau. In the statistical bulletins prices were stated in the money which had been agreed to in the contract of sale: that is in paper marks or in foreign money. Declarations relative to sales effected in foreign money were retained as worthy of attention. It is necessary to state that in Germany there was a system of detailed control over exports until September 1923. Numerous "Aussenhandelstellen," whose business it was to issue export licences, fixed with extreme detail the "minimum prices" of exports. It was then easy for the control to see that the exporter, in the statistical declaration paper, had stated a price at least equal to the minimum fixed by the Control Office, which was reported in the "export licence."

Declarations stating prices in paper marks still represented at the end of 1922 more than 50 per cent of the total number (although in reality about 90 per cent of sales abroad were now made in foreign money). These statements in paper marks were the source of very serious errors in the German trade statistics, either because of the negligence of exporters or for the two reasons following:

(*a*) Owing to delays due to various causes not all the bulletins relating to the exports of a given month can be utilized for the compilation of statistics referring to that month. A part of the exports effected in a month is, therefore, attributed by official statistics to the following months. At a time of a stable exchange no inconvenience is derived from this inaccuracy. But at a time of the depreciation of the mark the error could be very serious. Let us suppose that some exports effected in October 1921 for 1,000 million paper marks have been registered in November. In October those exports were worth about 28 million gold marks; in November scarcely 16 million.

The Statistical Bureau of the Reich eliminated this cause of error from the beginning of February 1923. According to the correction, the value of exports increased by 20 per cent as compared with the uncorrected figure.

(*b*) A varying interval of time—sometimes weeks, sometimes even months—generally passed between the time of the order given by a foreign customer and the time when the article crossed the German frontier. For example, an article had been ordered in September 1921: the total value agreed upon was 10,000 paper marks=400 gold marks. It was exported in the following November: its price was reduced to 160 gold marks. Now, if the German exporter had actually received no more than 10,000 paper marks in November the statistics are correct. But they become inaccurate if the exporter had, in reality, sold for foreign money, or if payment had been made in advance at the time the order was given, or if he had obtained from his customer a surcharge on the original price. The existence of this surcharge would not be declared in order that a surcharge on the exportation tax and the furnishing of a greater quantity of foreign bills to the Reich should be avoided.

**17.** According to official statistics, German exports in 1922 were worth four milliard gold marks. If the goods had been sold at 1913 prices the value of exports would have surpassed six milliards. It cannot be admitted that in 1922 Germany was selling at prices equal to scarcely two-thirds of the 1913 prices. The official statistics certainly exaggerated the depression of German prices.

The Statistical Bureau of the Reich recognized the justice of the criticism which had been made against the trade statistics in Germany itself. An enquiry made towards the end of 1922 among forty-four firms which had declared prices in paper marks showed, in the first place, that only four of them had actually sold in paper marks; in the second place, that the conversion of paper marks into gold marks on the basis of the rate of exchange existing at the moment of the declaration, made the gold prices equal to scarcely 60 per cent of those actually paid to the firms. Other cases cited by the Statistical Bureau show that the conversion of paper marks resulted in gold prices equalling scarcely a tenth of the world price!

For these reasons the Statistical Bureau ceased to reproduce, in its Annual Reports, figures which had been given for exports and imports in the preceding months' publications. Instead of those figures the Bureau preferred to publish some hypothetical figures, which indicated the value of exports and imports, supposing the prices of 1920, 1921, and 1922 equal to those of 1913. But for 1923 the Statistical Bureau endeavoured to give exact values both for imports and exports. The values of exports were calculated on the basis of statements made by exporters for sales effected in foreign currencies, sales which now represented the majority of the exports. Statements regarding sales in paper marks were neglected. The Bureau arrived at the conclusion that prices obtained for exports in 1923 were, on an average, 15 per cent higher than those of 1913.

## XI. THE INFLUENCE OF THE DEPRECIATION OF THE MARK ON PRICES OF EXPORTED GOODS

**18.** First it is necessary to take account of the influence of the depreciation of the exchange on the value of exports already effected but not paid for. This case, which was considered by Goschen,* was very important for Germany at certain times. In the eight months from May to December 1921 the sales effected at prices fixed in paper marks, according to official returns, represented 75 per cent of the total value of the exports. When there was a sudden fall in the German exchange in the autumn of 1921 many exporters, who had sold goods whose prices were fixed in paper marks, suffered heavy losses. Naturally, German exporters, taught by the experience of the autumn of 1921, hastened later to remedy their situation.

The means of protection were of various kinds. Above all, if the exporter often suffered a loss because he received a sum of paper marks having a lower value than that at the time of selling, he had, on the other hand, been free to choose his time for paying his debts in a depreciated currency, an advantage which compensated for the loss. The exporter might have bought, on credit, goods from an industrialist at a fixed price. Or he might have bought the goods with money borrowed from a bank.†

Also exporters purchased foreign bills to secure themselves against eventual losses caused by the depreciation of the mark. Let us suppose that in October an exporter had sold a certain quantity of goods, fixing the price in paper marks, and that the sum was payable in the following November. At the time of making the contract the exporter bought

* *Op. cit.*, p. 151.

† See footnote on p. 78.

foreign exchange corresponding in value to the sum of marks he was to receive. In November, if in the meantime the mark had depreciated, he lost on the sale of the goods, but gained a similar sum by reselling his foreign exchange.

The enormous fluctuations of the German exchange raised insurmountable technical difficulties to the organization of a forward market in foreign exchange. But hedging operations were, at certain times, frequent enough.

Often exporters, seeking to protect themselves from risks due to the depreciation of the mark, sought to avoid them by inducing the purchaser to advance the greatest part possible of the sum due.

Industrialists and merchants began to abandon the method of fixing sale prices on the basis of the cost of production. They accustomed themselves to including in the price a certain supplement which represented the premium for the risk of the depreciation of the paper mark between the time of the sale and the time of payment. Or they had recourse to the system of variable sale prices. Towards the end of 1921, in spite of the fact that the mark had depreciated rapidly in October and November, the method of fixed prices was still widespread. But it was already obvious that the principle of fixed prices could no longer be maintained. At the beginning of 1922 industry generally adopted the system of the "sliding scale"; a system which was still further developed in the summer of the same year.

This system of the sliding scale was applied in many different ways. The price often resulted from two factors, one of which was the basic price and the other a coefficient (the so-called key) varying according to a combination of determinate elements: wages, price of raw materials, exchange rate, etc. Sometimes the total price was formed from two elements: the cost of raw materials, which was calculated in foreign money, and internal expenses incurred in paper marks. At last, some time later, exporters, almost universally, gave up fixing sale prices in paper marks. They stabilized them thenceforward in an appreciated foreign currency (dollar, pound sterling, Dutch florin, Swiss franc) or even in gold marks.

**19.** Curve AB (Diagram XIV) shows the foreign demand for German goods. Along the Y axis are measured gold prices of a bale of German exported goods (in Marshall's sense); CD is the supply curve of German products, *supposing supply prices computed in gold.*

In a previous chapter it was seen that for a long time there was a tendency for the price of foreign exchange to increase at a greater rate than the internal prices of goods, and wages. This means that the supply curve CD tended to *fall*, dropping, for example, to C′D′.

Consequently, the gold price of exported goods diminished. Obviously the fall is the greater, other things being equal, the less elastic is the curve AB. In every case, however, the fall in gold prices is less than the

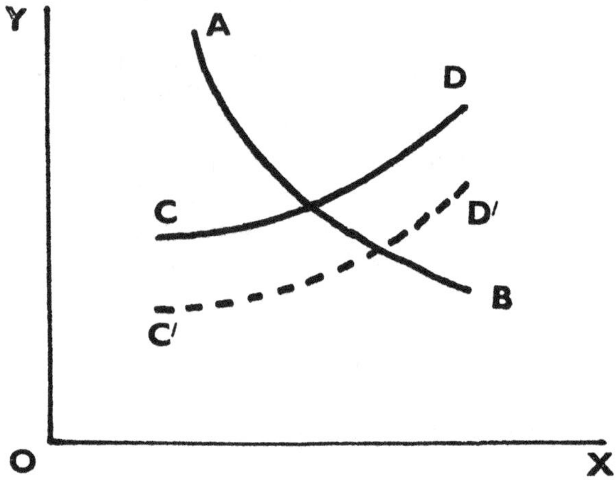


DIAGRAM XIV

fall of the costs curve and it is from this divergence that a profit was derived for the exporter.

The influence which the depreciation of the exchange exercised on the *total value in gold* of exports is different according to whether the elasticity of the curve AB is greater or lesser than unity. The fall in the unit gold price of exported goods is accompanied in the first case by a rise, and in the second by a fall in the aggregate value of exports.

## XII. CERTAIN STATISTICS OF EXPORT PRICES

**20.** German writers have frequently observed that the depreciation of the exchange was to Germany's disadvantage in that it induced her to sell her goods at unduly low prices. The phenomenon had been previously observed by Wagner in the Russian case. In his researches into the Russian exchange Wagner asserts that in consequence of the depreciation of the rouble, since internal prices had not increased in exact proportion to the premium on foreign exchange, Russian exporters sold their grain at gold prices which were below those of the world market. That, concluded Wagner, constituted a loss for the Russian economy, which in that way made a present of part of its production to foreign countries, although the exporters continued to make a profit.

The table on p. 248 shows the *average prices in gold marks* of a quintal of goods exported from Germany in the various months of 1919, 1920, 1921, and 1922. The figures in paper marks which appear in the sources (publications of the Statistical Bureau) have been converted into gold marks by reference to the monthly average rate quoted for the dollar on the Berlin Bourse.

From what I have said earlier it will be realized that the figures in this table cannot be considered as exact. They give unduly low values for German exports. But the tendency, which is apparent in the table, for the average prices of goods exported to fall in the periods of rapid depreciation of the mark and to rise in the periods of improvement or comparative stability of the foreign exchange value of the mark, accords with the facts. This is confirmed by numerous facts recorded in the German Press. According to statistics referred to by Dalberg, in 1921 the minimum prices, fixed in paper marks by the Foreign Trade Control Office, were not increased in proportion to the depreciation of the mark, and consequently the prices in terms of gold declined considerably.

(*a*) From May 1919 to February 1920, i.e. in a period during which the dollar rate rose rapidly (average rate 12·8 paper marks in May 1919; 99·1 paper marks in the following February), the average gold price of a quintal of exports decreased sharply, to 9·6 gold marks in the month of maximum divergence between the internal and external values of the paper mark.

(*b*) From February 1920 to July of the same year, i.e. in a period of improvement in the paper mark (average rate for the dollar fell to about 39 paper marks in June and July 1920), the average gold price of exported goods was much increased (from 9·6 gold marks in February to 31·4 gold marks in July).

(*c*) From July 1920 to November 1921 the depreciation of the mark was renewed. Formerly it had been slow and interrupted by short periods of improvement, but the decline was accelerated in the autumn of 1921. In November 1921 the average dollar rate was 263 paper marks. The

TABLE XXVII

*Value (in millions of gold marks) of German Exports and Average Prices (in gold marks) of a Quintal of Goods exported**

| | 1919 | | 1920 | | 1921 | | 1922 | |
|---|---|---|---|---|---|---|---|---|
| | *Total value* | *Average price* | *Total value* | *Average price* | *Total value* | *Average price* | *Total value* | *Average price* |
| January | — | — | 209·3 | 13·7 | — | — | 325·4 | 16·0 |
| February | — | — | 184·0 | 9·6 | — | — | 297·9 | 17·0 |
| March | — | — | 211·7 | 11·6 | — | — | 324·0 | 15·0 |
| April | — | — | 376·6 | 17·3 | — | — | 327·0 | 15·0 |
| May | 319·9 | 59·5 | 602·9 | 20·8 | 308·8 | 26·8 | 416·2 | 19·9 |
| June | 506·9 | 48·0 | 633·2 | 23·6 | 326·3 | 21·6 | 427·9 | 22·8 |
| July | 157·5 | 14·5 | 658·3 | 31·4 | 339·5 | 21·7 | 336·3 | 20·5 |
| August | 160·3 | 13·3 | 530·2 | 27·7 | 334·2 | 18·3 | 254·8 | 18·1 |
| September | 138·9 | 14·7 | 467·0 | 25·4 | 298·3 | 15·9 | 290·9 | 18·3 |
| October | 170·2 | 13·8 | 400·0 | 26·7 | 273·2 | 13·9 | 291·4 | 18·9 |
| November | 141·9 | 10·7 | 430·3 | 24·3 | 192·6 | 10·1 | 255·2 | 16·4 |
| December | 364·9 | 12·5 | 449·6 | 25·5 | 318·5 | 16·5 | 423·0 | 24·1 |

* For a more exact calculation of average prices it would be necessary to take account of the known variations in the composition of the export totals. But from tested facts it appears that in 1920, 1921, and 1922 these variations did not much influence the average price.

average price of exports fell continually during 1921 until it was 10·1 marks in November of that year.

(*d*) In December 1921 the paper mark improved somewhat. But in March 1922 once more the average exchange rate had risen to 284 paper marks. There followed—in the four succeeding months—a period of relative stabilization at about 300 marks per dollar.

From November to December 1921 the average price of exports rose sharply (from 10·1 to 16·5 gold marks); and in the following months it rose slowly until in June 1922 it was 22·8 marks.

(*e*) In July 1922 a new phase of a rapid depreciation of the mark began. The average rate for the dollar was 493 paper marks in July, 1,135 in August, and 7,183 in November. The average price of exports declined continually until it was 16·4 gold marks in November 1922.

It can be seen from the table that there was a clear tendency for the total gold value of exports to fall in periods of the most acute depreciation of the German exchange. From that, however, one could not conclude that the foreign demand for German goods was inelastic. The fall in the total export figures, computed in gold, was probably due to the causes shown in Section x of the present chapter.

## XIII. COMPARISONS BETWEEN PRICES IN THE WORLD MARKET, IN THE GERMAN MARKET, AND PRICES OF GOODS EXPORTED FROM GERMANY

**21.** Here I shall refer briefly to the results of an investigation carried out under my direction at the Berlin Office of the Reparations Commission with the object of ascertaining the prices of goods exported from Germany. The investigation was particularly concerned with the German exports to England. For a certain number of trades statistics were calculated of the average prices of articles supplied by Germany, and these prices were compared with the average prices of similar goods sold by other countries. The table on p. 250 shows the ratios, multiplied by 100, between average German prices and the prices of the world market (Germany excluded).

Owing to the obvious difficulties of the investigation and to the fact that it could not be extended to cover all goods, but only about a third of those imported from Germany, it is impossible to be sure that the results are accurate in every particular. But certain general results are sufficiently established. Firstly, if we calculate the average of the index numbers of the first column (1913), 101 is the result; in other words, the prices of German goods were then about equal on the average to those in the outside world. For the second half of 1922 we have, however, the index number 76·4. In the second place, the *dispersion* of the individual price ratios around their average was much greater in 1922 than in 1913. Ignoring the extreme figures, we can say that in 1913 German prices varied between 90 per cent and 115 per cent of world prices, whilst in 1922 they ranged from 50 per cent to 105 per cent of world prices. This is indeed a proof of the dislocation of the German price system which was caused by the inflation.

TABLE XXVIII

| | 1913 | *Second quarter of 1922* |
|---|---|---|
| Iron and steel goods | 93 | 69 |
| Other metal goods | 100 | 88 |
| Knives, hardware, utensils, instruments | 82 | 54 |
| Machines | 102 | 61 |
| Electric goods | 80 | 68 |
| Glass, porcelain | 114 | 58 |
| Cotton yarn and cloth | 92 | 77 |
| Wool yarns and cloth | 98 | 102 |
| Other textile goods | 105 | 63 |
| Confectionery | 96 | 78 |
| Chemical and paint products | 87 | 95 |
| Leather goods | 127 | 49 |
| Paper | 133 | 83 |
| Sundry articles | 107 | 124 |

22. The investigation, the results of which I have summarized, was concerned also with the prices of German exports from 1921 to the middle of 1922. The prices of some hundreds of German goods exported to England and Switzerland were examined for that purpose. These prices were represented by index numbers (base, 1913) and weighted aggregate indices were then calculated. In Table XXIX the aggregate indices are compared with the index numbers of general prices in Germany, England, and Switzerland.

This table shows that: (*a*) prices of goods exported from Germany were higher than prices generally in Germany, but appreciably lower than those in the importing countries; (*b*) the level of Swiss prices was, in the period under consideration, higher than the English, and also prices of German goods exported to Switzerland were higher than those of goods exported to England. This was probably the effect of the policy followed by the Control Bureaux which tended to fix prices for German goods higher or lower according to the price level of each importing country; (*c*) from the comparison of the index numbers of prices of exported goods and the prices in the outside world it may be concluded that, during the period of inflation, the terms of trade between Germany and foreign countries were turned against Germany.*

TABLE XXIX

*Index Numbers of Gold Prices* (1913 = 100)

| | GERMAN PRICES† | GERMAN GOODS EXPORTED TO | | GENERAL PRICES | | |
|---|---|---|---|---|---|---|
| | | *England* | *Switzerland* | *English*‡ | *Swiss*§ | *American*‖ |
| 4th quarter, 1921 | 66 | 97 | 124 | 138 | 176 | 141 |
| 1st quarter, 1922 | 81 | 102 | 122 | 142 | 171 | 140 |
| 2nd quarter, 1922 | 93 | 114 | 124 | 145 | 163 | 147 |
| 3rd quarter, 1922 | 80 | 113 | 136 | 143 | 162 | 154 |
| 4th quarter, 1922 | 75 | 113 | 130 | 146 | 167 | 155 |
| 1st quarter, 1923 | 82 | 115 | 130 | 153 | 175 | 157 |
| 2nd quarter, 1923 | 78 | 115 | — | 153 | 169 | 156 |

## XIV. THE RATIO OF INTERCHANGE BETWEEN GERMAN AND FOREIGN GOODS

**23.** The preceding investigations show that the inflation tended to turn the terms of trade against Germany. But since gold prices which were found in German statistics of goods exported from Germany are certainly much lower than the actual price realized, it is impossible to calculate, on the basis of these statistics, the losses which Germany suffered in her export trade during the depreciation of the mark. On the other hand, it must not be forgotten that a part of the goods imported by Germany was purchased with paper marks. It is calculated that in 1919 alone (in that year the sale of marks to foreigners was conspicuous) the excess of imports over exports had been 5 milliard gold marks.

* According to the calculations of the Statistical Bureau of the Reich, gold prices of imported goods had increased in 1923 on the average 26 per cent compared with 1913 and prices of exported goods only 14 per cent. (It may be observed, however, that the composition of Foreign Trade was not the same in the two years concerned.)

† Index numbers of the Statistical Bureau of the Reich.

‡ Averages of the index numbers of the *Economist*, *Statist*, *The Times*, and the Board of Trade.

§ Index numbers of Lorenz.

‖ Index numbers of the Labour Bureau.

Thanks to the depreciation of the mark, Germany actually procured gratuitously from abroad large quantities of raw materials and foodstuffs.

It is obviously impossible to determine, even approximately, the losses of foreign possessors of German marks. An idea of their order of magnitude is given by Singer. He calculated that about the middle of 1922 foreigners possessed 60 milliard paper marks, purchased probably at an average price of 25 gold pfennig for a paper mark. The depreciation of the mark had reduced the gold value of that mass of marks to a twentieth of the average purchase price, causing a loss abroad of 14 milliard gold marks. "Even in the unlikely hypothesis," continues Singer, "that those 60 milliard paper marks had been bought at 10 gold pfennig a paper mark, they would still have represented a value of 6 milliard gold marks. At the existing dollar rate of exchange this value was reduced to one-eighth: i.e. foreign possessors of paper marks or of deposits in German banks and foreign creditors whose claims were in terms of marks had still suffered a loss of 5 milliard gold marks, a sum triple that paid by Germany in foreign exchange on account of reparations."*

In the celebrated McKenna Report the profit received by Germany from the sale of marks (banknotes or credit in marks at German banks) from the Armistice onwards, was estimated between 7·6 and 8·7 milliard gold marks. On the other hand the sale of houses on a large scale to foreigners at ridiculous prices and other items would have to be taken into consideration in striking a balance—a very difficult task—of the losses and profits which the depreciation of the mark brought to Germany in her dealings with foreigners.

* "Die deutsche Auslandsverschuldung" in *Wirtschaftdienst* of July 7th, 1922.

CHAPTER VII

# The Course of Prices of Industrial Shares during the Paper Inflation*

## I. METHODOLOGICAL OBSERVATIONS

**1.** Economists have often investigated the relations existing between inflation and the prices of goods and the divergences between the purchasing power of a depreciated money in terms of goods in the home market and the purchasing power of the same money in the international market.

From a scientific point of view the influences of the inflation on the prices of investments have been studied less. There is one kind of investment—industrial shares—which acquires a special importance in countries with a much depreciated currency.

It is obvious that even the prices of investments (material goods or securities which represent them), expressed in a depreciated currency, cannot but show the effect of the increase in the paper circulation. Indeed, common observation shows that in the periods characterized by a depreciation of the currency there exists a continual process of revaluation of investments, a process which is more or less rapid and complete according to the various categories of investments. As regards the industrial shares which are quoted officially the revaluation occurs in the leading Stock Exchanges. From a certain point of view, it is a means by which the economic organism of a country is defended against the effects of the monetary depreciation. Otherwise, shares and other investments would be bought at an extremely low price by those (especially foreigners) who possessed "appreciated" foreign exchange.

But the revaluation of investments—which in countries where the currency depreciates rapidly becomes sometimes a veritable revolution in values—presents peculiar characteristics in contrast to the rise of the value of goods, provoked by the continual issues of paper money.

I will examine the relations between the depreciation of the currency and the prices of industrial shares, taking the facts manifested in the

* A memorandum published under the same title in the *Giornale degli Economisti*, 1925.

decade 1914–24 in Germany, which in this field also, as in many others, where the deep and disturbing action of monetary depreciation was felt, presents an extraordinary variety of phenomena, well worth attention.

2. In this investigation I have used the *index numbers* of German shares, calculated by the Statistical Bureau of the Reich.

The Statistical Bureau collected the quotations of 300 shares quoted in the Berlin Bourse, selecting them in such a way that the most important groups of industries were represented, in the total index, by a number corresponding to the number of companies existing in Germany. For example, of the 300 companies selected, 23 were of the "mixed" firms (mining, metallurgical, engineering), 31 were makers of machines, locomotives, and automobiles; 16 were in the coal industry; 16 were electrical concerns; 20 were chemical firms; 4 paper firms; 2 glass; 3 wood, etc.

The distribution of the three hundred companies among the various kinds of industries practically corresponds to the distribution of total nominal share capital among the same categories (according to the position on December 31st, 1920). Also in the selection of the companies belonging to a given group the Statistical Bureau sought to apply correctly the principles of sampling. In 1923 it introduced a small modification in the calculation of the index. In the banks group it discarded the quotations for five institutes of little importance and instead counted twice the quotations for the so-called D banks (Deutsche Bank, Diskonto-Gesellschaft, Dresdner Bank, and Darmstädter Bank) and of the Reichsbank.

As the *base* of the index numbers the 1913 annual average (i.e. the arithmetical average of the quotations at the end of each month) was taken as 100. The Statistical Bureau also calculated three other series of share index numbers, by dividing the quotations expressed in paper marks (1) by the average monthly exchange rate of the gold mark, (2) by the monthly index numbers of wholesale prices, and (3) by the monthly index numbers of the cost of living. The first series allows us to find out to what extent the prices of shares were adapted to the fall in the external value of the paper mark. But in the first phases of the inflation the entire structure of prices and of internal values was still based on the paper mark, the purchasing power of which decreased more slowly in the home market than in foreign exchange. It is therefore worth comparing the quotations for shares also with the prices of goods in the home market, as well as with the price of the gold monetary unit.

It is obvious that if one wishes to construct a correct index number of share prices it is necessary also to take account of the issues of *new* shares, which, when offered at a lower price than the Stock Exchange quotations, depress these last. In other words, it is necessary to take account of options. This was done by the Statistical Bureau of the Reich. In Germany this circumstance has a particular importance, because during the inflation all companies, with rare exceptions, continually increased their capital. By means of these new issues of shares, the progressive transformation of the original gold capital into paper capital was effected. The effective quotations for shares, expressed in paper marks, were, therefore, much lower than those prices which would have been established, following the monetary depreciation, if the original capital had not been "diluted."

The preceding methodological observations show the significance of Table XII in the Appendix, which indicates the movements of the index numbers of shares (1913=100) from 1918 until the end of 1923, i.e. until the monetary reform which stabilized the German exchange.

It must be remembered that the average quotations of shares in 1913 were above par, at 178·66 per cent of the nominal value of shares.

In the first column of the table for each year the prices of shares are shown *expressed in paper marks* and in the following columns the index numbers which were obtained by using as the coefficient of conversion: (*a*) the average exchange rate of the gold mark expressed in paper marks; and (*b*) the average index number of wholesale prices.

During the period August 1914–November 1917 there were no quotations in the share market.

## II. THE COURSE OF SHARE PRICES IN 1919

**3.** As the table shows in the first half of 1918 the share prices, expressed in paper marks, had risen more than the dollar exchange rate. That was also a consequence of various facts, analysed above, which damped the rise of exchanges during the war.

On the other hand, the index number of share prices had increased less than that of wholesale prices.

During the world conflict the rise in the quotations for industrial securities was considerable, especially for shares of companies engaged in the mining, metallurgical, and engineering industries. This was the natural consequence of heavy war profits.* For the "mixed firms" group, which included the shares of the most powerful industrial groups of the Ruhr and Upper Silesia, the index number expressed in gold in May 1918 reached 125 (1913 = 100).

But already some months before the end of the war the rise in share prices was arrested. From May to August 1918 the increase, in terms of paper marks, was very slight (from 138 to 143). The highest index number in gold for all shares was in May (112·7); in the following months it continually fell so that in September it had declined to 86·0. The paper index showed a maximum in August; then it fell.

Do these figures prove that the Bourse had already begun in May 1918 to discount an unfavourable end to the war?

We cannot give a certain answer; but it is clear that pessimistic expectations were reflected in the share prices at least as early as the beginning of August 1918.

**4.** In October 1918, the outcome of the war being decided, share prices fell considerably. The fall continued after the Armistice and in the first months of 1919. Owing to the very rapid depreciation of the mark, which in February 1920 was worth less than 5 gold pfennige (although in October 1918 it had still been worth 60 per cent of its pre-war value), the prices of shares, in terms of paper, increased in the second half of 1919; but the rise was very much less than proportional to the monetary depreciation. *The index number in gold fell from* 69·3 (*October* 1918) *to* 8·5 *in February* 1920. The fall appears less if the prices of shares are expressed in terms of the internal purchasing power

* Using the official figures published in the *Vierteljahreshefte zur deutschen Statistik*, the following table has been compiled:

PROFITS IN GERMAN INDUSTRY DURING THE WAR

(*Ratios between Net Profits and Capital Plus Reserve: Joint-Stock Companies*)

| | *All industries* | | *Iron and steel industries* | | *Chemical industries* | | *Average of wholesale prices* |
|---|---|---|---|---|---|---|---|
| | (*a*) | (*b*) | (*a*) | (*b*) | (*a*) | (*b*) | |
| 1913–14 | 7·96 | 7·96 | 8·33 | 8·33 | 5·94 | 5·94 | 100 |
| 1914–15 | 6·25 | 5·00 | 7·12 | 5·69 | 6·79 | 5·43 | 125 |
| 1915–16 | 8·74 | 5·90 | 14·87 | 10·00 | 14·34 | 9·69 | 148 |
| 1916–17 | 10·24 | 6·52 | 22·90 | 14·58 | 18·55 | 11·81 | 157 |
| 1917–18 | 10·76 | 5·41 | 19·61 | 9·60 | 21·65 | 10·88 | 199 |
| 1918–19 | 6·77 | 2·63 | 2·36 | 0·90 | 10·45 | 1·87 | 257 |

Column (*a*) shows the profits expressed in *paper marks*; the figures in column (*b*) are the ratio between these profits and the average index number of wholesale prices.

of the mark. According to the index number of wholesale prices, in February 1920, shares were still fetching about 12 per cent of their 1913 value, and according to the index number of retail prices about 24 per cent. Obviously the sharp fall of share prices which occurred in 1919 was in a very large part the consequence of the political and social disorganization of Germany, of the economic crisis, and of the lack of confidence which spread among the people when the advent of Bolshevism seemed imminent.

But gradually the internal situation improved and a social revolution seemed more and more improbable. Also, towards the end of 1919 and in the beginning of 1920, the depreciation of the mark had given a strong stimulus to exports; the wheels of industry began to move round again, and the number of unemployed rapidly decreased. The divergence between home prices and world prices was very great: wages remained low and consequently one may assume that profits in certain branches of production must have been pretty considerable. The public once more began to have confidence in shares. Also, having learned from the very rapid depreciation suffered by Government securities, mortgages, and debentures—in short, all securities with a fixed yield—the public began to consider shares as the representatives of an "intrinsic" value, of a gold value (Goldwert), whose price in paper marks must increase when the German exchange depreciated. As the depreciation of the mark proceeded, this phenomenon began to be understood by the public, who, for a long time, assured by official explanations, had attributed the decline in the purchasing power of the paper mark, not to the continuance of note-issues, but to the rise in prices caused by the war, the revolution, and the economic crisis. The public now saw that the paper mark could no longer fulfil the function of the "store of value." In 1919 there began that speculative fury which characterized the Bourse during almost the whole of the inflation period. In Berlin the Bourse authorities were obliged at that time to limit business to three days a week. Considerable purchases of German shares by foreigners were noted. Because of the dearness of living which lowered real incomes, many classes of people were forced to try to supplement their incomes by speculation on the Bourse. Also industrial and commercial firms considered the purchase of shares not only as a form of investment for reserve capital, but also as a temporary use for liquid resources—a use which guaranteed the preservation of the working capital which was threatened by the continual monetary depreciation.

### III. THE CLOSE CONNECTION BETWEEN SHARE PRICES AND THE DOLLAR RATE IN 1920 AND 1921

**5.** Table XXX and Diagrams XV and XVI show that in 1920 and 1921 the index number of share prices expressed in paper marks varied in close relation with the exchange rate of the dollar.

At times of rapid depreciation of the mark, as e.g. in the autumn of 1921, the index number showed a sharp rise. All shares, and not only particular groups, shared in the ascending movement.

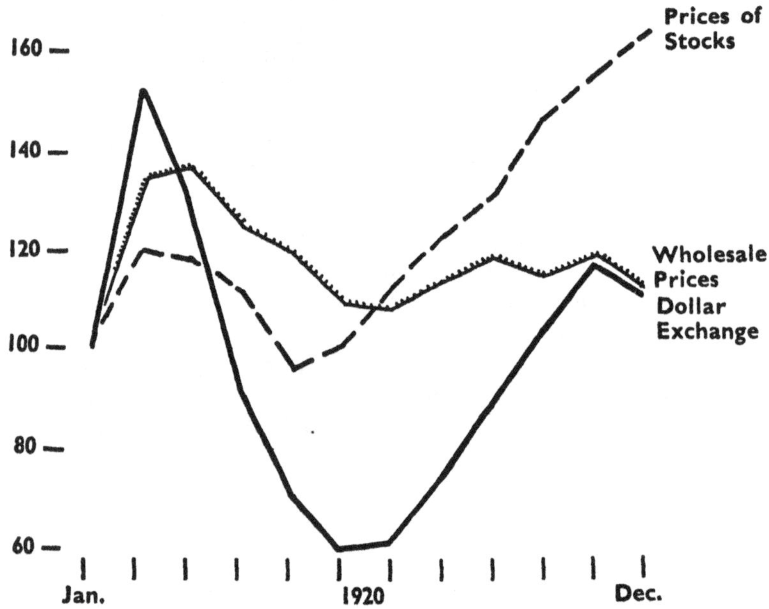


DIAGRAM XV.—Basis for all curves: January 1920 = 100

It was observed in Germany, as also, indeed, elsewhere, that the circle of speculators was greatly enlarged. Shares were held by speculators in a much larger measure than formerly, when they for the most part had been held longer by investors, who considered them as permanent investments. But in 1920 and 1921 shares passed rapidly from hand to hand, and oscillations of their prices were much more frequent and more violent than formerly.

The impulse to this movement began with the variations of the value of paper money, which kept the industrial securities' market in a state of continual instability.

It was in the autumn of 1921 that business on the German Bourse reached such a condition as to "put in the shade even the classical examples of the most violent fever of speculation." The technical

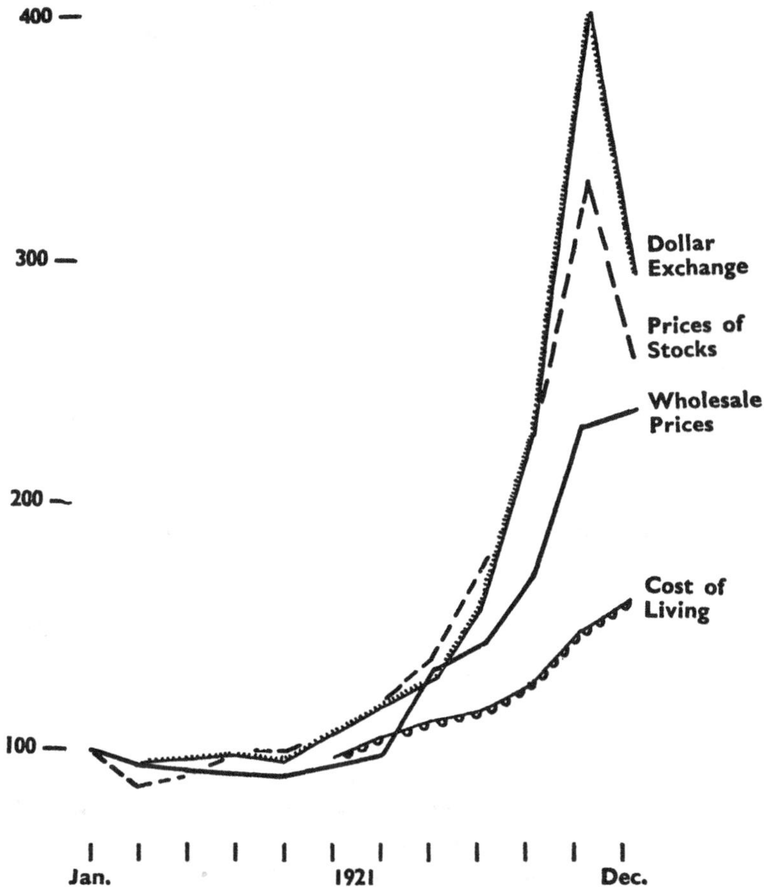


DIAGRAM XVI.—Basis for all curves: January 1921 = 100

equipment of the German exchanges was insufficient for the increasing mass of transactions. Speculation on the Bourse also necessitated an extension of banking equipment; the existing banks were obliged to increase continually the numbers of their employees; and many small new banks, whose sole object was the receiving and executing of

Bourse business, sprang up all over the place. In those days a financial newspaper wrote: "To-day there is no one—from lift-boy, typist, and small landlord to the wealthy lady in high society—who does not speculate in industrial securities and who does not study the list of official quotations as if it were a most precious letter."

At the same time the Bourse was perpetually supplied with new

TABLE XXX*

| | 1920 | | | 1921 | | | |
|---|---|---|---|---|---|---|---|
| | (*a*) | (*b*) | (*c*) | (*a*) | (*b*) | (*c*) | (*d*) |
| January .. | 100 | 100 | 100 | 100 | 100 | 100 | 100 |
| February .. | 153 | 120 | 134 | 94 | 93 | 96 | 97 |
| March .. | 130 | 118 | 136 | 96 | 95 | 93 | 96 |
| April .. .. | 92 | 111 | 125 | 98 | 99 | 92 | 95 |
| May .. .. | 72 | 96 | 120 | 96 | 100 | 91 | 95 |
| June .. .. | 60 | 101 | 110 | 107 | 107 | 95 | 99 |
| July .. .. | 61 | 113 | 109 | 118 | 121 | 99 | 106 |
| August .. | 74 | 123 | 115 | 130 | 140 | 133 | 113 |
| September .. | 90 | 132 | 119 | 162 | 177 | 144 | 117 |
| October .. | 105 | 148 | 116 | 231 | 232 | 171 | 128 |
| November .. | 119 | 157 | 120 | 405 | 337 | 237 | 151 |
| December .. | 113 | 165 | 114 | 296 | 263 | 242 | 163 |

material, thanks to the mass of new shares which were issued continually in 1920 and 1921 as a consequence of industry's need for capital.

**6.** Owing to the close connection between the dollar exchange rate and the prices of industrial shares, which was established in 1920 and 1921, the prices of securities had ceased to be the barometer of the general political and economic situation.

Political events of great importance (such as the partition of Upper Silesia) had scarcely any influence on share prices, and what effect they did have often was exactly opposite to what would have been expected under normal conditions. Events which were unfavourable to Germany, by causing a fresh depreciation of the mark, indirectly caused a rise in the prices of industrial securities.

Thanks to the adaptation of share prices to the depreciation of the currency, industrial shares, in 1920 and in 1921 (until December 1st), were well suited to be a "store of value." The detailed investigations

* In the Table are shown the percentage increases (*a*) in the exchange rate of the dollar; (*b*) in the index number of share prices; (*c*) in that of wholesale prices; and (*d*) in that of the cost of living during 1920 and 1921.

of the *Frankfurter Zeitung* show that those people who bought shares at the beginning of 1920 not only succeeded (in contrast with the unlucky holders of fixed interest securities) in escaping the losses involved in the depreciation of the mark, but even made some real profit.

But the conclusion is very different if one compares the share prices of 1920 and 1921 with those of 1913. As appears in Table XII (Appendix), the gold index number was in August 1921, 19·36 per cent; and in October 18·0 per cent of the 1913 level. The index numbers calculated on the basis of wholesale prices are higher; but the fact of an enormous decline still remains. Thus it is true that in 1920 and in 1921 share prices were adapted to the fluctuations in the value of the currency; but they varied round about a level much below that of 1913.

7. What were the causes of so great a depreciation of shares at a time when German industry was experiencing a phase of prosperity as was generally agreed and as numerous symptoms (among them the low unemployment figures) appeared to confirm?

It was often stated in Germany that the profits of industry were only "apparent" profits, profits "on paper," due mainly to the insufficiency of the sums set aside for the maintenance of equipment. Companies thought they were distributing profits, but actually they were distributing their "substance" and were working at a loss.* The depreciation of the shares must, it was thought, be the expression of the capital losses suffered by German industry.

One must admit that cases of this kind did occur in the early stages of the inflation. Moreover, it is certain that small industrialists or retailers were not aware, for a long time, of the losses which the increasing monetary inflation involved them in. But it is equally certain that the more important and better directed companies quickly learned to distinguish "apparent" profits from "real" ones, and that if their accounts showed profits, these could be considered as effective. Also, judging from many facts referred to by German financial papers, not a few companies realized considerable profits in the years 1920–22.

At the most it must be admitted that, in part, these profits were not "real" in the sense that they were derived from the decline in the capital of or from the restriction of the consumption of numerous other

* This is the theory maintained by Mering (*Erträgnisse deutscher Aktiengesellschaften vor und nach dem Krieg*, Berlin, 1923). The theory of "apparent" profits was elaborated in an interesting manner by two German economists, Prion and Schmalenbach, in a work published in 1922 (*Zwei Vorträge über Scheingewinne*, Jena, 1922).

classes of society. During the inflation the profits of industry had lost that significance which they have under normal conditions as indices of general prosperity. The favourable situation of some industries, whose fiscal burden was greatly lessened by the inflation, contrasted also with the desperate state of the national finances.

On the other hand, from an examination of the accounts of joint-stock companies, it would seem that, allowing for the monetary depreciation, in 1920 and 1921, the profits of German industry were in total lower than those realized before and during the war. According to the detailed calculations made by Mering from the accounts for 1921 (or for 1920–21) of 1,458 German companies, the net gains scarcely reach (supposing 1 gold mark equal to 10 paper marks) 28·81 per cent of the net profits of the financial year 1913–14: that is 3·04 per cent of the capital invested (share capital plus published reserves) compared with 10·55 per cent in the last year of peace.

Against these calculations it may be said that it is very difficult, even for experts, to ascertain from the published accounts what were the total profits realized by German industry during the inflation. Many accounts were compiled by assuming the existence of the profit it was desired to show and then adapting other items to it. Even the financial papers stated that it was now impossible to interpret balance sheets, because of the multiplicity of difficulties arising from the depreciation of money, aggravated by the lamentable disposition of companies not to give a fair picture of their situation and real profits. Even this deterioration in commercial morality was an index of the unhealthy conditions of German economy.

**8.** Leaving aside the insoluble question of profits effectively made by German industry during the inflation, let us limit ourselves to recording one certain point: the sum of the dividends distributed was much lower than that paid in 1913, and the fall of dividends, owing to the policy followed by the companies, was even greater than the fall of net profits which the accounts showed. Examining the accounts of the great iron and steel companies for the year 1920–21, the *Bergwerkszeitung* (No. 2, January 3rd, 1922) observed: "Again on this occasion the companies have given proof of their prudence in the distribution of dividends. The programme of big industry is always that of limiting dividends in order to reinforce continually the internal structure of the firms." In fact, thirteen iron and steel companies examined in the article cited had realized in 1920–21 a net profit of 383·6 million marks and had paid out only 160·1 million. The difference was added to the reserves.

We have seen that in 1920 and 1921 the gold prices of shares was round about 20 per cent of the average price of 1913. If it is remembered that, even at a time in which shares were considered above all as a means of conserving the savings and the liquid resources of firms, the height of the dividend paid to the shareholders is always one of the principal forces which determine the price of shares, there is for the low level of the index number of German shares in 1920 and 1921 a plausible explanation.

## IV. THE FALL IN THE PRICES OF INDUSTRIAL SHARES IN 1922

**9.** After February 1922 the evolution of the share market was quite different from that which had been observed in 1920 and 1921. Instead of the parallel between the exchange rate of the dollar and the price of shares, there appeared an increasing divergence between the curve of the index number of share prices and that of the exchange rate, and in the market for securities an unusual calm followed the frenzied speculation of the preceding months (see Diagram XVII).

In the second half of 1922, after the relative stability of the first months of that year, the depreciation of the currency proceeded with great rapidity. On an average the gold mark was worth 76 paper marks in June, 117 in July, 758 in October. The prices of shares followed only some way after the movement of the dollar exchange rate and of prices. The index number in paper was 8·2 in June (1913=1); and 20·6 in October. *When the paper index number is converted into gold terms, according to the exchange rate of the dollar, the index number for October* 1922 *is* 2·72 (1913 = 100). Based on wholesale and retail prices we have the indices 3·64 and 9·34.*

In October 1922 the index number was at lowest level known at any time since 1914. At the beginning of November the prices of the shares of a certain number of firms, whose capital had not been "diluted,"

* According to *Wirtschaft und Statistik* the market value of the capital invested in German companies was, at the following dates (according to the exchange rate of the dollar):

| | *Million gold marks* |
|---|---|
| End of 1913 | 31·2 |
| End of 1921 | 9·9 |
| End of 1922 | 4·9 |
| April 1923 | 9·6 |
| July 30th, 1923 | 12·8 |

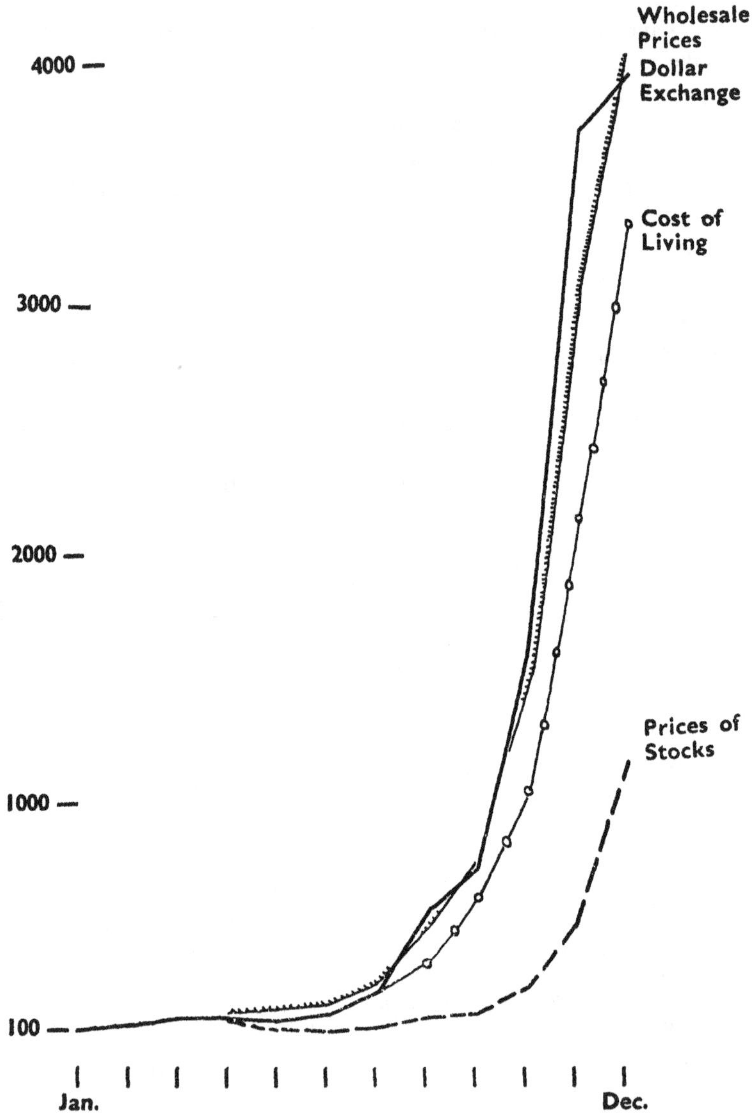


DIAGRAM XVII.— Basis for all curves: January 1922 = 100

had increased 89 times compared with 1914, while the value of the dollar had increased 1,525 times, the price of coal 1,250 times, the price of bar iron 2,000 times, and the index number of wholesale prices 945 times.

This enormous drop in share prices caused some odd situations. For example, all the share capital of a great company, the Daimler, was, according to the Bourse quotations, scarcely worth 980 million paper marks. Now, since a motor-car made by that company cost at that time on an average three million marks, it follows that "the Bourse attributed a value of 327 cars to the Daimler capital, with the three great works, the extensive area of land, its reserves and its liquid capital, and its commercial organization developed in Germany and abroad." The Bourse value of the sixteen great Tietz shops equalled the total price of 16,000 suits.

The undervaluation of German shares, which was one of the most remarkable phenomena of the German economy in 1922, was the object of lively discussions. It affected even the shares of important companies which possessed large works, seemed founded on a very solid economic and financial basis, were wisely managed, and which were working, if not at full pressure, certainly at a satisfactory rate. "The intrinsic value of the plant," observed an economic periodical, "is not the principal element in the valuation of a share; the fundamental element is always the capacity of the firm to produce. Now, since the production of German industry in 1922 was only 70 per cent of peace-time production, a proportional reduction in the price of securities would be perfectly comprehensible; actually the depreciation was far greater. How can this be explained?"

**10.** From the study of the columns of some reputable financial papers and from personal observations made in Germany, I have assembled the following points in explanation of the failure of the prices of shares to adapt themselves to the monetary depreciation.

After the ominous "black Thursday" (December 1st, 1921) the public, badly hit by the fall of share prices, realized that not even the purchase of shares was a safe means of investing their savings. Until then many believed that the risk of buying shares was less than that of possessing foreign exchange or foreign money, because they were able to judge more easily the conditions of this or that industry, rather than the whole political situation, which, as they believed, determined the exchange rates. But the events of December 1921 showed that even the prices of shares could suffer sudden and great oscillations independently of the situation of various industries. In the first months of 1922 there appeared an increasing tendency on the part of industrialists, merchants, bankers, and private investors to invest available sums in foreign exchange and goods, rather than in industrial shares.

**11.** But another cause even more potent helped to depress still further the prices of industrial securities, and that was the alteration in the conditions of the money market. During the whole of 1921 the paper inflation was accompanied by an abundance of money in the market. But in 1922 a scarcity of the means of payment began to be felt which more and more seriously disturbed industrial and commercial circles. Deposits in the banks diminished rapidly because of the progressive depreciation of German money. That obliged the banks to restrict credits. The new taxes, approved in the spring of 1922, helped to limit the liquid resources of industry. It was foreseen, in particular, that the forced loan of 70 milliard paper marks would be a serious burden on the money market.

The low price of shares was also in keeping with the following facts. Even during a great part of 1921 internal prices of goods, for well-known reasons, remained at a relatively low level, and numerous obstacles impeded their quick reaction to the increase in note-issues and to the rise in foreign exchange rates. But during 1922 the sensitiveness of internal prices increased. In Table XXXI it may be seen that from January to December 1922 the exchange rate of the dollar increased from 100 to 3,956; the index number of wholesale prices from 100 to 4,024; and the cost of living from 100 to 3,360. Persistent propaganda in industrial and commercial circles in order that sale prices should be fixed and adapted to "world-prices," "prices of repurchase," or to the "cost of reproduction" of goods, hastened the movement for the adaptation of internal prices to exchange rates. As a result of that, each new depreciation of the international value of the mark—we must remember that in 1922 the sudden rises in the dollar exchange rate were caused by political events rather than the preceding increases in the note-issues—immediately provoked a rise in all internal prices. The new note-issues were quickly absorbed in general business.

When the prices of raw materials, wages, etc., followed immediately the rise in foreign exchange rates, the need for working capital or for credit on the part of industrialists and merchants increased, and these classes, who were the most important among those who took part in business on the Bourse, had available only a limited purchasing power for use in the share market.

TABLE XXXI

1922

| | *Exchange rate of the dollar* | *Prices of shares* | *Wholesale prices* | *Cost of living* |
|---|---|---|---|---|
| January .. | .. 100 | 100 | 100 | 100 |
| February .. | .. 108 | 113 | 112 | 120 |
| March .. | .. 148 | 133 | 148 | 142 |
| April .. | .. 152 | 138 | 173 | 168 |
| May .. | .. 11 | 117 | 176 | 186 |
| June .. | .. 165 | 111 | 192 | 203 |
| July .. | .. 257 | 121 | 274 | 264 |
| August .. | .. 591 | 156 | 524 | 380 |
| September .. | .. 764 | 170 | 783 | 652 |
| October .. | .. 1,658 | 277 | 1,544 | 1,081 |
| November .. | .. 3,744 | 548 | 3,140 | 2,185 |
| December .. | .. 3,956 | 1,209 | 4,024 | 3,360 |

**12.** One must add that the increase of note-issues of paper money, which occurred in the first six or seven months of 1922, really appear moderate when compared with the fantastic increase of note-issues which characterized certain later periods. The quantity of money in circulation increased by 65 per cent from January to July 1922. As we stated in an earlier chapter, the German Government had seriously attempted, in the first six months of 1922, to restore the equilibrium of the national finances, by reducing expenditure and by increasing taxes and tariffs, and its efforts had actually been crowned with rapid success, so far as the ordinary account was concerned.

The scarcity of money was especially noticeable in July, after the renewed sharp rise in the price of the dollar, which had provoked a veritable revolution in internal prices. The depreciation of the exchange left the prices of shares unmoved. The financial journals in the summer of 1922 said that the prevailing influence exercised by money market conditions exceeded all those other considerations which had been making the purchase of shares appear attractive.

The relations between exchange rates and prices of shares appear to be reversed. While in 1920 and 1921 as a rule a rise in the price of shares followed each depreciation of the exchange, in 1922 it was often noticed that a rise in the dollar exercised rather a depressing influence on the price of industrial securities, because every sudden depreciation of the mark recalled great masses of paper money to the foreign exchange and goods market.

**13.** Several other causes, besides the conditions of the money market, helped to depress the prices of industrial shares. Already in the spring of 1922 the Bourse began to discount the approaching end of the period of relative prosperity of German industry, which had begun with the depreciation of the mark and with the establishment of a great divergence between the internal value and the international value of the German currency. It was realized that the artificial stimulus given to German industry by the continuous increases in the foreign exchange rates could not act indefinitely. In the summer this feeling was accentuated by the consternation about the internal political situation, aggravated after the assassination of Rathenau, and by the reparations crisis, which France, the Conference of London having finished without result, now threatened to determine by arms. It is certain that a great lack of confidence spread among the German people in the summer of 1922, a lack of confidence which provoked feverish purchases of foreign exchange, and consequently suddenly increased the dollar exchange rate, while the share market was neglected.

Abroad for a long time the conviction was held—and manifested in the purchases of fabulous sums of paper marks—that the German economy would be rapidly revived. But in the summer of 1922 even foreign confidence in the economic future of Germany was at last shaken, after the collapse of the mark, after which unmistakable signs of an imminent crisis were multiplied, and the indefatigable German official propaganda had announced the imminent catastrophe of the German economic system. Lack of confidence was shown even in the relatively low quotations in foreign stock exchanges for the shares of companies who had considerable interests in Germany.

Purchase of shares by foreigners in the summer of 1922, after the renewed fall in the German mark, were only moderate in amount, and were based not so much on a desire to speculate in German shares, but rather on an effort, on the part of foreign holders of paper marks, to salvage at least a part of their possessions.

Perhaps foreigners would have bought German shares more freely if by such means they had obtained control over some important firms. But that was impossible because of the means of protection invented *ad hoc* by the German companies. They issued a certain number of shares endowed with a plural vote, which assured to their possessors undisputed power in the firm. The purchase of German shares by foreigners could only have been made with the object of speculation or of employing liquid resources; and then the risk was very great.

**14.** Together with the lack of confidence in the political and economic situation of Germany, the low income from shares certainly helped to keep the prices of them low during 1922. The public knew very well that the dividends which would be paid in 1922 would be nominally higher but actually lower than those of 1921. Indeed, according to an investigation made by the *Industrie- und Handels-Zeitung* (December 27th, 1922), 120 companies had paid dividends equal, on the average, to 0·25 per cent of the prices of the shares! The companies continued the system of diverting a considerable part of their profits—which even in 1922 were very often "real" and not "apparent," and in many cases considerable—to the enlarging of their plant.

The German Press quoted some typical examples of very low dividends indeed paid by important companies. For example, the sum total of dividends paid in 1922 by "Ilse" scarcely equalled the amount of wages paid to the workmen of that company for only one day's work. Another typical case was that of the company which fixed a dividend equal to four bottles of mineral water, as compared with the pre-war dividend equivalent to 2,800 bottles.

Now, as an economic paper observed, "the shareholder, not receiving a sufficient income from his shares, thought that it would be better to invest his money in other ways. Even when speculative motives are dominant, there will come a time when the shareholder will sell his shares if he receives almost nothing from them. These last few years have shown that the increase in the price of shares has been impeded by insufficient yields; and to-day it is obvious that serious shareholders, in very considerable numbers, are withdrawing from the industrial shares market." For the same reasons even foreigners were no longer stimulated to buy German shares. It is true that, as has been observed, a Dutchman who, at the end of 1913, had to pay 1,000 florins to buy a single share in Harpeners, could in 1922 buy nine of them with the same sum. But in 1922 the return was so unfavourable that the Dutchman did not feel stimulated to profit from the high purchasing power of his money.

Also the "invisible mortgage" weighing on German industry because of the payment of reparations contributed to the uncertainty of the future income from shares. It was known that in the end German industry would have to adapt itself to bearing its share of the burden. How much would this lessen the future net profit of industry? Would the German Government succeed in obtaining a tolerable solution to the hoary question of reparations?

### V. THE INCREASE IN THE PRICE OF SHARES TOWARDS THE END OF 1922 AND DURING 1923

**15.** Towards the end of October and at the beginning of November 1922 the situation in the money market once more changed rapidly.

The rise in the price of shares which occurred so suddenly in the second half of October and whose violence recalled the frenzied bull speculation in the autumn of 1921,* was closely connected with the Foreign Exchange decree of October 12th, which fixed strict limits to the purchasing of foreign exchange. Numerous classes in whom was fixed the habit of investing their available resources in foreign

TABLE XXXII

| | *Index number of exchange rate of the dollar* | *Index number of price of shares* | *Index number of wholesale prices* | *Index number of the cost of living* |
|---|---|---|---|---|
| October 1922 .. | 1 | 1 | 1 | 1 |
| November 1922 .. | 2·3 | 2·5 | 2 | 1·5 |
| December 1922 .. | 2·4 | 4·4 | 2·6 | 2·7 |
| January 1923 .. | 5·6 | 10·8 | 4·9 | 5·0 |
| February 1923 .. | 8·8 | 21·9 | 9·9 | 12·0 |
| March 1923 .. | 6·7 | 16·3 | 8·6 | 12·9 |
| April 1923 .. | 7·7 | 24·3 | 9·2 | 13·4 |
| May 1923 .. | 15 | 46 | 14 | 17 |
| June 1923 .. | 34 | 171 | 34 | 35 |
| July 1923 .. .. | 111 | 654 | 13 | 171 |
| August 1923 .. | 1,452 | 6,049 | 1,668 | 2,655 |
| September 1923 .. | 31† | 257† | 42† | 68† |
| October 1923 .. | 7,911† | 83,085† | 12,540† | 16,580† |

* Here are the prices of some of the principal German shares (in paper marks):

| | *October 4th* | *November 3rd* |
|---|---|---|
| Gelsenkirchener .. .. | 3,350 | 24,000 |
| Harpener .. .. .. | 5,600 | 40,000 |
| Badische Anilin .. .. | 1,770 | 9,500 |
| Hochster Farben .. .. | 1,440 | 7,000 |
| A.E.G. .. .. .. .. | 895 | 5,300 |
| Siemens und Halske .. .. | 2,100 | 12,500 |
| Deutsche Bank .. .. .. | 660 | 3,750 |

† Thousands.

exchange, could do nothing but return once more to the share market, because the decree of October 12th had caused a heavy fall in the supply of foreign exchange. Those who possessed foreign exchange refrained from selling it, not knowing if it would be possible to repurchase it later.

One must add that in the last quarter of 1922 tension in the money market was somewhat relaxed by the unduly liberal credits granted by the Reichsbank. That was shown by the rapid increase in note issues. In the quarter October–December 1922, the note issues increased as from 100 to 267, that is in the same proportion in which they were increased during the first nine months of 1922.

**16.** Later, in January 1923, the foreign exchange and share markets were influenced by the occupation of the Ruhr. The dollar, which was quoted at 7,260 marks on January 2nd and 10,000 on January 9th, had risen to 22,400 on January 22nd, and to 49,000 on the 31st. After a short period of uncertainty—caused by the disparity of opinions on the probable effects of the occupation (some foreseeing a fall in quotations because of the economic crisis, others expecting a rise in proportion to the inevitable continual depreciation of the mark)—the entire market moved decidedly for a rise. The share market fell once more into an almost exclusive dependence on the dollar exchange rate. The flight from the mark became general.

In 1923 the habit of purchasing industrial shares spread even in rural parts. "In 1923 the telephone lines which connected Berlin with the agricultural districts were always congested at certain hours, because the country folk sought information on the latest dollar exchange rate and gave Stock Exchange orders to their bankers."*

As new decrees surrounded the purchase of foreign exchange with greater difficulties, the public bought shares, which they once more considered as "real values." The index number of shares increased from 8,981 in December 1922 to 22,400 in January 1923, and to 45,200 in February. A pause occurred when the Reichsbank began its policy of supporting the mark, imposing on the market an artificial exchange rate of the dollar. But that policy, which obviously was destined to be short-lived, finished unsuccessfully in the second half of April 1923, and the dollar exchange rose once more. There was now no longer any curb on note-issues. The quantity of paper money increased with a continually rising rhythm, mainly because of the expenses incurred for

* Lewinsohn, *Die Umschichtung der europäischen Vermögen*, Berlin, 1925, p. 154.

"Passive Resistance." By such means certain classes of society secured an enormous amount of purchasing power, which they employed in buying shares. It was noticed that for a long time orders to buy came especially from the occupied territories, whither were directed the subsidies which the Government was paying with excessive generosity.

**17.** In the first half of 1923 the prices of shares not only reflected the dollar exchange rate, but actually rose more rapidly than the latter. The index number, in terms of gold, was 5·24 in January, 8·61 in April, and 16·03 in July. This was the first time since the war that there had been such a decided rise. And this occurred while the political situation created by the occupation of the Ruhr continued and while Germany was threatened by an economic crisis, the gravity of which was widely realized, and the onset of which was marked by the rising unemployment figures.

The market showed a definite preference for the shares of the Rhenish mining and metallurgical companies, as it was supposed that these companies had profited greatly from the subsidies handed out by the Government.

The paradoxical situation in the securities market is revealed in the following extract from an article published by a leading financial review (*Plutus*, July 1923, p. 175): "There have been extraordinary *rises* in the quotations for all shares, the chief cause being the *catastrophic* change in the economic situation"!! It was thought that an economic catastrophe would annihilate the value of the mark, while perhaps a part of the resources invested in shares would be saved.

**18.** In the summer of 1923, when the price of the dollar jumped in the course of a few days to 1, 2, and then 5 million paper marks,* the paper mark ceased to perform its function as the "standard of value." The practice, already initiated in certain branches of industry and commerce, of calculating prices in terms of gold or some practically stable currency, spread widely. The Reichsbank was considering the possibility of opening accounts in terms of gold, against deposits of foreign exchange, which accounts should be the basis of a system of payments in stable money; and in the meantime, after much hesitation, it decided to restrict credits in paper marks, adopting instead the principle of "stable value credits." Working-class leaders were considering

* August 3rd, 1,000,000 marks; August 6th, 1,650,000 marks; August 7th, 3,300,000 marks; August 8th, 4,860,000 marks.

methods of computing wages which would guarantee to the worker a stable wage. The Ministry of Finance thought of changing the system of assessment and collection of taxes by putting the whole on a gold basis. The accounting of the entire economic system was thus rapidly revolutionized, the principle of valuation in gold being generally adopted. The veil—thick for the majority, but transparent for a minority of shrewd people—which the inflation had cast over all economic phenomena, was now rent aside and it became apparent that the enormously inflated paper prices often signified, when reduced to terms of gold, prices much below those of 1913. And then the watchword for the securities markets became: revaluation of shares, and speculation anticipated a rapid rise in quotations, which were thought to be much below the "intrinsic" worth of the shares. It was probably for this reason that the prices of shares, like the prices for goods, rose considerably during the final phase of the inflation. The index number of shares in terms of gold, which had been 16·0 in July 1923, jumped to 22·6 in September 1923, to 28·5 in October, and to 39·4 in November. Never since 1919 had the figure been so high. The over-valuation of shares, relatively to their yields, was colossal.*

At the beginning of November 1923—on the 3rd—there was an extraordinary situation: the index number of share prices, in terms of gold, rose above the pre-war level. The explanation is this: in those days the Bourse was using as its criterion for the valuation of shares in paper marks, not the Berlin quotation for the dollar, which was held artificially low, but the quotations of foreign markets, which at that time were much higher. This was only a passing phase; the prices of shares declined rapidly when, after the stabilization of the mark, foreign quotations once more approximated to the official Berlin rate. The average quotation for December 1923 was 26·9 (1913 = 100).

In a case before the Supreme Tribunal at Leipzig, the facts recounted offered a typical example of the extraordinary variability of the prices of securities towards the end of 1923. On October 29th, 1923, a person had given a bank an order to buy 40,000 marks of 3½ per cent East Prussia Mortgage Bonds. On that day bonds of the nominal value of 40,000 marks were worth, at the Bourse quotation, 39 gold marks. The bank did not execute the order until November 23rd, when it

* Certain shares had risen to even higher prices. The index number for the mining and metallurgical group was 25·5 in July, 47·3 in September, 49·3 in October, and 65·7 in November. This index number fell back to 39·5 in December. In *Wirtschaft und Statistik*, 1923, the reader can find, besides the monthly averages, the index numbers calculated for certain days.

bought the bonds for a price equivalent to 14·413 gold marks. The client having protested, the bank resold the securities on December 13th, receiving 2,915 gold marks.*

### VI. THE QUESTION OF THE "GOLD BALANCE SHEETS"

**19.** During 1924 the question of the gold balance sheets was the centre of all discussions relating to the Bourse and to the industrial situation. The decree of December 28th, 1923, had compelled industrial companies to compile new balance sheets, valuing their assets and liabilities in "gold marks." What criteria had to be adopted in making these estimates? Industrialists could not make up their minds about the answer to this question. For how could new balance sheets, which must show the financial state of companies, be compiled at a time when all values were unstable?

On the subject of the valuation of the assets of companies two opposing currents of thought were manifested. Some wished to apply the test of "intrinsic value" (Substanzwert) and others supported the test of "earning capacity" (Ertragswert).

The Deutsche Bank was an authoritative representative of the first opinion.† According to this institution the criteria of "real" or "intrinsic" value of buildings, plant, etc., which may be judged by their cost (taking account of wear and tear) must prevail in the drawing-up of the balance sheet. The low productivity of industry in 1924 was a transitory phenomenon. Besides, the object of the decree of December 28th, 1923, was only the elimination of the effects of the monetary depreciation from the balance sheets of industrial companies. A "deflation" in the various assets of the balance sheet must therefore be effected in relation to the monetary deflation which occurred with the return of the gold mark as the measure of prices. New investments of capital made in the depreciated currency, at different stages of the depreciation, must be reduced to their gold value, and the material losses, due to the inflation, had to be taken into consideration. But to determine the value of the assets of a company on the base of its actual profitability was equivalent to taking account not only of monetary influences, but of all the causes—defeat, political revolution, economic crises, the occupation of the Ruhr, etc.—which had contrib-

* On the prices of German shares from 1924 to 1931, see the author's study: *Le previsioni economiche*, Turin, 1932 (Collana di Economisti Italiani e Stranieri).

† See *Wirtschaftliche Mitteilungen*, published by Deutsche Bank, September issue, 1924.

uted to reducing the income of certain industries. Such a method lost sight of the connection between the inflation and the transformation of balance sheets to a gold basis, as desired by the said decree, and proceeded, instead, to a general revision of the position of German industry.

Others observed that a very heavy reduction of capital, which would have been the consequence of the application of the earning capacity criterion, would have rendered difficult the future issue of debentures, etc., which would have to be secured on the company's capital.

Besides, to reduce capital meant increasing dividend percentages, while the valuation of capital according to their "intrinsic" value implied that dividends would remain low. The latter, it was said, would be a stimulus to managements to persevere in their efforts to increase the profitability of their firms. It was also argued: if the capital is drastically reduced, in the near future, when industrial conditions will be improved, companies will have to distribute excessively high dividends, provoking the intervention of the Exchequer and the jealousy of the working classes.

It may also be added that a policy of excessive contraction of nominal capital would have given a picture the reverse of reality, indicating that Germany was using capital in relatively modest proportions, and it was yielding well; whilst actually there was invested in German industry a very large amount of capital but its productivity was rather low.

The small shareholders were especially opposed to any marked reduction in the capital of companies.

**20.** The supporters of the earning capacity criterion argued that an "intrinsic" value of capital did not exist. What did it matter that a company possessed extensive works, modern and costly machinery, if it could use only a part of its productive capacity? The unused works had no economic value or, at the most, had no more than a "break-up" value. Now, German industry found itself in precisely this state; for, as a result of the war and later of the inflation, established works were extended disproportionately to the permanent commercial possibilities of the products. Consequently, in the gold balance sheet the value of the works of those firms who were not in a position to employ fully their proper capacity for production must be reduced in proportion.

The application of the earning capacity criterion also offered several practical advantages. By reducing the capital by the appropriate amount, it became possible to distribute reasonable and regular dividends to the shareholders, to restore normal conditions in the determination of the value of the shares, to revive the interest of investors in the shares, and to help the security markets back to the fulfilment of their normal functions. If the dividends were increased in the future, the prices of the shares would rise beyond par, and that would make it easier for the companies to proceed, if necessary, to increase their capital, for confidence in the productivity of German industry would spread once more among the investing public.

But, accepting the earning capacity criterion, the question arose: at what rate of interest should the net profit of companies be capitalized? At the normal rate in force before the war or at that much higher rate existing at the end of the inflation? Given the rate of interest prevalent in 1924, in order to maintain the shares of a company at par a dividend of about 10 per cent would be necessary, while before the war 5 per cent was enough.

**21.** There is no doubt that the yield of industry ought to be the fundamental criterion for the determination of the gold value of a company's capital. But this criterion must be applied with due regard to circumstances.

Valuing assets on the basis of the 1924 yield, which was very low, partly for transitory causes, would have shown an exaggerated reduction in the capital of a company.

It was necessary to take account also of the probable *future* productivity. Indeed, only those works which it was certain would never be used in the future were valueless.

Often unused works had a potential value, which in the future would become actual, because of the possibility of an increase in production. Similarly, interest was very high in some months of 1924, through causes which for the most part were exceptional. It was not possible to foresee with accuracy what the productivity of firms and the rate of interest would be in the following years and, therefore, every calculation of the value of capital invested in industry necessarily contained some elements more or less arbitrary.

In practice, the criteria followed by companies in the valuation of their assets varied. For example, while the Deutsche Bank, out of respect for its principles, valued its assets generously, another bank, the Berliner Handelsgesellschaft, proceeded to a very great reduction of its capital.

Generally, it may be stated that companies, in the valuation of their capital, were mainly preoccupied with the ability to distribute dividends not too low relatively to the prevailing rate of interest, and which, therefore, would bring the price of the shares back to par.

## VII. PRINCIPAL RESULTS OF THE NEW "GOLD BALANCE SHEETS"

**22.** It is natural to try to compare the new gold balance sheets of 1924 with those of 1913, to see in what way the war and the inflation had modified the financial situation of firms, and in particular to measure the losses of assets suffered by German industry, which according to the opinion firmly held in official circles must have been considerable.

But the comparison between the balance sheets of 1913 and 1924 was generally very difficult and for many firms impossible. The figures of 1913 and 1924 were not of the same kind. A fall in the assets figures can be due to two very different causes (confusion of which has often given rise in Germany to erroneous conclusions): (1) *material losses* suffered by the works and plant of the company, and (2) a *fall in value* suffered by factories materially intact and even increased. The material losses might be caused by cessions of territory, forced liquidation, sequestration, destruction of buildings effected by orders of military commissions, the deterioration of plant imperfectly reconstructed during the inflation period, and by the contraction of working capital as a result of the depreciation of the currency. It seems to me that the amount of material losses has been much exaggerated. On the whole, in 1924 works were more extensive than in 1913. But there remains the fact of the fall in value suffered by these works, if they were valued on the basis of a productivity lower than pre-war, and at a higher rate of interest.

After 1913 many important companies were enlarged, annexing other smaller firms. To the capital possessed by companies in 1913 it would be necessary to add that of firms later absorbed. That would involve a study of the evolution of each company from 1913 onwards, a study which it is not always easy to make.

In 1913 industrial shares were generally quoted above par. Now should the actual capital of a company be compared with its nominal capital in 1913 or with the value of its capital computed according to the market quotations for its shares? The nominal capital of the Höchster Farbwerke was, in 1912, fifty million marks; in 1924, after the revision of its balance sheet, the nominal capital was 176 million marks. But in

1913 the market priced the shares at four times their nominal value; the total market valuation therefore amounted to 200 million marks. It is not sufficient, in order to secure reliable results, to add the reserves to the capital. In the case of the Höchster Farbwerke the capital *plus* reserves amounted in 1913 to 70 millions; in 1924 to 196 millions. The contrast between these various results is enormous. This is because the market valuation takes account of secret as well as published reserves. It would seem on the whole more correct to take the securities' market valuation for purposes of making comparisons—always bearing in mind, however, that these valuations are often influenced by purely ephemeral causes.

**23.** The principal results derived from the comparison of the new gold balance sheets with those of 1913 are as follows:

(*a*) Generally the value of the *total capital invested in industry* (the companies' own capital, that is share capital plus reserves, and loan capital) was less. According to an investigation, made by the Statistical Bureau of the Reich, concerning 478 companies already in existence before the war, the value of the capital invested fell from 1,941 to 1,512 million gold marks.

(*b*) Typical was the decline, large or small according to the company, of *working capital* (bank deposits, cash, stocks of goods, liquid resources). For several companies this had been the principal cause of the reduction of nominal capital. The balance sheets showed the disproportion between fixed and floating capital which occurred in Germany because of the inflation, and which was one of the principal causes of the "stabilization crisis."

(*c*) Whereas the total capital had generally decreased, the contraction of proprietors' capital and reserves was less, and even in some cases the proprietors' capital had increased. This fact was the consequence of the very great reduction of debts (mortgages, debentures, etc.) caused by the monetary depreciation. "Gelsenkirchener A.G." provides an example. In 1913 the value of the plant was 268 million marks; according to the new gold balance sheet it was 140 millions. But, on the other hand, the value of mortgages and loans, which had been 74 millions, was reduced to 13 millions. That allowed capital to be reduced by a lower proportion than the fall of assets: from 180 to 130 millions.

(*d*) A comparison of the balance sheets of 1924 and 1913 shows that generally the companies were conservative in the valuation of their assets, especially their plant, buildings, land, etc. For example, some companies estimated the new works acquired or constructed after 1919 according to the purchase price (or cost of production) converted to gold on the basis of the dollar exchange rate. By such means, in certain cases, the works were undervalued, because during the inflation the purchasing power of the paper mark was for a long time considerably higher than its value in terms of dollars.

Thus it may be assumed that in many cases the balance sheets must have concealed considerable secret reserves.

**24.** Four classes of companies undoubtedly suffered heavy *material* losses: they were *shipping companies*, *ordinary credit banks*, *mortgage banks*, and *assurance companies*.

It is well known that under the Treaty of Versailles the shipping companies were compelled to give up almost the whole of their fleets. Out of 5 million tons which they possessed before the war they kept no more than 400,000 tons, of which, at the most, 100,000 tons were suitable for deep-sea traffic. The indemnities paid by the German Government were only sufficient to reconstruct a small part of the lost fleets.

It is necessary to recognize that after the end of the war the companies devoted much energy to the reconstruction of the fleet, employing the large profits they had made thanks to the inflation. Also the replacement of the German fleet was hastened by certain favourable circumstances: for example, the German shippers, profiting by the freight crisis, were able to buy back in England, at extraordinarily low prices, about 700,000 tons of German ships.

In 1925 the principal companies which had transformed their balance sheets showed a meagre 1,673,000 tons (in 1913, 4,350,000 tons). An almost proportional reduction of capital (from 455 to 186 million marks, 59 per cent decrease) in the balance sheets corresponded to this 62 per cent reduction in tonnage. Experts, however, observed that the valuations of the merchant service were extremely conservative; the effective value of the vessels, all of very recent construction, was obviously above the figures entered in the new gold balance sheets.

**25.** Even the banks suffered heavy losses of capital through the war (as a result of forced closures and liquidation of foreign branches, sequestration of securities and property held abroad). But in all probability the most serious losses were, in general, caused by the inflation.

According to the new gold balance sheets, the leading seven Berlin banks possessed a capital of 474 million marks and 185·2 millions reserve. In 1913 the total capital was 1,590 millions and the reserve 474 millions (including the capital and reserves of those banks which, in the meantime, had been absorbed by these seven institutions). Thus the gold capital had been reduced by 70·2 per cent and the reserve by 61 per cent.

Here are some individual figures for the various banks which have been calculated on the basis of the data contained in the *Frankfurter Zeitung* of December 7th, 1924 (No. 914).

TABLE XXXIII

(*Millions of marks*)

| | 1924 | | 1913 | |
|---|---|---|---|---|
| | *Capital* | *Reserve* | *Capital* | *Reserve* |
| Deutsche Bank .. .. .. | 150 | 50 | 353 | 157 |
| Diskonto-Gesellschaft .. .. | 100 | 45 | 344 | 120 |
| Dresdner Bank .. .. | 78 | 22 | 294 | 79 |
| Darmstädter und Nationalbank | 60 | 40 | 283 | 52 |
| Commerz und Privatbank .. | 42 | 21 | 145 | 23 |
| Berl. Handelsgesellschaft .. | 22 | 5 | 110 | 35 |
| Mitteldeutsche Kreditbank .. | 22 | 2·2 | 60 | 8 |

From other calculations of the *Frankfurter Zeitung* it appears that the value of the share capital of the great banks computed by the market valuation of December 1924 was barely a *fifth* of the 1913 value (taking account in the calculations of the banks absorbed after 1913).

TABLE XXXIV

*Value of the Banks' Share-Capital calculated according to Prices quoted for Shares*

(*Millions of marks*)

| | *End of* 1913 | *December 5th,* 1924 | *Percentage* |
|---|---|---|---|
| Deutsche Bank .. .. .. | 773 | 177 | 23 |
| Diskonto-Gesellschaft .. .. | 551 | 113 | 21 |
| Dresdner Bank .. .. .. | 418 | 81 | 19 |
| Darmstädter und Nationalbank.. | 328 | 71 | 22 |

The proportion of the reduction of capital and reserves varies much from bank to bank. A great impression was made in financial circles, in the summer of 1924, by the publication of the gold balance sheet of the Berliner Handelsgesellschaft, which reduced its private capital, nominally not increased after 1914, in the proportion of 5 to 1. This bank, guided by a genial financier, Carl Fürstenberg, had followed a prudent policy during the inflation, refusing to allow itself to be caught in the expansion movement which was typical of banking institutions during that period. It was believed therefore that the Handelsgesellschaft must have succeeded in saving at least a very great part of its proprietors' capital.

There was a discussion in the German Press as to which was the phase of the inflation in which the banks suffered the greatest losses. Some held that the last phase of the inflation especially, when the depreciation was very rapid, had been fatal to the banks. Since the legal method of payment was always with paper money, the banks had to hold available in their tills considerable sums of paper money, the value of which rapidly diminished. It should be observed that, in granting credits to customers the banks had to use not only their deposits but also their own capital, which by such means was dragged into the vortex of the monetary depreciation.

Others, however, maintained that the banks had suffered the heaviest losses, without realizing it, in the first phases of the inflation when the phenomenon of the monetary depreciation had not yet been properly understood by the majority of bank directors. The more acute of the big and little speculators rushed to the banks, from which they obtained credits which they repaid with money whose value was always depreciating. Compared with other business firms the banks adopted defensive methods against the effects of the depreciation of money—in their case the raising of the rate of interest and of commission charges—too late, and these measures were often of little use.*

**26.** Besides the ordinary credit banks, the *mortgage banks* lost a great part of their capital, which the law obliged them to invest in certain ways. They were ruined by the collapse of the mark and of Government securities. In 1913 all the German mortgage banks had at their disposal a capital of 712 million marks and a reserve of 240 millions. According to the gold balance sheets in 1924 the capital was reduced to 154 millions and the reserves to 32 millions.

* Diskonto-Gesellschaft, *Report*, 1923, p. 12.

The *assurance companies* also saw a great part of their capital disappear, which they were obliged by law to invest in mortgage loans on land, etc., and in Government securities. It was not until July 1923 that a new law permitted these companies to choose different investments, better adapted to avoiding the influences of the monetary depreciation. But it was too late.

### VIII. THE CAPITAL OF THE PRINCIPAL GERMAN INDUSTRIAL GROUPS IN 1924

**27.** So far as the principal industries were concerned the results of the revaluation of capital did not, on the whole, fulfil the pessimistic expectations of the German official world. Generally the great companies of the mining and iron and steel industry, and the electrical and chemical industries, have preserved or increased their capital, compared with 1913.* It is true that this was often due to the growth of firms after 1913, owing to the absorption of smaller firms, and to the reduction of mortgages, debentures, etc. However, the fact is always important because it proves that the great German companies were able to resist the tempest loosed by the war, the defeat, the revolution and the inflation. Examples of important companies which had been forced to reduce greatly their pre-war capital are not frequent.† Examination of the gold balance sheets shows that in the years 1914–23 there was a great concentration of capital in the iron and steel, chemical and electrical industries. In other branches of industry the process of concentration was less marked.

According to the calculations of Katona‡ the capital (plus published

* Of course, this would not justify the conclusion that inflation was favourable to German economy as a whole. Account ought to be taken of the lot of thousands of small businesses and, moreover, of the unfavourable influences of inflation on production which are described in Chapters V and X.

† The following cases may be quoted: Gesellschaft für elekt. Unternehmungen, Rombacher Hütte, Hohenlohe Werke. Another case of considerable loss of resources is that of three companies forming the so-called "Metallbank" group ("Metallgesellschaft," "Metallbank," "Scheideanstalt"). The proprietary capital of these three companies (capital and reserves), which in 1914 amounted to 108 million gold marks, was reduced in 1924 to 68 millions. The shrinkage of working capital was particularly great. It is certain, even in such cases, that the estimates were very conservative; buildings and lands like the industrial shares have been estimated according to 1924 prices, which were exceptionally low.

‡ *Wirtschaftskurve der Frankfurter Zeitung*, 1925, part i. In the table the heavy reduction of capital of the A.E.G. is worth noticing. The balance sheet did not indicate how much war losses, the depreciation of credits and securities, the contraction of liquid resources, and the criteria for valuation of actual capital respectively contributed to the shrinkage. Several electrical companies suffered losses during the inflation

reserves) of certain great companies was as shown in the following table.

TABLE XXXV

(*Millions of marks*)

| | *Pre-war* | *Beginning of 1925* | |
|---|---|---|---|
| Krupp | 209 | 200 | |
| Phönix | 120 | 180 | |
| Gelsenkirchen | 220 | 168 | |
| Deutsch-Luxemburg | 130 | 127 | |
| Bochumer Verein | 50 | 72 | * |
| Siemens und Halske | 87 | 168 | |
| Siemens-Schuckert | 90 | 105 | |
| Klöckner-Werke | — | 118 | |
| Rheinische Stahlwerke | 58 | 124 | |
| Mannesmann | 90 | 115 | |
| Harpener | 120 | 102 | |
| Ilse | 21 | 88 | |
| Rheinische Braunkohle | 36 | 70 | |
| A.E.G. | 248 | 172 | |
| Rhein.-West.-El. Werke | 54 | 156 | |
| Bad. Anilin | 83 | 235 | |
| Elberfelder Farben | 79 | 195 | |
| Höchster Farben | 70 | 196 | |
| Linke Hoffmann | 22 | 72 | |
| Deutsche Erdöl | 41 | 105 | |

N.B.—The electro-iron and steel trust was dissolved during the stabilization crisis. But the amalgamation of the three iron and steel firms was permanent.

The figures of the nominal capital shown in the table do not include the so-called "reserve shares" at the disposal of the managements and not yet issued.

The large increase of capital of the great chemical companies is worth noticing. The same phenomenon is met with again in the minor companies (e.g. "Agfa": Capital plus reserve in 1913 = 25 million marks; in 1924 = 64 million).

The figures referred to show that many industrial companies had, at the end of the inflation, proprietors' capital far greater than that of the great banks, which had in 1913 had the largest capital. Another

because many communes denounced existing contracts, thus getting the possession of power stations for which they often paid derisory sums in paper marks. Elsewhere companies profited from the reduction of the value of the debentures which they had issued, generally for large sums.

* Electro-Iron and Steel Trust. Total 640 million marks.

notable fact, shown in an official statistical report published in 1925, was the great concentration of the capital of joint-stock companies.*

IX. CONCLUSION

**28.** The foregoing facts have shown how varied were the causes which influenced the prices of German shares after the end of the war. Some writers have attempted to reduce these causes to the following simple formula: during the paper inflation the prices of shares were dominated by the "intrinsic value" of the share as representing "material wealth"; whilst in stable monetary conditions the price is fixed by the yield of the share capitalized at the current rate of interest.

Our investigations have shown that this formula is not entirely accurate. It is true that in the last phase of the inflation, i.e. in 1923, there was a tendency to overvalue shares, i.e. there was a disequilibrium between their price and their yield. But on the whole, even during the monetary depreciation, the yield exercised a great influence; and the prices of shares, though fluctuating at certain times (1920, 1921, 1923) with the dollar exchange rate, were always well below the pre-war level.

Many other facts show that the yield was one of the guiding elements in the valuation of capital even in periods of monetary depreciation. Why did houses, even the modern and expensively built houses, situated in the best quarters, have such silly prices during the inflation? They were still "material" wealth. Their prices were so low precisely because of the low yield. On the other hand, why did the prices of certain securities, which did not represent material wealth, but only a right to receive a fixed sum, increase with the monetary depreciation, as did

* From an article published in the *Berliner Tageblatt* (No. 343, July 23rd, 1926) the following summary is reproduced:

| | 1904 | | 1925 | |
|---|---|---|---|---|
| *Capital of German Joint-Stock Companies* | *Percentage of total number of companies* | *Percentage of total capital* | *Percentage of total number of companies* | *Percentage of total capital* |
| Up to 100,000 .. .. | 7·9 | 0·2 | 38·6 | 0·7 |
| 100,000–500,000 .. .. | 26·1 | 3·6 | 29·1 | 3·0 |
| 500,000–1 million .. .. | 15·1 | 4·3 | 11·5 | 5·0 |
| 1 million–5 millions .. | 42·5 | 34·0 | 16·2 | 25·8 |
| 5 millions–10 millions .. | 4·6 | 13·6 | 2·5 | 12·8 |
| 10 millions–20 millions .. | 1·9 | 11·8 | 1·0 | 11·5 |
| Over 20 millions .. .. | 1·9 | 32·5 | 1·0 | 41·2 |

The companies with a capital above 5 million marks were scarcely 4·5 per cent of the total number in 1925, but they possessed more than 65 per cent of the total capital. Compared with 1904 the concentration of capital had increased considerably.

the "stable value" securities? Because these securities were productive of a constant real income, owing to the fact that the nominal interest increased proportionately to the rise in the price of gold or some other material (coal, corn, potassium, sugar). It was observed in Germany that the prices of shares of those companies which had more or less extensive foreign interests ("Valutapapiere")* were more sensitive to the monetary depreciation. That was because of the greater demand for these securities, the public thinking that companies whose receipts consisted partly of profits realized in foreign currencies would be in a better position to raise their nominal dividends.

The vicissitudes of share prices were the cause of heavy losses for some, and of conspicuous chance profits for others, during the inflation. The movement of share prices contributed very much to those serious displacements in the distribution of wealth which occurred during the years of the paper inflation.

* Strictly speaking the "Valutapapiere" were securities issued in a foreign currency, whose prices must obviously vary with the dollar exchange rate. But during the inflation there was a tendency to enlarge the conception of "Valutapapiere" and this character was also attributed to the securities of German companies which had foreign interests. For example, for a certain time, even the shares of the Deutsche Bank became "Valutapapiere," after this bank had acquired interests in the petroleum industry, which had foreign interests.

# CHAPTER VIII

# Social Influences of the Inflation*

## PART I

### I. WAR PROFITS

**1.** The social effects of the inflation in Germany were not substantially different from those which had occurred in the past whenever the circulating medium had depreciated, nor from those which during and after the World War were apparent, to a greater or lesser degree, in all countries with a depreciated currency. Inflation was always a terrible instrument for the redistribution of wealth. It is not possible to study the influences of the inflation separately from those of other causes which acted at the same time, e.g. the war. But it may be said that on the whole the inflation generally favoured the entrepreneurs and the owners of material means of production, especially strengthening the positions of industrial capitalists; that it caused a lowering of the real wages of workmen; that it decimated or destroyed altogether the old middle class of investors, possessors of those securities which now could only, ironically, be said to show a fixed income; and that it created a new middle class of intermediaries, traders, small speculators on the Bourse, and small profiteers of the monetary depreciation.

However, if the social effects of the inflation present fundamental features common to various countries, there were between concrete cases certain differences worthy of attention. The longer or shorter duration, the greater or less intensity of the inflation, and the varied economic and social structures of the various countries were largely responsible for these differences. It is obvious that the redistribution of wealth must have been greater in a country with a highly differentiated structure such as Germany, in whose great and wealthy cities lived a substantial middle class of capitalists, than in predominantly agricultural countries, such as the Balkan States.

Besides, in the various countries the effects of the inflation were combined with effects deriving from different sources and were by them, according to the case, either strengthened or weakened. It appears

* This chapter includes two memoranda: "Influenza del deprezzamento del marco sulla distribuzione della ricchezza" (*Economia*, 1925), and "Movement of Wages in Germany, 1920–1928" (a paper read before the London Royal Statistical Society on April 16th, 1929, and published in the *Journal* of that Society, 1929).

that in some States, as in Hungary, the bankers drew great profits from the monetary depreciation; whilst in others, as in Germany, they suffered more or less serious losses. In several countries landed proprietors gained by the inflation, which freed them from heavy mortgage burdens; but where, after the war, new agrarian laws compelled the appropriation or division of lands the inflation harmed the great landowners, because it depreciated the compensation they received.

In contrast to other countries, whose money was relatively stable at the beginning of 1920, Germany experienced after 1919 violent and profound movements in the social structure, such as had never occurred in the past. Especially in the post-war years, at a time of low productivity, the inequality in the distribution of wealth was accentuated. Outstanding concentrations of capital were accumulated, which outside Germany were often interpreted as indices of German economic prosperity, whilst, at least in great part, they were only the consequence of a transfer of wealth, i.e. of the appropriatory powers exercised by some plutocratic groups, favoured by the inflation, to the disadvantage of those classes of society who had not been able, or did not know how, to defend themselves against the influence of the depreciation of the mark.

2. As could be easily foreseen, the war helped very much to increase the income of those entrepreneurs who had been in a position to supply in great quantities the goods demanded by the military authorities. Particularly the application of the "Hindenburg programme" ensured magnificent profits to the industries concerned in the production of war materials.

Sources of outstanding profits suddenly appeared; and acute individuals, even if destitute of capital, were able to make large profits.*

* On the sudden wealth created by the war in Germany see Schultze's book, *Not und Verschwendung*, 1924. On profits from war industries see Lewinsohn, *Die Umschichtung der europäischen Vermögen*, Berlin, 1925, pp. 44 and following. That the distribution of income became more unequal in Germany during the war is confirmed by Prussian statistics, which give the results of the general tax on income. On the basis of those returns I have calculated the "relative average deviation from the average income" (which can be assumed as an index summary of the inequality of distribution).

| | RELATIVE AVERAGE DEVIATION | |
|---|---|---|
| | 1913 | 1918 |
| | *Percentage* | *Percentage* |
| Incomes over 900 marks .. .. | 65·4 | 74·7 |
| All incomes .. .. .. | 73·5 | 78·2 |

Figures regarding incomes over 900 marks are more accurate because the lower

The inflation was beginning to make its influence felt. The incomes of many classes of society were diminished because of the rise in prices, which was due to the scarcity of some consumption goods and to the progressive depreciation of the currency.

It would be erroneous, however, to say that the influences of the war contributed solely to increasing the inequality of the distribution of incomes and property. For though on the one hand huge fortunes were made owing to great unmerited "contingent profits," on the other hand the sudden closure of foreign markets which cut down exports, the sequestration of part of the merchant navy, the stoppage of maritime traffic (except in the Baltic Sea), the loss of foreign investments, and the displacements in the internal demand for goods decimated numerous considerable fortunes. Hamburg, for example, was seriously stricken by the war. Elsewhere, though some of the working classes suffered, others obtained higher wages; and though some of the middle classes which possessed Government securities, debentures, loans, etc., declined, a new middle class of small merchants, intermediaries of all kinds, small industrialists, and small rural landowners drew profits from the favourable circumstances.

II. THE POST-ARMISTICE SOCIAL REVOLUTION

**3.** As the magnificent war profits diminished a new and abundant source of exceptional profits began to open up during 1919. In the course of that year the monetary depreciation was greatly accentuated. The paper mark, which in October 1918 was still worth about 60 per cent of its pre-war value (in terms of gold), in December 1919 was worth, on the average, 9 per cent of its gold parity. The leaders of the Socialist Party, who had risen in the revolution of November 1918, had neither the strength nor the ability to impose on the monied classes the taxes necessary for balancing the National Budget. They could do nothing but increase the issues of paper money, abundantly serving, by such means, the interests of those bourgeois groups which, after a short period of confusion caused by the revolution, exercised a prevailing influence on the economic and financial policy of the Reich.

In the following years in Germany the inflation revealed itself as an unsettling and revolutionary influence much more powerful than the war itself. The displacements it produced in the German social

incomes were estimated by the Prussian Statistical Bureau on the base of disputable criteria. A tendency towards an increasing inequality in incomes during the war is also clearly shown in Saxon statistics.

structure were much more radical than those occasioned by the long war. Unsuspected sources of profits appeared and huge fortunes were rapidly accumulated, while the poverty of many classes of society increased and the total income of the German people remained below the pre-war income.

**4.** There was nothing unusual in the phenomenon of increasing inequality of income in pre-war Germany. It was natural, given the socio-economic structure, that the greater part of the increase in production and total income should fall to the lot of those who, as organizers of industry, commerce, transport, and banking, had given the impetus to the adoption of technical improvements and more rational use of the natural resources and personnel of the country, and so had magnificently developed those resources.

As Schmoller justly observed, only a puerile optimist, unsupported by any historical example, could suppose that a time of economic and technical progress had in itself a tendency towards a less unequal distribution of wealth.*

Similarly, it would not have been strange if the wealth of the classes directing German economic life had increased after the war in a victorious Germany. As a German author (Pinner) writes, the world conflict was not, as regards Germany, the war of the German *people*, but the war of industrial "expansionism." The great industrialists, putting into action the intentions clearly expressed in the famous memorandum of the six economic associations, would have despoiled the conquered without mercy, securing for their own benefit that indemnity of war which, according to Helfferich's celebrated phrase, "would have been a heavy ball of lead tied to the feet of future generations of the Allied countries."

**5.** But it is most astonishing that huge private fortunes and imposing concentrations of capital were amassed in the years 1919–23: years which were not, on the whole, a time of general economic prosperity. The fact is certainly surprising, although the surprise is lessened if we consider that even in the past times of economic regressions, of social dissolution, and of profound political disturbances have often been characterized by a concentration of property. "In those periods the strong recovered their primitive habits as beasts of prey."† Often

* Schmöller, *Principes d'Economie politique*, Paris, 1907, vol. iv. p. 456.

† Schmöller, *op. cit.*, p. 463.

social and political crises have seriously harmed, at first, a great number of small landowners, industrialists, merchants, or capitalists, whilst the big men for some time have resisted and profited from the crisis, and actually increased their personal property.

In Germany itself it was observed that industrial and banking concentration made particularly rapid progress during the crises of 1900 and 1907, because a number of small industrial firms or banks which found themselves in precarious positions were readily absorbed by stronger firms.

### III. THE ORIGIN OF THE GREAT PRIVATE FORTUNES AMASSED DURING THE INFLATION

**6.** In the years of the inflation the name of Stinnes became almost legendary: it was synonymous for concentration of wealth, industry, and power.* From him there spread out threads, visible and invisible, which regulated a great part of German economic life. But Stinnes did not reign alone. Everyone knows the names Thyssen, Klöckner, Stumm, Otto Wolff, Herzfeld, etc.

Even before the war the "windfall profits" deriving from especially favourable circumstances had largely contributed to the accumulation of large fortunes. But nevertheless, if the origin and growth of great properties based on industry and trade are examined, it must be acknowledged that the great captains of German industry had some eminent qualities. The origin of their fortune was sometimes a technical discovery of great importance (e.g. Krupp, Siemens, Mannesmann); or they owed their success to having created new forms of economic organization (e.g. Emil Rathenau, the founder of A.E.G.); or they opened new routes for German commercial expansion, creating the banking organizations necessary for penetration into foreign markets, as did Georg von Siemens, the founder of the Deutsche Bank. Thyssen, a great industrialist, had applied on a vast scale the principle of "vertical concentration" of firms, i.e. the combination of coal, iron, and finished products. Even in the great firms of Krupp the mining of iron and coal, the furnaces, the metals, steel plates, and machine works were united in a complete economic organism. Kirdorf founded the "Gelsenkirchener Bergswerksgesellschaft," a grandiose union of mining firms, and later

* On the German "new rich" see, besides Lewinsohn's book already cited, Pinner, *Deutsche Wirtschaftsführer*, 1924; Ufermann, *Könige der Inflation*, 1924; Ufermann and Hüglin, *Stinnes und seine Konzerne*, 1924; besides numerous articles in the principal financial and political journals.

gave his name to the famous Rheinisch-Westphälisches Kohlensyndikat. Others continually improved maritime transport, creating a system of lines which connected Germany with the most remote regions of the world.

7. In short, the great leaders of the German economy were producers. Their wealth had its roots in the general prosperity of the country, to which they had contributed by continually improving the productive equipment, and by perfecting the banking, industrial, and commercial organizations—and even by promoting that progress in agriculture which was due to the employment of scientific methods.

It is true that there are some examples of "conjuncture profits." Schmoller quotes the example of the peasants of Schöneberg, who quite unexpectedly became millionaires, thanks to the rapid increase in the value of their land. But there were, perhaps, no examples of great fortunes amassed exclusively by speculation, gambling on the Bourse, or by clever exploitation of circumstances. In general, that is to say, the accumulation of great fortunes had not, in the past, meant the transfer of wealth from one to another.

But the new men of the post-war period were not generally creators of new industries or new forms of economic organization (the principle of "vertical concentration," of which so much was heard after the war, had already been applied here and there in pre-war German economy). The new men were for the most part very clever speculators, combining their knowledge of business with the strategy of the Bourse and of high finance. And, above all, their successes were intimately connected with the inflation.

In post-war Germany the spirit of speculation spread in all classes of society as a result of the inflation. For the inflation made all values unstable, and obliged many of the working classes and those with small incomes to seek profits on the Bourse in order to supplement their incomes which were continually being reduced by the monetary depreciation. But even industrialists were diverted from productive work and became speculators on the Bourse: it being obvious that fortunate dealings in securities and foreign exchange could be much more profitable than the constant hard work involved in trying to improve production. The great speculators—such as Herzfeld—were only the more refined expression of the spirit of speculation which inspired the entire population.

Those who in Germany in the post-war years considerably increased their own fortunes or who became new possessors of huge fortunes, were mainly those men who understood before others the phenomenon of the inflation,* and who, foreseeing the continual depreciation of the German currency, used this knowledge in all their financial operations.

A German author (whose interesting observations have helped the writing of the present chapter) justifiably writes that the new captains of the German economy "derived their power from the destructive forces of their time and became rich not with the increase of general prosperity, but with the increase in the poverty of their people," which in a large measure was caused by the depreciation of the currency.†

**8.** To understand the phenomenon of the rapid accumulation of large fortunes, it is necessary to take account of these two circumstances: on the one hand, for a number of reasons some individuals secured enormous liquid money capital; on the other, exceptionally favourable circumstances occurred, owing to the depreciation of prices, for the employment of those sums of money.

During the war great profits were realized in munitions, financial transactions of various kinds, in the plundering of occupied territories, and in foreign trade, which, thanks to the limitations and prohibitions imposed by the Government, assured substantial profits to those who could obtain permits to import or export. After the end of the war new and sometimes more important sources of wealth were opened up to enterprising spirits. Firms of Cologne acquired a huge collection of war material which flowed into that city during the retreat of the German troops. By such means Otto Wolff, for example, considerably increased the fortune he had amassed during the war.

The German Press has described the complicated financial transactions, the confusion of interests, and the frauds which for years ranged round the famous dump of war residue in Hanau. That dump, whose creation had already given rise to several large fortunes during the war, extended for miles. Speculators of every faction took part again and again in the long chain of buyers and sellers along which ownership of the dump passed.

* Even in Austria (where more still than in Germany the fortunes of the new rich were made in speculation) during the war some people concerned with high finance and industry had begun the "flight from the crown," and the habit was already established in those circles of reckoning in Swiss francs and of investing in foreign exchange.

† Pinner, *Wirtschaftsführer*, 1924, p. 32.

**9.** Others enriched themselves by operations in foreign exchange, in markets with which Germany gradually opened up connections. Others again made big profits by importing raw materials. Some made money out of the export trade, buying up huge quantities of German goods and selling them at higher prices abroad. Foreign trade provided opportunities for securing plenty of foreign exchange. Many people knew how to profit by the exceptional conditions of the immediately post-war period when the low level of home production, the obstacles in the way of imports, and the transfers which had to be made to the Allies, combined to create a great scarcity of coal, iron, timber, and many other primary and semi-manufactured goods. Whoever possessed such goods could secure a monopoly price, far above the cost of production; and the goods passed from one speculator to another, through a long chain of middlemen.

Before the war great merchants would often be faced with the competition of powerful syndicates, who designed to subject the merchants to themselves. But in the period immediately following the war the pressing need for goods in Germany and the necessity for re-opening connections with foreign countries were favourable conditions for the great wholesale merchants. It was by no mere coincidence that certain great merchants rose rapidly in those post-war days. The most typical example was Otto Wolff, a merchant in iron goods, who was before the war quite a small man and who after the war succeeded in extending his influence over many firms, among the largest of them being Phönix, and the steel firms of Zypen, Rheinische Stahlwerke, and Defrieswerke.* But Stinnes, Sichel, and Röchling were all more or less merchants.

**10.** Thanks to another circumstance, peculiar to Germany, some great business firms, after the war, amassed large liquid resources in foreign exchange or in German money. Numerous metallurgical and mining firms, such as Stumm, Stinnes, Kirdorf, etc., possessed mines, furnaces, and steel works in Lorraine, the Saar territory, and in Luxemburg. The firms in Lorraine were liquidated under the terms of the Treaty of Versailles, and the German Government indemnified the owners; Stumm, for example, received 112 million paper marks at the beginning of 1920. Those in the Saar and in Luxemburg were sold entirely or in part to French syndicates. The Stumm business, for

* For a description of the Otto Wolff Groups, see *Konzerne der Metallindustrie* (published by the Metallurgical Workers' Union, Stuttgart, 1924), p. 222.

example, sold to France a 60-per-cent share in its works in the Saar, receiving, it is said, 200 million French francs, equal to 100 million gold marks.* Kirdorf and Stinnes, under advantageous conditions, sold the iron and steel works in Luxemburg to France for francs. These operations of some of the great industrialists, who had always advocated the war *à outrance* and had been violently nationalist, were severely criticized in Germany.

**11.** The great industrialists and speculators operated only in part with their own means. They soon realized how profitable it would be at a time of continuous monetary depreciation to borrow other people's money. It became one of the rules of good management to contract as many debts as possible: debts which were repaid later with depreciated currency. Great profits were made from the inflation by knowing how to exploit bank credits wisely. On this point one may read in the report of the "General Association of German Banks and Bankers" for 1923: "Thanks to the aid of the banks, German industry and commerce were given immediately after the war the means not only to preserve their resources but also to increase them in a considerable measure. Industry rapidly recognized that it was economically more advantageous to incur the highest possible debts at the bank rather than to keep large deposits."

Either because they had not yet understood the consequences of the monetary depreciation, or because they were under the dominating influence of certain people or certain industrial groups, the credit banks became one of the principal instruments for the enrichment of speculators during the rising wave of the inflation.

**12.** After the end of the war the price of industrial shares suffered a heavy depreciation. The fear of Bolshevism induced many capitalists to sell what shares they possessed dirt cheap; but a minority of industrialists and financiers justly foresaw that the social upheavals would be only temporary and hastened to buy industrial shares. This was the origin of some of the great "groups" which were formed in Germany in the post-war years.

Stumm's, for example, used the francs received from the sale of firms in the Saar and the indemnities received from the German Government to purchase shares of the companies they wished to annex to their group. Otto Wolff also laid the foundation of the group which

* Lewinsohn, *op. cit.*, p. 125.

took his name by buying cheaply immediately after the war shares of the leading companies. Generally the post-war profiteers were buyers of shares, firms, securities, and merchandise; in short, of all material wealth, in which they invested both the foreign exchange received from export trade, sea traffic, etc., and the money they were able to borrow.

### IV. SPECULATION ON THE BOURSE DURING THE INFLATION

**13.** The purchase of shares was sometimes made directly by industrial groups and sometimes by speculators who specialized in such operations. They, realizing the importance which the possession of the majority of the shares of particular companies could have for certain groups, bought them and later sold them in blocks to the highest bidders. Many still recall the surprise aroused in the financial world of Berlin in 1922 by the news that a Roumanian speculator, Cyprut by name, until then unknown, had succeeded in buying on the quiet about 35 per cent of the shares of a great Berlin bank, the Berliner Handelsgesellschaft. The whole lot was offered to Stinnes and was bought by him.

But on the remarkable scene of the Berlin Bourse for some time the most notable and also the most interesting personage was Herzfeld. He was distinguished from the mass of ordinary speculators on the Bourse not only by the grandiose nature of his operations but also because he sometimes subordinated them to his object of making possible a more rational combination of firms. Probably Herzfeld's most brilliant operation was the acquisition of the majority of the shares of a great iron and steel firm, the Bochumer Verein. The shares were bought by Stinnes, who co-ordinated the works of the Bochumer Verein with others of the great Rhein-Elbe Union group. Another great transaction of Herzfeld was the purchase of the shares of Mansfeld, the most important German company producing copper. The shares were sold to the Wolff and A.E.G. enterprises, which could proceed with the economic and financial reorganization of that great firm, until then managed on somewhat old-fashioned lines. Finally, by the acquisition of the shares of the Salzdetfurth, Leopoldshall, and Westeregeln firms, Herzfeld created a huge "trust" in the potash industry, thus contributing to the resurrection and reorganization of an industry which passed through a serious crisis after the war.

The activity of Herzfeld was variously judged in Germany. Some approved of the advantages derived from the development of the national economy by Herzfeld's operations; whilst others observed that a serious disturbance in the markets and the concentration of the shares of great firms in the hands of a few people were the consequences of those speculations.

**14.** Now these purchases which contributed so much to the concentration of capital and industry were narrowly connected with the phenomenon of the inflation and the depreciation of the mark. Before the war similar transactions had required enormous capital and probably would not have been possible, because the prices of shares would have increased so rapidly as to render the purchase of them too expensive. After the war the prices of shares, expressed in paper marks, had increased very much, but in a much lower proportion, than that of the depreciation of the currency. Besides, if the shares were paid for at a date later than the time of purchase and, in addition, with borrowed money, the continual monetary depreciation still more reduced the real purchase price. But expressed in *paper marks* the prices of shares seemed very high. This exercised a psychological influence on the great mass of shareholders. Deluded by the apparently high prices, even the most cautious shareholders were induced to sell their securities; and only much later, when the veil of the inflation had been torn aside, did they realize that they had made a very bad bargain!

### V. THE GREAT "INFLATION PROFITEERS"

**15.** The fact that the most successful profiteers of the inflation period were speculators rather than producers implied a marked distinction between the new rich and the old rich. The typical leaders of the great German industries in pre-war days had built up their fortunes by devoting themselves to the development of a given enterprise. It is true that the original firm would be continually enlarging its field by absorbing new manufactures. But the development was natural and harmonious. The new plant would be integrated with the old and the completed firm would form an economic "organism." The development of the firms of Thyssen, Krupp, A.E.G., etc., was typical.

But the typical post-war "profiteer" did not confine his attentions to a single industry. Opportunities of profit-making were, thanks to the post-war currency depreciation, varied and continually changing. Sometimes foreign trade promised a wide margin of profit, thanks to a sudden divergence between internal and external prices of goods;

sometimes the purchase of blocks of shares of certain companies was lucrative business; sometimes there was a boom in one industry, sometimes in another. Whoever was seeking large and quick profits had to get his profit from favourable conditions wherever they appeared. And he had to make up his mind quickly, because everything changed so quickly in the conditions created by the inflation—prices to-morrow would not be the same as those of to-day. The profiteer's field of activity was continually widening. The industrialist became a *brasseur d'affaires* who bought up all sorts of firms, even those which had no connection with his original business. The profiteers surrounded themselves with a numerous clientele: the number of directors, attorneys, etc., increased.*

**16.** The typical business man of this kind after the war was Stinnes, around whom were grouped all sorts of businesses: coal, lignite, petrol, iron-mining, blast-furnaces, steelworks, engineering works, electrical works, shipyards, forests, cellulose and paper manufacturers, banks and insurance companies, transport, ocean and inland shipping, merchant firms, newspapers, and inns. The name which an Austrian inflation profiteer gave to his business meant "Everything."

Another characteristic of the new wealth was the rapidity with which it was accumulated. Stinnes had already considerable wealth just before the war—about thirty millions; it increased rapidly during the war; but it was during the brief period 1919–23 that he added enterprise to enterprise. Minoux, one of the general directors of Stinnes, after breaking away from his chief in the summer of 1923, made in a few months quite a large fortune for himself, succeeding even in profiteering from the final phase of the depreciation of the mark. Another typical example was Jacob Michael. Like many other fortunate post-war speculators (Kahn, Mannheimer, and Steinberg in Germany and Bosel in Austria) he was in 1924 scarcely thirty years old. His case was interesting because, unlike the other new rich, Michael made the greater part of his money in the period immediately following stabilization. He threw over the principle which had ruled during the inflation, when the watchword had been "fly from the mark and buy material goods." Michael shrewdly foresaw that the first effect of the stabilization

* Some typical examples of the "inflation" of directors were quoted in the German Press. There were eighty-two directors in the firms of the "Aniline group." A handbook of directors of the big companies contained 70 per cent more names than before the war. The huge number of directors was an obstacle to rationalization of the companies after the inflation.

would be the appearance of a scarcity of capital, which had been hidden until then by the continuous issues of paper money. Consequently, in the first period of stabilization, when everybody was jealously holding on to the real goods bought during the inflation, Michael sold the majority of his own shares, and, at a time when the ordinary sources of credit were almost dried up, had at his command enormous sums of money, which he lent out at extremely high rates of interest.

### VI. UNFAVOURABLE EFFECTS OF THE WAR AND THE INFLATION ON CERTAIN CLASSES OF GREAT WEALTH

**17.** If in the post-war years some people were raised up by that wheel of fortune, the monetary inflation, others with great wealth suffered severe falls. The diminution of the fortune of the house of Krupp was a direct consequence of the war. It lost much through the destruction of part of the works at Essen. Giving evidence of very great tenacity, Krupps, having ceased producing war materials, reorganized in a marvellous manner for the production of other goods.

The annihilation of public debt securities and the heavy fall in the price of shares struck a blow, not only at the mass of small and average investors, but also at great capitalists, who had invested their personal wealth in marketable securities.

Some German cities, such as Frankfort-on-Maine, were mainly inhabited by "rentiers"—holders of securities. In the city the "old" rich suffered particularly. It also seems that many private bankers, who before the war possessed large capital, have suffered serious losses. The prosperity of some banking houses during the inflation period was only apparent; business increased very much, but when they came to reckon up their positions after stabilization, they realized that they had sacrificed part of their capital. For example, the German financial papers related the fall of the old banking house of Frankfort, de Neufville, which before the war had a capital valued at anything from 10 to 15 million gold marks.

Although the fates of the various banks differed according to whether their managers realized sooner or later the significance of the monetary depreciation, it may be stated with certainty that the "financial capital" was not favoured by the inflation, as was capital invested in industry.

Some old well-established merchant-firms in the provinces, alien to speculation, also saw some of their working capital evaporate during the inflation period.

**18.** Agriculture differed from industry in that no progress towards the concentration of farms or of property occurred. On the whole the various classes of agriculturists maintained their positions. The number of transfers of property did not increase during the inflation. Even small and middle-size cultivators profited from the increase in prices of agricultural products and from the decline in mortgage burdens, so that even in the most trying times of the inflation and of the economic crisis, when unemployment and pauperism were swamping the cities and industrial areas, the agricultural classes continued to enjoy blessings which contrasted strongly with the poverty of many other classes.

Some great properties in Silesia—formerly some of the richest estates in the country—were broken up by the partition of Upper Silesia. But on the whole the great landed properties were maintained after the war, having been treated with all respect by the young German republic. Neither the abolition of feoffment of trusts nor "internal colonization" appreciably affected the great estates. Thanks to the inflation the great standard properties were almost completely freed from heavy mortgage debts.

On the other hand, serious changes occurred in the ownership of house property. The inflation and the regulation of rents policy without doubt caused a concentration of property of this kind. In 1922 and 1923, because of the rapid depreciation of the mark, the old house-rents became ridiculous. Consequently the value of houses fell considerably. Many landlords, for whom houses were now valueless because the rents did not cover maintenance expenses, were forced to sell them. Recent German statistics show that during the inflation period the frequency of changes in house property was much higher than that known before the war. Besides foreigners, German speculators also bought a great many houses.*

* Eulenberg, "Die sozialen Wirkungen der Währungsverhältnisse," in the *Jahrbücher für Nationalökonomie*, 1924. The foreign purchasers of houses were chiefly those people who possessed German marks. Their purchases were especially frequent in the second half of 1922 when foreigners, finally persuaded that the German currency would remain depreciated, sought to invest their marks in material wealth. After November 1923, when the German exchange was stabilized, the buying of houses by foreigners ceased almost completely and in 1924 the opposite movement began, i.e. the repurchase of houses by Germans.

PART II

## I. GERMAN STATISTICS OF WORKING-CLASS WAGES

**1.** We will now discuss the influence of the depreciation of the mark on the situation of the working classes, so far as that is indicated by the movement of wages. Owing to the deficiency of statistics (which has also been lamented by the International Bureau of Labour)* our analysis is necessarily incomplete and is limited to the discussion of certain broad tendencies.

The principal source of statistics about wage rates in Germany from the end of the war onwards is in the collective contracts.† Before the war these had been of no great importance, since they regulated the wages of scarcely 1·5 million workmen (about a tenth of the total number of workmen). This figure fell to 0·9 million towards the end of 1917; but directly after the revolution of November 1918 the system of collective contracts spread rapidly, so that towards the end of 1923 they applied to 14·2 million workers (i.e. about 75 per cent of the total). In the years following 1923 the importance of collective contracts once more declined somewhat. Towards the end of 1927, eleven million people were subject to them.

A considerable proportion of the working classes remained outside the collective contracts all the time, but there is no doubt that these agreements exercised a great influence, especially on the rate of wages and the hours of work, even on the conditions of the work of people who were not directly subject to them.

The wage rates fixed in these contracts were: (*a*) rates per working hour; (*b*) piece-rates. Piece-rates were regulated by estimating the amount of work normally done by a man in an hour and the payment for such a quantity was fixed accordingly. The workman was then paid according to the theoretical number of hours represented by the work which he had done.

Wages fixed in the collective contracts are a rough index of the income of the working classes. Exact calculation of working-class income would necessitate taking account of the other elements which are included in the total wage and also of the influence of unemployment. These agreed wage-rates do not even measure exactly the wages actually

* *Les conditions de la vie des ouvriers dans les pays à change déprécié*, Geneva, 1925, p. 11.

† See the official publication *Die Tarifverträge im Deutschen Reich*, Berlin, 1928.

paid per hour. For in the expansion phases of the economic cycle the rate of wages fixed by the collective contracts often only represented minima which were exceeded in practice.

2. With regard to *real* wages I recall that, after an attempt made in December 1919, the Statistical Bureau of the Reich published a cost-of-living index at the beginning of February 1920. This publication was called for by the necessity of securing a statistical measure of the cost of living which would serve as a basis in the wage agreements between employers and employed.

The index was calculated by the following method. The quantity of goods normally consumed by a family of five persons (parents and three children aged respectively 12, 7, and 1½ years) was fixed. At first the index covered only food, rent, fuel, and light; then in 1922 clothing was also included, and the index was revised for the preceding months.

War-time conditions of price regulations and control of consumption goods were continued in 1920. In calculating the theoretical expenditure of a working-class family the quantities consumed were multiplied by the official prices; but if the quantities included in the normal consumers' purchases exceeded the rations which an individual could buy at the official prices, the excess quantities were multiplied by the free market prices, or sometimes by the "black market" prices.

The method adopted by the Statistical Bureau was thus that of the normal fixed budget. In order to lessen the rigidity of this method the Statistical Bureau modified the standard budget from time to time by making adjustments to allow for great seasonal variations in consumption. Other changes in the standard budget became necessary as the systems of rationing and price regulation of various articles were relaxed. The changes were made in such a way as to leave unchanged the total number of calories represented by the various classes of goods. These changes were in total of relatively slight importance and the Statistical Bureau therefore believed that the comparability of the various figures was unaffected.

The index was based on prices ruling in 1913–14. The data was collected in seventy-two German towns, selected as representative. For each town a separate index was calculated. The total index for the Reich was an average of these town indices weighted according to the populations of the various towns.

At first prices were indexed once a month, later (beginning from 1922) twice a month, and then in March 1923 the rapid depreciation of the mark made it necessary to calculate the indices every week.

The method here described was followed during the whole of the inflation period. In spite of its defects this index was considered by distinguished German statisticians as a sufficiently satisfactory measure of the variations in the cost of living from the beginning of 1920 until the end of 1923.

## II. THE CALCULATION OF THE REAL WAGES DURING A TIME OF RAPID MONETARY DEPRECIATION

**3.** The measurement of real wages at a time of the rapid depreciation of the currency (as occurred in Germany in 1923) presents interesting statistical problems.

The workman spends his wage on the days following pay-days. Let $C_1$, $C_2$, $C_3$ . . . be the cost-of-living indices in successive weeks, and $S_1$, $S_2$, $S_3$ . . . the nominal wages paid at the end of each week. Since, normally, the wage paid at the end of each week is spent during the following week, the index of the real wage is not $\frac{S_1}{C_1}, \frac{S_2}{C_2}; \ldots;$ but $\frac{S_1}{C_2}, \frac{S_2}{C_3}$. If the monetary depreciation is slow the correction is not of much significance, but at a time of rapid increase in prices the purchasing power of the *spent* wage can be considerably lower than the purchasing power of the same wage at the time of payment.

In some studies of wages in Berlin during 1922 and 1923, Meerwarth constructed an index of real wages by comparing the wages paid on the Friday with the index number of the cost-of-living calculated for the period between the Saturday and the following Friday.*

**4.** The experiences of 1923 showed that not even this method gave satisfactory results. Mommer† objected that it was hardly likely that in the period of rapid depreciation the workmen would distribute the spending of their wages over the following week. It was much more likely that they would hasten to make all necessary purchases the moment they were paid. Besides, during 1923, the methods of paying wages were often modified, and they varied much from industry to industry. In the summer of 1923, following the demands of the working

* Meerwarth, "Zur neuesten Entwicklung der Löhne" (*Zeitschrift des preussischen statistischen Landesamts*, 1923).

† Mommer, "Löhne und Gehälter im Jahre 1923 und ihre Kaufkraft" (*Vierteljahresberichte des Thür. Stat. Landesamts*, 1923, p. 183).

classes, it became the custom to make an advance of wages on Tuesday the balance being paid on Friday. Later, some firms used to pay wages three times a week, or even daily.

These various methods of payment seriously influences real wages. In the weeks preceding the monetary reform, for example, it made a difference to the workman whether he received his wage in the morning or the afternoon.

For the reasons mentioned, it is impossible to calculate with sufficient accuracy the real wages of German workmen during 1923. Even official figures must be accepted with reservation.

**5.** The stabilization of the mark made necessary a reform of the cost-of-living index number. Thanks to the rapid improvement of the standard of living of the working classes which occurred in 1924, the composition of the "normal budget" was very different from real conditions. The consumption of better quality goods than those considered in the normal budget increased. Besides, it was desirable to complete the budget by adding "miscellaneous expenses," which had been neglected, as of little importance, during the inflation period, when consumption had necessarily been very restricted. But the new index numbers took no account of taxes or of insurance contributions.

When the index number was revised, a very detailed investigation was made into pre-war prices, about 15,000 separate prices being ascertained. The new index, which has resulted from the revision, shows figures about 10 per cent above those calculated by the old method. The new index number was published from February 1925 onwards; but the indices for the months from January 1924 were recalculated by the new method, so that in fact the series goes back to January 1924. The need for weekly indices being much less than it was during the inflation period, the new index has been monthly only.

## III. THE EFFECTS ON WAGES OF THE POLITICAL UPHEAVAL OF NOVEMBER 1918

**6.** In Germany, as in other countries, the war period was on the whole one of relative shortage of labour. Thanks to the intense demand for workers for war industries, the reserve of industrial labour was absorbed, including that part which is normally constituted by women,* and unemployment practically vanished. But the effect of the scarcity

* Kessler, "Die Lage der deutschen Arbeiterschaft nach 1914," in the book *Strukturwandlungen der deutschen Volkswirtschaft*, 1928, vol. i, p. 438.

of labour in raising wages was neutralized by other circumstances, especially by the continual monetary depreciation.

In Germany, as elsewhere, during the war inaccurate ideas about the high level of wages were freely held. Statistics show that, except in the munition industries, real wages were considerably below the pre-war standard.* Below are shown the index numbers of real wages, as calculated by the Statistical Bureau of the Reitch.

TABLE XXXVI

*Indices of Real Wages*

| | GOVERNMENT WORKERS | | | |
|---|---|---|---|---|
| | *Skilled* | *Unskilled* | *Ruhr Miners* | *Printers* |
| 1913 | 100 | 100 | 100 | 100 |
| 1914 | 97·2 | 97·2 | 93·3 | 97·2 |
| 1915 | 79·7 | 80·8 | 81·3 | 77·3 |
| 1916 | 69·2 | 73·8 | 74·4 | 60·6 |
| 1917 | 63·9 | 74·2 | 62·7 | 49·4 |
| 1918 | 83·3 | 99·8 | 63·7 | 54·1 |
| 1919 | 92·2 | 119·8 | 82·4 | 72·3 |

7. The revolution of November 1918 brought political and moral advantages to the working classes. In the famous Labour Magna Charta (as some German writer called it) which was signed on November 15th, 1918, by representatives of the industrialists and the working classes, fundamental rules were laid down which in the new republic were to regulate the relations between capital and labour; i.e. recognition of the trade unions as representative of the workers; the determination of working conditions, for each industry, by collective agreements between industrialists and workers; the formation of works councils for the task of supervising the application of the collective contracts; the acceptance of the principle of the eight-hour working day; the re-organization, on an equal representation basis, of managing committees; conciliation committees for individual industries, formed from employers and employed equally; and the creation of a central commission, also on equal representation basis, to settle disputes regarding different professional groups.

The principles set forth in the "Labour Charter" were afterwards, in a great part, embodied in legislation. Article 165 of the Constitution of Weimar recognizes the workmen's right to collaborate with the

* Wilbrandt, *Die moderne Industriearbeiterschaft*, 1926, p. 128. Quante, "Lohnpolitik und Lohnentwicklung im Kriege," in the *Zeitschrift des preussischen Statistischen Bureaus*, 1919.

entrepreneurs, on an equal footing, for the solution of questions concerning their work. We must also mention the laws and decrees on the eight-hour working day, works councils, social insurances, unemployment, collective contracts, committees of management, etc.*

As a result of the importance assumed by the Socialist trade unions ("freie Gewerkschaften") after the revolution there was a great influx of new members. The number of members, which in 1913 was 2½ millions, fell to 1·7 millions towards the end of the war, rose to 5·5 millions in 1919 and to 7·9 millions in 1920.† At the same time even employees in private industry were organizing themselves with a swing to the left. The three principal unions of State and private employees included 1·6 million members in 1920.

The working classes became the principal support of the new German State constituted at Weimar. The Constitution of Weimar attempted an agreement between parliamentarianism and syndicalism, by means of a "social liberalism" (as it was called): i.e. a moderate liberal system taking account of the powerful movement of the working classes, of their powerful unions and of their aspirations.

From our point of view the first consequence of the revolution was a considerable increase of wages. It may be recalled that often in Germany the trade unions were reproved for having considered the revolution solely as a means for obtaining higher wages.‡ But, because of the inflation, these increases in wages were soon lost to the working classes. From the end of 1919 until the end of 1924 the wage of the German worker was mainly influenced by monetary causes, that is by the inflation until November 1923 and later by the monetary stabilization.

## IV. THE INFLUENCE OF THE INFLATION UNTIL THE SUMMER OF 1922. THE FALL IN REAL WAGES AND INCREASE IN EMPLOYMENT

**8.** The inflation influenced wages in different ways at different stages of the depreciation of the mark. Until the summer of 1922 the principal effects were as follows:

(*a*) The increase in nominal wage rates was slower than the increase in prices caused by the monetary inflation. In other words, real wages fell.

* See *Denkschrift über die seit dem 9, November 1918 auf dem Gebiete der Sozialpolitik getroffenen Massnahmen*, Berlin, 1919 (Drucksachen der Nationalversammlung, 215).

† See *Jahrbuch des Allgemeinen Deutschen Gewerkschaftsbundes*, 1927, p. 245.

‡ Wilbrandt, *op. cit.*, p. 128.

(*b*) As far as it concerned the workers' incomes, this effect was partly offset by the decline in unemployment which accompanied the depreciation of the mark.

The curves of Diagram XVIII represent: (A) index of the dollar exchange rate (1913 = 1); (B) index of wholesale prices (1913 = 1); (C) index of the cost of living (1913 = 1); (D) index of the nominal wages of miners (1913 = 1); (E) the percentage of unemployed among the members of the trade unions; and (F) the real wages of miners expressed as a percentage of the 1913 wage. The first four curves are on a logarithmic scale.

At the beginning of 1920 the exchange rate of the dollar rose suddenly from 15·43 to 23·60 paper marks. Internal prices having also risen, the consequence was a fall in real wages; but at the same time unemployment declined. There followed a brief period of considerable improvement in the mark (the price of the dollar fell to 9·32 marks in June 1920), during which the industries, particularly in the export trade, experienced serious difficulties. Unemployment once more rose appreciably. Real wages showed a tendency to revert to the level existing at the beginning of the year.

A fresh depreciation of the mark in the second half of 1920 brought an improvement in the conditions of the labour market. Unemployment rapidly fell once more (except for a recrudescence of a seasonal character) when towards the end of 1921 a rapid increase in the dollar exchange rate was begun. From about 15 marks in the middle of 1921, the dollar rose to 350 in September 1922. Commercial papers of the end of 1921 and of the first six months of 1922 show, as we have seen, intense activity in many industries and in particular in those producing exports and production goods. *In that period real wages fell appreciably*. The real wages of miners, which in the middle of 1921 were about 90 per cent of the pre-war level, were scarcely 50 to 60 per cent of the same at the end of 1922.*

**9.** The connection between the two effects of the inflation (the fall in the rate of real wages and the increase in employment) has been explained in a preceding chapter. The abundance of money capital which existed during an early phase of the inflation, stimulated the

* From Meerwarth's studies (art. cited) it appears that towards the end of 1922 real wages were, in the industries studied by the author, less than the subsistence minimum.

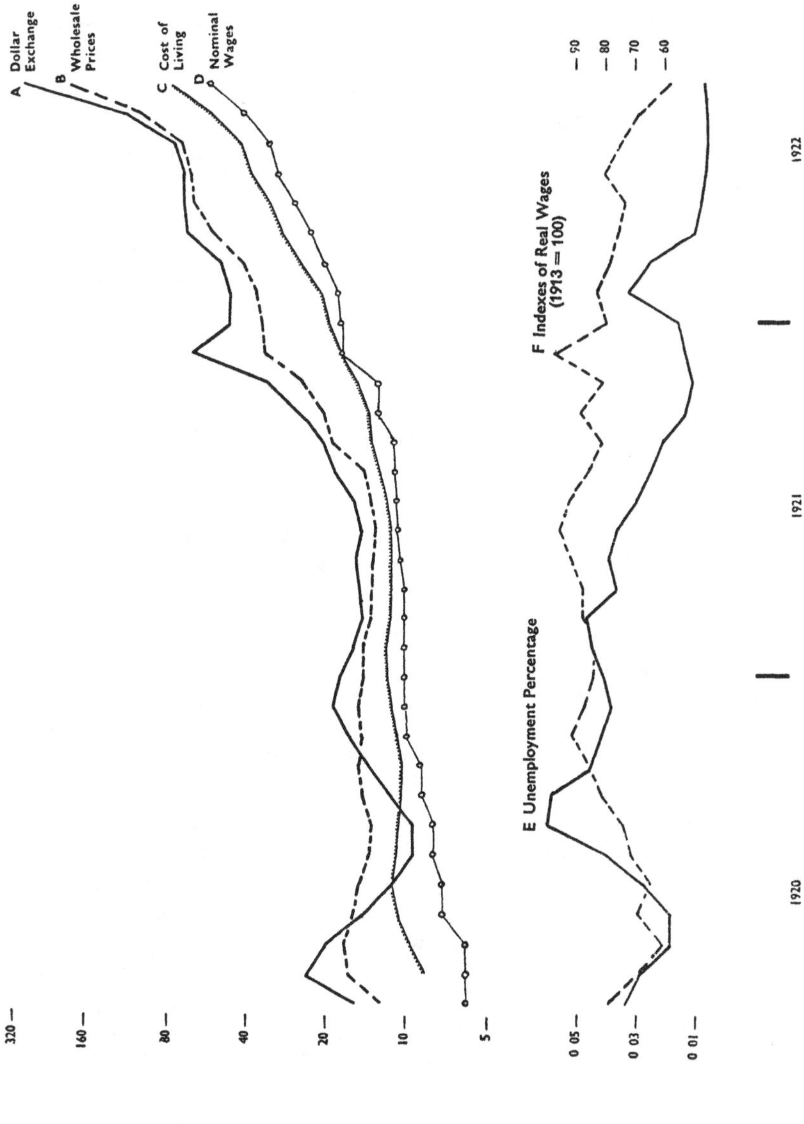


DIAGRAM XVIII.
Working-class Income and the Inflation.

demand for labour. The additional workers were mainly used in the industries making productive goods.

It is true that the rise in the number of workers employed was dependent on the availability of other factors of production, such as foreign raw materials and coal. The supply of coal was somewhat inelastic owing to the difficulty of rapidly increasing production (from this point of view indeed the technical conditions in the lignite industry were more favourable) and to the obligations imposed on Germany by the Treaty of Versailles concerning reparations in kind. But in spite of the rigidity of the supply of other elements of production required for use with labour checking the expansion of the demand for labour, the facts show that this demand was, on the whole, rather elastic during the depreciation of the mark.

The rise in the demand for labour tended to provoke an immediate rise in nominal wages; but this effect was quickly offset by new rises in prices which were the consequence of new issues of paper money on the Government account, and the rates of real wages continued to remain low.*

### V. REAL WAGES AND UNEMPLOYMENT IN THE LAST PHASES OF THE DEPRECIATION OF THE MARK

**10.** The following period (from the end of 1922 to the end of 1923) was characterized by an enormous rise in nominal wage-rates; which increased even more rapidly than wholesale prices and the dollar exchange rate—in marked contrast to the preceding years. This is shown in Diagram XIX. The curves in this diagram show: (A) the movement of the dollar exchange rate; (B) nominal wages of miners; (C) the percentage of unemployed among the members of the trade unions; and (D) the real wages of miners expressed as a percentage of the 1913 wage. The first two curves are on a logarithmic scale.

The enormous rise of nominal wages was due, in a great part, to the influence of the trade unions which, concerned at the decline in the standard of living of wage-earners which occurred in 1922 because of

* A consequence of the fall in real wages was the continual fall in the ratio of wages to the total cost of production. For example, according to the results of an official inquiry in the textile industry, for most products the percentage of wages in the total cost of production was, towards the end of the inflation, much lower than the figures calculated for 1913. This percentage had fallen: in dyeing from 36·9 per cent to 27 per cent; in the manufacture of men's clothing from 18·3 per cent to 15 per cent; in cotton spinning from 63 per cent to 42·7 per cent; and in shirt-making from 29 per cent to 19·8 per cent, etc.

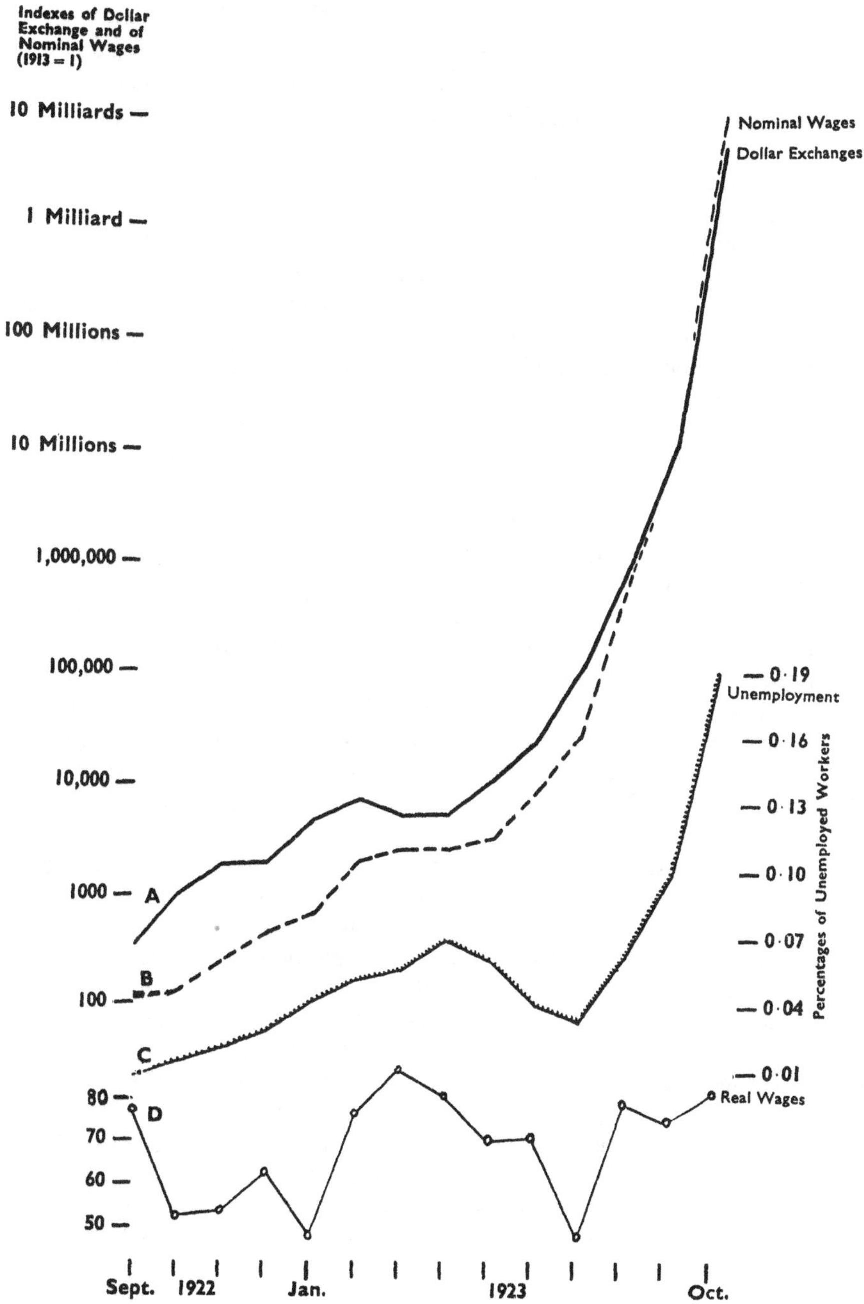


Diagram XIX.—Indexes of real wages (1913 = 100)

the monetary depreciation, attempted the application of various systems with the object of securing workers a real wage independent of the fluctuations of the value of the mark.

**11.** In the summer of 1923 the system of fixing wages on the basis of the cost-of-living index number calculated by the Statistical Bureau of the Reich became general. But not even this system could protect the working classes against the influences of the monetary depreciation at a time when this was very rapid. In fact, wages were fixed on the basis of an index number of prices which, at the time of payment, no longer represented actual conditions. Therefore in the last phase of the depreciation for the "multiplier" represented by the index number of the cost of living there was substituted, in some industries, a multiplier deduced from the exchange rate of the dollar at Berlin on the day the wages were paid. This system was much easier than that based on the index number of prices, the calculation of which required some days; but it also was rendered illusory by the growing velocity of the depreciation of the mark, because the wage received by the workers on a given day was spent on the following days when prices had risen further. According to the agreements between representatives of the working classes and those of the employers (towards the end of August 1923) the principle was settled that wages must be fixed on the basis of prices expected in the week in which the wages would be *spent*. The multiplier must be calculated, therefore, on the basis of *forecasted* prices. In the event of a forecast proving inaccurate, a correction would be made by supplementing the wages or by deducting from the wage of the following week. The difficulties of the practical application of this system are obvious. And whilst this system increased the unproductive work of firms, it failed to assure stable real wages to the working classes. In fact, one of the most characteristic phenomena which appear in the statistical data is the extreme variability of real wages during 1923.

Each renewed sharp depreciation of the German mark (e.g. in January 1923, after the invasion of the Ruhr, and in May, after the breakdown of attempts by the Reichsbank to stabilize the exchange rate) provoked a fall in real wages. The working classes reacted by demanding an increase in nominal wages and thus succeeded sometimes in obtaining relatively high real wages almost equal to pre-war ones. But sooner or later a new collapse of the mark considerably reduced real wages; there followed further demands from the working classes, and so on.

VI. THE VARIABILITY OF WORKERS' INCOMES DURING THE INFLATION

**12.** According to the Statistical Bureau of the Reich, the wages of miners were 47·7 per cent of the pre-war wage in January 1923, 86·2 per cent in March, 47·6 in July, and 81·2 in October. Even greater and more frequent differences may be seen by an examination of real weekly wages, as shown in Diagram xx, in which is represented the movement of real weekly wages (time-rates) of workers employed in the metal industries of Thuringia, according to data accurately calculated by a German writer.*

Owing to the great variability of wages, the loss of economic welfare

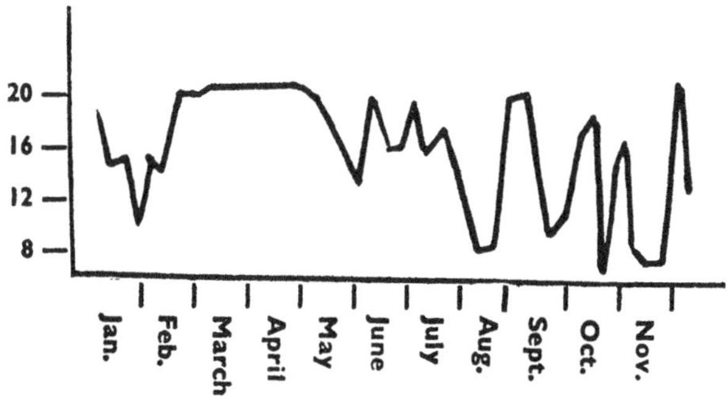


DIAGRAM XX.—Weekly wages of workers (metal industry) in Thuringia in 1923, in gold marks (nominal wages in paper marks divided by the index of cost of living)

suffered by the working classes as a result of the depreciation of the currency was even greater than that resulting from the difference between the average real wage during the inflation and the average pre-war real wage.

The influence of unemployment on the income of workers must also be taken into account. In contrast to what happened in the preceding years, at the beginning of the second half of 1922 the depreciation of the mark and the increase in prices were accompanied by an *increase* in unemployment, as will be seen in Diagram IX.†

**13.** It may seem strange that the same cause (the monetary depreciation) gave rise to different effects. The apparent contrast is explained if one remembers that the monetary depreciation stimulated the demand for labour when there was a time-lag between the rise in wholesale

* Soecknick, *Die Löhne in der Nachkriegszeit*, 1926, p. 37.

† This was also shown in other countries with a depreciated currency after the rise in prices had reached a certain limit (see art. "La Crise du Chômage" in the *Revue Internationale du Travail*, 1924).

prices and the rise in wages; but it ceased to have this influence when wages, becoming more sensitive, rose simultaneously with prices.

If the unemployment curve is compared with the curve of the ratio between the index number of nominal wages and the index number of wholesale prices, it is seen that there is a valid statistical relation for

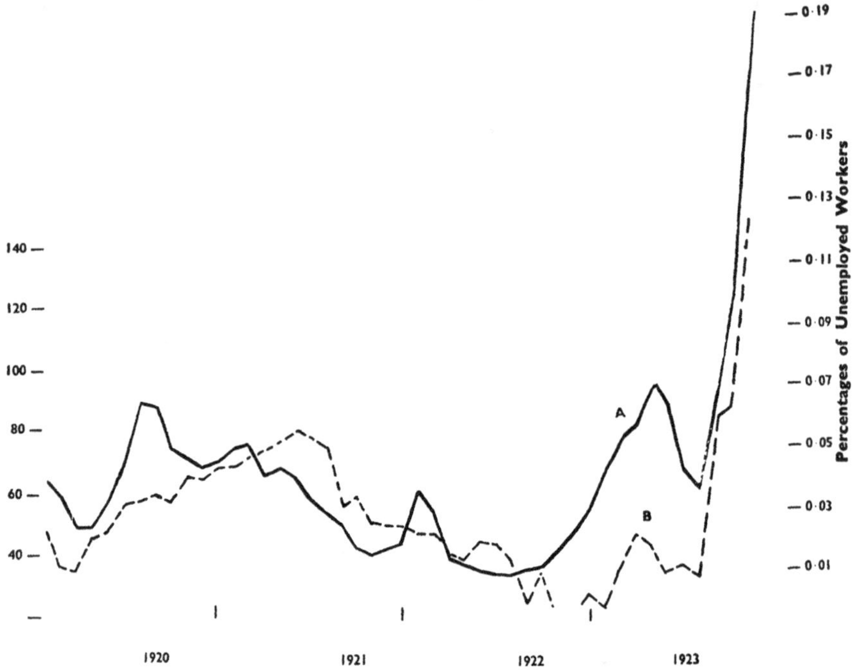


DIAGRAM XXI.—A. Unemployment. B. Rates of wage-rates to wholesale prices

the whole period of the inflation as shown in Diagram XXI. It is apparent that for the most part unemployment tended to decline at times when the ratio between the index number of nominal wage rates and the index number of prices fell, while it increased when that ratio rose.*

**14.** The calculation of the *income* of workers during the inflation cannot be attempted. The uncertainty of some of the elements which

* I do not intend to argue from this that the rise in nominal wages was the only or even the most important cause of unemployment in 1923. It was the result of the serious disorganization of the German economy, which was provoked by economic causes such as the depreciation of the mark and by political causes such as the occupation of the Ruhr.

must be taken into account is too serious. We must content ourselves with mentioning that the International Bureau of Labour, in the work already cited, arrived at the similar conclusion that the income of workers, which increased from 1920 to 1921, decreased in the course of 1922 and 1923. This conclusion is confirmed by the statistics of consumption, to which we shall refer below.

### VII. THE TENDENCY TO EQUALITY OF WAGES OF DIFFERENT CLASSES OF WORKERS

**15.** Another characteristic phenomenon of the inflation period was the lessening of the differences between the wages of different classes of workers (skilled and unskilled; young and old; men and women).

The causes of this phenomenon, which was not peculiar to Germany, are well known.* Because of the depreciation of the mark the real wages of unskilled workers very quickly approached the subsistence minimum and therefore, as the monetary depreciation continued, the nominal wages of these classes of workers were perforce increased, whilst the real wages of the skilled workers were still allowed to fall. Moreover, after the war large numbers of unskilled workers joined the trade unions and so increased their relative bargaining power. One must also remember that, as Meerwarth observes, either because the migration from the country to the towns and industrial centres had diminished (it had consisted mainly of unskilled workers) or because until the middle of 1922 there was an intense demand for labour, the pressure exercised on wages before the war by an abundance of unskilled labour was absent.

The figures in the footnote show that the ratio between the wages of skilled and unskilled workers diminished from 1914 to 1922, from 145·9 to 106·8.†

Furthermore, the trade unions used their influence to reduce the margin between the wages of young and adult workers, as they wished to deter industrialists using the services of young workers in preferenceto the old.

* See the publication of the International Labour Organization, *Fluctuations des salaires dans différents pays de 1914 à 1921*, Geneva, 1922.

† Based on the figures contained in the publication *Zahlen zur Geldentwertung*, I have calculated the following ratios relating to railway workers.

*Wages of Skilled Workers (wages of unskilled workers* = 100)

| | | | |
|---|---|---|---|
| 1913 .. .. .. | 145·8 | 1919 .. .. .. | 112·2 |
| 1914 .. .. .. | 145·9 | 1920 .. .. .. | 109·2 |
| 1915 .. .. .. | 143·8 | 1921 .. .. .. | 108·5 |
| 1916 .. .. .. | 136·2 | 1922 .. .. .. | 106·8 |
| 1917 .. .. .. | 125·6 | 1923 (January–October) | 105·5 |
| 1918 .. .. .. | 121·8 | | |

## PART III

### I. THE POSITION OF OWNERS OF MARKETABLE SECURITIES

**1.** German wealth was to a very great extent "marketable," i.e. it had taken the form of industrial shares (thanks to the continual transformation of firms into limited companies), debentures and bonds issued by central and local governments and mortgage bonds of the mortgage institutes. The entrepreneur, i.e. the organizer of production, was becoming more and more distinguished from the capitalist, who was satisfied by an income in the creation of which he took no active part. This phenomenon was, of course, common to all countries who were in conditions analogous to those of Germany, but in Germany it was particularly marked as statistics of various kinds show.

According to an estimate of Eulenburg, the total marketable capital before the war amounted to 162·7 milliard marks, i.e. to rather less than half the total capital of the German people, according to the estimates of Helfferich.* There was thus in Germany before the war a large class of "rentiers." They suffered very much from the effects of the inflation, which we shall now examine.

**2.** Among these capitalists, the owners of *industrial shares* played an important part before the war, since in 1913 the value of the share capital of the German companies was estimated at 31 milliard marks, according to the Bourse quotations.

If the share prices of the first months of 1924 are compared with those of 1913 it is seen that the old shareholders, i.e. those who had held shares before the war and had kept them, had saved only a very small part of their former capital. In September 1924 a reputable financial journal calculated the sums invested in fourteen companies by shareholders on the assumption that they had bought the securities in 1914 and had taken up the new shares issued in the following years. It compared these sums with the amount of share capital in 1924, after the revision of balance sheets. In aggregate it showed that the gold capital of the companies was scarcely 25 per cent of the capital originally invested by the shareholders; hence the old shareholders had lost 75 per cent of their investments.

These losses were not, however, suffered in equal measure by large and small shareholders. During the inflation the decline in the (gold)

* "Die sozialen Wirkungen der Währungsverhältnisse," in *Jahrbücher für Nationalökonomie*, 1924, p. 225.

prices of shares was not, for the most part, the expression of a real and permanent decline in the value of industrial equipment, but it was the consequence of transitory circumstances, such as the fall in industrial productivity or the conditions of the money market. There was also the influence of the dividend policies followed by companies which used to distribute to shareholders only a part of the often considerable profits, preferring to employ them in enlarging their plant. Small shareholders urged by necessity to realize their capital, now more timorous because of the further falls in share prices, sold their shares, while the big shareholders were, on the whole, able to keep their shares and wait for better times. With the help of some figures on the distribution of Phönix shares, Lewinsohn has given us an interesting example of how the shares, formerly mainly in the hands of small holders, gradually came to be concentrated in the hands of a small group of large shareholders.

Often, later, the big shareholders were able to compensate themselves in various ways for the drop in share dividends, e.g. with the fees which they received as members of supervision boards. The Press did not hesitate to show up the generous fees often paid by companies which had not paid out a farthing in dividend to their shareholders.

### II. THE LOSSES SUFFERED BY SMALL SHAREHOLDERS

**3.** The fall of share (gold) prices was also partly the effect of a definite "confiscation" policy followed by big shareholders to the disadvantage of small ones. The most important financial papers have often shown up and complained severely of the abuses committed during the post-war years by the small oligarchy of financiers and big industrialists which dominated the joint-stock companies. One of the means by which, during the great inflation, the progressive expropriation of small and average shareholders was accomplished was by the increase in capital of the companies. Often new shares—which were issued at a much lower price than the market price—were only offered in part on option to shareholders. The latter, deluded by the apparently valuable option, it being reckoned in paper marks, did not realize that actually they had lost a part of their capital. Some of the new shares were bought by syndicates, generally consisting of large shareholders, and these re-sold them, thus realizing vast profits, or kept them for other purposes. Sometimes new shares, not offered to shareholders, remained at the disposal of supervision boards, which used them for financial operations concerning amalgamation with other companies. It seems that the creation of these so-called "Verwertungsaktien" particularly had led sometimes to a scandalous enrichment of certain plutocratic groups to the disadvantage of the majority of the shareholders. Besides, the holding of a great quantity of these reserve shares made it possible for a group of big shareholders to undermine the control of the shareholders' meeting.

In December 1923 a decree was passed obliging the companies to compile new balance sheets, giving a fresh estimate, in gold currency terms, of their assets and liabilities. This provision was in itself perfectly reasonable and opportune, because the inflation had made the balance sheets expressed in paper marks altogether unintelligible and senseless. But in several cases the transformation of the balance sheet in terms of paper into one in terms of gold, and the consequent reduction of the nominal capital of the companies, became the means by which some powerful groups sought to further their own ends to the disadvantage of small shareholders.

The supporters of a heavy reduction in share capital maintained that it was a matter of perfect indifference to the shareholder whether the *nominal value* of the shares was fixed in one figure rather than the other. What was important was the *effective* value and this was, in substance, determined by the dividend and by the current rate of interest. From the theoretical point of view this argument was quite sound. But one must not forget that all are not "Economic Men" and that, on the contrary, people often act irrationally. In fact, the announcement that companies intended to make a heavy reduction in nominal capital often provoked panic among small shareholders, who hastened to sell their securities. In this way the better informed shareholders, realizing the true financial state of companies, were supplied with an opportunity to buy shares very cheaply.

**4.** But the question at once arises: Why did the small shareholders agree to the decisions of the general meetings of the companies, when those decisions were so much against their interests? The answer is that certain groups, although they held only a minority of the shares, could dominate the companies by securing the privilege of plural voting. The practice of issuing a class of privileged shares to which was attached a plural vote (sometimes twenty, thirty, or even more votes) was unknown before the war. The Aniline group was the first to issue shares with plural votes, in 1920. The example was quickly followed by other companies. The meetings of shareholders were induced to approve of the creation of this type of privileged share, because its supporters maintained that it was a necessary defence measure against the invasion of foreign capital, which threatened to secure control of the great German companies. But, in fact, the attempts made by foreign groups to secure control of German industries were very rare. That the danger of foreign control really existed was in most cases questionable; but the concentration of economic power in the hands of a few people soon became an obvious reality.

The shares with plural votes, which ought to have checked such a development, actually helped to secure the concentration of firms in the hands of fewer and fewer organizers. The mass of small shareholders were practically deprived of their power to vote. Indeed, some groups assumed a despotic control over companies, securing for themselves a power and influence over German economy quite disproportionate to their own capital. The German Press often denounced the abuses which were the consequence of the issues of shares with plural votes. On the other hand, it was said that to increase the influence of supervision committees as compared with that of shareholders' meetings, by issuing preferential shares with plural votes, meant giving a privilege to *service* as opposed to *capital*. But practice has shown, in Germany, that plural votes shares did not generally serve to create a special position for those who have dedicated their services to developing the firm, but that they were simply the means by which a certain small group of financiers and industrialists could maintain their position relatively to other groups.

The abuses to which we have referred are an example of the moral deterioration caused by the inflation. After the monetary stabilization the abuses largely disappeared.

### III. THE HOLDERS OF THE FIXED INTEREST SECURITIES AND MORTGAGE BONDS

**5.** In Germany the holders of fixed interest securities and of various kinds of bonds were very numerous. According to official estimates, in 1913 the outstanding loans of the Reich amounted to 4,806 million marks, those of the States to 16,197 millions, and those of the municipalities to 6,341 millions. War loans added 51,148 million paper marks. Later the premium loan of 1919 (3,840 millions) was added.

According to the *Memorandum on the Revaluation*, published by the

Minister of Finance at the beginning of 1925, the value of mortgages existing in 1913 amounted to 65 milliard marks. A part of these mortgages constituted the guarantee of the mortgage bonds issued by the mortgage institutes, which amounted to 17,051 million marks. The total mortgage debt was roughly distributed thus: three-quarters was urban and one-quarter rural. The value of industrial debentures, etc., amounted to 4,606 million marks in 1913.*

The depreciation of the mark completely dislocated another source of national saving, i.e. life assurances.†

The influence of the inflation must also have been particularly serious for co-operative societies and the savings banks. These could only employ their capital and deposits in a limited way in the purchase of foreign exchange, which was the most efficacious method of protection against the depreciation of the national currency. For example, Schultz-Delitsch co-operative societies which had before the war a capital of 428 million marks, lost it almost entirely during the inflation. Moreover, the members of these societies lost the major part of their deposits, which had amounted to 1,600 million marks in 1913.

According to Eulenberg the deposits accumulated by the savings banks, banking and insurance institutes, and co-operative societies amounted in the aggregate in 1913 to about 44 milliards.

**6.** The preceding figures are an index of the very great importance of capital in the form of fixed income securities, mortgage loans, and various kinds of credits. This enormous mass of marketable capital was completely upset by the inflation. It is no exaggeration to state that the depreciation of the currency caused in Germany the vastest expropriation of some classes of society that has ever been effected in time of peace.

The public debt of the Reich was practically cancelled and even partly by law, in 1923. In fact, the law of May 19th, 1923, on the liquidation of small amounts of stock inscribed in the public debt register fixed the minimum limit for holdings at 5,000 marks. As it was observed in the report which accompanied the proposal of the law, there were 920,000 holdings in the war loan alone which were less than 5,000 marks. The owners had to choose between reimbursement

* Incalculating the total sum of money capital it is important to avoid double counting. For example, one cannot add the value of mortgage credits to savings deposits because part of the mortgages (13 milliards) were held by the savings banks themselves, which had invested part of their deposits in that way.

† See p. 282.

at nominal value (! !) (150 per cent of the nominal value for the 5 per cent war loan) and the acceptance of a document recognizing the debt. Thus this law completely sacrificed the small subscribers.

In September 1923 the Management of the Reich Debts and of the Prussian Debts declared that, since the interest payments were now so small and much lower than the cost of paying them, they were obliged to stop paying the said interest, although the rights of owners of securities remained unrepudiated.

**7.** The effects of the expropriation of owners of securities or of monetary capital differed according to the nature of that capital. In the case of contract loans between private persons, debentures issued by industrial firms and mortgage securities, the annihilation of the value of the mark meant the confiscation of the lender's wealth to the advantage of the borrower. By such means agricultural landowners, for example, freed their lands from mortgage. Since, in Germany, agricultural lands are in the majority of cases farmed on a business basis, the owners could by increasing prices adapt their income to the monetary depreciation. In 1922 they were freed from the obligation to sell part of their cereals at the maximum prices (which had been lower than market prices).

But owners of houses did not benefit in this way during the inflation, because, though their mortgage liabilities virtually vanished, rents were reduced to pitifully small figures, as we have already remarked.

It is often difficult to trace the direction of the transfer of wealth which the inflation effected. In the case of houses the person to benefit was not the owner, who was the mortgage holder, but the tenant. But the low rents paid by workers resulted in a low level of nominal wages, and that meant a fall in the cost of production for the entrepreneur and an increase in his profits in cases where he had succeeded in maintaining high selling prices. But often foreigners took advantage of the inflation by purchasing German goods at a very low price.

**8.** The consequence of all these transfers of purchasing power from one class of society to another was probably an increase in the concentration of wealth. In fact, those who were in a position to benefit from the inflation were far fewer than the victims of the depreciation. Holders of debentures, etc., issued by one private entrepreneur could be counted by hundreds and thousands. In the savings banks there were sums belonging to very many depositors, but the number of those to whom these savings were lent out was comparatively low. A proprietor of rural or urban land had often burdened his property with more than one mortgage, thus securing for himself sums of money from different lenders.

Naturally, in practice there were many offsetting changes. For example, it may be that A owns at the same time land burdened by mortgage and some Government securities. But, on the whole, it is certain that there was in Germany a numerous middle class which possessed the fixed-interest securities or loans which provided the greater part of their incomes or at least an income which supplemented a professional income. These classes were the principal victims of the inflation.

Besides those who possessed wealth in the form of securities or credits, there were numerous other individuals who lived totally or partly on a fixed money income; those receiving assurance payments from private companies, old people or those disabled by accidents, the war-disabled, or parents of the fallen, and pensioners of the State and private institutions The depreciation destroyed what was often the sole income of those individuals. They were reduced to the most abject poverty.

The inflation also destroyed the wealth of charitable institutions, of religious societies, and of scientific or literary foundations. In Berlin, for example, there were about sixty charitable institutions whose endowment, which was invested in mortgage and securities, amounted to 56 million gold marks. This was almost entirely lost, being after the "revaluation" as little as a million and a half marks.

## IV. THE QUESTION OF THE "REVALUATION" OF OLD CREDITS EXPRESSED IN PAPER MARKS

**9.** For a long time in Germany, as elsewhere, holders of industrial securities, mortgages, or other loans were not conscious of the injustice done them when they were reimbursed with depreciated currency. For a long time the phenomenon of the depreciation was ill understood by the masses. The fall in the purchasing power of money was attributed to the rise in prices caused by the war, the revolution, the scarcity of goods, and by the destruction of capital; and it was confidently expected that when these abnormal conditions disappeared prices would fall and the mark would return to its old parity.

But towards the end of 1921 and still more during 1922 and 1923 the gold value of old securities expressed in marks became a very small fraction of the original value. The ruin of investors was manifest and public opinion was agitated. For a long time the ruling classes cleverly contrived to divert the irritation of the classes ruined by the monetary depreciation with propaganda aimed at showing that the financial burdens imposed on Germany by the Treaty of Versailles had caused the ruin of the mark. These notions, spread and continually repeated by the daily papers, by the agrarian parties, and by the great industrialists, convinced most people. But eventually the enrichment of some classes at the expense of others became all too obvious. At the same time the democratic and Socialist Press was collecting irrefutable evidence showing the very grave responsibility of the great industrialists who had favoured the depreciation of the mark.

Moreover, the ruling classes, even those who had profited from the monetary depreciation, began to feel a certain discomfort. The breakdown of the contractual system caused by the depreciation was too blatant, and the violation of property rights too obvious, and these are the bases of civilized society. The apparently most solid guarantees by which the law protected the rights of creditors were, in practice, rendered illusory; for example, the real value of a mortgaged property provided no protection for the creditor.*

The Nationalist parties were afraid of losing the large following which they had among the small capitalists, rentiers, and Government officials, who had been seriously harmed by the monetary depreciation. By a clever move they pledged themselves to *revaluation*, and in 1923 took the initiative in the proposal for a law in favour of creditors.† For obvious reasons it was especially the cause of mortgage creditors which seemed just.

**10.** Even at the end of 1922 (i.e. when the paper mark was worth less than a thousandth of a gold mark) the German judiciary constantly reiterated the principle: mark = mark, thus sanctioning the ruin of creditors. But at the beginning of 1923 some judges began to take account of the spirit as well as of the letter of the law. A new orientation of justice began with the well-known decision of the Court of Appeal

* Another typical example was the virtual inversion of the law preferring the interests of holders of debentures to those of shareholders; for, owing to the monetary depreciation, the former lost all while the latter saved at least a part of their capital.

† See the projected law presented to the Reichstag by Deputy Düringer in March 1923. Another project, presented by Deputy Strathmann on July 4th, provided for a modest revaluation of individual debentures.

at Darmstadt on March 29th, 1923. It was justly observed that according to the Civil Code a debt must be paid according to equity and good faith, and that to reimburse the creditor after the depreciation of the currency with the identical nominal sum received was contrary to good faith, as the debtor still kept the property which guaranteed the loan.

At first the Government had intended to prohibit by law all revaluations of credits, thus stopping the growth of a legal system which interpreted the existing laws in a sense favourable to creditors. But after decisions of various kinds had been made by German tribunals, the supporters of the theory of revaluation of mortgage credits obtained a decisive victory in the judgment of the Supreme Tribunal of Leipzig (November 23rd, 1923).

### V. THE DECREE OF FEBRUARY 14TH, 1924, AND THE LAW OF JULY 16TH, 1925, ON "REVALUATION"

**11.** After this judgment a solution of the problem of revaluation was prescribed by legislation. Exercising the exceptional powers conferred on it, the German Government regulated the situation by the decree of February 14th, 1924 (Dritte Steuernotverordnung). This decree (which recalled measures taken by the French Directorate after the liquidation of the assignats)* was, together with that on the revision of the balance sheets of joint-stock companies, one of the corner-stones of the legislation which reorganized German life after the turbulent period of the inflation. In spite of the criticisms which it has aroused, the decree of February 14th, 1924, represents an interesting and original attempt to restore in part those economic relationships which had been profoundly disturbed by the monetary depreciation.†

The most important kinds of private credits among the ten covered by this decree were industrial debentures and mortgages, which were revalued at about 15 per cent of their original gold value. Mortgage bonds, savings bank deposits, and obligations arising from life assurance contracts were revalued at a rate corresponding to the revaluation of mortgages and other claims held by the Land Credits Institute, assurance companies, and savings banks. For example, in Prussia the deposits in savings banks were revalued (according to a decree of December

* On this and other historical experiences see Hargreaves, *Restoring Currency Standards*, 1926.

† Poland followed the example of Germany in the decree of May 14th, 1924, on the revaluation of private loans.

1930, which finally regulated the matter) at a rate varying between 17 per cent (Berlin) and 29 per cent (Upper Silesia) of the original value of the deposit.

**12.** But although the conception of the decree of February 14th, 1924, was praiseworthy, its practical application was undoubtedly very limited. The agitation of unsatisfied creditors did not cease. It induced the German Government to announce a new plan which became law on July 16th, 1925. The chief provisions of the new law were as follows: (*a*) The normal rate of revaluation of mortgages was raised to 25 per cent of the original gold value; (*b*) the law had retrospective effect for extinct mortgages, if the creditor had accepted the reimbursement with a reservation; (*c*) for mortgages taken up after June 15th, 1922, the law had retrospective effect even if the reimbursement had been accepted without reservation; (*d*) the payment of sums due on the basis of this law could be demanded after January 1st, 1932: in the meantime debtors paid interest at 1·2 per cent after January 1st, 1925, 2·5 per cent after July 1st, 1925, 3 per cent after January 1st, 1926, and 5 per cent after January 1st, 1928; (*e*) the debtor could obtain a reduction in the rate of revaluation to 15 per cent in cases of straitened economic conditions; (*f*) those who had bought industrial debentures before July 1st, 1920, received (besides 15 per cent of the gold value of the security) a small share in the dividends of the company; (*g*) for securities taken up after January 1st, 1918, there was used, as a coefficient for the transformation from paper value to gold value, an average between the dollar exchange rate and the index number of wholesale prices.

According to official estimates the gold value of mortgages subject to revaluation according to the law of July 16th, 1925, amounted to about 40 milliard marks.

### VI. SPECIAL TAXES ON INFLATION PROFITS

**13.** The decree quoted above also included some noteworthy provisions for the imposition of special taxes (for the Reich or the States) on the extraordinary profits arising out of the inflation conditions. It created a tax, in favour of the Reich, on profits made from the monetary depreciation, and three other taxes in favour of the States.

The tax for the Reich was imposed on profits made from the depreciation of industrial debentures and others similar. It was fixed at about 1·7 per cent of the original gold value. Securities which, at the time of the imposition of the tax, had already been redeemed at a rate lower than 15 per cent of the original gold value, were further inflicted with a tax equal to the difference between the amount reimbursed and the amount corresponding to 15 per cent of the original value. This supertax was payable at a half-yearly rate of 2 per cent of the original gold value of the securities.

The States taxes, on profits derived from the depreciation of the mark, were as follows:

(*a*) *A tax on rents*, which was earmarked for the States. It was decided to free house-rents gradually from the restriction system. Rents were raised progressively, so that they slowly approached pre-war rents. In this way owners of houses, freed from mortgage burdens (which had either been redeemed during the inflation, or, if still existing, were revalued at the rate of about 25 per cent of their pre-war gold value), enjoyed unjust enrichment. A part of the increased rents was therefore absorbed by the new tax, which was fixed in such a way that house-owners received at least 30 per cent of the pre-war rent.

(*b*) *A tax on owners of rural property*. This tax, earmarked for the States, was designed to strike at profits made from the progressive shrinkage of mortgage debts. It was very small: 1·7 per cent of the original maximum gold value of the mortgage in the case of revalued mortgages; and in the case of mortgages already extinct, the difference between the amount, in gold, effectively restored to the creditor and the amount corresponding to the rate of revaluation of mortgages. It is not clear whether this tax has yet been collected.

(*c*) The States were also authorized to tax, at the rate of 20 per cent, the profits made by those who had bought wood from the administrators of State properties, paying for it after the consignment, and who had thus profited largely from the monetary depreciation which had occurred in the interval.

Other provisions of the decree of February 14th, 1924, authorized the Minister of Finance to attack by a special tax the "inflation profits" made from credits granted by the banks, and from the issue of emergency money by private persons during the depreciation of the mark. These provisions have, however, only remained on paper, because of the serious difficulties of practical application, which were well described in a memorandum of the German Government.

## VII. THE REVALUATION OF GOVERNMENT SECURITIES

**14.** The decree of February 14th deferred an eventual revaluation of public loans issued by the Reich, the States, and the municipalities, until the reparations obligations should be completely satisfied. But the agitation for the revaluation of public securities continued. It gave rise during 1924 to a violent speculation on the Bourse* which caused the prices of Government securities to suffer serious fluctuations. The agitation was supported, for political reasons, by the German Nationalist party and by some groups of speculators who had bought great quantities of Government securities to sell again; while on the other hand the great industrialists and great landowners tenaciously fought every proposal for the revaluation of *private* credits beyond the limits already fixed by the decree of February 14th, 1924.

The German Government published on May 26th, 1925, a project for the revaluation of public loans which, after many vicissitudes, became law on July 16th, 1925.

The chief provisions of this law were as follows: (*a*) Old securities were converted, at the rate of a new security of 25 marks, for an old one of 1,000 marks; (*b*) for securities bought after July 1st, 1920, the payment of interest on new securities would begin after the payments made by the Reich for reparations had ceased; (*c*) to "old holders," i.e. to those who had bought Government securities before July 1st, 1920, was given a lottery right. All the new securities held by them would be drawn by lots in a period of thirty years from the beginning of 1926. The drawn security would be redeemed by the payment of a sum equal to five times the nominal value of the new security (i.e. to 12½ per cent of the nominal value of the old security). To this was to be added interest on this sum, at 4½ per cent, calculated as from January 1st, 1926; (*d*) the "old holders" (excluding foreigners) whose total annual income did not exceed 800 marks should receive a "priority yield" to the amount of 80 per cent of the nominal value of the new securities. The yield was to be increased by 50 per cent for those holders who were seventy years of age and renounced their "lottery right."

* At first the speculation was concentrated on the 3-per-cent consolidated loan of the Reich, and on the 3-per-cent Prussian, because it was thought that the probability of revaluation was greater for these two loans as they were quoted in foreign markets and were partly held by foreign capitalists. But during 1924 speculation centred particularly round War Loan, and on some days that almost monopolized attention on the Berlin Bourse.

According to estimates of the German Government the amount of public securities which were still in the hands of original holders was by no means insignificant, probably amounting to 15–20 milliard paper marks. The actual figure, resulting from the applications of bondholders, consequent upon the law of July 16th, 1925, is still higher, but this was partly the result of frauds.

These various laws refer to the loans of the Reich and the States, and are also applied, with certain modifications, to the local government loans.

### VIII. THE INCOMES OF GOVERNMENT EMPLOYEES AND OF THE PROFESSIONS DURING THE INFLATION

**15.** Something must be said of the flunctuations in the incomes of Government employees and professional men during the inflation.

Before the war the salaries of Government employees were regulated by the law of July 1st, 1909. This was considerably modified, during the inflation, by the law of April 30th, 1920. Further modifications, rendered necessary, first by the continual depreciation of the mark and, later, by the monetary stabilization, were made in the following years.

On the basis of the figures published by the Statistical Bureau of the Reich,* I have constructed Diagram XXII, which shows the real salaries of upper class (curve A), middle class (curve B), and lower class (curve C) employees. The salaries have been changed from nominal into "real" by means of the index number of the cost of living (till 1920 that of Calwer; for the following years, that of the Statistical Bureau of the Reich). The diagram shows that for all classes of employees during the war and the inflation real salaries remained below the pre-war level. But the fall was proportionately greater for the upper and middle classes than for the lower class.

In September 1923 the upper-class employees had only 44·5 per cent of their pre-war salary, the middle class 57·6 per cent, but the lower class had 80 per cent. But as with the wages of workmen, so also with the real salaries of employees, there was very great variability during the period of the rapid depreciation of the mark, beginning in the autumn of 1921.†

**16.** There are no statistics about the incomes of professional men. But it is generally recognized that the economic situation of a large part of this class (doctors, private teachers, artists, and other intellectual workers) during the inflation was even more serious than that of the

* *Zahlen zur Geldentwertung*, p. 43.

† The Statistical Bureau states that, as from 1920, real salaries were calculated on the basis of the cost of living in the period during which the salaries were spent; in the last phase of the inflation the method of payment was also taken into account (advance, supplements, etc.). In spite of that the results remain largely approximate.

working class and of Government employees.* Doctors, for example, had relatively little work from private patients, and health insurance

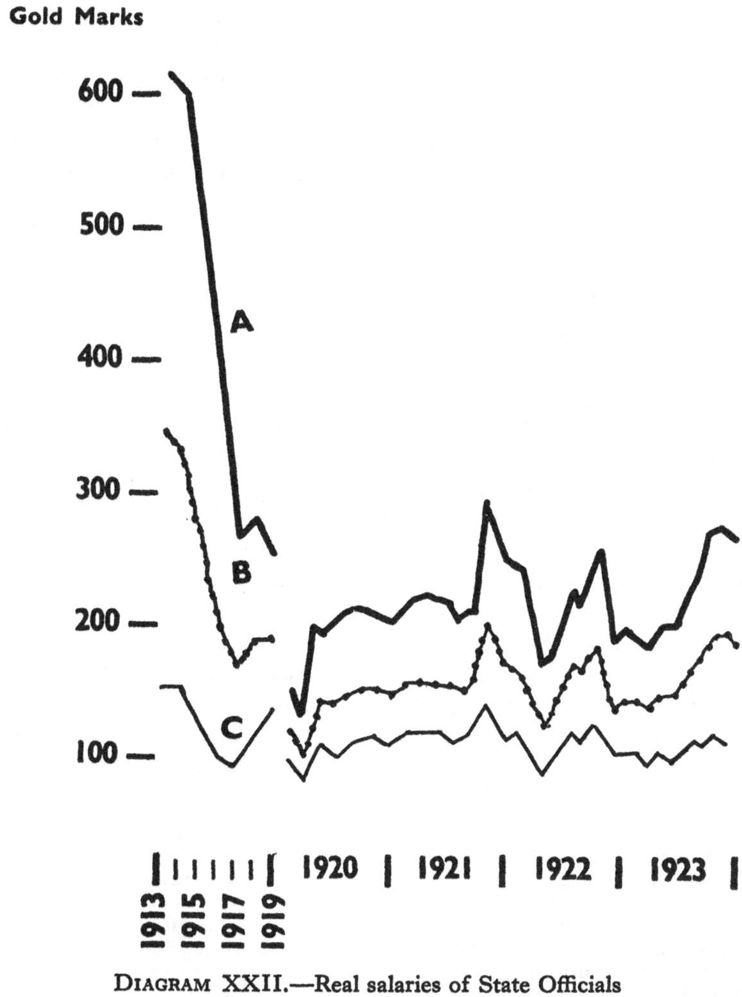


DIAGRAM XXII.—Real salaries of State Officials

companies, in the depths of a financial crisis caused by the depreciation

* H. Guradze and K. Freudenberg, in the article "Das Existenzminimum des geistigen Arbeiters," *Jahrbücher für Nationalökonomie*, 1923, calculated that in 1922 and 1923 the income of the brain-worker was below the subsistence minimum.

of the mark, paid fees very much below those of pre-war days.* Expenditure on medical and other personal services (e.g. teaching) is very elastic. From some statistics of the budgets of some Hamburg families it appears that families with incomes of less than 2,500 marks spent 1·63 per cent of their income on doctors' fees, and families with incomes of more than 7,000 marks spent 7 per cent. During the inflation the average income of numerous classes of society fell, but the cost of food was less elastic. The money spent on the services of doctors and other professionals was therefore reduced considerably. Thus the income of these classes fell by a greater proportion than did the general average income.

### IX. THE POVERTY OF CERTAIN SOCIAL CLASSES DURING THE INFLATION

**17.** The poverty of certain German classes during the inflation which contrasted with the foolish extravagance and provocative ostentation of inflation profiteers,† was mainly the result of the monetary depreciation. In fact, the period of most acute and widespread poverty was 1923, that year in which the dollar exchange rate rose from 10,000 to 4,200 milliard paper marks! An indication of that poverty is given by statistics about individuals who received small subsidies or pensions from national or local governments. Excluding the unemployed, they amounted to 5,632,000 towards the end of 1923, according to the statements of the minister Brauns. Naturally there are no statistics about those people who were reduced to a life of penury and misery among the professional and academic classes: students, tutors, writers, artists, and scholars.‡ But many in the working classes also suffered dire poverty; they were the unorganized workers, and especially domestic workers of both sexes, both in the great cities and in some agricultural regions.

* Gunther, "Die Anpassung der Sozialversicherung an die Geldenwertung und Lohnsteigerung," in the *Jahrbücher fur Nationalökonomie*, 1923.

† As is well known, the same contrast was observed in Austria and other countries with a much depreciated currency. "It seems that in Vienna the extravagance and dissipation of the profiteers know no limits, and they increase in the same proportion as the currency falls in value. The most striking characteristic of Vienna is the contrast between a small group of people living in luxury (they were those who had been known to defend themselves from the depreciation and to gain advantage for themselves) and a strata of society living in the most abject poverty. The old middle class has completely disappeared" (*Bergswerkszeitung* of January 1st, 1922).

‡ Schreiber writes in a moving way of the decadence of the intellectual classes during the inflation period (*Da Not der deutschen Wissenschaft und die Geistesarbeiter*, Leipzig, 1924). But the author is wrong in representing this poverty as a result of the Treaty of Versailles!

**18.** The poverty of the German people was the subject of much discussion for a long time. It was exaggerated by Germans with ill-directed patriotic spirit, and was denied by their adversaries. From personal observation it appears that the poverty of the German people was certainly not general, but it was limited to certain classes, in fact to those which had been most severely hit by the inflation. The poverty was revealed by many symptoms, some of which are measurable by statistics: the condition of children (underweight, spread of tuberculosis and rickets); lack of clothing; the lowered feeding standards (fall in the consumption of cereals, meat, butter, milk, eggs, etc., and the substitution of poorer foods, as, e.g., the substitution of rye for wheat, margarine and other inferior fats for butter, and all sorts of substitutes for coffee); the very poor condition of houses; the excessive work of women; the appearance of certain maladies formerly almost unknown in Germany, such as acne and scurvy; the rise in the number of suicides due to the lack of means of subsistence; deaths through malnutrition (which were very rare before the war); and the rise in the number of pauper funerals because relatives could not pay the expenses, although a decree by the Minister of the Interior permitted the substitution of pasteboard shells for wooden coffins, which were too dear!

The statistics of meat consumption reveal some curious details which throw an interesting light on social conditions in Germany in 1922 and 1923. While the consumption of the better quality meats (bullocks, calves, pigs, and sheep) declined, the consumption of horse-flesh and, still more, of dogs increased: obvious proof, as *Wirtschaft und Statistik* wrote, of the increasing poverty of the German people. From the last quarter of 1921 to the last quarter of 1922 the number of pigs killed fell from 1,416,051 to 1,131,148, while the number of horses increased from 30,967 to 47,652. During 1923 the fall in the consumption of pork continued, and at the same time the conditions of some classes became so bad that they were eventually obliged to reduce their consumption of horse-flesh. But consumption of dog-flesh increased. Statistics show that 1,090 dogs were slaughtered in the third quarter of 1921; 3,678 in the third quarter of 1922, and 6,430 in the third quarter of 1923. Directly after the stabilization the consumption of pork increased, whilst that of dogs and horses declined. In the third quarter of 1924 the number of dogs butchered was only 841.

Another direct index of the worsening of the economic conditions of many classes was the increase in both open and clandestine prostitution. A typical symptom of the sad condition of the old middle classes was also given by the very great number of little shops which sold furniture, *objets d'arts*, jewellery, carpets, etc., belonging to very many families who, once well-to-do, were now living on the proceeds of the sale of their personal property.

That the poverty which crushed so many classes in 1923 was really a consequence of the inflation was also shown by the fact that it declined rapidly after the stabilization of the mark. This decline was essentially due to the cessation of the process of continual centralization of the social income by a small minority of inflation profiteers.

### X. SOME POLITICAL, DEMOGRAPHIC, AND MORAL CONSEQUENCES OF THE INFLATION

**19.** It would be interesting to trace the various psychological, moral, social, and political influences exercised by the inflation; but in the present volume, which has a strictly economic character, we must limit ourselves to a somewhat rapid survey.

At first, perhaps, the political and social effects of the inflation were not altogether unfavourable. In the period of the serious social and political disturbance which followed the military defeat, the presence of acute unemployment would have been a cause of trouble. The inflation made possible the rapid absorption of the unemployed at the expense of the small capitalist classes. Later, however, the depreciation of the mark provoked continual agitation among workers, who demanded increases in wages; in 1923 discontent spread further and further among other classes of society. Among the old middle classes, ruined by the inflation, extreme nationalist propaganda was started and made rapid headway, and among the workers communist ideas spread.

**20.** The paper inflation, by reinforcing the economic position of those classes which formed the backbone of the "Right" parties, i.e. the great industrialists and the great financiers, encouraged the political reaction against democracy.

The old political order collapsed on November 9th, 1918. The old régime, founded on bureaucracy and the exaggeration of the hierarchical principle, had not survived the supreme test of the Great War, the victors in which had been the more liberal States.

It is recognized in some quarters that the men of the Socialist party, who were raised up by the revolution of November 1918 to govern the nation, had given proof of moderation and political wisdom. In 1919, at a time when Germany was profoundly disturbed by separatist and communist movements and by reactions of the militarist spirit, there flocked to the banner of Liberalism the best minds of those parties who wished to save Germany from economic ruin and political dissolution. They concentrated all their efforts on creating a constitution which would be the expression of democratic and liberal ideas and at the same time affirm the principle of representation as opposed to the Soviet system. But the new republic, fiercely opposed by the leading classes of the old régime, was actually supported only by the working classes and by a few intellectuals in the Democratic party—not a very solid foundation.

In the war years the scarcity of goods, and other causes intimately connected with the war, had placed the owners of the means of production in a monopolistic position and had weakened the authority of the Government. The following years completed what the war had begun. The power of the great industrialists and of great war and inflation profiteers increased. There was established what Rathenau called the dictatorship of heavy industry—an industrial feudalism pitted against the nation.

The great industrialists and landowners were enabled, by the profits obtained from the monetary depreciation, to finance generously the propaganda and the campaign against the Republic. It was carried on chiefly through the Press. The depreciation of the currency had created very serious difficulties for many papers, because of the enormous rise in the price of paper, of telegraph rates, and of the expense of maintaining their foreign correspondents, etc. Many papers were bought up by the controllers of the heavy industries. Besides this, they were astute enough to become masters of the most important news agencies which, by supplying news even to independent papers, were an effective instrument for influencing public opinion. The very numerous small provincial papers which, taken together, had a great importance because they were read by the country population, were in the hands of the agrarian parties.

Large amounts of money were also used for the formation and maintenance of numerous national institutions of a military character which openly opposed the Republican-Liberal régime. As a Liberal paper wrote:* "The years of the inflation, so advantageous for agriculture, have made it possible to create a model party organization. While the great landowners pay taxes to the Government in depreciated

* "Der Landbund—Terror in Pommern," in the *Berliner Tageblatt* of August 15th, 1924.

paper, they give to the *Landbund* a contribution of stable value, calculated according to the extent of their possessions. By such means enormous sums have been collected, and have been well used. In all Pomerania there does not exist a paper of any importance which does not belong to the *Landbund*."

Whilst the monetary depreciation favoured some powerful classes hostile to the new Democratic-Liberal régime, it continually weakened its supporters. The funds collected by the big trade unions and by the Socialist party evaporated. The working classes were beaten by the inflation, and then was exposed the error of their leaders, who in the early years had not energetically opposed the inflation—probably because they were deluded by some immediate advantage which the depreciation had brought to the workers. The depreciation of the currency also weakened those intellectual classes who supported the democratic and liberal ideal and the conception of a Government as protector of general interests, and not the slave of the classes which were economically dominant.

Thus the currency inflation was also responsible for the Liberal régime always showing a weak front to the new industrial and agrarian feudalism which was constantly threatening the basis of the new Republic.

**21.** Even population statistics show the influence of the inflation and the succeeding stabilization. The very marked increase in mortality from pulmonary tuberculosis, between 1921 and 1923, is typical. This increase was followed by a sharp fall in the following years. The statistics of diseases also show an improvement in health conditions after 1923. Emigration increased after 1920 and reached its highest figure in 1923; then it dropped, in spite of the increase in unemployment in Germany.

From many symptoms, some of which may be measured by statistics, it may be seen that the inflation generated a profound moral disturbance. The most significant indices are those concerning crime. The inflation provoked a wave of crime which subsided directly after the monetary stabilization. Table XXXVII is based on official statistics.*

The influence of economic conditions on crime is obvious from an analysis of statistics, which show that 1923 reached a maximum of thefts,† misappropriation, and illicit receiving. But crimes against the person (major and minor assault and homicide) lessened considerably

* See "Kriminalstatistik für 1925" (*Statistik des deutschen Reichs*, vol. 335).

† The following is a characteristic fact: metal plates had to be removed from several monuments to prevent them from being stolen.

during the inflation—perhaps because of the decline in the consumption of alcoholic beverages?—and increased once more in the following

TABLE XXXVII

*Index Numbers of Crime*

(Total number of criminals, i.e. "Verbrechen" and "Vergehen." 1882 = 100)

| | 1913 | 1921 | 1923 | 1924 | 1925 |
|---|---|---|---|---|---|
| Total number of crimes .. | 117 | 136 | 170 | 150 | 122 |
| Crimes committed by men .. | 123 | 137 | 179 | 158 | 129 |
| Crimes committed by young men .. .. .. .. | 125 | 173 | 212 | 153 | 87 |

years. The stabilization had a favourable influence on certain forms of crime, causing a heavy fall in those crimes which had their roots in poverty; but those of other kinds, such as social crimes, continued to show an alarming increase.

# CHAPTER IX

# The Monetary Reform of November 1923*

## I. CHARACTERISTICS OF THE MONETARY REFORM

**1.** Whoever studies the recent economic history of Europe is struck by a most surprising fact: the rapid monetary restoration of some countries where for several years paper money had continually depreciated. In some cases the stabilization of the exchange was not obtained by a continuous effort, prolonged over a period of years, whose effects would show themselves slowly in the progressive economic and financial restoration of the country, as occurred before the war in several well-known cases of monetary reform. Instead, the passing from a period of tempestuous depreciation of the currency to an almost complete stability of the exchange was very sudden.

At Vienna the dollar exchange rate was quoted at 11,175 crowns on June 1st, 1922; it rose to 20,675 on July 4th; 50,875 on August 2nd; and to 83,600 on the 25th of the same month. It fell to little more than 70,000 crowns towards the end of December 1922. From then onwards the exchange rate of the dollar suffered only inconsiderable oscillations.

The dollar was worth 160,000 paper marks on July 3rd, 1923, on the Berlin Bourse; 13 million on September 4th; 420 milliard on November 20th. From then onwards the exchange rate of the dollar at Berlin remained invariable; and so also did the ratio of the value between the new rentenmark and the dollar (1 dollar=4·2 rentenmarks). During 1924 the German and Austrian exchanges were the most stable in Europe. The depreciation of the Hungarian crown also ceased abruptly in June 1924.

**2.** Some writers have considered the monetary reform, introduced by the decree of October 15th, 1923,† on the creation of the "Rentenbank" and the issue of the "rentenmark" as a "revaluation" of German money; whilst others have spoken of the "stabilization" of the German Exchange; and still others of the legal reduction of the value of the currency. It is a question of terms and points of view. Some writers refer to the paper mark, others to the rentenmark.

* First published in *Giornale degli Economisti*, 1925, under the title "Considerazioni su alcune recenti esperienze monetarie."

† The reader will find a translation of the decree of November 15th, 1923, in the *Memorandum sur les banques centrales*, Geneva, 1924, League of Nations, p. 84.

Some confusion arises from the existence of these two kinds of currency. The paper mark was not revalued in the sense which is commonly attributed to this term. It would have been "revalued" if, by a reduction in the quantity of the circulation, its purchasing power in terms of foreign exchange and goods in the home market had been raised after November 15th, 1923. Instead, on November 20th, 1923, the value of the paper mark was simply "stabilized" at the rate of 4,200 milliard marks for a dollar, i.e. 1,000 milliard paper marks for a gold mark.

New currency was issued, and the new unit, the rentenmark, was given the value of one gold mark. This value of the rentenmark was not stated officially but resulted indirectly from the promise to the holders of rentenmarks that on demand 500 rentenmarks could be converted into a bond having a nominal value of 500 gold marks.

It was not the decree of October 15th, 1923, but the monetary law of August 30th, 1924 (coming into operation on October 11th, 1924) which sanctioned the legal reduction of the value of the paper mark. Under this law paper marks could be converted into the new currency at the rate of 1 billion paper marks for a "Reichsmark" (a billion = $1{,}000{,}000^2$).

The official rate of stabilization—4,200 milliard paper marks for one dollar—in November 1923 gave the mark a higher value, in dollars, than it commanded in the free market (as shown by the quotations abroad). Only in this very limited sense can it be said that the monetary reform of 1923 involved a "revaluation" of the paper mark. After the stabilization of the exchange, foreign quotations moved back to those ruling at Berlin.

In another sense there was a "revaluation" of the old paper mark: certain loans expressed in paper marks were partly revalued by the "third extraordinary fiscal decree," as was shown in a previous chapter.

## II. THE POSITION IN GERMANY AT THE TIME OF THE MONETARY REFORM

**3.** When the decree of October 15th was published the effect of it was extremely uncertain. According to Helfferich the experiment with the rentenmark was made without having created the conditions for a monetary recovery, i.e. the solution of the reparations question and the improvement of the economic and political situation. The attempt was a "leap over a ravine the other edge of which was obscured by clouds." Even the minister Luther, the author of the decree of October 15th, 1923, described his work as that of one "who builds a house, beginning with the roof."

Consequently, the unhoped-for success of the monetary reform, which was accompanied by a rapid re-establishment of the equilibrium of the national budget and by an appreciable and obvious improvement in the living conditions of the German people, was considered miraculous. "The miracle of the rentenmark" became a common expression. Actually the improvement occurred so rapidly that people unaccustomed to systematic observation of economic factors could not easily find an explanation of it. The deficit in the Reich budget had risen to enormous figures during 1923. The floating debt increased by 906 million gold marks in August 1923; 1,506 in September; 860 millions in October, and by 1,249 millions in November—altogether more than four and a half milliards in the course of four months. At the beginning of 1923 the gold reserve of the Reichsbank amounted to a milliard gold marks. In the course of the year it was continually reduced, and amounted scarcely to 444 millions on October 15th, 1923. The Reichsbank possessed then only a trifling amount of foreign exchange. In November 1923 it could satisfy only a very small part of the demands for it. Given the political and economic situation it was not possible for the German Government or private persons to obtain loans abroad. Above all, because of the monetary crisis, in September and October 1923 the economic and social conditions of Germany were rapidly deteriorating. Trade was arrested, factories closed, unemployment figures rose continually, and the provisioning of towns and industrial centres was seriously menaced. Whoever was in Germany in those days will know that Luther did not exaggerate when he wrote: "The effective starving of the towns and the impossibility of continuing economic activities on the basis of the paper mark was so obvious in the days preceding November 16th that a dissolution of the social order must have been expected almost from hour to hour."*

The beneficial influence of the stabilization of the exchange made itself felt immediately. Commerce revived, the food situation in the cities was eased, the purchasing power of many classes was increased,

* It is interesting for the foreign student to consider what great differences of opinion were held in Germany with regard to the rentenmark. While the foreign Press spoke of the "miracle" worked by the rentenmark, and even some German economists wrote that "the issue of the rentenmark was a milestone in the financial history of Germany, a *volte-face* which was a sign of the beginning of a recovery in the grand style" (Bräuer in *Wirtschaftsdienst* of July 25th, 1924), Professor Harms wrote that the creation of the rentenmark was "the climax of the misunderstanding of monetary phenomena," which provoked an economic crisis, a great increase in prices, and an unhealthy expansion of certain industries at the expense, in particular, of agriculture.

the factories re-opened, unemployment declined rapidly, and a refreshing wave of confidence revived the energies of the German people.

### III. SOME EXPLANATION OF THE "MIRACLE" OF THE RENTENMARK

**4.** What were the causes of the sudden stabilization of the German exchange?

Inspired by the Quantitative Theory, some economists have affirmed that the success of the German monetary reform was dependent on these conditions: the cessation of issues of paper marks, strict limitation of the quantity of the new money, and the calling-in of paper marks in proportion to the issues of new money, according to a certain ratio of value between the old and the new. Therefore, it was thought, if the rentenmark were *added* to the existing paper marks there would have been a new inflation and, consequently, a further depreciation of the German currency.

In reality the facts worked out only partly according to this theoretical scheme. It is true that at first there were thoughts of fixing a legal ratio of conversion between the rentenmark and the paper mark. But later the idea was abandoned. The paper mark was not only preserved, but it remained the only legal tender money until October 11th, 1924 (the date of the coming into operation of the new monetary law which instituted the "Reichsmark"). The rentenmark was only "a legal means of payment." The new rentenmarks, which were first issued as from November 16th, 1923, were added to the circulating medium already existing. It is true that on November 16th the discounting of Treasury bills by the Reichsbank was stopped, i.e. the issuing of paper money for the Government. That was a fact of fundamental importance. But the issuing of paper money for commercial purposes continued after November 16th. At that date the quantity of paper marks in circulation amounted to 93 trillions (a trillion = $1{,}000{,}000^3$). By November 30th it had already passed 400 trillions; it reached 496 trillions on December 31st; 690 trillions on March 31st, 1924; 927 trillions on May 31st; and 1,211 trillions on July 31st following.

At the same time the issues of new rentenmarks increased, and their circulation amounted to 501 millions on November 30th, 1923; 1,049 millions on December 31st; 1,760 millions on March 31st, 1924; and 1,803 millions on July 31st following.

It is well, then, to remember this: the stabilization of the German exchange was not obtained by means of contraction, or even by a stoppage of the expansion of the circulation of *legal* currency. On the contrary, the quantity of the legal currency rose considerably.

**5.** Impressed by the great increase in the circulation during 1924, Professor Harms (of Kiel University) criticized the German monetary policy severely. He held that the introduction of the rentenmark was accompanied "by the most colossal monetary inflation ever recorded in the history of the world."*

We shall see in the following pages how, in reality, in the first months following the introduction of the rentenmark, the extreme liberality of credit by the Reichsbank had already begun to disturb the equilibrium of the exchanges and to provoke a rise in the prices of goods in the home market. But, on the whole, the criticism of Harms is beside the point. He did not recognize that the phenomenon, really surprising at first sight, of the continual expansion of the circulation at a time of the stabilization of the exchange was not peculiar to Germany, but that it occurred also in other countries who were experiencing similar monetary conditions. The most typical example was given by Austria. On August 31st, 1922, the Austrian circulation amounted to 1,353 milliard crowns. It was 2,971 milliards on October 31st; 3,133 milliards on November 23rd, five days after the suspension of the issues for the Government; 4,080 milliards on December 31st, 1922; 4,459 on March 31st, 1923; 5,433 milliards on June 30th, and 7,126 milliards on December 31st. Similarly in Hungary and Poland there was a marked rise in the circulation of legal tender currency during the period of the stabilization of the exchange.

**6.** Even the Dawes Report did not give a satisfactory solution of the "enigma" of the stability of the German exchange. The experts mentioned the rentenmark only in passing as they considered it as an absolutely precarious and artificial solution of the German monetary problem. According to expert opinion the rentenmark scheme lacked the elements of a stable equilibrium "because the liquid cover for this money was entirely insufficient to guarantee a permanent system." Therefore they advised the calling-in of the rentenmark and the substitution for it of a guaranteed and convertible bank-note. The German Government and the President of the Reichsbank accepted the experts' proposal, which involved the elimination of the rentenmark. The explanation is that they probably thought that, since Germany was in dire need of foreign loans, it was necessary to create a monetary system which would command the confidence of potential foreign creditors.

On the causes of the stabilization of the German exchange the

* *Wirtschaftsdienst*, August 1st, 1924, No. 31.

experts wrote: "The temporary equilibrium of the German exchange has been ascribed to various causes by different authorities; some lay stress upon psychological factors, and in particular a renewal of confidence, the exact basis of which it would be difficult to determine, but which took account of the efforts being made by the German Goverment to balance its budget, and of the appointment of the Committees of Experts by the Reparation Commission; others refer to a decrease in internal consumption which with the lack of credit, accompanied by what was probably an excessive restriction in importation, reduced the demands both for the circulating medium and for foreign currencies."*

The authorities who attributed the equilibrium of the exchange to the confidence spread among the German people were directing attention to a factor which was certainly of considerable, if not of dominating, importance. On the other hand, the second explanation (the decrease in consumption) has no foundation. Indeed, many facts show that the first effect of the stabilization of the currency was an *increase in consumption* by many classes of society, i.e. by those classes—salary and wage-earners—whose purchasing power had formerly been reduced by the rapid depreciation of the sums received as salaries or wages. Owing to the rise in the home demand, some industries—especially the textile industry—entered on a new phase of prosperity. Imports increased considerably: especially those of luxury goods. The unfavourable balance of trade was in January 1924, 136 million gold marks; in February 1924, 232 millions; in March, 236; April, 312; and in May, 354.†

* *The Experts' Plan for Reparation Payments*, published by the Reparation Com mission, Paris, 1926, p. 41.

† The following figures are extracted from German official statistics:

*German Imports (quintals)*

| | *1st half* 1923 | *1st half* 1924 |
|---|---|---|
| Bananas | 829 | 102,325 |
| Oranges, mandarins | 106,449 | 1,283,689 |
| Dates | 70 | 13,724 |
| Pineapples | 65 | 8,339 |
| Apricots, peaches, prunes | 90,769 | 312,687 |
| Champagne (bottled) | 75,458 | 781,002 |
| Butter | 5,234 | 181,655 |
| Eggs (thousands of) | 1,630 | 494,081 |
| Silks, fabrics | 180 | 1,404 |
| Men's silk hats | 1,068 | 3,671 |
| Skin gloves (pairs) | 4,164 | 39,961 |
| Shoes of fine leather (pairs) weight less than 600 gr. | 6,331 | 190,128 |
| Furs for coats | 2,962 | 5,036 |

Contrary to the statements of some economists and especially of some practical men, who for years repeated that the *sine qua non* of the monetary stabilization was the equilibrium of the balance of trade, the German exchange was stabilized just at a time when this balance was markedly unfavourable.

A typical example of the rise in consumption was the craze for foreign travel which suddenly possessed some classes of the German people in the first months of 1924. Being concerned for the stabilization of the exchange, the German Government intervened in April 1924 to stop the exodus of Germans, with a drastic measure raising the cost of passports to 500 gold marks per person.

7. The stability of the value of the rentenmark could not be due to the possibility of converting the latter into mortgage securities. As stated above, with 500 rentenmarks one could obtain at any moment a bond with the nominal value of 500 gold marks, which was guaranteed by a legal mortgage on German property and which yielded a rate of interest at 5 per cent *in gold* (actually payable in paper at the exchange rate of the gold mark).

This ingenious system could, at the most, curb, but could not prevent altogether, the depreciation of the rentenmark at a time when the market value of the mortgage bonds was lower than the nominal value. The market rate of interest was then much higher than 5 per cent. Indeed, during 1924 the prices of the so-called "stable-value loans" were so low that sometimes they yielded an effective interest of as much as 15 to 20 per cent. Besides, the increase of the issues of rentenmarks would continually add to the Government's burden on interest on mortgage bonds, for which the public would exchange increasing quantities of rentenmarks; and therefore, in a precarious financial position, the uncertainty of the Government being able to continue the payment of interest would increase.

Before the introduction of the rentenmark there had already been another monetary experiment, little known outside Germany. This was the issue, to the amount of 500 millions of gold marks, of the Gold Loan Bonds (Goldanleihe), which were to serve as a medium of exchange. Now the value of the "Goldanleihe" was kept stable in terms of dollars, despite their having no cover. Moreover, the existence of cover for the rentenmark, though it might have had some influence in creating among the public an atmosphere of confidence and special favour for the new money, could not explain how the value of the paper mark was maintained constant in the face of continuous and considerable increase in issues.

## IV. THE SUBSTITUTION FOR LEGAL TENDER CURRENCY OF OTHER MEANS OF PAYMENT DURING THE LAST PHASE OF THE INFLATION

**8.** In order to understand the sudden stabilization of the exchange in Germany and other European countries with greatly depreciated currencies, it is necessary to take into account the monetary and financial phenomena which prevail in a very advanced stage of the depreciation of a currency. The systematic and comparative description of conditions in Germany, Poland, Russia, Hungary, and Austria, when made, will form an interesting chapter in the theory of monetary depreciation. Economists' theories, until now, have been modelled on phenomena observed in countries where the currency was not so enormously depreciated as in the above-mentioned countries after the end of the World War. It is true that in the latter countries were repeated some of the phenomena which occurred during the depreciation of the French assignats and of the currency of the American Colonies. But in those two cases the depreciation took place in social and economic circumstances very different from those of our time; the economic and social structure was very much simpler than that, for example, of modern Germany. Much more interesting, and fruitful from a scientific point of view, than those remote experiences (which in any case are not, owing to the insufficiency of statistics, susceptible to any detailed investigation) were the experiments made in that huge laboratory of monetary facts which some countries became after the war.

In spite of differences in details (to which the depreciation of the currency in each country owed its peculiar aspect), even the last phase of the monetary depreciation in the various countries—Germany, Austria, Poland, Hungary, and even Russia—presented certain fundamental uniformities.

**9.** In this last phase the legal paper money was replaced by other monies (which had no legal recognition), not only as "a store of value" and as "a standard of value," but also as a means of payment. Little by little foreign money, or the old national metallic money (which had been hoarded), or new money created by private firms, entered the circulation. The legal money was rejected by the public.

This phenomenon had appeared in earlier episodes, when monetary inflation had reached the point of destroying confidence, in the national money. As White* records, about 1780 (i.e. during the last phase of the inflation of the paper money issued by the American Colonies in their struggle with England) coined money, partly obtained from private hoards and partly from the army and from English and French ships, was put into circulation. The same phenomenon also appeared in France during the assignat period. Whilst the value of the paper money rapidly decreased, silver reappeared in circulation. Thiers writes that in the southern provinces the piastre circulated, having come from Spain. "Metallic money rapidly re-entered the channels of the circulation and performed all the functions of money."† More recently this phenomenon appeared in Russia during the Bolshevik régime.

In the Report of the Sokolnikoff Finance Commission it was stated that "following the catastrophic depreciation of the rouble, certain goods have been used as a means of exchange; even gold and foreign money have satisfied the need for money."‡ In spite of the prohibitions of the Soviet Government commerce was using the old gold money, still possessed by the population (there were still about 400 million roubles left in the summer of 1923), which was gradually being taken from hiding-places. By such means while the legal paper money rapidly depreciated, in the internal economy of Russia "there was an increasing transition to, or rather a re-establishment of, the old gold monetary system."§ Ordinary business was itself responsible for laying the foundation-stone of a restored gold currency. The paper rouble was rejected, especially by the peasants, who were unwilling to sell their grain for paper money. In the end the Soviet Government had to give way, even in the monetary field, to the requirements of economic life, and was obliged to make a series of concessions.

**10.** The replacements of the legal money by other monies in Germany developed in an interesting way. In the summer of 1922 at a time when the external value of the mark was falling rapidly, causing a revolution of internal prices, the most important industries, one after another, adopted the practice of expressing prices in a foreign "appreciated" money (dollars, Swiss francs, Dutch florins, etc.) or in gold marks. The Press of those days cited the example of a cloth-making syndicate, and firms making velvet, leather, porcelain, china, lace,

* *Money and Banking illustrated by American History*, Boston, 1895, p. 142.

† Falkner, *Das Papiergeld der französischen Revolution*, Leipzig, 1924, p. 85.

‡ Bernatzky, *Der Zusammenbruch der russischen Währung*, Leipzig, 1924 (Schriften des V.f.S., 165 Band), p. 65.

§ Bernatzky, *op. cit.*, p. 66.

cars, etc. Later the paper mark continually lost importance as a means of payment also. Wholesale trade, which badly needed a means of payment, resorted to foreign exchange.

In the summer of 1923, the need for a circulating medium being at times very acute, because of the rapid fall in the total real value of paper marks, the "emergency monies" (which had from time to time appeared in the circulation, and which had been regulated by the law of July 17th, 1922) were multiplied. State and local governments, industrial associations, chambers of commerce, and private traders issued great quantities of paper "money." Sometimes the issues were authorized and came under certain guarantees (see the decree of October 26th, 1923), but most were illegal issues, which, thanks to the rapid depreciation of notes, yielded considerable profits to the issuers. Illegal issues were especially frequent in the occupied territories. It is said that in the autumn of 1923 there were two thousand different kinds of emergency money in circulation! The abuses which arose from these issues constitute one of the most unhappy chapters in the history of the mark.

**11.** Towards mid-October 1923 it was obvious that the monetary chaos could not go on any longer without involving the entire economic system in complete catastrophe. On October 13th the law granting full powers was passed, and on October 15th the decree which instituted the "Rentenbank" provided for the issue of a new money, the rentenmark, beginning from November 15th, 1923.

But, in the meantime, among the German population the need for a stable-value currency had become greater than ever. The working classes especially declared further delays to be intolerable and imperiously demanded a means of payment with *a stable value*. It being impossible, for technical reasons, to anticipate the date of the issue of the rentenmark, it was necessary to look elsewhere for an immediate solution of the urgent monetary problem, in order to avoid the dangers arising from the threatening attitude of the working classes. The Government put into circulation some small denominations (up to a tenth of a dollar) of "Gold Loan" and some "Dollar Treasury Bonds." However, as the notes immediately available were very limited, the Government authorized and even encouraged the issue of "emergency monies with a constant value" (wertbeständiges Notgeld).

The issuers—who were principally the provinces, towns, and chambers of commerce—had to cover completely the paper money issued by depositing an equivalent sum in Gold Loan securities or by a special type of Gold Treasury Bond, which was created for the purpose (see decree of October 26th, 1923, and successive modifications, published by the Press on November 4th).

The railway administration was authorized to issue "emergency monies with a constant value," up to the amount of 200 million gold marks, which were "guaranteed" by a deposit of Gold Loan and of Gold Treasury Bonds of equivalent value.

**12.** It is unnecessary to state that the guarantee of the so-called "money with a stable value" was purely fictitious. Actually the Gold Loan and the Gold Treasury Bonds were mere paper without any cover.

Indeed, the law of August 14th, 1923, on the Gold Loan of 500 million gold marks, contained only this limited promise: "In order to guarantee the payment of interest and the redemption of the loan of 500 million gold marks, the Government of the Reich is authorized, if the ordinary receipts do not provide sufficient cover, to raise supplements to the tax on capital, in accordance with detailed regulations to be determined later." These vague words constituted the entire guarantee behind the Gold Loan! Nevertheless, the Gold Loan Bonds and the notes issued against the Gold Loan deposits did not depreciate in value. The public allowed itself to be hypnotized by the word "wertbeständig" (Stable-value) written on the new paper money. And the public accordingly accepted and hoarded these notes (the Gold Loan Bonds almost disappeared from circulation) even whilst it rejected the old paper mark—preferring not to trade rather than receive a currency in which it had lost all faith.*

**13.** Together with the introduction of foreign currencies and exchange, the creation of the "emergency money" (which became important in the German circulation in the autumn of 1923—indeed, the total value of the emergency money became considerably higher than the total value of the legal tender money) was evidence of the

* It is not possible to estimate the value of the "emergency money" which circulated in Germany just before the introduction of the rentenmark, because the illegal issues cannot be estimated. According to official estimates, the *authorized* "Notgeld" and "Goldanleihe" amounted to 728 million gold marks on December 31st, 1923. According to an estimate of the Statistical Bureau of the Reich (see *Wirtschaft und Statistik*, 1924, p. 121) the issue of unauthorized subsidiary money amounted, at its maximum, to 332 trillion paper marks. In its *Report* for 1923 the Reichsbank gave a considerably higher figure: 400–500 trillion paper marks.

spontaneous reaction of the economic organism against the depreciation of the legal currency.*

It is impossible to show in any precise fashion the amount of foreign exchange circulating in Germany before the introduction of the rentenmark. Estimates vary very much. According to an estimate of the Cuno Government the foreign exchange and currencies in Germany in December 1922 amounted to 3 milliard gold marks. But the amount effectively circulating is not known. Accepting the opinion of some business men, Schacht estimated in October 1923 at 1½ to 2 milliards the amount of foreign exchange and currencies circulating in Germany. According to Professor Hirsch, in the inflation years much foreign money entered Germany, part being hoarded and part being used as a means of payment. He maintains that this reserve of exchange in the autumn of 1923 was worth between three and four milliard gold marks.† However, all these estimates are unreliable.

### V. CIRCUMSTANCES WHICH FAVOURED THE SUCCESS OF THE GERMAN MONETARY REFORM

**14.** Another characteristic of an advanced stage of the inflation, which I have illustrated in an earlier chapter, was that the depreciation of the paper money proceeded more rapidly than the rise in the quantity of money in circulation. From this there arose a phenomenon which was at first sight surprising, and which led to erroneous interpretations, i.e. the continual depreciation of the total "real" value of the notes in circulation, which in the end was reduced to a small fraction of the value of the circulation in normal times. Towards the end of October 1923 the total sum of paper marks issued in Germany equalled scarcely 150 million gold marks. As I have already explained, the phenomenon was a consequence of the very great increase in the velocity of circulation.

**15.** In the case of Germany it is necessary to consider also the following circumstances: (*a*) for a long time the existence abroad of a

* According to Professor Hirsch the phenomenon of the "repudiation" of the paper mark was clearly apparent towards the end of June 1923, at first in the occupied territory and later in other parts of Germany. Instead the "Goldanleihe" was accepted by the country people. A considerable part of the harvest of 1923 was bought by consumers with Gold Loan securities (*Die deutsche Währungsfrage*, Berlin, 1924, pp. 121, 129). But in the cities, as the present author discovered personally, the paper mark was not rejected, although the "appreciated" foreign currencies were more willingly accepted.

† See the article "Wirtschaftsbereinigung" in the *Vossische Zeitung* of April 9th, 1924, n. 170.

great quantity of marks and at home of important credits in paper marks in favour of foreigners in German banks (the total in paper marks towards the end of 1920 was said to be 30 milliards) was a circumstance which imperilled the success of attempts at the stabilization of the German mark. But thanks to the depreciation which occurred in 1923, the value of paper marks possessed by foreigners was practically reduced to zero; (*b*) the existence of a great mass of short-term floating debt is a very important circumstance which must be taken into account when the stabilization of a currency is attempted. Now, every difficulty of this kind had been eased in Germany by November 1923; the entire floating debt having been reduced to scarcely 200 million gold marks.

**16.** The facts expounded in the preceding paragraphs explain the "miraculous" event of the sudden stabilization of the German exchange. The most important factor was *the continual fall in the real value of the quantity of paper marks in circulation*. Already towards the end of 1922 this real value had become less than the value of the gold reserve of the Reichsbank.

Similarly, in certain other countries, where the legal currency fell to very low levels, the gold cover of the notes (the gold being valued according to the foreign exchanges) was much greater than in countries where the currency depreciation had not gone to such lengths.*

From that arose the apparently paradoxical result that it became easier to redeem or convert paper money the more rapidly the paper inflation proceeded. In Germany in the second half of 1922, if the management of the Reichsbank had not obstinately refused to touch the gold reserves —of which later a large part was wasted during the "Passive Resistance" —it would have been possible to stabilize the exchange, re-establishing the convertibility of notes. Because of the great need for circulating medium few notes would have been actually presented for conversion. Naturally, the fundamental condition for the success of this operation would have been the suspension of note-issues for the Government.

* The figures below illustrate this point (source: *Memorandum sur les banques centrales*, League of Nations, Geneva, 1924, p. 32):

*Gold Reserve of Banks of Issues (percentage of the total real value of notes)*

| End of .. | 1913 | 1918 | 1920 | 1921 | 1923 |
|---|---|---|---|---|---|
| France .. .. | 61·6 | 11·9 | 30·8 | 24·4 | 35·8 |
| Italy .. .. | 60·2 | 10·9 | 29·6 | 24·9 | 28·8 |
| Belgium .. .. | 23·3 | 9·3 | 13·1 | 10·8 | 15·1 |
| Germany .. | 45·1 | 20·1 | 25·9 | 40·4 | 95·0 |
| Poland .. .. | — | — | 3·7 | 8·1 | 97·4 |

In the autumn of 1923 the monetary situation was as follows: There was a great quantity of paper marks, whose nominal value increased at a fantastic rate, but which in reality, despite the great increase in the velocity of the circulation, were sufficient only for a part of the transactions in German internal business. In the total circulation legal money now only played a secondary part, and the need of a circulating medium was largely satisfied by "emergency" means of payment, or by illegal currencies.

When a paper money is generally accepted by the public and it has filled all the channels of circulation, fulfilling perfectly the function of a medium of exchange, it is necessary, if it is desired to proceed with a monetary reform by issuing a *new* money, to call in an equivalent amount of the old money. When, however, the circulation of the old money is limited, the new money can circulate alongside the old (in the place of non-legal means of payment, of various auxiliary monies, etc.) without the new issues causing a fresh inflation.

**17.** In Germany, in the autumn of 1923, the question was complicated by the fact that the G9vernment could not suddenly give up procuring new resources for itself by manufacturing notes. A foreign loan—as in the case of Austria, and later of Hungary—was not then possible. It was calculated that in the transition period, during which the National Budget would be balanced, the Government would need 1,200 million gold marks, of which 300 would serve to redeem Treasury bonds in paper marks. It might appear to be a matter of indifference whether the Government created 1,200 *million* rentenmarks or 1,200 *trillion* paper marks (since November 20th 1 rentenmark equalled a billion paper marks); in other words, whether it put into circulation, for example, 1,200 million pieces of paper on each of which was stamped 1 *rentenmark*, or 1,200 million pieces of paper on each of which was stamped *a billion paper marks*.*

But it was necessary to take account of a psychological element. In October and in the first half of November lack of confidence in the German legal currency was such that, as Luther wrote, "any piece of paper, however problematical its guarantee, on which was written 'constant value' was accepted more willingly than the paper mark." If the Government had been able to suspend the issues of paper money for the State, probably confidence in the mark would have revived, as had happened in the case of the Austrian crown, and as occurred later

* A billion = $1{,}000{,}000^2$; a trillion = $1{,}000{,}000^3$.

with the Hungarian crown. But think what would have been the psychological effect of the Government announcing that it would issue more paper marks to about ten times the value of the total amount of paper circulating on November 15th, 1923! No one would have had any faith in the promise of the Government that later the issues would be stopped. The precipitous depreciation of the paper mark would have continued. But on the basis of the simple fact that the new paper money had a different name from the old, the public thought it was something different from the paper mark, believed in the efficacy of the mortgage guarantee and had confidence. The new money was accepted, despite the fact it was an inconvertible paper currency. It was held and not spent rapidly, as had happened in the last months with the paper mark.

Undoubtedly this confidence, thanks to which the rentenmark could enter the channels of circulation immediately, would have been quickly dissipated if the public had been led to expect that, despite the obligation imposed on the Rentenbank by decree, the Government would exceed the pre-arranged limit to issues.* An attempt to violate these obligations was made by the Government in December 1923, but it was confronted by a determined refusal by the management of the Rentenbank. The incident helped to strengthen confidence in the new money. The limitation of the quantity was then of primary and fundamental importance.

**18.** It is not difficult to explain why the monetary reform had been accompanied not by a *contraction* but by an actual *increase* in the quantity of legal money in circulation. The lack of confidence in the paper mark being lessened, consumers, producers, and merchants ceased to be pre-occupied with the necessity of reducing their holdings of paper marks to the minimum. In other words, the *velocity of circulation of paper marks declined.* That helped to create the need for a new circulating medium, so that new paper marks could be issued within the limits of this need, without imperilling the stability of the exchange.

Besides, *the rentenmark and the new paper marks took the place of the various auxiliary monies, legal and illegal, which had been issued in the autumn of* 1923 *and of foreign exchange.*

In fact, from German monetary statistics it appears that the circulation of the "Notgeld" and of the "Goldanleihe" notes fell continually after

* According to the Decree of October 15th, 1923, the maximum issue of rentenmarks was fixed at 2,400 million, including 1,200 million to be put at the disposal of the Government.

the introduction of the rentenmark. The amount of authorized emergency money, of railway emergency money and of Gold Loan notes in circulation, which was 728 million gold marks on December 31st, 1923, was reduced to 348 millions on March 31st, 1924, and to 38 millions on July 31st following.

At the same time the Reichsbank energetically set about eliminating illegal emergency monies from circulation. According to an enquiry made by the Central Statistical Bureau, at the end of January 1924, the circulation of unauthorized money was reduced to about 160 trillions (132 of which were in occupied territory) and to 105·6 trillions at the end of February of the same year.

A secondary cause responsible for the contraction of the circulation of legal German money had been the spread of French francs in occupied territories. In February 1924, confidence in German money being renewed on the one hand, whilst on the other the franc was depreciating, German money slowly took the place of the French.

The increase in the circulation of legal money which occurred after the introduction of the rentenmark can be explained, up to the amount of 1,100–1,200 million marks, by the substitution of rentenmarks and paper marks for the various kinds of auxiliary monies.*

The phenomenon of the replacement of foreign exchange by German money showed itself in the balance sheets of the Reichsbank, which showed a continuous and noticeable rise in the item "other assets," in which, as experts know, was included precisely that foreign exchange.† It shows that the public sold foreign exchange to the Reichsbank for German money.

The cessation of the depreciation reduced the demand for foreign exchange; while scarcity of money resulting from the cessation of the inflation made it necessary for industrialists and merchants to liquidate their superfluous reserves of foreign exchange.

## VI. MONETARY AND BANKING POLICY DURING 1924

**19.** Let us now turn our attention for a moment to the monetary and banking policy followed in Germany after November 1923.

* According to the statements made by the President of the Reichsbank on May 26th, 1924, at Hamburg, on January 1st, 1924, there was still 1,157 million gold marks of auxiliary money circulating in Germany; at the end of May of the same year it was reduced to 152 millions.

† According to the balance sheets of the Reichsbank, "other assets" amounted to 18·8 million gold marks on November 15th, 1923; to 285·8 millions on January 7th, 1924; 702·3 millions on June 30th; and 1,183 millions on October 31st, 1924.

As from October 25th, 1923, the Reichsbank imposed a uniform rate for foreign exchange on all the German Bourses. The Reichsbank continued to exercise a rigorous control over foreign exchange business, allocating it according to a scale of needs and often reducing the quota assigned to a very small percentage of the demand. It is doubtful whether this policy of strict rationing of exchange was really effective. It did not prevent in the first half of 1924 the importation of unnecessary goods from increasing considerably. Besides, business in foreign exchange in the occupied territories escaped the control of the Reichsbank.

**20.** At first the exchange rate of 4,200 milliard paper marks for a dollar, which was fixed for the first time on November 20th, 1923, was an arbitrary rate not corresponding to the quotations which were made in the free market, in the occupied territories and abroad. But during December 1923 the quotations for the paper mark abroad moved round about the official rate at Berlin.

However, in February 1924 there occurred again a depreciation of the exchange. On February 9th at New York a billion paper marks was quoted for 20·40 cents (parity 23·82 cents). At the same time domestic prices—which had fallen in December, particularly because of the abolition of the "surcharge against the risk of the depreciation of the currency"—once more began to rise.*

Actually in the first quarter of 1924 monetary conditions had not yet returned to normal. It is true that the Reichsbank kept the dollar exchange rate invariable; but the official rate was partly nominal,

* (1913 = 100)

| *Official Index Number of Wholesale Prices* | | *Index Numbers from the "Frankfurter Zeitung"* | |
|---|---|---|---|
| November 1923 | 139·0 | November 29th, 1923 | 165·0 |
| December 1923 | 126·2 | December 13th, 1923 | 156·5 |
| January 1924 | 117·3 | January 17th, 1924 | 145·4 |
| February 1924 | 116·2 | February 14th, 1924 | 144·6 |
| March 1924 | 120·7 | March 13th, 1924 | 149·4 |
| April 1924 | 124·1 | April 15th, 1924 | 152·3 |
| May 1924 | 125·2 | May 1st, 1924 | 151·9 |
| | | May 15th, 1924 | 148·5 |

*Average quotations for the paper mark at New York (for 1 billion: parity, 23·82)*

| | | | |
|---|---|---|---|
| December 1923 | 23·72 | April 1924 | 22·59 |
| January 1924 | 23·92 | May 1924 | 23·41 |
| February 1924 | 22·67 | June 1924 | 23·94 |
| March 1924 | 22·44 | | |

because whoever needed foreign exchange obtained only a part of what he required from the Reichsbank. Buying foreign exchange in other ways was more expensive. In the exchanges of the occupied territories (Cologne), which had not adopted the official Berlin rate, the dollar exchange rate in paper marks was generally higher by one-tenth than the Berlin quotation.

The demand for foreign exchange increased so much—as generally happens at times of monetary instability—in February that the Reichsbank could only satisfy it to a very small extent. On February 8th its quotas were only 3 per cent for sterling and 2 per cent for dollars. The fear of not being able to obtain all the foreign exchange which they needed led business men to accumulate reserves of foreign exchange over and above their immediate needs. Anticipation of very low quotas being distributed also tended to raise the nominal demand.

Some industrialists and merchants, especially in the textile industry, persisted in the practice of making their clients pay in foreign exchange. With the object of obtaining foreign exchange some industrial firms and even retail merchants allowed a discount on the price, in cases where payment was made in foreign money.

**21.** The stability of the German exchange was thus once again in danger in February and March 1924. As was unanimously agreed in Germany, the cause of the new monetary disturbance was the credit policy of the Reichsbank which was not strict enough. There is in fact no doubt that symptoms of a new "inflation" appeared in the first quarter of 1924. The Reichsbank had not dared to adopt a strict restriction of credits immediately after the introduction of the rentenmark, for fear of provoking a very serious crisis in German business. Short-term credits allowed by the Reichsbank amounted to—on November 30th, 1923, 364 million gold marks; December 31st, 1923, 600 millions; January 31st, 1924, 1,102 millions; February 29th, 1,482 millions; and March 31st, 1915 millions. Of these 2 milliards, 800 millions represented loans to agriculturists.

The excessive grants of credit on the one hand freed many holders of foreign exchange from the necessity of selling it in order to obtain working capital for their business, and on the other stimulated the speculative purchasing of foreign exchange. In short, in various ways tension was created in the foreign exchange market and there was a depreciation of the exchange in the free market. In the internal market the liberality of the Reichsbank created a fictitious prosperity in some industries, especially in textiles and leather goods, provoking a rise in prices.

On April 7th, the Reichsbank, now convinced that it was heading for a fresh inflation, which would cause a new depreciation of the paper mark and the rentenmark, decided to restrict credits, limiting the total outstanding to the figure which had been reached at the end of March.

**22.** The salutary effects of the new Reichsbank policy on the foreign exchange market and on domestic prices were not slow in showing themselves.

The shortage of money, which occurred in Germany after the contraction of credits by the Reichsbank, caused a supply of hoarded foreign exchange and induced exporters to deliver, more quickly than formerly, to the Reichsbank the foreign exchange obtained from sales abroad. At the same time the demand for foreign exchange on the Berlin Bourse declined considerably. On June 3rd, for the first time in 1924, the Reichsbank could entirely satisfy demands.

Other things which contributed to this favourable situation in the foreign exchange market were the foreign credits conceded through the new Discount Bank (Golddiskontbank)* or coming from private sources, and the return of German capital which had been sent abroad during the inflation period. But throughout 1924 the demand for and the supply of foreign exchange were, at least in great part, dependent on the credit policy of the Reichsbank.

The causal connection between the abundance of credit and the depreciation of the exchange in the first quarter of 1924, and between the credit restriction and hardening of the mark in the succeeding months, was quite obvious, and was recognized even in official papers, which had earlier generally shown little sympathy with the ideas of the Quantity Theory.

It is not difficult to see why the credit policy of the Reichsbank necessarily had a dominating influence. Working capital having been destroyed in the last phases of the inflation, and deposits in credit and savings banks having been reduced to very low figures, the demands for credit on the part of business men were necessarily directed exclusively to the central bank of issues.

* This bank, founded in accordance with the law of March 13th, 1924, had the object of making possible foreign purchases, for which rentenmarks could not be used; the rentenmarks not having the character of international money. The law is reproduced in *Memorandum sur les monnaies*, League of Nations, Geneva, 1924, p. 96.

As a result of the contraction of credit by the Reichsbank and the consequent improvement in the foreign exchange market, the quotations of the mark abroad and on the Bourses in occupied territories continually improved from the middle of April onwards. In May the average quotation at New York was 23·41 and in June 23·94. In Germany itself the "free market" premium over the official foreign exchange rate, which had existed in the early months of the year, now disappeared. Now it could be said that the German exchange was truly stabilized.

Control over the foreign exchange market was gradually relaxed. The "Foreign Exchange Commissioner" ceased to function. Nevertheless, certain restrictions (based on the decrees of October 31st and of November 8th, 1924) continued in force. They were principally concerned with: (*a*) the buying of means necessary for making foreign payments (which had to be done through an authorized bank); (*b*) the prohibition of forward contracts in foreign exchange; (*c*) the prohibition of the buying or selling of foreign exchange at a higher rate than the official rate at Berlin; and (*d*) the obligation of banks to furnish the authorities with information on foreign exchange business concluded in their own names or for a third party. All obligations to deliver foreign exchange to the Reichsbank was abolished.

**23.** An important measure which was used in support of the new money, the rentenmark, must be mentioned. The Rentenbank, in granting loans—which were not given directly but through the Reichsbank—imposed on customers the so-called "constant value clause,"* i.e. the obligation to repay the loan in as many gold marks as represented its original value. According to the President of the Rentenbank, this measure was an efficient protection for the new money, saving it from the speculators. The memory of recent experiences was still keen; they had shown that the depreciation of the German currency had been aggravated by the action of powerful groups of speculators, who were interested in lessening the real value of the sums they had borrowed.

## VII. THE NEW GERMAN CURRENCY: THE REICHSMARK

**24.** According to the law of August 30th, 1924, from October 11th, 1924, the German currency was the "reichsmark," whose ratio in value with the old mark (1 reichsmark = 1 billion paper marks) was fixed

* With the application of the new monetary law (October 11th, 1924) the clause was abolished by the Reichsbank, which wished to make it clear that the stability of German money was assured.

by law. Its ratio of value with the rentenmark was also fixed (1 reichsmark = 1 rentenmark). The old paper mark was withdrawn from circulation and it ceased to be legal tender on June 5th, 1925.

The fine gold content of the reichsmark was the same as that fixed for the old mark by the banking law of March 14th, 1875 (1,392 marks = 500 grams of fine gold).* The new banking law reproduces, with a few minor modifications, the well-known proposals made by experts for German monetary reform. In the first place the convertibility of notes at the Reichsbank remained suspended. In substance, the system established after November 1923 continued, inconvertible notes circulated internally, and the Reichsbank guaranteed the stability of the exchange by foreign exchange operations. Actually, the German monetary system was on a dollar exchange standard.

In accordance with the experts' recommendations, which were accepted in the law on the liquidation of the Rentenbank on August 30th, 1924, the withdrawal of the rentenmarks was to be achieved in ten years at the latest. About 2,070 million rentenmarks were outstanding. In the third week of November 1924 the Reichsbank began to pay back to the Rentenbank the loans which the latter had granted it for private business.

In the following years the last restrictions placed on foreign exchange business were removed. Until August 23rd, 1926, the Reichsbank kept the exchange rate of the dollar invariable in German marks; from then onwards it abandoned this system and allowed the dollar exchange rate to vary with market conditions. Finally, in April 1930, the Directors and General Council of the Reichsbank revived Article 31 of the banking law of August 30th, 1924 (until then suspended) which obliged the Reichsbank to convert notes, at its discretion, into German gold money, gold ingots, or foreign exchange.

During the years between 1925 and the financial crisis of 1931 the fluctuating amounts of foreign loans were the dominating influence in determining the value of the mark in terms of other currencies. For long periods the persistent supply of foreign exchange arising from long or short-term loans had the effect of maintaining the exchange favourable to Germany. Moreover, the Reichsbank was able to replenish its gold reserves rapidly.†

* Until the second half of 1927 the Reichsbank paid a premium of 6 marks for each kilo of gold.

† On these influences of foreign loans in Germany see a memorandum by the present author, *Inductive Verification of the Theory of International Payments* (Publications of the Egyptian University, Cairo, 1933).

## VIII. FINANCIAL POLICY IN 1924

**25.** The stabilization of the German exchange showed, as did that of the Austrian crown, this characteristic: The exchange was stabilized *before* there existed the conditions (above all the equilibrium of the Reich Budget) which alone could assure a *lasting* recovery of the monetary situation.

But in Germany the balance of the Reich Budget was quickly established—to the general amazement. What were the causes of this phenomenon? It was essentially a question of two causes: (*a*) the strict cutting down of expenses; and (*b*) the introduction of new taxes and the revaluation of existing taxes and tariffs.

On October 15th, 1923, the German Government took the energetic step of completely suspending loans for Passive Resistance. As has been seen in a previous chapter, the excessively generous subsidies granted by the German Government were the principal cause of the enormous deficit in 1923. Also in the autumn of 1923 the German Government tried to free the Budget temporarily from the burden of reparations by putting the burden on to private industry. On November 23rd, 1923, the "Micum" (Mission Interalliée de Contrôle des Usines et des Mines) and the leading heavy industries concluded an agreement about the supply of coal on reparations account. Analogous agreements were concluded later with representatives of other German industries. Afterwards the new reparations arrangements, fixed in the London Agreement, conceded a respite to Germany, allowing her to make payments to German industrialists, occasioned by deliveries in kind, out of the proceeds of a foreign loan.

The expenses of civil administration were reduced by dismissing a great number of employees. The financial recovery of the railways eliminated another important cause of the deficit in the Reich Budget.

In Germany, after the war, the heaviest item in the Reich expenditure was the service of public loans. Of the 17½ milliard marks estimated expenditure for the financial year 1919, interest on loans of the Reich represented a good 10 milliards.*

But the monetary depreciation caused the pre-war debt and those contracted during and after the war to disappear almost completely. The consolidated debt of the Reich (58·5 milliard gold marks)† was entirely annulled. The floating debt in paper marks, which amounted

* Lansburgh, *Die Politik der Reichsbank*, Leipzig, 1924, p. 24.

† End of March 1918.

to 197 trillion paper marks on November 15th, 1923, was paid by the transfer to the Reichsbank of 197 million rentenmarks lent by the Rentenbank, the Reich not paying any interest. Taking into account debts contracted after the introduction of the rentenmark, the public debt of the Reich on October 31st, 1923, amounted to barely 3,265 million gold marks (including 926·4 million for the foreign loans contracted in 1924). In the Budget estimates for 1924, expenses for the interest and ammortization of the public debt were estimated at 156 million gold marks, out of a total expenditure (in the ordinary account) of 4,942 million gold marks, i.e. little more than 3 per cent of the total expenses!

**26.** As we have seen in another chapter, beginning from the second half of 1922, the rapid depreciation of the German mark caused a progressive fall in ordinary receipts. They were reduced to 14·5 million gold marks in October 1923.*

Experience showed that the various attempts to reduce the deficit in the National Budget by new taxes would not be successful until the exchange was stabilized. The incessant monetary depreciation also continually reduced the real yield of new taxes; while a large part of the national expenditure increased in immediate proportion to the monetary depreciation. Moreover, owing to the great flexibility of prices, new taxes generally tended to be reflected at once in price increases, therefore adding a new stimulus to the increase of issues of paper-money.

Once the exchange rate was stabilized, the yield of taxes increased rapidly. From 14·5 million gold marks in October 1923 it increased to 63·2 millions in November, 312·3 millions in December 1923, and 503·5 millions in January 1924. Thanks to this marked increase in receipts, receipts and expenditure were balanced in January 1924, for the first time since the outbreak of the war. In September 1923 the Reich had been obliged to resort to loans (discounting of Treasury bills) to the extent of 1,560 million gold marks. In January 1924 it obtained only 1·9 million gold marks by borrowing.

It is true that included in the yield of taxes in the first two months following the stabilization there was a considerable sum on account of taxes paid once only and also certain extraordinary taxes imposed with the object of rapidly increasing the receipts of the Reich (the total

* Taking as a basis not the exchange rate of the paper mark, but the cost of living index, the income from taxes amounted in October 1923 to 23·9 million marks.

was 167·5 millions in December 1923 and 121·9 millions in January 1924). However, the increase in receipts was mainly due to the higher yield of existing taxes. In February 1924 extraordinary taxes yielded only 8·2 per cent of the total sum.

**27.** The conditions of the Budget appeared so favourable in November 1924 that the Government, yielding to the insistence of interested persons, was induced to lighten the tax burden. The decree of November 10th, 1924, reduced advance payments on income and corporation taxes; raised the taxable minimum of wages to 60 marks a month; and lowered the rate of the turnover tax from 2 per cent to 1·50 per cent.

In the financial year 1924–25 there was a considerable surplus of receipts over expenses: the effective receipts having exceeded the estimates by about 2 milliard marks. However, so considerable an increase in receipts was obtained at the price of a fiscal burden which was generally held to be out of proportion to the contributive capacity of the German people.

The favourable state of the Budget soon induced the Government to relax the rigorous economy of public expenses which had been practised at the beginning of 1924.*

The documented history of German public finances from 1924 to the financial crisis of 1930, may be found in the Reports of the Agent-General of Reparations.†

* A curious consequence of the extraordinarily favourable financial state of the Reich was the intervention of the latter in the money and capital markets. Thanks to the abundance of liquid resources which the Reich possessed, it had become a financial power of the first order in a country where the lack of working capital for private industry was seriously felt. Through numerous banks created by the Reich itself, funds which had accumulated in the Reich or State Treasuries were put at the disposal of German business as short-term loans. But the Reich and States often granted directly special long-term loans to industry and agriculture; or else invested money in the purchase of firms, industrial shares, etc. The inconveniences of the system, aggravated by the lack of sufficient control, by public opinion, over these financial operations, were obvious.

† According to these reports (see especially the *Report* of the Agent General for Reparation Payments, May 21st, 1930), the expenses and total receipts (i.e. the ordinary and extraordinary Budgets) of the Reich were as follows:

*(Millions of gold marks)*

| *Financial Year* | *Expenses* | *Receipts* | *Balance* |
|---|---|---|---|
| 1924–25 | 7,220 | 7,757 | + 537 |
| 1925–26 | 7,444 | 7,334 | − 110 |
| 1926–27 | 8,543 | 7,690 | − 853 |
| 1927–28 | 9,316 | 8,961 | − 355 |
| 1928–29 | 10,888 | 9,751 | − 1,237 |
| 1929–30 | 10,846 | 10,061 | − 785 |

[*Footnote continued overleaf.*

*Footnote continued from previous page.*

The burdens due to the war were as follows:

| | (Millions of gold marks) | | |
|---|---|---|---|
| *Financial year* | *Reparations* | *Internal expenses on war account* | *Total* |
| 1924–25 | — | 2,108 | 2,108 |
| 1925–26 | 291 | 1,513 | 1,804 |
| 1926–27 | 550 | 1,496 | 2,046 |
| 1927–28 | 899 | 1,560 | 2,459 |
| 1928–29 | 1,220 | 1,915 | 3,135 |
| 1929–30 | 1,075 | 1,752 | 2,827 |

The expenditure in "reparations" include the contribution included in the Reich Budget and the yield of taxes on transport besides some minor items; the "Internal Expenses" include war pensions, payment for war damages, and other less important items.

According to German financial statistics, the total expenses of the Reich and State and Local Governments (excluding, however, social insurances and analogous self-supporting public services) amounted in 1925–26 to 14·5 milliard marks; in 1926–27 to 17·2 milliards; in 1927–28 to 18·8 milliards; and in 1928–29 to 20·9 milliards.

# CHAPTER X

# The Stabilization Crisis*

## I. THE SCARCITY OF WORKING CAPITAL IMMEDIATELY AFTER THE MONETARY INFLATION

**1.** The word "stabilization" came into current use after the end of the war, but besides being much misused it did not express the phenomena to which it referred. It could mean that after the monetary inflation had finished, the various phenomena were "stabilized" in the positions reached during the inflation itself. But, as Professor Del Vecchio rightly observes, stabilization is a dynamic and not a static process. "In the inflation period the entire monetary system was out of equilibrium precisely because the various elements of the system did not move together. Then when the time for stabilization comes, the various elements must be put in equilibrium, which must certainly be a dynamic action."†

A salient characteristic of the economy of several countries, which have stabilized their money after a more or less lengthy period of inflation, was the lack of working capital for business. This deficiency, it may be said, is the essence of the "stabilization crisis."‡ It manifests itself in the high rate of interest. If a table is compiled of the rates of interest ruling in the autumn of 1925 in the various European countries, an obvious correlation is shown between the height of interest and the intensity of the inflation through which the various countries had passed. In other words, in the countries considered the disequilibrium between the demand and supply of capital was, usually, greater the

* This article was published for the first time in the *Giornale degli Economisti*, 1926.

† *Lezioni di economia pura*, Padua, 1930, p. 361.

‡ See Fürstenberg's book *Ein Land ohne Betriebsmittel*, Berlin, 1925. The title clearly indicates what was the fundamental characteristic of the German economy after the stabilization.

During the Bankers' Congress of September 1925 Wassermann, general manager of the Deutsche Bank, said: "Our real property, agriculture, mines, and factories all remain, fortunately, for the most part in good condition, though some are obsolete; but all are without sufficient working capital to revivify them and to render them productive in the highest degree possible."

more extreme had been the monetary depreciation.* On the central phenomenon of high interest rates turned (and were explained by it) many other phenomena which were observed during the stabilization: e.g. the closing of many relatively unproductive firms, the suspension of the construction of new plant, the constant attempts to rationalize production, and the influx of foreign loans.

2. In the first phases of the inflation the rate of interest tended to rise in Germany, as always happens at a time of monetary depreciation. But for a long time the rise in interest rates was appreciably less than the rate of currency depreciation. Subsequently the rate of interest became more sensitive to the influence of the currency depreciation. As the depreciation became even more rapid, the premium for the creditor's risk was bound to increase, and consequently in the final phase of inflation the rate of interest was extremely high. At the beginning of November 1923 the rates for "call money" rose as high as 30 per cent per day! In this connection the decree of October 10th, 1923, is interesting. It authorized the Reichsbank to charge different rates of interest according to whether or not loans were granted with the "valorization clause." Following this decree an interest of 10 per cent was fixed on loans carrying the above-mentioned clause.

In December 1923 complete confidence in German money was not yet re-established and the premium for the risk of depreciation remained, although it was lower. In the same month, according to the statements of a well-known banker, on day-to-day loans in paper marks an interest not lower than 3–5 per cent per day was paid on the average.† On the other hand, for rentenmark loans with a clause which guaranteed the lender against the risk of the depreciation of the rentenmark itself, interest of 1 to 1½ per cent per month was asked.

* Below are the official discount rates in certain countries at the beginning of October 1925 (it is well known, however, that in some countries, such as Germany and Austria, the market rates of interest were higher than the official discount rate):

| | *Per cent* | | *Per cent* |
|---|---|---|---|
| Poland (advance 14 per cent) | 12 | Sweden .. .. .. | 4½ |
| Germany (advance 11 per cent) | 9 | Switzerland .. .. .. | 4 |
| Austria .. .. .. | 9 | England .. .. .. | 4 |
| Hungary .. .. .. | 9 | Holland .. .. .. | 3½ |
| Finland .. .. .. | 8 | United States (Federal Reserve Bank of New York) .. | 3½ |
| Czechoslovakia .. .. | 7 | | |

Other figures are in *Memorandum sur les monnaies et les banques centrales* (Geneva, 1925, League of Nations), vol. i, p. 42.

† Urbig, *Die deutsche Währung vor und nach der Stabilisierung* (an address given at the Bankers' Congress of September 1925).

During 1924 the highest rates of interest were registered in April and May. From April 28th to May 10th the rate for the "Monatsgeld" rose in Berlin to a level corresponding to 72 per cent per annum. The very great difference between the rate for loans in marks and the rate paid for loans from foreigners in foreign currency was typical. (The latter rate was 15–16 per cent per annum in the period to which we refer.) Thus arose a situation which favoured the great industrialists, who, thanks to their connections, were able to obtain credits abroad, in contrast to those industrialists who had to look for money at home. Later the influence of foreign loans greatly reduced the rates of interest, which towards the end of October 1924 were 13 per cent per annum for loans in marks and 7·2 per cent for loans in foreign currencies.

The money and capital markets, even after the stabilization, were in completely abnormal conditions. The fundamental cause of the disturbance was the divergence between the official discount rate and the market rate. In normal times the latter was lower than the rate fixed by the Reichsbank; but in 1924 the situation was reversed, for after the stabilization the official rate was fixed at 10 per cent. The consequence was that the Reichsbank could not satisfy all the demands made on it for loans, but had to fix arbitrarily a contingent maximum. But that made the reconstitution of an unofficial discount market impossible, for in order that it would work properly it was necessary that bills should be discounted at any moment, in case of need, at the Central Bank.

**3.** Why was there a great dearth of capital after the inflation?

The reply generally given to this question in Germany was not satisfactory. It argued thus: The working capital of a firm necessarily assumes the form of money at a given phase of its cycle of turnover. If during that phase the currency depreciates, the entrepreneur no longer possesses sufficient capital to replenish his stocks of raw materials, to buy machinery and pay wages, so that production has to be reduced. Besides, it often happens during the inflation that selling prices are not completely adapted to the fall in value of the paper money, e.g. because of the limits imposed by public authorities. Many retail merchants saw their working capital fall in this way, to the advantage of the consumers.* Some German writers assure us that the same thing

* Löffler, "Einfluss der Gesetzgebung auf die Kapitalsaufzehrung" (in the volume *Geldenwertung und Stabilisierung in ihren Einflüssen auf die soziale Entwicklung in Österreich*, published in *Schriften des Vereins für Sozialpolitik*, 1925).

happened in Germany and Austria to a certain number of small and average industrial firms. That may be true; but it is only fair to add that generally the big firms, thanks to their superior administration and to their stronger position in the market, were able to safeguard their working capital by rapidly increasing selling prices. However, it is certain that some mistakes were made, especially in the first phases of the inflation.

According to some German writers the most obvious sign of the decrease in working capital was the very great contraction of the aggregate value of the German circulation in the last phase of the inflation, when the entire mass of paper money was scarcely worth 100–200 million gold marks, whilst in 1913 the value of the gold and notes in circulation had risen to 6 milliard marks. It is unnecessary to observe that this is an obvious sophism.*

On the other hand some writers have at last been reduced to stating that the phrases "lack of capital," "lack of liquid resources" were void of sense in the case of Germany. From the point of view of social economy, Professor Hahn writes,† "liquid resources" are not money but raw materials and semi-finished and finished products. Now two basic materials, iron and coal, were at certain times very plentiful. In June 1925 about ten million tons of coal had accumulated at the pit-heads; similarly large stocks of iron and steel goods remained unsold.

A clear proof of the fact that Germany did not need "capital" was given, according to some other writers, by the foreign trade statistics. The analysis of German imports showed that foreign loans had been used for a great part "unproductively," i.e. they had been used chiefly for importing foodstuffs rather than "capital goods."

According to Professor Hahn the causes of the stabilization crisis must be sought in the realm of the *circulation* of goods. The crisis was a "crisis of markets" due to the disequilibrium existing in the quantities of the equation of "exchange." It appeared as a "working-capital" crisis because the capital of industry remained embodied in unsold goods.

It is clear that the question has practical as well as theoretical importance, for measures appropriate for overcoming the crisis will differ according to the explanations given of the shortage of capital. Those who believe that the lack of capital signifies a deficiency of certain

* See Chapter IV of the present volume.

† "Kapitalmangel" in *Bank-Archiv* of December 15th, 1925.

commodities will advise the filling of this gap by stimulating the production of those goods, or by using foreign loans which will allow them to be imported; whilst these provisions will seem useless, or even dangerous, to those who accept a purely monetary explanation of the phenomenon of the shortage of capital.

### II. THE "CONVERSION OF CIRCULATING CAPITAL INTO FIXED CAPITAL" DURING THE INFLATION

**4.** Paper inflation is the cause of a series of disequilibria in the economy of a country. Its effects are analogous to those of certain illnesses which cause in the human body an abnormal and strange growth of certain muscles while other groups of muscles are atrophied. Inflation prevents the various parts of the economy of a country from developing in a harmonious manner; and it follows that some parts are over-developed whilst other are undeveloped. A typical example of this under-development is given precisely by the shortage of working capital. This shortage is not a monetary factor but the consequence of the excessive "immobilization" of capital which occurs during the inflation. "What is the significance," asks Professor Cabiati, "of the paper castle erected during the war and in the years immediately following it? A gigantic immobilization of national wealth."*

"Immobilization" means the displacement of the economically most advantageous ratio between "fixed capital" and "circulating capital"; in the direction of an excess of the former over the latter. It is a phenomenon analogous to that which occurs in the expansion phases of the Trade Cycle. The Italian economist, Ferrara,† records that in the well-known articles of Wilson is expounded the theory that the English crisis of 1847 and the disappearance of floating capital were due to the immobilization of enormous wealth in railway concerns.

To the classical economists, "the conversion of circulating capital into fixed capital" meant essentially a fall in the subsistence goods destined for the working classes relatively to the total investments of entrepreneurs. According to Mill, that which had been spent on the construction of a railway, "when once expended, is incapable of ever being paid in wages or applied to the maintenance of labourers again; as a matter of account it is that so much food and clothing and tools have been consumed, and a country has got a railway instead."‡

* "Il ritorno all'oro" in the *Annali di Economia*, 1925, p. 199.

† *Raccolta delle prefazioni*, Torino, 1890, vol. ii, p. 250.

‡ *Principles of Political Economy*, edited by Ashley, London, 1926, p. 744.

However, according to Mill, the production of new fixed capital generally happens gradually and is not disadvantageous to the working classes. It would be so if it took place suddenly to a great amount, "because much of the capital sunk must necessarily in that case be provided from funds already employed as circulating capital."*

Also, according to Cairnes the introduction and extension of fixed capital is, as a general rule, "effected through the agency of fresh savings rather than by withdrawal from the support of labour funds already thus employed."† But Cairnes continues that at certain times the conversion of circulating capital into fixed capital is done on so large a scale that "it may be productive of even disastrous results." The example given by Cairnes is the "extensive conversion of tillage-lands to pasture," which happened in England during the sixteenth century, which "issued in the remarkable phenomenon of a rapidly growing national capital, with improved industrial processes and extended trade, accompanied by a sudden and portentous development of pauperism."

To the classical doctrine it has been objected that a "fund" of consumption goods for the subsistence of the workers during the period of production—which would be, according to Jevons, capital in a disinvested form—does not exist in a system of continuous production. Cannan observes: "To support the labourers . . . is the office, not of the accumulated stock of produce, but of the supply of produce."‡

This is true; but the phrase "conversion of circulating capital into fixed capital" ("a somewhat imaginary process," says Cannan)§ expresses in a crude way a genuine fact—a change in the direction of production, under the influence of certain circumstances (inflation in our case), the production of final consumption goods declining absolutely or relatively whilst the production of certain capital goods increases. In substance what happens under the influence of inflation is *a change in the composition of the stock of capital goods*. The quantity of lower order "intermediate goods" (i.e. those near to the finished goods for direct consumption) diminishes; the quantity of higher order intermediate goods (e.g. iron) increases, and plant for the production of these latter commodities is extended.

The abnormal production of capital goods is financed in the last

* *Principles of Political Economy*, edited by Ashley, London, 1926, p. 97.

† *Some Leading Principles of Political Economy*, London, 1814, p. 210.

‡ *Theories of Production and Distribution*, London, 1924, p. 120.

§ *Op. cit.*, p. 114.

analysis by the "forced saving" of the people who have had to restrict their consumption of final goods. Under the influence of the inflation, the profits of the entrepreneurs rise faster than the voluntary savings of other classes of society. A typical index of this may be found in the German statistics regarding the distribution of the subscribers to various war loans according to the individual amounts subscribed. When the results for the various loans are compared, an obvious feature is the increasing concentration of savings. That is, the most important subscribers furnish an increasing proportion of the total amount of the loans; which, as Professor Rist remarks, was due to the formation of exceptional war profits (rather than to propaganda) whilst, on the other hand, the savings of many classes were reduced because of the high cost of living.*

### III. THE CAUSES OF THE SHORTAGE OF CAPITAL

**5.** A shortage of capital was not felt for a long time in Germany. The entire war period was characterized by great liquidity in the money market. It continued in 1919, 1920, and 1921, as may be read in the reports of the great German banks. In those years it was easy for entrepreneurs to procure capital by issuing shares and debentures, in order to enlarge their plant, and there was no scarcity of liquid resources.

A symptom of the abundance of capital in the German market was that for a long time German entrepreneurs, on the whole, felt no need of foreign loans—in marked contrast to what happened *after* the monetary stabilization. "The inflation," observed a banker during the congress of German bankers in 1925, "gave industry and commerce the opportunity to do without foreign loans." "So long as loans could be obtained in Germany which amortized themselves, thanks to the depreciation of the mark, there was no recourse to foreign credits. A firm who had debts abroad, which had to be repaid in full, was in an inferior position compared with his rivals who had contracted debts at home."†

Also, German entrepreneurs became creditors abroad during the inflation, since the equivalent in foreign money of part of the goods exported was left abroad.

* Rist, *op. cit.*, p. 96.

† Löb, *Auslandskredite und Auslandsbeteiligung in der deutschen Wirtschaft* (paper read at the Congress of Bankers in September 1925).

**6.** So long as the workers adapted themselves to the fall in real wages, which was a result of the inflation, entrepreneurs experienced no "shortage of capital." The flow of subsistence goods for the working classes was very much reduced; but it was sufficient to maintain the workers during the productive process.

So long as there is great unemployment, the workers generally accept the fall in the rate of real wages; but when unemployment ceases the position of the workers is strengthened and they demand higher wages. But when the workers demand that real wages should return to the previous level, before the production of consumption goods can, thanks to improvements in the producing apparatus, be increased in proportion, the flow of consumption goods becomes insufficient and a shortage of capital appears.

The German financial papers agree that the symptoms of a shortage of capital were apparent from the second half of 1922. It was then that the resistance of the workers to the reduction in real wages (which was the result of the depreciation of the currency) became more and more insistent. The working classes sought to re-establish the earlier level of real wages and to keep it stable. The profits which entrepreneurs derived from the inflation decreased. They began to experience difficulties in financing their businesses. It is well known that from the beginning of the second half of 1922 there was an increasing demand for bank advances for entrepreneurs; a demand which the commercial credit banks, whose deposits were continually falling, were incapable of satisfying. The shortage of capital began to be felt, with the consequence that production was limited.*

It was then that the Reichsbank intervened by extending enormously its short-term loans. Thanks to these loans the shortage of capital was temporarily evaded. Employers were able to pay higher money wages; but the prices of all kinds of consumption goods increased immediately, and the attempt of the working classes to increase real wages came to nothing. They then obtained a fresh rise in money wages; there followed a new expansion of credit and a further rise of prices and of money wages. The consequence was a formidable increase in the volume of Reichsbank loans. It was observed in Austria as well as in Germany that the inflation proceeded with quickened pace especially after the so-called "system of the index" was applied to wages, i.e. after the workers had obtained money wages which varied with the index number of the cost of living.

* Diskonto-Gesellschaft, *Report* for 1922, p. 10.

The last phase of the German inflation—from the summer of 1922 till November 1923—was notable for the way in which periods of capital shortage alternated with periods when—as after the occupation of the Ruhr—enormous issues of paper money created the appearance of abundant capital.

**7.** It was after the stabilization of the mark and the monetary reform of November 1923 that the shortage of capital became really very serious. "Stabilization" meant the end of the process which had provided the entrepreneurs with abundant financial means, at the expense of the owners of liquid capital, house-owners, small shareholders, salaried workers, and wage-earners. Once stabilization had been achieved, it was impossible to continue the financing of business by "forced saving." "Voluntary" saving, which was extremely rare, became the sole source of "capital."

A German financial paper rightly said how after the monetary reform "finance became the most difficult business of a commercial enterprise, whilst during the inflation it was the easiest." Profits from the inflation having disappeared, German entrepreneurs had to moderate the pace of expansion of their firms, to abandon great financial plans, and to rely entirely on themselves. It was no longer possible for them to free themselves from debt by repaying depreciated money. Numerous entrepreneurs had bought, in apparently favourable conditions, firms which, when the currency was stabilized, proved unproductive because of defective technical apparatus or commercial organization.

**8.** I will now elucidate some of the principal causes which made the shortage of working capital appear almost immediately.

(*a*) In the last phases of the inflation entrepreneurs had granted continual increases in nominal wages, which the giddy depreciation of the mark always rendered illusory. But after the inflation those increases became effective; in fact, one of the immediate and most typical consequences of the monetary stabilization was the sudden rise in the purchasing power of the working classes.

Another important circumstance was the rise in legal rents. As is well known, in 1923 expenditure on rent had practically disappeared from family budgets. After the stabilization legal rents were raised rapidly, so that towards the end of 1924 they had reached 70 per cent of their pre-war level. This rapid increase must obviously have had reactions on wages. Reading the German economic papers one discovers that the payment of wages constituted one of the principal financial difficulties in which were involved the many firms struck by the crisis.

(*b*) As has been shown, in the last phase of the inflation, interest rose to very high rates; it obviously contained a high premium against the future depreciation of the currency. Real interest was low or more often negative. But after the stabilization interest pressed heavily on business because, the psychological influences of the inflation still continuing, even rates of interest on new debts remained very high for some time.

(*c*) After the monetary stabilization the fiscal burden of industry increased enormously and suddenly. During the inflation the rate of taxes had been incessantly raised. Actually, thanks to the rapidity of the depreciation, the rates were ineffective and the fiscal burden was reduced almost to zero. Furthermore, entrepreneurs profited in many ways from the depreciation, because the levy on wages, the processing taxes, etc., were turned over only slowly into the State Treasury. In the autumn of 1923 the inflation was practically the only form of taxation and it weighed almost exclusively on capitalists, workers, and private and Government salaried employees.

But after the stabilization the high direct taxes became effective. Also new extraordinary taxes were introduced with the object of rapidly restoring the equilibrium of the National Budget. From the extreme position deplored during the inflation, things went to the opposite extreme; the fiscal burden became disproportionate to the contributive capacity of German business. For 1925–26 it amounted to a good 11 milliard gold marks, taking account of the Reich, State, and Local Government taxes; that was very much higher than the pre-war figure.

The rise in the public receipts also had consequences of a political character, i.e. the financial power of the Reich was reinforced. In a certain sense it may be said that the financial strength of the Reich increased as that of the great groups of industrial firms decreased.

Possessing a bigger income, the Reich, State, and Local Governments could, during 1924 and 1925, considerably increase the salaries of officials, civil and war pensions, contributions to assurance societies, unemployment subsidies, and other expenses of a social character.* According to official figures the total annual expenditure (Reich, State,

* In particular the "beneficial" expenditure of Local Governments increased considerably. Calculations made for sixty-seven Rhine municipalities show that expenditure per inhabitant rose from 10·20 marks in 1924 to 12·34 marks in 1925 (in 1914 it was 3·17 marks).

and Local Government) for salaries and pensions amounted in 1925 to about 4,600 million gold marks—very much more than that spent during the inflation.

(*d*) To the heavy fiscal burden which was imposed on industry immediately after the monetary stabilization, it is necessary to add new charges of a social character (social insurance and unemployment contributions). According to official estimates, in 1924 they amounted to 1,692 million marks. The employers and the workers paid about a half each. In 1925 the charge was raised probably to 2,220 million marks.*

### IV. THE POST-STABILIZATION FALL IN THE DEMAND FOR INSTRUMENTAL GOODS

**9.** Owing to the insufficiency of working capital, industries were obliged to reduce their demand for instruments of production very much. This decline in the demand for instrumental goods was one of the fundamental characteristics of the situation in Germany after the monetary reform. To take a random example from the many referred to in the German Press: "The Phönix company has suspended the construction of new plant owing to lack of money. Only essential repairs are now being carried out."

Moreover, the various State departments restricted or suspended orders for materials for new plant. The sudden fall in the demand for the means of production meant crises in the engineering, iron and steel, and coal industries. It was these groups of industries which bore the brunt of the stabilization crisis.

At the same time, for reasons formerly explained, there was an increase in the demand for goods for final consumption by the working classes, salaried workers, capitalists, and house-owners, who had a greater purchasing power than before.

As a result of the change in demand there appeared simultaneously an over-production of instrumental goods and an under-production of goods for direct consumption.

The most obvious sign of the former phenomenon was the accumulation of stocks of unsold coal and iron.† In some months of 1925 the

* "Deutsche Wirtschafts und Finanzpolitik" (in the *Veröffentlichungen des Reichsverbandes der deutschen Industrie*, 1925, p. 45).

† The *Bericht des Reichskohlenverbandes* for 1924–25 contains some interesting particulars about the coal crisis and its causes. It shows especially a fall in production, the closing down of mines, and the dismissal of workmen. The daily output, which amounted to 470,000 tons in January 1925, was reduced to 417,300 tons in May of

unsold stocks of coal and coke represented an immobilized capital of about 150 million gold marks. In the struggle for the acquisition of minerals which there had been during the inflation, more attention was paid to the quantity than to the quality of production. A competent judge writes on this point: "The prosperity of the industries consuming coal, which had been dependent on the inflation, caused rapid development of all the mines. Thousands of new workers were employed and millions of gold marks were invested in new plant. Not even Hugo Stinnes saw through the veil raised by the inflation; the artificial prosperity deceived him about the future of coal; indeed, all his declarations and forecasts expressed an unconditional confidence, almost fanatical, in the future of coal." Overtaken by the stabilization crisis the mining industry found itself heavily burdened by firms, with very small returns, which produced coal of poor quality which was therefore no longer saleable. Between the end of 1923 and October 1925, 63 mines in the Ruhr area were closed.

On the other hand, stocks of goods for direct consumption were very scarce at the beginning of 1924, as an official enquiry showed. The replacement of these stocks, either by increased home production, or by using foreign credits (see below) was one of the first concerns of industry.*

## V. THE MOVEMENT OF THE WORKING CLASSES TOWARDS INDUSTRIES PRODUCING GOODS FOR DIRECT CONSUMPTION

**10.** After the monetary stabilization the working classes were moving in a direction opposite to that which had occurred during the inflation. The number of men employed in the mining and iron and steel industries decreased and they turned instead to agriculture and the building industries. Miners who had come originally from the eastern agricultural districts began to return to their old homes and former occupations. From some mining districts of the Ruhr emigration was so great that some towns were almost depopulated. Towards the end

the same year. Among the causes of over-production which in 1924 followed the scarcity, against which Germany had been struggling until the end of 1923, the Report cites the following: "The fall in the demand of the iron and steel industry (also caused by the preference which this industry had now for Swedish iron ore rather than for French, which required larger quantities of coke); the improvement in the technical methods of using coal; and the fall of disposals to the Allies after the application of the Dawes Plan."

* *Kapitalbildung und Investitionen in der deutschen Volkswirtschaft*, Berlin, 1931 (publication of the Institut für Konjunkturforschung), p. 19.

of September 1925 the total number of Ruhr miners was reduced to little more than 400,000 (from 562,174 at the end of 1922), which was even lower than the 1913 figure (at the end of the year: 420,000).

The same phenomenon appeared in the iron and steel industry. According to the statistics of the "north-west group of the Iron and Steel Union," in 1925 the number of workers had fallen from 260,000 in 1913 to 190,000 and that in spite of the entry of new companies into the Union. During 1925 the raw steel syndicate was obliged to reduce the quota assigned to each firm, at first by 10 per cent (January), later by 15 per cent (March), 20 per cent (June), and finally by 35 per cent (September).* Even the non-ferrous metal industries proceeded to close firms and discharge workmen, but to a much less degree than in the iron industry.

Another example is the number of men employed in the shipyards: in the principal ones in 1913, 49,744 men were employed; more than 100,000 in 1921; 33,456 in 1924, and 27,812 in 1925.

These are only examples of special cases. But in a more general way the movement of the working masses is revealed by the following figures:†

TABLE XXXVIII

NUMBER OF MEN EMPLOYED IN

| | *Industries producing means of production* | | *Industries producing direct-consumption goods* | |
|---|---|---|---|---|
| | | *Percentage* | | *Percentage* |
| 1913 | 6,732,354 | 70·4 | 2,829,632 | 29·6 |
| 1922 | 7,277,795 | 72·3 | 2,787,565 | 27·7 |
| 1923 | 6,262,079 | 73·5 | 2,253,159 | 26·5 |
| 1924 | 6,143,302 | 68·5 | 2,800,780 | 31·3 |

In 1922, compared with 1913, the number of workers employed in the industries for goods for direct consumption had fallen, and that of men in the first broad class of industries had risen. In 1923, as a result of the serious general economic crisis in both of the categories the number of workmen fell, but comparatively less in the industries

* According to statements of representatives of the pig-iron syndicate, in August 1925 already half the furnaces in Germany had been extinguished and the quantities sold represented scarcely 70 per cent of sales in the previous January. Stocks of iron goods accumulated. See also the interesting *Report of the Essen Chamber of Commerce for 1925*.

† The figures have been compiled by the Institut für Konjunkturforschung. The "means of production" industries include: mines and quarries, metals, engineering, chemicals, building, and timber. The "goods for direct consumption" include: textiles, leather, clothing, food producing, printing, and paper industries.

producing the means of production. In 1924 the opposite movement began and the number of workers employed in the industries producing direct-consumption goods suffered a considerable increase, both absolutely and relatively.

### VI. THE CRISIS IN THE GREAT INDUSTRIAL GROUPS FORMED DURING THE INFLATION

**11.** The crisis of the coal and iron and steel industries was also shown in the weakening or, occasionally, in the disintegration of the great groups formed during the depreciation of the mark. Those groups, which in the past years had followed a policy opposed to speculation and excessive expansion, such as Krupp, Thyssen, Harpen, and Gelsenkirchener, could contend with the crisis. On the other hand the "Sichel" group, which had developed largely during the inflation, after having attempted in vain to save itself, by retreating to its original sphere (the iron trade), was forced into bankruptcy. The "Lothringen" iron and steel group was able to give up rapidly a series of industrial participations and so to overcome the crisis. Those struck more or less heavily by the crisis were the firms of Giesche's Erben, Rombacher Hütten, "Rheinmetall," and the engineering firms of the Kahn group (grown up during the inflation). The important "Hannoversche Waggonfabrik" had to declare a moratorium; and the difficulties of the great Stumm group could not be overcome in spite of prompt intervention by the great banks. I will not cite the well-known case of Stinnes. Above all, there occurred a disintegration of the overgrown groups which had been formed during the inflation, and which had been hailed on their formation as happy combines of finance with production.

Experience showed that the groups which grew up because of the deficiency of certain raw materials did not maximize in normal conditions technical and economic advantages. This industrial concentration in many cases only increased the dead weight of German business, being the result of unwise capital investments and of a reorganization of industry which did not meet the needs of national economy.

The time for easy profits had finished, and the necessity arose for analysing accurately the costs of production and for eliminating unproductive work. A serious defect in the "vertical" groups became more obvious: this was the increasing complexity of organization and the prevalence of a bureaucratic spirit, causing lack of adaptability, tending to reduce the quality of output and to increase production costs.

Some groups abandoned the connections existing between the various firms. Cases were not rare of firms detaching themselves from the group to which they belonged and re-purchasing their independence. The obligation of the firms of a group to accept raw materials or goods produced by the other members became in many cases an intolerable restriction on production, and caused an increase in costs. The scarcity of raw materials which was one of the principal causes of concentration in the post-war years had now ceased. Goods became abundant and firms often found it more convenient to buy from firms not belonging to the group. Taking account of altered circumstances some groups modified their constitution and adopted more elastic rules. For example, the new contract of community of interest, concluded in January 1925 between the firms in the Kahn group, was limited to recommending individual members to obtain their requirements *preferably* from their fellow members. The recommendation only became an obligation when the demand for a given commodity surpassed the immediate possible production.

**12.** The crisis in the groups formed and enlarged during the inflation was not limited to the iron and steel and engineering industries. Even in the textile industry, with the return to less abnormal conditions of producing and selling, some groups which had been created during the inflation by the concentration of financial capital found themselves in serious difficulties. They were composed of elements which were too heterogeneous to be successfully controlled by a single head. Groups which had been formed with the object of including all the stages of production, from spinning to the finished product, could not be maintained. In several cases firms left the group and regained their independence.

It is interesting to observe how after the monetary stabilization economists as well as business men considered the advantages of vertical concentration with much greater scepticism than they had during the inflation.

To sum up, it may be said that the stabilization of the currency did not affect the position of groups which were soundly organized and rationally managed. Indeed, these groups showed a tendency to further concentration, the object being to reduce the costs of production by closer connection of firms making the same goods. On the other hand, the stabilization of the currency made things very difficult for those groups which were merely a mixture of firms. And while the power of some great iron and steel and mining groups declined, the situation of some great industries, such as the chemical and electricity, was strengthened. The struggle of the Aniline group with the great raw material trusts is an interesting example. In August 1925 the Aniline group secured a victory by buying the shares of the Riebeck petroleum and mining companies, which belonged to the Stinnes group.

On the whole the good fortune of the great speculators, who had profited largely from the inflation, was of short duration. No new aristocracy of captains of industry arose from it. After the monetary stabilization the direction of German industry and commerce was once more in the hands of the old captains, or of their heirs and successors.

### VII. THE PROGRESS OF HORIZONTAL CONCENTRATION AFTER THE MONETARY STABILIZATION

**13.** During the inflation vertical concentration had in many cases impeded horizontal concentration and had thus led to the missing of the advantages of this second form of organization. That was obvious in the iron and steel industries. These firms had, on the one hand, bought coal mines and on the other acquired or constructed steelworks, furnaces, and other plant, for the production of finished iron goods. Thus the iron and steel industry became divided into a certain number of vertical sections (the Thyssen, Rhein-Elbe-Union, Phönix, Krupp, Rheinmetall, Klöckner groups, and a few others), in each of which was produced all or almost all kinds of semi-finished articles: pig-iron, steel in various shapes, steel plates, tubes, etc. As long as the demand for these goods was brisk and the profits of the industry considerable, the defects of the system did not appear. They became obvious when the stabilization crisis began. Then the necessity was realized by effecting a specialization of production, by concentrating the manufacture of given articles in those groups which could produce them at the lowest cost. An attempt to apply this principle was the exchange of the production quotas which were assigned to each group, for every article, by the iron syndicate.* In other words, each of the groups *A* and *B* produced articles *a* and *b*. If *A* has favourable conditions for *a*, and *B* can produce *b* at a lower cost, then *A* gives *B* its quota of the share in the production of *b*, *B* giving *A* in exchange the right to produce *B*'s own quota of *a*. The application of this system in practice took a

* E.g., in the summer of 1925 the Phönix group exchanged with the Hoesch firm a part of its quota of pig-iron for a corresponding quota of iron-plates.

long time and did not fully achieve its object, which was to accomplish a rational division of labour among the groups. It was necessary for the groups to be placed under a single management. This was achieved by founding the great steel trust "Vereinigte Stahlwerke."*

We have here, then, a new proof of the false direction which the inflation had given to the working world; anti-economic combination of firms; multiplication of the number of similar firms; apparently an intense activity, but with a practically useless or even negative result.

That is why in post-stabilization Germany there was a redistribution of industrial control, in order to secure more economical combinations of firms. This movement developed in two apparently opposite directions—*decentralization* of groups created during the inflation, and *concentration* of similar firms. The contradiction is apparent only, since the impetus to the first and second movements alike came from the need to organize industries rationally, so reducing the costs of production.† Horizontal combination came to the forefront after the stabilization.

**14.** The great profiteers of the inflation had engaged in a struggle against the cartels in the years after the war. They were able, in the years of serious difficulties for many firms, to extend their dominion, thanks to the preponderating weight of their capital and to the banking facilities at their disposal. The majority of students of economic facts in those years held that the era of cartels had finished. And, indeed, the progressive disintegration of the great coal syndicate and the end of the iron syndicate seemed to support their opinion. The principal motive which had conduced to the formation of the coal syndicate, i.e. the desire to reduce competition between mines at a time of over-production, had disappeared in the time of scarcity which followed the war.

Later, however, it happened that the few firms which issued victoriously and much enlarged from the inflation period found it advantageous to reunite into syndicates. The formation of these received a fresh impulse during 1924. The most important instance was the creation of the new steel syndicate (Rohstahlgemeinschaft). The

* Nominal capital: 800 million marks.

† In 1925 the concentration movement was progressing so rapidly that people spoke of a new stage in the economic evolution of Germany. This movement was simply a struggle to increase the productivity of industry. The most important two cases of horizontal reorganization in 1925 were the fusion of the firms in the Aniline group (this being a colossal concentration of capital—1,100 million marks) and the fusion of the petroleum firms.

production quotas assigned to the associated firms amounted to a total of 14·7 million tons. I should also mention the renewal of the Rhenish-Westphalian coal syndicate and that of Lower Silesia, the creation of the syndicate for semi-finished iron and steel goods and of those for tubes, steel plates, etc.

### VIII. THE SITUATION OF INDUSTRIES PRODUCING CONSUMPTION GOODS

**15.** Whilst the industries producing instruments of production and the raw materials used in these industries were involved in a crisis, one may say, broadly speaking, that the industries producing goods for direct consumption, or the raw materials especially used by these industries,* enjoyed conditions of relative prosperity.† This contrast between the situation of the two great groups of industry was revealed in several characteristic facts. For example, during 1925, the depression of share prices was especially marked for the mining and iron and steel industries, and for some branches of the engineering trade such as that of making railway goods. It was felt less by certain industries producing direct consumption goods, such as textiles and beer.

Another example, not without interest, is the distribution of "protested" bills. During 1925 the share in the total number of protests of the production goods industries increased from 37·5 per cent to 46·2 per cent, whilst that of the consumption goods industries fell from 62·5 per cent to 53·8 per cent. These figures show that industries of the former group had suffered a serious weakening of their financial situation, whilst those in the second group had shown an improvement due to the increase of the purchasing power of many classes of consumers.

**16.** An examination of the circumstances of the principal German companies in 1924 and 1925, made by the present author, shows that the firms which escaped the stabilization crisis belonged, on the whole, to the following industries: brewing, artificial silks, generation and transport of electricity, gas and water supply, tramways, opticians' goods, building, commonly-consumed textile goods, paper, glass, cellulose, oil, cinematographic films, large shops, construction of roads and canal works, mills, the potash industry, and, in general, the chemical and pharmaceutical industries, cement industries, and brickworks,

* It is obvious that many raw or subsidiary materials served for the production of instrumental goods as well as for goods for direct consumption, e.g. iron, cement, coal. The building of dwelling-houses involves some consumption of iron; but the impulse deriving from the increase in the building of houses was more than counterbalanced by the cessation of construction of industrial plant.

† *Wirtschaft und Statistik*, No. 14 of 1925.

the construction of plant for gas, water, and electric current, and the manufacture of trams. As may be seen, these were mainly firms producing direct consumption goods.

The position of German industries was reflected in the dividends paid for the financial year 1924 (or 1924–25). According to data contained in the *Statistical Annual for Germany*, which were calculated on the basis of the balance sheets of 7,666 companies with a total capital of 14 milliard gold marks, the dividends (expressed as a percentage of capital) were as follows:

TABLE XXXIX

| | |
|---|---|
| Breweries | 7·16 |
| Gas, water, and electricity firms | 6·27 |
| Textile industries | 5·66 |
| Rubber industries | 5·44 |
| Games and musical instruments | 5·31 |
| Theatrical and sports firms | 5·20 |
| Paper manufacturers | 5·14 |
| Leather manufacturers | 5·10 |
| Chemical industries | 5·52 |
| Electric industries | 4·91 |
| Engineering industries | 3·02 |
| Metallurgical industries | 1·93 |
| Coal | 1·16 |
| Mixed coal and iron and steel firms | 0·53 |
| Lignite industry | 7·51 |
| Banks | 6·49 |
| Insurance companies | 6·05 |

Except for certain cases, to which we shall return later, the table brings out the contrast between the industries producing production goods and those producing consumption goods.

## IX. CHANGES WITHIN THE CONSUMPTION TRADES

**17.** Among the consumption goods industries there were a few which were involved in the crisis, as a result of the redistribution of consumption which followed the stabilization. The demand for goods for popular consumption increased, whilst the demand for luxury goods declined.* This was obvious even to those who visited Germany immediately after the monetary stabilization.

* Certain relevant changes in the textile industry illustrate this. In 1925 the cotton industry experienced a considerable fall in the sale of factories which produced chiefly luxury goods. Sales fell in the mining districts because of the coal crisis. "But on the whole the level of employment in the cotton industry is high. The weaving and

The changes occurring in the demand for consumption goods are minutely documented in a report of the Hamburg Chamber of Retail Merchants. There was a fall in the sales of furs, perfumes, fine soaps, high-class cigars, flowers, high-priced sticks, high-class china and crystal, costly carpets, jewels and goods in ivory, bronze, gold, and silver. Orders for clothes made to measure declined. Furniture sales were generally satisfactory; but the public showed a decided preference for simple furniture, and therefore makers who had formerly specialized in elegant furniture had to turn to making lower-priced articles. Ordinary writing-paper was sold without difficulty, but the finer qualities found few buyers. The sale of rare books also fell. There was a good demand for low-priced musical instruments such as guitars and harmoniums, but it was difficult to sell costly pianos. *Objets d'arts* and antique furniture were little in demand; but low-priced imitations of antique articles were widely bought. The German public preferred moderate-priced inns and avoided luxury hotels.*

The little luxury theatres, expensive cabarets, and cafés, which had sprung up in Berlin during the inflation, closed one after another, or became ordinary teashops. On the other hand, huge popular restaurants, vast cinemas, public baths, and stadiums were built. The motor manufacturers bewailed the slackness of their markets and devised various systems for stimulating purchases; but the number of motor-cycles ("the car of the *petit bourgeois*") increased rapidly.

"After the stabilization," observed the manager of one of the big Berlin shops, "the purchasing power of the public increased. The inflation profiteers satisfied their needs on a grand scale; but now purchases are distributed among more numerous classes. The custom of the middle classes is established once more."

The statistics of consumers' co-operatives, which included in round

spinning establishments have sufficient orders for full-time work until the first quarter of 1926 and even after that. The printed fabrics and cotton velvet factories are also working busily. On the other hand, the linen industry laments the drop in sales of fine goods and pure linen. The customers who formerly bought these goods are now content with goods of half linen or cotton. In the woollen industry the situation is, on the whole, good. The spinners are fully occupied for many months. Even the condition of the hosiery trade continues to be satisfactory. The large shops experience good business, so that several have begun important extension works (e.g. Wertheim at Berlin)." See the report "Die Lage der Textilwirtschaft" published in the *Frankfurter Zeitung*, p. 786, of October 21st, 1925.

Another example of the crisis produced by the change in consumption was the difficult situation of the margarine industry, which had developed during and after the war when the consumption of butter had almost ceased.

* *Jahresbericht der Detaillistenkammer zu Hamburg*, Hamburg, 1925.

figures 1,700,000 members, showed a continual increase in sales. The weekly average purchase of each member rose to 2·74 marks in January 1924; 3·22 in July of the same year; 3·65 in January 1925, and 4·14 in July 1925.*

The consumption of meat, which before the war had reached 52 kg. per person, was reduced to 22 kg. in 1923, and rose again to 41 kg. in 1924. Immediately after the monetary stabilization the consumption of beer, tobacco, sugar, and coffee also increased, as Diagrams XXIII to XXV show, and as is confirmed also by statistics about the fiscal

DIAGRAM XXIII

A. Tobacco consumption B. Meat consumption

receipts which, under the Dawes Plan, guaranteed the payments of the German Government.

An analysis of the import statistics for 1924 and 1925 reveals some facts which show, not only an increase, but also an improvement in popular consumption. Wheat was substituted for rye, butter for margarine, higher grade meat for lower grade; and imports of cheese, eggs, vegetables, and fruit increased.

While the consumption of electricity by the civil population was greatly reduced during the inflation period—despite the relatively low charges—after the stabilization there was a sudden rise in the demand.

Another example is the rise in the uses of personal service. The rise in the original incomes of numerous classes of society was also reflected on some kinds of "derivative" incomes; e.g. the services of doctors

* Professor Sering also stated at a meeting of the Reichswirtschaftsrat that the consumption of food by the German people increased considerably during 1924 (see *Verhandlungen des Zolltarifausschusses über die Agrarzölle, Vorläufiger Reichswirtschaftsrat*, 1920–25, p. 8).

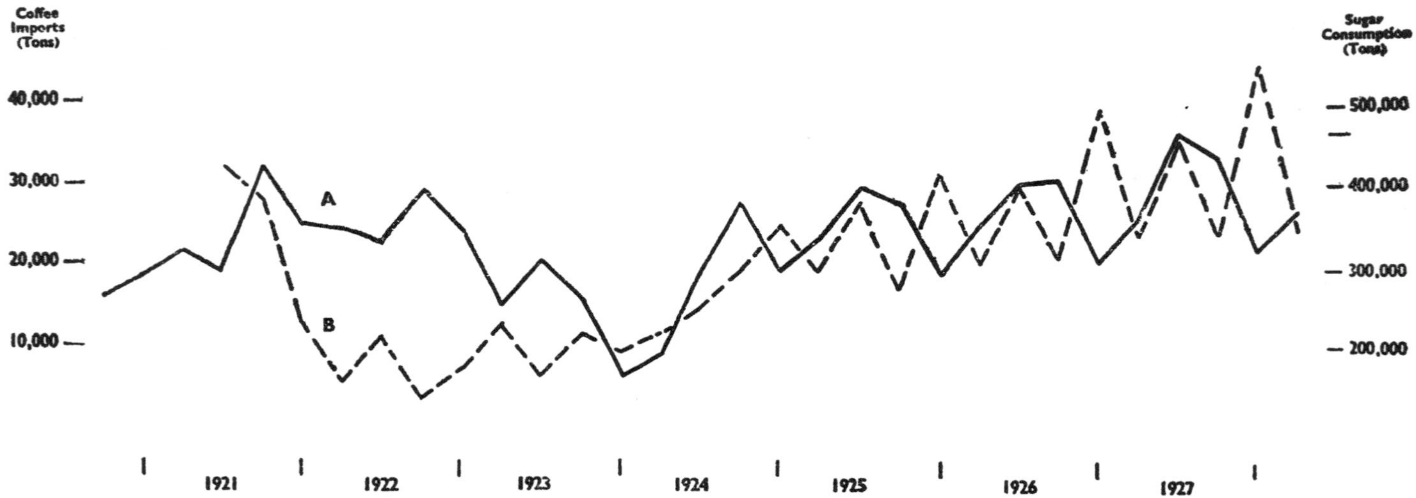


DIAGRAM XXIV

A. Sugar consumption B. Coffee imports

and private tutors were much more in demand and were better paid after the stabilization than during the inflation; hence the old middle professional and intellectual class began to be reinstated.

Agriculturists struggled against the adverse circumstance of a shortage of working capital, and sought to re-establish the conditions necessary for an increase in production.* This was shown in the remarkable increase in the consumption of chemical fertilizers.† Indeed, thanks to increased employment of labour and of fertilizers, agricultural production, which had been depressed during the inflation, increased

DIAGRAM XXV.—Beer consumption (quarterly)

rapidly after the stabilization. Even in the building up of the country's depleted livestock population satisfactory progress was made.

**18.** A typical example of the recovery of the production of "direct" goods which occurred immediately after the monetary stabilization was the construction of dwelling-houses. During the inflation the building trade was practically limited to the building of mansions for the profiteers of the monetary depreciation (as could be seen by passing through the environs of Berlin); but in 1924 there was a decided revival of the building of houses for the working and middle classes. Also "there was a recovery on a large scale of works of restoration and

* Similarly in Austria there was an intensification of agricultural production after the currency stabilization, as the sons and daughters of the peasants were turned away from industry in the crisis and returned to the paternal farm. At the same time greater activity was noticed in the building trade (*Geldentwertung und Stabilisierung*, etc., p. 194). The inflation, on the other hand, had led to an increase in uncultivated land and therefore to a decline in agricultural outputs (*ibid.*, p. 472).

† According to statistics published by the Potash Syndicate home sales amounted to a monthly average of 41,874 tons in 1924, and in 1925 to an average of 64,396 tons.

improvement, and of reconstruction of old houses, so that the long period of inactivity, which had lasted a decade, now seemed over and new life entered the building trade."*

The building of small houses in agricultural regions and in small towns particularly showed a lively recovery. Worth noting, too, is the considerable, and perhaps exaggerated, expenditure of towns on works for the benefit of the middle and working classes, such as grandiose stadiums, theatres and public baths, youth hostels, crèches, moderate-priced nursing homes, hospitals, etc. All that had been neglected during the inflation period.

**19.** As some previously given figures show, not all the "means of production" industries suffered from the stabilization crisis. That can be explained by the following considerations. Broadly speaking, the productive energies of a country are employed for two different purposes. They are partly directed towards the production of goods which satisfy directly the needs of consumers, and indirect goods—raw materials and machinery—from which direct goods are ultimately manufactured. Industries which are occupied in the various stages of production are organically connected, according to definite proportions. If an increase in demand stimulates the production of direct goods,

* *Jahrbücher für Nationalökonomie*, 1924, p. 724. Statistics of requests for permission to build houses (according to the review *Bauwelt* of 1925):

*Number of Requests*

| | 1923 | 1924 | 1925 |
|---|---|---|---|
| January | 483 | 687 | 2,447 |
| February | 441 | 675 | 2,401 |
| March | 516 | 1,263 | 4,345 |
| April | 383 | 965 | 4,338 |
| May | 638 | 1,778 | 3,573 |
| June | 741 | 1,698 | 3,454 |
| July | 612 | 1,408 | 4,270 |
| August | 549 | 1,487 | 2,755 |
| September | 412 | 1,708 | 2,997 |
| October | 579 | 2,805 | 4,598 |
| November | 296 | 2,087 | 2,740 |
| December | 308 | 1,647 | 3,971 |

Also from 1923 to 1925 the ratio of the building of dwelling-houses to the erection of buildings other than houses increased.

According to the *Statistisches Jahrbuch für das deutsche Reich*, the net increase in the number of houses was as follows:

| | | | |
|---|---|---|---|
| 1924 | 106,502 | 1926 | 205,793 |
| 1925 | 178,930 | 1927 | 288,635 |

the production of indirect goods also increases in a certain proportion.

But the productive energies of a country are partly employed in the manufacture of certain instruments of production whose connection with the consumers' demand for direct goods is much less close; although, in the last analysis, the object of indirect goods is always that of satisfying the future needs of consumers. For example, the construction of a dyke which will facilitate the irrigation of uncultivated land; a railway line; ports; shipyards; industrial plant for the exploitation of recent scientific discoveries; and renewal on a large scale of existing machinery.

During the stabilization crisis the execution of industrial work of this second category was stopped. But on the other hand the expansion of the demand for certain direct consumers' goods, which was the consequence of the increased purchasing power of large classes of consumers, did stimulate also the production of certain indirect goods. For instance, the increased demand for electric current rendered necessary the construction of new generating plant, and stimulated certain branches of the electrical engineering industry and at the same time the lignite industry. The increase in agricultural production stimulated the demand for and production of artificial fertilizers. The intensified building of houses gave an impulse to the cement industry, the making of pipes, etc. The prosperity of the tramways caused larger orders of material to be given.

### X. THE REACTION OF ENTREPRENEURS TO THE SHORTAGE OF CAPITAL

**20.** Entrepreneurs reacted in various ways to the shortage of capital which occurred after the monetary stabilization.

(*a*) At first they attempted to lower wages, which they declared were too high.* The offensive had already been begun by an article by Stinnes, published in the *Allgemeine Zeitung* of October 25th, 1923, in which he declared that German industry could only withstand foreign competition by lowering wages.

At the same time there was an energetic attempt by the Employers' Union to suppress the eight-hour day law, which the workers considered the most important achievement of the political revolution of November 1918. It may be said that the proclamation of the eight-hour day, which was made on November 12th, 1918, was the first act of the six popular Commissaries, and was the realization of a long-lived aspiration

* Later, however, wages rose again, as will be shown below.

of the working classes. The National Assembly confirmed, on March 1st, 1919, the decrees of the Commissaries.

The agitation of the industrial classes provoked the provisional decree of November 17th, 1923, which did not abolish, it is true, the principles of the eight-hour day, but did practically suspend its application.*

Immediately after the promulgation of that decree industrialists hastened to lengthen the working day.† They profited from the favourable situation created, mainly, by the great increase in unemployment and the decline of the syndicalist organizations, whose capital disappeared during the last phases of the monetary depreciation. The workers, conscious of their weak position, generally docilely accepted the terms of the industrialists; and even the leaders of the workers, whatever their political feelings, were unanimous in recognizing that the struggle for the return of the eight-hour working day would not have success.‡

(*b*) Another method was the limitation of dividends; indeed, there were many cases of joint-stock companies ceasing to pay dividends, declaring that they preferred to invest the money in the firm because of the great shortage of working capital, for which, otherwise, they would have to contract debts on onerous terms.

Also the German industrialists were obliged to reconcile themselves to using their reserves of foreign exchange which they had deposited in foreign banks during the depreciation of the mark. The increase in imports which occurred immediately after the stabilization of the exchange was closely connected with this.

(*c*) At the same time entrepreneurs sought to increase their working capital by having recourse once more to bank credits, i.e. in substance, by financing their firms at the expense of other classes of society. In the first months of 1924 the Reichsbank, fearing that a rigorously restrictive banking policy would be too severe a blow for German business, once more granted loans to industrialists, thus seriously

* The new decree on the length of the working day came into force on January 1st, 1924.

† From notices referred to by the German Press it seems, e.g., that in the potash industry the length of the working day was fixed at 10 hours on the surface and 8 hours in the mine; that metallurgical labourers worked 54 hours a week in Berlin, and elsewhere even longer; that in the lignite mines working time had been raised to 62½ hours weekly, etc.

‡ There were similar developments in Austria. In the second half of 1922, i.e. during the first months of the monetary stabilization, entrepreneurs began a struggle against the workers and social legislation on the pretext of making possible a "production policy" (see *Geldentwertung und Stabilisierung*, etc., p. 236).

imperilling the monetary reform of November 1923. Some German economists believed that, on the strength of a series of special conditions which is too long to enumerate, in the first months of 1924 German industry was able to finance itself and keep up a state of apparent prosperity mainly at the expense of the agricultural classes.* However that may be, this source of new capital was definitely closed in April 1924 when the Reichsbank fixed maxima for credits, which maxima could on no account be surpassed. Thus was established the principle, afterwards followed faithfully, both by the Government and by the Director of the Reichsbank, that the stabilization of the value of the currency was a necessity which had precedence over any other matter whatever.

(*d*) During the inflation the central bank, the Reichsbank, had become the sole source of credit. It was the instrument through which the "forced" saving, by means of note-issues, was transmitted to the entrepreneurs. The ordinary credit banks simply served as intermediaries between their customers and the Reichsbank. But after the stabilization of the German currency, the relations between the great banks and industry changed once more. Whilst during the inflation industry had enriched itself at the expense of banking capital, and later in many cases it could finance itself without having recourse to the credit banks, after the stabilization the latter began to regain their old influence.† It was the great banks who during 1925 intervened to support or liquidate some of the big industrial groups which had grown up during the inflation.

(*e*) But industry's need for credit could be satisfied only imperfectly by the available capital in Germany. After the final acceptance of the Dawes Plan large foreign credits were granted to German business. We can obtain some idea of their extent by considering the unfavourable balance of German external trade, which was as high as about 4·8 milliard marks from July 1st, 1924, to December 31st, 1925.

## XI. THE RECONSTITUTION OF WORKING CAPITAL BY FOREIGN LOANS

**21.** From the preceding considerations it appears that if the deficiency of working capital meant in particular a deficiency in the flow of subsistence goods, foreign credits would have to be employed, either

* Harms in *Wirtschaftsdienst* of April 25th, 1924.

† Especially in Austria, a country where the dependence of industry on the banks had always been greater than in Germany, the stabilization sealed the supremacy of the banks which possessed liquid capital (*Geldentwertung und Stabilisierung*, etc., p. 63).

N

directly or indirectly, for the purchase abroad of goods for direct consumption, or of raw materials easily transformable into these goods.

German trade statistics fully confirm this deduction. Indeed, the most typical feature of German foreign trade in 1924 and 1925 was the enormous increase of imports of food and finished goods, as the figures in the footnote show.* These imports, which from 3,095 millions in 1913 had fallen to only 1,228 millions in 1923—(the year of the maximum contraction of the "subsistence fund")—had risen again to 1,691 millions in the second half of 1924 (and they then represented 36·1 per cent of the total imports against barely 29 per cent in 1923) and to 1,949 millions in the first half of 1925.

The necessity for importing, above all, products for immediate consumption in order to build up quickly the subsistence fund, rather than raw materials, was also shown by a very detailed analysis of the statistics of imports of agricultural products. According to some calculations published in *Wirtschaft und Statistik* of August 1st, 1925, the excess of imports over exports amounted in the first half of 1925 to, for forage, 194 million marks (401 in 1913); but for cattle and meat, 158 (108); for butter, milk, eggs, and cheese, 386 (201). Thus Germany preferred to import pastoral products instead of forage.

For the same reasons, imports of finished industrial goods—especially textiles and clothing—also increased suddenly after the stabilization of the German exchange (822 millions in the whole of 1923; 924 millions in the first half alone of 1924; 857 millions in the second half of 1924; 1,069 millions in the first half of 1925). In the second half of 1925 imports of food and finished goods rose altogether to 54·4 per cent of the total imports, against 33·4 per cent in 1923.

* Imports of food, beverages, and livestock into Germany:

| | *Millions of gold marks* | *Percentage of the total imports* |
|---|---|---|
| 1913 | 3,095 | 28·7 |
| 1923 | 1,228 | 20·0 |
| 1924 (1st half) | 1,078 | 24·2 |
| 1924 (2nd half) | 1,691 | 36·1 |
| 1925 (1st half) | 1,949 | 30·5 |

Imports of fully manufactured goods:

| | *Millions of gold marks* | *Percentage of total imports* |
|---|---|---|
| 1913 | 1,413 | 13·1 |
| 1923 | 822 | 13·4 |
| 1924 (1st half) | 924 | 20·8 |
| 1924 (2nd half) | 857 | 18·3 |
| 1925 (1st half) | 1,069 | 16·7 |

However, it would be more accurate for our purpose to consider separately, among the finished products, those which were direct consumption goods, and to add to them the raw materials from which they are made. Now from calculations made from German statistics it appears that for textile products (raw materials and finished goods), for skins and leather, the unfavourable balance of trade was so great in the first half of 1925—608 million marks for the former category, 94 for the latter—that it was a long way above all the figures for preceding years. The desire to profit from the special facilities granted by the Treaty of Versailles until January 10th, 1925, for imports from Alsace-Lorraine, the Saar and Luxembourg, only partly explains this enormous increase.*

**22.** In analysing exports we discover movements corresponding to those which we have noted in the imports. Since the home demand for finished goods for direct consumption, constituting part of the subsistence fund, was very intense in 1924 and 1925, exports remained stationary, or at the most showed a barely susceptible increase. It is certainly typical that in 1923, a year of very serious crisis for German business (the occupation of the Ruhr), finished goods to the value of 5,200 million marks were exported (85·7 per cent of the total exports; in 1913 the proportion of finished products was 63·3 per cent); while in 1924, in which year there was, on the whole, a sharp recovery in production (as was shown by the big drop in unemployment), exports of finished goods amounted to 5,191 millions (80 per cent of the total exports). In the first half of 1925 the percentage dropped further (to 75·8 per cent), closely approaching that of pre-war days. On this point it was often observed in the German Press that many industrialists and producers of direct consumption goods, who during the inflation had concentrated their attention on foreign markets because the home market could not absorb their products, after the stabilization cared little for exports, because the capacity of absorption of the home market increased considerably.

Not so the producers of instruments of production and of raw materials necessary for the manufacture of these instruments, i.e. coal and iron. The fall in the home demand made them look to foreign markets for an outlet for their surplus. Unfortunately the excessive production of iron was a world phenomena and not peculiar to Germany;

* See the *Report* of the "Reichskreditgesellschaft" on the economic situation of Germany in the first half of 1925.

besides, German exports also met with serious difficulties because of the "exchange dumping" practised by the French industry. The only article of which the German industrialists succeeded in forcing the exports in 1925 was coal. In the coal trade the situation of exporters was completely reversed. While in 1922 the intense internal demand for instruments of production had provoked big imports of coal and created an unfavourable trade balance in coal, in the course of 1925 imports fell and exports were stimulated, and the balance of trade in that commodity became favourable once more.* In a less degree there was an increase in the exporting of iron goods and machines.†

## XII. THE "RATIONALIZATION" OF GERMAN INDUSTRY

**23.** Foreign loans could only be a temporary remedy for the shortage of capital. That persuaded German entrepreneurs that they must think seriously of reorganizing their business in a more rational manner, to increase productivity and to render possible the building up of their working capital.

Under the influence of the inflation an increasing disorganization had been manifest in many branches of German industry.‡ There was a mania for grandiosity, everyone being able to pay with a depreciated

* See *Report* of "Reichskohlenverband" for 1924–25. The coal exports which in 1922 (second half) amounted monthly to 200,000 tons and in 1923 to 160,000, rose to 267,000 tons in January 1924, to about a million tons in September of the same year, and to about 1·4 millions in January 1925. The monthly average of the first half of 1925 was 1·1 million tons. Coal imports which had reached 878,000 tons in January 1925, fell in the course of that year and rose later because of the English dumping; but on the whole the 1925 balance was favourable.

† See *Monatliche Nachweise des Auswärtigen Handels*, 1924 and 1925.

‡ The situation of the motor-car industry is typical of this: "This industry thinks of good times past. The advantages of the inflation (inexhaustible credit at the Reichsbank, low wages and freights) had created favourable conditions for production. Thanks to a big demand and to the lack of foreign competition the industry had the monopoly of the home market. The situation changed with the stabilization of the currency. In these last years the industry had developed independently of the world market. It had not known a crisis since the war, as had the companion industries in other countries, and it had been able to consolidate considerably its financial position by paying off its debts with depreciated money. The result was that the factories developed in a disordered manner and entrepreneurs ignored the new technique of trade organization adopted abroad in the meantime. In the motor-cycle industry also there was the same waste of capital and the same dissipation of energy; the number of factories increased in a few years from 20 to 70, but of these only a few could hold the field. . . . Only defects of organization can explain why the automobile industry worked at such high costs; the price of raw materials was the same in Germany as abroad; German wages were, as is well known, very low, and the fiscal burden in the other countries who had been involved in the war was as heavy as in Germany" (*Frankfurter Zeitung*, No. 492, July 5th, 1925).

currency, which was the cause of frequent "bubbles." Very many new firms were started without any solid or rational organization, their sole object being to take rapid advantage of the favourable situation, making as it were a "cultivation of rapine" in the field of national economy. Another important phenomenon already mentioned in a previous chapter was the way in which entrepreneurs became accustomed to speculating as a matter of habit on the Bourse, hoping by fortunate speculation to make larger profits than those obtained from the normal work of managing firms. This mentality lasted for some time in Germany among industrialists and helped to impede a rapid recovery of normal conditions. "Rational production" was therefore the slogan of German industry in 1925 and 1926.* Firms dismissed many unproductive workers who had entered them during the inflation. Even the numbers of general managers and other high administrative officials became smaller, although less rapidly.

**24.** Often radical alterations were necessary in order to establish the equilibrium between fixed or working capital. As we have seen, the monetary inflation had provoked a vast "immobilization" of capital in fixed plant, and in certain raw or subsidiary materials. These two forms of immobilization were not identical in their final effects. Stocks of iron and coal could be sold gradually and the working capital of the firms reconstituted. But it was necessary to realize that part of the huge plant constructed during the inflation had no economic value. The myth of the "intrinsic value" and of the "real value" was finally exploded after the monetary stabilization. When the joint-stock companies compiled their new gold balance sheets in 1924, they had to eliminate a considerable part of their assets.

It was not only a question of writing down the value of plant. In some cases superfluous plant was actually destroyed. In the Ruhr basin, for example, several mines whose closure was at first hoped to be temporary, were definitely abandoned and made useless. At the congress of engineering industrialists which met in December 1925 it was decided to adopt the same methods in the iron and steel and engineering industries.

* "It is necessary to make the maximum effort to organize rationally production and commerce. Every pfennig must be considered in the calculation of cost and profit; and intermediaries must be eliminated, without mercy, by means of competition. We must abandon the principal error of syndicates which fix prices according to the costs of production of the weakest. The weakest must not be maintained, but eliminated" (*Frankfurter Zeitung*, No. 624 of August 27th, 1925).

The outspoken words of an industrialist during that congress are worth quoting: "We have some very extensive factories which are nothing but *rubbish*. Therefore it is not sufficient, if we wish to restore our business, to close these establishments, in the hope of reopening them later. Even factories not working cost money; e.g. the Rheinische Metallwarenfabrik spends half a million marks per annum on a locomotive factory which is closed. Therefore our slogan must be: *Demolition! We must consider as finally lost the capital unwisely invested in those factories*. Certainly this is a unique occurrence in the industrial history of Germany; it is a recognition of very grave mistakes committed during the inflation."

The importance of these statements is obvious. Rarely do great industries such as mining and iron and steel adopt such a serious measure as the destruction of works.* But the consequence of this energetic method was a fall in the cost of production. One of the chief causes of the high costs, which were typical of German industry after the inflation, was certainly the serious disproportion between fixed capital and working capital.†

Here are some facts significant in the judging of the theory of the "inflationists," who declared that the monetary depreciation reinforced the equipment of the country. In the potash industry a good 118 mines were closed or definitely abandoned; "now since the average cost of a mine is about 5 million marks, it may be seen what an enormous sum of national capital has been uselessly invested."‡ The cement syndicate of northern Germany closed and practically demolished seventeen factories (*Frankfurter Zeitung*, December 12th, 1925).

It was affirmed that three-quarters of the existing plant in the shipyards was useless; and that superfluous equipment must be partly destroyed (*id*., December 30th, 1925). Also the agricultural industry suffered from an excess of land relatively to working capital. Consequently many big proprietors had to sell a part of their land; by such means and thanks to the fall in the prices of real property capital (as the Deutsche Bank observed in its economic bulletin of November 1925) there was re-established in agriculture a normal ratio between "fixed" and "circulating" capital.

* Einaudi shows that the mining industry generally prefers to work continually at a loss rather than close the mines (*La rendita mineraria*, Turin, 1900, p. 528).

† The German Industrial Confederation also clearly stated in a memorandum "the necessity for reducing the productive apparatus of Germany in proportion to the contraction of working capital" (*Deutsche Wirtschafts und Finanzpolitik*, 1925, p. 7).

‡ *Annual Report* (1925) of the Damman Bank, Hanover.

## XIII. THE MONETARY STABILIZATION AS A PREREQUISITE OF ECONOMIC RECONSTRUCTION

**25.** Experiences in Germany in those years showed the obvious error of those economists, politicians, and representatives of big industry who for a long time had insisted that the stabilization of the value of the mark would be the *consequence* of the recovery of the economic situation and that, therefore, it was vain to think of monetary reform before the economic premises were established.

In vain did Germany for years await the arrival of these "premises." In the meantime the disequilibrium produced in the German economy by monetary instability was more and more aggravated.

But the facts proved right those who considered stabilization as the condition necessary for economic recovery. The monetary reform of 1923 and that of 1924 (which based the note-issue on gold) made it possible for the restorative forces which would re-establish economic equilibrium to come into operation.

Stabilization of the value of the currency is not a simple monetary fact: as Professor Cabiati justly observed in his acute essay on the return to gold, this is to "mistake the shadow for the substance." The monetary incident of stabilization implies a change in the orientation of production, a deflation of the productive apparatus, of the overgrown banking organization* and of the enormous groups whose origin was due to the depreciation of the mark; it implied also a rigorous revision of the costs of production and a simplification of the organization of firms, the forming of combinations and integrations according to economic and technical considerations, and the elimination of relatively unproductive firms;† it implied a decline in the number of unproductive workers

* It has been calculated that more than a hundred thousand bank employees were discharged during 1924 and 1925 (*Frankfurter Zeitung*, No. 683, September 12th, 1925). Many small banks which sprang up during the inflation disappeared after stabilization.

† According to official returns the number of firms included in the commercial register fell in 1925 by 14,728. The continual transformation of public companies into private is also noteworthy. During the inflation the opposite process had been operating.

The following figures are taken from official sources:

| | NUMBER OF | |
|---|---|---|
| | *Public companies* | *Limited liability firms* |
| 1913 | 4,773 | 25,448 |
| 1922 | 9,490 | 58,934 |
| 1923 | 16,362 | 71,343 |
| 1924 | 17,074 | 70,631 |
| 1925 | 13,010 | 64,398 |
| 1926 | 12,343 | 57,338 |

(small traders, and more or less "legitimate" intermediaries), and the abandonment of purely speculative activities, such as gambling on the Bourse in securities and foreign exchange, in favour of some truly productive activity. The rise in interest rates was a powerful stimulus to the selection of the fittest firms—a process which had been suspended by the inflation.

Consequences of a social character must be added; thanks to the monetary stabilization, the distribution of the national income became less unequal; the financial plutocracy of inflation profiteers disappeared;* the conditions of salaried workers, artisans, and small capitalists improved, co-operative societies† and other institutions for the security of the middle classes were reorganized; savings banks, social insurances, and charitable institutions were reconstituted.

**26.** Experience of the stabilization showed how much in error those people had been who, in 1919 and the following years, believed that the rapid reconstruction of German business would be helped by the incessant printing of notes. It must be admitted that a part of the enormous mass of the "forced" saving of the German population which was directed by means of the inflation towards the capital goods industries was usefully employed. But the disadvantageous effects of the inflation quickly surpassed the advantages. The inflation crisis was not, as has been erroneously supposed, a purging of the economic organism. On the contrary, when the currency had been stabilized, economic reconstruction had still to be accomplished, and, owing to the acute scarcity of working capital, it had to be accomplished in conditions vastly less favourable than those prevailing in any previous year.

There is ample evidence to support the view that the productivity

* An example suggestive of the ephemeral character of some profits derived from the inflation is given by agriculture. This issued from the inflation completely free from mortgage burdens which before the war had amounted to 16 milliard marks, according to official estimates. At the most this burden, under the law of July 16th, 1925, on the revaluation of mortgages, amounted to about 3 milliards. Now, the shortage of working capital which occurred also in agriculture, after the stabilization of the exchange—and which was aggravated by the low price of agricultural products—obliged agriculturists to contract debts under onerous conditions (the average rate of interest for mortgages was 12 per cent; before the war $3\frac{1}{2}$ to 4 per cent; the average interest on personal loans was 14 per cent); so that it was calculated that towards the middle of 1925 the total burden of interest corresponded to a pre-war capital of 8·4–9·2 milliards.

† A sign of the re-establishment of the middle classes was the reorganization of private insurance companies whose capital had been almost completely destroyed during the inflation (see *Jahrbuch des deutschen Genossenschaftsverbandes*, 1927, and the book *Fünfzig Jahre Raiffeisen, 1877–1927*, 1928).

of labour increased rapidly after stabilization. In June 1926, in the Ruhr coal area, 389,037 employees (salaried workers and wage-earners) produced more coal, and of better quality, than that produced by 581,054 workers in 1923. This was due to the introduction of new improved machinery, to the better selection of workers, and to the improved organization of labour, to the closing of the less productive mines, to the reduction in the number of workers on the surface, to the increased intensity of work and to technical improvements of various kinds (e.g. in the new central coke ovens scarcely a quarter of the number of workers employed in 1922 were now engaged).* Similar progress was made in the iron and steel industry, in which the average production per worker increased considerably after 1924. The average monthly production for each blast furnace, which had been more or less stationary from 1920 to 1923 (at little more than 40,000 tons), rose to 76,000 tons in September 1925 and to 101,000 tons in 1926.

If we study the evolution of German business during 1924 and 1925, we shall see that it shows obvious progress despite the crisis which in a particularly serious manner struck the important industrial groups. Taken on the whole production made considerable headway at the beginning of 1924 and eminent German economists maintain that in 1925 it had surpassed not only the production of 1923 (in which year German business felt the consequences of the inflation crisis and of the occupation of the Ruhr) but also that of 1922, which, it was estimated, had been the most prosperous year between 1918 and 1924.

Certainly the long and painful business of the reconstruction of an economy, on which for ten years inflation had been imposed, could not be accomplished speedily.

## XIV. THE INFLUENCE OF THE MONETARY STABILIZATION ON THE SITUATION OF ORDINARY CREDIT BANKS

**27.** Thanks to the monetary reform there was, together with the reconstruction of productive equipment, a progressive though gradual adjustment of the capital market. Inflation had given a distorted direction to the flow of new saving, whether the internal saving of the firms themselves or that of the public. The speculation induced by the inflation put the securities market in a state of continual agitation which upset savers; they bought at random, no longer guided by the criteria of the productivity of firms, as in normal conditions, but

* See *Wirtschaftskurve der Frankfurter Zeitung* for 1926, Heft III.

deluded by the belief that shares, representing "material wealth," had an "intrinsic value." Part of the public savings were lost to the national economy.

The havoc wrought in the delicate and complex mechanism of the capital market was among the most serious disadvantages inflicted by the inflation on the national economy. The recovery of the normal functions of that market could only take place slowly, and, in the meantime, the disorganization accentuated the lack of capital.

One of the most important consequences of the stabilization was the gradual return of the credit banks to their normal functions. The principal assets and liabilities of the six chief Berlin banks were as follows:

TABLE XL

(*Millions of marks*)

| | *December* 31, 1913 | *January* 1, 1924 | *December* 31, 1925 | *December* 31 1926 |
|---|---|---|---|---|
| Bills .. .. .. .. | 1,779 | 37 | 1,249 | 1,556 |
| Advances on goods .. | 509 | 74 | 443 | 457 |
| Advances on securities .. | 760 | 17 | 122 | 718 |
| Current loans .. .. | 2,949 | 518 | 2,301 | 2,771 |
| Deposits and other creditors | 4,373 | 905 | 3,585 | 4,936 |

These figures show how the assets and liabilities of the banks were reduced at the time of the monetary stabilization. In the following years deposits grew rapidly (thanks also to the influx of foreign money) and the banks were able to expand their lending operations.*

XV. WAGES AFTER THE MONETARY STABILIZATION

**28.** Among the social influences of the monetary stabilization those affecting wages have a particular importance.

As from January 1924 the Statistical Bureau of the Reich began to publish statistics about the rates of wages fixed under collective contracts in twelve groups of important industries. They are the highest rates paid to adult workers (including allowances for wife and two children) in the most important centres of the industries considered. The Statistical Bureau itself has calculated separately the weighted average of wage-rates for skilled and for unskilled workers.

This material forms a very important source for the study of the

* For particulars see P. B. Whale, *Joint-Stock Banking in Germany*, 1930, Ch. VIII.

movement of wages from the beginning of 1924 onwards. Diagram XXVI shows:

A. The nominal wage-rate per hour;
B. The index of the real income of workers.*

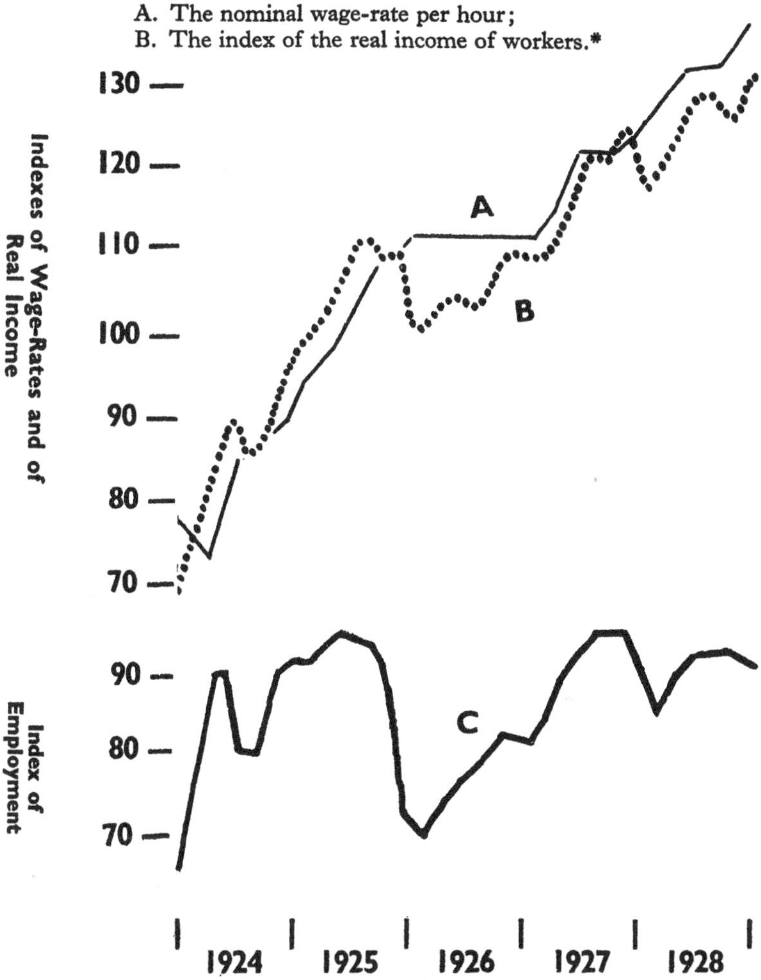


Diagram XXVI

A. Money wage-rates: unskilled workers (1924–26 = 100)
B. Real income of unskilled workers (1924–26 = 100)
C. Employment (percentage of employed workers among the members of the Workers' Associations)

* I have explained the method I adopted in calculating the real income of workers in the article "Movement of Wages in Germany, etc.," p. 394.

In these two curves the average of the years 1924–26 has been taken as 100. I have taken the wages and income of unskilled workers. Similar results may be obtained by examining the data relating to skilled workers.

Curve C of the diagram shows the degree of employment (percentage of employed workers among members of trade unions, taking account of partial unemployment). Curve B must be considered with the reserve arising from the hypothesis on which it has been calculated. In it no account was taken of some important elements in total wages, and in particular of income from overtime or piece-work.

**29.** The remarkable increase in wages in the first months of 1924 was a reaction against the excessively low wages which had been fixed at the beginning of the monetary stabilization. From the second half of 1924 onwards, the German currency being now finally stabilized, currency movements ceased to have a dominant influence on the movements of wages. Thenceforward wages appeared to be dominated in their general movement by the progressive adjustment of German business which resulted in an increase of the average production per workman, and in the more ephemeral movements, by the cyclical fluctuations of German business.

In the period under consideration hourly wage-rates rose from 42·2 to 77·6 pfennige. The rise in real wages was less; but nevertheless quite considerable.

As the diagram shows, workers' incomes were more variable than wages-rates. But through the fluctuations may be seen a definite upward trend. The index of real incomes (1924–1920 = 100) rose from 68·1 (January 1924) to 124 in June 1928.

During 1924 the big increase in the average income of workers was the combined effect of the rise in wage-rates and the fall in unemployment. But from 1925 to 1928 the general movement of workers' incomes was principally influenced by the rise in wage-rates. In June 1925, in which month unemployment figures were very low (4·6 per cent of the members of trade unions), the index of workers' incomes was 110·8, while in June 1928 it had risen to 124, despite the fact that the percentage of unemployed was much higher (7·5 per cent).*

* After stabilization the rise in wage-rates was greater for skilled workers than for unskilled. This was partly due to the decline in the influence of unskilled workers on the policy of the trade unions. Because of extensive unemployment millions of unskilled workers ceased to be members of the trade union movement. The ratio between the

On the basis of the information at our disposal we cannot be absolutely sure whether the average income of the workers increased more or less than that of other classes of society or than the total national income, but on the whole one can say that the economic progress of Germany after the monetary stabilization brought substantial benefits even to the working classes.

wages of skilled workers and those of unskilled workers was 131·4 in January 1924. It rose in the course of the year to about 140 and afterwards maintained more or less at this figure.

## CHAPTER XI

# Conclusion

**1.** Germany's monetary experiences have been interpreted in many ways. Some have seen in them a confirmation of the Quantity Theory of Money. Others have maintained that actually the experience of Germany and other countries during the great inflation showed that the quantity theory is not logically satisfactory for the interpretation of concrete facts, but rather that it leads to erroneous conclusions.

It has been stated that, contrary to the quantity theory, prices were not the passive element in the exchange equation. Prices rose under the influence of factors outside this equation, i.e. the exchange rate, and the rise of prices provoked the rise in the quantity of the circulating medium.*

According to Professor Mitchell† it is wrong to consider the quantity of money as a given fact controlled by the authority by which it is issued, and to which producers and consumers must adapt themselves. On the contrary, in case of need, if the quantity of money issued is disproportionate to the level of prices, the business system itself creates new money or new systems for the fuller use of the existing money, so that the high level of prices which prevails after a depreciation of the exchange is maintained. Mitchell quotes the example of Treasury bonds, which, according to circumstances, are simply an investment or can be used as a circulating medium.

I do not associate myself with this point of view. Rather, German experiences show us the fundamental importance in the determination of the level of internal prices and of the currency's external value, of the quantity of money issued by the Government. It was only the continual increase in the issues of legal money which made possible the incessant rise in prices and the continual fall in the external value of the mark, as has been demonstrated in the course of this book. The systems invented from time to time for the better use of the money, to which I have alluded in Chapter II, only had a limited effect. The best empirical demonstration of the influence of the financial and

* Nogaro, *La monnaie et les phénomènes monetaires contemporains*, Paris, 1924. De Bordes, *The Austrian Crown*, London, 1924, p. 198.

† *History of the Greenbacks*, Chicago, 1903, p. 308.

banking policy as a fundamental cause of the depreciation of the mark was given by the German Government itself, when it found at last, in November 1923, the necessary energy to proceed with a monetary reform. As soon as the Government issues had been stopped the exchange and prices were stabilized and no external influence on the exchange equation was of effect in provoking a depreciation of the money. Thanks to rigorous control over the quantity it was possible for the German Government to keep stable the value of the rentenmark which had no gold cover.

But in the course of this volume I have recorded much data on the period immediately preceding the monetary reform, which is of interest from a theoretical point of view. In that period the German mark was completely repudiated. It ceased to perform its functions as the monetary unit. Wholesale traders adopted the practice of fixing prices in gold, and producers and merchants took as their basis the pre-war prices, which they increased in accordance with a certain coefficient, in order to allow for the depreciation of gold. A general increase in prices was the outcome of this system. Actually in that period business men themselves attempted to create the money which they needed. The means of payment which they used were based on deposits of foreign money which they held in foreign banks; also large quantities of illegal emergency money (Notgeld) were put into circulation. But even at that time the rise in the issues of legal money still exercised a great influence. The need for a circulating medium was especially felt because entrepreneurs had to pay the wages of workers, which they certainly could not do with foreign exchange. If the Reichsbank had resisted the pressure of the industrialists it would have stopped the depreciation of the exchange. As for the illegal money issued by the industrialists for paying wages, the Reichsbank would have been able to avoid the spread of it and to overcome the abuses arising therefrom if it had applied from the first the rigorous measures which it adopted only towards the end of 1923.

Facts observed during the inflation in Germany show that each time the Reichsbank caused a relative scarcity of means of payment, German industrialists and merchants were obliged to sell their foreign exchange in the market, and therefore the mark exchange improved. This happened in February 1923 when the Reichsbank initiated its action for the support of the mark. Also in August 1923 the big rise in prices provoked such a demand for paper marks, that the exchange, after a sharp fall, once more improved somewhat. A considerably higher price than the official rate was willingly paid for paper marks in order that entrepreneurs might have the means to satisfy their own current needs. But the improvement was temporary as the issues of paper money were continued.

After the monetary reform the Reichsbank was twice obliged to defend German money by a drastic contraction of credits; the first occasion was in April 1924 and the second in May 1929 during the crisis of the discussions about reparations. In both these cases it was shown to be possible for a central bank, by restricting credits, to arrest immediately the demand for foreign exchange, to raise the value of the national currency and to revive confidence in it.

In the first edition of this book, before the banking crisis of July 1931, I wrote: "Although without doubt there arose from the dependence on foreign credit a certain weakness in the monetary system, it would be incorrect to conclude that the Reichsbank has lost control over the value of the mark. Indeed, the value of the mark does not depend on the metallic cover but on the quantity of marks in circulation; and the Reichsbank, by limiting issues, could always stop, despite temporary oscillations, a fresh depreciation of the German currency."

Subsequent events have confirmed this observation. It is true that the stability of the mark exchange was obtained by a rigorous control and by a limitation of payments abroad; but, on the other hand, those measures would have been ineffective (as analogous measures had been during the inflation) if at the same time the Reichsbank had increased the issues of notes.

After 1933, the execution of the vast public works plan for relieving unemployment and, later, the great programme for the re-armament of Germany, made it necessary to abandon the policy of deflation which was begun after the banking crisis of 1931. It has become increasingly difficult for the Reichsbank to maintain a stable value of the mark while it favours an expansion of credit.

**2.** It seems that certain critics of the quantity theory have not grasped the fundamental conception on which this theory is based. It is as follows: the limitation of the quantity of money is necessary for the stability of the price structure. The conception is thus expressed by Ricardo: "there is no point more important in issuing paper money than to be fully impressed with the effects which follow from the principle of limitation of quantity."

The significance of this principle is clearly shown by an examination of Walras' equations which describe economic equilibrium. Walras' analysis of the problem of exchange shows that, on the hypothesis of a commodity money—and making $m$ the number of goods exchanged and $n$ the number of individuals who take part in the exchange—the number of the unknowns is as follows: $m-1$ prices, and $n\ m$ the quantities exchanged. There are $m - 1$ and not $m$ prices to be determined because obviously the price of the goods which functions as money is equal to unity. Walras shows that the number of conditions (equations) of the problem is exactly equal to $m - 1 + n\ m$, so that the problem of the exchange is determinate in the case of commodity money.

But when the standard of value is not a commodity but paper money there are not $m - 1$ but $m$ prices to be determined. Therefore the number of the conditions in the problem is less than the number of unknowns. *One equation is missing.* It follows that prices are unstable. Now, if the quantity of money in circulation is limited to a certain figure by a central monetary authority, that gives the condition which was lacking and the problem is determinate once more.

From that it is obvious *that the limitation of the quantity is one of the conditions of economic equilibrium.* This was vaguely felt by those who, taught by experience, stated in Germany that the monetary reform could not be the consequence of economic reconstruction but that, on the contrary, the prerequisite of economic stabilization was the stopping of the inflation. The German example is particularly instructive because it shows that, if the monetary authority—inspired by the erroneous idea that the issues of notes made in response to the demands of commerce are legitimate—does not put some limit to the issues of paper money, prices continue to rise until astronomical figures are reached.*

* It was pleasant to observe, in Professor Graham's book, *Exchange, Prices, and Production in Hyper-inflation: Germany 1920–1923* (Princeton, 1930), the similarities between many conclusions of this economist and those arrived at by the present author in articles published between 1923 and 1929, of which, presumably, Professor Graham was unaware. The chief points on which there is some disagreement between us are: (*a*) I insist more firmly than Graham on the financial and monetary policy of Germany as the fundamental cause of the fall of the internal as well as of the external value of the mark and, in contrast to Graham, I attribute less importance to the payment of reparations; (*b*) contrary to Graham, I do not believe that the depreciation of the mark was, on the whole, advantageous to German economy. If that was so, why was the eventuality of a new depreciation considered almost with terror in German official circles, which from 1931 onwards have made some desperate efforts to keep the mark exchange stable?

**3.** The critics of the quantity theory observe also that even admitting that the quantity of money in circulation depends on the will of the Government, the second monetary factor of the exchange equation, i.e. the velocity of circulation, is not susceptible to control.

The velocity of circulation of money is connected with the habits of consumers or producers in holding available in the form of money a certain part of their income or capital; the larger is this part the less rapid is the circulation of money, and *vice versa*. Normally these habits on which the velocity of the circulation of money depends, change slowly. During the inflation in Germany and in various other countries, the velocity of the circulation sometimes increased suddenly in the panic created among holders of paper money by a sharp fall in the exchange, followed by a big rise in prices. But many experiences also show that if Governments and banks of issue hold fast and refuse to increase the issues of paper money, the crisis of lack of confidence passes, the exchange returns to its former level, and the rise in the velocity of circulation is temporary. Conditions experienced after the monetary stabilization of November 1923 are significant on this subject. The velocity of circulation of money (which was enormous in the last period of the depreciation of the mark, because no one wished to keep in the form of paper marks even a small part of their available resources) fell immediately when the issue of paper marks by the Government was suspended and when the public realized that it was the firm intention of the Government not to increase, for any reason whatever, the issues of rentenmarks beyond the limit fixed by law.

The following is another case worth mentioning. After the banking crisis of July 1931 many Germans were seized by panic and feared a depreciation of the mark, the convertibility of which into gold had been suspended owing to the serious diminution of the gold reserves of the Reichsbank. Deposits in savings banks fell and a wave of hasty purchasing of goods occurred, i.e. the velocity of the circulation of money rose. But the phenomenon was purely temporary, the public soon being convinced that the Government had firmly decided to oppose monetary inflation and to maintain stable the mark exchange.

Confidence is certainly an important element which must be taken into account in a study of the variations of the value of money. Many times I have pointed out in this volume psychological causes of the fall of the mark. Recent monetary history includes several cases in which confidence in a currency was re-established by energetic declarations or measures of a Government and the process of depreciation was stopped at once. One must observe, however, that confidence based on such declarations and acting as a powerful support to the value of the currency, even diverting speculation from direct operations against it, is maintained and strengthened only if the public knows that the issues of money are strictly limited; if they are continued the wave of confidence is quickly broken. At the beginning of the inflation, when the public still did not understand the phenomenon of monetary depreciation and attributed the rise in prices to other causes, confidence in the depreciated money was maintained for a time in spite of the rise in the issues; but in a later phase each new issue weakened confidence more and more.

**4.** That the stabilization of the value of the mark, thanks to the limitation of the quantity, must be considered not as the *end* but as the *starting-point* of the process of economic reconstruction is clearly confirmed by economic events after 1923. The years following 1923 were characterized by a considerable increase in total economic production, which was higher than during the inflation period, despite the apparent feverish activity of that time.

The German experiences throw much light on the effects of the inflation on economic production. The argument which many economists use against the inflation, according to which inflation does not stimulate the production of new resources, but only causes a redistribution of existing resources, no longer seems tenable in the light of recent experiences. If we consider the problem from a dynamic point of view, it appears that inflation, by imposing a restriction on consumption on many classes of society, allows a part of the productive energies of the country to be employed in the manufacture of new instruments of production. But at the same time, as the example of Germany shows, so profound a disequilibrium is created in the economic organism that on the whole, except in particular cases, the national economy gains little from the creation of this new capital. A large part of the new fixed capital was, later, revealed as useless, as was the case in the iron and steel and engineering industries. During the inflation the quantity rather than the quality of the instruments of production was raised.

Those large concerns, such as the great chemical industries, the electrical firms, and the potash industry, which followed a policy of adjustment and concentration during the depreciation probably profited in a lasting manner from the inflation. But these great businesses are not the whole of the German economy!

The inflation retarded the crisis for some time, but this broke out later, throwing millions out of employment. At first inflation stimulated production because of the divergence between the internal and external values of the mark, but later it exercised an increasingly disadvantageous influence, disorganizing and limiting production. It annihilated thrift; it made reform of the national budget impossible for years; it obstructed the solution of the Reparations question; it destroyed incalculable moral and intellectual values. It provoked a serious revolution in social classes, a few people accumulating wealth and forming a class of usurpers of national property, whilst millions of individuals were thrown into poverty. It was a distressing preoccupation and constant torment of innumerable families; it poisoned the German people by spreading among all classes the spirit of speculation and by diverting them from proper and regular work, and it was the cause of incessant political and moral disturbance. It is indeed easy enough to understand why the record of the sad years 1919–23 always weighs like a nightmare on the German people.

APPENDIX

# German Economic Conditions from the end of the Inflation until 1931

## I. THE DIFFERENT PHASES OF THE STABILIZATION CRISIS

**1.** The principal aspects of the stabilization crisis which accompanied the monetary reform were studied in Chapter x.

In this crisis four phases can be distinguished (it will be appreciated that distinctions of this kind are always somewhat arbitrary):

(1) The first phase includes the months from November 1923 to April 1924. In contrast to what happened in other countries where the currency had depreciated less than in Germany, the *immediate* effect of the monetary stabilization was not an economic crisis. On the contrary, there was a remarkable improvement over the economic conditions of the last phase of the inflation, which had disorganized the entire economic system.

The reports of German chambers of commerce, the trade papers, and the reports of private companies agree in stating that after the introduction of the rentenmark and the stabilization of the exchange, the circulation and economic production slowly revived. Typical of this were the conditions in the textile industry, in which, in the last phase of the depreciation of the mark, sales and production had almost completely stopped. After the introduction of the rentenmark the industry awoke from its torpor. The first symptoms of a new activity appeared in the retail trade; later, confidence in a continual improvement of market conditions caused the textile and clothing industries to receive a large number of orders from wholesale merchants.*

The increase in economic production is apparent in the decline in unemployment. The number of workers working short-time, which was 1·8 millions in November 1923, fell to 251,500 on February 15th, 1924, and to 90,133 on March 15th, 1924. The number of workers completely unemployed and in receipt of unemployment benefit was 1,307,034 on February 15th, 1924, and 988,752 on March 15th, 1924.

(2) At the end of 1923 and in the first months of 1924 the issue of the new rentenmarks and the credits somewhat generously granted by the Reichsbank relieved the scarcity of circulating capital. But in April 1924 the Reichsbank abruptly ceased the expansion of credit which was threatening the stability of the currency. Following this change of policy the stabilization crisis began to develop; the rate of interest rose, unemployment increased again, stock market prices, the volume of production, new company promotions, and imports of

* Similarly in Poland, in the period immediately following the stabilization of the exchange, the textile industry experienced a sudden prosperity, thanks to the fact that numerous classes of society, who during the rapid depreciation of the currency had for a long time been obliged to forgo some purchases, now began to purchase clothing. Later, however, the effects of the stabilization crisis became obvious.

raw materials all declined; and the number of bankruptcies and of firms subjected to creditors' control rose very considerably. But as a result of the contraction of credit, prices fell and exports were stimulated, so that the balance of trade was once again favourable in July and August 1924.

(3) After the London Agreement on the Dawes Plan, foreign credits began to flow to Germany. The influences exercised by them were very complex. Without doubt they relieved the crisis, as was shown by the fall in unemployment, the relatively small number of bankruptcies, the fall in interest rates, etc.; but at the same time, they prolonged the condition of *malaise* of German business, quite apart from the fact that frequently the employment of foreign credits was anything but rational. In the last months of 1924 and in the first months of 1925 there was a brief period of respite in German economic conditions. The index number of production rose from 82 (third quarter of 1924) to 102 (first quarter of 1925) (1913 = 100).

(4) But in the summer of 1925 the respite ended and there began, at last, the crisis of the adjustment of German economic conditions. It was loudly heralded by the collapse of some of the great industrial and financial groups which had sprung up during the inflation. From the third quarter of 1925 until the end of the second quarter of 1927 there were 31,183 bankruptcies; and the voluntary liquidation of firms exceeded the establishment of new ones by 19,586. The crisis upset many old-established firms; but for the most part the bankruptcies and voluntary liquidations concerned businesses which had been established during the inflation. At the same time unemployment spread rapidly: the number of workers unemployed, which in June 1925 was 195,099, rose to more than a million on December 15th in the same year. It is estimated that in March 1926, when unemployment was at its maximum, there were altogether about three million people out of work.

Rightly, the Deutsche Bank wrote in its *Report* for 1926: "This crisis is not due to a change of circumstances, but is essentially a phase of the process of deflation which German economic conditions is undergoing after the monetary stabilization."

Thus the stabilization crisis passed through alternate stages and lasted a long time. That is clear also from the fact that there was not in reality a rapid deflation. At first the Central Bank hesitated; later it granted discounts, although in limited quantities, at a much lower rate than the market rate; and eventually the Government intervened many times, directly or indirectly, to support tottering industries.

### II. THE ECONOMIC REVIVAL OF 1926 AND ITS CAUSES

**2.** The summer of 1925 was a period of great monetary tension (see Diagram XXVII). The resources of the great banks were for the most part employed in supporting certain big industrial groups, or in seeing that their liquidation (as in the case of Stinnes) occurred without being too serious a jolt for the economic condition of the country. The great banks also, fearing for their liquidity, proceeded to a rigorous restriction of credits, which immediately exercised a serious influence on industry. The first to be hit were the production goods industries, which dismissed part of their workers. At the beginning of 1926 the credit crisis of 1925 apparently developed into a crisis of overproduction and, following the American example, there were many suggestions for the financing of consumers.

In the meantime the monetary tension relaxed. At the beginning of 1926, owing to the coincidence of several circumstances, there was a plentiful supply of funds in the money market. The liquidation of stocks and the progressive reorganization of business freed a large amount of money capital. Owing to the economic depression part of the working capital of firms went into the banks. In consequence of a financial policy which was often criticized, enormous

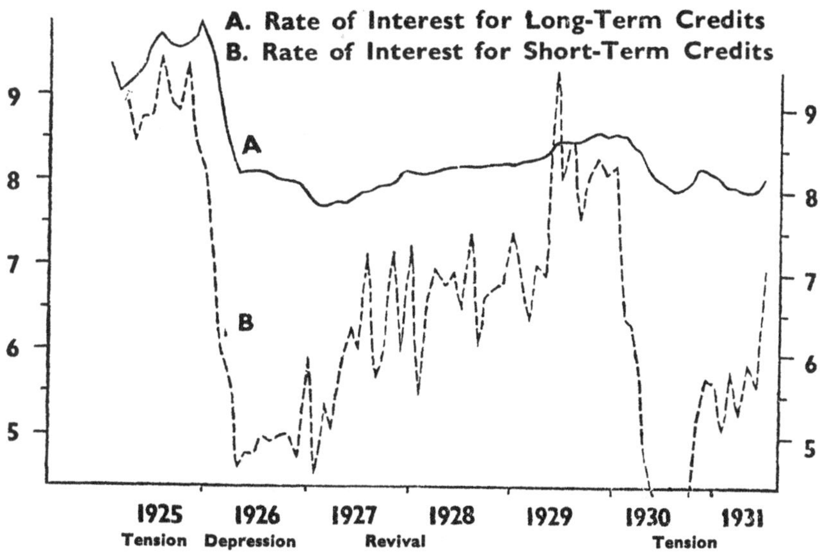


DIAGRAM XXVII

sums of "public money" accumulated and sought temporary employment in the money market. Also money accruing from foreign loans, whilst awaiting permanent use, was temporarily invested in short-term loans.

The amount of money seeking employment in short-term loans was then so great that considerable sums were temporarily invested abroad, especially in the London money market.

The changed conditions of the money market made it possible for the Reichsbank to terminate finally, at the beginning of 1926, the regulations about the limitation of credits, and to reduce the discount rate, in accordance with the open market rates. The discount rate (which had been 9 per cent at the end of 1925) was reduced to 8 per cent on January 12th, to 7 per cent on March 7th, to 6·5 per cent on June 7th, and to 6 per cent on July 6th. The advances rate was reduced from 11 per cent to 7 per cent during the same period. But even so, the official discount rate generally remained, during the whole year 1926, above the open market rates.

The movement of certain interest rates is shown in the following table:

| | *Day-to-day money* | *Rate for commercial bills* | *Actual yield on mortgage bonds* | |
|---|---|---|---|---|
| | | | *5 per cent* | *8 per cent* |
| October 1925 .. | 9·41 | 8·89 | 8·02 | 9·64 |
| November 1925 | 8·49 | 8·66 | 8·21 | 9·71 |
| December 1925 .. | 8·20 | 8·61 | 8·15 | 9·90 |
| January 1926 .. | 7·13 | 7·68 | 7·53 | 9·52 |
| February 1926 .. | 6·04 | 7·03 | 6·98 | 8·88 |
| March 1926 .. | 5·70 | 6·46 | 6·56 | 8·47 |
| April 1926 .. | 5·64 | 5·80 | 6·08 | 8·13 |

In accordance with the changed conditions of the money market the commercial banks also lessened the rates for loans on current account* and relaxed the almost prohibitive conditions for the cover of loans which had been fixed during the summer of 1925.

The abundance of money which appeared in the money market modified the conditions of the capital market, as also did the operations of the Reichsbank, which, at the beginning of 1926, commenced systematic purchases of mortgage debentures on its own account and for customers.

The facility with which new bonds could be placed in the market induced mortgage banks to lower the rate of interest for mortgage loans. The expenses for a mortgage credit (interest, commission, and other expenses) amounted to about 15 per cent of the nominal capital at the end of 1925, to about 12 per cent in March 1926 and about 10 per cent in the summer of the same year.

One of the first effects of the fall in the rate of interest was the rise in the prices of shares. Independently of any improvement in economic prospects, a rise in share prices occurs in the depression as soon as the rate of interest has fallen low enough to be below the yield of the shares themselves. Now the rise in the price of shares, although simply the expression of a new valuation of capital corresponding to the variation of the rate of interest, probably has considerable psychological effects on entrepreneurs and capitalists, who interpret that rise as a sign of a future improvement in the economic situation.

3. The fall in the rate of interest on long-term loans had more direct effects on business activity—in the first place, on the building industry.

The income from the ownership of houses is little influenced by economic fluctuations. Therefore the building of houses is stimulated in the phases of the depression, when it is possible to obtain mortgage loans at a favourable rate of interest, and, on the other hand, it is discouraged in an advanced phase of economic expansion, when interest rates have risen appreciably.

According to German statistics, the correlation between the variations of the rate of interest and the building of houses was very close before the war. After the inflation it was disturbed by numerous interventions of the Government, but it continued to exist in part. Indeed, the curve of house-building

* It was calculated that during 1926 the cost of credit had fallen by 4½ per cent of the capital loaned (*Dresdner Bank, Geschäftsbericht für 1926*, Berlin, 1927).

permits, which was depressed towards the end of 1925, already showed a recovery at the beginning of 1926, i.e. at a time of general economic depression.

A symptom of the renewed activity in the building trade was the sharp rise in the shares of the chief industrial construction firms, of companies for building houses, for the production of cement, and of companies owning building land. If the prices of shares of the principal companies on January 2nd, 1926, were put equal to 100, the index would be seen to have risen to 175 on June 29th and to 239 on August 20th of the same year.*

The variations in the activity of so important a trade as building (according to the census of 1925 it employed 1,433,734 workers in Germany) exercised a series of repercussions on other industries, among them being the iron and steel industry. But on that industry and generally on industries producing instrumental goods the fall in the rate of interest for long-term loans had, in 1926, even more direct and important effects. It helped to increase the advantage of a series of technical innovations and it facilitated, or often rendered possible, their execution.†

One must also add the influence of the progressive liquidation of stocks of goods. In September 1926 the commercial papers showed that by then the process of absorption of stocks was completed as far as the principal industrial commodities were concerned, particularly in the textile industry which had been seriously hit by the collapse of markets. It was observed that now, therefore, there existed the necessary premises for an economic recovery. Actually, foreseeing the exhaustion of their stocks, merchants began to renew orders to industrialists.

Finally, among the factors which in 1926 gave an impulse to a new phase of expansion must be included the influence of the 1925 harvest. As the bad harvest of 1924 had probably contributed to the monetary tension of 1925 by stimulating imports, so the abundant harvest of 1925 favoured economic recovery by influencing in a favourable manner the balance of trade. The total harvest of cereals rose from 8·3 million tons (1924) to 11·4 millions; and therefore imports dropped considerably.

### III. THE INFLUENCE OF THE ENGLISH COAL STRIKE OF 1926

**4.** The English strike (May–November 1926) also had an important influence on certain basic German industries. The immediate consequence of the strike was the disappearance of English coal from German coastal regions where British exporters had been selling about 300,000 tons a month. Also German exports received a strong impetus. It was largely due to the English strike that exports of German fuels in May–November 1926 increased by 225 million marks as compared with the same period of the preceding year.‡ Stocks of coal diminished rapidly and, later, production was also stimulated. The financial

* See *Frankfurter Zeitung*, No. 621, of August 21st, 1926. While the variations of the rate of interest quickly influenced that part of the building trade which was concerned with building houses, the construction of industrial buildings was subject to the influence of expectations of future profits besides that of the rate of interest.

† Reichs-Kredit-Gesellschaft, *Bericht des Vorstandes über das Geschäftsjahr, 1926*, Berlin, 1927.

‡ *Report of the Agent-General for Reparation Payments* June 10th, 1927, p. 92.

situation of coal companies, no longer oppressed by useless immobilization of floating capital, improved considerably.

The coal strike caused a great contraction in the production of English iron and steel firms. The drop amounted, according to German industrialists, to 3·5 million tons of pig-iron and to 4·5 million tons of steel. The increased demand for the products of continental iron and steel firms provoked several months' work for the German industry.*

As the Diskonto-Gesellschaft wrote in its *Report* for 1926: "The improvement in the situation of the two basic industries (coal and iron) was gradually transmitted to the other industries with which business connected them. Those two industries opened the way for a general expansion, which towards the end of 1926 began to extend to an even greater part of German business." Dismissals were suspended in the coal and iron industries and new workers were taken on; the rate of wages was increased, although only a little, and the increased purchasing power of the working classes gave a stimulus to industries producing direct consumption goods. Workers in the Ruhr, Upper Silesia, and the lignite mining districts were able to increase their consumption of bread, margarine, beer, and tobacco and finally to make purchases of domestic utensils and various other commodities.

To these effects were added other psychological influences of much more importance. The economic improvement caused by the English coal strike helped very much to create an atmosphere of confidence and optimism in industrial circles.

### IV. THE TRANSFORMATION OF THE PRODUCTIVE EQUIPMENT OF GERMAN INDUSTRY

**5.** However, the English strike was neither the sole nor the principal cause of the economic expansion. As we have seen, symptoms of recovery were visible even before the strike occurred.

In the past vast applications of new technique, which caused a considerable production of fixed capital, often gave the impulse for a phase of expansion. The economic history of the nineteenth century offers many examples of this; as, for instance, railway construction, the transformation of the iron and steel industry after the application of the Thomas process, and the exploitation of electricity towards the end of the nineteenth century and at the beginning of the twentieth.

In the case of Germany, the expansion which began in 1926 was not caused by great new technical discoveries. There arose, however, new industries, and certain branches of existing industries were developed owing to technical progress (e.g. the chemical and electrical industries, and those producing artificial silk, radios, cinematographic apparatus, nitrogen, automobiles, cosmetics, and sports goods).† But more important, in its effects on economic expansion, was the vast process of rational transformation of Germany's

* Statements of Dr. Reichert before the "Verein deutschen Eisen und Stahl-Industriellen" (December 1926).

† See the volume *Erzeugungs- und Absatzbedingungen der deutschen Wirtschaft* (published by the Committee of Inquiry into the economic situation of Germany), p. 145.

productive equipment, which commenced in 1926; its influence was the same as that exercised in other cases by important inventions.

Also the new expansion phase in German business was characterized by large investment in fixed capital, as was shown in the consumption of steel.* It is difficult to understand, at first sight, why, in reorganizing production, German industry had to proceed to new investment in fixed capital. Does it not appear, from the facts detailed in this volume, that industrial plant was excessively developed during the war and the inflation years? Even the Dawes Committee had stated, in its celebrated report,† that Germany possessed an impressive productive equipment.

The contradiction is only apparent. During the inflation many industries had enlarged, but had not perfected, their machinery, so that after the inflation German business found itself possessing vast industrial plant which was defective, and whose productivity was low compared with the equipment of other great industrial countries, especially America. The Krupp Company, after having referred, in its *Report* for 1928, to the new buildings completed by it, wrote: "It is not a question of an *extension* of our plant but of an intensification of production." It was precisely this "intensification" which characterized the new phase of expansion into which Germany entered towards the end of 1926, in contrast to that which had occurred in the years of the inflation. Technical progress was considerable, particularly in the coal, iron and steel, electrical and chemical industries, and also in the motor trade. In the industries producing direct consumption goods progress was generally slower, because, among other things, of the great number of firms and of the variety of goods demanded by consumers.

**6.** The facts which have been mentioned cannot be dissociated from psychological elements. As the "Danatbank" aptly remarked in its *Report* for 1926, "the recent great industrial transformations could only have taken place in an atmosphere of optimism, from which industrialists gained confidence that the new great investments would increase the productivity of firms." In 1926, according to the same bank, "confidence in a progressive development of German business is spreading in industrial circles."

**7.** It is necessary to notice that, beside the industrial demand for instrumental goods, there was a large demand for *public works*. The variations of this second demand, after the monetary stabilization, certainly constituted one of the predominating factors of the economic situation. According to German statistics, the value of the new plant erected in Germany in the years 1924–28 amounted to 26·8 milliard marks. Now, of this sum only 7·7 milliards was attributable to agriculture, industry, and commerce. The value of the new

* Consumption of steel according to Reichs-Kredit-Gesellschaft (in thousands of tons):

| | 1926 | 1927 |
|---|---|---|
| January .. .. | 676·8 | 1,236·0 |
| June .. .. .. | 840·9 | 1,513·6 |
| November .. .. | 1,168·0 | 1,651·4 |

† *Documents relatifs à l'application du plan des experts*, p. 34 (Paris, Alcan, 1926).

permanent investments made directly by public authorities amounted to 5·7 milliards marks; 5·4 milliards—provided mainly by taxes on rents, and distributed under the control of the public authorities—were invested in dwelling-houses; the new plant of firms supplying gas, water, and electricity, which are usually under the control of local authorities, absorbed 2·6 milliards; and the improvement of means of communication (especially railways) required 4·4 milliards.*

**8.** An interesting particular which is revealed in German statistics and which occurred in the first phase of the expansion period which began towards the end of 1926, together with the creation of new plant, was an accumulation of stocks of consumption goods. But, later, the increase in the stocks of goods of this category slowed down, and new investments predominantly took the form of new fixed plant, while at the same time the increase in the stocks of raw materials for instrumental goods industries continued. In fact, in 1927, stocks of food, clothing, and other consumption goods increased by 3,256 million marks; while in a later phase of the expansion, i.e. in 1928, the rise was only 1,859 millions. The value of new plant in those two years was, respectively, 7,168 and 7,263 million marks, and the existing stocks of the instrumental goods industries increased, respectively, by 609 millions and 627 millions. On the whole, in the years 1924–28 the value of new real capital created amounted to 39·3 milliard marks (excluding the gold reserve of the Reichsbank), distributed thus: new plant, 26·8 milliards, and increase of stocks, 12·5 milliards.†

## V. THE EXPANSION OF BANK CREDIT AND OF THE MONETARY CIRCULATION

**9.** The economic expansion was accompanied by the creation of new purchasing power by the banks, as the following summary shows:

*Assets of Six Large Banks (millions of marks)*

| *End of* | *Bills* | *Advances on goods* | *Loans and advances on securities* | *Current account loans* |
|---|---|---|---|---|
| October 1926 .. .. | 1,413 | 388 | 718 | 2,771 |
| February 1927 .. .. | 1,427 | 514 | 857 | 3,193 |
| October 1927 .. .. | 1,509 | 619 | 530 | 3,892 |
| February 1928 .. .. | 2,022 | 815 | 536 | 4,084 |

In the period covered by this summary the increase in current account loans and of advances on goods was especially noticeable. Security Loans fell for reasons which I shall discuss below. After a set-back in May and June 1927, caused by a restriction of loans to the Stock Exchange,‡ the expansion of credit continued in the following months.

* See *Kapitalbildung und Investitionen in der deutschen Volkswirtschaft*, Berlin, 1931 (publication of the Institut für Konjunkturforschung).

† Data drawn from *Kapitalbildung, etc.*

‡ See *Report of the Agent-General, etc.*, p. 114, December 10th, 1927, where will be found many other notes about the expansion of credit in 1927.

Short-term credit of the Reichsbank (bills of exchange and advances on securities), which amounted to little more than a milliard marks in August 1926, reached 2,900 million marks in September 1927. Later they declined somewhat, in consequence of the rise in the discount rate (from 6 to 7 per cent) and in the rate for advances (from 7 to 8 per cent). Between the end of August 1926 and the end of September 1927 the circulation of Reichsbank notes rose from 3,225 and 4,182 million marks.*

The expansion of bank credit during the revival was made possible by a complex of conditions which had been developing during the preceding phase of economic depression. These conditions may be summarized thus:

(*a*) *An increase in the gold or gold exchange reserves of the Reichsbank.*

| *End of* | *Gold and foreign exchange (millions of marks)* | NOTE CIRCULATION (*millions of marks*) *Reichs-marks* | *Renten-marks* | *Total note circulation* | *Ratio of reserve to total circulation* |
|---|---|---|---|---|---|
| January 1926 .. | 1,673 | 2,649 | 1,450 | 4,099 | 40·8 |
| March 1926 .. | 1,972 | 3,160 | 1,108 | 4,268 | 46·2 |
| July 1926 .. | 1,987 | 3,106 | 1,363 | 4,469 | 44·4 |
| September 1926 | 2,120 | 3,251 | 1,369 | 4,620 | 45·9 |
| December 1926 | 2,350 | 3,735 | 1,164 | 4,899 | 48·0 |

The ratio of reserve to circulation (including the Rentenbank notes) increased during 1926 from 40·8 to 48 per cent.† According to a statement by the President of the Reichsbank, the increase in the circulation during 1926 was due mainly to the influx of foreign exchange, provided by the foreign loans, which were exchanged for notes at the Reichsbank. It was this continual rise in the circulation, which had no connection with a corresponding increase in German production but simply with the transfer of foreign loans, which aroused the attention of the Reichsbank and induced it to put obstacles in the way of foreign borrowing. We shall consider the question of foreign loans later. For the present I shall emphasize this point: in the summer of 1926, at a time when production on the whole was still lower than that of the summer of 1925, there was a considerably larger quantity of circulating medium than had existed a year earlier. The effects of this increase of circulation in stimulating business and propelling German economy into a phase of expansion were bound to be felt before long.

Moreover, in spite of the increase which occurred in 1926, the circulation was susceptible to further expansion without any danger to the stability of the mark, as the high percentage of notes covered showed. In the first half of 1926 the Reichsbank, with the object of partly neutralizing the influence of foreign loans, had considerably reduced its own short-term loans, by maintaining the official discount rate at a higher level than the market rate.

* For further particulars see the *Report of the Commissioner of the Reichsbank*, Berlin, December 7th, 1927.

† In addition to foreign exchange earmarked as cover for notes, the Reichsbank held other foreign exchange, the amount of which was not shown in the weekly returns.

(*b*) *The increasing liquidity of the assets of the ordinary banks.*

German financial papers used to calculate a "coefficient of elasticity" of the credit banks, which is the ratio between *liquid* assets (i.e. cash, balances with other banks—including foreign banks—commercial bills, securities quoted on the Bourse, and loans and advances on securities) and the sight liabilities (deposits, current account balances, and acceptances). The coefficient of elasticity varies in the following manner for the six great banks.

| *End of* | | *End of* | |
|---|---|---|---|
| December 1924 .. | 63 | February 1926 .. | 56 |
| February 1925 .. | 54 | April 1926 .. .. | 56 |
| April 1925 .. .. | 55 | June 1926 .. .. | 59 |
| June 1925 .. .. | 54 | August 1926 .. | 58 |
| August 1925 .. | 50 | October 1926 .. | 59 |
| October 1925 .. | 53 | December 1926 .. | 61 |

It can be seen from the preceding summary that the coefficient of elasticity, which dropped considerably during the monetary tension of 1925, increased from 50 to 61 from August 1925 to December 1926.

During 1926 "current account debits" had increased relatively little. But deposits increased. According to the calculations of the Institut für Konjunkturforschung* deposits at various credit institutions (ordinary credit banks, savings banks, public banks, etc.) increased by 1·3 million marks from the end of 1925 to the beginning of September 1926.

Although saving was continued even during the depression, it is not probable, according to the above-mentioned Institute, that the expansion of deposits during 1926 was entirely due to new saving by the German people. In part the money deposited represented disinvested working capital. It is, besides, very likely that part of the new deposits was created by the influx of foreign exchange, Generally in 1926 foreign loans were not quickly used in the purchase of foreign goods. In fact in that year, in spite of foreign loans, the balance of trade remained favourable. According to the financial Press, part of the loans available internally were probably kept for some time in the form of money, and were not immediately invested in production. In part the new long-term loans simply replaced short-term bank loans which had been contracted in the preceding phase of expansion. Besides, according to the financial Press, local authorities and firms of a public character hastened to take up long-term loans, taking advantage of the favourable situation of the money market before the projects to be financed by the loans were completed. Money, temporarily uninvested, was often left on deposit at the banks. The statistics of the Institut für Konjunkturforschung show the existence of a great disequilibrium between saving and investments in 1926. New savings (deposits at the savings banks and ordinary banks, assurance company reserves and the reserves of the social insurance societies, receipts from the tax on house-rents) amounted to 10·7 milliards of marks, whilst new investments, including stocks, amounted to only 3·3 milliards.

* *Vierteljahrshefte, etc.*, fasc. 3, 1926.

*(c) The increasing liquidity of commercial enterprises*

In 1925 the increasing accumulation of stocks held by speculators, big merchants, and producers had created a dam in the economic circulation, and helped to provoke a shortage of capital and a rise in the rate of interest; while during the depression of 1926, the progressive liquidation of stocks, some sold in the home market and some exported, increased the liquidity of commercial enterprises, lessened the demand for capital, and contributed to the fall of the interest rate and the improvement of the balance of trade.

Financial papers of 1926 show a continual improvement in the financial situation of businesses and considerable progress in the economic reorganization of commercial enterprises.

Hence, it appears from the preceding analysis that during the depression of 1926 changes both on the side of the supply of credit and on that of the demand, combined to create a series of conditions which made possible the expansion of credit in a successive phase of economic recovery. These conditions may be summed up in a single expression: the general increasing liquidity of the central bank, of big commercial banks, and of most industrial concerns. Towards the end of 1926, on the one hand, the banks were in a position to increase the supply of loans, while on the other private firms could extend their debts to banks by offering them acceptable security.

VI. "FORCED SAVING" DURING THE EXPANSION

**10.** The situation of the money market, described in the preceding paragraph, was one of the pre-requisites of economic recovery. But the development of industry is subject to the existence of an adequate supply of "capital," not in the financial sense, but of material means for production (including the subsistence of the working classes). According to Professor Spiethoff "every initiation and every extension of capitalistic production pre-supposes the existence of available material goods or of unemployed workers . . . which *expansion cannot create but must find.*"*

Now, the facts referred to above prove that, even in the recent case of Germany, the idea that expansion is fed by stocks of economic goods which have accumulated during the depreciation is unfounded. It is certain that in a great country like Germany, with highly developed industry, with intensive agricultural production and with a considerable volume of trade with other countries, there always exists some very important stocks of raw materials, agricultural products, and semi-finished or finished articles. In past years the amount of these stocks has sometimes been estimated at a good 30 milliard marks. But statistics do not show that these stocks assumed exceptional dimensions before the expansion phase; but rather the contrary. In fact, according to the statistics of the Institut für Konjunkturforschung, there was a *minimum* of stocks just at the beginning of the expansion period (end of 1926), and then stocks increased during the expansion itself. During the depression not only stocks of indirect goods (coal, iron, etc.), but also stocks of industrial articles ready for consumption, declined.

Nor does it appear that in 1926 there was a surplus of machinery fit for

* Art. "Krisen" in the *Handwörterbuch der Staatswissenschaften*, last edition, p. 74.

production, since the expansion received one of its principal impulses precisely from the need to construct new machinery.

Thus at the time of the economic recovery there was not an accumulation of "idle" material wealth. Instead, there was a great abundance of available forces of labour. In January 1927 the number of unemployed receiving benefit still amounted to about two millions.* Without doubt this was, if not a necessary condition for expansion, at least a circumstance which much facilitated recovery. During 1927 a large number of the unemployed were re-engaged in production, which increased very considerably.

But whence came the sustenance for the workers newly taken into service?

According to a theory which has recently had some support, in the first phase of the expansion the rise in prices, which is the consequence of the expansion of bank credits and of the circulation, provokes a reduction in the consumption of those classes whose money incomes increase less than prices increase, or are totally insensitive to the rise in prices (wages, salaries of many classes of the employed, interest, rents, etc.). Hence in order to make an expansion possible it is not necessary to accumulate at first a subsistence fund for the new workers. This fund, or, better, this flow, is created during the expansion itself, thanks to the "forced" saving of many other individuals.

It is difficult to say if recent German statistics confirm this theory; but they do not seem to be incompatible with it. During the economic recovery of 1926 the nominal rate of wages remained almost stable; the volume of employment increased considerably; and the rate of real wages diminished.† Hence it seems that actually in that first phase of the economic recovery there was indeed "forced" saving on the part of the working classes. But since (as other calculations show‡) the real income of the working classes increased slightly during 1926 owing to the fall in unemployment, we must conclude that in the case considered here the expression "forced saving" must not be understood as a fall in consumption, but in the sense that labourers worked more, receiving the same real wage as formerly or a real total wage not increased in proportion to their efforts.

It is possible that in former economic cycles forced saving played an important part.§ But in the case I am considering I have the impression that its influence in making economic recovery possible, even if present, was superseded by that of another much more relevant factor, i.e. the great influx of foreign capital. This was the principal characteristic of the economic cycle now being studied.||

* On unemployment towards the end of 1926, see the *Report of the Agent-General for Reparation Payments*, Berlin, June 10th, 1927.

† According to the *Report of the Agent-General, etc.*, Berlin, December 10th, p. 165, the index of real wages (1925 = 100) fell from 109 (March 1926) to 104 (February 1927).

‡ See Chapter x of the present volume.

§ According to Aftalion (*Les Crises périodiques de sur production*, ii, p. 376, 1913), "la prosperité est une période de privation où on se résigne à satisfaction imparfaite des besoins présents en vue d'accroître la richesse des années à venir."

|| Estimates for the amount of foreign capital which entered Germany from 1924 to 1929 vary, mainly because of the difficulties of estimating the amount of short-term loans. At the end of 1929 long-term loans amounted to more than 6 milliard marks; those at short notice were estimated at 8 milliard marks; other long-term investments

**11.** Germany is an interesting example of a debtor country which did not import foreign capital in the form of instruments of production, as generally happened with debtor countries before the war. And this is natural, because Germany is herself a great producer of steel, machines, and other "instruments." Foreign capital was chiefly imported in the form of foodstuffs and raw materials, used in the manufacture of direct consumption goods.* Part of the foreign credits were used for the direct purchase of foreign raw materials or semi-finished goods. The part not spent in this way was substantially used as wages, directly or indirectly (i.e. through the purchase of raw materials or other German intermediate products). The increase in the purchasing power of the working classes stimulated the imports of foodstuffs and foreign finished goods, or of foreign raw materials necessary for the manufacture of articles demanded in bigger quantities at home. A typical example was the textile industry. In the course of 1927 the rise in the demand for clothes, which was due to the rise in wages, provoked an increase in prices and gave a great impetus to the import of raw cotton; but imports of yarn and finished goods also increased considerably. The favourable "conjuncture" of the German textile industry even stimulated the industries of neighbouring countries, especially Czechoslovakia and France.

Briefly, the economic effects of foreign loans can be summarized in the following way. As we have seen, the labour of a part of the German workers was employed in the transformation of the productive apparatus of German industry. Now, the German people could not have saved enough to support this extraordinary need of capital in addition to the ordinary needs of industry. Foreign loans, forming a part of the flow of subsistence for the working classes, permitted the intensification of the production of machinery.

Thanks to foreign loans Germany was able to reconstruct her own equipment. Naturally, in order that the foreign loans should be definitely useful, it was necessary that the new plant should be really productive and not a mere "immobilization" of capital. Now, it must be recognized that the facility for contracting foreign loans, by paralysing the action of the check which prevents a disequilibrium between the production of direct consumption goods and of instrumental goods—i.e. the increase in the rate of interest—can tend to cause an overproduction of instrumental goods. And how this occurred in Germany we shall now see.

## VII. ECONOMIC ACTIVITY DURING 1927–28

**12.** The years 1927 and 1928 were characterized by great economic activity. All the principal indices—production, popular consumption, wages, volume of

made by foreigners in Germany (purchases of shares and debentures, mortgages, private loans, etc.) reached about two to three milliards. The effects of foreign loans on Germany have been analysed by the present author in the paper *Inductive Verification of the Theory of International Payments* (Publications of the Faculty of Law of the Egyptian University, No. 1).

* Trade statistics show that in 1927 imports of foodstuffs and finished products, compared with 1926, increased sharply, which was in consonance with the movement in foreign credits.

internal trade, Government receipts, and foreign trade—provide evidence concordant with the imposing development of German economy during that period. It appears from the statistics, besides, that very probably in no other important country was economic progress so rapid in those years as in Germany. Some measure of this progress is to be found in the growth of the national income, which jumped, according to official estimates, from 54 milliards of marks in 1925 to 62 milliards in 1927 and to about 70 milliards in 1928. The real income of the workers was in 1928 about 19 per cent higher than in 1925. The index of total production rose from 76·6 in 1925 to 100 in 1928. Economic expansion did not mean solely intense production of instrumental goods, for the consumption goods industries were also developed considerably. The consumption of meat, beer, sugar, coffee, and textile products increased markedly.

**13.** On January 12th, 1927, the Reichsbank decided to reduce the rate of discount from 6 to 5 per cent. This cheap money policy was much criticized, since, it was argued, it contributed to an unhealthy development of business. One of the reasons for adopting this policy appears to have been the desire to check the import of foreign capital by reducing the rate of interest in Germany. This reduction of the discount rate was followed by rapid expansion in short-term loans at the Reichsbank and in the note circulation. According to statements by the President of the Reichsbank, the latter, in the course of a few months, put at the disposal of German business credits amounting to $1\frac{1}{2}$–$1\frac{3}{4}$ milliards of marks. This credit expansion helped to cause a great increase in imports, while exports remained almost unchanged, the increase in production being absorbed by the rising home demand. Consequently, the balance of trade became unfavourable, and the Reichsbank in the first months of 1927 lost about a milliard of gold and foreign exchange. As the note circulation had not declined, the ratio of reserve to circulation (including the Rentenbank notes) fell from 49·9 per cent in January to 38·7 per cent in June.

Meanwhile, the market rate of interest, after the great depression of 1926, had again begun to rise (see Diagram XXVII).* As happens in every expansion

| * 1927 | *Day-to-day money* (1) | *Commercial bills* (1) | *Yield of fixed interest securities* (2) | *Mortgage loans* (2) |
|---|---|---|---|---|
| January .. .. .. | 4·33 | 4·66 | 6·79 | 8·45 |
| February .. .. .. | 5·41 | 4·42 | 6·37 | 7·60 |
| March .. .. .. | 5·11 | 4·88 | 6·76 | 7·79 |
| April .. .. .. | 5·84 | 4·88 | 6·83 | 7·92 |
| May .. .. .. | 6·31 | 5·00 | 7·24 | 8·19 |
| June .. .. .. | 6·04 | 5·67 | 7·50 | 8·49 |
| July .. .. .. | 7·16 | 6·00 | 7·51 | 8·77 |
| August .. .. .. | 5·74 | 6·00 | 7·66 | 9·28 |
| September .. .. .. | 6·07 | 6·22 | 7·81 | 9·58 |
| October .. .. .. | 7·32 | 7·08 | 7·99 | 9·68 |
| November .. .. .. | 6·05 | 7·27 | 8·40 | 9·84 |
| December .. .. .. | 7·26 | 7·37 | 8·23 | 9·83 |

(1) According to the Institut für Konjunkturforschung.
(2) According to the Reichskreditkgesellschaft.

phase, the rise in the rate of interest was greater for short-term loans than for long-term loans. Whilst at the beginning of 1927 the rate of interest for commercial bills stood at 4·66 per cent and the yield of fixed interest securities at 6·79 per cent, the difference between these two rates was much less towards the end of the year (7·37 and 8·23 per cent).

To keep in touch with the conditions of the money market the Reichsbank also, during 1927, had to change the official discount rate. It was raised to 6 per cent on June 10th, 1927, and to 7 per cent on October 4th. On this latter date the rate for advances on securities was raised from 7 per cent to 8 per cent.

During 1926 and at the beginning of 1927 the Mortgage Credit Institute had gradually substituted interest rate offered on newly issued bonds from 8 per cent to 9 and 6 per cent, and finally thought that in the near future a 5-per-cent rate would correspond more to the conditions of the capital markets. But during 1927 it had to return to the 8-per-cent bonds. The rate for mortgage loans, which in February hovered about 7·60 per cent, was once more raised to 9·83 per cent in December.

While, on the one hand, the demand for loans increased owing to the industrial expansion, on the other hand, in the first months of 1927, some factors had an unfavourable influence on the quantity of monetary capital available. I refer to the loan of 500 million marks raised by the Reich in February 1927, which absorbed a part of the available capital, and to the obstacles raised by the Reichsbank and by the German Government to the negotiation of foreign loans. From January to March 1927 foreign loans were kept within modest figures. It is true, however, that foreign capital, repulsed from the long-term loan market, flowed to that for short-term loans, where it fed the very active speculation on the rise of industrial securities.

The formation of new German monetary capital which is shown, though imperfectly, by deposits in savings banks and ordinary banks and by the statistics of note issues, slowed down during 1927. Also in the first months of 1927 the bank balance sheets showed a tendency of short-notice deposits to increase relatively to those at long notice; which probably meant that, in the event of future monetary restrictions, business men wished to be able to withdraw the deposited money at any time.

**14.** On May 13th, 1927, the President of the Reichsbank took the draconian step of compelling the commercial banks to reduce by 25 per cent their loans to speculators. This was meant to divert to industry and commerce the monetary capital which, it was said, was being absorbed by speculation on securities. The sudden intervention of the Reichsbank had the opposite effect. It caused confusion in the monetary capital market. It upset the function of the speculator which was to buy, anticipating public saving, new shares with the aid of bank credit and to sell them again later to capitalists. Because of the difficulty of placing new shares with the public, which after the crash of May 13th, 1927, had been seized by panic, many companies had to give up the idea of increasing their capital. Statistics of issues of shares and debentures show, indeed, a heavy drop after May 1927.

The disturbance spread from the share market to that for mortgage bonds. The difficulty of placing new bonds with the public obliged banks to reduce mortgage loans. The building industry quickly felt the repercussions—as may be seen from the fact that the number of building permits, having risen considerably from January to May, fell rapidly after July.

In conclusion, towards the end of the second quarter of 1927 various symptoms showed that in all probability the expansion phase, so recently begun, was already approaching its end. The rise in the rate of interest, the fall in the prices of shares, the rapid increase in the portfolio of the Reichsbank, and the contraction of the gold reserve,* the tightness of credit at ordinary banks, the drop in the issues of shares and debentures, and the change in the composition of deposits—short-notice deposits increasing relatively: these and other factors showed that the situation of the capital market was changed. There was, besides, the danger that slackness in the building trade would exercise a heavy pressure on other branches of industry.

Despite the situation of the home capital market the expansion phase still continued for some time, thanks to foreign capital, which flowed in again after the Reichsbank and the German Government had removed the obstacles previously opposed to it. Foreign loans, which from January to May 1927 scarcely reached 150 million marks, rose to about 1,400 millions from May to December. At the same time also a large quantity of foreign money came in for short-term employment. The big banks showed a large increase in deposits from abroad. The balance sheets of the Deutsche Bank and of the Därmstadter und Nationalbank (the only two banks which published information on this point) showed that foreigners' deposits increased in 1927 from 643 to 1,130 millions, while home deposits only increased from 2,193 to 2,306 millions.

### VIII. THE CHECK TO ECONOMIC EXPANSION

**15.** If it is true that the foreign loans, by satisfying the need for capital, tended to prolong the expansion phase, it is necessary to remember that industrialists took foreign capital on loan because they believed that they could use it profitably. When in an advanced stage of the expansion the prospect of profit deteriorated, it was of little use that foreigners were still ready to put new capital at their disposal: the expansion itself would be checked sooner or later. One must also add that an expansion which is not founded on the solid base of internal saving but on capital borrowed from abroad (especially if the loans are short-term) must necessarily include uncertain and unstable elements. The immobilization of short-term loans, which firms had often employed for permanent investments, could present some difficulties.

The figures in the following table show that the consumption of iron and steel products reached a maximum in Germany in 1927 (monthly average

*

| 1927 | *Reserve of gold and gold exchange* (*millions of marks*) | CIRCULATION *Reichs-marks* (*millions of marks*) | *Renten-marks* | *Total circulation* | *Ratio of Reserve to total circulation* |
|---|---|---|---|---|---|
| End of January .. | 2,256 | 3,410 | 1,108 | 4,518 | 49·9 |
| End of February | 2,037 | 3,465 | 1,114 | 4,579 | 44·5 |
| End of March .. | 2,054 | 3,589 | 1,096 | 4,685 | 43·8 |
| End of April .. | 2,020 | 3,676 | 1,060 | 4,736 | 42·6 |
| End of May .. | 1,894 | 3,719 | 1,033 | 4,752 | 39·8 |
| End of June .. | 1,869 | 3,815 | 1,017 | 4,832 | 38·7 |

1·45 million tons) and fell again in 1928. But total industrial production continued to increase in 1928, and was maintained, on the whole, at a high level even in 1929.

| | 1926 | 1927 | 1928 | 1929 |
|---|---|---|---|---|
| Percentage of workers employed* .. | 77·3 | 90·4 | 90·1 | 86·8 |
| Total production (1928 = 100) .. | 71·5 | 97·2 | 100·0 | 101·3 |
| Goods carried by railways (million tons) | 31·8 | 36·2 | 36·1 | 36·3 |
| Coal†— | | | | |
| (*a*) Production .. (million tons) | 14·7 | 15·6 | 15·7 | 16·9 |
| (*b*) Home consumption (million tons) | 11·0 | 12·8 | 13·1 | 14·0 |
| Steel‡— | | | | |
| (*a*) Production .. (million tons) | 1·17 | 1·55 | 1·39 | 1·54 |
| (*b*) Home consumption (million tons) | 0·91 | 1·45 | 1·24 | 1·29 |
| Wages§ .. .. .. .. .. | 66·6 | 71·5 | 78·5 | 82·9 |
| Co-operative societies' turnover‖ .. | 5·11 | 6·95 | 8·31 | 9·30 |
| Index number of cost of living (1913 = 100) .. .. .. | 141·1 | 147·6 | 151·6 | 153·8 |

Certain characteristic phenomena highly relevant to trade cycle theory are brought out by an examination of the economic situation in 1928 and 1929. Statistics of consumption of foodstuffs and of some industrial products—such as clothing, shoes, furniture, and various domestic utensils—show that consumption on the whole increased considerably even in 1928. Then the consumption of luxuries began to decline, owing to the decline in the profits received by the industrial classes¶ but popular consumption can be said to have begun to diminish appreciably only in 1930, i.e. after the symptoms of depression were already apparent.** Later—in 1931 and 1932—when the crisis entered a new and more developed phase and unemployment was rapidly increasing, consumption contracted sharply.

* Percentage of employed workmen among members of trade unions (the partially employed workers were represented by a theoretical number of fully employed men).

† Lignite has been reduced to terms of coal. Calculations of the Reichskreditgesellschaft. Monthly average.

‡ Calculations of the Reichskreditgesellschaft. Monthly average.

§ Average wage-rate (in pfennig) according to collective agreements for an hour's work by an unskilled workman.

‖ Value, in marks, of weekly purchases made on an average by each member.

¶ *Report of the Agent-General for Reparation Payments*, p. 291, May 21st, 1930.

** Much data on this is to be found in the publication of the Berlin Institut für Konjunkturforschung and in the Reports of the Agent-General for Reparations and of the Reichskreditgesellschaft. Some of the relevant figures are given below:

| | *Retail sales (clothing, furniture and household goods)* | CONSUMPTION (QUANTITIES) *Sugar* | *Meat* | *Beer* | *Tobacco* |
|---|---|---|---|---|---|
| | | (1925–27 = 100) | | | |
| 1925 | 100·0 | 94·6 | 91·3 | 98·8 | 95·8 |
| 1926 | 102·5 | 98·7 | 97·1 | 97·0 | 100·3 |
| 1927 | 113·4 | 106·7 | 111·6 | 104·2 | 103·9 |
| 1928 | 120·2 | 110·9 | 123·5 | 106·6 | 115·5 |
| 1929 | 116·3 | 111·8 | 122·0 | 110·0 | 118·3 |

These facts point to the conclusion that the decline in consumers' purchases of final goods was not the cause of the depression.

**16.** In 1929 the prosperous economic situation of certain important countries, such as the United States and France, had favourable repercussions on German business, checking the depression there. In that year German exports increased considerably. Foreign demand especially stimulated exports of steel goods and of machines and, therefore, for some time, compensated the production goods industries for the contraction in the home demand. The curve of total steel production definitely changed its direction only at the beginning of the second half of 1929.

Since 1930 the German economic depression was closely connected with the world crisis and was seriously affected by it. Until then there had been a certain contrast between the fluctuations of the German economy and the economic conditions of the outside world. The depression of 1926 and the rapid expansion during 1927 constituted, at least in part, phenomena peculiar to Germany.

German economic conditions depreciated rapidly during 1930. Clear indications of this were—the big drop in total production, and particularly that of steel; the rise in unemployment, which reached unheard-of proportions (more than four million unemployed at the end of December); the fall in popular consumption, especially of beer and tobacco; and the enormous reduction of imports, whereby the balance of trade, which in the years of expansion had been unfavourable, became favourable.

## IX. CAUSES OF THE DEPRESSION. TWO THEORIES: "CRISIS OF RETURNS" OR "SHORTAGE OF CAPITAL"?

**17.** What caused the check to expansion in 1928, the slump and the deepening of the depression in the following years?

The German crisis had two aspects. It was a part of the world crisis and, on the other hand, it was the reflex of causes peculiar to Germany. I will study the second aspect only.

By examining the abundant economic literature in Germany on the crisis—reports of banks, of the great joint-stock companies, and of chambers of commerce; articles in reliable financial papers; official and private publications, and by talking with competent persons, the author has seen, underlying all others, two fundamental ideas: Some insist on the causes which checked the initiative of German entrepreneurs (particularly some define the crisis as a "crisis of returns" in industry and agriculture); while others consider the shortage of capital as a fundamental factor. But often the opinions expressed have not been clear and they oscillate between the two ideas. There are a few who consider as the only or at least as the principal cause of the crisis—and not only in Germany but also in the world—the payment of reparations; an opinion which I can only describe as too one-sided.*

According to the Reichskreditgesellschaft (whose periodical reports on economic conditions in Germany are rightly much appreciated), "every

* An important aspect of the German crisis, illustration of which the limits imposed on the present work do not permit, is the agricultural depression.

worsening of the ratio between the cost of new investments and the expected income diminished the volume of investments which entrepreneurs thought it advantageous to make."* In 1929 and 1930 the disposition to make investments or improvements in plant was generally slight. The contraction of investments and stocks induced business men to repay a part of their loans, especially those which had been obtained abroad to finance German imports. Also demands on the home capital market declined, as is shown by the fall in issues of debentures or shares.

The bank quoted above, examining the fluctuations of German economy, therefore attributed an important part to the variations of the *demand for capital* by German industry, which in its turn was determined by changes in the prospects of profit offered by possible new investments.

The second of the two ideas, which was mentioned above, is found, for example, clearly expressed in the announcement made by the Government of the Reich at the beginning of October 1930, in which the alternations of the expansion phase and of the depression is explained by the variations in the *supply of capital*, i.e. a period of great influx of foreign capital was followed by a period of export of capital from Germany, which caused a shortage of money at home and a rise in the rate of interest.

The two theories are not so sharply contrasted as appears at first sight. It can be said that the fluctuations in the influx of capital, by creating uncertainty about the future supply, induced entrepreneurs not to commence the construction of new plant, which they were not sure of being able to finish. It was observed in that period in Germany that the contraction of the flow of capital available for the building industry made entrepreneurs so hesitant that eventually the employment of the scanty capital supplied was difficult and the appearance of an abundance of capital was created, although there was really an appreciable shortage.

**18.** There is no doubt that in 1928 and even more in 1929 the spirit of enterprise among entrepreneurs was weakened. The profits of joint-stock companies, which had increased considerably from 1926 to 1927, were maintained in 1928 at much the same level as 1927, and declined in 1929. Probably, in view of the forecasted fall in future profits, the expansion in the volume of business was already slackening at the beginning of 1928, as certain statistics show. Imports of raw material for industry—which had increased rapidly during 1927—reached their maximum in the first months of 1928. From then onwards imports slowly declined. At the beginning of 1925 this fall had also been an index of an approaching depression. Another typical index was given by the so-called "sensitive prices index."† The index number, which was 109·9 in May 1926, rose in the following months and reached the maximum level (140·9) in January 1928. From that time it fell continually; while the index number of general prices continued to rise during the whole of 1928 and began to move definitely downwards only in 1929. The Institut für Konjunkturforschung has also constructed an index of the orders given to

* *Deutschlands wirtschaftliche Lage an der Jahreswende*, p. 32, 1930–31.

† Prices of the following articles: scrap-iron, pig-iron, steel, and brass; lead, steel plates; skins; wool; hemp and flax.

industry. This shows a rapid increase in 1926 and early in 1927; but after that the steep rise was checked.

The weakening of the spirit of enterprise was not a transitory phenomenon. On the contrary, after 1928 lack of confidence and pessimism were decidedly uppermost. The causes of this phenomenon were of various kinds: economic, political, and psychological.

As we have seen, German business from the end of 1926 until the end of 1928 had experienced extraordinary development. It was impossible for economic progress to continue at so fast a pace. The wave of optimism which had prevailed at the beginning of the expansion phase (and the most obvious symptoms of which had been the very great increase in the prices of shares) passed, and it was succeeded by the spread of calmer and more objective ideas of economic possibilities. A steadier rhythm had to be impressed on economic activity. The development of the programme of rationalization having already made remarkable progress in several important industries—and, moreover, the practical results of the vast industrial transformation in many cases not having been up to expectations—the demand for capital and labour was no longer so intense as formerly.

## X. THE CONNECTION BETWEEN UNEMPLOYMENT AND THE RATIO BETWEEN NOMINAL WAGES AND SALE PRICES

**19.** But these considerations, which can explain how towards the middle of 1928 German economy entered a phase of slower development, do not explain the causes of the deep economic depression in which the expansion phase was swallowed up.

Probably one of the principal causes which acted in an unfavourable way on the prospect of profit and provoked unemployment and a fall in production was the increase in wages. In the first edition of this work I wrote: "There is now announced (March 1928) a denunciation by the trade unions of numerous collective agreements affecting several million workers. A new general rise in wages, by obliging entrepreneurs to restrict their demands for instrumental goods, may seriously endanger the continuation of the prevailing activity."

Actually the rise in real wages continued throughout 1928 and even in the succeeding years, as the figures in the footnote show.* The reports of the

* Wages of skilled workers:

| | *Weekly wages in marks* | *Index of Real wages* (1925–27 = 100) |
|---|---|---|
| 1925 | 42·31 | 95·9 |
| 1926 | 45·45 | 102·1 |
| 1927 | 47·53 | 102·0 |
| 1928 | 51·07 | 106·7 |
| 1929 | 53·35 | 109·9 |
| 1930— | | |
| January | 53·89 | 112·7 |
| February | 53·89 | 113·6 |
| March | 53·89 | 114·9 |

(See *Report of the Agent-General, etc.*, Berlin, May 21st, 1930, p. 302.)

great banks and of the big industrial companies for 1929 were almost unanimous in expressing the opinion that the exaggerated rise in wages, imposed by the trade unions through the collective agreements, and the considerable contributions paid by entrepreneurs to the various social insurance funds, seriously reduced the returns of businesses and prevented entrepreneurs from making new investments. Later, the depression having begun, it was again unanimously stated that the quasi-insensitiveness of nominal wages to the change of the

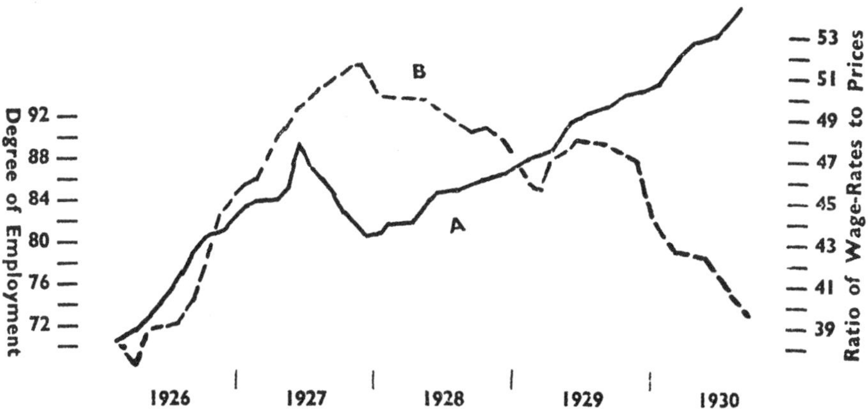


DIAGRAM XXVIII

A. Ratio of wages-rates for unskilled workers to prices of consumption goods
B. Percentage of occupied workers among members of the Workers' Associations (part-time work is also taken into account)

conjuncture—so that the wage-earner was almost changed into a salaried worker—was one of the principal causes of the length and severity of the crisis. It was observed, for example, that the rise in salaries paid by the railway administration obliged it to reduce considerably its orders for materials. Stegerwald, the Minister for Labour, often called attention to the unduly high wages of workers employed in the industries producing for the home market. These increases in wages were partly the result of foreign loans, whose yield was spent almost exclusively in Germany itself. The wages of workers employed in the export industries were not raised so high, because of the struggle against foreign competition.

The German crisis is so vast and complex a phenomenon that it would be useless and unscientific to attempt to ascribe it to a single cause. The point of view of some German entrepreneurs is too one-sided; and the offensive opened by them against the trade unions aggravated a situation already very tense. Nevertheless, wages statistics supply something towards the explanation of the depression.

In Diagram XXVIII the continuous curve represents the ratio of nominal wage-rates to the index number of prices of direct consumption goods, and the dotted curve shows the percentage of unemployment. The diagram suggests three distinct periods: (*a*) in the first period, from the beginning of 1926 until the middle of 1927, the ratio of nominal wages to selling prices increased, especially as a result of a drop in the latter. In spite of this, unemployment declined. That may be explained by remembering that in that period the drop in selling prices was the effect of the progress of industrial organization and did not imply a decline in profits; (*b*) in the second period, which included the second half of 1927, the trade unions obtained big increases in nominal wages, but owing to the inflation of prices those increases could be supported by industry, and unemployment continued to fall; (*c*) at the beginning of 1928 the situation changed rapidly. The rise in selling prices continued, but not at a sufficient rate to compensate for the rise in wages. Unemployment increased. In the succeeding years, in spite of the crisis, the level of real wages continued to rise and unemployment grew continually.

**20.** There is at any given moment a normal rate of wages, depending on all the conditions of the economic equilibrium. If the entrepreneur is then obliged to pay a higher rate, the repercussion of this disturbance of the equilibrium is a rise in unemployment. Diagram XXVIII suggests the conclusion that probably the extreme rises in wage rates disturbed the equilibrium in 1928. It is, of course, true that the proof offered by the diagram is somewhat vague, and that the interrelationship of wage rates and unemployment needs more rigorous and profound statistical analysis, which the deficiencies in the data do not permit. Besides, the demonstration of a correlation between phenomenon A and phenomenon B naturally does not exclude the existence of other correlations between A and C, A and D, etc. In the present case, besides the rigidity of wages—on which the attacks of the industrial classes were concentrated—it is also necessary to take account of the high interest which, because of the huge dimensions assumed by fixed capital, weighed heavily on firms, and of the taxes and numerous other elements of cost, such as railway charges. An accurate analysis of the causes which provoked a rise in the costs of production after 1924 may be found in a work published by the Commission of Inquiry into the economic conditions of Germany.*

None the less, it seems that the forsaking of the policy of rigid wages by the trade unions (the policy being based on the erroneous theory that high wages in periods of crisis, by maintaining the demand for consumption goods, stimulated economic activity) and the consideration of a system which would allow for variation of real wages according to the phases of the economic cycle in the last analysis would have been profitable to the working classes themselves, since such a system would have curbed the spread of unemployment.

**21.** While capitalists attacked the high wages theory of the trade unions, the representatives of the working classes attacked the cartels, maintaining that their policy of rigid prices prevented that fall in prices which, thanks to the stimulus it would have given to demand, would have made way for revival. The great raw material syndicates impeded the fall in the cost of production

* See *Erzeugungs- und Absatzbedingungen der deutschen Wirtschaft*, especially pp. 91–136, Berlin, 1931.

for the manufacturing industries, which formed the backbone of German economy and, among others, contributed largely to exports. These observations are certainly quite correct. A comparison between "free" and "controlled" prices is interesting at this point. In the "free" prices which were influenced by world prices, there was from the beginning of 1928 until the end of 1931 a fall of about 50 per cent, whilst in the controlled prices of the big syndicates—pig-iron and semi-finished steel, certain non-ferrous metals, coal, artificial manures, benzine, cellulose and paper, and building materials—the drop from the highest level (end of 1929) was at the end of 1931 scarcely 11 per cent.*

Generally, it can be said that the formerly quasi-elastic system—when wages, costs of production, and prices fell rapidly in times of depression—was replaced by an almost rigid system; and certainly this was one of the causes which prolonged the depression.†

But in the case of Germany one must take account of other circumstances which had weakened the spirit of enterprise; chief among these were the question of reparations, the condition of the national finances, and the internal political situation.

I must add that the German experiences do not support the theory according to which in the last phases of the expansion, because of the increase of production due to the extension and improvement of productive apparatus, prices fall; and, it is argued, it is this fall in prices which causes the end of the expansion and the beginning of the depression. In Germany, in 1928, prices were kept at a high level, and in many cases were increased; and according to many authoritative views, among which is that of the Reichsbank,‡ it was precisely these high prices which had an unfavourable influence on the expansion and hastened its end. These high prices showed that, owing to mistakes, the transformation of the productive apparatus had not brought about the anticipated fall in production costs. A fall in prices, if it had been the result of that fall in costs which was the principal object of rationalization, would not have created financial difficulties for industry.

### XI. OTHER FACTORS IN THE DEPRESSION: THE REPARATIONS PROBLEM, THE GOVERNMENT FINANCIAL POSITION, AND THE INTERNAL POLITICAL SITUATION

**22.** In November 1928 the stoppage in the iron and steel industries caused a considerable disturbance in German business. Also the winter of 1928–29 was unusually severe; in that period transport was almost paralysed and there was a great recrudescence of unemployment. At the beginning of 1929, the difficult negotiations at Paris about the definitive regulation of reparations

* See *Vierteljahrshefte zur Konjunkturforschung*, part 3, p. 49, Berlin, 1931.

† The German Government issued (December 8th, 1931) an exceptional decree, which imposed a considerable cut in wages and salaries on non-governmental employees (the rates had to be brought to the level of January 10th, 1927); in prices of goods; rents, tariffs for railway transport and for supplies of gas, water, and electricity; and interest on loans contracted by public bodies, on mortgage bonds, on debentures issued by joint-stock companies or by private firms, and on mortgages. For entirely peculiar reasons, the policy of deflation, began in 1931, did not have the success anticipated.

‡ See *Report* for 1928.

created a state of uncertainty and *malaise*. When later, in April of the same year, it appeared that the negotiations had not had any positive result, a serious psychological crisis spread in Germany. Large quantities of foreign exchange were bought for speculation, money due from abroad was not transferred to Germany, and the savings banks showed a sudden drop in deposits. The dollar exchange rate increased until it reached the gold export point. In the two months January and February the Reichsbank parted with more than 200 millions' worth of foreign exchange. In March it had to begin selling gold, too, and in less than two months it lost about 960 million marks in gold. To put a stop to the contraction of its reserve the Reichsbank, on April 25th, increased the discount rate (from 6·50 to 7·50 per cent) and later adopted a more energetic measure, i.e. a rigorous restriction of credit.

In the summer of 1929 the acute psychological crisis had passed, and some people began to hope for a recovery which would signalize the beginning of a new economic cycle. This forecast was based on the expectation of a new influx of foreign capital, on the hope that the economic expansion of other countries would be the basis of a growing demand for German goods, and on the great force of resistance of which German economy had given proof during "the acid test" of the Conference of Paris.

Succeeding events showed that this forecast was too optimistic. The acute stage of the psychological crisis was overcome, but, since the solution of the reparations question was not considered satisfactory in industrial and banking circles, there remained "an atmosphere of pessimism and of hopeless resignation" (as the *Darmstädter und Nationalbank* wrote) quite unfavourable to the conception of optimistic and constructive projects.

The condition of public finance also helped to aggravate continually the lack of confidence. The expenses of the Reich, of the States, and of the local authorities had shown an impressive increase after 1924. The very severe criticisms to which, in Germany itself, the financial policy of public bodies was subjected were of no avail. The result of the exaggerated expenses and of the dissipation of public money was a fiscal burden which weighed heavily on the economic apparatus of Germany and weakened the spirit of enterprise.*

Taxes always tended to fall more heavily on the profits of industry and capital rather than on consumers. From 1925 to 1928 the yield from taxes on income, companies, capital, and land rose from 1,341 to 2,752 million marks; while the total yield of customs and taxes on wages, on sales, on consumption, and on transport, rose considerably less, i.e. from 5,062 millions to 5,414 millions. The yield of the tax on wages in 1928 was scarcely equal to that of 1925, although in the meantime both nominal and real wages had increased considerably. It was especially due to the increase in unemployment, which was relieved by unduly high doles, that the conditions of public finance worsened during 1930, the various remedies devised being manifestly inadequate. In 1930 and 1931 the gravity of the financial situation was one of the principal factors of the economic depression, for its influence was both material and psychological.

* In all honesty one must recognize that later the German Government made great efforts to establish equilibrium in the Reich budget, by considerably reducing expenses and demanding heavy sacrifices from the German people.

Another important factor in uncertainty and in the lack of confidence was, at one time, the internal political situation. When after the election of September 14th, 1930, the great progress made by extreme political parties (the Nationalists and Communists) was apparent, a new psychological crisis occurred. It was revealed materially in the sudden drop in the prices of German shares, in the flight of German capital abroad, in the panicky sale of German securities in foreign markets, and in the fall in the reserve of the Reichsbank. The spirit of enterprise among entrepreneurs was paralysed and unemployment increased. The Minister Stegerwald declared that the election of September 1930 caused the dismissal of 500,000 workers.

The causes to which I have referred must necessarily have lessened the demand for capital for new investment by entrepreneurs. Add to that the influence of the drop in orders from public bodies, who were in a critical financial condition, and the consequence was inevitably a deep depression in the production goods industries.

XII. THE VARIATIONS IN THE SUPPLY OF CAPITAL. INTERNAL SAVING

**23.** But the fluctuations in the demand for capital are not sufficient to explain the German crisis. When the demand for capital slackens because of the blackening of the prospect of profits, the rate of interest, other things being equal, must fall. If, instead, it rises, as happened in Germany during 1928 and 1929 (see Diagram XXVIII), it may be said that some changes also occurred in the supply of capital, and that it is necessary to take account of them in order to have a complete picture of the causes of the economic depression.

In the past years the supply of capital had come from two sources: (*a*) internal saving; (*b*) foreign loans, both long term and short term.

The indices we possess show that during 1928—after the effects on the capital market of the events of May 13th, 1927, formerly discussed had been overcome—issues of new securities were maintained at a high level, and that deposits at the savings banks increased considerably. From the examination of the balance sheets of joint-stock companies it seems probable that in 1928, despite the rise in wages, the "internal saving" of firms did not appreciably decline.

In the following years there was a slackening in the flow of saving, which was the consequence rather than the cause of the depression. And at the same time there were noted some important qualitative changes in the supply of capital. The lack of confidence in the internal political situation of Germany provoked a contraction in the supply of capital for long-term investments. Capitalists preferred to hold their savings available in the form of bank deposits on demand or at short notice, contenting themselves with a low interest rate. Thus there came about a very big divergence between interest rates for long- and short-term loans. To that must be added the influence of the flight of German capital, which was caused by various psychological crises mentioned a little earlier. Also, because of the critical financial situations of the Reich, the States and the local authorities, these bodies were often obliged to have recourse to bank credits, thus reducing the volume of credit available for private business and helping to harden the rate of interest.

**24.** But the changes which occurred in the supply of foreign capital were particularly important.

From 1925 onwards the influx of foreign capital into Germany was subject to the influence of two kinds of causes: (*a*) the variations in the need for capital by German business; (*b*) the situation of the international markets and other conditions of a psychological and political character, which made foreign capitalists more or less willing to invest their money in Germany.

In Diagram XXIX the movement of the rate of interest for short-term loans at Berlin is compared with the movement of the rate of interest for loans of the same kind in the international markets, i.e. at New York and London.*

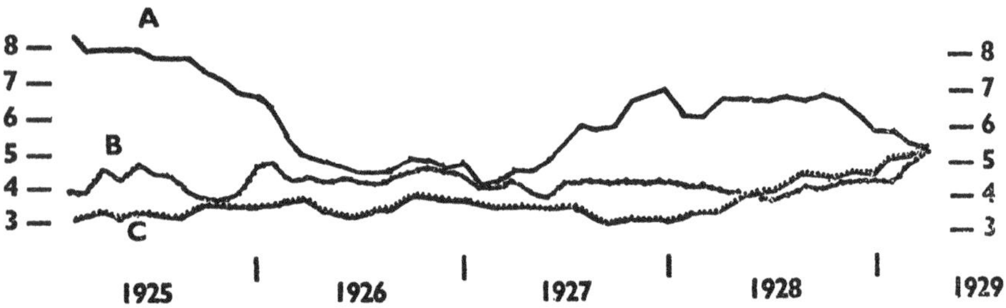


DIAGRAM XXIX

A. Rates of interest for short-term loans in Berlin
B. Rates of interest for short-term loans in London
C. Rates of interest for short-term loans in New York.

The diagram shows that the rate of interest remained more or less at the same level in the years 1925–27 in the international money market, while it fluctuated considerably in Germany, where it declined from the end of 1925 until the second half of 1926. Then from the beginning of 1927 until the end of the same year it once more increased perceptibly. It is reasonable to suppose that these fluctuations were mainly the reflection of the variations in the demand for capital by German industry. The supply of foreign capital followed the fluctuations of the demand and was seen to be completely elastic.

But at the beginning of 1928, for well-known reasons, the situation of the money market at New York changed. During 1928 and for a large part of 1929 New York attracted a large amount of capital and increasing monetary tension—of which the rising rate of interest is an expression—was manifest in the international market. German business had to pay a higher price for the use of foreign capital, which it needed to supplement the insufficient internal saving, and this rise in the interest rate, which occurred at a time when the prospects of profit were declining, was certainly a curb on economic expansion. Since the conditions of the American market—which until then had chiefly financed the German expansion—made the arrangement of new long-term loans difficult, the German banks began borrowing continually larger sums of money

* The diagram is based on the data contained in the various *Reports* of the Agent-General for Reparations Payments.

at short term. Thus was a situation full of uncertainties and dangers not only prolonged but incessantly aggravated, as future events showed.

In the years after 1928 the increasing lack of confidence among foreign capitalists made them more and more hesitant about investing their savings permanently in Germany. The total amount of new long-term loans fell from 1·7 milliards in 1928 to 0·6 milliard in 1929. On the other hand, new short-term loans probably amounted in 1929 to more than two milliard marks (net inflow).* In the years 1924–28 foreign loans, besides covering reparations payments and the service of the loans themselves, also made possible the reconstitution of the gold reserve of the Reichsbank, and covered a considerable excess of imports over exports (i.e. they were transformed into working capital for German business, as I have already stated). But in 1929 the net amount of new foreign loans, both short and long term, was little higher than the sums paid by Germany for reparations. Imports and exports were practically balanced. In 1930 the balance of short-term capital movements was unfavourable to Germany. The total influx (700 millions) was considerably less than the sum owed by Germany for reparations and for interest payments (2·5 milliards). The difference was met to a great extent (1·5 milliards) by an excess of exports over imports. Imports fell by 3 milliard marks compared with the previous year. Thus the stoppage of the influx of foreign capital—which entered principally in the form of raw materials and food—corresponded with a patent contraction of the working capital at the disposal of German industry. This in the last analysis meant a contraction of the flow of subsistence goods for the working classes, which, provided that wages did not fall, was bound to cause an increase in unemployment.

It has been calculated that in the first six months of 1931 the unfavourable balance of total capital movements amounted to 3·5 milliards. Consequently the excess of exports over imports increased. This state of the balance of trade was thus anything but a favourable symptom; it was, on the contrary, the most obvious symptom—incidentally confirmed by the high rate of interest—of the lack of capital which troubled German business.

### XIII. MISTAKES MADE IN THE INVESTMENT OF CAPITAL

**25.** In the preceding paragraphs I have referred to the vast process of reorganization, transformation, and concentration of firms which began in Germany after the monetary stabilization. "Rationalization" was necessary for German industry, which after the inflation was in a condition inferior to that of industries in other countries. But it is obvious now that in many cases entrepreneurs, seized by an excessive optimism and being able to carry out their grandiose schemes because of the facility with which foreign loans or bank credits could be obtained, developed their fixed investments in an exaggerated manner. Rationalization of firms in many cases did not achieve its object. Considerable capital was invested in the amplification and improvement of plant without there being the corresponding increase in sales which would have provided the expected profits.

* See data referred to in *Report of the Committee Appointed on the Recommendation of the London Conference*, Annex iii, 1931.

"Recent events," writes Professor Bonn,* "have shown that the captains of industry completely lacked the qualities necessary to those who direct the business of a country. Those qualities are the capacity to foresee, clearly and in time, future events, and to take the steps most appropriate to their anticipations. The present crisis is, above all, the result of mistakes made in investments in fixed capital."

On this point, the conclusion of the Committee of Enquiry into German economic conditions is especially interesting. It stated that in the iron and steel industry the considerable increase in producing capacity was effected with a view to a future rise in the demand for iron and steel products, which, however, did not materialize. Hence a part of the invested capital must be considered as lost. It is true that these conclusions met with outspoken opposition from the industrialists, who denied having been extravagant in the construction of plant.† But the people best informed about German business generally maintain that in the iron and steel and other industries excessive investments have caused heavy capital losses. That this was also the opinion of the Bourse is shown by the big drop in the prices of shares in 1930 and 1931. In appraising the value of shares, the Bourse began to take account of the losses of capital. Later, companies (including the Steel Syndicate) acknowledged these losses, reducing their nominal capital correspondingly.

## XIV. THE BANKING SITUATION AND THE RESTRICTION OF BANK CREDITS

**26.** The difficulties in which many industries found themselves—following erratic speculations made, with extreme boldness and complete disregard for the interests of investors, by certain captains of industry, who wanted to create unduly complex financial-economic organizations—could not but have serious repercussions on the situation of the banks, as is clearly seen in their reports for 1929 and 1930. The situation was characterized by the fall in the reserves of foreign exchange—caused by the withdrawal of foreign capital—and by the worsening of the so-called "coefficient of liquidity."‡ A part of the credits

* "Deflation der Panik" in the *Berliner Tageblatt,* of October 4th, 1931, n. 468. In the volume *Erzeugungs- und Absatzbedingungen der deutschen Wirtschaft,* p. 151 (published by the Commission of Enquiry into the Economic Situation of Germany), the causes which led to the mistakes of many German industrialists are analysed. In many cases the desire of technicians to create perfect plant prevailed over considerations of an economic character.

† "That the new investments have not reaped the expected profits is explained by the fact that the increase of productivity obtained by perfecting technique was more than offset by the increase in the cost of production, which was the result of a continual rise in wages, salaries, social insurance payments, and taxes. Compared with the first working year (1926) the costs of the company increased altogether in the four succeeding years by 308 million marks as a result of the decrees of the Government concerning wages, social insurance payments, and the increase in taxes" (*Report* of the Steel Syndicate for 1930).

‡ "Coefficient of Liquidity" for:

| | | *Percentage* | |
|---|---|---|---|
| | 1928 | 1929 | 1930 |
| Darmstädter und Nationalbank .. | 51·5 | 45·5 | 38·6 |
| Dresdner Bank .. .. .. | 50 | 43·5 | 36·6 |
| Commerz- und Privatbank .. .. | 47 | 46·7 | 41·4 |

granted to industry and commerce for financing the construction of new plant was "frozen." As one may read in the various bank reports, this obliged the banks to be very cautious in the granting of new loans. At the beginning of 1931 it was apparent that the policy of the banks was inspired not so much by the desire to secure a certain amount of profit, as by preoccupation with liquidity and the security of loans. They were induced to refuse even secure credits in order to increase their available liquid resources, to examine strictly the guarantees offered for credits, and to restrict unsecured credits.

Diagram xxx (constructed on a logarithmic scale from data published by

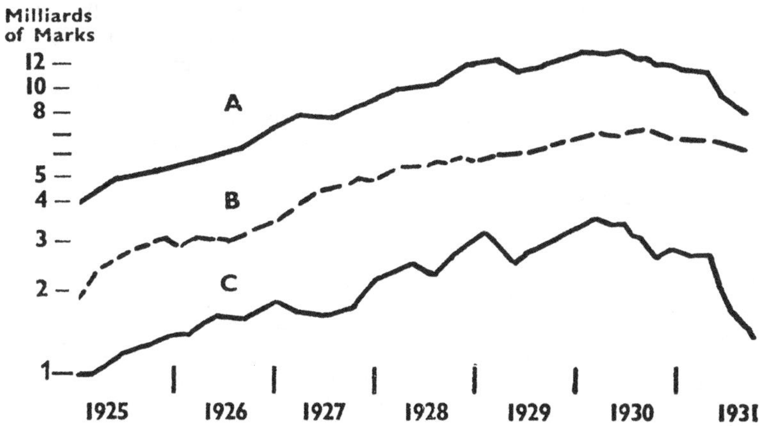


DIAGRAM XXX

A. Aggregate deposits with German banks
B. Credits in current account
C. Bills discounted

the Institut für Konjunkturforschung) shows the movements of deposits, of loans on current accounts and of bills, at the big German banks. They reveal certain facts worthy of attention: Deposits increased very much from the beginning of 1925 (3·8 milliard marks) until the end of 1928 (11·1 milliards). We know that to a great extent (for any large bank 30 to 40 per cent) they were deposited by foreigners. In 1929 the increase stopped, and, after March, owing to political and psychological factors previously mentioned, deposits even declined perceptibly. In the first months of 1930 money once more poured into the banks; but later the decline began again. The loans curve showed a similar movement. Loans on current account rose rapidly during the revival and the first phase of the expansion.

Serious mistakes were made not only by entrepreneurs but also by the banks during the phase of economic expansion. As some notorious cases revealed, creating surprise and indignation among the public, they granted unduly generous credits to large firms, favouring extravagant development, and also did not supervise, as they should have done, the use of the loans.

The most typical case was that of the "Norddeutsche Wollkämmerei" of Bremen; the failure of this large firm—as against liabilities of 235 million marks there were assets of scarcely 39 millions—showed with what carelessness some big German banks had dispensed huge loans in the years of expansion. The "Danat-Bank" (which had a capital of 60 millions, plus 40 millions reserve) had granted loans to the above-mentioned firm to the amount of 40 millions; other banks supplied altogether more than 80 millions.

During the expansion period interest rates fixed by the banks were, on the whole, too low. It follows that, bank loans being relatively cheap, borrowers had no proper inducement to replace them, as soon as possible, by long-term loans issued in the capital market. As it was easy to finance the holding of stocks with bank credit, these increased extravagantly; until, a sudden restriction of credits being imposed, there followed a sharp drop in prices.

The banks were also too generous in financing, with the aid of funds entrusted to them at short notice, business which normally would have had to be provided for by long-term loans in the market. This extravagant lending was partly the result of competition between the banks and of the fact that, there being no central office for the control of loans, no bank knew exactly what sum of money a firm had already taken on loan from other banks.

## XV. THE BANKING CRISIS OF THE SUMMER OF 1931

**27.** At the beginning of 1930 there occurred a reaction against the pessimism prevailing in the previous months. Some people foresaw that the capital, which could not find employment in America and other countries because of the crisis, would come to Germany in the form of long-term loans, and would stimulate economic recovery. In the first months of 1930 the money market experienced conditions of extraordinary liquidity (see Diagram XXX). The prices of shares increased; the "barometer" of the Bourse announced a new phase of expansion. The situation appeared to be analogous to that which had existed at the beginning of 1926.

The example is interesting because it shows the fallacy of superficial barometers. The apparent outward similarities concealed very great differences between the situations of 1926 and 1930. In 1926 the process of industrial and banking liquidation was already far advanced; the financial situation was promising; the internal political situation did not cause consternation, and the international situation was considerably improved (thanks to the peaceful policy of Stresemann), and the foreign markets were ready to give generous financial help for the economic reconstruction of Germany. But at the beginning of 1930 liquidation was hardly begun; the condition of public finance was growing continually worse, and the political situation was anything but clear. Indeed, the rise in the price of shares was of short duration.

**28.** Also at the beginning of 1931 the conviction began to spread—not only in Germany—that the most severe phase of the crisis was already passed. At the meetings of the principal joint-stock companies a certain optimism was shown by some of the great industrialists. It seemed that the internal political crisis, which had been the result of the election of September 14th, 1930, had been relieved. The winter, during which the increasing unemployment figures had given rise to serious anxiety, had passed without too much misery. The renewed confidence in the political stability of Germany (of which the gradual return of fugitive capital from abroad and the increase in the price of German loans at New York were symptoms) prepared an atmosphere favourable for future economic revival. In Germany certain signs of increased activity—which apparently was not due solely to seasonal causes—were noticed, according to the March Report of the Prussian Chamber of Commerce, in the textile, shoe, chemical, and automobile industries. From January to April prices of shares on the Bourse rose considerably; but, as before, the Bourse was again a false barometer of the economic situation.

Other more important facts clearly showed that the depression continued. The situation of the production goods industries deteriorated, as the statistics of the Steel Trust show. The Institut für Konjunkturforschung correctly maintained that there the prerequisites of economic recovery—in particular a definitive re-establishment of confidence in the German internal situation and in the international political situation, the recovery of the Government finances and a sufficient supply of long-term capital—did not yet exist. Despite the abundance of money, the rate of interest for long-term loans continued to remain much higher than rates in foreign markets. Indeed, it was calculated that the interest paid to mortgage banks for loans secured by a first mortgage amounted in general to 9·50 per cent. The hope which had risen in the spring of the previous year, when the mortgage banks once more attempted to introduce a class of 7-per-cent mortgage bonds, had proved a delusion. Even the supply of long-term money by insurance companies, savings banks, and other public institutions continued to be scarce.

In fact the following months showed that those who had anticipated an early end of the depression had been mistaken. Above all, they had not attached sufficient weight to the financial condition of the Reich, the States, and the local authorities, which was rapidly worsening. The decree of June 5th, which contained draconian financial provisions, revealed to everyone the gravity of the financial situation. At the same time the collapse of the "Credit-Anstalt" of Vienna aroused in foreign markets the fear that the position of the big German banks was also seriously disturbed. Adding to the spread of lack of confidence was the realization of the critical situation of some of the big German companies (the great shops of the "Karstadt," the insurance company "Nordstern" and the "Nordwolle": this last case, which I have mentioned before, especially made a very great impression).

The result of the German election of September 1930 was the signal for a hurried withdrawal of foreign short-term credits from the German banks. The withdrawal of capital, which at times in the first months of 1931 seemed to have stopped, began again with renewed energy at the beginning of June of that year. The quantity of foreign exchange which the Reichsbank had to sell daily assumed alarming proportions: fifty, a hundred million marks and more. In the afternoon of June 12th it was announced that that morning the Reichsbank had had to exchange 200 million marks for foreign exchange. On the following day the losses amounted to 100 millions. The increase in the rate of discount from 5 to 7 per cent gave only a temporary relief. In order to protect the reserve, which was rapidly approaching the extreme limit allowed by the banking laws, the Reichsbank once more began to apply the policy of restriction of credits, which twice in the past, in similar though much less serious conditions (i.e. in May 1929 and September 1930) had achieved good results.

Hoover's well-known declaration succeeded in postponing the threatened tempest. The demand for foreign exchange declined and could be satisfied without the intervention of the Central Bank. The Reichsbank announced that it would not apply the restriction of credits rigorously. It was only a "bright interval"; after a few days the demand for foreign exchange revived, and the commercial banks which could not liquidate their assets quickly had recourse to the Reichsbank.

The influence of the withdrawal of foreign capital was aggravated by the flight of German capital from the interior, which became more and more serious. At the beginning of July it was calculated that the Reichsbank had lost in the last weeks about a milliard and a half of gold or foreign exchange. To this figure must be added about 500 millions in foreign exchange paid out by the ordinary banks. At the same time, the anxiety of German depositors, provoked by the failure of the Nordwolle, was increased, as it became known that some big banks, especially the Danat, were largely involved. The deposits of this latter bank fell rapidly, and on the morning of July 13th it was announced that it had closed its offices. Thus began the most acute phase of the crisis.

## CONCLUSIONS

From this lengthy analysis it appears that the variations of the supply of capital certainly had a very great influence on the fluctuations of German economic activities. Already in 1927, when the German economy was rapidly developing, there appeared, as we have seen, some difficulties over the supply of capital. But the fact that changes occurred in the supply of capital is not enough to explain the check to expansion; it is also necessary to analyse the causes which influenced the spirit of enterprise among entrepreneurs. After the stoppage of the expansion and the beginning of the depression, causes of a psychological order acquired, for the reasons given, very great importance. A wave of pessimism struck Germany and dominated the minds of entrepreneurs as well as of the investing classes. At first it was manifested in a growing lack of confidence in the rulers of the country, in the political system based on the Weimar Constitution, and in the effects of the economic policy adopted in post-war years. On the other hand, the public was losing confidence in the great industrialists, and the German economic crisis acquired the dangerous significance of "a crisis of the capitalist system," which it was declared had proved itself totally incapable of resolving the economic and social problems resulting from the Great War. This lack of confidence provoked what Bonn called "the revolt of the capitalists," i.e. savers either withdrew their money or hoarded it or placed it abroad, or offered their savings in the form of short-term loans, refusing to employ it in permanent investments. This profound and widespread psychological disturbance was, in Germany as elsewhere, one of the most typical features of the economic crisis and increased the gravity of the objective facts of the crisis itself.

# APPENDIX OF TABLES

## TABLE I*

*Income and Expenses of the Reich*, 1919–23

(*in millions of gold marks*)

| 1919 | *Income* | *Expenditure* | *Increase in floating debt* |
|---|---|---|---|
| April | 306·5 | 1,439·4 | 1,132·8 |
| May | 330·0 | 1,346·3 | 1,016·2 |
| June | 299·7 | 1,212·6 | 914·0 |
| July | 320·2 | 1,063·7 | 743·5 |
| August | 256·5 | 947·8 | 691·4 |
| September | 207·8 | 635·3 | 426·0 |
| October | 242·6 | 660·5 | 417·9 |
| November | 140·3 | 418·8 | 278·5 |
| December | 136·5 | 232·4 | 95·2 |
| January | 116·4 | 239·2 | 122·5 |
| February | 73·8 | 105·9 | 31·8 |
| March | 128·8 | 257·8 | 129·2 |
| | 2,559·1 | 8,559·8 | 5,999·0 |

| 1920 | *Income* | *Expenditure* | *Increase of floating debt* |
|---|---|---|---|
| April | 52·0 | 307·9 | 247·8 |
| May | 102·2 | 694·8 | 584·5 |
| June | 193·5 | 1,441·6 | 1,240·0 |
| July | 256·1 | 1,279·3 | 1,015·1 |
| August | 191·7 | 791·7 | 591·9 |
| September | 176·8 | 817·2 | 632·3 |
| October | 197·8 | 348·8 | 142·9 |
| November | 241·1 | 629·1 | 379·9 |
| December | 411·3 | 722·7 | 303·3 |
| January | 434·9 | 613·5 | 170·5 |
| February | 460·3 | 899·4 | 431·9 |
| March | 460·4 | 782·9 | 314·4 |
| | 3,178·1 | 9,328·7 | 6,053·6 |

* The figures after 1919 have been taken from the official publication, *Deutschlands Wirtschaft, Währung und Finanzen*, Berlin, 1924, p. 31. Those for 1919 are deduced from Jessen's work, *Staatsfinanzen 1914–22* (Berlin, 1923). They also include the income derived from postal and railway administration, while beginning from 1920 the figures in Table 1 include only taxes.

TABLE I (*continued*)

| 1921 | *Income* | *Expenditure* | *Increase of floating debt* |
|---|---|---|---|
| April .. .. .. | 352·3 | 773·2 | 416·9 |
| May .. .. .. | 411·8 | 686·0 | 270·2 |
| June .. .. .. | 350·3 | 862·3 | 508·0 |
| July .. .. .. | 304·8 | 617·8 | 309·0 |
| August .. .. | 256·3 | 863·2 | 602·9 |
| September .. .. | 196·5 | 506·0 | 305·5 |
| October .. .. | 173·0 | 384·5 | 207·5 |
| November .. .. | 112·5 | 254·6 | 138·1 |
| December .. .. | 175·3 | 626·5 | 447·2 |
| January .. .. | 192·6 | 388·2 | 191·6 |
| February .. .. | 194·2 | 342·4 | 144·2 |
| March .. .. | 207·8 | 346·5 | 134·7 |
| | 2,927·4 | 6,651·3 | 3,675·8 |

| 1922 | *Income* | *Expenditure* | *Increase of floating debt* |
|---|---|---|---|
| April .. .. .. | 190·3 | 321·8 | 129·8 |
| May .. .. .. | 254·9 | 376·9 | 120·3 |
| June .. .. .. | 235·1 | 313·8 | 77·0 |
| July .. .. .. | 183·4 | 208·5 | 23·4 |
| August .. .. | 116·4 | 205·1 | 86·9 |
| September .. .. | 90·8 | 434·9 | 342·5 |
| October .. .. | 66·2 | 269·5 | 201·6 |
| November .. .. | 60·6 | 199·8 | 137·5 |
| December .. .. | 73·4 | 438·0 | 362·9 |
| January .. .. | 65·9 | 204·6 | 137·0 |
| February .. .. | 50·8 | 279·0 | 226·5 |
| March .. .. | 100·3 | 698·9 | 596·9 |
| | 1,488·1 | 3,950·6 | 2,442·3 |

| 1923* | *Income* | *Expenditure* | *Increase of floating debt* |
|---|---|---|---|
| April .. .. .. | 150·6 | 466·6 | 316·0 |
| May .. .. .. | 123·3 | 284·7 | 161·4 |
| June .. .. .. | 48·2 | 496·4 | 448·2 |
| July .. .. .. | 48·3 | 473·9 | 425·6 |
| August .. .. | 78·1 | 1,013·1 | 914·7 |
| September .. .. | 55·6 | 1,661·8 | 1,564·1 |
| October .. .. | 14·5 | 881·8 | 860·1 |
| | 518·6 | 5,278·3 | 4,690·1 |

* The figures for 1923 are somewhat uncertain because of the difficulty of converting sums expressed in paper marks into gold marks at a time of rapid depreciation of the money (see Appendix to Chapter III of this volume). The gold figures for October were calculated by the Statistical Bureau of the Reich by dividing the sums of paper marks by the average exchange rate of the gold mark calculated for every ten days.

TABLE II*

*Total Value of Treasury Bills Discounted by the Reichsbank (milliards of paper marks)*

| *End of month* | *1914* | *1915* | *1916* | *1917* | *1918* | *1919* | *1920* | *1921* | *1922* | *1923* |
|---|---|---|---|---|---|---|---|---|---|---|
| January .. .. .. | — | 4·3 | 6·8 | 15·0 | 32·5 | 58·6 | 88·3 | 155·5 | 255·9 | 2,082 |
| February .. .. | — | 5·9 | 8·9 | 17·7 | 35·8 | 61·6 | 89·0 | 161·8 | 263·0 | 3,588 |
| March .. .. .. | — | 7·2 | 8·6 | 18·7 | 33·4 | 63·8 | 91·6 | 166·4 | 272·1 | 6,601 |
| April .. .. .. | — | 3·1 | 4·8 | 13·8 | 31·5 | 67·2 | 95·1 | 172·7 | 281·1 | 8,442 |
| May .. .. .. | — | 3·8 | 5·9 | 15·6 | 34·7 | 70·4 | 101·6 | 176·7 | 289·4 | 10,275 |
| June .. .. .. | — | 5·2 | 7·2 | 18·3 | 38·4 | 73·4 | 113·2 | 185·1 | 295·3 | 22,020 |
| July .. .. .. | 0·3 | 6·7 | 8·8 | 21·4 | 41·8 | 76·1 | 122·7 | 190·8 | 308·0 | 57,849 |
| August .. .. | 2·1 | 8·2 | 10·9 | 24·7 | 46·0 | 78·2 | 129·4 | 202·9 | 331·5 | 1,196† |
| September .. .. | 2·7 | 8·6 | 11·5 | 26·0 | 48·0 | 80·6 | 138·3 | 210·5 | 451·1 | 46,717† |
| October .. .. | 1·0 | 3·6 | 8·3 | 22·9 | 48·2 | 83·3 | 140·6 | 218·0 | 603·8 | 6·9‡ |
| November .. .. | 1·6 | 4·1 | 9·9 | 24·8 | 51·2 | 85·2 | 147·6 | 226·7 | 839·1 | 191·6‡§ |
| December .. .. | 2·9 | 5·7 | 12·6 | 28·6 | 55·2 | 86·4 | 152·8 | 247·1 | 1,495·2 | 1·2‡ |

* Sources (for this and following tables, where not otherwise stated): Official publications: *Zahlen zur Geldenwertung in Deutschland 1914 bis 1923*; *Deutschlands Wirtschaft, Währung und Finanzen*, 1924; *Wirtschaft und Statistik* (periodical publication of the Statistical Bureau of the Reich); *Statistisches Jahrbuch für das deutsche Reich.*

† Billions of marks (a billion = $1{,}000{,}000^2$). ‡ Trillions of marks (a trillion = $1{,}000{,}000^3$). § November 15th.

TABLE III

*Circulation of the Reichsbank (milliards of paper marks)*

| *End of month* | *1914* | *1915* | *1916* | *1917* | *1918* | *1919* | *1920* | *1921* | *1922* | *1923* |
|---|---|---|---|---|---|---|---|---|---|---|
| January | 2·1 | 4·7 | 6·5 | 7·9 | 11·1 | 23·6 | 37·4 | 66·6 | 115 | 1,984 |
| February | 2·0 | 4·9 | 6·6 | 8·1 | 11·3 | 24·1 | 41·0 | 67·4 | 120 | 3,513 |
| March | 2·4 | 5·6 | 7·0 | 8·6 | 12·0 | 25·5 | 45·2 | 69·4 | 131 | 5,518 |
| April | 2·1 | 5·3 | 7·0 | 8·3 | 11·8 | 26·6 | 47·9 | 70·8 | 140 | 6,546 |
| May | 2·0 | 5·3 | 6·7 | 8·3 | 12·0 | 28·2 | 50·0 | 71·8 | 152 | 8,564 |
| June | 2·4 | 5·8 | 7·2 | 8·7 | 12·5 | 30·0 | 54·0 | 75·3 | 169 | 17,291 |
| July | 2·9 | 5·5 | 7·0 | 8·9 | 12·7 | 29·3 | 55·8 | 77·4 | 190 | 45,594 |
| August | 4·2 | 5·6 | 7·1 | 9·3 | 13·6 | 28·5 | 58·4 | 80·1 | 238 | 663* |
| September | 4·5 | 6·2 | 7·4 | 10·2 | 15·3 | 29·8 | 61·7 | 86·4 | 317 | 28,229* |
| October | 4·2 | 5·9 | 7·3 | 10·4 | 16·7 | 30·9 | 63·6 | 91·5 | 469 | 2·5† |
| November | 4·2 | 6·0 | 7·3 | 10·6 | 18·6 | 31·9 | 64·3 | 100·9 | 754 | 400·3† |
| December | 5·0 | 6·9 | 8·1 | 11·5 | 22·2 | 35·7 | 68·8 | 113·6 | 1,280 | 496·5† |

* Billions of marks. † Trillions of marks.

## TABLE IV

*Monthly Average Exchange Rate of the Gold Mark expressed in Paper Marks**

| *Months* | *1914* | *1915* | *1916* | *1917* | *1918* | *1919* | *1920* | *1921* | *1922* | *1923* |
|---|---|---|---|---|---|---|---|---|---|---|
| January .. .. | — | 1·10 | 1·27 | 1·38 | 1·24 | 1·95 | 15·4 | 15·5 | 45·7 | 4,281 |
| February .. .. | — | 1·12 | 1·28 | 1·40 | 1·26 | 2·17 | 23·6 | 14·6 | 49·5 | 6,650 |
| March .. .. | — | 1·15 | 1·32 | 1·39 | 1·24 | 2·47 | 20·0 | 14·9 | 67·7 | 5,047 |
| April .. .. | — | 1·16 | 1·30 | 1·54 | 1·22 | 3·00 | 14·2 | 15·1 | 69·3 | 5,825 |
| May .. .. | — | 1·15 | 1·24 | 1·56 | 1·22 | 3·06 | 11·1 | 14·8 | 69·1 | 11,355 |
| June .. .. | — | 1·16 | 1·26 | 1·69 | 1·28 | 3·34 | 9·3 | 16·5 | 75·6 | 26,202 |
| July .. .. .. | — | 1·17 | 1·31 | 1·70 | 1·38 | 3·59 | 9·4 | 18·3 | 117·5 | 84,186 |
| August .. .. | 1·00 | 1·17 | 1·33 | 1·70 | 1·45 | 4·48 | 11·4 | 20·1 | 270·3 | 1,100,632 |
| September .. .. | 1·00 | 1·15 | 1·37 | 1·72 | 1·57 | 5·73 | 13·8 | 25·0 | 349·2 | 23·5† |
| October .. .. | 1·04 | 1·16 | 1·36 | 1·74 | 1·57 | 6·39 | 16·2 | 35·8 | 757·7 | 6·10‡ |
| November .. .. | 1·10 | 1·18 | 1·38 | 1·65 | 1·77 | 9·12 | 18·4 | 62·6 | 1,711·1 | 522·3‡ |
| December .. .. | 1·07 | 1·23 | 1·36 | 1·35 | 1·97 | 11·14 | 17·4 | 45·7 | 1,807·8 | 1,000·0‡ |
| Yearly average .. | 1·02 | 1·16 | 1·31 | 1·57 | 1·43 | 4·70 | 15·0 | 24·9 | 449·2 | — |

* See *Wirtschaft und Statistik*, 1923, p. 413. † Millions. ‡ Milliards.

TABLE V

*Prices in Germany*

(*a*) Index Numbers of Wholesale Prices in Paper

(Monthly average) 1913 = 1

| *Month* | *1914* | *1915* | *1916* | *1917* | *1918* | *1919* | *1920* | *1921* | *1922* | *1923* |
|---|---|---|---|---|---|---|---|---|---|---|
| January | 0·96 | 1·26 | 1·50 | 1·56 | 2·04 | 2·62 | 12·6 | 14·4 | 36·7 | 2,785 |
| February | 0·96 | 1·33 | 1·51 | 1·58 | 1·98 | 2·70 | 16·8 | 13·8 | 41·0 | 5,585 |
| March | 0·96 | 1·39 | 1·48 | 1·59 | 1·98 | 2·74 | 17·1 | 13·4 | 54·3 | 4,883 |
| April | 0·95 | 1·42 | 1·49 | 1·63 | 2·04 | 2·86 | 15·7 | 13·3 | 63·5 | 5,212 |
| May | 0·97 | 1·39 | 1·51 | 1·63 | 2·03 | 2·97 | 15·1 | 13·1 | 64·6 | 8,170 |
| June | 0·99 | 1·39 | 1·52 | 1·65 | 2·09 | 3·08 | 13·8 | 13·7 | 70·3 | 19,385 |
| July | 0·99 | 1·50 | 1·61 | 1·72 | 2·08 | 3·39 | 13·7 | 14·3 | 100·6 | 74,787 |
| August | 1·09 | 1·46 | 1·59 | 2·03 | 2·35 | 4·22 | 14·5 | 19·2 | 192 | 944,041 |
| September | 1·11 | 1·45 | 1·54 | 1·99 | 2·30 | 4·93 | 15·0 | 20·7 | 287 | 23·9* |
| October | 1·18 | 1·47 | 1·53 | 2·01 | 2·34 | 5·62 | 14·7 | 24·6 | 566 | 7,095* |
| November | 1·23 | 1·47 | 1·51 | 2·03 | 2·34 | 6·78 | 15·1 | 34·2 | 1,154 | 726† |
| December | 1·25 | 1·49 | 1·51 | 2·03 | 2·45 | 8·03 | 14·4 | 34·9 | 1,475 | 1,262† |

* Millions. † Milliards.

TABLE V (*continued*)

(*b*) Index Numbers of Wholesale Prices in Gold (monthly average)

(1913 = 100)

| *Month* | *1914* | *1915* | *1916* | *1917* | *1918* | *1919* | *1920* | *1921* | *1922* | *1923* |
|---|---|---|---|---|---|---|---|---|---|---|
| January | 95·8 | 114·8 | 117·8 | 113·1 | 164·4 | 134·2 | 81·1 | 93·1 | 80·2 | 65·0 |
| February | 95·9 | 118·6 | 118·0 | 113·0 | 157·6 | 124·2 | 71·4 | 94·3 | 82·9 | 84·0 |
| March | 96·0 | 121·2 | 112·0 | 114·7 | 159·7 | 110·7 | 85·6 | 90·0 | 80·3 | 96·8 |
| April | 95·1 | 122·6 | 114·8 | 105·6 | 167·5 | 95·3 | 110·4 | 87·7 | 91·7 | 89·5 |
| May | 97·1 | 120·7 | 121·6 | 104·6 | 165·8 | 97·1 | 136·3 | 88·2 | 93·4 | 71·9 |
| June | 99·2 | 119·7 | 120·3 | 97·5 | 163·8 | 92·3 | 148·3 | 82·7 | 93·0 | 74·0 |
| July | 99·1 | 128·2 | 123·1 | 101·1 | 150·8 | 94·4 | 145·4 | 78·2 | 85·6 | 88·8 |
| August | 109·2 | 124·7 | 119·8 | 119·5 | 162·0 | 94·1 | 127·6 | 95·5 | 71·0 | 85·8 |
| September | 111·3 | 125·5 | 112·7 | 116·0 | 145·6 | 86·1 | 108·5 | 82·7 | 82·2 | 101·7 |
| October | 113·1 | 127·2 | 112·7 | 115·8 | 148·8 | 88·0 | 90·3 | 68·8 | 74·7 | 117·9 |
| November | 112·1 | 124·7 | 109·7 | 122·8 | 132·4 | 74·3 | 82·1 | 54·5 | 67·3 | 139·0 |
| December | 116·6 | 120·3 | 110·9 | 150·5 | 124·2 | 72·1 | 82·8 | 76·3 | 81·6 | 126·2 |

TABLE V (*continued*)

(*c*) Cost of Living Index Numbers in Paper (1913 = 1)

| *Month* | *1920* | *1921* | *1922* | *1923* | *1923** |
|---|---|---|---|---|---|
| January .. | — | 11·8 | 20·4 | 1,120 | 1,366 |
| February .. | 8·5 | 11·5 | 24·5 | 2,643 | 3,183 |
| March .. | 9·6 | 11·4 | 29·0 | 2,854 | 3,315 |
| April .. | 10·4 | 11·3 | 34·4 | 2,954 | 3,500 |
| May .. | 11·0 | 11·2 | 38·0 | 3,816 | 4,620 |
| June .. | 10·8 | 11·7 | 41·5 | 7,650 | 9,347 |
| July .. | 10·6 | 12·5 | 53·9 | 37,651 | 46,510 |
| August .. | 10·2 | 13·3 | 77·6 | 586,045 | 670,485 |
| September | 10·1 | 13·7 | 133·2 | 15·0† | 17·3† |
| October .. | 10·7 | 15·0 | 220·7 | 3·66‡ | 4·3‡ |
| November | 11·2 | 17·7 | 446·1 | 657‡ | 862‡ |
| December | 11·6 | 19·3 | 685·1 | 1,247‡ | 1,512‡ |

(*d*) Cost of Living Index Numbers in Gold (1913 = 100)

| *Month* | *1920* | *1921* | *1922* | *1923* | *1923** |
|---|---|---|---|---|---|
| January .. | — | 69·2 | 39·9 | 24·2 | 31·9 |
| February .. | 29·7 | 70·8 | 44·6 | 36·2 | 47·8 |
| March .. | 40·9 | 69·1 | 39·0 | 52·0 | 65·6 |
| April .. | 64·5 | 67·5 | 45·8 | 47·4 | 60·1 |
| May .. | 88·1 | 68·4 | 50·1 | 31·0 | 40·6 |
| June .. | 102·3 | 63·5 | 50·0 | 26·6 | 35·6 |
| July .. | 99·5 | 61·6 | 42·5 | 39·6 | 55·2 |
| August .. | 78·0 | 59·4 | 26·0 | 46·2 | 60·9 |
| September | 63·8 | 48·5 | 32·6 | 56·1 | 73·6 |
| October .. | 58·2 | 36·6 | 25·7 | 54·3 | 71·6 |
| November .. | 54·3 | 25·4 | 23·4 | 121·2 | 165·0 |
| December .. | 60·2 | 38·2 | 33·8 | 118·2 | 151·2 |

* Food only. † Millions. ‡ Milliards.

## TABLE VI

*Ratios between Index Numbers of German Prices in Paper Marks and Index Numbers of American Prices ("Price Parities")*

| *Month* | *1914* | *1915* | *1916* | *1917* | *1918* | *1919* | *1920* | *1921* | *1922* | *1923* |
|---|---|---|---|---|---|---|---|---|---|---|
| January .. .. | — | 1·27 | 1·31 | 1·02 | 1·10 | 1·32 | 5·39 | 8·5 | 26·6 | 1,785 |
| February .. | — | 1·33 | 1·29 | 1·00 | 1·06 | 1·40 | 7·26 | 8·6 | 29·1 | 3,557 |
| March .. .. | — | 1·39 | 1·23 | 0·97 | 1·05 | 1·40 | 7·30 | 8·6 | 38·3 | 3,074 |
| April .. .. | — | 1·42 | 1·22 | 0·94 | 1·07 | 1·44 | 6·39 | 9·0 | 44·4 | 3,277 |
| May .. .. | — | 1·38 | 1·23 | 0·89 | 1·06 | 1·47 | 6·10 | 9·0 | 43·6 | 5,237 |
| June .. .. | — | 1·39 | 1·22 | 0·89 | 1·08 | 1·52 | 5·69 | 9·6 | 46·9 | 12,670 |
| July .. .. | — | 1·49 | 1·29 | 0·91 | 1·05 | 1·60 | 5·67 | 10·1 | 64·9 | — |
| August .. .. | 1·08 | 1·45 | 1·25 | 1·06 | 1·16 | 1·95 | 6·28 | 13·5 | 123·9 | — |
| September .. | 1·08 | 1·44 | 1·18 | 1·06 | 1·11 | 2·35 | 6·63 | 14·7 | 187·6 | — |
| October .. .. | 1·21 | 1·42 | 1·12 | 1·09 | 1·15 | 2·66 | 6·95 | 17·3 | 367·5 | — |
| November .. | 1·26 | 1·40 | 1·03 | 1·10 | 1·15 | 3·12 | 7·70 | 24·2 | 737·8 | — |
| December .. | 1·29 | 1·36 | 1·01 | 1·11 | 1·22 | 3·60 | 8·04 | 24·9 | 945·4 | — |
| Yearly average .. | 1·08 | 1·40 | 1·20 | 1·01 | 1·12 | 2·01 | 6·57 | 13·0 | 229·4 | — |

TABLE VII

*"Coefficients of Divergence" between the Internal and External Values of the Paper Mark*

(*a*) Ratios between American Prices and Prices in Gold in Germany

| *Month* | *1914* | *1915* | *1916* | *1917* | *1918* | *1919* | *1920* | *1921* | *1922* | *1923* |
|---|---|---|---|---|---|---|---|---|---|---|
| January .. .. | — | 0·87 | 0·97 | 1·35 | 1·13 | 1·48 | 2·86 | 1·83 | 1·72 | 2·40 |
| February .. .. | — | 0·84 | 0·99 | 1·40 | 1·19 | 1·55 | 3·25 | 1·70 | 1·70 | 1·87 |
| March .. .. | — | 0·83 | 1·07 | 1·43 | 1·18 | 1·76 | 2·73 | 1·72 | 1·77 | 1·64 |
| April .. .. | — | 0·82 | 1·06 | 1·64 | 1·14 | 2·08 | 2·22 | 1·69 | 1·56 | 1·78 |
| May .. .. | — | 0·83 | 1·01 | 1·75 | 1·15 | 2·08 | 1·81 | 1·64 | 1·58 | 2·17 |
| June .. .. | — | 0·83 | 1·03 | 1·90 | 1·18 | 2·20 | 1·64 | 1·72 | 1·61 | 2·07 |
| July .. .. | — | 0·78 | 1·01 | 1·87 | 1·31 | 2·24 | 1·66 | 1·80 | 1·81 | — |
| August .. .. | 0·92 | 0·81 | 1·06 | 1·60 | 1·25 | 2·30 | 1·81 | 1·49 | 2·18 | — |
| September.. .. | 0·92 | 0·80 | 1·16 | 1·62 | 1·41 | 2·44 | 2·08 | 1·70 | 1·86 | — |
| October .. .. | 0·86 | 0·82 | 1·21 | 1·60 | 1·36 | 2·40 | 2·33 | 2·06 | 2·06 | — |
| November .. | 0·87 | 0·84 | 1·34 | 1·50 | 1·54 | 2·92 | 2·39 | 2·58 | 2·32 | — |
| December .. .. | 0·83 | 0·90 | 1·35 | 1·22 | 1·61 | 3·09 | 2·16 | 1·83 | 1·91 | — |
| Yearly average .. | 0·94 | 0·83 | 1·09 | 1·55 | 1·28 | 2·34 | 2·28 | 1·92 | 1·96 | — |

TABLE VII (*continued*)

(*b*) Ratios between Gold Prices of Goods imported into Germany and Gold Prices of Goods produced in Germany

| *Month* | *1914* | *1915* | *1916* | *1917* | *1918* | *1919* | *1920* | *1921* | *1922* | *1923* |
|---|---|---|---|---|---|---|---|---|---|---|
| January .. .. | — | 1·01 | 0·93 | 0·90 | 0·69 | 1·12 | 2·84 | 1·34 | 1·50 | 1·99 |
| February .. .. | — | 0·94 | 0·93 | 0·89 | 0·71 | 1·08 | 3·36 | 1·26 | 1·54 | 1·78 |
| March .. .. | — | 0·90 | 0·96 | 0·88 | 0·71 | 1·06 | 3·21 | 1·26 | 1·48 | 1·51 |
| April .. .. | — | 0·88 | 0·93 | 0·86 | 0·69 | 1·06 | 2·89 | 1·22 | 1·37 | 1·57 |
| May .. .. | — | 0·90 | 0·92 | 0·85 | 0·69 | 1·03 | 2·00 | 1·20 | 1·43 | 1·92 |
| June .. .. | — | 0·94 | 0·92 | 0·87 | 0·67 | 1·04 | 1·71 | 1·21 | 1·46 | 1·83 |
| July .. .. | — | 0·91 | 0·85 | 0·83 | 0·67 | 1·04 | 1·51 | 1·26 | 1·49 | — |
| August .. .. | 0·92 | 0·98 | 0·88 | 0·69 | 0·59 | 1·01 | 1·45 | 1·01 | 1·96 | — |
| September .. .. | 0·94 | 0·96 | 0·92 | 0·71 | 0·60 | 1·33 | 1·65 | 1·35 | 1·67 | — |
| October .. .. | 0·95 | 0·96 | 0·93 | 0·71 | 0·89 | 1·63 | 1·80 | 1·60 | 1·81 | — |
| November .. | 1·05 | 0·95 | 0·93 | 0·69 | 0·90 | 2·06 | 1·76 | 1·91 | 2·25 | — |
| December .. .. | 1·06 | 0·94 | 0·94 | 0·69 | 1·18 | 2·38 | 1·53 | 1·60 | 1·89 | — |
| Yearly average .. | 0·98 | 0·94 | 0·92 | 0·80 | 0·75 | 1·32 | 2·14 | 1·35 | 1·65 | — |

TABLE VIII

*Gold Reserves of the Reichsbank (millions of gold marks)*

| | | | |
|---|---|---|---|
| July 23rd, 1914 .. .. | 1,356·8 | December 31st, 1920 .. | 1,091·6 |
| December 31st, 1914 .. | 2,092·8 | December 31st, 1921 .. | 995·4 |
| December 31st, 1915 .. | 2,445·2 | December 31st, 1922 .. | 1,004·8 |
| December 31st, 1916 .. | 2,520·5 | October 15th, 1923 .. | 443·9 |
| December 31st, 1917 .. | 2,406·6 | December 31st, 1923 .. | 467·0 |
| December 31st, 1918 .. | 2,262·2 | October 15th, 1924 .. | 613·6* |
| December 31st, 1919 .. | 1,089·5 | December 31st, 1925 .. | 1,208·2† |

* Plus 204·5 millions of "foreign exchange" included in the reserve.
† Plus 402·5 millions of "foreign exchange" included in the reserve.

TABLE IX

*Foreign Trade of Germany**

(*a*) German Imports (thousands of tons)

| *Month* | *1919* | *1920* | *1921* | *1922* | *1923* |
|---|---|---|---|---|---|
| January .. .. | 200 | 1,129 | — | 2,309 | 4,743 |
| February .. .. | 159 | 1,475 | — | 1,475 | 3,166 |
| March .. .. | 249 | 1,357 | — | 2,645 | 5,220 |
| April .. .. | 373 | 1,224 | — | 2,889 | 6,396 |
| May .. .. | 613 | 1,485 | 1,534 | 3,810 | 4,013 |
| June .. .. | 884 | 1,737 | 1,824 | 4,029 | 4,807 |
| July .. .. | 1,298 | 1,739 | 1,925 | 4,798 | 4,160 |
| August .. .. | 1,531 | 1,512 | 2,111 | 4,676 | 4,120 |
| September .. .. | 1,277 | 1,680 | 2,533 | 4,829 | 3,420 |
| October .. .. | 1,240 | 1,758 | 3,005 | 5,552 | 2,915 |
| November .. .. | 1,018 | 1,757 | 2,535 | 4,551 | 3,370 |
| December .. .. | 1,081 | 2,007 | 2,086 | 4,326 | 2,850 |

(*b*) German Exports (thousands of tons)

| *Month* | *1919* | *1920* | *1921* | *1922* | *1923* |
|---|---|---|---|---|---|
| January .. .. | 323 | 1,523 | — | 2,027 | 1,311 |
| February .. .. | 397 | 1,923 | — | 1,747 | 1,096 |
| March .. .. | 583 | 1,826 | — | 2,153 | 938 |
| April .. .. | 641 | 2,170 | — | 2,176 | 1,029 |
| May .. .. | 538 | 2,895 | 1,145 | 2,093 | 930 |
| June .. .. | 1,055 | 2,680 | 1,509 | 1,880 | 890 |
| July .. .. | 1,085 | 2,004 | 1,558 | 1,636 | 1,053 |
| August .. .. | 1,202 | 1,910 | 1,828 | 1,407 | 1,074 |
| September .. .. | 944 | 1,837 | 1,871 | 1,587 | 1,143 |
| October .. .. | 1,231 | 1,494 | 1,973 | 1,539 | 1,183 |
| November .. .. | 1,324 | 1,768 | 1,908 | 1,551 | 1,005 |
| December .. .. | 2,762 | 1,758 | 1,930 | 1,756 | 1,104 |

* Sources: For 1919, *Sammlung von Aktenstücken über die Verhandlungen auf der Sachverständigenkonferenz zu Brüssel vom 16 bis 22nd December, 1920*; for the following years the monthly publication *Monatliche Nachweise* on the foreign trade of Germany. Figures for January–April 1921 have never been published.

## Table X

*Unemployment**

(Unemployed Members of Trade Unions; Percentage of the Total Number of Members)

| *Month* | *1919* | *1920* | *1921* | *1922* | *1923* |
|---|---|---|---|---|---|
| January .. .. | 6·6 | 3·4 | 4·5 | 3·3 | 4·2 |
| February .. .. | 6·0 | 2·9 | 4·7 | 2·7 | 5·2 |
| March .. .. | 3·9 | 1·9 | 3·7 | 1·1 | 5·6 |
| April .. .. | 5·2 | 1·9 | 3·9 | 0·9 | 7·0 |
| May .. .. | 3·8 | 2·7 | 3·7 | 0·7 | 6·2 |
| June .. .. | 2·5 | 4·0 | 3·0 | 0·6 | 4·1 |
| July .. .. | 3·1 | 6·0 | 2·6 | 0·6 | 3·5 |
| August .. .. | 3·1 | 5·9 | 2·2 | 0·7 | 6·3 |
| September .. .. | 2·2 | 4·5 | 1·4 | 0·8 | 9·9 |
| October .. .. | 2·6 | 4·2 | 1·2 | 1·4 | 19·1 |
| November .. .. | 2·9 | 3·9 | 1·4 | 2·0 | 23·4 |
| December .. .. | 2·9 | 4·1 | 1·6 | 2·8 | 28·2 |

* Source: *Reichsarbeitsblatt*, March 1st, 1924.

TABLE XI

*Wages*

(*a*) Nominal Wages of a Coal-miner (Hewer) in the Ruhr District* (1913 = 1)

| *Year* | *Yearly average* | *Month* | *1920* | *1921* | *1922* | *1923* |
|---|---|---|---|---|---|---|
| 1914 | 1·0 | January .. | 6·0 | 10·0 | 18·1 | 696 |
| 1915 | 1·1 | February .. | 6·0 | 10·0 | 20·3 | 2,115 |
| 1916 | 1·3 | March .. | 6·0 | 10·0 | 23·3 | 2,430 |
| 1917 | 1·6 | April .. .. | 7·2 | 10·4 | 26·1 | 2,430 |
| 1918 | 2·0 | May .. .. | 7·3 | 10·7 | 30·4 | 3,067 |
| 1919 | 3·4 | June .. .. | 7·9 | 10·8 | 32·7 | 7,640 |
| | | July .. .. | 7·9 | 10·9 | 41·0 | 27,621 |
| | | August .. | 8·7 | 11·0 | 55·4 | 844,187 |
| | | September .. | 8·7 | 12·7 | 106·5 | 22·1† |
| | | October .. | 9·8 | 12·8 | 133·8 | 10·9‡ |
| | | November .. | 9·9 | 17·6 | 261·8 | 493·8‡ |
| | | December .. | 9·9 | 17·8 | 452·3 | 862·0‡ |

* From 1914 to 1919 average annual earnings in cash; from January 1920 until November 1922, average monthly earnings in cash according to statistics of the mining authorities; from December 1922 onwards, wages according to the scales operating in the Rhine-Westphalia province (including allowances for a wife and two children, but excluding the coal supplied to the workmen).

† Millions. ‡ Milliards.

(*b*) Real Wages of a Coal-miner (Hewer) in the Ruhr District* (1913 = 100)

| *Year* | *Annual average* | *Month* | *1920* | *1921* | *1922* | *1923* |
|---|---|---|---|---|---|---|
| 1914 | 93·3 | January .. | 80·0 | 84·4 | 83·1 | 47·7 |
| 1915 | 81·3 | February .. | 70·2 | 87·3 | 78·8 | 75·6 |
| 1916 | 74·4 | March .. | 62·7 | 88·0 | 76·3 | 86·2 |
| 1917 | 62·7 | April .. | 69·3 | 92·2 | 73·8 | 79·9 |
| 1918 | 63·7 | May .. .. | 66·4 | 95·9 | 80·7 | 69·6 |
| 1919 | 82·4 | June .. .. | 72·6 | 92·9 | 75·7 | 70·8 |
| | | July .. .. | 74·4 | 86·5 | 69·5 | 47·6 |
| | | August .. | 84·6 | 81·9 | 59·1 | 78·5 |
| | | September .. | 85·9 | 89·9 | 75·6 | 74·7 |
| | | October .. | 91·6 | 82·2 | 51·6 | 81·2 |
| | | November .. | 88·4 | 97·5 | 52·6 | 55·7 |
| | | December .. | 85·3 | 90·5 | 62·2 | 73·3 |

* Calculated from the beginning of February 1920 on the base of the official index number of the cost of living in the period in which the wages were consumed (that is, a nominal monthly wage divided by the index number of the cost of living from the 8th of the same month to the 7th of the next month). From September 1923 account was also taken of the methods of payment of wages.

TABLE XI (*continued*)

(*c*) Average Wage per Hour (in Pfennig, Unskilled Workers)

| *Month* | *1924* | *1925* | *1926* | *1927* | *1928* |
|---|---|---|---|---|---|
| January .. .. | 44·2 | 54·9 | 65·1 | 66·0 | 73·7 |
| February .. .. | 43·3 | 55·5 | 65·2 | 66·1 | 73·9 |
| March .. .. | 42·4 | 56·8 | 65·2 | 66·7 | 74·1 |
| April .. .. | 44·8 | 58·3 | 65·2 | 69·1 | 75·5 |
| May .. .. | 48·0 | 59·5 | 65·2 | 71·5 | 77·4 |
| June .. .. | 50·2 | 60·6 | 65·0 | 71·7 | 77·6 |
| July .. .. | 50·1 | 62·0 | 65·0 | 71·7 | 77·6 |
| August .. .. | 50·4 | 62·9 | 65·0 | 71·7 | 78·3 |
| September .. .. | 50·5 | 63·5 | 65·6 | 71·9 | 79·7 |
| October .. .. | 51·4 | 63·7 | 65·7 | 72·6 | 80·4 |
| November .. .. | 52·9 | 64·9 | 65·7 | 72·8 | 80·4 |
| December .. .. | 54·2 | 65·1 | 66·0 | 72·9 | — |

(*d*) Index Numbers of the Real Income of Unskilled Workers* (1924–26 = 100)

| *Month* | *1924* | *1925* | *1926* | *1927* | *1928* |
|---|---|---|---|---|---|
| January .. .. | 68 | 99 | 100 | 109 | 120 |
| February .. .. | 73 | 101 | 102 | 109 | 121 |
| March .. .. | 78 | 104 | 103 | 113 | 122 |
| April .. .. | 85 | 107 | 104 | 117 | 125 |
| May .. .. | 90 | 111 | 105 | 122 | 128 |
| June .. .. | 91 | 111 | 105 | 122 | 128 |
| July .. .. | 86 | 109 | 104 | 121 | 126 |
| August .. .. | 87 | 108 | 105 | 124 | 126 |
| September .. .. | 90 | 109 | 108 | 124 | 130 |
| October .. .. | 91 | 109 | 110 | 126 | 131 |
| November .. .. | 95 | 107 | 109 | 121 | — |
| December .. .. | 98 | 101 | 108 | 117 | — |

* Calculated by the author on the basis of wages per hour and taking account of the cost of living, of total and partial employment, and of subsidies paid to the unemployed.

TABLE XII

*Index Numbers of the Prices of German Shares* (1913 = 100)

| | 1918 | | | 1919 | | |
|---|---|---|---|---|---|---|
| | *In paper marks* | *Adjusted according to the exchange rate of the dollar* | *Adjusted according to index numbers of wholesale prices* | *In paper marks* | *Adjusted according to the exchange rate of the dollar* | *Adjusted according to index numbers of wholesale prices* |
| January | 126 | 101·55 | 62·38 | 97 | 49·68 | 37·02 |
| February | 131 | 104·32 | 66·50 | 98 | 45·57 | 36·30 |
| March | 132 | 106·48 | 67·00 | 97 | 39·20 | 35·40 |
| April | 133 | 109·23 | 65·52 | 96 | 31·99 | 33·57 |
| May | 138 | 112·75 | 68·32 | 91 | 29·74 | 30·64 |
| June | 137 | 107·36 | 66·18 | 96 | 28·77 | 31·17 |
| July | 137 | 99·34 | 66·50 | 100 | 27·85 | 29·50 |
| August | 143 | 98·53 | 61·64 | 99 | 22·08 | 23·46 |
| September | 135 | 86·03 | 59·47 | 112 | 19·56 | 22·72 |
| October | 109 | 69·28 | 46·88 | 124 | 19·41 | 22·06 |
| November | 95 | 53·72 | 40·60 | 125 | 13·70 | 18·44 |
| December | 88 | 44·63 | 35·77 | 127 | 11·40 | 15·84 |

TABLE XII (*continued*)

| | 1920 | | | 1921 | | |
|---|---|---|---|---|---|---|
| | *In paper marks* | *Adjusted according to the exchange rate of the dollar* | *Adjusted according to index numbers of wholesale prices* | *In paper marks* | *Adjusted according to the exchange rate of the dollar* | *Adjusted according to index numbers of wholesale prices* |
| January .. .. | 166 | 10·73 | 13·18 | 278 | 18·00 | 19·34 |
| February .. .. | 200 | 8·47 | 11·87 | 260 | 17·82 | 18·90 |
| March .. .. .. | 196 | 9·82 | 11·48 | 265 | 17·84 | 19·83 |
| April .. .. .. | 184 | 12·93 | 11·72 | 275 | 18·17 | 20·72 |
| May .. .. .. | 160 | 14·45 | 10·61 | 277 | 18·71 | 21·21 |
| June .. .. .. | 167 | 17·93 | 12·09 | 299 | 18·12 | 21·91 |
| July .. .. .. | 187 | 19·92 | 13·70 | 337 | 18·45 | 23·60 |
| August .. .. | 204 | 17·98 | 14·10 | 389 | 19·36 | 20·28 |
| September .. .. | 220 | 15·94 | 14·69 | 492 | 19·69 | 23·80 |
| October .. .. | 245 | 15·06 | 16·74 | 644 | 18·00 | 26·17 |
| November .. .. | 260 | 14·12 | 17·21 | 936 | 14·94 | 27·40 |
| December .. .. | 274 | 15·79 | 19·05 | 731 | 15·99 | 20·97 |

TABLE XII (*continued*)

| | 1921 *In paper marks* | 1921 *Adjusted according to the exchange rate of the dollar* | 1921 *Adjusted according to index numbers of wholesale prices* | 1922 *In paper marks* | 1922 *Adjusted according to the exchange rate of the dollar* | 1922 *Adjusted according to index numbers of wholesale prices* |
|---|---|---|---|---|---|---|
| January .. .. | 743 | 16·27 | 20·28 | 21,400 | 5·24 | 8·05 |
| February .. .. | 841 | 16·98 | 20·49 | 45,200 | 6·79 | 8·09 |
| March .. .. .. | 986 | 14·57 | 18·16 | 33,600 | 6·66 | 6·88 |
| April .. .. .. | 1,018 | 14·69 | 16·02 | 50,200 | 8·61 | 9·63 |
| May .. .. .. | 873 | 12·63 | 13·50 | 95,100 | 8·38 | 11·64 |
| June .. .. .. | 823 | 10·89 | 11·71 | 352,000 | 13·44 | 18·17 |
| July .. .. .. | 897 | 7·63 | 8·92 | 1,349,400 | 16·03 | 18·04 |
| August .. .. | 1,156 | 4·28 | 6·02 | 12,474,300 | 11·33 | 13·21 |
| September .. .. | 1,262 | 3·61 | 4·40 | 531,300,000 | 22·56 | 22·08 |
| October .. .. | 2,062 | 2·72 | 3·64 | 171,322* | 28·47 | 24,13 |
| November .. .. | 5,070 | 2·96 | 4·40 | 23,680,000* | 39·36 | 32·63 |
| December .. .. | 8,981 | 4·97 | 6·09 | 26,890,000* | 26·80 | 21·27 |

* Millions.

## Table XIII

### *Statistics of Consumption**

#### (*a*) Consumption of Meat (tons)†

| | 1921 | 1922 | 1923 | 1924 |
|---|---|---|---|---|
| First quarter .. .. | — | 470,623 | 383,595 | 504,868 |
| Second quarter .. .. | — | 378,868 | 360,966 | 480,159 |
| Third quarter .. .. | 453,752 | 355,221 | 305,911 | 527,423 |
| Fourth quarter .. .. | 538,633 | 430,949 | 391,553 | 649,256 |

| | 1925 | 1926 | 1927 | 1928 |
|---|---|---|---|---|
| First quarter .. .. | 621,805 | 651,226 | 709,322 | 807,782 |
| Second quarter .. .. | 583,273 | 579,323 | 682,168 | 718,462 |
| Third quarter .. .. | 615,646 | 614,659 | 685,192 | — |
| Fourth quarter .. .. | 653,235 | 734,044 | 833,111 | — |

* Calculated by the Berlin Office of the Reparations Commission.

† Carcases subject to control, plus net imports of meat and store cattle.

#### (*b*) Consumption of Sugar (tons)

| | 1920 | 1921 | 1922 | 1923 | 1924 |
|---|---|---|---|---|---|
| First quarter .. | — | 283,994 | 353,171 | 346,003 | 166,344 |
| Second quarter .. | — | 316,868 | 345,811 | 254,028 | 193,599 |
| Third quarter .. | — | 292,161 | 332,230 | 309,063 | 298,959 |
| Fourth quarter .. | 261,536 | 423,363 | 389,049 | 261,727 | 387,823 |

| | 1925 | 1926 | 1927 | 1928 |
|---|---|---|---|---|
| First quarter .. | 296,505 | 295,503 | 313,421 | 326,816 |
| Second quarter .. | 337,092 | 355,384 | 358,752 | 373,137 |
| Third quarter .. | 395,247 | 405,017 | 473,324 | — |
| Fourth quarter .. | 378,341 | 409,093 | 440,682 | — |

#### (*c*) Consumption of Beer* (thousands of hectolitres)

| | 1920 | 1921 | 1922 | 1923 | 1924 |
|---|---|---|---|---|---|
| First quarter .. | — | 5,807 | 7,182 | 5,646 | 5,685 |
| Second quarter .. | — | 8,352 | 9,862 | 8,026 | 9,807 |
| Third quarter .. | — | 11,267 | 9,439 | 8,560 | 10,605 |
| Fourth quarter .. | 5,039 | 6,764 | 5,566 | 4,038 | 8,442 |

| | 1925 | 1926 | 1927 | 1928 |
|---|---|---|---|---|
| First quarter .. | 8,662 | 9,951 | 9,994 | 11,495 |
| Second quarter .. | 12,900 | 12,407 | 13,427 | 14,536 |
| Third quarter .. | 14,111 | 14,461 | 15,231 | — |
| Fourth quarter .. | 10,187 | 11,213 | 11,094 | — |

* Production plus net imports.

TABLE XIII (*continued*)

(*d*) Consumption of Tobacco (tons)

| | 1920 | 1921 | 1922 | 1923 | 1924 |
|---|---|---|---|---|---|
| First quarter .. | — | 29,541 | 26,483 | 19,855 | 26,932 |
| Second quarter .. | — | 22,731 | 39,846 | 21,055 | 22,130 |
| Third quarter .. | — | 37,385 | 23,183 | 18,614 | 24,752 |
| Fourth quarter .. | 27,667 | 25,035 | 21,120 | 20,448 | 27,957 |

| | 1925 | 1926 | 1927 | 1928 |
|---|---|---|---|---|
| First quarter .. | 26,968 | 24,108 | 28,792 | 32,282 |
| Second quarter .. | 30,085 | 29,021 | 32,211 | 31,007 |
| Third quarter .. | 38,331 | 31,340 | 33,190 | — |
| Fourth quarter .. | 23,858 | 32,583 | 32,759 | — |

(*e*) Net Imports of Coffee (tons)

| | 1921 | 1922 | 1923 | 1924 |
|---|---|---|---|---|
| First quarter .. | — | 13,364 | 7,375 | 9,950 |
| Second quarter .. | — | 8,212 | 12,877 | 11,660 |
| Third quarter .. | 32,381 | 11,566 | 6,727 | 15,079 |
| Fourth quarter .. | 28,466 | 3,650 | 11,751 | 18,621 |

| | 1925 | 1926 | 1927 | 1928 |
|---|---|---|---|---|
| First quarter .. | 25,648 | 32,128 | 39,953 | 45,379 |
| Second quarter .. | 18,884 | 20,987 | 24,085 | 23,945 |
| Third quarter .. | 28,383 | 30,685 | 36,310 | — |
| Fourth quarter .. | 17,429 | 20,998 | 24,353 | — |

(*f*) Consumption of Sub-tropical Fruits (tons)

| | | | |
|---|---|---|---|
| 1913 .. .. .. | 298,579 | 1924 .. .. .. | 300,776 |
| 1920 .. .. .. | 79,144 | 1925 .. .. .. | 379,892 |
| 1921 (May–December) | 58,440 | 1926 .. .. . | 386,928 |
| 1922 .. .. .. | 52,006 | 1927 .. .. . | 420,541 |
| 1923 .. .. .. | 43,917 | | |

*Debits Passed by the Reparation Commission in respect of transactions outside the Dawes Plan**

*(Millions of gold marks)*

| | | |
|---|---|---|
| Cash receipts and sundry payments (including 1,691 millions paid in 1921 and 1922 in execution of the London Agreement) | | 1,924·4 |
| Deliveries in kind: | | |
| (*a*) In execution of Armistice Conventions | 1,025·3 | |
| (*b*) In execution of Treaty of Versailles† | 2,376·6 | |
| | | 3,401·9 |
| Reparation Recovery Acts | | 372·6 |
| Cessions of property belonging to the Reich and to the States | | 2,628·3 |
| Requisitions and supplies to the armies | | 752·7 |
| Receipts of the Ruhr | | 947·5 |
| Total‡ | | 10,027·4 |
| Payments in execution of the Dawes Plan | | 7,553·2 |
| Payments in execution of the Young Plan | | 2,800·0 |
| Grand total | | 20,380·6 |

* Figures as known on August 31st, 1928, calculated by the Reparation Commission.

† Including the value (711·5 millions) of the ships delivered by Germany.

‡ The figures of payments effected by Germany, according to the Reparation Commission, differ much from those indicated by the German Government. For the explanation of this divergence, see A. Antonnia, *Le bilan des réparations et la crise mondiale*, Paris, 1935, pp. 425 *et seq.*

# INDEX

*(Reference should also be made to the detailed Table of Contents, p. 7, to the list of Tables, p. 15, and to the list of Diagrams, p. 19.)*

FSC
www.fsc.org
MIX
Papier | Fördert gute Waldnutzung
FSC® C083411

Kolibri 360 GmbH
Ferdinand-Jühlke-Straße 7
99095 Erfurt, Deutschland
produktsicherheit@kolibri360.de